Authoritarian Politics in Modern Society

AUTHORITARIAN POLITICS IN MODERN SOCIETY

The Dynamics of Established One-Party Systems

Edited by

Samuel P. Huntington
and
Clement H. Moore

Basic Books, Inc., Publishers · New York · London

© 1970 by Basic Books, Inc.

Library of Congress Catalog Card Number: 78–94304

SBN 465–00569–1

Manufactured in the United States of America

The Authors

JEREMY R. AZRAEL is Professor of Political Science and Chairman of the Committee on Slavic Area Studies at The University of Chicago. His publications include *Managerial Power and Soviet Politics* and numerous contributions to symposia and professional journals.

HENRY BIENEN is Associate Professor of Politics and Faculty Associate of the Center of International Studies at Princeton University. He is editor and co-author of *The Military Intervenes: Case Studies in Political Development* and has written *Tanzania: Party Transformation and Economic Development, Violence and Social Change,* and numerous articles in scholarly journals. Mr. Bienen, in addition, is an editor of *World Politics.*

MELVIN CROAN is Associate Professor of Political Science and Associate Chairman of the Department of Political Science at the University of Wisconsin. He has published numerous scholarly articles on German, Soviet, and international communist politics in various professional journals and contributed chapters to several books dealing with communism in East Europe.

CARL J. FRIEDRICH is Eaton Professor of the Science of Government at Harvard University and until recently also held the position of Professor of Political Science at Heidelberg. He is now President of the International Political Science Association. He is author of *Europe: An Emergent Nation?, Constitutional Government and Democracy,* and *Man and His Government.*

GINO GERMANI is Monroe Gutman Professor of Latin American Affairs at Harvard University. Previously he has been Professor of Sociology and chairman of that department at the University of Buenos Aires. He has published several books and continues his research and writings in the fields of urbanization and modernization within Latin America and other developing countries, especially those with fascist leanings.

SAMUEL P. HUNTINGTON is Frank M. Thomson Professor of Government at Harvard University, where he is also a member of the Executive Committee of the Center for International Affairs. He is author of *Political Order in Changing Societies, The Soldier and the State: The Theory and Politics of Civil-Military Relations, The Common Defense: Strategic Programs in National Politics,* co-author of *Political Power: USA/USSR* and has contributed numerous articles in scholarly journals.

v

35990

ANDREW C. JANOS is Associate Professor of Political Science at the University of California at Berkeley. He is the author of *The Seizure of Power: The Study of Force and Political Consent* and numerous articles in the field of East European studies.

JUAN J. LINZ is Professor of Sociology and Political Science at Yale University and was last year Professor of Sociology at the University of Madrid. His publications include *Los Empresarios ante el Poder Publico*, "The Party System of Spain: Past and Future" in *Party Systems and Voter Alignments* by Lipset and Rokkan, as well as numerous articles in symposia and scholarly journals both in the United States and Spain.

CLEMENT H. MOORE is currently teaching at the American University in Cairo. His publications include *Tunisia Since Independence: The Dynamics of One-Party Government, Politics in North Africa, Tunisia: The Politics of Modernization* (co-author), and numerous articles in scholarly journals.

ERGUN ÖZBUDUN is Associate Professor of Government at the University of Ankara. His writings include *The Causes of Party Cohesion in Western Democracies, The Means of the Legislative Control of the Executive in the Parliamentary Government System,* "The Role of the Military in Turkish Politics," and other articles on comparative political parties and political development.

HUGH DOUGLAS PRICE is Professor of Government at Harvard University. He is author of *The Negro and Southern Politics* and of numerous articles on American government and politics. He recently completed a study of *Political Change in Middletown and Yankee City* and is currently engaged in a National Science Foundation project on "Modeling Complex Political Systems."

HUNG-CHAO TAI is Associate Professor of Political Science at the University of Detroit and is author of a forthcoming book entitled *Land Reform in the Developing Countries: A Comparative Analysis.*

JAMES R. TOWNSEND is Associate Professor of Political Science at the University of Washington, where he is also affiliated with the Far Eastern and Russian Institute. He has written *Political Participation in Communist China,* "The Revolutionization of Chinese Youth," and numerous articles in professional and scholarly journals.

M. GEORGE ZANINOVICH is Associate Professor at the University of Oregon, presently Visiting Associate Professor in the Department of Political Science and the Russian Institute, Columbia University. Among his publications are *The Development of Socialist Yugoslavia, Content Analysis: A Handbook with Applications for the Study of International Crises* (co-author), and several articles in symposia and professional journals.

Preface

How can one-party political systems adapt to socioeconomic changes, particularly to increasing economic affluence and social complexity? In one form or another, this problem confronts Spain and Yugoslavia, Mexico and Tunisia, Communist and Nationalist China, as well as many other communist and non-communist states. Our purpose in this volume is to shed some light and many perspectives on the subject. This effort is a part of the research program on Political Institutionalization and Social Change conducted by the Center for International Affairs at Harvard University with support from the Carnegie Corporation of New York. The project began with consultations between the two editors early in 1967 and then the preparation by Professor Moore of a general outline paper, "The Evolution of Established One-Party Systems: Statement of Purpose," which was circulated to the other project participants in the fall of 1967. Most of the chapters now in the volume were discussed at a conference in April, 1968 at Jenner, California, the sponsorship of which was shared by the Institute of International Studies of the University of California at Berkeley. Participants in the conference, in addition to the authors of chapters in this volume, included: Leonard Binder, Ulf Himmelstrand, Chalmers Johnson, John H. Kautsky, Michael Leiserson, Alfred G. Meyer, Robert Scalapino, Jan F. Triska, and Myron Weiner. Robert Jackson and Elena Venturini provided us with notes of the discussions. Revisions of the papers presented at the conference were generally completed by the late fall of 1968. In addition to those chapters that grew from papers discussed at the conference, we are delighted to be able to include in this volume the paper by Carl J. Friedrich on the Nazi experience and one by Andrew Janos on the group approach to communist politics. We are indebted to Mrs. Gloria Mims for assistance in connection with the conference and to Mrs. Betty Means and Christopher Mitchell for help in preparation of the manuscript for publication.

February 1970   Samuel P. Huntington
                                                        Clement H. Moore

Contents

Part I

ONE-PARTY SYSTEMS: THEORIES AND APPROACHES

1

Social and Institutional Dynamics of One-Party Systems

|| *Samuel P. Huntington*

Authoritarian Politics and Modern Society

The events of the 1930s led many people to question the future of democratic government. In somewhat similar fashion, the events of the 1960s led many people to question the viability of authoritarian governments. The communist dictatorship governing the world's largest country collapsed into chaos. In East Europe the Yugoslav and Czech regimes moved significantly toward greater liberalization and democratization. Throughout the communist world there seemed to be a conflict between the forces of the future reflecting economic rationality and political liberty and those of a disowned but still real Stalinist past. The Soviet system, one scholar argued, faced a choice between degeneration and fundamental transformation. In a similar vein, a Yugoslav observer held that the communist systems "will either have to relinquish power voluntarily as the result of free elections or try to retain their power by imposing open police dictatorships. . . ." [1] At the other end of Europe, the dictatorships in Spain and Portugal faced increasing opposition and dissent which heightened the prospect that they would not long survive their aging leaders. The fate of the revolutionary Cuban regime without Castro seemed as uncertain as that of the militaristic Taiwan regime without Chiang. While democratic systems of government clearly faced many problems, the very survivability of many authoritarian systems seemed to be in doubt.

Beneath these more immediate and specific premonitions of collapse was the more general feeling that authoritarian government could well be incompatible with a complex, highly developed, industrialized, modern society. Most rich countries are democratic countries. Is it not probable, even

3

inevitable, as societies become economically well off and socially complex, that their political systems will also have to become more open, participant, responsive? A few years earlier, as Raymond Aron pointed out, social scientists had pondered the question: How monopolistic can a monopolistic party be? More recently they were asking: How non-monopolistic can such a party become? At times the pessimistic view of the future of authoritarianism became a simple optimistic view of the inevitability of democracy.[2] "All versions of Communism are becoming decadent. They must inevitably change into a democratic society." [3] The theory of "convergence" popular among pundits and scholars in the early 1960s posited that: (1) societies with similar economic and social systems have similar political systems; and (2) complex, modern, industrialized societies have democratic political systems. Authoritarian politics, in short, is incompatible with modern society.

The primary purpose of this chapter—and, indeed, of this volume—is to examine these assumptions and propositions more concretely and systematically. Authoritarian systems obviously have existed throughout history and have assumed a variety of forms. Clearly also the political institutions of a society have some relationship to the level of development of that society. It seems reasonable to assume that the more traditional and simple forms of authoritarian rule (like the more simple and traditional forms of democratic rule) are impossible in a highly complex, modern society. Such societies are not likely to be governed effectively—or even governed at all—by absolute monarchs, personalistic dictatorships, or military juntas. These traditional and relatively simple types of political systems have recurred again and again throughout history. Substantial evidence plus common sense suggests that such political systems cannot indefinitely survive the modernization of their societies. The more important and interesting question concerns not the fate of these political systems but rather that of the principal modern form of authoritarianism: the one-party system.

One-party systems exist in great number and variety. Whatever their form, however, they are themselves the product of modernization. Their roots, as Clement Moore shows, can be traced to the Puritans and Jacobins. While they first emerged in the nineteenth century, they are preeminently a twentieth century political phenomenon, products of the convulsive processes of social, economic, and political change of that century: social revolution, world war, nationalist struggle. The one-party system is the principal modern form of authoritarian government. Quite clearly, however, a one-party system can cease to be a one-party system without ceasing to be authoritarian (by "reverting" to a more traditional, militaristic, or personalistic form of authoritarianism), and conceivably a one-party system can cease to be authoritarian without ceasing to be a one-party system (a possibility which is examined more closely in the last section of this chapter). But in general the fate of authoritarianism in modern society depends upon the viability of the one-party system in modern society. If increasing complexity, affluence, differentiation, and industrialization disintegrate one-party systems, they also shatter the future of authoritarianism—unless political innovators should develop new and more adaptable forms of authoritarian rule.

The issue is thus the viability in modern societies of the most modern form of authoritarianism. What are the dynamics of one-party systems? Under what conditions do they arise? Under what conditions do they survive? To what extent is it possible to distinguish among different types of systems and to discover different patterns of evolution in these systems? What can their evolution in the past tell us about their prospects for the future?

Political Authority: Strong and Weak One-Party Systems

Party systems are commonly classified by the number of parties in them. In these terms, a one-party system can presumably be distinguished from a no-party system and a pluralistic party system. A no-party system is typically a traditional system. Parties are the products of modern politics and, more particularly, the extension of social mobilization, the expansion of political consciousness, and the growth of mass political participation. Parties structure mass participation in politics. They did not exist anywhere before the democratic revolution of the last half of the eighteenth century, and they do not exist today in many places where political modernization is still in its early phases. At some point in this process factions and cliques become more stable, regularized organizations which engage in a continuous struggle for control over government. In the classic pattern, parties emerge out of legislative factions whose members find that they have to establish organizations in their constituencies in order to stay in office. The politics of factions and legislative cliques is, in a sense, multi-party politics in embryo. Different types of social structures and cleavages give rise to different types of pluralistic party systems. These systems may be dominant-party, two-party, or multi-party systems, and their parties may be cohesive, ideological parties of integration or loose, pragmatic parties of representation.[4]

In a one-party system, in contrast, other parties may exist—as, indeed, they do in Poland, China, and Mexico—but they have little effect on the course of events. They are like the minor parties in a two-party system. A one-party system thus differs from a dominant party system, where there is one major party capable of governing and several smaller parties which the major party cannot ignore in its political calculations. The line between the two systems cannot be precisely defined, but in the 1950s it presumably lay somewhere between Mexico and India. The Congress Party was the dominant party in India, but it could not govern in total disregard of what went on outside its ranks. The smaller parties served, in Rajni Kothari's phrase, as "parties of pressure" and, like pressure groups in a two-party system, they at times exercised significant influence on decisions on policy and leadership within the Congress Party.[5] In Mexico, on the other hand, the *Partido Revolucionario Institucional* (PRI) could and did virtually ignore the other parties. Someone who wished to protest in Mexico might join a minor party, but someone who wished to exert pressure would operate within the PRI. In a single-party system, interests are articulated within the party; in a dominant-party system they are articulated both within the dominant party and through the smaller parties. The difference between the two systems was well reflected in the distribution of votes. In Mexico the PRI almost never got less than 80 per cent of the vote in a national election; in India the Congress never got more than 50 per cent of the vote in a national election.

One-party systems can thus be distinguished from no-party and pluralistic party systems. To call a polity a one-party system, however, does not really tell us very much apart from that. The differences between any two one-party systems could conceivably be just as great as those between early eighteenth century England and the late twentieth century United States, both of which, it has been alleged, were two-party systems. One-party systems, like other types of party systems, have to be distinguished in terms of the role of the parties in the total political system. Every political system consists not only of parties but also of other institutions and groups. Each numerical type of party system can itself be subdivided according to the relative importance of the parties in the political system as a whole. What is the role, power, authority of the party or parties compared to legislatures, executives, bureaucracies, interest groups, and other political actors? Strong party systems can be distinguished from weak party systems by, among other things, the extent to which the party or parties monopolize: (1) the legitimation of the political system; (2) the recruitment of political leadership; and (3) interest aggregation and policy-making. Judged by these criteria, the American two-party system, for instance, is weaker than the British two-party system. More generally, it is possible to make a rough classification of party systems along numerical and power dimensions as in Table 1–1.[6]

TABLE 1-1   *Types of Party Systems*

Strength of Parties	Number of Parties				
	None	One	Dominant	Two	Multi
Strong					
Moderate					
Weak					

The relative strength of the party vis-à-vis other institutions and groups is particularly crucial in a one-party system. In pluralistic party systems, change is in large part mediated through the party system itself. The evolution of the society is mirrored in the fortunes of the parties in the system:

their origin and demise and the changing balance of power among them. In a one-party system, however, change is in part reflected in the shifting role of groups within the party, but it is even more reflected in the changing balance between the party and other institutions and groups. Reflecting theories of totalitarianism, writers often assume that in one-party systems the party is the only significant actor. They assume, in effect, that the scope of the political system is limited to that of the party system. This is far from the case. In strong one-party systems the party may to a large extent perform all three functions mentioned above, but it never monopolizes them completely. In weak one-party systems, there may well be only one party but that party may also play only a minor role in the political system as a whole. Most significantly, the importance of the party itself may change as the system evolves, and the relative importance of the other sources of power and authority which can challenge it may also change.

The other principal actors who may play roles in single-party political systems can be loosely grouped into five categories: personalistic actors, such as the charismatic political leader; traditional actors, such as the church or the monarchy; bureaucratic actors, like the state administration, the police, and the military; parliamentary actors, such as national assemblies, local government bodies, and associations; and functional social-economic groups, such as peasants, workers, managers, technical specialists, and intellectuals. In some systems the key non-party groups will be traditional; in others bureaucratic; in others parliamentary. In some one-party systems one or more of these groups may play dominant roles, eclipsing that of the party. In others there may be an uneasy balance of power between party and non-party groups. In still others the party may be the dominant institution on the political scene.

The evolution of a one-party system can, in some measure, be traced in the shifting roles of these other actors and forces that contest with the party for supremacy in the system. At any one time, a mixture of traditional, personalistic, bureaucratic, and parliamentary actors and associated social-economic groups may coexist with the party. In general, however, modernization in societies with one-party systems produces changes in the most significant non-party actors. The power of the traditional actors, if they are not completely overthrown by the revolutionary effort which brings the system into existence, tends to decrease. Personalistic leadership, particularly of the charismatic type, often plays a major role in the inauguration of one-party systems, but then declines as the operations of the system become formalized and institutionalized. Bureaucratic groups similarly pose challenges in the initial phases and either displace the party as the dominant force or arrive at an accommodation which usually means accepting a secondary role. Finally, while modernization in its first phase promotes the centralization of power and then the expansion of power, it often eventually leads to the dispersion of power. The problem then becomes reconciling parliamentary bodies with the continued primacy of the single party and providing for the representation of functional social-economic groupings within the party framework.

Clearly there is no easy or precise way by which to answer the question: How important is the party in a single party system? Experts on the Mexican political system differ drastically on the role which they assign to the PRI, on the one hand, and to the presidency and the "Revolutionary Family," on the other.[7] Keeping in mind the three criteria suggested above, however, it is possible to make rough comparisons and judgments between different systems and between different phases in the evolution of the same system. In the totalitarian systems of the 1930s, as Franz Neumann suggests, the party was more important than the state in the Soviet Union, the state was more important than the party in Italy, and the balance in Germany lay somewhere in between.[8] Clearly also in the Soviet Union the party was more important vis-à-vis the top leadership in the 1960s than it was in the 1940s during the heyday of Stalin's personal rule.

The differences between a strong one-party system and an extremely weak one are highlighted by the contrast between the post-Stalin Soviet Union and Franco Spain. In the former the party and its *apparat* was the preeminent group. The church and the traditional elite had all but been eliminated. Parliamentary and representative bodies had purely dignified roles. The social and economic elites were products of the system. The police had been subordinated to the party immediately following the death of Stalin. The army, after a brief excursion into politics in the mid-1950s, had resumed its more normal subordinated role. The state bureaucracy or managers, whom many observers had seen as the nucleus of a new ruling class, had displayed neither the unity nor the desire nor the talents to act as an independent political force. Finally, the seeming efforts by Khrushchev to expand his personal power had been brought to a sharp halt by his removal from power by the collective action of the Presidium backed by the Central Committee. In the Soviet Union, perhaps more than in any other state, the party did come close to monopolizing legitimacy, political recruitment, and the determination of policy. The Soviet Union, clearly, was a strong one-party system.

Franco Spain, on the other hand, was a weak one-party system, if, indeed, it even deserved to be called that. Insofar as it was a party system at all, it was a one-party system, but the party was a not very important part of the system, and the continued existence of many traditional and bureaucratic groups and institutions significantly weakened the party. In this "Mediterranean" syndicalist pattern of politics, as Kalman Silvert calls it,[9] the aggregation of power under any auspices, much less that of a single party, becomes very difficult. In Spain, the regime rested to varying degrees on support from the army, the church, the monarchists, the Carlists, the financial oligarchy, Opus Dei, and the Falange. The latter was only one pillar among many. During the Civil War the Falange had been an important force. Once the war was over, the level of political mobilization declined drastically and with it the influence and role of the regime's political party. For a generation old Falange types dreamed of the day when they would come into their own and the movement would become the system, but Franco was careful to insure that this would never happen. Temporary increases in Falange power were the products of Franco's manipulation and were designed to balance off increases in the power of other groups in order to enhance Franco's own. "Franco conceived of the FET," as Stanley Payne observed, "as the party of the state, but he never thought of his regime as a real party-state. The Falange, far from controlling the state, was no more than an instrument for holding the state together. Whenever its political pretensions threatened to disturb the internal equilibrium worked out by the Caudillo, he quickly cut the party down to size." [10] The party in Spain was a feeble rival to the army, the church, and even the monarchists, not to mention, of course, the Caudillo himself. As a result, when political consciousness and activity began to rise significantly in the late 1960s, the Franco regime was caught in a dilemma. If such political participation were channeled into the Falange it would disrupt the balance within the regime. But if it were not absorbed into some element of the regime, it would eventually threaten the system itself.

In the short run a reasonably stable and effective authoritarian system may exist with only a weak party. In the longer run, however, it would appear that the strength of an authoritarian regime will, in large measure, depend on the strength of its party. Significantly, when authoritarian regimes with weak parties confront crises, the party tends to reemerge as a more important actor. Nasser responded to three major crises—the need to consolidate power in 1954 after his victory over Naguib, the need to unify the Egyptian people behind him in 1957 after the Suez crisis, and the shift to a socialist policy in 1962—by attempting to create a mass political organization.[11] Somewhat similarly, crises in the evolution of the Franco regime were not infrequently followed by a new burst of life in the Falange. In both Egypt and Spain a crisis may generate new political interest and activity, and the authoritarian regime, which normally survives through popular indifference, suddenly discovers the need to have some organized and controlled structure through which otherwise potentially threatening political action may be channeled. Unless it can guarantee indefinitely a relatively low level of political mobilization, an authoritarian regime may have little choice but to organize and develop a political party as an essential structural support.

Social Bifurcation: Exclusionary and Revolutionary One-Party Systems

Party systems originate in the patterns of cleavage and alignment among social forces. Different relationships among social forces and different sequences in the development of cleavages among them give rise to different types of party systems. Once the systems take root, however, they develop a life of their own. The events and choices of one decade may thus have consequences for a century to come. The question here is: What type of social structure, what configuration of social forces furnishes fertile soil for the emergence of one-party systems? At one point in time, the southern United States, Nationalist China, and Soviet Russia were all one-party systems. Are there any social conditions that may serve to link together such otherwise disparate political forms?

Two theories are commonly made relating one-party systems to social structure. First, it has been argued, particularly by Africans, that party systems reflect the class structure of societies, and in a society where there are no pronounced differences among social and economic classes, there is no social basis for more than one party. Anglo-Saxon two-party systems, Julius Nyerere says, are "a reflection of the society" in which they developed and in which "there was a struggle between the 'haves' and the 'have-nots,' each of whom organized themselves into political parties—one party associated with wealth and the status quo, and the other with the masses of the people and change." The "idea of class," however, "is something entirely foreign to Africa," and a homogeneous society requires only one party. Or, as Madeira Keita put it, "there is no fundamental opposition among us" and hence why is "there any reason to remain divided and split into parties that fought one another?" [12]

A second rationale for one-party systems argues along just the opposite lines. Instead of the single party reflecting a homogeneous society, its justification is found in the need to counterbalance the fissiparous tendencies of a heterogeneous society. The source of the single-party system is in need rather than nature. It is, indeed, seen as an artificially created mechanism or institution to hold together a society which would otherwise fly apart. With some, if not wanton, disregard for logic, many African leaders have held this view simultaneously with the homogeneous society view, reconciling the two by the differences between class and tribe as social forces. Competitive elections, in Keita's words, oblige political leaders "to play on regionalism and what we have called internal racism." In this view, the political elite plays an innovative and autonomous role, using the party to correct the deficiencies in social structure and to impose unity on a divided society. "One-man one-party regimes," in Rupert Emerson's words, "are necessary in Africa precisely because the nations rest on such shaky foundations and are confronted by such urgent and monumental tasks of integration and development." [13]

Neither the homogeneous thesis nor the heterogeneous thesis is an adequate explanation of the emergence of viable one-party systems. The homogeneous argument is based on the Marxist premise of the direct correspondence between social class and political organization. It rationalizes the emergence of one-party systems in Africa with independence, but it hardly explains their collapse shortly thereafter. Nor does it explain the emergence of one-party systems in other societies that by no stretch of the imagination could be described as either homogeneous or consensual. Nor does it explain, assuming any validity to De Tocqueville and Louis Hartz, why the United States has two parties instead of one. The heterogeneous thesis, on the other hand, is more of a prescription than an explanation: it states why one-party systems should exist rather than why they do exist. It deals more with what are alleged to be the effects of one-party systems than with their causes. If the conditions that are otherwise required for the creation of strong one-party systems exist in Africa, the consequences of those systems for national integration may well be beneficial.

The social origins of one-party systems are to be found in neither homogeneity nor heterogeneity but in bifurcation. Societies in which the impact of modernization on traditional structures produces a complex pattern of cross-cutting cleavages typically evolve into pluralistic party systems. The democratic party systems of Western Europe, for instance, "reflect differences in the national histories of conflict and compromise" across the cleavage lines between center and periphery, state and church, land and industry. These multiple lines of cleavage gave rise to a variety of party systems, but in no case was there a sharp bifurcation of the society with all lines of social and political cleavage reinforcing each other. None of the countries of Western Europe, as Robert Dahl has observed, "closely approaches the pattern described . . . as full-scale political polarization, where sharp political, socioeconomic, and psychological dualisms all coincide." [14]

One-party systems, in contrast, tend to be the product of either the cumulation of cleavages leading to sharply differentiated groups within society or of the ascendancy in importance of one line of cleavage over all others. A one-party system is, in effect, the product of the efforts of a political elite to organize and to legitimate rule by one social force over another in a bifurcated society. The bifurcation may be between social-economic groups or between racial, religious, or ethnic ones. In the past in Europe, for instance, in those cases where intense religious, linguistic, and ethnic polarizations did develop, the result was either "a separation into different countries so that the cleavages became international rather than national, as with the separation of Ireland from Britain or Norway from Sweden" or "the creation of a one-party authoritarian or totalitarian states, as in the case of Fascist Italy, Nazi Germany, and Franco Spain." [15] One-party systems, in short, arise from pronounced bifurcations that cannot be resolved by secession and territorial separation. The breakdown of a traditional social order and the escalation of political participation in a revolutionary situation naturally lead to the polarization of social forces, to intense struggle and violence between revolutionary and counter-revolutionary groups, and so to the establishment of a one-party system. Such, at least, has been the outcome of twentieth century revolutions in Russia, Mexico, China, Turkey, Yugoslavia, Bolivia, Cuba, Albania, and Vietnam. On the other hand, one-party systems also tend to arise in situations of intense ethnic or religious division and conflict. Revolutionary societies and plural societies are the natural habitats of one-party systems. Each has a bifurcated social structure.

One-party systems have appeared in societies at almost all levels of social, economic, and cultural modernization. Yet the great bulk of one-party systems, and particularly those with the greatest staying power, come into existence in societies in the early and early-to-middle phases of modernization. There are good reasons for this. The sharp bifurcation of society, which is the prerequisite to the establishment of a viable one-party system, is most likely at that stage of change. The largest number of one-party systems are produced by social revolutions, and revolutions, in the grand sense, occur only at particular times in the process of modernization and development. The tendency to polarization comes with the breakdown of traditional society structures and the mobilization of new groups into politics. The single-party system is created by leaders of a more modern social force confronting a more backward social force. The constituency of the party becomes more highly mobilized, socially and politically, than the target of the party. That target, indeed, is usually either a traditional elite to be exterminated, a traditional mass to be modernized and assimilated into the party's constituency, or a less modernized, "inferior" race to be held in subjection.

One-party systems created in societies that have not reached the necessary level of development—and cleavage—are, as in tropical Africa, likely to be weak and fragile. Efforts to introduce a one-party system in a complex and differentiated society are also likely to fail. A strong one-party system cannot be created in a backward society because *all* organizations are weak and it cannot be created in a highly developed society because *other* organizations are strong. In the latter society, power is already so dispersed that its reconcentration into a strong single-party system requires a "permanent revolution" of accelerating mass mobilization against the existing complex social, economic, and political structures. The tensions created by such efforts are likely to drive the regime into expansionist foreign policies which, as with Nazi Germany, may undo it even if it is able temporarily to surmount the domestic problems. Dahomey in the 1960s was too backward to establish a stable one-party system; Germany in the 1930s was too advanced to do so.

A strong one-party system appears to meet certain functional needs for a society in the early to middle phases of modernization. In an era when modernization involves the expansion of political participation, the single party is the functional equivalent of the absolute monarchy of seventeenth century Europe. The absolute monarchy centralized power to promote modernizing reform, but it then proved incapable of expanding power to assimilate new groups into the political system. The one-party system, however, is unusual among political institutions in providing significant capacities for both the concentration and the expansion of power. It is thus peculiarly relevant in the later modernizing societies which, unlike the early modernizers, confront a highly telescoped modernizing process and hence face simultaneous needs to concentrate and to expand power.[16] Whether the one-party system also provides an effective means for dispersing power in the third phase of political modernization will be discussed in the latter part of this chapter.

TABLE 1-2   *Relative Capacities of Political Systems*

To Concentrate Power	To Expand Power	
	Low	High
Low	Praetorian system	Two-party system Multi-party system
High	Absolute monarchy Bureaucratic empire Military dictator "Modernizing autocracy"	One-party system Dominant-party system

Ideology plays a major role in the emergence of a one-party system, and ideology along with political mobilization and organizational discipline is a product of struggle and violence. The ideology of a one-party system identifies a chosen people or constituency, targets an enemy, proclaims the necessity for a struggle against the enemy, and holds forth the assurance of ultimate victory. Strong one-party systems come into being only when there is an explicit recognition of the difference between "we" and "they" and of the necessity for conflict between the two. The leaders of the party mobilize supporters from one social group for war against another group and its institutions. In its origins the one-party system must be intensely anti-capitalist, anti-traditionalist, anti-imperialist, anti-Semitic, or anti-something.

The creation of a one-party system redefines the scope of the political community. The basis of that community is the "chosen" social force, and other social groupings must either be assimilated to it or permanently excluded from the scope of politics. Legitimate political participation is limited to the members of the constituency social force, and the party which speaks for that social force monopolizes, at least in theory, legitimate political activity. Every one-party system comes into existence with a concept of the community of the chosen and of the party as the political expression of that community. The community may be in part a social fact pre-existing the creation of the one-party system, and it may also in part be the product of political action by the leaders of the party. If that community does not pre-exist the establishment of the party, the first task of the party is to bring it into existence.

The most appropriate theory of the one-party system is the Leninist theory. But it applies not just to the proletariat but to any dominant social force in a bifurcated society. "The dictatorship of the proletariat," in Lenin's words, "is the class struggle of the proletariat which has achieved victory and seized political power," and the dictatorship of the proletariat is "in essence, the dictatorship of its organized and class conscious minority," that is, the party.[17] The single-party system, moreover, is the product of struggle as well as cleavage. "The dictatorship of the proletariat is the fiercest, sharpest and most merciless war of the new class against its *more powerful* enemy, the bourgeoisie, whose resistance is increased *ten-fold* by its overthrow. . . . The dictatorship of the proletariat is a stubborn struggle —sanguinary and bloodless, violent and peaceful, military and economic, educational and administrative—against the forces and traditions of the old society." [18]

Experience suggests that the strength of a one-party system depends upon the duration and intensity of the struggle to acquire power or to consolidate power after taking over the government. "One party systems which emerge out of revolutions, consequently, are more stable than those produced by nationalist movements, and those produced by prolonged nationalist movements are more stable than those produced by movements whose struggle was brief and easy." [19] If a party that desires to establish a single-party system comes to power without a struggle, it must exacerbate social cleavages in order to consolidate its rule. The contrast between the communist regimes which took over government in the wake of the advancing Red Army and the African regimes which came to power in the wake of the retreating imperial powers is very marked. The communist regimes consciously and explicitly fired up social conflict in East Europe. During the late 1940s and early 1950s they were, in their terminology, in the phase of "people's democracy," which meant intensification of class struggle. Between 1948 and 1953, "the emphasis on class struggle made organized violence an integral characteristic of the people's democracy as a social system." [20] If the society was not polarized before the communists came to power, it certainly was afterward. The people's democracy phase, as another scholar has described it, was

> characterized as a process of highly intensified class struggle. Usually the fight was initiated shortly after the seizure of power. A newly installed Stalinist elite, unwilling to share authority or power with other political and economic factions, began to draw sharp distinctions between class friends and class enemies in the social structure of the people's democracy.[21]

This process of bifurcation gave the East European communist regimes a relatively secure hold on power.[22]

In the absence of pronounced bifurcation and struggle between social forces, efforts to establish one-party systems usually prove abortive. In many African states, the party came to power easily, without a major struggle, and consequently had no legacy of struggle upon which to live and no incentive to struggle by which to develop. Hence it withered in power. Political leaders only mobilize and organize masses when they have a real need—ideological or political—to do so. If they are already in power and have no ideological drive to split and to remake their societies, they have no reason to make the effort to develop and maintain a strong party. Indeed, after independence, African party leaders attempted to minimize social conflict, to emphasize national unity, and obscure or ignore the differences between the modernized elite and the traditional masses. The political elites became the victims of their own theories, all of which postulated, in one form or another, that "the CPP is Ghana, and Ghana is the CPP." In the event, their parties turned out to be as weak as their theories. They had no real function to perform. The one-party state, in Immanuel Wallerstein's phrase, became the no-party state, and its leaders were easily overthrown whenever military leaders had the inclination to do so.

In similar fashion an abortive one-party system may derive from the efforts of a regime in power to organize a party without dividing its society. As with Nasser and Ne Win, the effort is made to include everyone in the party. One indication of the strength of a one-party system, however, is the premium put on membership in the party. The more important the party is in the system, the more difficult it is to become a member and the more frequent are the purges expelling members. If party membership becomes universal, it becomes meaningless. Paradoxically, a competitive party system can be organized from the top down since the political elite has to create a strong party in order to stay in power. But a one-party system cannot be created this way because those in power lack the competitive impetus to develop and to maintain a strong party organization.

Successful one-party systems have their origins in bifurcation; the party is the means by which the leaders of one social force dominate the other social force. The party monopolizes or tries to monopolize all political activity. With respect to the cleavage and the subordinate social force, however, the political leaders can follow one or a combination of two policies. On the one hand, they can accept the bifurcation of the society and use the party as a means of mobilizing support from their constituency while at the same time suppressing or restricting political activity by the subordinate social force. In effect, the party maintains its monopoly over political participation by limiting the scope of political participation. Systems in which this policy is followed are *exclusionary one-party systems.* Alternatively, the party leadership can attempt to eradicate the bifurcation of society by shrinking society to correspond to its constituency through liquidation of the subordinate social force or by expanding its constituency to correspond to society by the assimilation of the subordinate social force. These systems are *revolutionary one-party systems.*

In one-party systems based on ethnic or racial bifurcation, the party usually follows an exclusionary policy. Exclusionary systems emerge out of competitive systems when a new ethnic or racial group appears to threaten a previously homogeneous society. In the oldest one-party system in the world, in Liberia, party competition prevailed until the 1880s. At that time, however, the settlers began to expand into the interior and to have more direct contacts with the indigenous Africans. As a result,

Americo-Liberians found themselves captives of the very situation they had created through expansion of the republic into the hostile tribal hinterland beyond the five coastal counties and the subsequent conflicts with the British and the French, who were coveting the same areas. It was the need for solidarity in meeting the twin threats to their supremacy, posed by tribal rebellion and foreign occupation, which convinced Americo-Liberians of the value of the single-party system.[23]

At about the same time the cousins of the Americo-Liberians in the New World were furnishing an impetus to the development of a one-party system in the American South roughly comparable to that which the tribal Africans were furnishing to the Americo-Liberians. In similar fashion, as South Africa increasingly became a bifurcated society between white and nonwhite, it also became more of a one-party system. With increasing emphasis on the need for common action by whites against the domestic and foreign foe, the support for the United Party dwindled away, and the Nationalists acquired an overwhelming predominance in the national and provincial legislatures. In 1965 the Minister of Justice, B. J. Vorster, suggested that the country would become a one-party state, and a cautious scholar the same year observed that South Africa was a "a two-party system, tending towards a one-party system, within an ethnic oligarchy or pigmentocracy." [24] Tribal and religious dualities similarly provide a basis for some single party systems in West Africa. In Northern Ireland religion is the source of bifurcation: the Ulster Unionists, the overwhelmingly dominant party, "unite Protestants, including many industrial workers who might otherwise be drawn to the Labour party, in opposition to the minority of Catholics favoring ties to Eire rather than Britain." [25]

Exclusionary systems do not necessarily, however, rest on a racial or religious base. In effect, the Republican People's Party in Turkey was such a system during the 1920s and 1930s: political participation was effectively limited to the westernized, urban classes and the mass of the traditional peasantry were excluded from power. "It is the essence of the Ataturk Revolution," Frederick Frey has observed, "that it *exploited* the communications bifurcation existing in Turkish society rather than lamenting it or immediately attacking it, as a number of other nationalist movements have done." During the same years, the Kuomintang followed a somewhat similar policy with respect to the Chinese peasantry, and after its removal to Taiwan a somewhat looser exclusionary policy was followed with respect to the bifurcation between mainlanders and islanders. In Colombia the bi-party agreement to alternate the presidency and to divide parliamentary seats was a less highly developed mechanism designed to achieve, however, basically the same purpose of excluding the lower classes from political power.[26]

The leadership of an exclusionary single party is thus dedicated to the indefinite maintenance of a bifurcated society and the indefinite exclusion of the subordinate group from politics. The leadership of a revolutionary single party, in contrast, is dedicated to the rapid end of the bifurcation of society through the elimination or conversion of the opposing social force. In most cases the constituency social force of a revolutionary one-party system is defined in class, occupational, or other economic terms. One notable case of a revolutionary one-party system which attempted to define an ethnic base is Nazi Germany. Indeed, it was precisely this combination of racial constituency plus revolutionary goals which was responsible for its uniquely frightening characteristics and which led straight to its genocidal policies.

TABLE 1-3 *Bifurcation and One-Party Systems*

Basis of Bifurcation	Policies Toward Bifurcation	
	Exclusionary	Revolutionary
Ethnic-Religious	Ulster	Nazi Germany
	Liberia	
Economic	Kemalist Turkey	Communist regimes
	Nationalist China	Mexico

More usually, the constituency social force in a revolutionary one-party system is defined in economic terms, and its political leadership attempts to induce, persuade, or coerce "nationalist bourgeoisie" or "peasantry" to adopt the proper "proletarian" code of behavior. It is a mobilizing, proselytizing movement dedicated to the creation of a society of equals—or a classless society—which will forever end social cleavage. Obviously it never achieves its goal completely, but obviously also revolutionary single-party systems do bring into existence societies in which the ideal is equality and in which the fact is far greater homogeneity and equality than ever existed in the pre-one-party society.

From Monopoly to Competition: The Democratization of Exclusionary One-Party Systems

In an exclusionary system a single significant political organization representing the interests of the dominant social force monopolizes power and the subordinate social force is indefinitely excluded from political roles. The system is a modern version of a two-class or two-caste society. The aristocracy of birth or wealth, however, is formalized and organized through a party structure. Modern forms of political organization are used to maintain a non-modern pattern of society. Societies with more modern social structures, in contrast, typically have either revolutionary one-party systems or competitive party systems. The maintenance of an exclusionary one-party system depends on: (1) a sympathetic or indifferent international environment that does not challenge the legitimacy of the system; (2) a significant difference in political consciousness and political mobilization between the constituency and excluded social forces; and (3) a relatively high degree of unity within the political elite of the constituency social force.

Social and economic modernization, in the long run, undermines these conditions. To the extent that the society is open to influence from the world community, the two-class system will gradually lose its legitimacy. A modern society implies at least formal equality among citizens. The maintenance of a bifurcated social system increasingly loses support among the elite of the system and the system itself becomes open to sanctions and pressures from the more modern societies with which it becomes involved. At this point the society may withdraw from the international community and, like South Africa, attempt to return to a modern version of the "splendid isolation" by which Sparta maintained its two-class system. Or, if isolation is impossible, the system may have to adapt to the political, moral, and ideological pressures brought to bear on it from outside. In 1945 the Turks felt the need to progress toward a more democratic politics in order to conform to the model of the victorious western powers in World War II and to be accepted into the United Nations. Two years later the need for U.S. military and economic assistance reinforced these tendencies. As Adnan Menderes, the future leader of the Democratic Party, remarked in 1946:

> The difficulties encountered during the war years uncovered and showed the weak points created by the one-party system in the structure of the country. The hope in the miracles of one-party system vanished, as the one-party system countries were defeated everywhere. Thus, the one-party mentality was destroyed in the turmoil and fire of the second World War. No country can remain unaffected by the great international events and the contemporary dominating international currents. This influence was felt in our country too.[27]

In similar fashion, the independence of other African countries impelled President Tubman to remove the formal distinctions between Americo-Liberians and natives, and the economic and social incorporation of the South into the American national community brought increasing pressures against its racial bifurcation and single-party systems.

Modernization of the society also tends to produce changes in the excluded social force, such as increasing literacy, urbanization, and education, which lead to increased political consciousness and mobilization. Economic and social change also tends to diversify the social and political elite, to introduce potentially disruptive antagonisms within the single party and the constituency social force, and eventually to produce new, more complex lines of cleavage cutting across the previously dominant bifurcation.

The political leadership of an exclusionary system can react to these challenges in one or a combination of three ways. It can attempt to slow down social and economic change and to channel it in ways that will minimize conflict within the existing elite and hamper the development of political consciousness by the excluded social force. In Liberia, for instance, government policy encouraging foreign investment tended and in part was designed to prevent the emergence of a Liberian entrepreneurial elite controlling relatively autonomous sources of economic power. For many years, in the American South, educational policies tended to slow down the development of higher economic and political aspirations on the part of Negroes. Secondly, the political leaders can resort to repression to contain elite disunity and mass dissatisfaction on the part of the excluded social force. Increasing use of police, population control measures, internal passports, and informer systems among the excluded social force mark the gradual evolution of the one-party system into a full-scale garrison-police state. More repression of the excluded social force may also require more participation by the constituency social force in the control functions. The constituency population is armed and organized into militia and self-defense units. As the system becomes increasingly authoritarian with respect to one social force, it becomes increasingly populistic with respect to the other. Through these means the political elite may well be able to postpone —perhaps indefinitely—the breakdown of the political system that guarantees its authority. It will, however, always remain vulnerable to the potential mobilization of the excluded social force by an effective counterelite, and if this social force is equal in size to or larger than the constituency social force, such mobilization can well destroy the system through either secession or revolution. The Chinese Communists, capitalizing on long-standing peasant grievances and the politicizing impact of the Japanese occupation, successfully mobilized the peasants and overthrew the exclusionary Nationalist regime in mainland China.

A third course for the political leadership of an exclusionary one-party system is to accept both modernization and its political consequences (elite disunity and excluded social force mobilization) and to attempt to adapt their political system to these developments. One segment of the political elite, for instance, may downgrade the importance of the existing bifurcation and appeal to the previously excluded social force for support in its struggle with the other segments of the political elite. Conceivably, this mobilization could take place within the established single-party and both constituency social force and previously excluded social force could articulate their interests through the same political framework. In fact, however, this does not happen. The party system presupposes bifurcation. The dissident segment of the political elite that appeals to the excluded social force usually forms a new political vehicle for that purpose. Alternatively and less frequently, the dominant leadership group in the established party takes the lead in appealing to the excluded force and the dissident segment of the political elite forms a new political organization based on the previously dominant social force. Or, conceivably, two or more parties come into existence that appeal along new lines of cleavage to elements of both the previous constituency and excluded social forces. A portion of the previously dominant political elite may thus preserve its authority at the expense of the political institutions with which it was once identified. But the shift is still made from a single-party system to a competitive-party system.

The elite within an exclusionary system is often preeminently a political elite. Its power derives from its control over the governmental and party apparatus; its members see politics as the preferable and natural career for themselves. In Turkey during the 1920s and 1930s the political system was dominated by military officers, bureaucrats, and others who generally disdained private careers and carried over into republican Turkey many of the identifications characteristic of the Ottoman bureaucracy. In Liberia the decline of commercial enterprise on the part of the Americo-Liberians in the latter part of the nineteenth century coincided with the emergence of the single-party system; "government, politics and law became the only respectable ways of getting a living, and so they have remained until very recently." [28] In the American South traditionally there was a similar preference for legal and governmental skills compared to commercial and industrial ones. On Taiwan the mainlanders who dominated the higher echelons of the Kuomintang played little role in the tremendous expansion of the private economic sector in the 1950s and 1960s.

In all these cases not only did the elite of the constituency social force monopolize political leadership positions, but, like Spartans, they also tended to eschew other career opportunities. To the extent that members of this elite did go into business enterprises, they were typically enterprises closely associated with the government and the capital for them typically came, legally or illegally, from the public treasury. The principal threat to the maintenance of this type of system comes from the diversification of the elite resulting from the rise of new groups controlling autonomous sources of economic power, that is, from the development of an independently wealthy business and industrial middle class. In the Ottoman Empire, for instance, commercial activities had been the preserve of Greeks, Armenians, and other minorities. The republic eliminated these groups by migration or massacre, and it was almost a generation before their places were taken by new Turkish entrepreneurs. These years "saw the rise for the first time in history of a Turkish business class." [29] Many members of this class emerged out of politics, using political connections as stepping stones to economic independence. Others made their way purely through the economic realm and only entered politics after achieving economic success. In any event, businessmen of both types played leading roles in the events of the mid-1940s, which transformed Turkey from a single to a multi-party system.

The shift to a competitive party system in Turkey in 1945 and 1946 was led by members of the existing political elite, representing the interests of middle-class business and entrepreneurial groups who were unhappy with the economic policies of the Republican Peoples Party (RPP) government.

"These new Turkish business men and managers," as one scholar has noted, "were self-confident, self-reliant, and ambitious; they were becoming very resentful of the controls and restrictions imposed upon them by what they had begun to regard as the dead hand of officialdom. The civil servant was falling from the dizzy eminence that he once occupied in the Turkish social hierarchy. . . . The appearance of a new and flourishing commercial class was radically changing the political balance of forces in the country, and affecting even her traditional social ethos."[30] The first opposition party was founded in July, 1945 by an extremely wealthy Istanbul industrialist. In January, 1946 it was displaced as the leading opposition by the Democratic Party founded by four leading political figures of the Republican Peoples Party. Significantly, the principal leader in the formation of the Democratic Party in 1945 was Celal Bayar, a bureaucrat turned banker; the dominant figure in its successor party, the Justice Party, in the 1960s was Suleyman Demirel, a bureaucrat turned businessman. The Democratic Party endorsed five of the six principles of Kemalism, but attacked the policy of etatism and advocated a shift toward a more liberal reliance on private enterprise.[31]

The emergence in Turkey of an entrepreneurial middle class and of a segment of the political elite which identified with that class confronted the leadership of the RPP with three possible choices. They could, conceivably, adopt a policy of repression, using the power of the state to confiscate or reduce the autonomous centers of economic wealth and to purge and imprison the dissident political leaders. Such a course, however, would have had harmful effects on economic development and also would clearly have injured Turkey's somewhat probationary standing in the post-war Allied-dominated international community. Alternatively, the RPP leaders could have attempted to contain this emerging social force and the dissident political leadership within the framework of the dominant party. This, however, would have required some major changes in the thrust of government policy and, more importantly, a sharing of power and office with the dissident leadership (one of whom, Bayar, was a former premier and a potential replacement of Inonu as President). From the viewpoint of the RPP leadership, a third course was clearly preferable: respond to international pressure and domestic development by permitting the dissident elements to organize one or more opposition parties. Such a course would involve some costs in terms of political criticism and opposition, but the position of the RPP was so overwhelmingly dominant it was hard to conceive of it being dislodged from power.

If this was the calculation, it was wrong. The events of 1946–1950 demonstrated the extent to which the dynamics of competition can transform a political system. The Democratic Party attracted almost all those elements who for two decades had accumulated grievances against the RPP. The gradual penetration of communications media into the countryside in the 1930s and 1940s made it possible for the new party to break down the pre-

viously existing bifurcation between urban elite and rural peasantry. Combining appeals to the traditional religious values and to the concrete economic interests of the farmer, the Democratic Party was able to mobilize the peasantry into politics as a massive voting bloc on its side.

Turkey is the most clear-cut instance of the shift from an exclusionary one-party system to a competitive system. In somewhat more complex fashion, however, the same processes of external pressure, elite diversification, and social mobilization have been responsible for the gradual breakdown of the one-party systems in the American South. In these cases, too, a crucial role has been played by the emergence of an indigenous business and industrial elite, which is more concerned with promoting economic growth than with preserving the racial status quo and which consequently does not hesitate to follow its economic predilections and identify itself with the Republican Party. In Taiwan in the 1960s the development of a prosperous islander middle class posed problems of adaptation for the Kuomintang (KMT) leadership comparable to those which confronted Turkey in the 1940s. The KMT faced a rising opposition vote in the urban areas; in 1964 it elected mayors in only two of the five major cities on the island. Like the RPP leadership, that of the KMT had the choice of suppressing this opposition, assimilating it into the KMT, or permitting it to continue to develop. In the 1960s it did in some measure it a little of all three. Perhaps most significantly, unlike the RPP, it made some efforts to incorporate the new groups into the party. In the fall of 1968 the KMT leadership announced a policy of achieving greater separation between party and government and appointed prominent businessmen to head the party in the two main cities on the island.[32]

In Liberia, in contrast, the political leadership adopted policies designed to maintain the existing system. After his first election to the presidency in 1944, Tubman announced a "unification" policy that would abolish the previous distinctions between Americo-Liberians and natives. Some changes were, indeed, made in the representation of the natives in the legislature, in reducing compulsory labor and the confiscation of tribal lands, and in providing better educational and welfare facilities. These measures were, in large part, required by the growth of African nationalism in the rest of West Africa and, as a result, it no longer became acceptable "in Liberia publicly to make distinctions between civilized and uncivilized elements of the population or, indeed, to use the traditional designations of Americo-Liberians and Natives." The changes, however, did not affect fundamentals. "The fiction of equality receives official sanction; but in matters of structure and substance, it remains fiction."[33] While acquiescing in the rhetoric of equality between constituency and excluded social groups, the government also pursued economic policies designed to minimize diversification among the elite. Tubman's so-called open door policy with respect to foreign investment maintained a distinction between economic and political power. Foreigners were allowed to invest but were not allowed to

become citizens or to own land. Foreign investment, in turn, precluded Liberians themselves from amassing fortunes except through government channels. Economic neocolonialism, in a sense, thus underwrote the exclusionary political system. The political elite remained united and secure in its monopoly of power. For the Americo-Liberians, "it is the ethic of Mississippi that most nearly characterizes their outlook: to retain power in traditional fashion and to keep the Natives in their place." [34]

From Revolution to Institution: The Emergence of Established One-Party Systems

In the exclusionary one-party system the breakdown of the bifurcation of society means the breakdown of the system. Conversely, if the party system changes, the bifurcation is also undermined. One is the corollary of the other. It would be wrong, however, to generalize this pattern of evolution to revolutionary systems. Exclusionary one-party systems change when they fail; revolutionary one-party systems change when they succeed. In both cases, the end of the bifurcation undermines the basis of the system. but in the revolutionary system the end of bifurcation is the goal of the system. The result is change but a different pattern of change from that which characterizes the exclusionary systems. The end of the bifurcation leads not to the emergence of a pluralistic party system but instead to what may be termed an established one-party system. The system is adapted to changed circumstances, much as ruling monarchies eventually became constitutional ones or the aristocratic two-party system of late eighteenth century England eventually evolved into the mass-party system of the twentieth century. The established one-party system is also the descendant of the revolutionary one-party system, but it is also a new type of system with different characteristics and must be judged by different criteria. It reflects the needs of a relatively consensual society rather than those of a sharply divided one.

The revolutionary one-party system is a familiar phenomenon to social scientists. Its social dynamism, autocratic and charismatic leadership, disciplined party, highly developed ideology, stress on propaganda and mass mobilization combined with coercion and terror, and its commitment to the destruction of existing institutions have been fully delineated in, among others, the Friedrich-Brzezinski model of totalitarianism and the Tucker model of the movement-regime.[35] Both models offer appropriate standards by which to analyze revolutionary one-party systems. They are inappropriate to the analysis of exclusionary one-party systems, a limitation which Friedrich-Brzezinski recognize but Tucker does not. More significantly, both models are inappropriate for the analysis of one-party systems that have evolved from the revolutionary phase reflecting the bifurcation of society to the post-revolutionary phase based on a high degree of homogeneity in society. Friedrich-Brzezinski argue that the future of totalitarian re-

gimes is ''unclear,'' although some ''internal transformation'' is possible and ''an increasing recognition of law and legal restraints'' could provide the way to greater stability. Tucker says that movement-regimes may lose their ''revolutionary momentum eventually'' and become what he terms ''extinct' movement-regimes,''—surely a classic case of semantically duck-ing the issue, since his phrase implies that the movement-regime is dead, but gives no indication of what may have taken its place.

Lack of a model of a post-revolutionary one-party system encourages the tendency to judge such systems by the standards of their predecessors. One-party systems are evaluated by their deviations from the revolutionary, totalitarian, or movement-regime model, and when they do deviate, as they must, are judged to be verging on ''degeneration'' or ''extinction.'' In effect, the achievements of the child are judged by the standards of the parent. This may be appropriate if the child attempts to duplicate the achievements of the parents. But if the child responds to different needs and has different goals—as in the Buddenbrooks-Rostow dynamics, he is almost certain to have—then his performance must be analyzed and evaluated in terms of a different model. Such a model of an ''established one-party system'' may differ from the revolutionary one-party system as much as the latter dif-fered from the traditional Tsarist, Porfirian, Manchu, or colonial autocracy which it succeeded.

The evolution of a revolutionary one-party system into an established one-party system goes through three phases, which may be usefully labeled *transformation, consolidation,* and *adaptation.* These phases are analyti-cally distinct. They may overlap in practice, but a minimum sequence is maintained in that a revolutionary one-party system enters the transforma-tion phase before it enters the other two, and it enters the consolidation phase before it begins the process of adaptation. In each phase the party and its political leadership confront the consequences of their successes in the earlier phase. They may not deal successfully with those consequences; they may, indeed, like the leadership of China in the 1960s, attempt to stop the transition from one phase to another. But, in general, there are no inherent reasons why a revolutionary one-party system cannot evolve into an established one-party system.

Revolutionary one-party systems usually achieve in their early phases a fairly high level of organizational and institutional development, combining mass participation and a strong party organization, which creates the possi-bility of adapting the system to changing requirements of its environment. In this respect, a striking difference exists between a strong, revolutionary one-party system and a weak, abortive one-party system. In Franco Spain, for instance, even those most active in the political system had little hope for the adaptation of the system from within. Consequently, those who wished to change the system withdrew from the system. ''I no longer saw hope of democratic evolution,'' said one former cabinet minister explain-ing why he left the government.[36] The expectations in Spain during the

last years of the Franco regime were that change would be brought about after the death of Franco by the emergence of new political leaders and forces who had not been identified with the system. In East Europe, in contrast, in the 1960s it became clear that modifications of the system could take place and were taking place as a result of the initiative of key participants within the system. Significant economic reforms were introduced in many East European communist states; important adaptations of political institutions took place in Yugoslavia and, briefly, in Czechoslovakia; the displacement of Novotny by Dubcek demonstrated that an important change in leadership could be mediated through the institutional processes of a one-party regime. In East Europe, apparently, change of the political system could come from within the system; in Spain, it would come from outside the system.

Transformation

The conquest of formal authority by the revolutionary party inaugurates a phase in which the principal aim is the transformation of society: the destruction of the old order and its replacement by new political institutions and social patterns appropriate for a homogeneous rather than a bifurcated society. The nature and success of these efforts, in large part, depend on the level of social and political development achieved in the pre-revolutionary society. In a highly complex society like the Germany of the 1930s, "Gleichschaltung" will necessarily be violent and extreme and even then not entirely successful. In a less developed society, the revolutionary transformation may be much more all encompassing.

The familiar revolutionary, movement-regime, and totalitarian models of one-party systems stress the monistic tendencies toward the atomization of society and the subordination of all groups to party control. In the transformation phase of a revolutionary one-party system these tendencies dominate. The survival of the system may well depend upon the ability of the party to assert itself against fissiparous tendencies of autonomous interest groups. In Bolivia, for instance, the worker and peasant organizations were created independent of the party and maintained substantial autonomy through the period of MNR rule. They were often able to defy the government, and the independence of the miners was, indeed, one factor leading to the overthrow of the MNR regime in 1964. This experience may be contrasted with that of the Neo-Destour. In Tunisia the business and farmer organizations were created by the party and in large part led by party workers whose loyalties were first to the party and then to their organized group. The labor federation, on the other hand, had developed with a high degree of autonomy from the party but was effectively brought within the party after the struggle between Bourguiba and Ben Salah in 1956. Similar assertions of the control of the party over interest associations have taken place in most of the one-party states of tropical Africa.[37]

The strongest resistance against the process usually comes from the most entrenched conservative institutions, of which the church is most important. Where the Catholic church has existed for an extended period of time, as in Poland and Mexico, the revolutionary party may well have to settle for accommodation with it rather than elimination of it.

In the transformation phase the party organization is the leading force for innovation and change. In its efforts to destroy and to reconstruct, it inevitably clashes with the state bureaucracy inherited from the previous regime. In Russia, for instance, the bifurcation of the society was, in some measure, reflected in a bifurcation between party and bureaucracy. The bureaucracy was essentially a part of the old order, and the party had to develop an elaborate system of political commissars and other forms of control to guard against its potentially anti-Soviet actions. Subsequently the party brought into existence new schools and other institutions to create Soviet military officers, managers, experts, and bureaucrats. The bifurcation between party and bureaucracy was eased, and in due course the extreme forms of party control over the bureaucracy could be moderated or abandoned. Throughout these phases, however, the party was the generator of change and the bureaucracy the defender of continuity.

The struggle with the old order and the effective destruction of its institutions typically require the concentration of revolutionary authority in a single autocratic leader. Some political orders are the work of many men, but one-party systems seem to be more the work of one man than other types of systems. Lenin, Mao, Hitler, Mussolini, Tito, Paz Estenssoro, Castro, Bourguiba, Nkrumah, Toure, Nyerere, created their parties, and for a while, system, party, and man tended to be identified one with another. The party is the organizational instrument of the leader; the leader is the charismatic embodiment of the party. The core of the party is the lieutenants of the leader, and the identity of interest between party and leader in the conquest of power and the destruction of the old order is virtually complete. The disappearance of the traditional sources of authority creates the opportunity and the need for charismatic leadership to fill the vacuum.

For similar reasons ideology also plays a legitimating role during the revolutionary phase. It defines the goal, identifies the enemy, and justifies the struggle. It furnishes a plan to guide the intellectual leadership of the party and a means of mobilizing popular support and participation in the efforts to destroy the old political institutions and old social structure.

Consolidation

The reconstitution of society is thus guided by and legitimated by an ideology and a leader. Initially, both of these serve the ends of the party. Once the old order, however, has been substantially destroyed and the social basis laid for a new one, both ideological commitment and charismatic leadership tend to become dysfunctional to the maintenance of the new system. The consolidation of that system requires the establishment of the supremacy of the party as the source of legitimacy and the source of power against the leader and the ideology which earlier played indispensable roles in the liquidation of the old order.

Ideology is often identified as necessarily playing a major role in one-party systems. In actuality, of course, ideology is linked not to any particular form of organization but rather to the process of change. In periods of intense, rapid, and violent change and conflict, ideology naturally plays an important role. Once the society settles down, the need for ideology declines, and the ideology itself begins to "erode." In a bifurcated society, ideology is essential; in a consensual society, it is superfluous. It is no longer required to legitimate the system, and, indeed, a stress on ideology and its role may threaten the existence of the system.

Unless the party leadership makes strenuous efforts to prevent it, ideology tends to become less important and less relevant in revolutionary one-party systems. In East Europe, as H. Gordon Skilling observes, there has been "a diminution of faith in the official theory despite persistent efforts to impose it on the minds of men." Ideology, as another scholar has put it, is "gradually being replaced by pragmatism." In the Soviet Union, similar trends were observed in the 1950s and 1960s. "Marxist-Leninist doctrine for some time," it was argued in 1966, "has had little effect on the attitudes and feelings of the people of the U.S.S.R. . . . Most party members are mere careerists who use Marxist doctrine only as a shield to defend their own actions and as a sword against their rivals." [38] Party leaders often respond to the decline in ideology by promoting greater efforts by their propaganda and agitation departments to inculcate new generations in the old faith. The result is self-defeating, as the concepts and slogans that play useful roles in the transformation of society are found to have little relevance to the consolidation of that society. "What do these phrases mean?" as one young activist at Moscow State University asked the head of the CPSU's ideological commission. "If they mean something, please tell us; if they don't mean anything, why do you keep on saying them?" [39]

The key question concerns the effects of ideological erosion on the system. The argument here is that the decline of ideology in one-party systems is a sign not of decay but of stability—an indicator not of the weakness but of the strength of the regime. Historically ideology is clearly linked to conflict and cleavage. In modern societies, indeed, any serious cleavage takes on ideological overtones. The decline of ideology consequently would be impossible if the one-party were threatened by serious social tensions. It may, indeed, become increasingly in the interests of the regime to promote this decline. The erosion of ideology, in short, goes hand in hand with the acceptance, stability, and long-term vitality of the system.

The relation between ideological emphasis and institutional weakness is clearly visible in non-communist one-party systems. In the mid-1960s the weaker, the more tentative, the more fragile the system, the greater the emphasis the leaders of the system placed on ideology. The efforts to formulate and propagate an ideology on the part of people like Nkrumah, Sukarno, Toure, Nyerere, and others varied more or less directly with the instability of their systems. In contrast, in the two most firmly established non-communist one-party systems, those of Mexico and Tunisia, ideology received much less attention. In Mexico the myths and symbols of the Revolution were regularly invoked by all political groupings to justify their actions, but no one seriously claimed that the Revolution had an ideology or tried to develop one. In Tunisia, Bourguibism was the local label for pragmatism and a synonym for gradualism. The more stable communist one-party systems may also be those in which ideology receives the shortest shrift. In the 1960s Yugoslavia was probably the least ideological of the communist states. Yet was it not also probably the most stable? Renewed stress on ideology, as in China, in contrast, is usually a portent of social tension and political conflict.

Except in the special, limited sense in which Karl Mannheim used the term, ideology almost always implies a critique of the existing situation and of existing institutions. A new system of political institutions may well be legitimated in ideological terms. In due course, however, this becomes increasingly difficult. Existing institutions may be rationalized and defended in terms of a conservative ideology, but they cannot be effectively justified by an "ideational" ideology, whether socialist, Marxist, or liberal. The justification of the political system comes increasingly to rest on its institutional rather than its ideological characteristics. Indeed, as Carl Beck suggests, as with the American system, sheer "historical givenness" may well become the most persuasive legitimation of the system.[40]

At some point in the consolidation of a one-party system, ideology ceases to be a way of achieving consensus and instead becomes a threat to consensus. In Poland in the late 1960s, for instance, various ideological groups played significant roles. These included orthodox Marxist-Leninist-Gomulkaists, Stalinists, Maoists, "liberal" Marxists, non-Marxist socialists, and the non-Marxist Catholics of the Znak group. On the ideological level, these groups divided sharply and even profoundly. None of them, however, challenged the legitimacy of existing Polish political and economic institutions. The Catholic intellectuals of Znak, for instance, "accept the existing political and social system and the foreign and domestic policies of the regime," and they played active roles in the Sejm and the State Council. Yet they also "reject Marxism, proclaim openly their adherence to a Catholic world view, and defend their religious interests in legislative matters." In the words of one of their leaders, "Despite differences in world outlook between Catholics and Marxists, we desire within the framework of the socialist system to co-operate in everything which is good, moral and creative for the individual and the community, in all which can lift the social masses to a higher level of economic, cultural and moral life." [41] In such a situation, the interests of the regime are to minimize its ideological rationale, which would clearly alienate erstwhile supporters on both left and right, and instead to stress its justification in the realities of the situation and in the operating effectiveness of its institutions. The regime gains by down-playing its own ideology as well as everyone else's. Similarly, in Mexico, the leaders of the PRI have little interest in maintaining ideological purity if this means antagonizing foreign and domestic business interests with which they must do business. Support for the regime—or at least acceptance of the regime—is broader than acceptance of the theoretical rationale behind it. Just as in the United States or other western societies, many individuals and groups with varying ideological beliefs—explicit and unarticulated—may accept the existing system. In this sense, Kolakowski was undoubtedly right when he argued that in Poland "the word 'Marxist' no longer means a person who recognizes a definite, meaningful view of the world, but a person of a definite intellectual make-up who is distinguished by his readiness to recognize the views established institutionally." [42]

The relationship between leader and party changes in a similar way. In the initial struggle for power, the interests of the party and leader are virtually identical. The movement or party is an extension of the leader. This identity of interest continues at least for a while after the leader and party have acquired the formal attributes of power. The party is then the means by which the leader extends his control over existing social and governmental institutions or attacks and destroys those institutions. A parallel identity of interest between party organization and aspiring leader may also occur during succession struggles within the one-party system. In the Soviet case Stalin and Khrushchev identified their interests with those of the party *apparat* and their conquest of power also represented a victory for the party organization against its personal and institutional rivals.

Once the leader and party are securely in power, however, their interests begin to diverge. The leader wishes to maximize his own power, which means that he must avoid becoming the prisoner of any particular institution or group. Unlike the president or premier in a constitutional system, he does not have any institutional basis of authority. He may hold many offices or none at all, but his power clearly is personal, not institutional. He thus necessarily opposes the development of institutions that could restrain his power. He tries to reduce the authority of the party and to balance it off against the army, the bureaucracy, the police, mass organizations, and other groups. The leader comes to see the party as more and more of a challenge to his personal authority as leader.

Eventually, the leader goes beyond his efforts to subordinate the party by balancing it with external checks and attempts to weaken and perhaps even to destroy the party internally. At this point, the leader explicitly articulates the contrast between his personal, charismatic authority, and the routinized, bureaucratic authority embodied in the party. The leader typically attempts to revive the enthusiasm, the dynamism, the egalitarianism, and primitive austerity that characterized the movement in its earliest phases. Literally and symbolically, Mao returns to Yenan, Castro to the Sierra Maestra, Ben Gurion to the Negev, and Nyerere to the bush. In Tanganyika alone, however, was this effort to restore revolutionary dynamism linked to efforts to strengthen the party. Elsewhere, the drive to "keep the revolution going" was a drive to expand popular mobilization and to reduce party institutionalization, in short, to undermine the stability of the one-party system. In Cuba, Castro continuously resisted Soviet urgings that he strengthen and institutionalize the party organization; he wanted to keep it at a low level of institutionalization. In China, the relatively high level of institutionalization achieved by the Chinese Communist Party required Mao to resort to the frenzied activities of the Cultural Revolution to reduce the authority of party from both within and without.

The extent to which the party consolidates its authority vis-à-vis the leader can be measured in terms of three criteria. One is the extent to which the party monopolizes access to the top leadership position. Where the authority of the party is strong the top leader will be a product of the party and will be a party careerist, having worked his way up through the ranks of the party organization. This is the situation in both Mexico and the Soviet Union. Where party authority was weak, the top leader may be a party member, but he may, more importantly, be a product of the military or civil bureaucracies or of a populist mass movement not dominated by the party. A second criterion of party strength vis-à-vis the leader is the extent to which the party monopolizes the process by which the top leader is chosen. If military, religious, labor, or other groups or leaders play a key role in the selection of the top leader for the political system, clearly the authority of the party is weak vis-à-vis that leader (and those other groups). In this sense, as Merle Fainsod has suggested, the extent to which the removal of Khrushchev and the emergence of his successors was handled entirely within the CPSU structure was an indication of the strength of the party in the 1960s as compared to its weaker position in the 1950s when the secret police, managers, and army played roles in the post-Stalin succession struggle.[43] Finally, the authority of the party is enhanced to the extent that the formal office which the leader occupies is a party office. If the top leader is President of the Republic, the Osagyefo, Der Fuehrer, or Il Duce, he has claims to authority transcending those which he derives from the party.

Perhaps the gravest threat to stability in a one-party system is the problem of succession. In a non-party, traditional monarchy, succession was institutionalized through heredity. In competitive party systems, succession is institutionalized within the system by the alternation of parties in office and within the parties by their own rules and procedures for selecting officers and candidates. In a one-party system succession has to take place within the party and the way in which succession is arranged goes directly to the heart of the problem of the relationship between the leader and the party. With one exception all one-party systems are the product of the twentieth century and most the product of the mid-twentieth century. In almost all systems—communist and non-communist—the founding leader remains in office until he dies. The only clear-cut exceptions to this rule are the two Latin American one-party systems in Mexico and Bolivia and two of the East European systems, Poland and Hungary, where, however, the founding leader was less important than in other systems because of the foreign influences responsible for bringing it into being. In all other one-party systems the founding leader either died in office or was in office in 1968. The creation of a succession system, consequently, normally has to wait until the death of the leader, and normally, of course, the leader has little interest in attempting to develop a means for providing a successor.

In most political systems, unlike the American system, the death of the top leader produces a succession struggle. A political system, however, which allows the tenure of its top leaders to be determined by health and accident is not a particularly highly developed one. Presumably more adaptable and complex systems have ways of changing leaders under other circumstances and through other means. The development of such techniques is a major turning point in the consolidation of one-party systems. The means of regularizing and providing for NDIO (non-death-in-office) successions differ significantly for those one-party systems where electoral competition retains some reality and for the communist systems where it does not. In Mexico and Bolivia (as in Liberia) the presidential term was set at four to six years, and in all three countries constitution or custom limited tenure to one or two terms. This pattern was broken in Liberia after 1943 when Tubman was regularly reelected to office; Paz Estenssoro also broke it in Bolivia in 1964, thereby contributing to the events which led to the overthrow of him and his party. In Mexico, on the other hand, six NDIO successions occurred on schedule between 1934 and 1968. In all three countries the choice of a successor for the incumbent president was made through the party machinery. In Liberia generally and in Bolivia open struggles for the succession were resolved in the party's convention. In Mexico the process of *auscultación* was more closed and oligarchical with the incumbent president in effect playing the major role in the selection of his successor in consultation with former presidents and the other principal leaders of the party.

In communist one-party systems the NDIO problem is more difficult to resolve since the position of first secretary or general secretary carries no fixed term of office. As of 1968 communist one-party systems had undergone fourteen successions, eight of which were NDIO successions. One was the removal of Khrushchev. The other seven communist NDIO successions occurred in the East European communist states. Intervention by the Soviet Union, however, played a decisive role in four of these successions (Poland, 1948; Czechoslovakia, 1951; Hungary, July and October 1956); and a partial role in one of them (Bulgaria, 1954). Only the voluntary replacement of Ochab by Gomulka in Poland in 1956 and the involuntary replacement of Novotny by Dubcek in Czechoslovakia in 1968 were NDIO successions determined almost entirely by in-system influences. In 1968 communist systems were thus still evolving procedures for the peaceful removal of first secretaries. The ousters of Khrushchev and Novotny, however, provided possible models for the way in which this could occur.

In general the institutionalization of leadership in a one-party system requires that it be limited in tenure, limited in power, collectivized, or subjected to some combination of these changes. If tenure is limited the leader may exercise extensive power during his term of office and, as in Mexico, have the dominant say in the choice of his successor. If the power of the leader is limited, the penalties for losing power will also be limited, and the way will be opened for irregular but frequent changes in the top leadership without disrupting the system and with the possibility that people will be able to move in and out and back again into leadership positions. The struggle will, in effect, be regulated by rules of the game.[44] Finally, if the leadership is collectivized in a council or bureau, changes can take place in its membership gradually, again without disrupting the system. The authority of the council may be absolute, but the authority of each of its members is limited and a majority of the council can renew itself by coopting new members and purging old ones.

The inherent conflict between personal leadership and party institutionalization produces a tendency toward bureaucratic and oligarchical leadership in one-party systems. In both Mexico and the Soviet Union, certainly, the top leaders have tended increasingly to be products of the party bureaucracy: "mediocre *apparatchiki,*" Zbigniew Brzezinski calls them in the Soviet Union; "managerial specialists" Robert Scott calls them in Mexico.[45] In Mexico the office of the president has become increasingly institutionalized at the same time that the tenure of its occupants has remained strictly limited. In the Soviet Union the tendency is toward oligarchy and to bring into existence "an institutional collective leadership, designed to prevent any one leader from using a particular institution as a vehicle for obtaining political supremacy." [46] The institutionalization of power in a one-party system would appear to lead either toward the division of power among several men for an indefinite period of time or the concentration of power in one man for a limited period of time.

Adaptation

The change from a revolutionary to an established one-party system involves struggles between the party organization and a Weberian sequence of opponents. In the initial transformation phase, the party destroys the traditional sources of authority. In the second phase, it consolidates its authority as an organization against the charismatic appeals of the founding leader. In the third, adaptive phase, the party deals with legal-rational challenges to its authority which are, in large part, the product of its earlier successes. The creation of a relatively homogeneous society and the emergence of new social forces require the party to redefine its roles within that society. Four developments which the party must come to terms with are: (1) the emergence of a new, innovative, technical-managerial class; (2) the development of a complex group structure, typical of a more industrial society, whose interests have to be related to the political sphere; (3) the reemergence of a critical intelligentsia apart from and, indeed, increasingly alienated from the institutionalized structures of power; and (4) the demands by local and popular groups for participation in and influence over the political system.

INNOVATIVE TECHNOCRATS In a revolutionary one-party system the party is clearly the principal source of social, economic, and institutional innovation. In an established one-party system, the party plays a very different role. As a result of modernization and economic development, the society and the economy are more complex; organizational and functional units are more numerous. What is required is no longer a general staff directing the fundamental change from one type of society and economy to another but rather a coordinating staff relating to each other the various initiatives taking place within the society. Once a new technical bureaucracy develops identified with the one-party system, it becomes the source of innovations designed not to destroy the system but to improve it. The innovators are not the reds but the experts. The party apparatus, on the other hand, becomes a gyroscope rather than a motor.

Many social scientists see the managerial and technical bureaucracy as a second New Class on the verge of preempting the position and power of the party *apparatchiki*. Such theories represent the application to the one-party state of Veblen's concept of a soviet of engineers, Burnham's theory of the managerial revolution, and Lasswell's projection of a garrison state ruled by military or police specialists. These theories are all, in a sense, the latter day counterpart of Engels' view that the "governing of men" would be replaced by "the administration of things." They all posit the resolution of the conflict between the political generalist and the technical specialist by the displacement and disappearance of the former. Such theories are unhistorical and apolitical. The conflict between political generalist and managerial specialist is built into modern society just as the conflict between church and state was built into medieval society. This conflict is inherent but limited. A complex society requires both increased functional autonomy for managerial specialists *and* increased political authority for the central political leadership. Meeting this latter need is the principal function of the party *apparat*. It is as essential to the system as the expert bureaucracy.

In such a system the conflict between the political generalists and the managerial specialists continues, but it is a conflict between complements, the existence of each of which is necessary for the existence of the other. The erosion of ideology tends to reduce the differences between political needs as seen by the party elite and technical-administrative needs endorsed by the managerial specialists. The conflict becomes unbearable only when the top political leadership, as in China, refuses to adapt to the increasing complexity of society and instead attempts to maintain the original social dynamism of the revolutionary movement. In such a situation, to be revolutionary is to be reactionary. In one-party systems like those in Mexico, East Europe, and the Soviet Union, on the other hand, the managers have been able to exercise increasing initiative in their specialized areas because the principal function of the party organization is now not to change the system but to integrate it. The reversal of roles between party and bureaucracy was explicitly recognized by the Czech party newspaper, which declared: "We are now at the threshold of the scientific-technical revolution. The main initiative and responsibility for its realization is in the hands of the intelligentsia, which has thus become the guarantor of social progress. In this sense, it has become the most revolutionary factor in society." [47]

In an established one-party system party membership, consequently, becomes more and more heterogeneous as more specialized and diverse elite groups join; in due course these groups also play more important roles in the middle and upper echelons of the party bureaucracy. In 1945, for instance, intellectuals made up less than 10 per cent of the 210,000 members of the Polish Communist Party. In 1960, intellectuals comprised 43.5 per cent of a total membership of 1,155,000. Within the "intellectual" category about 25 per cent of the total membership consisted of technical and managerial specialists.[48] At the same time, however, the functions of the party activists become even more distinctive and specialized. In this respect, the middle ranks of the party apparatus tend to become increasingly conservative and resistant to change. The pattern tends to develop in which the technical and managerial specialists become the proponents of change, the middle-level *apparatchiki* the opponents of change, and the top-level party leaders the arbiters and mediators of change.

INTEREST GROUPS   In established one-party states professional, industrial, commercial, labor, and other socioeconomic groups play a more and more important role in society and increasingly require some definition of their relationships to the political system. In the East European communist states theorists like Dordjevic and Lakatos have stressed the natural role of interest groups in a complex socialist society, and official dogma has also been altered to recognize the legitimacy of specialized interest groups articulating their own needs. In 1966, for instance, the Hungarian Communist Party Congress explicitly stated that within the "broad national unity" that prevailed "with regard to the most important political issues, the building of socialism, and the defense of peace . . . there may appear, for objective and subjective reasons, in some cases temporary but with respect to certain issues even more lasting differences between certain social strata, groups, or between local and public interests generally." These "contradictory interests and differences of opinion" are appropriately expressed in debates and are to be taken into consideration by the party in the formulation of policy.[49] In East Europe generally it is likely that representative bodies "may indeed seek increasingly to embody, not the 'public will,' but the specialized and expert views of various segments of society." [50] This willingness to permit interest groups to articulate their needs presumably goes hand in hand with the assumption that the party apparatus will remain the arbiter among these interests.

The theory and analysis of interest groups in politics originally developed in the United States and has had its primary applicability there. In varying degrees, efforts have been made to extend interest group analysis to Western Europe and to the modernizing countries of Asia, Africa, and Latin America. In fact, however, it would appear that the interest group approach is more relevant to established one-party systems—communist and non-communist—than it is to multi-party systems or to the transitional political systems of modernizing societies. A focus on interest groups implicitly assumes a high degree of consensus on fundamental issues in the society and hence the greater importance in political affairs of the conflicts among specific groups over particular interests. The appeal of interest group analysis to East European theorists is an accurate reflection of the nature of politics in those societies.[51]

People associate interest groups with pluralism, and pluralism with liberal democracy. But pluralism can take a corporate form as well as a liberal one, and it would seem to be precisely this pattern that is characteristic of the established one-party in both Mexico and East Europe. Old theories of functional representation, guild socialism, syndicalism, and even Beer's Old Tory and Old Whig theories of the representation of the fixed, corporate interests of the Kingdom seem to find new relevance in the established one-party systems.

Group interests may be related to the political system in one or more of three ways. In Mexico the sectoral organization of the party provides for the representation of interests directly within the party structure. In communist systems the tendency is to maintain the purity of the party and to provide for group representation in either the legislature or through a front coalition. Formal legislative representation is most highly developed in Yugoslavia with its five-chambered National Assembly including, in addition to a territorial Federal Chamber, chambers of Economy, Education, Social Welfare and Health, and a Political-Administrative Chamber. Legislation is passed either by the Federal Chamber alone or by the Federal Chamber and one of the functional chambers. The whole structure suggests the late medieval systems of estates, such as prevailed in Sweden until 1865, with its parliament composed of four chambers representing nobles, clergy, bourgeois, and peasants. Czechs have suggested the possible desirability of adapting the Yugoslav system to their country. Lakatos recommended that interest groups nominate candidates for the representative assemblies and that the people be able to choose among them in competitive elections. A third channel for the articulation of group interests may be furnished by a front organization dominated by the Communist Party but including spokesmen for other parties and groups. In Czechoslovakia in the spring of 1968, for instance, the National Front included the Communist and four other parties, plus thirty-four other organizations including labor, youth, student, professional, literary, women's, consumers' cooperative, producers' cooperative, and nationality groups. There was, as one observer commented, "something of the representation-by-guild idea about it all—curious kin to the nonparty formations proposed by the French, Italian, Spanish and Latin American syndicalists in 1900–1914 to serve as law-giving trade-union councils in lieu of corrupt parliamentary parties, an idea seized upon and prostituted by Benito Mussolini when he came to power and tried to fake a corporate state." [52]

The advocacy of somewhat similar ideas of group representation in Hungary in the late 1960s produced a counter-tendency, in which influential party members were "worried about the erosion of the party's power and about the crystallization of social and economic interest groups which will eventually demand decision-making power." [53] There were, as one aide of the Czech Central Committee expressed it, "possible contradictions between specific group interests and the general, predefined aim of society." Groups must be allowed to express their conflicting views in the appropriate arenas in the state structure. At the same time the articulation of group interests does not reduce the need for guidance from the central political institutions. The "overall governmental political leadership," as Mlynar continued, "must not be allowed to be influenced by tendencies to place local or group interest above the needs of society as a whole." The party, of course, remains the exclusive guardian of the interests of society as a whole.[54] "Corporate centralism," Scott's phrase for the Mexican system, would seem to be equally relevant to Eastern Europe.

CRITICAL INTELLIGENTSIA   A revolution is a dramatic and violent expansion of political participation, involving the mobilization of peasant and worker masses by an ideologically motivated intellectual elite. At the close of the revolutionary struggle, popular involvement in politics subsides, but the involvement of the intellectual elite continues, since it is this group that furnishes the cadres to staff the new government. The subsequent history of the one-party system, however, involves marked changes in this pattern. The second generation of leadership comes out of the party apparatus and is largely composed of bureaucrats not intellectuals. The result is a widening gap between a regime responding to political and institutional needs and intellectuals who in a relatively stable society have lost all their functions except that of criticism. Criticism from intellectuals is the hallmark of any established political system including a one-party system. The stability of the system, in turn, depends upon the capacity of the political elite to mobilize the support of the masses against the intellectual elite.

The separation of the political elite from the intellectuals is signaled by the criticisms of the former by the latter. The concern of the intellectuals with ideology and with the reformulation of the original revolutionary ideology to give it new "meaning" intensifies in the same ratio in which the political elite becomes indifferent to ideology. Every revolutionary one-party state eventually produces both its New Class and its Milovan Djilas to lambaste the New Class. In Mexico, for instance, the typical political leader, in the words of Jesus Silva Herzog, became "the profiteer of the Revolution, concerned exclusively with personal profit." In Poland Kuron and Modzelewski made similar criticisms of the "central party bureaucracy" exploiting the workers.[55] In part, the conflict between the intellectuals and political bureaucracy reflects the differences in functional role; in part, also, it normally reflects differences in social origins. The intellectual critics are likely to come from middle-class, educated backgrounds; they may well, indeed, be children of the political elite. The political leaders, on the other hand, are likely to come from more humble backgrounds and to have made their way to the top through the new avenues of social mobility opened by the revolution. In part, it is precisely their earthiness, vulgarity, and populism that antagonizes the intellectuals. Alienation of the intellectuals, it has been said, is the precursor of revolution. But it is also the consequence of revolution.

The reaction of the political elite to the challenge by the intellectuals usually takes three forms. The direct response is, of course, the coercive one. Most prominent among the intellectuals' demands is that for intellectual freedom. The political elite typically responds to this by carefully circumscribing the permissible area of activity by the intellectuals and jailing the most notable dissidents. At the same time the political leaders attempt to divide the intellectual elite from the managerial elite. The managers' demands are usually concrete and limited; those of the intellectuals more diffuse and general. To grant the demands of the intellectuals would be to jeopardize the authority of the political elite and perhaps even the stability of the entire system. To grant the demands of the managerial elites for functional autonomy is to improve the efficiency and performance of the system without posing any real threat to the position of the political leadership. Hence, the political leaders frequently acquiesce in the various demands of the managerial elites and thus provide economic reform and decentralization as substitutes for political liberalization.

Finally, the political elite counters the challenge from the intellectuals by mobilizing against them segments of the masses. In contrast to the middle and upper strata, the lower classes tend to be less tolerant, less liberal, more ethnically and religiously prejudiced, and more favorably disposed to authoritarian solutions. In established one-party states, mass participation in politics thus serves the interest of the political elite. "By mobilizing the masses into social control organizations," as one study has suggested, "the regime attempts to limit and to suppress deviant behavior among other groups in the population." [56] Reliance on such organizations appears to depend on the extent of the challenges to the regime. "The more unstable the regime," as Gyorgy has pointed out with respect to East Europe, "the more extensive the proliferation of these organizations; the smaller the 'core' or 'cadre' of the Party, the larger their size and the broader their professional base." In Albania, Bulgaria, and Czechoslovakia during the 1950s, where there was little effective opposition, mass organizations played a little role. In Hungary and Rumania, they were more important, while in the German Democratic Republic they "displayed a truly phenomenal range and variety in their scope and activities." [57] To support their position, the political elite also often has recourse to populistic appeals of a chauvinist character, such as anti-Semitism, for use against the intellectuals.

POPULAR PARTICIPATION   In the first phase of a revolutionary one-party system, the party leadership attempts to mobilize its constituency to play a major role in the destruction and reconstruction of economic, social, and political institutions. In the consolidation phase, mass participation declines sharply as the ideological and charismatic factors connected with it tend to disappear or to become routinized. With the weakening of the bifurcation in society and the effective reconstitution of society, the original need for substantial popular participation in political affairs disappears. Most importantly, the party elite loses its interest in stimulating such participation.

The evolution of the system from the consolidation to the adaptation phase produces the social basis for new forms of political participation. In contrast to participation in the reconstitution phase, the legitimation of this new participation derives not from the extreme conflict of interest between two social forces but rather from the absence of major conflicts of interests within the society. It is premised on basic harmony in society rather than fundamental bifurcation.

During the transformation phase popular participation is generally expressed through the social-mobilization organization in which people are enlisted to achieve goals prescribed by the party leadership. In the adaptation phase, in contrast, participation may also assume a more spontaneous form and electoral participation tends to play a more meaningful role. In the transformation phase elections enable the party to legitimate its activities and to identify the populace with its goals. In the adaptation phase, the fundamental identity between the populace and the system tends to be assumed, and the elections enable the populace to make choices between individuals for party and governmental posts. The rationale is simple—and almost unavoidable: If the domestic enemies of the system have been eliminated, why then should not the populace have the opportunity to choose among competing individual candidates all of whom share the same fundamental commitment to the party and the system? If some enemies appear to still exist, electoral competition may also be one way of mobilizing mass sentiment in support of the party against the criticisms of the intellectuals about its "undemocratic" character.

Electoral competition, however, also poses at least a potential threat to the existing party *apparat* whose members have achieved their positions through bureaucratic rather than electoral processes. Consequently, electoral competition is more likely initially to develop for governmental than for party positions. Its inauguration also may be aided by the extent to which the initially dominant founder-leader has been able to survive and see it in his interest, as well as the party's, to introduce electoral competition. The way in which Tito and Nyerere have been able to shake up their party cadres through the mechanism of elections may, in some measure, reduce incentives to accomplish similar results outside the party through either a Stalinist terror or a Maoist Cultural Revolution.

A fairly significant amount of electoral competition among individuals has already developed in several one-party systems. In Yugoslavia in 1965 there were twice as many candidates as seats in the elections for the commune assemblies, and a total of 1,653 candidates ran for the 1,196 seats in the federal parliament. In the 1967 elections, 25 per cent of the seats in the federal assembly were contested by more than one candidate. In 1965 in Poland 617 candidates contested 460 seats in the national assembly. In Hungary in February, 1965 Janos Kadar spoke of the desirability of multiple candidates for elected bodies, and in November, 1966 the Hungarian parliament passed a law permitting voters to have a choice between two candidates.[58] In Tanzania intraparty elections produced substantial turnover not only in candidates for the legislature but also in party regional chairmen and members of the National Executive Council.

In Mexico a system of party primaries, inaugurated in 1946, was abandoned in 1950 largely because of opposition from labor groups and from the "dangerous public demonstrations of internal party conflict" it encouraged.[59] Fifteen years later the problem of popular participation in the nominating process was still with the PRI. Carlos Madrazo, elected party president in 1964, made major efforts to democratize the internal functioning of the party. A year later he resigned in protest due to the opposition from the party bureaucrats. The issue came to a head in Sonora in December, 1966 when the party organization authorized five candidates to campaign freely for the nomination for governor of the state. In February, 1967, however, the party leadership shut off this competition and announced its choice of the candidate. The result was riots and disorder as students and other urban groups protested this action. While the PRI pioneered in the development of mechanisms for group representation within the party, it was much slower in developing the mechanisms for popular electoral participation through the party.

Intraparty electoral competition among individual candidates furnishes an effective means of identifying local groups with the party and of promoting turnover in low-level and middle-level party and governmental posts. It also, however, poses two potential threats to the single-party system. Electoral competition has consequences for group identification and intergroup relations. In Tanzania, Yugoslavia, and elsewhere, it added incentives for candidates to make tribal and nationality appeals that the one-party system without competition had tended to suppress. Where electoral competition does take place, consequently, such appeals are usually formally prohibited, although obviously not prevented. In addition to activating communal identifications and rivalries, individual electoral competition could lead to the formation of blocs and continuing political organizations or subparties within the single party. Conceivably such a system could become multiparty in all but name, as individuals with similar interests and policies in different parts of the country coalesced together for the mutual promotion of their political futures. It might well be argued, indeed, that a system of individual electoral competition is inherently unstable and must eventually give way to competition between organized factions, blocs, and political machines.

Such a development is possible but not inevitable in an established one-party system. The experience of other societies demonstrates quite conclusively that electoral competition can exist for indefinite periods of time with little or no continuing political organization. There is no law that personal politics and loose factional politics must give way to more organized forms of political competition. The widespread failure of electoral competition to generate enduring coalitions and broad-based organizations in non-communist modernizing societies is a sign of the potential success of such competition in communist and other established one-party systems.

The Stability of Established One-Party Systems

The established one-party system that emerges from the process of transformation, consolidation, and adaptation differs from a revolutionary one-party system in six ways.

1. Ideology is less important in shaping its goals and the decisions of its leaders; pragmatic considerations are more important.
2. The political leadership tends to be oligarchical, bureaucratic, and institutionalized rather than personalistic, charismatic, and autocratic.
3. The sources of initiative are dispersed among technocratic and managerial elites instead of concentrated in the party elite; the party *apparat* becomes the mediator between change and stability.
4. A plurality of important interest groups exist, giving rise to a corporate social structure, with the party *apparat* becoming the aggregator and regulator of competing special interests.
5. The intellectuals criticize the system instead of ruling it.
6. Popular participation in the system is less the product of mobilization by

the party and more the result of competition through elections within the party.

In addition, the most significant difference between established and revolutionary one-party systems concerns the scope of politics. In a revolutionary system the ideology of the leadership encourages it to assign political meanings to almost all types of social behavior and to attempt to subject this behavior to political control. Politics is monopolized by the party and society is dominated by politics. The transformation of society requires the politicization of society. In due course, however, the increasing complexity of society compels changes in the relations among these three elements. The effective functioning of an established one-party system requires relaxation of the political controls on the increasingly complex and diversified activities in society. Economics, technical, social units require greater degrees of autonomy in order to accomplish effectively the ends of the system. As in Yugoslavia in the 1960s, "depoliticization" becomes the order of the day.

The extent to which the party continues to monopolize politics in an established one-party system depends upon the extent to which politics plays less of a role in society. The continued subjection of all major sectors of social life to political controls is beyond the capacity of the party in a way which was not true of the transformation and consolidation phases. Consequently, the failure to restrict the scope of the political system can leave other elements—interest groups, bureaucratic groups, the military—with no choice but to play political roles because the decisions of primary concern to them are made on political rather than technical or functional grounds. If school curricula, factory organization, and tactical doctrines are determined primarily by political criteria, then pedagogues, managers, and colonels will want a role in shaping those criteria. If, on the other hand, such issues are defined as essentially "non-political" and are decided primarily on "functional" grounds, then by restricting the scope of politics, the party is better able to maintain its authority over politics.

That authority, in turn, depends upon the extent to which the party monopolizes the legitimation of the political system, the recruitment of political leadership, and the formulation and implementation of policy. In a revolutionary one-party system, the party comes close to exercising exclusive control over all these functions. In an established one-party system, its control over them varies from one to the other. The emergence of interest groups and the restriction of the scope of political decision-making gives the party a less monopolistic although still important role in the aggregation of interests and the formulation of policy. Policy initiatives may come from many different sources, but only the party *apparat* is in a position to mediate the conflict of interests that the diversification of society produces. In a welter of special interests, it alone can lay some claim to represent the interests of the whole.

In an established one-party system the party maintains firmer control over political recruitment than over policy formulation. The crucial question here concerns the extent to which individuals may rise to high positions of political leadership through bureaucratic or popular channels outside the party organization. Conceivably, for instance, top-ranking military officers or industrial managers could come to the top of their respective hierarchies and then either be coopted into or force their way into the top positions of political leadership. The extent to which such lateral entry into politics does not take place depends on: (1) the degree to which the various functional bureaucracies are isolated from politics, that is, the effectiveness of "depoliticization" in the society; and (2) the relative status and skill of those political bureaucrats who come up through the party hierarchy. For the party the latter involves the problem of how to maintain the status of the political career in a diversified society and how to attract to that career both the children of nonpolitical elite groups and the upwardly mobile children of non-elite groups.

The other potential source of challenge to the party monopoly of political leadership recruitment might come from individuals alienated from or never a part of the party *apparat* who are able to win wide popular support in the society. The likelihood of such a populist challenge, however, is relatively remote. Party control over the media of mass communication and the maintenance of guidelines, if not outright censorship, over the bounds of legitimate political discourse make it difficult for a dissident figure to develop a popular appeal outside the party without being treated as a traitor to the entire society. Even in as relatively an open one-party system as Mexico, a dissident like Carlos Madrazo, for instance, affirmed his intention of working through the party rather than against it. In addition, to the extent that the party internalizes a system of electoral competition, it provides openings for potential dissident leaders to rise up through the party structure and presumably be assimilated into that structure.

Of most significance to the continued stability of an established single party is the maintenance by the party of its monopoly of the legitimation of the system. In a revolutionary one-party system, the party reconstructs society by reducing the existing bifurcation and expanding its constituency social force to encompass, at least in theory, all elements of the society. In an established one-party system the legitimacy of the system continues to depend upon the identity of interest between party and society. The party can countenance all sorts of groups representing and expressing special interests, but it cannot permit another group to promote a competing general interest, a competing image of the good society, or a competing view of the moral basis of political authority. It is precisely for this reason that the party elite cannot tolerate the existence of "real" opposition parties.

In the development of an established one-party system, the party may play a declining role in the day-to-day workings of society, through the reduction of the scope of politics, and a declining role in the day-to-day workings of government, through the increased initiatives assumed by interest groups and functional bureaucracies. The immediate power of the party can be limited in this way, however, only because its ultimate authority is unchallenged. The party has no alternative but to reserve to itself the right to speak for the society as a whole: it was, indeed, this right which it established for itself in the revolutionary process. In the mid-1960s the Yugoslav League of Communists seemed to be moving in this direction. The party, it was said, would give up its "commanding role in Yugoslav life" and instead devote itself to the ideological and moral guidance of the society. The communists, as Zaninovich interprets it, would become "a sort of overriding Brahmanic caste, in that they immunize themselves from the 'dirty business' of politics and become the exclusive (and priestly) guardians of socialist morality." Another analogy might be the Supreme Court of the United States, with the party, like the Court, being the final arbiter of what is and is not permissible within the constitutional principles and institutional framework of the political system. "We talk of the withering away of the state," Tito said, "but the withering away of the League (party) is not to be considered." [60]

The need for the party to maintain its position as the source of political legitimacy sets the limits of permissible dissent. A Mihajlo Mihajlov who bases his argument for an opposition journal on the provisions of the Yugoslav constitution is either naive or disingenuous. The source of legitimacy in Yugoslavia is not the constitution but the party, and any effort to invoke the constitution as a source of legitimation against the party is clearly not tolerable. The limits of dissent are set by the fundamentals of the system, of which the party's monopoly of ultimate authority is the most sacrosanct. As one journalist commented with respect to Yugoslavia: "The press is nominally free but does not exercise the liberty to criticize the party, its top leaders or its program. Churches are free to hold religious services, but not to run schools or participate in politics. People are free to associate in non-party groupings as long as they are not politically oriented. Speech is free except that statements against the party from a public platform are punishable." [61] Similarly, the parliaments in communist one-party systems may assume a more significant role in shaping policy and even in forming governments. Yet such efforts are tolerable only so long as they do not threaten the ultimate supremacy of the party. If parliamentary deputies were to claim to be sovereign representatives of the will of the people, the established one-party system would confront a constitutional crisis.

Many efforts have been made to identify the types of dissent and opposition that may exist in political systems, including one-party systems. In most instances, opposition is categorized on substantive grounds. Distinctions are made between opposition to the personnel of government, to specific policies, to the political structure, and to the social-economic system. In a somewhat similar vein, Skilling distinguishes integral opposition to the system itself, fundamental opposition within the system to basic policies, and specific opposition to aspects of the system.[62] In an established one-party system, however, the more important consideration is not what is opposed but where it is opposed. Opposition articulated through the one-party system can be much more sweeping in its criticism than opposition expressed outside the system. As in any relatively stable political order, procedural regularity furnishes the dissenter with his opportunity and his opiate. In an established single-party system, as in a democratic, competitive party system, political stability is measured by the degree to which the system possesses the institutional channels for transforming dissenters into participants.

‖ Notes

1. Mihajlo Mihajlov, *A Historic Proposal* (New York: Freedom House, 1966), p. 7; Zbigniew K. Brzezinski, "The Soviet Political System: Transformation or Degeneration," *Problems of Communism,* XV (January–February 1966), 1–14.
2. To keep things simple, an authoritarian government is defined as a non-democratic one. A democratic government is one whose principal leaders are chosen at regular intervals through competitive elections in which the bulk of the adult population has the opportunity to participate.
3. Raymond Aron, "Can the Party Alone Run a One-Party State?" *Government and Opposition,* II (February 1967), 165; Milovan Djilas in C. L. Sulzberger, "A Conversation with Yugoslavia's Djilas—'We are Going Toward the Death of All Isms,'" *New York Times Magazine,* June 9, 1968, p. 112.
4. See Seymour Martin Lipset and Stein Rokkan, eds., *Party Systems and Voter Alignments* (New York: The Free Press, 1967), esp. pp. 1–64, and Sigmund Neumann, ed., *Modern Political Parties* (Chicago: University of Chicago Press, 1955).
5. Rajni Kothari, "The Congress 'System' in India," *Asian Survey,* IV (December 1964), 1161–1173.
6. Cf. my *Political Order in Changing Societies* (New Haven: Yale University Press, 1968), pp. 420ff.
7. Contrast Robert E. Scott, *Mexican Government in Transition* (Urbana: The University of Illinois Press, 1959), chap. 5 and Frank Brandenburg, *The Making of Modern Mexico* (Englewood Cliffs, N.J.: Prentice-Hall, 1964), pp. 142–145.
8. Franz Neumann, *Behemoth: The Structure and Practice of National Socialism, 1933–1944* (New York: Oxford University Press, 1944), p. 67. See Also Carl Friedrich, ch. 7 of this volume.
9. Kalman Silvert, ed., *Expectant Peoples* (New York: Random House, 1963), pp. 358–361.
10. Stanley G. Payne, *Falange: A History of Spanish Fascism* (Stanford: Stanford University Press, 1961), p. 200.
11. See Leonard Binder, "Political Recruitment and Participation in Egypt," in Joseph LaPalombara and Myron Weiner, eds., *Political Parties and Political Development* (Princeton: Princeton University Press, 1966), pp. 218–219.
12. Paul E. Sigmund, ed., *The Ideologies of the Developing Nations* (New York: Frederick A. Praeger, 1963), pp. 175, 198.
13. *Ibid.,* p. 172; Rupert Emerson, "Parties and National Integration in Africa," in LaPalombara and Weiner, *op. cit.,* p. 296.

14. Robert A. Dahl, ed., *Political Oppositions in Western Democracies* (New Haven: Yale University Press, 1966), p. 385.
15. *Ibid.,* p. 386.
16. See Frederick W. Frey, *The Turkish Political Elite* (Cambridge: MIT Press, 1965), chap. 13, and Samuel P. Huntington, "The Political Modernization of Traditional Monarchies," *Daedalus,* XCV (Summer 1966), 766–772.
17. Lenin, quoted in Joseph Stalin, *Problems of Leninism* (New York: International Publishers, 1934), pp. 36–37.
18. Lenin, *'Left' Communism: An Infantile Disorder,* quoted in Joseph Stalin, *Foundations of Leninism* rev. trans. (New York: International Publishers, 1932), p. 47.
19. Huntington, *Political Order in Changing Societies,* p. 425.
20. Zbigniew K. Brzezinski, *The Soviet Bloc: Unity and Conflict,* rev. ed. (Cambridge: Harvard University Press, 1967), p. 90.
21. Andrew Gyorgy, "The Internal Political Order," in Stephen Fischer-Galati, ed., *Eastern Europe in the Sixties* (New York: Frederick A. Praeger, 1963), p. 162.
22. A similar policy of deliberately firing up social conflict was adapted by Cárdenas in Mexico and had similar results in strengthening the single-party system and redefining the political community. "Cárdenas accomplished the feat of bringing off a class war, while at the same time subordinating it to the overriding theme of Mexican nationalism. Major surgery was performed upon economic and social institutions of long standing. Social realignments and change in stratification arrangements took place, and national sentiment and unity triumphed in these changes. Modern evolutionary Mexico was ready to emerge based upon the twin assumptions of nationalism and modernization as the overriding values of the future." L. Vincent Padgett, *The Mexican Political System* (Boston: Houghton Mifflin, 1966), pp. 39–40.
23. J. Gus Liebenow, "Liberia," in James S. Coleman and Carl G. Rosberg, eds., *Political Parties and National Integration in Tropical Africa* (Berkeley: University of California Press, 1964), p. 451.
24. Leonard M. Thompson, *Politics in the Republic of South Africa* (Boston: Little, Brown, 1966), p. 151.
25. Leon D. Epstein, *Political Parties in Western Democracies* (New York: Frederick A. Praeger, 1967), p. 54; B. J. O. Dudley, "Traditionalism and Politics: A Case Study of Northern Nigeria," *Government and Opposition,* II (July–October 1967), 509ff.
26. Frederick W. Frey, "Political Development, Power, and Communications in Turkey," in Lucian Pye, ed., *Communications and Political Development* (Princeton: Princeton University Press, 1963), p. 313. For comparison of the Colombian Front to one-party systems, see Robert H. Dix, *Colombia: The Political Dimensions of Change* (New Haven: Yale University Press, 1967), pp. 392–399.
27. Quoted in Kemal H. Karpat, *Turkey's Politics: The Transition to a Multi-Party System* (Princeton: Princeton University Press, 1959), p. 140n.
28. Merran Fraenkel, *Tribe and Class in Monrovia* (New York: Oxford University Press, 1964), p. 18.
29. Dankwart A. Rustow, "Politics and Development Policy," in Frederick C. Shorter, ed., *Four Studies on the Economic Development of Turkey* (London: Frank Cass, 1967), p. 12.
30. Bernard Lewis, *The Emergence of Modern Turkey* (New York: Oxford University Press, 1961), p. 467.
31. Karpat, *op. cit.,* pp. 148ff.; Rustow, *op. cit.,* p. 24.
32. *The New York Times,* October 13, 1958, p. 16.

33. George Dalton, "History, Politics, and Economic Development in Liberia," *Journal of Economic History*, XXV (December 1965), 585.

34. *Ibid.*, p. 584.

35. Carl J. Friedrich and Zbigniew K. Brzezinski, *Totalitarian Dictatorship and Autocracy*, 2nd ed., rev. by Friedrich (New York: Frederick A. Praeger, 1966), esp. pp. 375–378; Robert C. Tucker, "Towards a Comparative Politics of Movement-Regimes," *American Political Science Review*, LV (June 1961), 281–289. See also Brzezinski's later critique of Soviet adaptation, "The Soviet Political System," pp. 1–14.

36. Quoted in J. H. Huizinga, "Franco and the Spanish Furies," *Interplay*, I (April 1968), 17.

37. See Immanuel Wallerstein, "Voluntary Associations," in Coleman and Rosberg, *op. cit.*, pp. 337–339, and Elliot J. Berg and Jeffrey Butler, "Trade Unions," *ibid.*, pp. 341, 366; Clement H. Moore, in Charles A. Micaud, et al., *Tunisia: The Politics of Modernization* (New York: Frederick A. Praeger, 1964), pp. 86, 104; Clement H. Moore, "Mass Party Regimes in Africa," in Herbert J. Spiro, ed., *Africa: The Primacy of Politics* (New York: Random House, 1966), p. 105; Douglas E. Ashford, *The Elusiveness of Power: The African Single Party State* (Ithaca: Cornell University Center for International Studies, 1965), pp. 11–14.

38. H. Gordon Skilling, *The Government of Communist East Europe* (New York: Thomas Y. Crowell, 1966), pp. 210–211; Joseph R. Strayer, "Problems of Dictatorship: The Russian Experience," *Foreign Affairs*, XLIV (January 1966), 272–273.

39. Quoted in Peter Grose, "The Communist Party Is the Rear Guard of Russia," *New York Times Magazine*, March 27, 1966, p. 131.

40. See my "Conservatism as an Ideology," *American Political Science Review*, LI (June 1957), 454–473, and Carl Beck, "Bureaucracy and Political Development in Eastern Europe," in Joseph LaPalombara, ed., *Bureaucracy and Political Development* (Princeton: Princeton University Press, 1963), pp. 299–300.

41. Skilling, *op. cit.*, p. 129; Jerzy Zawieyski, quoted in Richard Hiscocks, *Poland: Bridge for the Abyss?* (New York: Oxford University Press, 1963), p. 326.

42. Quoted in Brzezinski, *Soviet Bloc*, p. 310.

43. Merle Fainsod, "The Dynamics of One-Party Systems," in Oliver Garceau, ed., *Political Research and Political Theory* (Cambridge: Harvard University Press, 1968), pp. 221–246.

44. See Jerome M. Gilison, "New Factors of Stability in Soviet Collective Leadership," *World Politics*, XIX (July 1967), 571–572.

45. Brzezinski, "The Soviet Political System," p. 5; Robert E. Scott, *op. cit.*, p. 216.

46. Brzezinski, "The Soviet Political System," p. 4.

47. *Rude Pravo*, quoted in Morton Schwartz, "Czechoslovakia: Toward One-Party Pluralism?" *Problems of Communism*, XVI (January–February 1967), 24.

48. Richard F. Starr, *Poland, 1944–1962: The Sovietization of a Captive People* (Baton Rouge: Louisiana State University Press, 1962), pp. 174–179.

49. Quoted in Paul Lendvai, "Hungary: Charge vs. Immobilism," *Problems of Communism*, XVI (March–April 1967), 14.

50. Skilling, *op. cit.*, p. 231.

51. See, generally, H. Gordon Skilling, "Interest Groups and Communist Politics," *World Politics*, XVIII (April 1966), 435–451.

52. Albert Parry, "Why Moscow Couldn't Stand Prague's Deviation," *New York Times Magazine*, September 1, 1968, p. 47.

53. Lendvai, *op. cit.*, p. 16; Schwartz, *op. cit.*, p. 22; Skilling, *Communist East Europe*, pp. 133, 231.

54. Schwartz, *op. cit.*, p. 25.

55. See Michael Gamarnikow, "Poland: Political Pluralism in a One-Party State,"

Problems of Communism, XVI (July–August 1967), 4–6; Stanley R. Ross, ed., *Is The Mexican Revolution Dead?* (New York: Alfred A. Knopf, 1966), pp. 17, 22–23.

56. Zbigniew Brzezinski and Samuel P. Huntington, *Political Power: USA/USSR* (New York: Viking, 1964), p. 99.
57. Gyorgy, *op. cit.,* pp. 185–187.
58. Lendvai, *op. cit.,* p. 14; Skilling, *Communist East Europe,* pp. 131–132; M. George Zaninovich, *The Development of Socialist Yugoslavia* (Baltimore: Johns Hopkins Press, 1968), pp. 152–155.
59. Scott, *op. cit.,* p. 142. See also Ozbudun, ch. 12 of this volume.
60. Zaninovich, *op. cit.,* p. 145; Ghita Ionescu, *The Politics of the European Communist States* (New York: Frederick A. Praeger, 1967), pp. 244–248.
61. David Binder, *The New York Times,* May 29, 1966.
62. Dahl, *op. cit.,* p. 342; H. Gordon Skilling, "Background to the Study of Opposition in Communist Eastern Europe," *Government and Opposition,* III (Summer 1968), 297–301.

2

The Single Party as Source

of Legitimacy

‖ Clement H. Moore

The political party, unlike factions within a traditional ruling group, is a distinctively modern phenomenon, for it involves "stable organization" [1] enjoining some degree of mass membership or support. Indeed, for Joseph LaPalombara and Myron Weiner, parties arise in response to one or a number of crises of political modernization, those of legitimacy, participation, or "integration." "It is in this context of an erosion of traditional belief patterns, particularly as they affect the individual's relationship to authority, that political parties and other types of politically relevant organizations emerge." [2] It is in this context, too, that the single-party phenomenon can be understood.

Whether or not party history always begins as in England (under James I) with a single party (the Puritans) contesting the legitimacy of the tradiional order,[3] the rise of parties has usually been associated with crises of legitimacy as well as participation. One possible response, since the Bolshevik Revolution of 1917, has been the established one-party system. The party not only regulates participation but advances a claim to be the sole source of legitimacy. Of course the very concept of a "single-party system" appears paradoxical, as Sigmund Neumann and others have pointed out,[4] for party implies a plurality of parties. But the paradox merely reflects the failure of Puritans, Jacobins, and other incipient single-party vanguards in the West to achieve hegemony, so that norms of party competition, supplementing other bases of legitimacy, historically preceded the establishment of one-party systems. This evolution helps to explain why some hegemonic parties do not claim to be an exclusive source of legitimacy, for the Western norm of party competition, virtually unquestioned by modernizers before the World War I, was transmitted to other settings. However, the breakdowns even of some Western systems which adapted this norm lent greater international currency to Bolshevik and fascist models. In countries simultaneously facing crises of legitimacy and participation, the single-party "solution" has often been imposed.

Of course not all established single-party systems may be viewed in this perspective. One must exclude dominant one-party systems, even those in which the leading party regularly gains massive majorities, if the legitimacy of the system derives primarily from some other source, such as a widespread commitment to constitutional procedures that the party may therefore not transgress.[5] Thus Democratic Party machines in southern states, even those displaying the continuous organization of a party as distinct from a faction,[6] cannot usefully be compared with single parties which seek to build legitimacy, for the machines have operated in the context of an established constitutional order. Similarly, the True Whig Party of Liberia has held power since 1877—making it the oldest established one-party system in the world—without altering the traditional order until very recently. After its founding in 1869, in the heyday of a vigorous two-party politics within the Americo-Liberian community, it came to reflect the interests of this oligarchy facing the twin threats of foreign intervention and rebellion by a native population outnumbering it twenty to one.[7] In contrast to this established and clearly defined oligarchy, new black bourgeoisies in Africa must seek legitimacy for themselves and their emerging post-colonial regimes. If there is any source of legitimacy, apart from "charisma," it will be the single party, not status within the all-too-new oligarchy. That is why studies of American or American-type party machines can shed only limited light on the political processes of other established one-party systems. They do not face comparable problems. Machines generate power but not legitimacy.

On the other hand, it makes little difference in our perspective whether the party is dominant or unique, that is, whether or not it tolerates marginal opposition parties. What counts is whether the dominant party is committed to other sources of legitimacy or subordinates them to its claim. In a number of communist countries other parties are permitted a nominal existence. So also in Tunisia, rival parties were tolerated until recently, though legitimacy derives from Bourguiba and his ruling party rather than his tailor-made constitution or any other source.[8] In Mexico, by contrast, the priority of legitimating principles is less clear-cut than in either Tunisia or communist countries, on the one hand, or Liberia and Byrd's Virginia on the other. As implied in its very name, the *Partido Revolucionario Institucionalista* is the institutional custodian of the Revolution of 1910—contemporary Mexico's founding myth—yet Mexican political leaders possibly pay more than lip service to the Constitution of 1917—another expression of revolutionary values and one which antedates the party or its predecessors.[9] It is quite conceivable that the National Action Party, which won elections in two provinces in 1968,[10] may eventually destroy the

PRI's monopoly, just as opposition parties in India wore down the Congress Party. Similarly, the commitment of Republican People's Party leaders, especially Ismet Inonu, to constitutional principles took clear precedence over party loyalty in the late 1940s, permitting Turkey's transition to a two-party system.[11] But as in Mexico today, it would have been difficult ten years earlier to have predicted such an evolution; in fact in 1935 Interior Minister Recep Peker appeared bent on consolidating the RPP as the exclusive source of legitimacy justified by an explicit ideology. Had the Germans and Italians won World War II, Peker's alternative would probably have triumphed over Inonu's.

Thus the Turkish and certainly the Mexican single-party experiences are properly included in our perspective; indeed, the respective parties confronted legitimacy crises inherent in the breakup of the Ottoman Empire and in the praetorian politics of post-revolutionary Mexico. It is as instructive to discuss why the RPP "failed" to generate the fascist structures that might have ensured its survival as a monopolistic party as it is comparatively to analyze the alternatives that African, fascist, communist, and for that matter the Mexican established single parties face. For, whatever the intentions of the political actors, whether they be tutelary democrats or budding Stalinists, their parties have to generate or maintain legitimacy if the established one-party system is to survive. Unless the Mexican PRI, for instance, can continue to justify itself as the institutional embodiment of the Revolution, Mexico will acquire a multi-party system. Conversely, the PRI's "success" to date in the face of commitment to another, potentially contradictory legitimating principle only underlines the RPP's "failure" in the face of similarly conflicting commitments.

Even the True Whig Party will perhaps join in the single-party search for legitimacy. For President Tubman has taken modest steps toward opening the oligarchy to native tribesmen. Hence, if multi-party politics is to be avoided, the True Whig Party after Tubman's retirement will either have to reverse this tendency or develop a new legitimating principle incompatible with that of Americo-Liberian obligarchy. Party, an intervening variable today, would have to replace social status as the independent variable determining the Liberian structure of authority. But then the True Whig Party would no longer be merely an American-style machine, for it would also be a source of legitimacy. To retain its political monopoly it would probably find it more necessary than the Mexican PRI to transgress the unwritten constitution—perhaps in the name of the written one—by suppressing an Americo-Liberian opposition.

To recapitulate the argument, most established one-party systems can best be understood as responses to simultaneous participation and legitimacy crises. The exceptions, party machines that establish themselves in the context of an already existing legitimate order, are museum pieces that cannot usefully be included in our subsequent analysis. Indeed, there is some doubt that they are real parties. V. O. Key points out that most southern states were one-party only in the two-party context of national politics, while within each state the Democratic Party masked a factional politics resembling two-party, multi-party, or more often no-party systems. Byrd's machine inside the Democratic Party of Virginia would probably come closest to qualifying as an established one-party system at the state level. The point, of course, is that if party is defined as a relatively stable organization, enjoining some degree of mass membership or support, designed for the purpose of putting candidates into office to serve the material or ideal interests of its members,[12] then most groups contesting Democratic state primaries to put their men in office would have to be called factions rather than parties. Groups durable enough to be called parties have usually engendered durable competition.

But there is more. It is perhaps not accidental that it was Virginia, the most oligarchical of the southern states, that sustained the closest approximation to an established one-party system. As in Liberia, formally competitive politics masked aristocratic privilege. The party machine in part reflected the determination of a traditional oligarchy to exercise its vocation of public service. But the machine was less durable than the True Whig Party, just as the oligarchy was less entrenched and did not even for its members enjoy an unchallenged title to rule. The comparison suggests that the party must be reducible to an established group, such as the Americo-Liberian oligarchy, if it is to survive without becoming a source of legitimacy. Conversely, a single party cannot be an autonomous agency for political recruitment over a long period of time, unless it becomes established as an independent source of legitimacy for the political system.

Yet the party cannot establish its legitimacy, it would seem, unless it acquires some autonomy as an instrument for recruiting top political leaders. Thus dictators who attain power through other bases of support often have difficulties creating a party to legitimate their regimes. Nasser has failed three times since 1954 to build such an organization.[13] For, relying on military cliques to stay in power, he was unwilling to grant the Liberation Ralley, the National Union, or the Arab Socialist Union any autonomy in selecting leaders or even any significant influence, for that matter, over policy-making. Egypt remains a no-party state. So also in Spain, Franco rose to power in alliance with traditional groups, notably the military establishment. As a matter of political convenience during the Civil War, he supported the Falange, a minor and divided anti-Republican party that had no prospects of attaining power or even exerting much influence under the previous regime. After its founding leader, Primo de Rivera, died in a Republican prison, it was easy for Franco to consolidate control over the Falange—the Caudillo's brother-in-law served as the key intermediary. By 1941 "there appeared to be nothing left of it but a noisy propaganda machine, an overgrown bureaucracy, and a few immature students. . . . Although it grew more artificial and more isolated with each passing season, it survived, like the regime, because its enemies could never agree among themselves on how to remove it or with what to replace it." [14] According to Stanley Payne, Franco "realized that he could never fully rely upon the party, because its own immaturity and the frustrations continuously imposed on it soon robbed it of any popular backing." Moreover, "had it not been for the delicate nature of the Caudillo's juggling act, the party would never have retained a semi-independent identity as long as it did." [15] What was true of Franco's Spain was even more true of Salazar's Portugal. There, too, the fascist model influenced the dictator's search for legitimacy, but the party was even less autonomous than the Falange, for Salazar continued to rely primarily upon the conservative groups that had put him in power. As a result, legitimacy, what there is of it, rests on other grounds, and it has not been possible either in Portugal or Spain to institutionalize, for instance, the "national syndicalism" and corporatist order advocated by the Falange.

While one would have had to juggle with definitions to call Spain a "no-party system" in 1941, there is an important theoretical distinction to be made between autonomous and heteronomous parties in one-party regimes. To be autonomous, a party must not only be a relatively stable organization enjoining some degree of mass support; it must also retain a significant role in the political recruitment process. This does not mean that the party may not be subordinated, as in fascist Italy, Nazi Germany, or Stalinist Russia, to its top leader, but the dictator must at least co-opt most of his key lieutenants through the party apparatus. Otherwise the party will no longer have significant functions to perform that a government propaganda ministry could not equally well carry out. There is in fact a tendency in Africa, as there was in Italy, Germany, and Russia, for one-party states to develop, in this sense, into "no-party" or heteronomous party states.[16] But what African leaders may gain in political convenience by depriving their parties of other functions they may well lose in their efforts to establish some legitimacy. For heteronomous parties quickly lose their identity and support and thus become unlikely sources of legitimacy for their regimes. On the other hand, it may well be, as Aristide Zolberg has suggested, that many of the African single parties are comparable to political machines.[17] Then they in fact retain their autonomy, so far as they continue to be the prime agencies of political recruitment, even though it is unlikely, if they are merely machines, that they can establish legitimacy. But if they do not acquire legitimacy, they are unlikely long to survive, for the new oligarchies they support, unlike that of Americo-Liberian community, have no other source of legitimacy. Thus the military has already jumped into the vacuum that single parties failed to fill in Ghana, Algeria, and Togo, to cite three instances where more or less organized mass parties had at least a quasi-autonomous existence.

It therefore seems useful to conceive of the evolution of *established* one-party systems as the articulation of new legitimating criteria derived by and for the party rather than any other social or political structures. The party is not only an organization; in the absence or decay of other institutions, its historic task has been to create a new political culture. Though few single parties have succeeded, it is possible in this perspective to compare failures as well as possible successes. The only cases to be excluded are heteronomous parties and the museum pieces which depended on an independently certified and established legitimating principle. In the remaining universe of established single-party systems, ideology and organization are the Janus-faced substance from which legitimacy is to derive if the system is to persist. And just as the organization and functioning of single-party states can be compared, so too can the ideologies the parties generate to legitimate their rule. Differences in ideology in fact reflect and help to explain significant structural variations in the established systems.

It may be generally misleading, and sometimes perverse, to discuss ideology outside the context of political organization.[18] Ideology is not an individual affair. For the ideology to be operative, it must embrace a community of believers organized to achieve their shared goals. And, reciprocally, in established one-party systems the party organization is especially dependent upon the belief systems of cadres and leaders. For the party to be the prime source of legitimacy, its organization must be, in Philip Selznick's terms, "infused with value"—either valued for itself as an institution or valued as a weapon for the goals it can achieve. Historically the second, or instrumental, mode of legitimacy precedes the first, intrinsic mode; the "administrative ideology" associated with what Selznick calls "institutionalization" is the result of deradicalization or ritualization of ideology in the more generic and genetic sense.[19] Ideology, by origin is radical ideology or, as Daniel Bell puts it, "a way of translating ideas into action." [20] In this sense the Bolsheviks were the first to successfully convert ideas into "levers" for transforming society, and it was no accident that their chief instrument was a vanguard party. But both partisan organization and radical ideology have earlier—and simultaneous—roots in Western political and intellectual history. Michael Walzer has persuasively reinterpreted Puritanism as the prototype of radical ideology even as others have seen in Puritan organization the prototype of the modern political party.[21] Though the Puritans, displaced by Cromwell's military, never established a single-party regime, their experience is worth recalling for the light it sheds on the functions of radical ideology.

Unlike more contemporary ideologists, the Puritan "saints" were more concerned with moral order than politics and, so far as they attended to politics, they did not focus exclusively or even primarily upon government at the state level. But, as Walzer suggests, "magistracy is a far better description of the saints' true vocation than is either capitalist acquisition or bourgeois freedom. It suggests most clearly the activist role that Puritanism called upon the saints to play in the creation and maintenance of a new moral order." [22] The Puritans were the first political entrepreneurs in Western history. Marginal men—marginal not in the sense that they were not sociologically competent but rather in that they were alienated from a traditional order that appeared on the verge of collapse—the saints were the first to harness conscience to work in the political arena. Seeking control, hence "government" over self—for their ethics, even their cosmology, was expressed in a political language of war and repression [23]—they externalized their moral and religious concern into an organized and sustained political activity which is perhaps the most startling innovation of the postmedieval world. Though their contemporaries viewed their sustained commitment as hypocrisy and their hard work as meddlesomeness, the Puritans were the prototype of the modern militant—"militant," in fact, in a special sense that can help us to clarify the nature of ideological activity.

Too often in contemporary political analysis "ideological" parties and individuals are contrasted to the "pragmatic" varieties, usually with bias in favor of the latter. But if we accept Walzer's description, the saints were more profoundly pragmatic in their approach to politics than any of their contemporaries. Having internalized as anxiety the Machiavellian *fortuna,* they were driven methodically and systematically—without any regard for established forms and hence "free to experiment politically" [24]—to approach their goals in a continual and impersonal way. Not only were they the first to organize voluntary political organizations and the first to present detached appraisals of the existing order; they also achieved programmatic expressions of their political discontent and aspirations. Thus, unlike the true believers of medieval chiliastic sects, they applied their aspirations to political reality, uniting theory and practice as subsequent militants were to do more explicitly.

Calvinism, of course, achieved a more explicitly political elaboration in the Jacobin Republic of Virtue. And as radical ideology developed, so too did political organization. Though the Jacobins, who attained power only for a very brief period at the height of the French Revolution, never elaborated a rationale for a single-party system, the Jacobin clubs were forerunners of the single party in established one-party systems. The organizational vehicle of the revolutionary ideology, they practiced periodic purges (*épuration*) and constantly intervened in the functioning of the state administration.[25] Jacobin social goals were limited, for it was assumed that the right political order would more or less automatically produce the right society, but the Republic of Virtue assumed citizens made virtuous through sustained moral introspection that was possible only in the context of a political organization that brought the general will to light. It remained for Lenin, however, to unite theory and practice by explicitly linking radical ideology to an organizational weapon. To the pure ideology of Puritans, Jacobins, and the many other modern radicals who externalize moral or religious concerns into sustained and purposeful political activity is added a practical ideology that legitimates the organizational vanguard as the source of "true" interpretations and determines its operative goals. Thus twentieth century ideology becomes, in Brzezinski's words, "an action program suitable for mass consumption, derived from certain doctrinal assumption about the general nature of the dynamics of social reality, and combining some assertion about the inadequacies of the past and/or present with some explicit guides to action for improving the situation and some notions of the desired eventual state of affairs." [26] To which one might add that a prime function of the ideology is to hold together the organization that implements its prescriptions.[27] Indeed some contemporary scholars tread dangerously close to defining ideology in terms of organization; thus for Friedrich, "as long as the organization continues, the presumption has to be in favor of the continuity of the ideology." [28]

But the radical pragmatist's "union of theory and practice" expresses a methodological aspiration, not an analytic proposition. Organization may survive though ideology no longer guides action, just as churches may survive losses of faith. And, conversely, radical ideologues do not always establish organization. Leninism constitutes only a paradigm for established single-party systems, in that it offers a vocabulary and a methodological postulate for justifying and legitimating party rule. Irrespective of the content of the pure ideology, whether Marxist or non-Marxist and whatever the goals, all single parties in search of legitimacy adopt the vanguard principle and try to justify their strategies and tactics in terms of their goals. But the proposed union of theory and practice that legitimates parties and their leaders can always be questioned. Even Lenin did not escape criticism and occasional reverses at the hands of his fellow Bolsheviks. Leninism as practical ideology imposes the obligation upon those who would use it as a legitimating principle to relate their political actions to the abstract goals posited by their pure ideology. Leninism, like Puritanism, demands a continuous elaboration of means and ends—at once pragmatic and programmatic—that generates a sustained purposiveness for political organization. There is never a final "proof" of the meeting of means and ends.

In practice there is always some disassociation between the pure and practical ideologies, between ends and means, even in the pragmatic Leninist system. But whereas Lenin and Stalin usually sought to bridge the gap by revising the pure ideology—and resorting to terror when rational articulation became impossible [29]—the Sorelian transposition of Marx suggests an alternative that is less painful and equally applicable to other ideological systems. Pure ideology, as Plato foretold, can be translated into myth, which by definition is impervious to rational criticism because it is not action-related and hence not subject to an ongoing appraisal of means and ends. The myth of the general strike is designed to moralize society by engendering proletarian solidarity, but it has no action consequences. In fact Sorel obligingly points out that such "social myths in no way prevent a man profiting by the observations which he makes in the course of his life, and form no obstacle to the pursuit of his normal occupations . . . [just as] . . . English or American sectarians whose religious exaltation was fed by apocalyptic myths were often none the less very practical men." [30]

The test of myth is not whether what it predicts is true but whether it can be believed. Thus the test of the myth Sorel proposes is "whether the general strike contains everything that the Socialist doctrine expects of the revolutionary proletariat, . . . [that is, whether it is] a body of images capable of evoking instinctively all the sentiments which correspond to the different manifestations of the war undertaken by Socialism against modern society." [31] An effective myth in this sense, synthesizing all the noble proletarian sentiments associated with past limited strikes, is "global knowledge" in need of no practical fulfillment. While the social analyst can presumably predict whether a myth will be effective and ineffective, on the basis of objective aesthetic criteria,[32] the political actions of the effective myth-maker can only be appreciated as they *express* the myth, not judged in light of their consequences. Action, in short, has consummatory rather than instrumental value.[33]

Antonio Gramsci criticized the "abstract" character of Sorel's conception of myth, but his *Modern Prince* points toward a richer and more concrete theory of the vanguard party than a pragmatic ideologist like Lenin would allow. The party is the modern "myth-prince," an organism "in which the cementing of a collective will, recognized and partially asserted in action, has already begun." [34] Though Gramsci apparently does not elaborate his own conception of myth—possibly to do so would be like Sorel to question the scientific character of Marxism—Mussolini of course in his crude and undialectical fashion had already extracted the Sorelian conception of myth from its syndical context and applied it to a national constituency. "That which I am," he claimed after attaining power, "I owe to Sorel." The myth of the Third Rome was designed to generate solidarity, expressed in the party's grandiose public spectacles. To be fair to Mussolini, he acknowledged that, in addition to utilizing myth, leadership "requires a specific knowledge that governs and is adequate for action. For those who conceive socialism in terms of Sorel's myth nothing obtains other than an act of faith." "Pragmatic realism"—in short, a practical ideology—is also needed, and in this sense Mussolini rejoins Lenin, though the goals realistically to be pursued of course diverge.[35] But despite his boasts of "totalitarian" government and a fully elaborated "doctrine" based on a neo-Hegelian philosophy, Mussolini's pronouncements never displayed the ideological rigor of a Lenin or Stalin and were "pragmatic" only in the sense of being opportunistic with respect to ends as well as means. Legitimacy depended on myth expressed by the party, not on a programmatic pursuit of goals. Few Italians took "ideology" literally as a lever for transforming society; the party propaganda machine was significant mainly as an expression of the myth of the totalitarian state rather than for its functional consequences. Despite his chiliastic rhetoric, Mussolini himself appears to have had few fixed goals, other than staying in power and displaying it.

Clearly ideology in the twentieth century can have expressive as well as instrumental functions. Though in theory as subject as Leninism to rational analysis, fascism in Italy was primarily expressive rather than instrumental and hence less vulnerable to rational criticism. All established single parties need to be infused with value to generate legitimacy for their regimes and rulers. But the ideologies of such parties vary significantly not only with respect to the nature of the goals they posit but also with respect to their function. The goals may involve either a total or partial transformation of society, and they may be treated either as expressions of party solidarity or as tasks to be performed. Thus for comparative purposes it is possible to generate a four-fold typology of one-party ideologies, along with examples of each type, as Table 2-1 indicates.

TABLE 2-1 *Single-Party Ideologies*

	Goals	
Functions	**Total Transformation**	**Partial Transformation**
Instrumental	totalitarian	tutelary
	Stalinist Russia, Maoist China, Nazi Germany, "Stalinist" East Europe	Tunisia, Tanzania, Yugoslavia, Ataturk's Turkey
Expressive	chiliastic	administrative
	Fascist Italy, Nkrumah's Ghana, Mali, Guinea, Cuba, Ben Bella's Algeria	Mexico

Real systems of ideology and organization, of course, are too complex to classify in this simplistic way, for the instrumental and expressive functions are not mutually exclusive. Even Stalin, when appealing to nationalism during World War II, was using ideology expressively as well as instrumentally, and Mussolini did, after all, make the trains run on time.[36] The four boxes only denote very general tendencies, on the bases of which some hypotheses can be drawn about the evolution of established one-party systems. One virtue of the classification, however, is that it includes non-revolutionary as well as revolutionary variants, in contrast to Tucker's typology.[37] Thus it is possible to discuss adaptive single-party systems as well as those which transform society; chiliastic and administrative systems can adapt like Tucker's "extinct movement-regimes" without being extinguished, since their legitimacy does not depend primarily upon goal achievement. It will also be possible to discuss the phenomenon of "deradicalization" or ritualization within a given ideological system.

Totalitarian systems are inherently unstable in that they attempt the logically impossible task, in Brzezinski's words, of "institutionalizing revolutionary zeal." [38] Totalitarian ideology is inherently incompatible with bureaucratic routine or legal order, for it demands the perpetual movement of permanent revolution. Whether the party absorbs other bureaucrats and technicians or creates its own, they will tend to undermine its revolutionary purpose unless they are periodically purged, in which case bureaucratic order is constantly jeopardized—even, and especially, within the party. Purges and terror may also be necessary to ensure the internal consistency of the ideology, and hence the legitimacy of the rulers, despite widening, and ultimately unbridgeable, gaps between the ideology and social reality. Without terror and widespread purges the pure ideology may become dissociated from the party's organizational goals, or practical ideology. This has happened in China, resulting in a temporary breakdown of the established one-party system.[39] It would seem that totalitarian systems cannot endure without terror or some functional equivalent; instead, the ideology "erodes" or changes in ways we shall subsequently discuss.

Despite their inherent instability, and though the Soviet Union is no longer totalitarian, these systems generate remarkable power to transform society. Problems which plague other established single-party systems are not permitted to arise. Thus party membership is kept closed and exclusive; even the Nazi ideology provided relatively clear-cut criteria for defining the vanguard. Party cohesion is not undermined by factionalism; indeed, with the striking exception of the Chinese Communist Party, even opinion groups are banished, and in theory all of society is regimented though guerrilla pockets of autonomous groupings, for the most part illegitimate, may persist outside the monolith. Social as well as political pluralism, in short, is abolished unless, as in Poland, totalitarian breakthrough was prevented.

The conceptual revolution went furthest in China, perhaps because the gap there was greatest between the Western ideology and the traditional society. If Marxism could, as Adam Ulam suggests, harness anarchic former peasants to industrial order,[40] the Chinese had the further cultural task of making a modern revolution "against the world to join the world, against their past to keep it theirs, but past," [41] whereas the other totalitarians already belonged to a modern European heritage. All totalitarian ideologies are communications systems employing at least two interrelated languages, an esoteric code for members of the organization and an exoteric set of slogans for the public.[42] The esoteric code serves as a shorthand for communicating political information upward, coordinating the organization, and expanding hierarchical power linkages even under decentralized conditions,[43] while the slogans are supposed to mobilize the public and generate popular support. A distinctive feature of the Chinese system, however, has been its effort to generalize thought reform, and hence the esoteric code, beyond the confines of the party. Mao has tried to command Chinese language and thought as well as reality and thereby break out of organizational barriers to revolution. But dialectically the effort is bound to fail for, if thought reform succeeds, minds become mere superstructure conditioned by the material factors of organization and brainwashing—vulnerable, in short, to what the Chinese call bureaucratic "commandism."

Despite its injunction to link theory and practice, totalitarian ideology cannot "predict" policy. That it makes a difference for policy-making seems to be either a self-evident or nonsensical proposition—self-evident in that without ideology the Russians would not have performed a revolution [44] and nonsensical in that only misguided philosophers or social scientists make Humean correlations between thought and action.[45] But not even the perfectly pragmatic ideologist can with certainty deduce a particular policy from the esoteric code. Rational disagreements among the ideologists are bound to arise, as the Chinese recognize by permitting opinion groups. Thus, as David Comey properly points out, "if Marxist-Leninism can equally well justify collectivization *and* increasing the private sector of agriculture, then it is no longer the consistent guide to action which some people claim it is." [46] Yet totalitarian legitimacy rests precisely upon this premise. It is of small consolation to the totalitarian to excuse inconsistency by recognizing with Barrington Moore that "the power of ideas does not depend upon their logical coherence alone, but also upon the social functions that they perform." [47] For that is already to invoke the antithetical principle of legitimacy of an expressive ideologist like Sorel or Mussolini. To be sure, abetted by confessions, brainwashing, or sheer terror, a totalitarian ideology can retain a semblance of consistency over a long period of time. But when "glaring inconsistencies are tolerated, the complete acceptance of the doctrine is endangered" [48] unless ritualization sets in. Revolutionary zeal embodied in a vanguard party then carries with it the seeds of its own decay and supercession by another type of ideology.

Chiliastic systems have the convenience of being immune to rational criticism, for ideology expresses solidarity but has no practical consequences and is therefore quite compatible with bureaucratic routine, even with the rule of law so far as this does not interfere with partisan whims. But the chiliastic myth is a highly unstable source of legitimacy, even though one of its expressions is an organized mass party. For the party lacks operative guidelines, a practical ideology of even limited goals to define its tasks, select its members, and coordinate its organizational networks. The Algerian Front of National Liberation is a perfect example—a "party of detached parts," according to one of its regional leaders who like most Algerian militants bemoans the absence of a practical ideology. Without ideological guidelines, the party is simply a vehicle for individualist patrimonialism, for the chiliastic goal justifies all "counter revolutionary" measures. Chiliastic parties are, in Frantz Fanon's words, "syndicates of individual interests." [49] In this way other social and economic forces acquire illegitimate access into political system. In fact chiliastic ideology, enjoining no concrete goals, is peculiarly vulnerable to social pressures. Hence the party expressively dedicated to total transformation is in fact the most flexible and "adaptive" of established single-party types. The myth rapidly loses its credibility, and even the vanguard becomes cynical. Imaginary threats of "neocolonialism" and the like become functional necessities, and military charades may become rituals expressing the new myths. But international miscalculations can be costly.

In the last analysis the stability of the chiliastic system depends not so much upon the plausibility of the myth as upon social forces outside the party. If these are weak and readily exploitable or strong but bought off or in other ways satisfied, the system may endure though its legitimacy is feeble, *faute de mieux*. But the party is likely not as in the totalitarian case to clash with bureaucrats and experts but rather to evaporate into a bloated party-state. The established single-party system, unable to build legitimacy, becomes a no-party system with a heteronomous party. Was it accidental, for instance, that Mussolini sent most of his best party cadres off to the front in 1941? The party was superfluous—even at the regime's most critical period. Without an ideological principle of exclusion, the party indeed becomes the nation—and hence nothing. If, on the other hand, the party remains a vanguard of expressive ideologists, attempting to intervene against other social forces, it is likely to be overthrown unless these forces are feeble as in Mali or Guinea. Where, as in Ghana, the private sector and the ex-colonial civil service were strong, the vanguard failed. And Mussolini, of course, was eventually deposed by the traditional groups with which he had compromised.[50]

In the face of social pressures, chiliastic parties may introduce "corporatist" structures for the articulation and aggregation of sectoral interests. But chiliasm is incompatible with institutional bargaining; the national myth presupposes a general will and hence cannot legitimate political pluralism, even though it masks a *de facto* social pluralism and dispersion of power. Hence the effort to build a structural source of legitimacy is bound to fail. As in totalitarian regimes, the various sectoral organizations lack plausibility as representative groups, but they furthermore fail to mobilize because they are not animated by practical ideology. Thus the party is unable to embalm its myth in legitimate institution; in fact corporatism can succeed only in the context of ritualized or administrative ideology.

The chiliastic myths of culturally deprived, that is, non-Western areas may for short periods engender intense solidarity and apparent revolutionary momentum. The Chinese Cultural Revolution is the most striking example; after the disintegration of practical ideology and organization, the chiliastic "thought of Mao Tse-Tung," elevated to the realm of pure ideology, has become a vital source of legitimacy even without any stable attachment to a political organization. So also in Guinea, the first Three Year Plan may have been "too thunderingly simple about its hopes for a revolutionary transformation of society," [51] but the myth was believed—for a time. For, though not conceptually reducible to individual neurosis, class interest, cultural strain, or any other analytic category of the social sciences, expressive ideology may—when traditional meanings lose their relevance—be likened to a cognitive map "to make autonomous politics possible by providing the authoritative concepts that render it meaningful, the suasive images by means of which it can be sensibly grasped." [52] Much of the Third World lives in an age of expressive ideology, but the new revolutionary Puritanism remains an aesthetic aspiration unless it also generates a practical ideology. Yet, as Franz Schurmann suggests, "nationalist movements tend to generate only pure ideology; although they give their members a sense of identity in the world, they do not furnish them with rational instruments for action." [53]

Expressive ideology usually, though not necessarily, distracts the ideological imagination from concrete tasks. Hence durable "tutelary" regimes are rare in the Third World. Here a limited, but instrumental, ideology of social engineering can justify single-party rule which is, therefore, as in the totalitarian case, vulnerable to rational criticism. Programmatic intentions are tailored to social reality, making the ideology more "adaptable" than the totalitarian type though less so than the chiliastic type. Typically such ideologies derive from one of the other types. Thus Bourguiba succeeded, so to speak, in rationalizing nationalist anticolonial chiliasm, by giving it concrete expression in "Destour Socialism." Stemming from totalitarian ideology, on the other hand, Titoism once could be viewed as "an attempt at depoliticization of the average citizen's life." [54] In each case the party is to have a limited set of goals whence its legitimacy derives and on the basis of which its performance can be judged. Thus a practical ideology coordinates organizational endeavor and provides the party members with a sense of mission. But retaining the vanguard may mean reifying the limited goals. Then practical ideology is dissociated from its original instrumental or expressive nexus and can no longer be a source of movement once the limited goals are achieved. Moreover, the legitimacy of the limited goals can always be called into question, yet neither ideological reasoning nor mythical recollection can provide justification. Nor can the party itself generate procedures, through corporatism, internally democratic processes, and the like, to legitimate the goals, for then externals supposedly "depoliticized" or pre-political forces would subvert them. As with the totalitarian and chiliastic systems, tutelary legitimacy is incompatible with institutionalized procedures.

As Ulam has noted in the case of Yugoslavia, tutelary ideologies are in a sense "an optical illusion." [55] For limited goals are necessarily confined to particular countries; there can be no claim to certainty based on the doctrine's universality. The method of "Bourguibism," the nationalized socialism of Tito, Nyerere's *ujamaa,* Ataturk's Six Arrows—none of these is an exportable ideology. Conversely, when a totalitarian ideology is no longer exportable, it may become tutelary: there seems to be a necessary connection between the "pluralism" of international communism and domestic evolution, even though for a time a country can, like Rumania, retain more or less Stalinist methods. Yet tutelary ideology also displays inherent contradictions. The party either, as in the case of Turkey, allows itself to be undermined by the social forces it did not absorb and domesticate, or it must institutionalize itself, that is, replace substantive instrumental legitimacy with legitimacy derived from a diffuse respect for its internal structure. Then, too, the party risks being swamped by other forces, but it is conceivable that an established party can flexibly absorb them while retaining its identity and its functions of recruiting and legitimating the top political leadership.

Like chiliastic ideology, administrative ideology consists of symbols and myths defused of programmatic significance. It is an expressive rather than an instrumental type of ideology, for sentimentalists rather than revolutionary pragmatists. But, since it does not posit an ultimate goal (however irrelevant the goal may be as a guide to action), administrative ideology is tolerant of a wide range of practical, partial goals. Pluralism and corporate representation are therefore explicitly acceptable as methods for reaching decisions. The party lacks a fixed practical ideology defining organizational purpose; like the chiliastic party it has only a sense of purpose rather than concrete purposes. Indeed, far from remaining a mere organization, the party becomes an institution with procedures which may be likened to the constitution of an established state. To be sure, it retains administrative cadres and a mass membership, but, like the Yugoslav League of Communists, it becomes progressively "divorced from power." [56] The analogy, however, is not with the Christian church but rather with Islam, which theoretically admitted no distinction between religion and politics. Classically, the religious scholars, "the 'men who fasten and loosen,' retain a right of continual supervision, not over the exercise of power, it should be noted, but over the conditions of validity of the Caliphate's part." [57] So also in Yugoslavia, communists may preserve the party and its procedures by recalling and reenacting the myths upon which it is founded.

So far as it retains organizational features, the party-institution resembles the chiliastic party in that the prime function of the organization is politically to socialize the mass membership, even as its procedures recruit top leaders and legitimate their decisions. Like constitutionalism, administrative ideology can be a viable principle of legitimacy—as long as the myths underlying it inspire a sense of purposiveness and respect for the procedures.[58] But paradoxically the stuff of politics within the context of the single-party procedures will acquire a factional or multi-party character. Only the infringement of formal rules justifies exclusion; hence the party is open to all sociologically competent groups and individuals. However, unless the myth of party stewardship underlying the procedures is believed by all politically active members of the society, the party is apt to split among "constitutional" and "anti-constitutional" forces, and the latter will either have to be suppressed (presumably on the basis of tutelary or chiliastic ideology) or tolerated as opposition parties. In either case the character of the established single-party system changes.

Thus each of the four types of established single-party systems—the totalitarian, the chiliastic, the tutelary, and the administrative—displays dialectical tensions contained in its principle of legitimacy. But, as we have indicated earlier, these are ideal types deductively generated from two dimensions of ideology—its instrumental or expressive character and the nature of the goals it posits. In the real world, however, ideology is a complex set of interrelated normative propositions and beliefs that mean different things to different people. Thus in any particular political system individuals and groups may display differences with respect to both the form and substance of their ideological activities: they may be pragmatic or expressive ideologues and they may be committed to either total or partial goals, to name only the key distinctions. Pockets of chiliastic, tutelary, and administrative ideologists, for instance, can be found in a totalitarian system, and of course uncommitted islands outside the ideological system exist in any society, just as do individuals and groups committed to other ideologies, even in totalitarian societies.

Given the tensions within each ideological type, ideologies change over time. Within our framework it is possible to analyze the "ritualization" of ideology, the process whereby instrumental ideologies become expressive and concrete goals fade away—possibly giving rise to a general sense of purposiveness. The older the organization, according to theorists of American bureaucracies, the less committed it becomes to any particular goal and the more committed it becomes to maintaining the organizational structure as such.[59] We cannot assume any such built-in organismic tendencies in the organizations of established single-party systems, for the party, far from operating in an American "pluralistic" environment, itself defines the political system.[60] But in a backhanded way organizational theorists can shed light on the institutionalization—not inevitable, to be sure—of established single-party systems.

Thus Philip Selznick's discussion of the evolution of the Tennessee Valley Authority is instructive. Understandably, discussing a mere organization rather than a political system, Selznick's perspective is that of the instrumental ideologist, or what he calls the "moral pragmatist," who never stops asking "whether the end he has in view or the means he uses are governed by truly operative criteria of moral worth." [61] He brilliantly shows how "ideology," or what we have labeled "expressive ideology," can mask an organization's adaptation, or surrender, to external pressures. Thus the "grass roots" doctrine of TVA, while it "simply verbalizes an administrative approach which any agency would follow out of necessity," [62] also masked the informal cooptation of conservative agricultural interests by the authority. Unanalyzed elements in the doctrine permitted "covert adaptation in terms of practical necessities," for, "since unanalyzed abstractions cannot guide action, actual behavior will be determined not so much by professed ideas as by immediate exigencies and specific pressures." [63]

More generally, organizations over time tend to acquire distinctive character and to adapt to conditions of their environment. Commitment to established patterns is generated, and established policy will be institutionalized as doctrine. Unfortunately from Selznick's view, however, "an official doctrine whose terms are not operationally relevant will be given content in action, but this content will be informed by special interests and problems of those to whom delegation is made. Hence doctrinal formulations will tend to reinforce the inherent hazard of delegation." [64] Thus expressive ideology is one defense mechanism whereby an organization adapts to its environment.[65] Another is cooptation: of the formal sort for establishing legitimacy to a relevant public and of the informal sort "when there is a need of adjustment to the pressure of specific centers of power within the community." [66] The ambiguities of expressive ideology can mask the surrender of organizational goals that informal cooptation may entail; indeed, creating an institution out of an organization usually involves the "elaboration of socially integrating myths." [67]

In any established one-party system, it would seem essential that the ideology be expressively as well as instrumentally applied, if the organization is flexibly to adapt to its environment. Tucker's discussion of the "deradicalization" of Marxist movements provides added evidence. Orthodox leaders may "modify the *tactical* part of the ideology by stressing immediate short-term objectives and nonradical means of attaining them," but they must reject the formal revisionism "that would disavow the radical principles or eschatological elements of the movement's ideology." In fact, "intensified *verbal* allegiance to ultimate ideological goals belongs to the pattern of deradicalization." [68] Conversely, however, there may covertly occur in a communist party as in TVA what Sidney Tarrow with reference to Italy has called "the institutionalization of strategy" [69] characteristic of tutelary ideology. That is, even while pledging verbal allegiance to irrelevant principles, a party may acquire a practical organizational ideology attuned to its environment—for a time, at least, despite the risks of reifying limited goals.

Much has been written about the "erosion" of totalitarian ideology, especially in the Soviet Union. But what appears as erosion, implying an "end of ideology," may perhaps be better analyzed as a complex set of changes permitting the ideological custodian—the established party—to adapt to its environment. Within our typology the Soviet Communist Party appears to have shifted from a totalitarian ideology to one blending tutelary and chiliastic components. Yugoslav communism has apparently progressed further, evolving a mixture of tutelary, chiliastic, and institutional characteristics. With ideologies as with Aristotelian forms of government, "mixtures" may prove to be more durable bases of legitimacy than the pure types. Just as the mixed polity has more than one principle of legitimacy, so too does the established single-party system with a mixed ideology.

Only totalitarian ideology contains within it the seeds of each other type. Ritualization does connote "erosion" in the sense that it is unilinear, a process whereby total goals are replaced by partial goals and ideological propositions lose their original instrumental meanings. A totalitarian ideology can become administrative, but an administrative one cannot become totalitarian (unless a new group seizes the institution). Therefore totalitarian systems have better prospects of evolving into mixed systems than do other types. It is conceivable, of course, that a country like Tunisia having a tutelary ideology can mix tutelary and administrative principles. But it would not be able to acquire totalitarian or chiliastic principles without a fundamental change of system. The more complex the mixture, however, the more durable the compound. Parties that retain a chiliastic sense of mission are liable to survive longer than those whose myths rest merely on practical accomplishments. Independence had chiliastic significance during Tunisia's independence struggle, but the vision is only faintly discernible in secular humdrum Destour Socialism.

Moreover, a post-totalitarian society may be more likely to have internalized the ideology and hence be more susceptible to the "socially integrating myths" of a party-institution. The totalitarian leveling of society ensures greater ideological congruence between the party and new social forces that it generated.[70] Hence an administrative principle of legitimacy is less liable to challenges than it would be in less fully "socialized" societies. But the post-totalitarian party is also more likely to retain an ideological capacity to generate goals and myths than parties which never acquired a totalitarian cast. It is therefore less likely to drift into the unconscious adaptation to social forces that organizational theorists as instrumental ideologists seek to avoid by invoking leadership (for this is the message of Selznick's classic, *Leadership in Administration*)—organizational drift being the price of administrative ideology and "institutionalization," for parties even more than for private or semipublic American institutions, as the Mexican PRI, little more than a tool for social forces, clearly illustrates.

How then are apparently contradictory principles of legitimacy blended? In a country like the Soviet Union with a highly complex ideological infrastructure the answer lies in different components of ideology acquiring different uses for different groups of people. Ritualization, in fact ideology generally, cannot be discussed outside the context of audiences, indeed organized audiences such as established parties. David Apter is overly optimistic with respect to expressive African ideologies but on the right track when he suggests that "ritualization allows a transition from consummatory to instrumental values." [71] Expressive ideologies lack the programmatic substance for "instrumental values," but the ritualization of an instrumental ideology can generate both goals and myths.

An instrumental ideology is ritualized as a result of internal inconsistencies that inevitably occur as ideological goals become demonstrably impossible to achieve or else irrelevant to a changed society. Of course terror can also resolve inconsistencies, but if terror is excluded, ritualization must occur—hastened by the decline of Puritan fervor within the vanguard and the rise of "respectable" interests. Ideological change can be expressed in a variety of ways discussed by Barrington Moore. A doctrine, like the equality of rewards in the Soviet Union, can be repudiated outright. But there are more circuitous routes. Goals can be postponed—and forgotten. Or they can be ritually incanted in order to reassure the devotees that principles are not forgotten; in this way an instrumental proposition can be used expressively while its cognitive content is forgotten or—in the case, for instance, of anti-authoritarian populist symbols in an authoritarian state—given new cognitive content.[72] But as long as an established party exists with a vested interest in sustaining it, ideology never simply fades away. Indeed, the need to sustain it generates the "sense of purpose, organizationally expressed," that guides the party's functioning.[73]

The ritualization of an ideology—that is, one which is acted on and which justifies action—is the process whereby it loses instrumental meaning. Ideological propositions may be clamorously invoked, but they are no longer a basis for action. "Building socialism" for instance, may still have positive connotations and hence expressive uses, but it is no longer instrumental if it is dissociated from a series of more concrete propositions indicating how the socialist edifice is to be constructed. "Building socialism" becomes a mere slogan, much like the expressive exhortations of "revolutionary transformation" adopted by some single-party chiliasts and segments of the New Left in America. But this is not all that happens. The "ideology" must be retained. Hence, party programs must contain elaborate descriptions of how socialism is to be built. But the program itself will have an expressive rather than instrumental function. Very little of the ideology will remain operative. As Richard Lowenthal has suggested, "Communist ideology will have an effective influence on the policy decisions of Soviet leaders when, and only when, it expresses the needs of self-preservation of the party regime." [74] Even ideological "consistency" will be a virtue often invoked and rarely practiced.

To preserve the party, practical ideology determining organizational objectives and coordinating its activities is essential. But the only activities that are essential, if the established single-party regime is to survive, are that the party organization perpetuate itself and that it continue to be the prime instrument for recruiting top political leadership. Hence, "ideology" becomes a crucial party activity, generating the impression of a political system that is "consciously striving toward an announced but not exactly defined goal." [75] For expressive ideological activity gives the organization something to do, a role through which organization can be perpetuated. Even though it loses many of its control functions, the party survives, and indeed its "ideological section" may become paramount. And so, due to increasing specialization, ideology gets separated from politics—politics, that is in the sense of struggle for office and decision-making. Ideological experts acquire autonomy and therefore there can, as Alfred Meyer points out, be a growing conflict in the Soviet Union between ideology and science, as the less ideologically inclined party leaders, the generalists, lose control over their specialists.[76] But the specialized discipline of ideology can no longer directly affect most policy decisions. Indeed even—and perhaps especially—under Stalin after terror was substituted for rationality, but also today, ritualized ideology should be understood "less as a genuine master plan than as a hollow scheme to which lip service is paid in order to deflect attention from current realities." [77] Yet neither the party leaders nor the ideologists need become cynical like the disappointed chiliast, for gaps between words and deeds are expected. The catechism, organizationally expressed in a complex educational bureaucracy, is there for all to see; it reassures the faithful, especially the top leaders who seek self-legitimation.[78]

Ritualization permits a totalitarian ideology in breaking down to acquire three dimensions: the chiliastic, the tutelary, and the administrative. While it is no longer philosophy's task to change the world, the chiliastic component remains, routinely embedded in the political culture that the party continues to articulate and be the main expression of. The symbols remain, engendering enthusiasm upon occasion but usually expressed in Fourth-of-July type rituals. Yet chiliasm is not the sole principle of legitimacy, and therefore the credibility of the myths is not subjected to the sharp aesthetic scrutiny which founders of myth must face. The party seeks to play more than an educational role, for education divorced from practice tends toward overspecialization—in political systems as in universities. The custodian of values, it on occasion seeks to implement them, invoking tutelary legitimacy. To the extent that policy is ideologically derived, the "correct" solution still exists and must be imposed; that is, the party retains some control functions, though in shrinking sectors of social and administrative activity. Where, however, "correct" solutions do not prevail, policies and leaders may acquire another type of legitimacy derived from the very party procedures that generate them. This, of course, is institutional legitimacy based on the administrative principle.

The major constituencies of the three principles of legitimacy overlap but differ sufficiently to obscure their logical incompatibilities. There is a little chiliasm for everybody: in post-totalitarian society most citizens may have absorbed the founding myths. But the party's educational task is important, for it ensures that active politicians and managers, even if they are not specialized ideologists, are more practiced in articulating the catechism —and suggesting concord between its values and their designs—than the average citizen. One task of statesmanship is to express the unattainable in concrete practical terms. But, given the differentiation in the party between generalists and ideological specialists, the statesman's concrete alternatives will not be bounded by the practical ideology of indoctrination. The major audience of the tutelary component will be the party hacks, especially the ideologists. The major audience of the administrative component, on the other hand, will be the sociologically and politically component generalists and spokesmen of other groups; respecting the party and its procedures as an institution infused with value, they may be relatively free to provide new goals and directions to the political community, so far as the set of procedures is detached from tutelary organization. The ideological specialists, however, can be a constructive check upon the politicians, for the tutelary principle corrects the inherent drift of established institutions.

Yet it would be presumptuous and over-hasty to conclude that the established single-party system is here to stay, buttressed by not one but three principles of legitimacy. "Mixed" government is not always durable, and dialectical tensions can be a source of disease as well as health to a body politic. But our task was not to predict specific developments in any established single-party system, only to suggest ways in which the party could be a source of legitimacy for this kind of system. That the party can be the principal source of legitimacy in three ways rather than one—through shared myths, agreed goals, and procedural traditions—is perhaps already to suggest the potential, as well as some of the "contradictions" inherent in this distinctively modern mode of government.

‖ Notes

1. Carl J. Friedrich, *Man and His Government* (New York: McGraw Hill, 1963), p. 508.
2. Joseph LaPalombara and Myron Weiner, eds., *Political Parties and Political Development* (Princeton: Princeton University Press, 1966), p. 18.
3. Friedrich, *op. cit.,* p. 514.
4. Sigmund Neumann, ed., *Modern Political Parties* (Chicago: University of Chicago Press, 1956). See also Harry Eckstein, "Political Parties," in *The International Encyclopedia of the Social Sciences* (New York: Crowell-Collier and Macmillan, 1968), in which single-party systems are deliberately excluded.
5. More generally with J. P. Nettl, "We must look to parties as *substituting* for the legitimacy function of the state" in societies having what he calls a "low incidence of stateness." See his article, "The State as a Conceptual Variable," *World Politics,* XX, No. 4 (July 1968), esp. 581, 588–589.
6. For a discussion of factionalism, see V. O. Key, *Southern Politics* (New York: Alfred A. Knopf, 1949), pp. 298–310.
7. J. Gus Liebenow, "Liberia," in James S. Coleman and Carl G. Rosberg, eds., *Political Parties and National Integration in Tropical Africa* (Berkeley: University of California Press, 1964), pp. 448–481.
8. Clement H. Moore, *Tunisia Since Independence* (Berkeley: University of California Press, 1965), pp. 41–104.
9. For a discussion of Mexican mythology and its relation to legitimacy, see L. Vincent Padgett, *The Mexican Political System* (Boston: Houghton Mifflin, 1966), pp. 1–8, 43–46.
10. See *The New York Times,* February 25, 1968.
11. Kemal H. Karpat, *Turkey's Politics: The Transition to a Multi-Party System* (Princeton: Princeton University Press, 1959) presents a detailed discussion.
12. For a discussion of definitions see Friedrich, *op. cit.,* p. 508.
13. And, as Leonard Binder adds, "If a popular organization is to be the repository

of legitimacy, such an organization cannot be frequently or radically changed without mitigating its legitimizing effect." See his "Political Recruitment and Participation in Egypt," in LaPalombara and Weiner, *op. cit.,* pp. 217–240.

14. Stanley G. Payne, *Falange: A History of Spanish Fascism* (Stanford: Stanford University Press, 1961), pp. 226, 237.

15. *Ibid.,* pp. 200, 267.

16. See Immanuel Wallerstein, "The Decline of the Party in Single-Party African States," in LaPalombara and Weiner, *op. cit.,* pp. 201–216.

17. Aristide R. Zolberg, *Creating Political Order: The Party States of West Africa* (Chicago: Rand McNally, 1966), pp. 159–161.

18. For a good critique of such discussions, see Samuel H. Barnes, "Ideology and the Organization of Conflict: On the Relationship Between Political Thought and Behavior," *Journal of Politics,* XXVIII (August 1966), esp. 514–520. The positivist tradition of ethical and sociological inquiry is equally irrelevant. See, for instance, Gustav Bergmann, "Ideology," *Ethics,* LXI, No. 3 (April 1951), 205–218, esp. 215: "If I am to be consistent, I must call ideology every rationale, no matter how explicit and articulate on the fact-value issue and other fundamental questions, that assimilates facts and values to each other in a way in which the tradition in which I stand insists . . . cannot be done."

19. Philip Selznick, *Leadership in Administration* (New York: Harper and Row, 1957) alludes to the need for administrative ideology but does not discuss how it might evolve out of the sort of ideology which shaped his *Organizational Weapon* (New York: The Free Press, 1960).

20. Daniel Bell, *The End of Ideology* (New York: The Free Press, 1960), p. 370.

21. See H. G. Koenigsberger, "The Organization of Revolutionary Parties in France and the Netherlands during the Sixteenth Century," *The Journal of Modern History,* XXVII (December 1955), 335–351. These parties were "the logical counterpart of the increased power of the state . . . they were nearly always the result of the efforts of determined minorities who tried to impose their views on the country by force . . . without such organization these minorities could not hope to succeed . . . they did succeed only where the government was temporarily weak. . . . The new factor which made possible these formidable parties was religion. Religious belief alone, no matter whether it was held with fanatic conviction or for political expediency, could bring together the divergent interests of nobles, burghers, and peasants over areas as wide as the whole of France" (pp. 335–336).

22. Michael Walzer, *The Revolution of the Saints* (Cambridge: Harvard University Press, 1965), p. 307.

23. For instance, "When God used angels in spiritual warfare, he chose them without reference to any preexisting hierarchy. He did not recognize their status, Puritans insisted, rather he appointed their offices. . . . For most Puritans, employment determined status and employment was at the will of God. The independent sphere of angelic activity had vanished. A system of temporary offices had replaced the old hierarchy; the chain of being had been transformed into a chain of command." *Ibid.,* pp. 165–166.

24. *Ibid.,* p. 318.

25. See Crane Brinton, *The Jacobins* (New York: Russell and Russell, 1961), also the same author's *Decade of Revolution* (New York: Harper and Row, 1935).

26. Zbigniew K. Brzezinski, *Ideology and Power in Soviet Politics* (New York: Frederick A. Praeger, 1962), pp. 4–5.

27. Carl J. Friedrich and Zbigniew K. Brzezinski, *Totalitarian Dictatorship and Autocracy,* 2nd ed. (New York: Frederick A. Praeger, 1965), p. 88.

28. Carl J. Friedrich, *Man and His Government,* p. 91. See also Franz Schurmann,

Ideology and Organization in Communist China (Berkeley: University of California Press, 1966), p. 18. On p. 22, Schurmann writes:

> "For us, every organization has its own ideology. Since there is no such thing as an organized world-wide Communist party, there is no such thing as a 'Communist ideology.' "

29. Alasdair MacIntyre, "A Mistake About Causality in Social Science," in Peter Laslett, *Philosophy, Politics and Society,* Second Series (New York: Barnes and Noble, 1962), p. 68.

30. Georges Sorel, *Reflections on Violence* (New York: Collier Books, 1961), p. 125 and n. 10.

31. *Ibid.,* p. 127.

32. Unsystematically, and without being philosophically grounded as is Ernst Cassirer's work in Kant's *Critique of Judgement,* Sorel seems to be suggesting objective aesthetic criteria for judging the plausibility of a myth.

33. Had David Apter tried to make such a distinction, his analysis of "mobilization systems" in *The Politics of Modernization* (Chicago: University of Chicago Press, 1965), which he relates to "consummatory values," would have been more sharply drawn. It is not only the content of the value (whether "instrumental" or "consummatory" in Apter's language) but also its relationship to politica! behavior that matters in such an analysis, as we shall attempt to show.

34. Antonio Gramsci, *The Modern Prince* (New York: International Publishers, 1967), p. 137.

35. The quotations are drawn from an unpublished manuscript on Italian fascism by James Gregor. See also his book, *Contemporary Radical Ideologies* (New York: Random House, 1968), pp. 120–165.

36. But as Gino Germani shows below, fascists who took the doctrine literally, that is, instrumentally, were disillusioned by the early 1930s.

37. Robert C. Tucker, "Toward a Comparative Politics of Movement-Regimes," *American Political Science Review* (June 1961), 281–289.

38. Brzezinski, *Ideology and Power in Soviet Politics,* p. 20.

39. Schurmann, *op. cit.,* p. 28, n. 7. The author kindly permitted me to see a draft of his new epilogue to a forthcoming edition, in which he indicates that China no longer has a "practical ideology," as well as the fact that Mao's "thought" has been promoted to the realm of "pure ideology."

40. Adam B. Ulam, *The Unfinished Revolution* (New York: Vintage Books, 1964).

41. Joseph R. Levenson, *Confucian China and Its Modern Fate* (Berkeley: University of California Press, 1965), III, 124.

42. See Gabriel Almond, *The Appeals of Communism* (Princeton: Princeton University Press, 1954). The esoteric code presumably corresponds to Schurmann's "practical ideology." This should not be confused with Nathan Leites's "operational code," discussed in his *Study of Bolshevism* and more systematically elaborated recently by Alexander L. George in *The "Operational Code": A Neglected Approach to the Study of Political Leaders and Decision-Making,* Rand Corporation memorandum RM–5427–PR (September 1967). Leites's work, well summarized and criticized by Daniel Bell in his "Ten Theories in Search of Reality," *op. cit.,* pp. 310–320, reduces ideology to psychological dispositions and national character and therefore has a static bias; George makes it clear that the "operational code" is, in part for psychological reasons, highly resistant to change (pp. 7, 45). Tied to organization, on the other hand, Schurmann's "practical ideology" demonstrates its flexibility in the Chinese setting.

43. See Schurmann, *op. cit.,* pp. 58–62. Also Frederick Frey discusses ideology as a sort of "programmed control" enhancing the flow of certain types of information. See *The Turkish Political Elite* (Cambridge: MIT Press, 1965).

44. Barrington Moore, Jr., *Soviet Politics—The Dilemma of Power* (New York: Harper Torchbook, 1965), p. 431.

45. MacIntyre, *op. cit.*, presents cogent arguments against the Humean (and Weberian) view. His own analysis strengthens Weber's stress of the importance of ideas and uses the connection between Protestantism and the rise of capitalism to illustrate his analysis.

46. David D. Comey, "Marxist-Leninist Ideology and Soviet Policy," *Studies in Soviet Thought,* II, No. 4 (December 1962), 305.

47. Moore, *op. cit.*, p. 224.

48. Comey, *op. cit.*, p. 309.

49. Frantz Fanon, *Les Damnées de la Terre* (Paris: Maspero, 1961), p. 127.

50. For some formal similarities between fascism and some of the African variants of "socialism," see A. James Gregor, "African Socialism, Socialism and Fascism: An Appraisal," *The Review of Politics,* XXIX, No. 3 (July 1967), 324–353.

51. Apter, *op. cit.*, p. 314.

52. Clifford Geertz, "Ideology as a Cultural System," in David E. Apter, ed., *Ideology and Discontent* (New York: The Free Press, 1964), p. 63.

53. Schurmann, *op. cit.*, p. 23.

54. Adam B. Ulam, "Titoism," in M. M. Drachkovitch, ed., *Marxism in the Modern World* (Stanford: Stanford University Press, 1965), p. 152.

55. *Ibid.*, p. 159.

56. For an extended discussion of the League's evolution, see chap. 16 of this volume.

57. Louis Gardet, *La cité musulmane, vie sociale et politique* (Paris: Librairie Philosophique J. Vrin, 1961), p. 177.

58. On the interpretation of Ben Halpern, in " 'Myth' and 'Ideology' in Modern Usage," *History and Theory,* I, No. 2 (1961), 129–149, Sorel traces the diffusion of myth through three historic phases, as a fully alive expression of a will to action, as "ideology . . . in such a rationalized form as to extend its communicability in time and space," and finally, as follows, as an aspect of what we call administrative ideology: "Ideology may develop into something beyond itself—a *faith.* The transition to this culminating historic phase of myth occurs when a system of proof (or explanation and justification) accepted by a restricted (or partisan) group becomes institutionalized as the conventional view of a whole people or church" (p. 140).

59. William H. Starbuck, "Organizational Growth and Development," in James G. March, ed., *Handbook of Organizations* (Chicago: Rand McNally, 1965), pp. 474–476.

60. In *Politics and Vision* (Boston: Little Brown, 1960), pp. 352–434, Sheldon Wolin discusses the implications of organizational theory for political theory. In societies where the legitimacy of the political order is not seriously questioned—as in America until very recently—the "sublimation of politics" is possible. But in the Third World the same conditions do not apply, and the "political" is in the process of creation. Single parties, unlike American organizations, are centrally concerned with the problem of legitimacy.

61. Philip Selznick, *TVA and The Grass Roots* (New York: Harper Torchbook, 1966), p. xii.

62. *Ibid.*, p. 55.

63. *Ibid.*, p. 59–60.

64. *Ibid.*, p. 257.

65. Ulf Himmelstrand, who also distinguishes between instrumental and expressive uses of ideology, agrees that the "politicians with an expressive concern for ideology will tend to use ideology for expressive purposes rather than for specifying the details of policy proposals. Since these details will have to be

specified anyhow, a politician with an expressive political concern must specify them on the basis of more or less coincidental values from any interests, pressures and traditional ways which happen to make themselves felt at the moment." See his article, "A Theoretical and Empirical Approach to Depoliticization and Political Involvement," *Acta Sociologica*, VI, No. 1–2 (Copenhagen, 1962), 92.

66. Selznick, *TVA and The Grass Roots*, p. 259.
67. Selznick, *Leadership in Administration*, p. 151.
68. Robert C. Tucker, "The Deradicalization of Marxist Moments," *American Political Science Review*, LXI (June 1967), 350, 358.
69. Sidney G. Tarrow, "Political Dualism and Italian Communism," *American Political Science Review*, LXI (March 1967), 41.
70. In this respect we could, with Chalmers Johnson, consider ideology "to refer to an *alternative* value structure" which "may evolve into a value structure if it is instrumental in resynchronizing the system." See his *Revolutionary Change* (Boston: Little Brown, 1966), p. 82, and Talcott Parsons, *The Social System* (New York: The Free Press, 1964), pp. 525–535. Obviously what we call an administrative ideology would be more durable if embedded in a Parsonian "value structure," but Parsons himself is vague, as he admits on p. 534, as to how and when, say in the Soviet Union, such a structure crystallizes. We therefore find it more useful to discuss different modes of ideology and their possible linkages than to presage the "end of ideology" in value structure.
71. Apter, *op. cit.*, p. 307.
72. Moore, *op. cit.*, pp. 422–424.
73. The quote comes from Brzezinski, *Ideology and Power in Soviet Politics*, p. 82, where, however, he is suggesting that the party must continue to "ideologize" society. But in his exciting subsequent article, "The Soviet Political System: Transformation or Degeneration," *Problems of Communism*, XV (January–February 1966), 1–14, he suggests that social integration need not and cannot be enforced through efforts to "ideologize" society, but rather through new procedures—while the party retains a vested interest in ideological vitality. The distinction between expressive and instrumental ideology would have enriched his analysis.
74. Richard Lowenthal, "The Logic of One-Party Rule," in Alexander Dallin, ed., *Soviet Conduct in World Affairs* (New York: Columbia University Press, 1960), p. 62.
75. Brzezinski, *Ideology and Power in Soviet Politics*, p. 76.
76. Alfred G. Meyer, "The Functions of Ideology in the Soviet Political System," *Soviet Studies*, XVII (January 1966), 281ff.
77. Comey, *op. cit.*, p. 315.
78. This is one of Meyer's main points, *op. cit.*, p. 280.

Part II

WEAK AND ABORTIVE
ONE-PARTY SYSTEMS

3

Rise and Decline of One-Party Systems in Anglo-American Experience

‖ *Hugh Douglas Price*

Introduction

Much of the recent work in comparative government suggests exciting perspectives for the analysis of American government and politics.[1] By now it is more or less commonplace to view the early United States as "a new nation," the Jacksonians as engaged in mobilization, the robber barons as a "modernizing elite," and various structures of American government as "political systems." Thus it would seem that the relatively low-pressure development of American politics has been conducive neither to the emergence of ideology on the part of participants nor to theoretical sophistication on the part of political science observers. What the study of American politics has had to contribute *to* students of comparative politics would seem to lie more in the area of technical and methodological skills (sampling, attitude scales, logic of survey analysis, and so forth). In Table 3–1 we attempt to summarize some of the ways in which American experience is being usefully reexamined in terms of some of the perspectives emerging from the study of comparative government and political development.

But is the one-party system a useful concept for comparison between the United States and current one-party systems abroad? Surely "the name's the same," but a comparison of the British "cabinet system," the U.S. executives who constitute "the cabinet," and Andrew Jackson's "kitchen cabinet" is not necessarily a good idea. Similar names may conceal quite different functions, and it is similarity of function that is of most value for comparative purposes.

This conference on one-party systems has been organized around a general model of the functioning of a one-party system which seems in accord

TABLE 3-1   *Some Comparative Government Perspectives Which Are Influencing the Study of American Government and Politics*

Role of economic development	Crucial to analysis of contemporary South, and highly important for historical comparison of comparative state politics, regional differences, and city politics.
Political mobilization	Jacksonian Revolution and Whig response (in 1840) are obvious; also relevant are big city mobilization of immigrants, and current organization of the poor and the Negro.
Political modernization	Criteria not yet clear, but should have some usefulness in comparing state political systems and city systems over time (for example, strong governor, well-apportioned legislature, professional bureaucracy, and so forth, are the "modern" trend in the United States).
Systems analysis	Proving to be a very useful perspective for analysis of Congressional committees as systems (Fenno on Appropriations Committee), the House and Senate as systems (see Nelson Polsby on "institutionalizing" of the House), state and city governments as systems (for example, T. J. Anton on budgeting in Illinois), government bureaucracies as systems, and so forth.
Anti-colonial movements	Useful emphasis for viewing American Revolution, as suggested by Louis Hartz (*The Liberal Tradition in America*), as corrective for view of all-out social revolution.
Institution building	May help sharpen our understanding of emergence of such central institutions as Supreme Court, which Marshall built up from nothing, or even the presidency, which Jackson rescued from near oblivion and transformed.
Costs of counter-insurgency warfare	U.S. "success" in the Revolution and War of 1812 rested crucially on absence of any central economic or political targets for British to concentrate on, plus difficulty of pacification and high cost of dealing with guerrilla warfare (Wellington was more pessimistic than Westmoreland).
Cross-cultural or cross-national survey	Obvious application to comparison of the fifty states, and to city governments.
Political culture	Crucial to understanding difference in style between various states, cities, or ethnic groups.

with Walter Goldschmidt's suggestions for comparative functional research:

1. Because each culture defines its own institutions there is always an element of falsification when we engage in institutional comparisons among distinct cultures, and
2. Because no causal analysis can be demonstrated with single cases, no matter how clearly developed or intellectually satisfying they may be,
3. Therefore, it is necessary to engage in the comparison of the performance of functions to determine:
    a. Whether they are universally performed, and
    b. If not, then whether there are any special circumstances or any special consequences of failure of performance.

4. Functions, however, are derived from a model of social organization, a model developed out of existing experience with societies.[2]

The model for this conference emphasizes that the one-party systems to be compared are autonomous organizations monopolizing recruitment to top political positions. This definition obviously casts some political systems into a no-party or other category, whereas a somewhat less rigorous definition of a one-party system might include them.

Statement of the model is useful, but it sharpens the question of whether much of the American "one-party" experience falls within the definition. One's initial offhand response may be that the United States has indeed had its one-party systems also. On further thought, however, this yields to the realization that "one-party" has been used in discussion of American politics for little more than the absence of close two-party competition at the polls. For American politics it has tended to be a *residual* category, based on the *absence* of a specific electoral criteria, and *not* the presence of a specific phenomenon such as a single organization monopolizing access to high office.

The difficulties of stretching this volume's definition of the one-party system (which seems quite appropriate and useful to me) to cover the American experience can be summarized as follows:

1. Most American research on one-party systems has dealt with state or local *subsystems*. These lack many of the powers of a national system, and in particular are required by the national system to hold elections, register voters without discrimination, and so forth. The extent of national involvement has varied, of course, but has always been present to some degree. And in general it has increased substantially over time.
2. Most American systems discussed under the rubric "one-party" turn out to be systems that lack two-party competition but do *not* have a single organization effectively monopolizing all access to higher office. Indeed, one of the tasks that has been sadly neglected in American government studies is the classification of various types of local systems that are not two-party.
3. The American *national* system has been highly competitive since the 1820s, and access to office was not monopolized by any one organization in either the Federalist or the Jeffersonian period. Stretching things a bit, one might consider the Continental Congress as a one-party system based on anti-colonialism, and the aspirations of Hamiltonian Federalists and the Radical Republicans of the post-Civil War years as inclining toward monopoly. But none of these resulted in a stable one-party system. And even Jefferson Davis' Confederacy seems to have been a "no-party" system.[3]

Since the overlap between one-party systems, strictly defined, and the U.S. experience is so limited this chapter will examine the subject within both a somewhat broader context as well as the narrower American emphasis on one-party electorates. The broader perspective will suggest that the central function of a one-party system—autonomous organization in a way to monopolize access to top political office—has been performed by a variety of institutions. In the Anglo-American experience it is worth considering, I think, the way in which this has been done by means of a strong monarchy and its court (Elizabeth I), by a modernizing elite such as Cromwell and his Puritans, or by an oligarchy of local influentials who are coopted into a central political institution such as the "unreformed" Parliament of the eighteenth century. It may well be that this broader context—which faces ultimate political questions—is of more relevance to the study of current one-party system than the rather tame analysis of one-party electorates (which is a far cry from the central issue of organizing power in an independent polity).

Functional Equivalents of the One-Party System: Broad Anglo-American View

The superficial analog to the established one-party regime of post-colonial experience is the one-party state, such as Senator Byrd's Virginia, or city, such as Richard Daley's Chicago. But these are subsystems, performing only a limited range of functions. We shall consider their fate, which is generally linked to the impact of social change rather than a guide to change, later. For true functional equivalents to recent one-party experience abroad one must go back much further in the history of Anglo-American politics. Although much of the particular structure of Anglo-American institutions is archaic,[4] seventeenth and eighteenth century England faced many of the same functional problems as do many of the developing areas. An "established" one-party system is one which has achieved *stability,* and the search for stability was long and difficult in the English experience. As J. H. Plumb has recently put it:

> The contrast between political society in eighteenth and seventeenth century England is vivid and dramatic. In the seventeenth century men killed, tortured, and executed each other for political beliefs; they sacked towns and brutalized the countryside. They were subjected to conspiracy, plot, and invasion. This uncertain world lasted until 1715, and then began rapidly to vanish. By comparison, the political structure of eighteenth century England possesses adamantine strength and profound inertia.[5]

The search for political stability in England required some sort of successful integrating solution to the functional problem of recruiting top political leadership. To the non-specialist in the complex subject of English history, at least three distinct efforts seem worth examining for their relevance to modern one-party systems: the Elizabethan monarchy, which centralized power formerly dispersed to the peers; the Puritan regime of Cromwell, which was not successful; and finally the emergence of the Whig oligarchy, which was to rule as either a one-party or a no-party system for almost a century after Sir Robert Walpole.

It is misleading to look at Anglo-American political experience from current perspectives and put great emphasis on the emergence of Parliament, rise of two-party system, and the strength of U.S. political institutions. Examined in their own historical contexts the immediate problems were much closer to those of today's developing areas. As Lawrence Stone succinctly puts it in his marvelous volume:

> The greatest triumph of the Tudors was the ultimately successful assertion of a royal monopoly of violence both public and private, an achievement which profoundly altered not only the nature of politics, but also the quality of daily life.[6]

As a measure of their success Stone suggests a striking contrast:

> The difference between a Duke of Buckingham in the early sixteenth century, with his castles, his armouries, and his hundreds of armed retainers, and a Duke of Newcastle in the mid-eighteenth century, with his Palladian houses, his handful of pocket boroughs, and his spreading political "connexion," is a measure of the change in English society.[7]

What may be of greatest interest to political science today is not the baseness of a Newcastle, and the need for reform of "rotten boroughs" (a nineteenth century "reform" perspective), but the successful centralization of power, first by the Tudors—who rid the country of rival military potential —and subsequently of Sir Robert Walpole and his Whig successors, who organized effective political control.

Indeed, the exciting aspect of British parliamentary history is not its formal structure (which has been unsuccessfully imitated in a variety of moderns contexts) but its *function*. It effectively monopolized access to high political office, and hence comes very close to being the functional equivalent of the contemporary one-party system. Students of the one-party system can learn little from parliamentary debates, but might learn a great deal from the manipulations of a Walpole or Newcastle. This, of course, assumes that open resort to armed force is no longer a serious problem. If it is a problem, then the parallels are in the earlier, Tudor period.

Stone summarizes the difficult problem faced by the Tudors from four angles:

> They tried first to control and then to reduce the size of the force of retainers that magnates were in the habit of attaching to themselves; they tried first to control and then to prevent the building of castles and their stocking with excessive quantities of modern weapons; they sought to change men's attitudes of mind, to persuade the nobility themselves that resort to violence

was not merely illegal and impolitic but also dishonourable and morally wrong; and to persuade the dependents and tenants of the nobility that loyalty to their lord should not extend to support of private quarrels by force of arms, much less to the taking up of arms against the sovereign. Far from being accomplished within a few years by mere legislative fiat of Henry VII, this was a task which could only be achieved by a hundred years of patient endeavour on a broad front using a wide diversity of weapons. It called for a social transformation of extreme complexity, involving issues of power, technology, landholding, economic structure, education, status symbols, and concepts of honour and loyalty. The story is not one of royal intentions, which are plain enough in the statute book, but of royal achievement, which can only be dug out of the obscure records of local and family history.[8]

The brilliant political achievements of Elizabeth I and her predecessors did not extend to her immediate successors on the throne. But for the student of one-party systems the important thing is not the cause of the English Civil War, but the example of Cromwell and his Puritan saints as an example of what Michael Walzer has termed "the earliest form of political radicalism." Walzer explicitly suggests that a model of radical politics based on the English Puritans "may serve to reveal the crucial features of radicalism as a general historical phenomena and to make possible a more systematic comparison of Puritans, Jacobians, and Bolsheviks (and perhaps other groups as well)." [9] Such is one task of this conference, since the Puritans constituted a significant one-party system (broadly construed).

Cromwell and his "New Model Army" need to be considered not just as moralizers, but as ardent modernizers with a new dedication to political goals. As Walzer emphasizes, their radicalism was such that they viewed themselves "as chosen men, saints, and who seek a new order and an impersonal, ideological discipline." [10] The acting out of sainthood then produces a new politics which is "purposive, programmatic, and progressive in the sense that it continually approaches or seeks its goals," and "is methodical and systematic." [11] This would seem to be a very promising line of comparison for analyzing various nationalist or communist elites.

But Cromwell was a more successful general than politician. If we are to learn about conditions for political success there is more promising terrain in the amazing way in which British politics finally was stabilized in the first quarter of the eighteenth century. Our traditional emphasis on constitutional history has tended to put too much emphasis on the Glorious Revolution of 1688, and not enough on the subsequent political manipulation which *made* that event appear, *in retrospect,* so successful. We have, of course, a similar phenomena in the case of American politics, where the Constitutional Convention of 1787 is praised in similar retrospect for things that were, in fact, accomplished *long after.*

The whole argument for the usefulness of the British comparison might be undermined by the point that England was exceptional in the sixteenth century by its lack of a large army and of a national bureaucracy. Both of these factors were to change sharply in the period after the Glorious Revolution. Between 1689 and 1715 the size of the British executive agencies increased sharply so that they far overshadowed the court offices in both number and importance. The treasury achieved its preeminent position in domestic affairs. Since Britain was involved in almost continual war the army and navy both reached unparalleled size—and cost. The supplying of these services required more effective taxes (the issue on which Charles I had lost his head), and the contracting for them meant that government orders and opportunities for profit reached a much greater range of the population. As Plumb concludes:

> Two factors, therefore, emerge. The years immediately following the Revolution witnessed a considerable extension of government activity and efficiency. . . . This, with victories in the field, gradually bred confidence in the political nation—in the ability of the government to govern and to win its wars.[12]

Despite this marked growth in the size, scope, and impact of the central government English politics did *not* achieve stability in the reign of either William III or Queen Anne. Nothing like a one-party system was to be found in this period, rather the "rage of party" conflict was to be found. As Plumb notes "between 1689 and 1715 twelve general elections were fought, only one less than for the rest of the eighteenth century" and "they were strongly contested."[13] Parliament had been preserved and was now the key both to local dominance, formerly exercised by the peers, and to a say in the growing stakes of the central government. Hence the costs of competing for office rose rapidly, even though the duration of a Parliament might be very brief and could not then exceed three years. And these costs related not only to the original election, but to the frequent need to challenge or defend the result (especially in terms of the franchise) in a contested election case within Parliament. Plumb argues it was *in the constituencies,* not in London, that the first signs of stability were to be found.

It is at this point that one must pick and choose among varying historical accounts of eighteenth century English politics. For the period around 1761 and the time of the American Revolution we have Sir Lewis Namier's immensely influential studies of the parliamentary elite.[14] What Frederick Frey has done for Turkey, Namier did for the British "political nation" of the late eighteenth century. At that time, of course, there was precious little evidence of organized parties as such. But, as Namier emphasizes, Parliament was highly "representative" of the chief *political forces* of England at that time: the country gentlemen of various regions, London merchants, generals and admirals, those involved in the West Indies, and so forth. This representativeness was achieved, of course, in large part because Parliament was so *unrepresentative* of sheer population (most of which was not politicized, and hence not a part of what Namier viewed as "the political nation"). Rotten boroughs and totally uninhabitated ones (especially those under water) provided opportunities for powerful spokesmen of various interests to become a part of the ruling elite in Parliament. Thus prior to 1832 Parliament is more interesting as an assemblage of those who monopolized access to high office—sometimes as a two-party system, sometimes as a one-party system, and on occasion as a no-party system—than as a modern "legislative" body.

But is this view also accurate for the *early* eighteenth century? Keith Feiling's important book, *A History of the Tory Party, 1640–1714,* put great emphasis on the tendency toward a clear two-party split in England after 1694, and on the intensity of party competition in the reign of Queen Anne. Feiling later sought to extend this analysis into the age of George III, and there fell afoul of the work of Namier. Clearly, for the period *after* 1725 England was *not* organized on competing parties, but had achieved stability under a powerful one-party oligarchy. By putting an end to the competition which had marked the earlier period, the Whig Oligarchy created the system which Namier later dissects. But, as J. H. Plumb argues, it is an equal mistake to read the conditions of 1761 into the more volatile era of 1694–1725. Unfortunately, something of this sort has been done by Professor R. R. Walcott.[15]

Thus it can be argued that British experience *since* 1800 is less suggestive for students of one-party systems than that of earlier eras of Elizabeth I or Cromwell or Walpole and Pitt. The latter were concerned with the basic functional problem of defining an autonomous political structure—whether monarchy, republic, or parliamentary-based oligarchy—that could effectively monopolize political recruitment. British political history after 1800 is concerned with the less relevant (though fascinating) problems of parliamentary reform, expansion of franchise, and other aspects of mobilization and modernization. But all this occurred *within* a framework which was never seriously in question—it is the definition and maintenance of such a framework which is problematic in most one-party systems (at least of those outside the Soviet bloc). Hence the great relevance of the seventeenth and eighteenth centuries, and the comparative irrelevance of the more familiar nineteenth century developments in England.

American Development: The Two-Party System as Norm

What about the strictly American case? It would be tedious to consider all the possible early parallels with one-party systems. Daniel Boorstin has brilliantly described the initial success, subsequent erosion, and final collapse of the Puritan "guided theocracy" (my term).[16] The Quakers met a similar fate in Pennsylvania. The American environment was not favorable to the establishment of a one-party system at the colonial stage, nor was it much more favorable to one at the national level after independence. Still, much of American state and city policies has been either "no-party" or so lopsided in electoral result as to be regarded as dominated by one party. But in the latter case the "one party" has generally not been a one-party system; indeed, it has often been even less than an American "party" in a two-party situation. Thus the "one-party" rubric conceals a wide range of American phenomena, running from no-party situations through loose factional or personal followings, to the opposite extreme of the powerful "machine," which does *approach* one-party system status, though within a limited context.

But a retrospective view of American development, as with the British, probably masks many of the weaknesses and problems of the pre-Civil War political order. Instead of a highly successful and stable system, in which 1860 was a deviant case, it may be more realistic to regard the system as a very rickety and unstable one that rocked along, protected after 1815 by accidents of geography but on the verge of sectional breakdown in 1820, again in 1850, and again in 1860.

Despite the impressive structural development of parties in the Jacksonian period there seems to have been extremely *little* development of stable party identification in the pre-1860 period. The Jacksonians were more "Jackson men" than "Democrats," and the Whigs managed to disappear virtually overnight. Massive third-party movements such as the Anti-Masonic Party, Know-Nothings, and Native American Party swept up millions of followers.[17]

In treating the pre-1860 development we can distinguish at least three analytic traditions. Oldest, and least interesting to modern perspective, is the combined Great Man-Constitutional Worship view. It took the framing of the Constitution as the great key to the presumed success of American institutions, and elevated the framers (a large portion of whom refused to sign that august document) to the position of demigods. If it is admitted that the system has faced serious problems and on occasion performed badly since 1787, then neither of these extremes need be embraced.

A second perspective is more recent, and more interesting, but still finds little of great challenge in the pattern of American development. It is essentially a view of "American exceptionalism," and can be found in a variety of guises. We may distinguish both the ideological version, which can be found in the work of Louis Hartz, and a more sociological version expressed by Seymour Martin Lipset in his *The First New Nation*.[18] For both Hartz and Lipset the American system began under such uniquely auspicious circumstances that success was virtually assured. There being no serious challenges, the system suggests little in regard to how basic challenges are managed.

For Hartz the absence of challenge is an ideological matter, but the ideology lack rests on a sociological fault. Lacking a feudal background, the Americans developed neither a socialist challenge nor a reactionary response. Living under conditions of substantial social equality and with much opportunity for mobility, both social and geographic, they showed little enthusiasm for far-reaching ideological schemes. Instead of violence and revolution the country produced Brook Farm and a few Utopian communities. Only the South produced a serious philosophical challenge, and the South was outgunned in the Civil War. And Hartz argues that even the South's position was but a slight modification of the federalist Constitution. If amount of bloodshed is usually correlated with depth of differences at issue—as is often the case—the Civil War again appears as something of a mistake.

Lipset's *The First New Nation* is too well known to require summary, but some comment may be in order. It obviously opens up a variety of fascinating possible comparisons of the early United States and recent emergent nations, but again in a context of American exceptionalism. Lipset follows the chronological development only to shortly after 1800, with most emphasis on the pre-1800 period. Thereafter the process is a more or less automatic working out of the favorable value orientations which Lipset sees as present from the beginning. As with Hartz, there is little to become excited about in the system so portrayed since it was so uniquely blessed in the beginning that success was inevitable.

To some degree the advantages suggested by Hartz, Lipset, and others must be granted. But they do not completely exhaust the range of problems that a political order must face. If geography, ideology, and values were indeed uniquely favorable, there were still massive problems of institution-building, economic development, urbanization, sectionalism, and slavery facing the nation after 1800.[19]

A third perspective seeks to look at the American scene in the pre-1860 period more in the way it appeared to contemporaries than as it does in the Burkean halo of a century of subsequent stability and development. Such classic studies as Roy F. Nichols on *The Disruption of American Democracy* on the 1850s or Bray Hammond on *Banks and Politics in America* achieve this on particular issues or problems.

Two recent volumes—both published in 1966—have gone a long way to open our eyes to the frailty and weakness of the pre-1860 American political system. These are Richard P. McCormick's impressive *The Second American Party System* and James S. Young's brilliant study of *The Washington Community, 1800–1828*. Past studies of political parties have tended to emphasize (and apparently create) continuity of the two-party system over time (Federalists become Whigs and Whigs become Republicans, while Jeffersonian Republicans become Democrats), and contrast differences between the parties. McCormick breaks with this approach and contrasts party systems, arguing that the two-party system which emerged in the 1830s was *not* a continuation or reactivation of the original Federalist versus Jeffersonian system (the "first" party system). The post-Civil War party system—which was quite different in a number of ways—can thus be regarded as the "third" major party system.

The one book which is most likely to make students of one-party systems in the developing areas feel a sense of rapport for American political development is surely James S. Young's *The Washington Community*. It is excellent anthropology, superb history, and exciting political science. We can trace many of our political practices—including most of party organization—more or less directly back to the Jacksonian period. And we know a great deal about the intentions of the framers in 1787, but it has remained for Young to reconstruct from primary sources a convincing picture of the pathetic and chaotic community of would-be rulers who huddled in the unhappy village of Washington, D.C., in the first quarter of the nineteenth century.[20] By the end of the first decade of the new century the presidency had been reduced to a virtually empty symbolic office, Congress was unorganized on any but a personal basis, party was lacking in meaning or organization in Washington and was soon to fade away in most states; and effective ties between the mass population and the national elected elite were almost wholly lacking. The sad state of American government over most of its first forty years sharply increases the importance of the changes wrought by the Jacksonian movement (and downgrades the miracles previously attributed to the founding fathers).

McCormick provides a brilliant state-by-state account of the often delayed emergence of party competition, and of the factors which finally generated organized competition between two organized parties. This development came quite late in most of "the new states" of Ohio, Indiana, Illinois, Alabama, Mississippi, Missouri, and Louisiana. McCormick provides a series of detailed propositions which can be quoted, in part, to summarize his contribution.

1. The second American party system can be conceptualized as a distinctive party system, differing in the circumstances of its origins and in many general characteristics from earlier and later party systems.
2. The second party system did not form at one point in time; its formation took place over a period of approximately *sixteen years*. New party alignments appeared first in the Middle States, next in New England, then in the Old South, and finally in the new states of the West and South.
3. Party formation was most directly conditioned *not* by divisions in Congress nor by explicit doctrinal issues but *rather by the contest for the presidency*.
4. The sequence of party formation from region to region can best be explained in terms of *the regional identifications of the presidential candidates*.
5. Under the second party system, the two-party style of politics was for the first time extended to the *South* and the *West*.
6. The second party system was peculiar in that it produced balanced parties in every region and in nearly every state. There were no "one-party" regions, as there had been before 1824 and were to be after 1854.
7. This "balanced" character of the second party system, produced by the particular circumstances associated with its formation, made it an "arti-

ficial" party system. It could survive only by *avoiding regionally divisive issues.*

8. The second party system was characterized by *similar* alignments of voters in both state and national elections in every state. Previously, a wide variety of party situations—"one-party," "no-party," and "dual-party," as well as "two-party"—had been maintained.

9. The most crucial development in the extension of the second party system was the abrupt emergence of a two-party South between 1832 and 1834. This development owed much to the substitution of *Van Buren,* a northerner, for Jackson as the prospective Democratic candidate in 1836.

10. In particular northern states, where the contests for the presidency did not, for local reasons, stimulate the formation of balanced parties oriented toward the major presidential candidates (especially between 1827 and 1834), the Antimasons flourished.

11. Party structures differed in form from region to region depending upon the local constitutional and legal environments. In general, however, the convention plan of party organization and management gradually replaced the caucus and earlier informal devices.

12. The new type of institutionalized parties that developed, with their elaborate organizations and corps of managers and activists, were something more than mere media for expressing the will of the electorate. They possessed interest *of their own;* they were *active*—rather than neutral —factors in the political process.

13. The second party system brought into general acceptance *a new campaign style that was popular and "dramatic."* This style can properly be regarded as a significant form of American cultural expression. It added to American politics a "dramatic" function that transcended concern with government, issues, or candidates and afforded a generalized emotional experience.

14. The rate at which voters participated in elections was directly related to the closeness of interparty competition rather than to the presumed charismatic effect of candidates or the urgency of particular issues.

15. Because parties do *not* form, but rather *are formed* by leaders, the fortunes of particular parties in the formative period were greatly affected by the capacity of individual party leaders.[21]

In considering the incidence of two-party competition in the United States it is important to distinguish between various levels of government. A close division of the popular vote for president can rest on a series of states all of which are 100 per cent for one candidate or the other, or it can rest on states each of which is itself closely divided. In turn, state averages can rest on a variety of substate patterns. In general, the smaller the units—given existing patterns of cleavage in the electorate—the less likely a close balance between the parties. Figure 3–1 shows how different the picture can be for differing levels.

The extent of difference in degree of competition between statewide and smaller areas is shown in Figure 3–2, which contrasts the vote for U. S. Senator with that for House districts in the eight most populous states. All

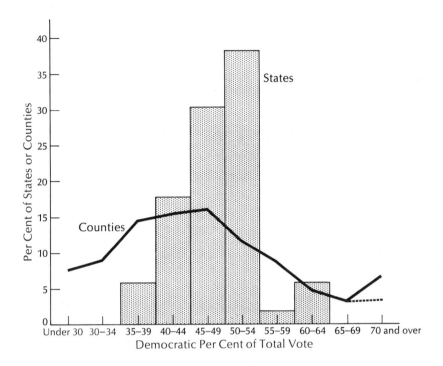

FIGURE 3–1. Extent of Two-Party Competition Is Relative to Size of Unit Considered: Comparison for States and Counties Where National Break Is Almost 50–50, Presidential Election, 1960

but one of these eight—Texas—have been quite competitive in recent years, but the competition does not exist uniformly over the state. Indeed, some writers on American politics have suggested that the existence of relatively safe one-party bastions is important to the maintenance of a party while out of power. As the theory goes, some of its leaders will always be able to survive in its electoral strongholds and this provides a basis for opposition to the majority party.[22]

An alternative view emphasizes the extent to which the one-party strongholds—the South for the Democrats and the farm states plus non-urban North for the Republicans—are atypical of the country and hence give undue influence to the less typical interests of the minority party. Under certain circumstances (sharp conflicts of interest between the one-party areas where a national minority retains control and those where it is out of office, plus either lack of information on electoral preferences or lack of desire to capture national office) the existence of a one-party base may indeed be disadvantageous to the chances of the minority at the national level. Obvious examples are Taft's renomination in 1912 on strength of southern Republican delegates, and Goldwater's 1964 nomination.

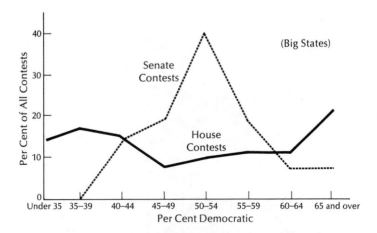

FIGURE 3–2. Party Competition in the Eight Most Populous States: Percentage Democratic for House Candidates in 1962 and for All Senate Candidates, 1958–1962 (includes New York, California, Pennsylvania, Illinois, Ohio, Texas, Michigan, and New Jersey)

Classification of units such as states by degree of competition seems easy but has produced a number of minor dilemmas.[23] The main problems of choice in developing an operational measure seem to involve the following points:

1. *Time period* to be covered: The mean value will obviously reflect any sharp changes occurring within a period. Moreover, the dispersion is important, since a shift from 10 per cent Democratic to 90 per cent Democratic would average out to a meaningless 50 per cent.
2. *Actual alternation* of majority: A strong minority that always polls 40 per cent to 49 per cent may differ substantially from a party that averages the same figure but has won office part of the time.
3. Definition of *offices to be covered*. This really depends upon the purpose of the index, which should be made specific.

   a. Presidential vote is most readily available, but tends to fluctuate more and shifts away from one-party status more rapidly.

   b. Governorship is ideal for dealing with state system, which may differ from presidential picture (especially if elections do not occur at same time). Senate vote is also useful for this purpose, but lacks long historical depth.

   c. Competition for House of Representatives may also be useful, though conclusions will be affected by frequent absence of any nominee for one or other party in some districts.

4. Treatment of *third parties*. The usual approach is to deal with the two-party vote, omitting such "deviant" years as 1912, or to take the vote of the major party that was least affected by third-party movements as the indicator.

An adequate classification system of American parties surely should go beyond the presence or absence of two-party competition. Whether there is an effective party organization present or not is one additional dimension. Duane Lockard has explored this, in part, by ranking states according to effectiveness of party in the legislature. Amount of differentiation between a state's presidential vote and the vote for state offices is itself a useful distinction. There is also the question of party competition that does *not* rest on the two national parties. This is a serious matter for Canada, and has been important for the United States until rather recently.[24] In situations where one of the major national parties is almost wiped out locally—as the Democrats were in Minnesota, Wisconsin, and North Dakota by entering World War I against Germany—a local third party may be organized and become a major factor at the state level. This happened with the Farmer-Labor Party in Minnesota, with the LaFollette Progressives in Wisconsin, and with the Non-Partisan League in North Dakota. In each case there was strong local opposition to the regular Republican Party, but the Democrats were in local disgrace.[25]

Among states lacking effective two-party competition there is great need for development of useful distinctions. V. O. Key explored the varying extent of bipartisan factionalism, largely on the basis of how close it came to a two-party situation (of which Louisiana, with its organized Long and anti-Long "slates," seemed the closest). The recent book of Donald Matthews and James Prothro [26] follows along this line, but fails even to make the basic distinction between "party in the electorate" and "party as organization." Some southern states seem to have relatively stable factional or sectional divisions of the electorate (a point missed by Matthews and Prothro) even in the absence of an organization which can dominate the nominating process to the extent that the Byrd machine has in Virginia. Thus Texas, Alabama, and Florida would all seem to have substantial elements of relatively stable factionalism *in the electorate,* though without a powerful factional organization.[27] Louisiana has often had both, and Virginia and North Carolina might be said to have the organization to a greater degree than the electoral base.

In the pre-Civil War period the no-party situation is of particular importance. There is substantial evidence that for most of the pre-1860 period "party" was of little meaning in Congress, where party identification of members was not even regularly listed until 1843 (for the House; the following Congress for the Senate).[28] For most of the period party lines did not even hold on elections to the speakership. And McCormick has shown in detail how state after state operated for thirty or forty years on a no-party basis. It is striking commentary on the modern two-party system that it operates to carry the national parties into previously one-party areas, or into no-party areas (of which there are few now left, other than nonpartisanship for some cities and suburbs), or to replace previous competition organized between a branch of the national party and a statewide local party.

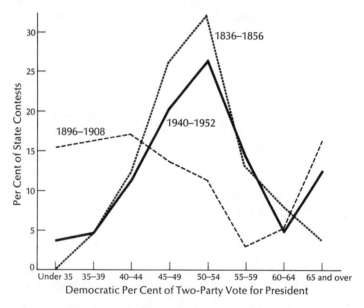

FIGURE 3–3. Statewide Competitiveness: Democratic Per Cent of State Vote for President in Three Contrasting Periods (omits three Free-Soil states in 1848, and four Dixiecratic states in 1948)

Complete data on gubernatorial and House elections has been hard to come by, but will shortly be available in standard form.[29] Figure 3–3 uses the presidential vote for the Democrats as a preliminary indicator of some of the sharp changes in extent of party competition in differing time periods. The most obvious point is that the Jacksonian party system (described by McCormick) and the current post-New Deal system are *both* quite highly competitive in contrast to the strong sectional pattern which prevailed after 1896.[30] Perhaps the biggest difference between the competitive system of the 1830s and that which emerged in the 1930s is that the former was a very fragile affair, reflecting the impact of various sectional presidential candidates and lacking any real party identification, whereas the modern system has a massive anchor of party identification (though this is gradually eroding, and is nothing like as strong as it was around the turn of the century).

This marked nationalization of modern politics is reflected in both the steady Republican advance in the South (which has so mystified the Survey Research Center, which is still enamored of the way that party identification under stable conditions effects voting choices), and the advances in Democratic strength in both the traditionally Republican farm states and upper New England. These changes have been brought about by a number of factors, of which the most obvious have been actual migration of people (for example, Republicans into the South and the steady spread of industry and urbanization into areas previously not directly affected by cleavages organized around these issues). Thus William Jennings Bryan symbolizes the older pro-agrarian Democratic tradition, which by 1896 no longer provided a winning coalition. Al Smith and Franklin D. Roosevelt led in the remaking of the Democratic Party on the basis of urbanism, unionism, and the immigrants, with the South in increasingly anomalous and unhappy alliance.[31]

The four most important factors in shaping the areas of two-party competition and, conversely, of one-party dominance seem to be the following:

1. The Civil War and Reconstruction. This was basic to the creation of strong party loyalties, which were to last for several generations (though with declining intensity). No such loyalties had been generated in the pre-Civil War era.[32] Some Democratic strength remained in the North, based either on southern migration patterns (along the Ohio River) or the loyalty of Irish-Catholic Democrats in the cities or traditional Protestant Democrats (who finally defected in large numbers in 1896). Whig leaders and Whig policies remained strong in the South, but the Republican Party was in a minority—but not an insignificant position—after Reconstruction. Final reduction of Republicans to a nullity was accomplished in the turmoil of the 1890s, when new "disfranchising" constitutions were pushed through in most southern states.[33]

2. The election of 1896. Bryan's polarization of the electorate brought some temporary gains to Democrats (silver states), but many permanent losses. The Democratic Party was a mere remnant in most of the Northeast and even much of the Midwest. At about this time the Republicans were being removed from contention in the South, and Congress began its conversion to a stable body based largely on seniority (the election of 1900 was the first in which freshmen House members were less than 30 per cent and the first in which average terms of service rose above 2.0). The policy and institutional effects of "the system of 1896" have been well summarized by E. E. Schattschneider.[34]

3. Conversion of the Democratic Party in the 1930s to an urban-working class-ethnic basis, replacing the old rural-farm-Protestant base except in the South.[35]

4. Steady shift of much of the country toward urbanism, industrial economy, and political participation by second generation immigrants and the Negro. These shifts have coincided with the shift in emphasis of the Democratic Party (or vice versa) to produce a standing Democratic *majority* in party identification since the 1930s, replacing what seems to have been substantial Republican predominance from the Civil War through the 1920s.

The special case of the big city "machine" is so well known that I refer the reader to the standard items, running from Ostrogorski, Lincoln Steffens, Robert Merton's functional chapter, down to Edward Banfield and James Wilson. The facts were evident by 1900, and the theories are mostly based on Chester Barnard. But it should be said that the "machine" may be a more useful model for students of one-party systems than the one-party electoral perspective. The successful machine at least involves management of political resources and has characteristics of autonomy and stability. The hallmark of most non-machine one-party electoral politics is the *absence* of autonomous or stable power centers and hence of centralized management of political resources.

One-Party States: Causes and Consequences

A good deal of research has gone into identifying the causes of two-party competition in the United States in recent times. Urbanization, per cent non-agriculture employees, per capita income, proportion foreign born, and proportion Catholic are all useful indicators for the emergence of Democratic strength outside the South. But these are *not* the indicators of two-party strength in the nineteenth century. For the period after the Civil War, and even more so after 1896, sectionalism seems to have been the overriding factor. Two-party states were the border states and those with populations that included substantial southern-oriented elements (as with Ohio and Indiana, as well as the more traditional "border" region). The "South" in the nineteenth century extended much farther north than in our day, including Maryland, most of Delaware, and much of New Jersey, plus substantial parts of Ohio, Indiana, Illinois, and Missouri. The modern South is not only less distinctive; it is also much less extensive.

Interest in the consequences of one-party electoral politics in the United States dates largely from V. O. Key's fascinating work in *Southern Politics*. One aspect of Key's argument was traced out by Duane Lockard in his *New England State Politics,* and this has subsequently come in for considerable criticism.[36] A number of recent writers have shown that most per capita dollar outlays of state governments are more closely related to level of state economic development than to degree of party competition or extent of electoral participation. But it may be useful to go back to Key's *original* propositions, which are *not* exhausted by contrasting level of aid to dependent children in Mississippi and Connecticut.

Key's basic concern and assignment was the analysis of southern electoral politics and its impact on public administration. State processes of politics and policy outputs were possible dependent variables, but the southern one-party system was the assigned independent variable. I doubt that it occurred to him that a subsequent decade would become excited over the successive discoveries that over 90 per cent of the variance in the size of total (*not* per capita) city budgets could be "explained" by the population size of the city,[37] or that—taking per capita figures—rich states spend more than poor states. At any rate, Key's assignment was the one-party South as an independent variable. As the author of the first comprehensive study of federal grants-in-aid, he was well aware of the impact these have on state spending levels,[38] and he was *not* concerned to explain why rich states spend more than poor states—a subject in the earlier book —but rather with how the presence of one-party politics might affect policy within the mostly poor states of the South.

His analysis comes very close to the heart of much current literature on political development. Just as many non-authoritarian one-party systems abroad seem *unable to sustain* effective development programs, so Key found the heart of one-party electoral politics in a sequence of processes which—he argues—rendered southern state governments *incapable of sustaining* effective programs, even *within* their financial capability. The analysis was complex and included consideration of the fluidity of factions, absence of continuing identification for either "in's" or "out's" and consequent emphasis on demagoguery and lack of substantive issues. As a result, state government was more open to favoritism, agencies were more unstable and tried to seek autonomy, legislatures were open to interest-group pressure (and rested on black-belt dominance through malapportionment and non-voting of Negroes). As a result, Key hypothesized, the "have-not's" tend to lose and the "have's" tend to gain (the latter being advantaged both in the private sector generally and within the interest group system of the weak state governments).[39] Figure 3–4 presents a somewhat simplified causal diagram of what seems to me to be Key's basic argument in Chapter 14 of *Southern Politics*. In the diagram the *rectangular* boxes indicate the hypothesized effects of politics based on highly fluid factions (a categorical variable quite different from percentage of vote going to a given party). To this I have added the *diamond*-shaped boxes to indicate the special impact in the South of the Negro, plus two *circles* (at the far right) to remind one of the limiting factor of state economic capability and the major consequences that can flow from federal aid and supervision (both discussed by Key at length in his earlier book).

If this makes for a rather complex diagram the responsibility rests in the complexity of the situation and the sophistication of Key's analysis (vir-

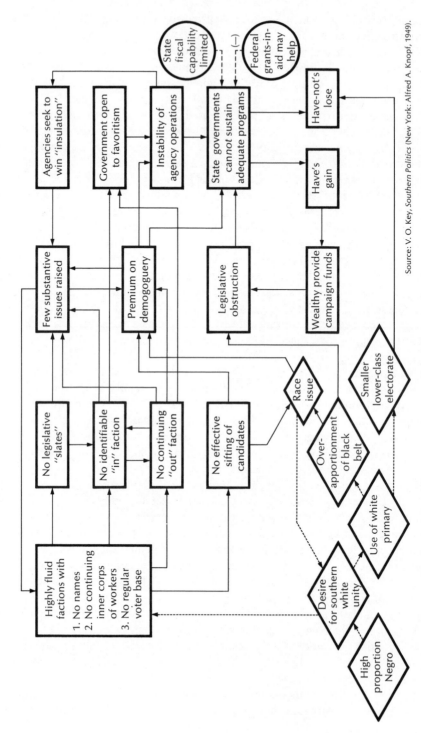

FIGURE 3–4. Causal Processes and Policy Effects on "Fluid Factionalism" in the South

Source: V. O. Key, *Southern Politics* (New York: Alfred A. Knopf, 1949).

tually none of which has been examined to date). Most of the recent critiques of Key on alleged one-party effects are pathetic caricatures which "disprove" a linear association (which Key did not suggest) between a dependent variable which was not Key's (percentage vote for one party) and an independent variable wrongly conceptualized (per capita spending, rather than per capita spending per $1,000 of available income, and after taking account of federal grants).

But after all is said and done, the recent spurt of activity on state policies has served the useful purpose of showing to what great extent sheer level of economic development (usually though *not* always industrialization) does determine many spending programs. Industrialism as a way of life does seem to have powerful imperatives across both state and national borders.[40] And the greatest changes in policy outputs do come with economic development. But political scientists need to keep in mind the customary distinction that economists have made for a generation between "policy" (or "instrumental") variables (which *can* be manipulated) and "environmental" variables, which are *not* subject to manipulation in the short run. Political factors may be less potent *predictors* of state or city spending than economic factors. But the political factors are much more subject to short-run human control. Mississippi voters can turn to a Republican candidate overnight—as they did in 1964, when Mississippi became *the* banner GOP state for Goldwater. But Mississippi *cannot* become as wealthy as Connecticut overnight. Moreover, if there is a national political decision to assume the greater part of the burden at the federal level, then the correlation between state economic status and welfare spending should drop close to zero (as happened in the case of state spending on highways when federal support became predominant several decades ago). After all, politics exists at levels other than those of the state capitol.

It is also vital to keep in mind that, for a developmental analysis over time, it may well be political factors that are crucial in bringing about changes in the economic situation. It is strange that at a time when students of comparative politics have sharply downgraded economics as a prime mover, students of American politics are moving to embrace a very simple and probably misleading version of the same idea. A reading of the literature on the role of state and federal funds in pre-Civil War canal and railroad construction quickly reveals the importance of *politics* for economic development. And Bray Hammond makes the same point in regard to banking and credit—he even titles his book *Banks and Politics in America*.

Untangling the interplay of economic and political factors will require analysis of time-series data, rather than just cross-sectional data. And it will probably involve non-recursive causal models that go well beyond the simple types analyzed by Blalock. Thus to explore the spread of industrial development (and consequent convergence of per capita income for regions and states) one might well consider the political effects of development as well as some of the institutional opportunities for using the federal government to promote development. Figure 3–5 spells out *one* very simple model of some of the processes that seem to have been at work in bringing about regional convergence in per capita income. But to deal with this question adequately would require a whole book on American political development, far exceeding the suggested limits for this volume.

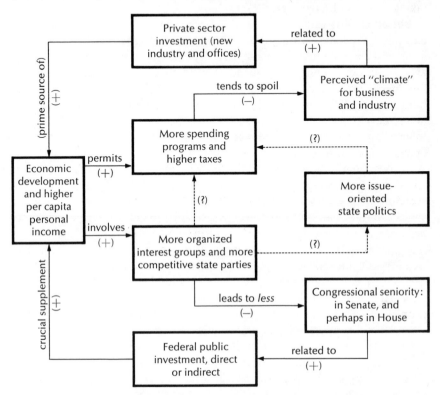

FIGURE 3–5. State Political Systems and Policy Outputs: Suggested Processes Involved in Spread of Industry, Income, Two-Party Competition, and State Spending Programs (dashed lines indicate relations at issue in recent cross-sectional debate)

The overall line of argument in this essay can be summarized, a bit abruptly, as follows:

1. Some of the basic functional problems of a one-party system *have* been dealt with in the Anglo-American experience, but at the national level, and in the period before 1800 for England, and before 1860 for the United States.
2. Most literature on one-party politics in America deals *only* with subsystems and concentrates largely on electoral politics. The consequences of one-party politics for policy are currently under debate, but all seem

agreed that one-party electoral politics is becoming rarer at the state or regional level.

3. Manipulation of political inducements by urban (or state) "machines" has been analyzed for decades, and *this* body of literature may be more useful for students of one-party systems abroad.

‖ *Notes*

1. I have argued this case in "Comparative Analysis of State and Local Governments: Potential and Problems" (Unpublished paper, American Political Science Association, 1963), and "Southern Politics in the Sixties: Notes on Economic Development and Political Modernization" (Unpublished paper, American Political Science Association, 1964).

2. Walter Goldschmidt, *Comparative Functionalism* (Berkeley: University of California Press, 1966).

3. See the fascinating comparison by Eric L. McKittrick, "Party Politics and the Union and Confederate War Efforts," in William N. Chambers and Walter Dean Burnham, eds., *The American Party Systems* (New York: Oxford University Press, 1967).

4. See Samuel P. Huntington, "Political Modernization: America vs. Europe," *World Politics,* XVIII (April 1966), 378–414.

5. J. H. Plumb, *The Origins of Political Stability* (Boston: Houghton Mifflin, 1967), p. xviii.

6. Lawrence Stone, *The Crisis of the Aristocracy* (Oxford: Oxford University Press, 1965), p. 200.

7. *Ibid.,* p. 201.

8. *Ibid.,* p. 201.

9. Michael L. Walzer, *The Revolution of the Saints* (Cambridge: Harvard University Press, 1965), p. 317.

10. *Ibid.*

11. *Ibid.,* p. 318.

12. Plumb, *op. cit.,* p. 126.

13. *Ibid.,* p. 71.

14. Sir Lewis Namier, *The Structure of Politics at the Accession of George III,* 2d ed. (London: Macmillan and Co., 1963), and *England in the Age of the American Revolution,* 2d ed. (London: Macmillan and Co., 1966).

15. R. R. Walcott, *English Politics in the Early Eighteenth Century* (New York: Oxford University Press, 1956).

16. Daniel J. Boorstin, *The Genius of American Politics* (Chicago: University of Chicago Press, 1953), chap. II.

17. See my essay on "Micro- and Macro-politics: Notes on Research Strategy," in Oliver Garceau, ed., *Political Research and Political Theory* (Cambridge: Harvard University Press, 1968), esp. pp. 105–109.

18. See Louis Hartz, *The Liberal Tradition in America* (New York: Harcourt, Brace, 1955), and Seymour Martin Lipset, *The First New Nation* (New York: Basic Books, 1963).

19. The importance of the slavery problem has been emphasized by Staughton Lynd in his *Class Conflict, Slavery, and the United States Constitution* (Indianapolis: Bobbs-Merrill, 1968).

20. James Sterling Young, *The Washington Community: 1800–1828* (New York: Columbia University Press, 1966).

21. See Richard P. McCormick, *The Second American Party System: Party Formation in the Jacksonian Era* (Chapel Hill: University of North Carolina Press, 1966), pp. 14–16.

22. For an examination of what happens in a state where most districts are competitive see Frank Munger, "Two-Party Politics in the State of Indiana" (Unpublished Ph.D. diss., Harvard University, 1955).

23. Fortunately the broad pattern of results is not much affected by such differences, since most existing measures are quite highly intercorrelated. See Richard E. Zody and Norman R. Luttberg, "An Evaluation of Various Measures of State Party Competition," *Western Political Quarterly,* XXI (1968), 723–724.

24. For an excellent analysis of this pattern in the Canadian case see Maurice Pinard, "One-Party Dominance and Third Parties," *Canadian Journal of Economics and Political Science* (1967), 358–373, esp. 369–370.

25. In the American South the party situation was, of course, the reverse, and hence facilitated the development of Populism in the 1890s.

26. Donald R. Matthews and James W. Prothro, *Negroes and the New Southern Politics* (New York: Harcourt, Brace and World, 1966).

27. The appropriate test for a stable faction in the electorate would be relative consistency of voting patterns in successive runoff campaigns, not degree of fragmentation in the first primary.

28. See Young, *op. cit.,* chap. 6.

29. For details consult the Inter-University Consortium for Political Research, P.O. Box 1248, Ann Arbor, Michigan.

30. The importance of the 1896 election is summarized by E. E. Schattschneider, "United States: The Functional Approach to Party Government," in Sigmund Neumann, ed., *Modern Political Parties* (Chicago: University of Chicago Press, 1956).

31. See David Burner, *The Politics of Provincialism: The Democratic Party in Transition, 1918–1932* (New York: Alfred A. Knopf, 1968).

32. The intensity of the post-Civil War loyalties is emphasized by numerous commentators, including Ostrogorski.

33. C. Vann Woodward, *Origins of the New South, 1877–1913* (Baton Rouge: Louisiana State University Press, 1951), chap. 12.

34. See n. 30, *supra.*

35. This was aptly emphasized by Samuel Lubell in his *The Future of American Politics* (New York: Harper and Brothers, 1951).

36. For an excellent review of the material through 1968 see John H. Fenton and Donald W. Chamberlayne, "The Literature Dealing with the Relationships between Political Processes, Socioeconomic Conditions and Public Policies in the American States: A Bibliographic Essay," *Polity,* I (Spring 1969), 388–404.

37. This finding was reported by Wood and Almendinger in Robert C. Wood, *1400 Governments* (Cambridge: Harvard University Press, 1961).

38. V. O. Key, Jr., *The Administration of Federal Grants to States* (Chicago: Public Administration Service, 1937), esp. pp. 335–336.

39. Key seems to have assumed that expanded state activity would be advantageous to the have-not's. This was probably more true twenty years ago than it is now.

40. See, for example, Clark Kerr et al., *Industrialism and Industrial Man* (Cambridge: Harvard University Press, 1961).

4

One-Party Systems in Africa

‖ *Henry Bienen*

Introduction

Various typologies have been constructed for the study of African politics, in order to differentiate party systems. However, what might be called subsystem variables which pertain to political parties have usually been omitted in the more general formulations of political types. This chapter is an attempt to come to grips with the meaning of one-party systems in Africa by shifting attention to factors of party operation, to the techniques for maintaining and exerting political power. This involves becoming more specific about political organizations and organizational techniques in Africa than the typologies have heretofore been which distinguish between mobilization and consociational systems [1] or revolutionary-centralizing and pragmatic-pluralist systems,[2] or even between mass and patron parties.[3] It also involves shifting to a different language than the one employed by the creators of these and other typologies for African politics.

The language of description, definitions, and typologies have had a peculiar importance in the study of African politics precisely because we have not had a great deal of evidence at hand about the workings of political parties. If we knew a great deal about political organizations in Africa from empirical studies, we could define parties in terms of a number of categories and then throw the specific parties into the various bins. But we would know, to begin with, that the bins were relevant because their relevance would have emerged out of the accumulated studies. The problem is that analysts have operated in somewhat of an empirical vacuum and the typologies they have constructed have been designed to seek out what was important about political organizations in terms of a wider set of questions for the society as a whole, for example, questions about mobilization of resources, control networks, economic development. But difficulties have been evident in moving from a concern with, for example, a *single* party as

99

a defining variable, or the ideology of a given party, to outcomes for economic development when we do not know how the parties operate at the grass roots or in the society as a whole. Moreover, typologies have had a tendency to be used (often by others than their creators) to explain political phenomena when they were meant originally as classificatory schemes. Somehow, it is assumed that the definitions actually explain. The rather sterile debates about democracy and one-party government in Africa or about economic development and single-party rule reflect both the aforementioned empirical vacuum and this tendency to move from definitions to explanations.

It is striking how dependent the typologies of one-party system in Africa have been for their language, images, and variables on characterizations of communist or socialist parties and in particular how derivative they are from a particular model of the Communist Party of the Soviet Union.

David Apter borrowed from Philip Selznick the concept of a mobilization system as one in which a party or regime engages in drastic and thorough reorganization of the society. The latter's work on the organizational weapon was concerned with studying Bolshevik strategy and tactics.[4] Another typology was designed by a specialist in Soviet politics to come to grips with the revolutionary nationalist regimes in order to compare them with communist regimes. I refer to Robert C. Tucker's revolutionary mass movement regime under single-party auspices, which he called the "movement-regime." [5] Tucker stressed revolutionary dynamicism as a basis of differentiation among types; he warned against trying to differentiate types primarily in organizational terms—a warning that was not heeded at least by political scientists concerned with Africa. Henry Bretton, for example, noting that Ghana might pass through a pronounced non-democratic "in all probability authoritarian-totalitarian regime," said that the form might be not only Marxist but fascist, although in a modified form "making allowances for organizational deficiencies." [6] Organizational deficiencies are themselves the crux of the matter; organizational forms are not.

Tucker did not address himself to specific African cases in any detail at all. Nor did other specialists on the Soviet Union or communist systems apply their analyses to Africa although there has been much discussion of African socialism, Soviet theories of "national democracy," and Soviet models for economic development.[7] Rather, what happened was that a generalized image of the CPSU was brought to the study of African one-party system, perhaps because they were, after all, one-party systems and the CPSU has been the most prominent, salient, long-lived one-party system going. There is a certain irony that those aspects of the CPSU which were contained in the totalitarian model—monolithic organization, hierarchical authority, organizational weapon in a word—were brought into the literature on African politics through typologies just when the totalitarian model was itself being called in question by analysts of the Soviet Union. A revisionist literature on Soviet politics is now stressing the prevalence of cliques in the system, the porosity of political structure of the system, the problem of extending central control to the peripheries, the existence of diversity of institutional forms at the local levels.[8]

It would not be earth-shaking to point out that cliques, family circles, and factions have abounded in African one-party systems, including the so-called mobilization ones as well as the parties of notables or patron parties although the idea has been resisted by some analysts and some African leaders as it was resisted by analysts of China's and the Soviet Union's communist parties. Once we would have said that all African one-party systems have factions, and even gone so far as to say that all are in some respects parties of notables, we would not have said either enough or the most useful things. We do not want to be guilty of overhomogenization here. Similarly, while I think the concept of political machine as applied to African politics is worth exploring, it seems to me that the concept of machine has not been an entirely successful one; it has remained a limited concept too broad in being applicable to all political organizations and too narrow in particularly suggesting corruption and patronage politics.

Thus, although I want to propose looking at the internal dynamics and adaptation of African parties to the exigencies of rule in the light of some ideas on American political machines and American single-party systems precisely because this literature focuses on localized politics, political patronage, individual self-interest, as well as social mobility of minority groups in a plural society, I am not trying to replace the term "party" with the term "machine." Nor am I interested in putting forward yet another typology of African politics, this time to be called the American political machine model. At this point, I am saying that some awareness of American party systems may be suggestive for thinking about African politics and that on the face of it, there has been much barking up the wrong trees with the Soviet-derived models, since the communist parties have usually been defined as a group around themes of monolithicness, dynamism, mobilizational abilities, cohesiveness, ideological commitment—all of which are organizing concepts that may be of limited use for studying African parties.

African Parties and Typologies of African Political Systems

It may be useful to be more explicit in criticizing the utility of the typologies which have had much currency in the study of African parties. To do this it is necessary to repair to recent African political history, as well as the history of the typologies themselves.

When I was asked to write on African one-party systems in the spring of 1967, I suspected that there might be a dwindling number by the time my thoughts were printed. When I later learned that this volume on one-party systems was to stress *established* one-party systems and that one criterion for membership in the category was that the systems had lasted at least ten years, I realized I was going to have a rather small universe of systems in

Africa. Before even trying to define African party systems, or to address myself to the question: At least ten years of what? I had to be generous in my construction of the ten-year period. We cannot ask for ten years of *rule* by single parties without immediately excluding almost all African political systems, since formal independence for most African countries is a phenomenon of the 1960s. If we add on a period of dominance by indigenous nationalist movements and one-party dominance, we can fulfill our obligation of ten years' longevity in a number of cases. But as we do this we must be aware that relative dominance of the soon-to-emerge-victorious nationalist movement over rival organizations differed greatly between countries. One-party states emerged in places where, on the basis of electoral performance, it looked as if at least a two-party system was being institutionalized in the terminal colonial period, for example Mali and Ghana.[9] Thus we cannot infer one-party dominance back into the nationalist movement period for all the systems which became independent under the aegis of a single party that identified itself with state and nation. We now have studies available which show how marginal advantages were used to consolidate one-party rule and which try to specify at what point in time and why a particular nationalist movement won out.[10]

The one-party systems that did emerge at independence were subsequently compared in terms of the differing party organizations by which the systems were defined. One such differentiation among one-party states was Ruth Schachter Morganthau's categorization of "mass" and "patron" parties.[11] Professor Morganthau noted that in 1956 the *Union Soudanaise* in Mali and the *Parti Démocratique de Guinée* (PDG) in Guinea defeated patron parties based on "chiefs," and that the mass parties consolidated their electoral victories as soon as they were in a position to do so.[12] Professor Morganthau, however, did not stress the marginal advantage of the mass parties. Rather, her political history unfolded as a contest between modernizers and traditionalists, although it did not specify as a necessary outcome the victory of mass parties (which after all were not victorious everywhere, for example, the Sawaba party in Niger), and it did doubt whether the distinction always remained valid after independence.[13]

The time variable is very relevant but not primarily because the popularity of given parties peaked near independence and then fell. It is important because given the short time that individual parties have been dominant, including a period in the pre-independence period, say from 1956 for the PDG in Guinea and the *Union Soudanaise* in Mali (the latter's dominance being less than the former's with respect to other political groups) from 1958 for the Tanganyika African National Union (TANU) and from 1956 for the Convention Peoples Party (CPP) in Ghana, and given their resources in terms of tasks to perform, time has been very short for African parties. There are no established one-party systems in Africa, south of the Sahara at least, and our need to fudge the ten years standard is one indication of this.

The typologies that proliferated in the 1960s for African political systems have been misleading for reasons other than neglect of a time factor. I have argued elsewhere that for all the concern for elaborating a number of distinguishing variables, the characteristics attributed to political systems in Africa were often based on images that African parties wanted to convey to the world and themselves.[14] Ideology emerges as a major distinguishing component in the various typologies. But it cannot be taken for granted that explicit ideologies in African states have descriptive relevance, and the few people who articulate these ideologies may not even be very close to the center of power within the party. The aspirations that certain elites have to transform their societies through a single party that penetrates all communities and social structures, and which mobilizes society's resources, may or may not be significant.

A further, though related, problem is that typologies may be based on relatively formal structures, that is, they relate to real phenomena but they are limited to an account of how they *would* work if they worked according to the normative expectations of the elites. They are not dealing with an empirical study of processes. They do not tell us the nature of relationships within the party; nor how the party relates to society as a whole and not merely to the modern, urban, or town sectors. We cannot tell from them whether or not normative expectations which may be stated in explicit ideologies at the center are shared throughout society.[15]

I am aware that analysts of African parties have been conscious of the "inexhaustible mixture" of differentiating elements. Nonetheless, the very existence of the typologies avows that their creators believe the units are not *sui generis* and are subject to useful generalization. And despite awareness of dilemmas in classifying complex political phenomena in Africa, I think the criticisms stand. Let us briefly consider other typologies.

The work of Coleman and Rosberg on "revolutionary-centralizing trends" and "pragmatic-pluralistic patterns" as two general tendencies in uniparty or one-party dominant states has ideology as its first differentiating factor. (Ideology receives the most elaboration of all the differentiating factors in terms of categories and subcategories.)[16] Other major differentiating factors are popular participation and organizational aspects. Parties are classified according to tendencies. The dominant parties in African states representative of the revolutionary-centralizing trend are said to be preoccupied with ideology, the content of which is programmatic and transformative regarding the socioeconomic modernization of contemporary society. They also tend to be ultra-popularistic and egalitarian and stress participation in affairs of party and state. Organizationally, it is said, the parties tend to be monolithic and centralized.[17]

This categorization is not derived from the ways parties work. It is an example of the aforementioned reliance on normative and formal structural differences. These normative and formal differences may be important but this has to be shown. We must make the same demands here with regard to stipulated institutional arrangements, constitutions, that are made in critiques of "formal-legal" studies in comparative politics of Western European countries and the United States.

The same criticism applies to David Apter's typologies of "mobilization" and "consociational" systems.[18] Apter states that a mobilization system usually contains a party of solidarity which either monopolizes power openly or in other ways makes all other groups dependent on it. The party network is, in effect, the structure of the new society. As he elaborated the system with reference to Africa, the party in the mobilization system demands fundamental commitment on the part of the individual; it can make quick changes in its alliances and alter its goals and targets. Power usually resides at the top of the organization, generally in a single leader who monopolizes legitimacy. The party or state will most often act on grounds of expediency and necessity, using ideology to give perspective and justification for what appears necessary. Thus hierarchical authority, claims for total allegiance, appearance of tactical flexibility, and party links to and domination of functional organizations and political groups seem to define the party of solidarity in the system.[19]

Of course, this typology is designed to help seek out the data that will tell us how much tactical flexibility parties have, or how hierarchical authority is. Nonetheless, this typology is dependent on formal structures and political rhetoric too. What we want to find out is how the central and local institutions work and how homogenous or heterogenous are the one-party systems. As we find out that the one-party systems even have a great deal of formal diversity of structures at local levels and that central organs cannot exact desired responses from regional and district bodies, we realize that there has been a focus on parties as if they were coterminous with the societies or territorial entities they purport to rule. If, in fact, all political parties in Africa have great difficulty in radiating out central authority, if authority is widely diffused, if one-party systems are vulnerable to military takeover, if power is dispersed, then it is not useful to pose a consociational model where authority is pyramidal (dispersed and shared between constituent units and a central agency) as compared to a mobilization system's hierarchical authority. If African countries are plural societies in the extreme, then is it heuristic to pose a consociational model where there tends to be a system of loyalties functioning on various levels as against the demand for total allegiance of the mobilization system's party? And what sense is there in postulating a unitarism of political organization when the local party organizations may constitute a political opposition to the center (as Apter himself has recently argued the CPP's constituency organizations did in Ghana) [20] or when this local organization shows deflection from the center's commands (as I have argued for TANU)?

Now the inventors of the categories "mass," "revolutionary-centralizing" and "mobilization system" did not insist that such parties as characterized these systems would necessarily best modernize a country or best solve the problems of ethnic heterogeneity. Indeed, Morganthau noted that conflicts among ethnic groups were often sharper in mass than in patron parties since "mass parties made a continuous attempt to propagate modern values and diminish the weight of ethnic exclusiveness," and were egalitarian by policy.[21] Moreover, she stated that mass party leaders sometimes institutionalized ethnic differences and played the ethnic arithmetic game.[22] For her, however, mass parties tried to blur the ethnic distinctions, although they sometimes failed.[23] Apter did not argue that a mobilization system would always be optimal for modernization but only that it was most successful in establishing a new polity and converting from later modernization to industrialization. In fact, his modernizing autocracies and neomercantilist societies were optimal political forms for long-term modernization and for the conversion from early to late stages of the modernization process.[24] Still, the very terminology shows that the revolutionary-centralizing, mobilization, and mass-party systems were seen as being more dynamic and tougher. But it is precisely this presumed strength that must be questioned, for this strength was thought to rest on the party's organizational coherence, which in turn rested on a mass base. Thus the mass party was thought to be linked to the countryside and able to exert itself there.

The crucial variable in differentiating mass and patron parties in Professor Morganthau's scheme was the way that elites related to non-elites.

> The main distinction between mass and patron parties lies not in the social origins of aspiring national leaders, and not in the scale of party organizations. It lies rather in the reply to the questions: How are the national leaders related to the rest of the population? On what groups and with what ideas and structures did they build parties? [25]

Her analysis rested on the view that mass parties reached out for all the citizens in the community in order to represent, lead, and rule them. Relative to patron parties they had an articulated organization and institutionalized leadership.

Indeed, there has been a seeming paradox in the treatment of leadership and party in Africa, for the application of the concept of charisma to the political analysis of African states has occurred for the mass single parties, not the patron ones, and the connection between personalism and mass popularity has been remarked on much more in analyses of so-called mass parties than of so-called patron ones. Discussion of politics in Ghana, Guinea, Mali, Tanzania has often been in terms of the political thought and personal characteristics of Nkrumah, Touré, Keita, and Nyerere.

Ghana's Convention Peoples Party qualified as a mass party in Morganthau's typology, and it was to Ghana that Apter strikingly applied the concept of charisma in order to explain institutional transfer from the colonial to the independent regime in terms of Nkrumah's leadership.[26]

And yet this is paradoxical when we consider that patron parties after all are supposed to be parties of personalities.[27] When Thomas Hodgkin and Morganthau discussed mass parties they stressed differentiation, strong articulation, organization in general, or what could be called relative institutionalization as compared to what were variously called patron,[28] elite, or cadre parties.

Morganthau explicitly states that mass parties had comparatively institutionalized leaderships, although these were not always collective leaderships. Patron parties had essentially personal leadership, although the mass party in the Ivory Coast, the *Parti Démocratique de la Côte d'Ivoire* (PDCI) after 1952 had essentially personal leadership too.[29] And the *Mouvement de l'Evolution Sociale de l'Afrique Noire* (MESAN) which dissolved opposition parties in 1962 to become a ruling single party in the Central African Republic has been described by one commentator as having broad popular support but being a personalistic organization.[30] It is at least terminologically strange that discussion of charisma centered on mass parties and their leaders and personalistic parties were not seen as having charismatic leaders.[31] But even more important is the peculiarity that the relatively institutionalized parties were seen as having charismatic leaders (this was particularly true for analysis of politics in Ghana and Tanzania), while charismatic leadership is by definition not institutionalized, although the leader's popularity may enhance the party's short-term strength. Granted, the term "charisma" was loosely applied to African leaders so that any popular leader with visibility and flamboyance came to be called charismatic.[32] Still, there is an anomaly in analyses that stress the mass characteristics of parties that reach out for a whole population through articulated organizations and analyses of charismatic leadership where the leader's direct ties to the population are stressed and his personal qualities rather than organizational ones are emphasized. (I do not want to explore the problems of the idea of charisma here but am interested in pointing to an anomaly in the writings on one-party systems.) [33]

As for the actual strength of the parties, perhaps when independence had been attained so recently, it was not really possible to say how successfully mass parties were leading, representing, and ruling their constituencies and society as a whole. But we might have been very skeptical of the statement, "In the single party states based on the mass parties there was at independence evidence of widespread consent. During at least a brief period the national and the party communities were indistinguishable; the mass party reflected the 'general will.' " [34] For even before there began to be studies of how national institutions, including single parties, functioned in the countryside, we might have asked: How could this be true, even at a moment of rejoicing and when parties were not yet called on to make good the pre-independence promises? For it should have been obvious that the apparatus of "modern" political life, on both the "input side" (parties, interest groups, voters, economic institutions) and the "output side" (bureaucracies, development corporations, legislative bodies, judiciaries, parties) were not very significant for large numbers of citizens. Many Africans operated in subsistence agricultural sectors; they were producing for or buying in markets only infrequently. Many did not vote in the elections that established majority parties (and still do not). Elections that were won by the ruling single parties were often to be participated in by less than half the potential voters.[35] Central and local government officials tried to widen the tax base and expended tremendous energy to collect taxes; but even now the bulk of the population in many African countries pay only local taxes or cesses; many people pay no tax at all because of exemptions, avoidance of registration, or the absence of any cash income.[36] Whether indigenous traditional institutions were comparatively weak or strong, neither personnel nor programs always existed to replace them. These things were known but neglected prior to the gathering of data on the operation of parties throughout their countries.

What I am suggesting is that there was an assumption made that political structures, "mass" parties in particular, operated uniformly throughout their society at least at the time of independence. Those like Professor Morganthau who saw a conjunction of national and party communities were emphasizing the absence of overt opposition. They saw popular regimes at a particular point in time. But this did not establish the nature of the relationships between party and society or within the party; it did not establish that parties were operating the same way in towns and countryside or operating everywhere in society.

As it became clear that even so-called mass and dynamic parties were not getting their economic programs across, that growth rates were not rising precipitously in Mali, Ghana, Guinea, or Tanganyika and as research was done outside the capital cities, it also became clear that the one-party revolutionary systems were not managing affairs well at local levels either. Central party organs were not exacting the responses they wanted from regional and district bodies. Plans and commands made at the center did not get implemented. One way to explain this would be to say that opposition rose again as parties had to do concrete things after independence when they took up the tasks of rule. This explanation is only partially satisfactory because it presumes that the structures were available for carrying out these tasks via central command.

If there was an exaggerated perception of the strength of some ruling single parties in Africa in the early 1960s, 1964–1965 marked a watershed in both the political history of Africa and the creation of typologies to encompass African politics. By 1964 most of the countries of tropical Africa were independent. When Zambia became independent at the end of that year, there were left the white minority dominated regimes of southern Africa and the soon-to-become-independent Gambia and the enclaves within South Africa. However, 1964 was the last year of civilian rule in a number of African states. True, armies had intervened in the politics of independent Africa prior to 1964. From independence in 1960, the Armée National

Congolaise had been prominent in Congolese politics; there were abortive coups in Ethiopia and the Somali Republic the same year. And the military was to be a factor in the Senghor-Dia conflict in Senegal in 1962 as it had been in the Senegal-Soudan breakup in 1960. In 1963, the military overthrew civilian regimes in Togo and Dahomey and was involved in negotiations on a new government after the fall of Youlou in Congo-Brazzaville. Also in 1963, there was a mutiny in Niger, but this was unsuccessful and civilian rule was restored in Dahomey too.[37] In 1964, army mutinies broke out in the East African countries (Uganda, Kenya, and Tanganyika), and there was a revolution in Zanzibar. However, no military regimes emerged.[38] It was in 1965 and 1966 that military coups swept civilians from office in Algeria, Congo (Leopoldville, now Kinshasa), Dahomey, Central African Republic, Upper Volta, Nigeria, Ghana, and Burundi. (There were also abortive coups in Togo and Congo-Brazzaville.)

These coups narrowed the universe of one-party systems in Africa for Algeria, the Central African Republic, Upper Volta, Ghana, and the northern and eastern regions of Nigeria were all one-party systems that could have been put in various categories. Ghana's Conventions Peoples Party qualified as a mobilization or mass typology, as did the *Front de Libération Nationale* in Algeria; the *Union Democratique Voltaique* was considered a patron party.[39] Just as the military coup in the Central African Republic removed a one-party system that might not have fit unambiguously into the mass-patron category, so the Nigerian military revolt removed two one-party dominant regimes that gave some difficulty in classification. The Northern Peoples' Congress (NPC) was not the only party in northern Nigeria. In the 1961 regional election, the NPC won close to 70 per cent of the votes and 130 out of 170 seats in the regional assembly.[40] There were other contenders, among them the Action Group and an alliance between the Northern (now Nigerian) Element's Progressive Union and the National Convention of Nigerian Citizens (NCNC). In the 1964 federal election, the NPC won by an increasing margin.[41]

As C. S. Whitaker describes the NPC, it is a party which after 1952 passed to the control of persons loyal to and dependent on the emirate bureaucracies of northern Nigeria. Membership in the northern House of Assembly became part of the patronage system of emirs.[42] Yet "clearly the NPC could not have remained dominant in an era of democratic elections if its support had been limited to a coalition of minority interests. The requisite mass support has been enlisted through appeals that make use of both associational and communal principles of participation on the one hand, and of both modern and traditional sentiments on the other." [43] In a complex situation, clients transfer their dependence on persons—their allegiance to individual traditional patrons—to the modern party of their patrons.[44] Organizationally, the NPC party authority is decentralized, a fact which reflects the traditional status of emirates as virtually autonomous states.[45] Yet the NPC strives for a mass following and wants to push down to the village level. It is able to do this by using the administrative apparatus of traditional emirate units. The NPC has a set of constitutional arrangements that establish a National Working Committee, annual conventions, annual elections of party officers, and so forth. Many of these arrangements establish structures similar on paper to those of TANU, the PDG, and the CPP. There are also ancillary bodies for youth and women, and trade unions, as there are for so-called mass parties. The constitutional arrangements would not be much of a guide to the practice and operation of party organs, but neither would they have been for TANU or the CPP in the past. The NPC, then, partakes of features of both "mass" and "patron" parties; it is a traditionally oriented party with wide support.

The NCNC has been the dominant party in the eastern region of Nigeria. It has been described as undergoing a transformation since elections in 1951 from a national front of affiliated groups into a political party in a stricter sense.[46] It too would be put in the mass party category. While many authors have noted the dependence of the NCNC on affiliated organizations, and especially Ibo ethnic associations, one recent paper has gone so far as to argue that ethnic associations in one county council area performed many of the functions normally assumed by political parties because the monopoly of the NCNC rendered the party unsuitable as an organizational base through which to compete for scarce economic resources and political offices. The clan became the group though which participants in the political system acted, and the party emerged as a holding company for local ethnic and clan organizations.[47]

As the military successfully intervened against political party rule, analysts had to again ask themselves what kinds of political animals these parties were. I have tried to suggest the complexity of the party situations and the variety of kinds of parties vulnerable to military intervention in this brief reference to the party types that the military replaced. But the very perception of party vulnerability, a perception growing out of increasing awareness that the parties were not everywhere the same within a country and deepened by the fact of military coups, led some analysts to move away from a focus on party and to argue that one-party states can perhaps better be described as no-party states.[48]

The argument for this designation can be briefly stated. Nationalist movements became parties of independence and then parties of rule in Africa. But as the victorious parties formed governments, they lost functional relevance and coherence. The growth of state agencies proceeded, and party functions atrophied. The party became largely an agency of the governmental bureaucracy or, at the expense of its rank and file, in certain cases it became a mere extension of the personality of a strong president or prime minister. No matter what roles parties have been assigned, almost everywhere in tropical Africa—whether in single party, multi-party, or non-party states—they perform few.[49]

One could point to a number of developments in support of this argument. Party leaders have become heads of state. They have not only formed governments but have also not drawn sharp distinctions between their party, the state, and the nation. Rulers have relied on the civil service, since civil servants are ordinarily better equipped for the problems of government than party cadres. Party members of influence and/or ability have entered government, not only at cabinet level but in the regular civil service. For example, TANU leaders in Tanganyika became permanent secretaries and foreign service officers; district party secretaries occasionally became civil servants in the regional administration. Across Africa, party agencies such as youth wings, student groups, and paramilitary wings have been transformed into adjuncts of state control. They have often been governmentalized in order to ensure their loyalty to government leaders, who could not rely on party mechanisms to ensure such loyalty. The major decisions on development policy, the drawing up of five-year-plans, programs to attract foreign investment, establishing proposed rates of growth, and means of financing plans—all these decisions have more often been taken in councils of state than in party caucuses or congresses or even in national executives and central committees. Foreign advisers may have much more to say about these matters than ostensibly important party figures.

If anyone could still doubt that parties no longer have primacy and centrality in African politics, the termination by the military of party rule and party existence in a number of African states can be mentioned again.

When all this has been said, the idea of the no-party state is not a satisfactory tool for the analysis of African politics, any more than the idea of authoritarian and dynamic mass parties. It is based on a description of those aspects of African politics most visible to outside observers. This is the politics of the capital city; of the "modern" sectors; of institutions that can be "seen" (because they have chains of command, rosters of personnel, constitutions that define their structure and goals) and can be "heard" (because we can more readily interview party officials and civil servants). The pendulum has swung too far away from the importance of party in African political life and from the empirically established importance of individual parties in specific polities.[50]

In order not to overhomogenize African politics, which is tempting to do when one is aware of significant economic constraints on the development of political structures, we need much more work on the operation of single parties at the grass roots and middle levels.[51] It is not really possible to say that the "staying power of single parties seems to be a function of the explicitness of an ideology, the degree of national isolation, and the degree to which the party concentrates on mobilizing and training middle cadres as agents of the center"[52] when we do not know how ideologies elaborated at the center are received, and when we do not know how middle-level elites function. Wallerstein maintained, "Today [1964–1965?] the party is an effective organism of power to some extent in some states, for example Guinea, Mali, Tanzania and Tunisia, and irrelevant in many others."[53]

But is party irrelevant when it does not qualify for being mass or mobilizational or even single-party in the system?

All this is not to say that we should stop searching for crucial variables across systems and cease asking general questions. And of course we must try to keep refining our definitions of one-party system and try to assess the importance of the existence of one-party systems. We do want to know whether it matters if a system is *de jure* or *de facto* single party and we want to know whether it matters if a country has a one-party dominant system or is ruled by a party without any other party opposition. We want to know whether it does make a difference to the operation of a single party within a unit that it also operates within a larger unit where it contends with other parties. There are a number of such cases. Tanzania is a *de jure* one-party system but TANU operates in mainland Tanzania and the Afro-Shirazi Party operates in Zanzibar. Similarly, when East and West Camerouns were linked, the smaller unit kept its separate single-party structure; this was true in Somalia too.[54] The one-party dominant regimes of Nigeria were also linked in a federal system. And in the Congo, at the end of 1963, some provinces had a dominant party.[55]

It is of more than passing interest whether or not a party becomes dominant through electoral manipulation, through bludgeoning its opponents with force and/or patronage power at its disposal, or whether it has direct and vast electoral support.[56] There is a rather vast literature on European and American parties that has addressed itself to the questions: Are one-party systems a different breed of animal from competing parties systems? What is the importance for a party configuration of registration laws, electoral districting, and the various ramifications of elections in general? There has been much speculation in the discussion of African parties about the former question, but on the latter one, there has been a tendency to dismiss elections because they appeared to be won rather overwhelmingly by the victors, were thought by observers to be obviously rigged and thus spurious, and sometimes data about them did not exist.

Africa gives us many different examples of the importance of elections, or their absence, in the politics of a country. There have been states where one-party system were *de jure:* the FLN in Algeria, TANU in Tanzania, the CPP in Ghana, the *Mouvement National de la Révolution* in Congo-Brazzaville. There are some where no party organization exists to compete with the ruling party (Guinea and Mali, Ivory Coast, Niger, Liberia), and others where the one party dominates and has all seats in the legislature (Mauritania, Tchad); there are still others where one-party dominance is almost complete in the parliament but where some opposition party seats exist (Malagasy Republic, Kenya, Uganda). There are various degrees of one-party dominance electorally, in terms of both final outcomes and percentage of votes. There have been multi-party systems where there is real bargaining in the legislature among parties (Uganda before mid-1965, Sierra Leone, and Somali Republic, for example). These lists are not exhaustive either as to category or membership within categories. I do not call attention to these as a set of party systems to be differentiated according to degree of one-party dominance. The Kenya African National Union may dominate the legislature in Kenya, but it faces organized opposition that can turn out a vote against it. Even more to the point is the irrelevance of absence of legislative opposition in certain countries. A number of one-party systems are what Finer calls ". . . hastily cobbled-up 'package' parties made up of the original competing factions" [57] as in Congo-Brazzaville up to 1963, Dahomey from time to time, Gabon, Togo on occasion, and some he does not mention, KANU at one point in Kenya, the Uganda People's Congress increasingly. If one pushes back into the pre-independence period some of the mass movements have a similar history.

Rather than point out the above for purposes of classification, I do so to suggest that the electoral process has been somewhat overlooked in the study of African politics. Once independence was achieved and a dominant party appeared to be ensconced, there was still much to be learned about the variety of one-party dominant regimes by examining electoral processes and not merely looking at the outcomes of elections as expressed in legislative majorities.[58] Although the presence or absence of minority parties may well be an important factor, we should not jump to the conclusion that systems can best be defined by this distinction.

We should be comparing political organizations with an open mind as to the importance of "one-partyness" for such things as electoral competition, amount and nature of coercion, kinds of rewards offered by parties, size and composition of the inner core of the organization, relationships between internal party hierarchies, formal structure, and ideology. Lest we fall into a new formalism, we should be careful not to make the initial assumption that the fact that only one political organization calls itself a party in a given country means a great deal for all the questions we can ask about the operation of that organization. It does mean, of course, that there is no challenging political party; but whether the ruling party can control village political organizations from some central power center, or implement economic plans made at the center, remain open questions.

Does this mean we are reduced to asking a set of ad hoc questions about political parties as they operate in society and thus must operate at a so-called low level of generality? I would not think so; we can frame propositions about the *operation* of political parties that would purport to hold true in all systems, or all African countries, or, for example, all countries with a certain ratio of subsistence to monetary sectors in their economies. I would focus on what I called subsystem variables that pertain to political parties. It might be asked, why choose electoral competition rather than size of administrative core at the party's headquarters? It has been precisely the difficulties posed by such questions that have thrown analysts back on very general formulations in the creation of typologies. But we are only going to be able to find out which particular factors are crucial for distinguishing among political parties by testing propositions relevant to the questions we ask. Our questions determine the kinds of propositions we should formulate. I am suggesting that, at this point, the most useful queries are those involving operation of political organizations in and for the political system.

Political Machines

I have argued that the application of Soviet-derived models to African parties has not been very fruitful. This is not to say that all comparisons with communist systems are useless. In fact, the wide variety of communist one-party systems that could be subgrouped into various types—East European and Asian; large scale and small scale; indigenous and imposed; and around other possible unifying themes—have not been taken into account.[59] There are also American one-party systems that can be classified according to area: southern, New England, and Midwest; degrees of one-party dominance; rural or urban, and so forth.

There has been a wide-ranging literature on American political machines. Machines have been defined as parties that rely characteristically upon the attraction of material rewards rather than enthusiasm for political principles.[60] A great deal flows from this understanding of a particular type of political organization. The party machine's central function is not to frame or to discipline its members in the framing of the policies of government. Elections are important but this is so because they are elections for jobs, and winning them gives access to more jobs; internal division over policy questions is supposed to play little part in elections. To say that a party is not policy oriented does not mean that policy issues never arise, but rather that cleavages within the party are not over policy issues.[61] In analyses that stress material rewards as a goal of a political organization and its members, patronage and corruption are also emphasized. At the top of the hierarchy of the organization, "glory," "power" and being on the "inside" can be put forth as motivations for political activity; "honest graft" is a factor too. At lower levels, corruption is required until precinct captains can be induced to work from other motives than personal gain.[62] Such is Banfield's well known description of the machine in its Chicago form.

None of the above, nor the emphasis on localism and self-interest in studies of machine politics, say anything about how democratic, representative, or noncoercive machines are. In fact, many descriptions of American political machines stress their toughness, their willingness to use coercion and to restrict popular participation at times.[63] Although I do not know the etymology of the word machine as applied to political organization, the term connotes a control mechanism: gears mesh; political units are cogs. In the American context, political machines are sometimes seen as maintaining an ongoing economic system by receiving economic benefits and distributing goods and services. Because the work on machines analyzes them as control mechanisms, they are often seen as status quo oriented organizations. Studies that do mention the innovating functions that machines perform treat these as latent functions.[64] We need to show, not assume, what kinds of parties will be innovative and/or coercive under different circumstances.

The justification for bringing the notion of political machine to bear on the study of African politics must be found in the attempt to come to grips with intraparty relationships and not because "machine" implies an American model as a "good thing." For that matter, the inner cores of parties, including Leninist ones, are machines in that the permanent party bureaucracy operates in terms of material rewards and all parties have what Michels called an "echeloned aspect." But since parties in the real world are concerned both with rewards and political principles, the need is to determine who is committed to what principles and especially to find out what principles various levels of and groups within parties hold. Furthermore, we can compare parties to see what kinds of recompense they give to members for services rendered and we can see what kinds of inner cores various parties have in terms of size and patterns of recruitment for paid officials. We could then call some political organizations "party-machines" if they met established criteria for size of cadres as a per cent of total membership and types of payment for various services. The point of this, however, is not to provide another label for political organizations but to focus on and understand the variety of organizations and organizational techniques manifest in African politics.

What we get from the literature on American machines is, above all, an understanding of the wide variety of organizations and organizational techniques and a sense of the heterogeneity of groups who can find common interest.[65]

A few more points about political machines made in the American context are relevant here. Leadership has been a prominent topic in the discussion of American political machines, but analyses have been made which feature the boss, not the charismatic leader. Mayor Daley and bosses Hague, Crump, and Pendergast have received a great deal of ink and attention. But their personalities have not been emphasized in attributions of success. No one has suggested a non-secular basis for that success. Consider some nicknames. "Hinky Dink" Kenna, "Bathhouse" John Coughlin, "Big" Bill Thompson, "Good Jelly" Jones have names that are chummy not by accident. These nicknames express the bosses' accessibility, their personal contact with constituents, at least to begin with.[66] The names "The Redeemer" Nkrumah, "Mzee" Kenyatta (*the* Old Man), "Mwalimu" Nyerere (*the* Teacher) do not express service for a price, which was the essence of bossism.[67] The machine, as personalized and typified by the boss, fulfilled, in Merton's words, "the important social function of humanizing and personalizing all manner of assistance to those in need." [68] The machine played this role through its agents because the official government machinery was often remote and bound down by legalistic restraints. In other words, the machinery was closer to the people than the bureaucracy. This was particularly true for immigrant groups, newly come to the big cities. In America, operating in a decentralized system, the boss was involved in the various levels of politics—city, county, state, and national—but his main concern was to maintain control over his own organization, his base of power, and to stay beyond the authority of higher echelons of power.[69] In Banfields's discussion of Chicago he says that ". . . a single actor—say the mayor of Chicago—can pursue a course of action only insofar as the formal decentralization is somehow overcome by informal centralization." The most important mechanism through which this is done is the political party or machine.[70] In their study *City Politics,* Banfield and Wilson see the machine as functioning to overcome a constitutional dispersion of authority typical of the separation of powers.[71]

The machine was many things to ethnic communities. Bosses were often the most prominent members of minority groups. The largest payoffs to voters in American cities were symbolic and material; party tickets were ethnically balanced.[72] The machine was a channel for upward social mobility through politics as a vocation for those of the immigrant groups who had political aptitude. When the new ethnic groups carried traditions from their home country, they were often the traditions of personalized government action; influence was a direct personal relationship.[73] Another point emerges in the literature on ethnic politics in America. Robert Dahl shows how ethnic characteristics serve as a kind of comprehensive symbol for class and other criteria. Analysts have argued over how important ethnic considerations really are or ought to be but few have quarreled with Dahl's observation on New Haven that politicians devised strategies on the assumption that whatever happened in elections could be adequately explained by shifts in ethnic voting blocks.[74] This kind of calculus has been evident in Africa too.

So far I have taken a number of points made about political machines in America out of a historical and social context in order to suggest that in thinking about leadership and ethnicity in Africa we might benefit from the work done on American politics. For reflection on politics to be useful in a comparative way, the things to be compared need not be held similar in time and place, although obviously we must be aware of what is indeed different about our situations. Thus, although nineteenth century America and mid-twentith century Africa are very unlike with regard to social, economic, and demographic characteristics, because of a contemporary African concern with the relationship of political centers to peripheries, we might consider the matter of the locus of one-party systems and political machines in America.[75] In other words, we might ask questions about one-party systems that are not really statewide (in the South) or nationwide (in some African countries) to see what we might learn about the operation of factionalized and localized organizations under very different conditions. The aim would be to try and find out if intraparty relationships are independent variables.

But even on a descriptive level, accounts of American political machines bear many more resemblances to politics in Africa than descriptions of one-party systems made in terms of what I have called the mass-party-derived terminologies and typologies. On the descriptive level, students concerned with adaptation of governing African single parties to the problems of rule in their societies and those who have described the internal dynamics of individual parties in fact have been telling us a story about bosses, corruption, honest graft, local satraps, the politics of ethnicity, decentralization of authority, and rural as well as urban based machines.

In my own study of Tanzania, I argued that "TANU itself is a congeries of regional, district, and sub-district organizations which communicate with each other and with Dar es Salaam only intermittently." [76] Rene Lemarchand says that the outstanding characteristic of all Congolese parties, whether mass or elite, was decentralization of the organization.[77] And this in what were often one-party provinces.

Zolberg has written a revisionist history of national movements and political parties on West Africa, arguing that the parties of Ghana, Guinea, Senegal, Mali, and the Ivory Coast did not need to be highly centralized and monolithic to achieve national independence under their banner and that, on the contrary, they reflected the pluralisms and lack of integration of their societies both before and after independence.[78] While African leaders have been described as charismatic leaders, we have also had implicit, or in some cases explicit, pictures of political bosses. Such was Zolberg's portrait of Houphouet-Boigny.[79] Henry Bretton's not very flattering account of Nkrumah as a political man also stressed his boss-like characteristics.[80] Concerning ethnic politics, we need hardly mention books; few studies of African politics do not treat political struggle and social change in terms of the movement of ethnic groups, the formation of ethnic associations in new urban areas, and ethnic conflict. Students of corruption in Africa have been many. Some have moralized about corruption,[81] while others have put forward a cost-benefit framework for analysis,[82] and have broadly examined the function of corruption, especially having in mind the political machine as an interest group.[83] We also have overviews of political machines in Africa that look at the rural and urban components. Some of these explicitly use the words "political machine" to describe what they are dealing with. But others who have used a different language have nonetheless provided a picture of the machine in action.[84]

Bretton titles two chapters in his recent book on Nkrumah, "Building the Political Machine." He says Nkrumah established himself as a political boss through a process of coercion, intimidation, and cooptation. He downplays the CPP itself ("The party possessed no independent power") and argues that Nkrumah had a personal political machine.[85] While the personal machine was entrenched, the CPP was still being extolled as the vanguard of the people, but the party *qua* party ". . . had been stripped of all power, potentialities, and initiative as thoroughly as the rest of the state apparatus." [86] Apter, too, has stressed the personal role of Nkrumah, but he has seen a charismatic leader who tried, and failed, to change the basis of public behavior by creating a new system of motivation. Apter has recently reaffirmed his view that the term charisma can be applied to Nkrumah, particularly during the years 1949–1954 and that charismatic leadership was important during a period of institutional transfer.[87] Apter also agrees that the CPP became an empty shell and that Nkrumah failed to create the new society he promised. But for Apter, the promise was important—in that it was an attempt to change the pattern of normative life and individual behavior. Nkrumah failed to restructure roles. He could not mobilize effectively. According to Apter, his failure was a structural one; that is, he could not build a political organization. But Apter, properly I think, stresses that the Convention People's Party, although never effective as such, kept changing, in both its role and its structure. "It lacked effective middle leadership, but its consequences, if only in negative terms, were for the people immense." Apter now emphasizes the orientational consequences of creating the first populist national body rather than the organizational context of the CPP *per se*. It remains to be demonstrated that the CPP has had this affect on Ghanaian society, but it is possible for it to have had such an affect without being well organized. We might note that American political machines, through their socializing activities, also changed patterns of behavior without necessarily being self-conscious or ideologically elaborate about this and without operating as strongly centralized national political organization or having charismatic leaders.

Bretton describes Nkrumah's rule as the acquisition of personal wealth. He does not stress the functionality of this for political organization building nor does he make Greenstone's argument that corruption can offset a decline in political capacity that sets in after independence in African states, although Bretton sees the political machine as a principal beneficiary of "private regarding interest." Bretton's notion of the political machine is very close to that of critics of American machines, in that in both cases the machine is seen as being against, not for, mass mobilization, since mass mobilization is construed as inevitably leading to rival centers of power. Thus machines restrict suffrage and social participation in general, except insofar as those phenomena are conducive to the machines' maintenance in power. It is generally understood that the machine exists to maintain itself, although it may perform action leading to other ends (the public good, economic development, and so forth) in the process. Bretton's descriptions of the use of the instruments of coercion also bear strong resemblances to descriptions of American machine coercion, although Bretton's comparisons are to Hitler's SS rather than to Boss Hague's thugs.[88]

A somewhat ambiguous portrayal of a political machine in Uganda has been made by Colin Leys. He describes the Uganda People's Congress as ". . . a coalition of local organizations, or rather local political systems, each with its own political elite, including a small number of leaders operating at the national level." This party, which became increasingly dominant between 1962 and 1965 is seen by Leys as being not ineffective, although the UPC was stronger generally at the local level than it was at the center.[89] Many of the national leaders, including the Prime Minister-become-President Obote, remained heavily dependent on their local political bases. Leys looks at politics in one Uganda district, Acholi, where the UPC dominated and ran a closed spoils systems. He shows how UPC leaders, both at the center and in Acholi, felt that *party* interest operated as a hidden hand that would facilitate good national outcomes—growth, development, unity. "The test to be applied to a parochial demand was where it fitted into the politics of securing party unity and party dominance. In other words, the significant moral boundary during these years (1962–1965) was between parties, rather than between the localities and the center." [90] Leys is not certain how many top UPC leaders had a clear objective of establishing a single-party regime, as opposed to reducing their political opponents to impotence. In any case, he says, the politics of party advantage were pursued so keenly that the rules of the game were rewritten in the process. Policy issues were systematically exploited for party purposes ". . . and party considerations were allowed to permeate into the fabric of rural life at almost every point." [91] The outcome of this spoils system was crises at national and local levels as the opponents could not continue to play by the rules of the game.

Whether this kind of system is functional for economic growth and/or national integration is an important question, of course. Leys himself is ambivalent and sees pluses and minuses. People are brought into contact with "modern" patterns of life via spoils systems improvements, that is, pork barrel projects. The party hierarchy establishes a novel and influential channel of communication between district and national elites. Yet the UPC remains a coalition of local interests, rather than a unitary structure, "and the vitality of local party organization to some extent militated against the vitality of national party organization. . . . The skills demanded of politicians in operating such a system were, moreover, integrative in a sense calculated to create a nation of competing sub-systems rather than an integrated national system." [92]

Zolberg, too, has been ambivalent about the machine, a term he applied to the *Parti Démocratique de la Côte d'Ivoire*. While this political organization was shown to be successful in getting control of the government and bringing the country to independence, its contribution to modernization was said to be more ambiguous.[93] "For the time being, the party remains essentially a political machine, capable of neutralizing many threats to its maintenance, capable of absorbing change, but not yet capable of constructing a new society." [94] Specifically, Zolberg shows how the PDCI reinforced ethnic cleavages as it tried to maintain itself. Zolberg was more positive about political machines in his later study of party-states in West Africa. He contends that the successes achieved by party-states stem from the retention of characteristics that can be described as those of a political machine—along with the persistence of bureaucratic institutions inherited from the colonial period.[95] His party-state emerges as a system where bureaucratic and patrimonial features coexist.[96] "The machine is particularly suited to govern small political communities in transition, and provides both flexibility and stability. . . . While retaining a great deal of flexibility, the machine can sustain a powerful central authority which will cope with certain community-wide problems if the boss is an enlightened one . . . a machine can coexist with a variety of economic arrangements. . . . Although it tends to redistribute income to the benefit of its own members, this membership basis tends to be broader than it would be in more hierarchical systems." [97]

Yet we must confront real questions that can be raised in a discussion of the utility of political machines, even if we agree that the one-party systems in Africa contain party-machines at their political core and can be defined in terms of the characteristics of these machines as they operate in society. One problem has to do with the decentralized nature of the political organizations. Among students of American parties, E. E. Schattschneider, took the view that the parties were loose confederations of state and local machines organized for limited purposes. Since the state and local parties bosses want patronage, and that is nearly all they want, they accentuate decentralization.[98]

Decentralization has usually been anathema in literature on political development in Africa, which has stressed the need for the centralization of authority for national integration. More recently, counterarguments have been made. W. Arthur Lewis has attacked claims that the single party is the appropriate vehicle for resolving regional differences by arguing that the one-party system cannot deal with the pluralisms inherent in African societies. He has stated that both strong centers and strong provincial governments are required and that federalism, broadly conceived as a reasonable degree of provincial devolution, is necessary in Africa.[99] Lewis has said that increases in taxes collected in Nigeria stemmed from decentralization and this is an answer to the people who claim that only highly centralized authoritarian governments can collect taxes.[100] Herbert Werlin has applied to the analyses of administration in Africa a federalist model, (garnered from Sayre and Kaufman) [101] in which "elasticity of control" operates. Werlin's model is one in which governmental units at different levels work in harmony; he stresses informal arrangements and lack of coercion. The central government's full authority is brought to bear only when absolutely needed. Power should be "persuasive rather than coercive." But in Africa power is inelastic, and political control does not increase or decrease in reaction to need.[102]

I have argued that highly localized determination of political life need not be synonymous with disorder, anarchy and chaos. In fact, it may be the only way to avoid these conditions in African circumstances. This localized determination may go hand in hand with the vigorous self-interest of elites and even with corruption.[103] Werlin is right when he says that the proper question in Africa is: How can there be more centralization as well as decentralization at the same time? Power here should not be conceived as existing in a zero sum game. The only way to build strong central institutions in Africa is to create local building blocks. (We should also note that local and central do not have an absolute meaning and that many national political units in Africa bear functional resemblances in terms of size, of politically involved population, budgets, government personnel, governmental capacity in general to counties or groups of counties in America.) [104] But local, as I suggested earlier, might not mean villages, but rather districts, or groupings of villages, or regions in different contexts.

In any case,

> Because the resources in the hands of central elites are few, the elites have a hard time centralizing authority over their own local party organizations. This holds true whether African leaders opt for the American machine model for their parties or for the model of the Communist party of the Soviet Union. So far, they have often equated modernity and political development with the construction of disciplined central organizations, first the ruling single-party and now the military. But the gap between image and reality cannot be closed by facades. And in African conditions there is no way of forcing central authority on the countryside.[105]

However, the low level of political capacity at the center might be offset by a modified and politicized version of the invisible hand working at the local level.

> The nation can be built in Africa through a congeries of regional, district, and subdistrict organizations that communicate with each other and the center. Each knows the others are there, but the organizations exist with full lives of their own. Political competition and decentralization are not, *per se,* inimical to development. In fact, if political development in Africa means creating effective political institutions, these are going to be political machines that are competitive and decentralized, whether within a one-party or multi-party framework.[106]

Conclusions

I have argued that typologies and definitions of African one-party systems derived from a literature that originally dealt with communist parties have been misleading. Research done on individual African one-party systems as well as multi-party systems shows us political organizations operating in terms familiar to students of American machine politics. I have suggested further that the machine may well be necessary in Africa. In passing I have argued that where parties do exist the no-party state appellation cannot be applied, although there may be much wearing of two hats, government and party, by politicians, and the civil service may carry out important functions. The party still can be the most popular institution and the most concrete expression of the nation.[107] It may be the only expression of government's authority in certain rural areas.[108] The party may be functionally diffuse and still struggling to identify its own mission, but at the same time its search for purpose and definition is linked to a national search for identity and definition. Even where a party may disappear it may have crucially affected the normative life of the nation; perhaps this is the case in Ghana now.

African single parties have had an organizational autonomy which has been derived more from parties' identification with a set of values, a group of leaders, a national history than on any administrative insulation of the party from state agencies or any isolation of the party from the encroachments of functionally linked organizations such as trade unions and youth groups. Moreover, single parties have been distinctive channels for recruitment in Africa even where some traditional leaders and some civil servants have been selected for posts precisely because of traditional status and administrative expertise. The point here is that party leaders have a choice among the civil servants and traditional leaders that they pick rather than having some chiefly or administrative hierarchy make choices for them. Nor should we forget that it is still a party organ that makes recruitment choices, although these choices may be taking place at a local level for both local posts and for national ones.[109]

If it is true that African one-party systems are decentralized political machines, it is also true that the machines may become so loose and decentralized as to no longer constitute a single party. The political organizations are not bound to become more centralized. A question arises that can be raised for all African one-party systems: How do you maintain cohesiveness where there is no party competition around which to enforce consensus and where central elites cannot enforce consensus by coercive means? One answer is that national elites must bargain with middle-level and local ones, using what patronage and moral suasion they have, and applying coercion selectively. This can all go on through a network of informal political arrangements. Another answer is that if it is difficult to maintain cohesion where there are no electoral challenges unless coercion is used internally in the party and by the party vis-à-vis other political groups, elections may have a crucial place within one-party systems. Competition for posts within the party might fragment the organization. On the other hand, such elections give the party a chance to define itself within the society and to assert party criteria in the recruitment process. Moreover, internal elections can provide a chance to discuss issues and to stress what Schattschneider has called the public personality of the party. This presupposes a party sufficiently disciplined to hold a certain line around issues during the election. In the presence or absence of meaningful elections, one-party dominance will depend on certain other features, which have not received enough attention: size of constituency in numbers and land area, structure of the economy, level of the economy and economic growth rates, rate of social mobility into various levels of party leadership. Thus although I have attempted to explore the meaning of one-party systems in Africa by focusing on what I called subsystem variables that pertain to parties and tried to use the concept of political machine toward this end, I am aware that an understanding of the meaning of one-party systems depends on delineating factors for social systems as a whole also.

‖ Notes

I am grateful to the Center of International Studies, Princeton University, for research support and aid in preparation of this essay and to Professor Clement Moore who made helpful criticisms of this essay.

1. See David E. Apter, *The Politics of Modernization* (Chicago: University of Chicago Press, 1966) and *The Political Kingdom in Uganda* (Princeton: Princeton University Press, 1961), pp. 22–24.
2. James S. Coleman and Carl Rosberg, Jr., *Political Parties and National Integration in Tropical Africa* (Berkeley: University of California Press, 1966), p. 5.
3. Ruth Schachter Morganthau, "Single-Party Systems in West Africa," *American Political Science Review*, LV (June 1961), 244–307 and *Political Parties in French Speaking West Africa* (Oxford: Clarendon Press, 1964), esp. pp. 330–358.
4. See Apter, *The Political Kingdom in Uganda,* and Philip Selznick, *The Organizational Weapon: A Study of Bolshevik Strategy and Tactics* (New York: The Free Press, 1960).
5. Robert C. Tucker, "On Revolutionary Mass-Movement Regimes," in Robert C. Tucker, *The Soviet Political Mind* (New York: Frederick A. Praeger, 1963), pp. 3–19.
6. Henry Bretton, "Current Political Thought and Practice in Ghana," *American Political Science Review*, LII (March 1958), 49–50, 57.
7. There have been no attempts I know of to take a close look at the lessons of Soviet political history, say from 1917–1933, in terms of the interactions of party with economy and the transformation of the CPSU as it undertook economic tasks in order to formulate propositions applicable to a wider universe.
8. Even before a recent revisionist literature on the Soviet Union, some authors had insisted that factions had persisted in Soviet politics even after Stalin's ascendancy. See especially, Franz Borkenau, "Getting at the Facts Behind the Soviet Facade," *Commentary*, XVII, No. 4 (April 1954), 393–400, where Borkenau describes a political patronage system or *sheftsvo*. Boris Nicolaevsky was another analyst who stressed that Soviet elite politics was a continuous struggle. In the 1960s, a "conflict" school has developed in the study of Soviet politics, as analysts now describe not only struggles at the top of the hierarchy but the clash of interest groups. Cf. Robert C. Tucker, "The Conflict Model," *Problems*

of Communism, XII (November–December 1963), 49–51; Sidney Ploss, *Conflict and Decision-Making in Soviet Russia* (Princeton: Princeton University Press, 1965); Carl A. Linden, *Khrushchev and the Soviet Leadership, 1957–1964* (Baltimore: Johns Hopkins Press, 1966).

9. Aristide Zolberg, *Creating Political Order: The Party States of West Africa* (Chicago: University of Chicago Press, 1966), p. 35.

10. Zolberg, *op. cit.*, and Zolberg's *One-Party Government in the Ivory Coast* (Princeton: Princeton University Press, 1964); Dennis Austin, *Politics in Ghana* (London: Oxford University Press, 1964).

11. Morganthau, "Single-Party Systems in West Africa," pp. 295–296.

12. Morganthau, *Political Parties in French Speaking West Africa*, p. 333.

13. *Ibid.*, p. 351, 354.

14. Henry Bienen, *Tanzania: Party Transformation and Economic Development* (Princeton: Princeton University Press, 1967), pp. 3–19; Bienen, "What Does Political Development Mean in Africa," *World Politics*, XX (October 1967), 128–141; and Bienen, "The Ruling Party in the African One-Party State," *The Journal of Commonwealth Political Studies*, V (November 1967), 214–230.

15. *Ibid.*, p. 216.

16. Coleman and Rosberg, *op. cit.*, p. 5.

17. *Ibid.*, pp. 5–6.

18. See Apter, *The Political Kingdom in Uganda.*

19. See Bienen, *Tanzania*, pp. 3–4.

20. A paper on Nkrumah will be forthcoming in *Daedalus.*

21. Morganthau, *Political Parties in French Speaking West Africa*, pp. 341–48. Zolberg, both in *One Party Government in the Ivory Coast* and *Creating Political Order* stressed that ethnic tensions were often exacerbated as political awareness rose. Crawford Young saw this too in *Politics in the Congo* (Princeton: Princeton University Press, 1965).

22. There are vivid illustrations of this in Young's work with regard to the MNC Lumumba and Zolberg's work on the *Union Soudanaise* in Mali and the *Parti Démocratique de la Côte d'Ivoire* in the Ivory Coast.

23. Morganthau, *Political Parties in French Speaking West Africa.*

24. Apter, *The Politics of Modernization*, p. 40.

25. *Ibid.*, pp. 336–337.

26. David Apter, *Ghana In Transition* (New York: Atheneum, 1963).

27. It is true that Morganthau saw some, but not all, mass-party top-level leaders, Sekou Touré in Guinea and Mamadou Konate in Mali (then the Soudan), as enjoying a type of charisma, one limited by constitutional procedure and the power exercised by groups and individuals within their parties. She also said that certain leaders of patron parties—Fily Dabo Sissoko in the Soudan and Sourou Migan Apithy in Dahomey—had a charisma comparatively unchecked by procedure though limited by the power of other patrons. Few others applied the concept of charisma to leaders of patron parties, and what the term means in Morganthau aside from extraordinary qualities ascribed to a leader is unclear to me. See Morganthau, *Political Parties in French Speaking West Africa*, pp. 339–340. Patron parties and parties of personality were terms employed by Thomas Hodgkin, in *Nationalism in Colonial Africa* (New York: New York University Press, 1957) and *African Political Parties* (London: Penguin, 1961), as Morganthau points out, *Political Parties in French Speaking West Africa*, p. 336ff. Hodgkin also used the term "elite" parties for patron parties in *African Political Parties*, pp. 68–69.

28. Both Hodgkin and Morganthau acknowledged their debts to Maurice Duverger's *Political Parties* (London: Methuen, 1954).

29. Morganthau, *Political Parties in French Speaking West Africa*, p. 339.

30. John A. Ballard, "Four Equatorial States," in Gwendolen Carter, ed., *National Unity and Regionalism in Eight African States* (Ithaca: Cornell University Press, 1966), pp. 261–279. Ballard says at one point that "MESAN was an entirely personal organization with each of its local agents responsible directly to Boganda (the leader until his death in 1959) himself" (p. 263). He also describes MESAN as a popular mass movement with direct ties between leader and members.

31. Of course, the looser the definition of charisma, the easier to apply it anywhere and everywhere. But since one component of charisma was that the leader had wide popularity, patron party leaders were probably excluded on the grounds of limited appeal. Morganthau allowed Lamine Kaba of the Kankan region of Guinea to be called charismatic although he "enjoyed charisma only within a locality considerably smaller than a territory" (*Political Parties in French Speaking West Africa*, p. 340).

32. Zolberg points out in *Creating Political Order,* p. 138, that Houphouet-Boigny, who does not possess this style, is believed by many of his countrymen to be among the elect, specially designated to rule over them.

33. There was a conference on leadership sponsored by *Daedalus* and the Institute of War and Peace Studies, Columbia University, held at the Sterling Forest Conference Center, Tuxedo, New York, October 19–21, 1967. The concept of charisma was discussed in a number of papers. Ann Ruth Willner has an interesting monograph, *Charismatic Political Leadership* (Princeton: Princeton University Center of International Studies, 1968).

34. Morganthau, *Political Parties in French Speaking West Africa*, p. 351.

35. The Tanganyika African National Union won a large majority of the votes cast in the 1960 election but the 885,000 registered voters represented about half of the estimated potential voters. And since less than one-seventh of the registered voters actually voted, the voting electorate was a small percentage of the possible one. In the presidential election Nyerere received over 1.1 million votes to his opponents's 21,276. The total vote was less than a quarter of the potential electorate. TANU claimed a membership at the time which was greater than Nyerere's vote. The more than 2.5 million votes cast in the presidential and national assembly elections in Tanzania in 1965 represented a marked increase. However, about 50 per cent of the possible electorate was voting. Austin, *op. cit.,* p. 174, shows similar figures for Ghana, where the Convention People's Party received about 15 per cent of the total potential vote in elections in 1954 and 1956. Zolberg, *Creating Political Order,* refers to similar phenomena in Guinea and Mali.

36. Again, some examples from Tanzania: the non-monetary sector still accounts for more than a third of total Gross Domestic Product (or £200 million out of £600 million). Ninety-eight per cent of the population pay taxes only to district councils, who levy a tax of about 1 to 3 per cent on the income of all adult males. But it is estimated that 15 per cent of all males are escaping registration for taxation before official exemptions begin. See E. Lee, *Local Taxation in Tanganyika* (London: Oxford University Press, 1965). Of course, taxes are hard to collect where communications are poor, means of coercion slight, and habits of this kind of payment not ingrained.

37. For a discussion of coups in Africa see Aristide Zolberg, "Military Intervention in the New States of Tropical Africa: Elements of Comparative Analysis," in Henry Bienen, ed., *The Military Intervenes: Case Studies in Political Change* (New York: Russell Sage Foundation, 1968).

38. See Henry Bienen, "Public Order and the Military in Africa: Mutinies in Kenya, Uganda, and Tanganyika," in Bienen, *The Military Intervenes.*

39. Morganthau, *Political Parties in French Speaking West Africa*, p. 320.

40. Richard L. Sklar and C. S. Whitaker, Jr., "Nigeria" in Coleman and Rosberg, *op. cit.,* p. 654.

41. C. S. Whitaker, Jr., "A Dysrhythmic Process of Political Change," *World Politics,* XIX (January 1967), 209.

42. *Ibid.,* pp. 9–20.

43. Sklar and Whitaker, *op. cit.,* p. 622. Only people of northern Nigeria origin may be members of the NPC.

44. *Ibid.*

45. *Ibid.,* p. 625.

46. *Ibid.,* p. 601.

47. Audrey R. Chapman, "Ethnic Unions and the NCNC in Mbaise, Eastern Nigeria" (Paper delivered to the African Studies Association, Tenth Annual Meeting, November 1–4, 1967, New York City).

48. For a discussion of this issue, see my article, "The Party and the No-Party State: Tanganyika and the Soviet Union," and R. I. Rotberg, "Modern African Studies: Problems and Prospects," *World Politics,* XVIII (1966), 571. See also I. Wallerstein, "The Decline of the Party in Single Party States" in J. LaPalombara and M. Weiner, eds. *Political Parties and Political Development* (Princeton: Princeton University Press, 1966), and Frantz Fanon, *The Wretched of the Earth* (New York: Grove Press, 1963).

49. See Bienen, "The Ruling Party in the African One-Party State," p. 216.

50. Ibid., pp. 216–217.

51. Work such as carried out by Nicholas Hopkins on Mali; see his "Government in Kita: Institutions and Processes in a Malian Town," (Ph.D. diss., University of Chicago, 1967), and by Colin Leys on *Politicians and Policies* (Nairobi: East African Publishing House, 1967).

52. Wallerstein, *op. cit.,* p. 214.

53. *Ibid.* The *Union Soudanaise* had its political bureau, dissolved in August, 1967, and President Keita of Mali assigned full powers over the party and government to the *Comíte National de Défense de la Révolution.*

54. *Ibid.,* p. 206.

55. *Ibid.,* citing Crawford Young, "The Congo Provinces Become Twenty-One," *Africa Report* (October 1963).

56. S. E. Finer, "The One-Party Regimes in Africa," *Government and Opposition,* II (July–October 1967), 491–492.

57. *Ibid.,* p. 495.

58. The 1965 Tanzanian election has been a rather obviously fertile field for ploughing as Lionel Cliffe has shown in his edited work, *One Party Democracy* (Nairobi: East African Publishing House, 1967). There are interesting uses of election data in Zolberg, *Creating Political Order;* Austin, *op. cit.;* Herbert Weiss, *Political Protest in the Congo* (Princeton: Princeton University Press, 1967); and Sklar and Whitaker, *op. cit.*

59. I have already said the political history of the CPSU could be of great interest if applied in comparative studies. The revisionist studies of communist parties which are calling into question the totalitarian model should be useful too.

60. Edward C. Banfield, *Political Influence* (New York: The Free Press, 1961), p. 237.

61. Bienen, *Tanzania,* p. 88.

62. Banfield, *op. cit.,* p. 257.

63. See Dayton McKean's *The Boss: The Hague Machine in Action* (Boston: Houghton Mifflin, 1940).

64. Robert K. Merton, "The Latent Function of the Machine," from *Social Theory and Social Structure* (New York: The Free Press, 1957), pp. 71–81.

65. See V. O. Key, *Southern Politics* (New York: Alfred A. Knopf, 1949). Key has

said of Boss Crump's Tennessee organization that ". . . his state organization was held together largely by prerequisites for office, the desire for office, the disciplinary tools inherent in the control of government and party machinery, and the capacity to trade with East Tennessee Democrats—and Republicans" (pp. 67–68). Key points to the internal controls the machine wields and its bargaining abilities, that is, organizational power and tactical flexibility. The bludgeoning and rewarding of local leaders is emphasized. In his discussion of the Byrd machine in Virginia, Key describes the machine as a system for recruitment and advancement of political leaders. It is not merely skilled management that produces a well-disciplined oligarchy, but selections through a process of cooptation and indoctrination (pp. 25–26). Through this process, the Byrd machine monopolized political talent, allowing loyal organization men to compete for the support of local leaders for state wide office (p. 23). In his description of Texas machines, Key notes how small-time bosses or *jefes* relied on traditional techniques in dealing with immigrant groups: counsel in solving personal problems; aid in economic distress; patronage; assistance before governing authorities. Key wrote that in Arkansas there were men of prominence who controlled votes and swung them not for money but for the "best man" (p. 196). Huey Long used outright thuggery sometimes, along with the means noted above, and had the loyalty of the masses, whom he reached via new channels of communication (p. 162).

66. As noted by Duane Lockard, *The Politics of State and Local Government* (New York: Macmillan, 1963), p. 219.

67. *Ibid.,* p. 220.

68. Merton, *op. cit.*

69. Lockard, *op. cit.,* pp. 223–224.

70. Banfield, *op. cit.,* p. 237.

71. Edward Banfield and James Q. Wilson, *City Politics* (Cambridge: Harvard University Press, 1963), p. 126.

72. J. David Greenstone, "Corruption and Self-Interest in Kampala and Nairobi," *Comparative Studies in Society and History,* VII (January 1966), 207.

73. Nathan Glazer and Daniel Patrick Moynihan, *Beyond the Melting Pot* (Cambridge: MIT Press, 1963), p. 224.

74. Robert A. Dahl, *Who Governs?* (New Haven: Yale University Press, 1966), p. 53.

75. Similarly, we might compare the interactions of party and economy in the USSR with patterns or interaction in very different contexts in Africa.

76. Bienen, *Tanzania,* p. 413.

77. Rene Lemarchand, "Congo (Leopoldville)," in Coleman and Rosberg, *op. cit.,* p. 588.

78. Zolberg, *Creating Political Order.*

79. Zolberg, *One Party Government in the Ivory Coast.*

80. Henry Bretton, *The Rise and Fall of Kwame Nkrumah* (New York: Frederick A. Praeger, 1966).

81. Ronald Wraith and Edgar Simpkins, *Corruption in Developing Countries* (London: Allen and Unwin, 1963).

82. J. S. Nye, "Corruption and Political Development: A Cost-Benefit Analysis," *American Political Science Review,* LXI (June 1967), 417–427.

83. Colin Leys, "What is the Problem About Corruption," *The Journal of Modern African Studies,* III (1965), 215–230; Greenstone, *op. cit.*

84. David Apter made interesting fusions of terminology and analysis when he referred to the CPP as ". . . a Tammany-type machine with a neutralist ideology." Yet organizationally, Apter saw the CPP as a composite of the British

Labour Party and a communist party as Zolberg points out in *Creating Political Order*, p. 22. See Apter's *Gold Coast in Transition*, p. 202.

85. Bretton, *The Rise and Fall of Kwame Nkrumah*, p. 46.

86. *Ibid.*, p. 61.

87. Apter's early ideas on Ghana were published in *The Gold Coast in Transition;* he then updated his study in *Ghana in Transition*. His most recent work on Ghana will be published in a forthcoming issue of *Daedalus*. I am grateful for Professor Apter's permission to use an early draft of "Nkrumah's Charisma and the Coup."

88. Bretton, *The Rise and Fall of Kwame Nkrumah*.

89. Leys, *Politicans and Policies*, pp. 10–11.

90. *Ibid.*, p. 101.

91. *Ibid.*

92. *Ibid.*, p. 104.

93. Zolberg, *One Party Government in the Ivory Coast*, p. 319.

94. *Ibid.*, p. 320.

95. Zolberg, *Creating Political Order*, p. 159.

96. *Ibid.*, p. 141.

97. *Ibid.*, pp. 160–161.

98. E. E. Schattschneider, *Party Government* (New York: Rinehart, 1958), pp. 129–169.

99. W. Arthur Lewis, *Politics in West Africa* (New York: Oxford University Press, 1965).

100. W. Arthur Lewis, "Random Reflections on Local Development in Africa with Special Reference to West Africa," in *Local Development in Africa* (Summary Report of a Conference Jointly Sponsored by The Foreign Service Institute of the Department of State, The African Subcommittee of the Foreign Area Research Coordination Group, and the Agency for International Development, Washington, 1967), pp. 30–35.

101. See Wallace S. Sayre and Herbert Kaufman, *Governing New York City* (New York: Russell Sage Foundation, 1965), p. 584.

102. Herbert Werlin, "Elasticity of Control: An Analysis of Decentralization" (Conference on African Local Institutions and Rural Transformation, Institute of African Government, Department of Political Science, Lincoln University, 1967). See also Werlin's "The Nairobi City Council: A Study in Comparative Local Government," *Comparative Studies in Society and History*, VIII (January 1966), 183–186.

103. Bienen, "What Does Political Development Mean in Africa," p. 140.

104. Aristide Zolberg, "Political Development in Tropical Africa: Center and Peripheries," in *Local Development in Africa*, pp. 14–15.

105. Bienen, "What Does Political Development Mean in Africa," p. 140.

106. *Ibid.*, p. 141.

107. As Zolberg has argued for West African party-states, pp. 123, 126, and I have argued in *Tanzania*.

108. Bienen, *Tanzania*.

109. As for example when members of parliament are selected in district polls in Tanzania or regional TANU conferences select members of the National Executive Committee.

5

From Falange to Movimiento-Organización: The Spanish Single Party and the Franco Regime, 1936–1968

|| *Juan J. Linz*

Introduction

A close examination of the single party in Spanish politics allows us to explore the functions of a single-party system in a semideveloped society and an authoritarian regime. The many transformations it has undergone as well as the basic continuity over time point out the inherent limits to change within the system. Comparing it with single-party systems that appeared before and after it in different parts of the world will tell us much about the distinctive features of Spanish society, but will also contribute to our understanding of characteristics common to non-competitive parties in general. I do not intend to analyze here the social structure of Spain; [1] or the nature of the Franco regime; [2] or the forces opposing it, demanding basic changes or its overthrow; [3] or its future, particularly after Franco. [4] My focus is on *one part of the system:* the only legal political organization existing since 1937 that, in theory, is the avenue for political participation of Spaniards in their government. Some would argue that in recent years its role has been so minor that we should speak of a no-party state rather than of a one-party system, while others would not give up the image of a totalitarian regime not far from the Nazi model. As we will see, neither description is adequate to the present reality nor were they adequate even at the stages in history when at first glance they may appear to be more appropriate. In one respect the Movimiento occupies a unique position among the single parties of the world; it is the only one that traces its origin to fascism, the last survival of the many single parties ruling in Europe between the 1920s and mid-1940s (the fascist component in the Portuguese system was so minor that it would not qualify). On the other hand it could be argued that despite the fascist component, it was—even in its origins and moment of greatest power—closer to the bureaucratic single party so well characterized by Andrew C. Janos [5] for East Europe in the interwar years. This ambiguity will allow us to explore further the conditions under which single parties take either the bureaucratic-semipluralistic form or the more revolutionary-totalitarian forms he distinguishes as polar types. Considering its totalitarian potential and ambition in the early years of its long history and its role in an authoritarian regime, with its limited pluralism, lack of well-defined ideology, and limited political mobilization,[6] the Spanish case will shed light on the conditions for both types of single party, as well as on the conditions facilitating the transformation from one into the other. The corporativist ideological elements and the pluralism in the society will lead us to explore the difficult question of why it did not evolve further in the direction taken by the Mexican PRI. This might help us to be somewhat skeptical about the possibility of transformation of other single parties in that direction. By considering the difficulties of fully institutionalizing the party as a source of legitimacy, as reflected in the growing opposition and, even more, in the inability to incorporate many sectors of the society identified with or tolerated by the Franco regime, we shall make explicit some of the problems faced by long-lived single-party systems. The unwillingness and inability of the leaders to make any move toward a competitive party system, despite external and internal pressures (in contrast to Turkey), will tell us something about the difficulties of transforming authoritarian regimes into multi-party democracies despite their limited pluralism, increased liberalization, and favorable economic circumstances. On the other hand, the unwillingness to give up the single party despite its discredit, foreign pressures, and reliance on other social forces, groups, and institutions for most basic political functions, may tell us something about the residual functions of such parties.

While there is almost no end to the questions that can be raised and their implications for the comparative study of single parties, there is great dearth of information on the party and its role owing to lack of research and the difficulties in obtaining much of the relevant information.

Spain: A Semideveloped Society with a Not Fully Successful Liberal Democratic Past

It is impossible to present here the social structure and modern history of Spain that serves as background of the regime established by the victory of Franco's armies in 1939.[7] Spain is not a new nation, since its present frontiers were settled early in the sixteenth century. It was once an imperial power that made a great contribution to Western civilization. It is also a country that failed to adapt to the modern world, as it emerged at the end of the eighteenth century, particularly to become a successful industrial-capitalist society. The loss of empire, the failure to create a modern economy and the consequent poverty of its masses, its absence from the nineteenth century carving of the world by European powers, its limited contribution to modern science, and so forth, created a deep feeling of frustration and a search for causes. This reaction is reflected in the intellectuals' queries about "Spain as a problem," the working class protest movements, and the regional nationalisms that threatened (or appeared to threaten) the unity of the state. Many Spaniards put their hopes in liberalism, secularization, and democracy, as early as the nineteenth century, while others turned their sights back to glorious days under a strong monarchy, Catholic unity, and closure to foreign ideas. The ideological and political struggle between two Spains, in one form or another, has raged since then and led to civil wars, *pronunciamientos,* and political instability and intolerance. However, in 1876 after the defeat of the Carlists and the disintegration of the republican-federalist left, the moderate liberals succeeded in establishing a constitutional monarchy. Under it a two-party system was able to give the country a moderately stable and increasingly liberal government for almost fifty years. Universal male suffrage was introduced definitively in 1889, perhaps prematurely in view of the economic development and the literacy level. The loss of the last colonies in 1898, the complex problems created by Catalan linguistic and administrative autonomy demands, anarcho-syndicalist terrorism, the discontent of the lower classes, and above all the effects of an unsuccessful, costly, and unpopular colonial war in Morocco led to the overthrow of constitutional government. This occurred despite its achievements (often underrated by the contemporary intellectuals, as were those of the Giolittian Italy at the same time) and the possibilities of evolution within the system. The coup of General Primo de Rivera in 1923 interrupted any possibility of evolutionary change, displaced a political class, and was unable to create a new regime. It left a vacuum after its fall that was filled by a new republic in 1931. The new regime was born with broad popular support, but with a limited organized base of leaders and followers committed to democracy, with the exception of the masses affiliated to the socialist trade union federation, the UGT. Its founders were mainly intellectuals turned politicians, as well as middle-class demagogues, mostly men with little administrative experience. With a mixture of reformist zeal and resentment politics, they centered the problems on the weakening of the church, the army, and the aristocratic landowners.

In the 1930s Spain faced simultaneously the following crises: (1) a crisis of participation—the integration of its urban and rural proletariat into political life; (2) a crisis of national integration, different from the one achieved under Castillian hegemony; (3) a crisis provoked by the secularism of intellectuals and anti-clericalism of the workers confronting an established church with considerable influence in large sectors of the middle class and the countryside; and (4) the general European economic crisis, compounded by a backward economy confronted with rising expectations of the masses. The accumulation of these four major crises probably would have been beyond the capacity of any regime to deal with, but the failures of leading men of the regime made a disastrous outcome almost inevitable. The Restoration monarchy ended in a *pronunciamiento,* the Republic in a civil war. In both cases part of the army, following a tradition that had emerged in the course of the nineteenth century, felt that it had to intervene and control all the conflicting ideological and social forces. Primo de Rivera considered his role temporary: a paternalistic dictatorship to carry out a "surgical operation" [8] to return afterwards to normality. Franco came to feel that a deeper change was necessary to exorcise what he called the distinctive "demons" of the country: "anarchic spirit, negative critique, lack of solidarity among men, extremism and mutual hostility." [9] This committed him to continue his rule and to attempt to institutionalize a regime based on the rejection of political parties. His regime was an anti-party system, based more on the rejection of all parties than on the belief in one as a movement or revolutionary party.

The "anti-party party," which has as its main goal to destroy parties, is obviously more characteristic of conservative regimes, of parties with a bureaucratic-military-monarchical origin than of those growing out of a mass movement. Such parties are not exclusionary in the long run—even when they are born in a bifurcated society (in the sense used by Samuel P. Huntington in this volume) or a politically fragmented one—since they do not require any tight discipline and cannot distinguish those identifying with the ideology from those just accepting the system. On the other hand, their capacity to eliminate (politically, not physically) opposing tendencies in the society and to convert and integrate rather than just co-opt or neutralize those not initially identified is more limited than that of the movement-revolutionary parties described by Huntington. Perhaps this point of departure explains why Spain can—depending on the standards used to define one-party system—be described as either a non-party or a one-party system.

The *Unión Patriótica:* A Stillborn Single Party, 1923–1929

Primo de Rivera and his supporters were not ashamed to call the regime they had created a dictatorship, expressing thereby its emergency and transitional character.[10] Primo first ruled with a military junta and later with the collaboration of civilians, mainly civil servants and technicians, among whom the Minister of Finance, Calvo Sotelo, stood out. The dictator came to power without the support of any party or faction in a party—even when some Catalan politicians were not fully unsympathetic to him—but thanks to the support of parts of the army,[11] to the apathy and alienation surrounding the liberal regime, and to the legitimacy granted by the monarch. The dictator attempted to get broad popular support by appealing to citizenship and vaguely stated traditional values while attacking the old political class. A collection of signatures in its support was its "referendum." Not unaware of the new force of Italian fascism, it made only a feeble attempt to create a single party, the *Unión Patriótica*.[12] The UP, like some parties created by the East European bureaucratic single-party regimes, had all the weaknesses of a party created from above, based largely on office holders and seekers, with little support of the young and the intellectuals. In contrast to them, it did not co-opt any major party nor important political figures. It was able to attract some of the youth of the Maurist faction of the conservatives and some of the socially minded Catholic lay leaders, but basically it was stillborn. A corporative chamber where the existing interests groups and key institutions would be represented [13] was the constitutional innovation in which the UP did not play a dominant role.[14] Men from the UGT—the socialist trade union federation—were appointed to that *Asamblea Nacional,* and even when they refused, the UGT was allowed to function and grow, while its leader became a member of the Council of State. After the fall of the dictator and of the interim regime, the *dictablanda* (soft-dictatorship that succeeded it), the UP with the establishment of the Republic in 1931 became for the small fascist groups the image of what a single party should not be.[15]

The Anti-Democratic Forces under the Republic, 1931–1936

The new regime born after the Republican victory in the municipal election of April 12, 1931 displaced completely the old two-party system. Its base was the PSOE (Socialist Party) and minor and improvised bourgeois groups. The old republican Radical Party, even after turning to the right, could not be the conservative opposition to the socialist left-republican left-regionalist alliance led by Azaña. The Catholic-conservative sectors of society had to improvise a non-partisan movement, the *Acción Nacional* (later called *Acción Popular*),[16] which ultimately led to the emergence of a spectrum of rightist and center right parties, among which the demo-Christian-CEDA became dominant and increasingly distinct from its initial monarchist allies. However, the hostility to political parties was in the air; fascism was on the march in Europe; the Catholic church felt ambivalent about demo-Christian and clerical parties and supported corporativism; the anti-democratic and anti-liberal intellectual influence of the *Action Française* made itself felt through *Acción Española;* and the revival of Carlism, once the liberal monarchy had fallen, was inevitable. They all planted the seeds for anti-party ideas. Many issues, however, divided those united in their hostility to democracy. There were those advocating a national-syndicalist revolution like the *Juntas de Ofensiva Nacional Sindicalista,* founded by Ledesma Ramos by a fusion of the *Juntas Castellanas de Ac-*

tuación Hispánica of Onésimo Redondo with his own group formed around a journal called *La Conquista del Estado,* with a left fascist program.[17] The JONS in turn fused in 1934 with Falange Española a fascist party [18] founded by José Antonio Primo de Rivera, the son of the late dictator, who with his nationalist oratory and personal attractiveness was appealing to more conservative sectors.[19] Those dreaming with the old *Comunión Tradicionalista* traced their loyalty back to the dynastic wars against the liberal monarchy in the first half of the nineteenth century. They all avoided studiously the word "party" in their names and appeals. However, the mass of conservative Catholics still followed Gil Robles into the CEDA, which was not willing to break with a multi-party democracy.[20] However, in the program of its youth affiliate, the *Juventud de Acción Popular* (JAP), the ambivalences of the time found expression.[21]

Among the bureaucratic, professional, military, and economic elites, anti-democratic, anti-liberal and anti-parliamentary ideas were diffused by the magazine *Acción Española* [22] and the supporters of the monarchist authoritarian *Renovación Española,* which joined with the traditionalists to form the right opposition to the Radical-CEDA governments. This party became the spearhead of the civilian activists hoping and working for a military uprising after the Popular Front electoral victory. If extremists in the government police had not assassinated him on July 13, 1936, Calvo Sotelo [23] might have been the civilian head of such a rightist, bureaucratic single-party state—probably a monarchy—along the lines familiar from East Europe.

The Civil War: From Military Apoliticism to the Creation of a New Single Party

The deep crisis of the Republic was due to the limited commitment to democracy and tolerance in too many quarters, from anarcho-syndicalist revolutionaries, communists and radicalized maximalist socialists to the Falangists and Carlists.[24] The hope for revolutionary change of the proletariat, the talk of revolution on one side and the fear of any change on the part of reactionaries on the other, combined with an economic crisis and weak leadership of the moderates to create an explosive political climate. The intervention of the army, almost inevitable given its conception of order, together with the assassination of Calvo Sotelo, mobilized most of the population on one or the other side for what would be almost a three-year-long Civil War. The bitter class struggle and terror after the uprising and the persecution of the church did not allow room for neutrals or moderates.

This is not the place to argue whether the conflict that divided Spaniards so deeply could have been avoided, or if one or the other side had greater popular support, or what weight to attach to foreign support to each side in the final outcome. The fact that the Franco regime and its single party was born in the course of a Civil War, however, is central to our purposes here. Other one-party states were born in the struggle for independence; others —like the Yugoslav—in the course of the fight against an invader; some imposed by a mass movement gaining power by a silent revolution in collaboration with allies within the power structure against stunned and divided opponents, as in Italy and Germany. Finally, others were created by the fusion of a variety of political forces under mostly military and bureaucratic leadership, in countries of low political or social mobilization, often after the breakdown of traditional regimes. Incidentally, no single party has reached power by obtaining a majority in a competitive election, except Peronism (and legally it did not become a single-party regime). The only single-party systems built in the course of a civil war have been in the USSR, China, and to some extent Cuba and pre-war Hungary, although Yugoslavia contained elements of it. Mexico, despite the links between the PRI and the prolonged fighting in the course of the revolution, created its hegemonic party only after the struggle had ended. The circumstances surrounding its birth undoubtedly have affected the regime and the party decisively; they have assured its persistence, based on the widespread desire for peace, as well as imposed serious limits to its capacity to change internally or transform itself.

The army officers started what some expected to be only a *pronunciamiento* without making commitments to the various anti-democratic factions or right-of-center politicians. They sought their support in view of the limited number of men at their disposal and the fighting spirit of the party militias available. The negotiations often were difficult and everybody tried to maintain his independence for the future while mobilizing his forces for the fight and the common cause.

The position of the army is well reflected in the proclamations of the state of war in the different garrisons, in the initial holding on to the Republican flag [25] and in the September 25, 1936 decree of the military junta outlawing "all political activities and the syndical activities of workers and employers of political character, while allowing professional organizations exclusively subject to its authority." [26] Its preamble said:

> The strictly national character of the Saving Movement, initiated by the army and enthusiastically supported by the people, requires an absolute avoidance of any political partisanship, since all Spaniards of goodwill, whatever their peculiar ideologies, are fervently united to the army, effective symbol of national unity.
>
> . . . the convenience to use valuable personal collaborations offered at the service of the Nation, without distinction of political shades, that in each case might characterize them, requires imperatively, on everybody's part, an absolute abstention from political activity and trade union activities that would signify inclination or partisanship in favor of certain ideologies or would lead to the misunderstanding that on the part of the National Defense Council

there should be preference for one or the other of the political or syndical organizations mentioned.

After threatening their destruction in the bud if necessary, even if they should be based on the highest motives, it ends saying:

> The day will arrive in which the government that rules the destinies of Spain will know how to develop the only politics and only unionization possible in any well organized nation: the politics and the unionization led and controlled by the directors [managers one could say] of the public weal, as depositories of the trust of the people.

Few texts reveal better the military mentality, its basic skepticism if not contempt for ideological diversity—even on their own side—its fear of party conflict, its belief in a well-meaning government ruling for the public interest turning to individuals willing to collaborate rather than to organizations for assistance. Only four days later, on September 29, 1936, the military leaders and their junta would transmit their powers to one of their peers, a young general, Francisco Franco. On October 1 he would create a provisional government named the *Junta Técnica del Estado,* in which, together with army officers and civil servants, we would find three men who had formed part of the Primo de Rivera Assembly. No Falangist would enter the government until January 30, 1938.

In the meantime the Carlists and the Falangists had mobilized their forces, and the latter in particular recruited the young and adventurous, and even some of those afraid of the repression among former members of the leftist mass organizations, to go to the front. While there are no reliable statistics, at the end of 1936 the Falange claimed 50,000 men serving at the front and 30,000 in the rear guard. Stanley Payne suggests a reversal of these figures.[27] In September, 1936, Manuel Hedilla claimed in an interview to a German correspondent that before the war the Falange had 80,000 members and sympathizers, but now had reached 120,000 on the front, with another 150,000 volunteers ready to follow a call, plus 320,000 non-mobilized members of which 80,000 were women.[28] Even considering some of these figures exaggerated and knowing the low level of political indoctrination of those members, a new political force had emerged.[29]

Obviously the prohibitions of political activity remained a dead letter even when the military often interfered, even brutally, against their political allies and trade union organizing by the Falangists encountered great difficulties.

To create a military-bureaucratic regime without a party, or with a state party created only from above, or a military-bureaucratic-monarchical regime like those of East Europe with a party based on individually coopted leaders and conservative politicians and experts, became increasingly difficult. Even so, men like the brother of Franco played with the idea. If

Calvo Sotelo had lived, he could have been the civil servant-financial expert type of authoritarian head of government like Oliveira Salazar in Portugal, Stoyadinović in Yugoslavia, and Bela Imrédy in Hungary, but his death deprived the regime of an outstanding and well-known leader of this type. The defeat of Gil Robles at the polls in February, 1936, with the subsequent disillusionment of many of his followers, and his unwillingness to commit his party to an insurrectionary course eliminated from the scene another potential civilian leader for an anti-democratic movement with army support. The CEDA did not act as a party, and its leader advised his supporters to act as individuals and to join the regular army rather than to create their own militia if they wished. However, the JAP formed some units under military command.[30] Anti-democratic monarchism did not have mass appeal, and Carlism could not expand far beyond its traditional Catholic conservative and regional constituency, even when the *Requetés* provided some of the best fighting units.

The Falange, with its rhetoric, its mixture of social demagoguery and defense of traditional and middle-class values, its aura of youthfulness, and its affinity with movements that had swept Europe and brought international recognition to two powerful nations supporting Franco, represented something new. Its emphasis on equality within a national community—reflected in the use of the term "comrade" and the *tu* rather than the formal *usted*—attracted much of the lower middle class, some of the workers (partly out of fear and opportunism), and reformist sectors of the middle class otherwise scared by the proletarian revolution. The absence of any reference to a monarchy also favored it. Some more intellectual sectors would find the less clerical outlook appealing. In the war years, the Falange would achieve a high level of political participation and mobilization, which for the first time extended to women—beyond traditional charity or voting for clerical candidates—and to middle-class youth. To a lesser extent the traditionalists achieved the same. Falangism soon was able to give to many with its symbolism, rhetoric, and aesthetics, largely copied from the Nazi and fascist models, a feeling of participating in the making of history that made a deep impression on the younger generation.

Years later Dionisio Ridruejo—the Djilas of the regime—would write about this period, in which he was one of the main propagandists and organizers of the party, in these bitter terms:

> The rhetoric fostering of this intoxication with style would allow [people] to call a police action [he means the repression of the working class] a revolution, and what is even more serious live it spiritually as if it were a revolution.[31]

This participation, mostly voluntary, however, took place within an authoritarian framework under the effective control of the military authorities. In the meantime the building of a trade union organization found enormous difficulties both among the workers and the conservative circles and the army. However, this growing party was practically leaderless, and none, except José Antonio, would have been acceptable to the army and conservatives, if any at all. The party had been practically outlawed by the Republicans on March 14, 1936, and nine of the twelve members of the *Junta Política* arrested. For a party in which the charisma of the leader was specially important, the imprisonment of José Antonio on that date, and the deaths of Onésimo Redondo and Ramiro Ledesma, among others, left the party without a single top leader until the appointment on September 3, 1936 of Manuel Hedilla as "leader of the provisional leadership Junta," a position he would hold until April, 1937, when, after a complex crisis, Franco decided to assume those powers himself. In this respect the loss of the three founders of Spanish fascism, early in the Civil War, placed the party in a very different position from the PNF or the NSDAP. To some extent it was like that of the Iron Guard after the death of Codreanu. However, in that case the leading lieutenant lived. Under General Antonescu the party there suffered a fate similar to that of the Falange. Only one of the members of the *Junta Política* and twenty-five of the provincial chiefs were initially in the area dominated by the uprising. The parallel would be the NSDAP without Hitler, Strasser, Goebbels, and Goering!

The first somewhat informal meeting of leaders in August 1, 1936, was followed by another one at the end of the month in which the head of the party militia of the Sevilla and Valladolid organizations seemed to emerge. But a party congress of national councillors and provincial chiefs on September 2, 1936, rejected this idea. The failure of a triumvirate after the fusion of FE with the JONS years back was too recent for it to be tried again. The meeting therefore approved a six-member leadership council with Hedilla as its head until the return of the founder, José Antonio. All the attempts to liberate him from jail failed and in the early morning hours of November 20, he was shot. Hedilla's task of organizing the party, particularly the beginnings of Falangist trade unions, and of defending it against the encroachments by the military was not easy. The influx of new members, the absence at the front of the activists, the lack of social status and professional qualifications of many militants, led newcomers to be appointed to party offices. At the local level the party activists often became subordinates of the military, and with some objection by their superiors, were engaged in the repression of their opponents. In a radio Christmas message, the new leader demanded social reform and "open arms to workers and peasants, exalting the nobility of work," saying, "there is only one class, Spaniards," asking for the extinction of those who do not work, and so forth. The party started organizing a welfare service, *Auxilio de Invierno,* which assisted many of the children of the victims of the repression. The news of the death of the founder coincided with the Third National Party Council, but the leadership decided not to announce it, probably moved by the vain hope that it was false. The myth of the *Ausente* (the absent one) was to continue to November 16, 1938, when the news would become official in Franco Spain. The party council could on the basis of its statutes have appointed a new leader according to Article 47 of the by-law that said: "The office of leader will last three years. After each period of three years the leadership will be extended for another three if the National Council by a vote of three-fourths of its members should not decide to celebrate a new leader election." This principle did not foresee a succession by designation by the leader, as the statutes approved in 1937 and in a more indirect way the present legislation established. At the November, 1936 meeting, the Council—in view of the circumstances of the war—prolonged its own existence and did not alter the mandate given to the Junta de Mando and Hedilla as its head.

In that same period, Franco, who had been appointed Generalissimo and head of the government and the state by the strictly military *Junta de Defensa Nacional,* was moving slowly but surely to gain control of the divergent political forces fighting on his side.[32] In December his headquarters, on account of the creation by the *Requetés* of a Royal Carlist Military Academy, demanded the instant emigration of Manuel Fal Conde, the national leader of the *Comunión Tradicionalista.* On December 22, the militias of the *Requeté* and the Falangists were made subject to military authority and discipline, and those who wanted to attain military rank had to attend training institutions created by the state. The men close to Franco did not like the style and manners of many of the Falangist leaders.

Nicolás Franco, brother of the general, thought of a Franquista party— along the lines of the *Unión Patriótica*—and former CEDA men were involved. The neo-Falangists, neo-traditionalists, and neo-monarchists certainly would not have been reluctant to join. The German ambassador did not view such a trend with pleasure. He argued that it would not be possible to win over the working class, especially of that part of Spain not yet conquered, for the national ideals and for social ideas that could be implemented, and to tie it to the new state, without the participation of the Falange (January, 1937). Another idea was to have Franco join the Falange and then be elected leader and make the party the state party.

The traditional non-monarchist, non-Carlist, Catholic middle classes were left without a party after the CEDA disintegrated. The younger generations among them largely joined the Falange, but they contributed to its change and facilitated its subordination to the army, somewhat as on the other side, the non-working-class Republicans who joined the Communist Party contributed to a slowdown of the proletarian revolution, put an end to the dispersion of authority, and helped in the reconstruction of a state apparatus. Whatever misgivings many officers, conservative elites and the church had about the Falange, the party and its militias were a reality to be reckoned with. Their problem was to control it and if possible use it for their own purposes, neutralizing the aspects each of them considered dangerous, and limit its influence. The social development of Spain, the lengthy war, the foreign influences, made a pure bureaucratic state single party impossible.

Both in Falangist and in Carlist circles the idea of a rapprochement, in part to avoid an imposed unification, gained ground. The Falangists stressed their acceptance of the Catholic tradition and noted that this was a substitute for the pagan cult of fatherland and race of similar foreign movements. These informal conversations took place in February, 1936, and both parties stated their very different conceptions of the political future of Spain and the role of a unified party in it. After the monarchical restoration, in the traditionalist conception any party would ultimately be supplanted by the king and an organic representation, which would also make the *Comunión Tradicionalista* dispensable. They seemed to have agreed, however, not to allow any third party to intervene in their affairs and to reject a civilian government not formed exclusively by both political forces. Traditionalists not unwilling to accept a restoration under Juan de Borbón, the son of the last king, Alphons XIII, and Andalusian Falangists with monarchist-UP ties also became involved.

At this point—February 20—Ramón Serrano Súñer [33] arrived in Salamanca. He would be architect of the single party in the form it essentially would have until 1945 and with only minor modifications until 1968. Thirty-five years old, brother-in-law of Franco, university classmate and friend of José Antonio, he had studied in Rome and Bologna, and became a practicing lawyer after he had successfully entered the elite corps of the Spanish civil service, the *Abogados del Estado* (the equivalent to the French Inspection des Finances).[34] He had been alternate vice president of the CEDA and twice deputy in the Republican parliament, where he had defended the contested election of José Antonio. The biographical sketch in itself contains many of the elements that would give a particular political character to the unified party and the regime. Here we have a man personally close to Franco (he would be called the *cuñadísimo,* the superlative of brother-in-law), with enough familiarity with Italian fascism to understand the contribution the fascist ideology could make to the regime, personal ties with the founder, considerable parliamentary and political experience, an identification with the clerical party that would make him acceptable to the church while it would arouse German suspicions; in addition, he was endowed with the ascriptive achievement of high civil service status that means so much to the Spanish middle classes. He was no outsider to the conservative middle-class system of values and stratification, but in contrast to most of his peers he had the sense to see the need for a modern ideology, an organization, and symbols capable of appealing to important sectors among the defeated, potentially useful to incorporate the working class, to justify a modicum of social reform, and to give the new regime a legitimacy in the international system. A military dictatorship or a nonconstitutional monarchy based on traditionalist-ultra-Catholic ideas could not have done this. The mimetic character of so many one-party system ideologies, determined largely by the international context at the time of their emergence, is obvious here as it is in Africa and the Arab world today.

The situation in 1938 was described by Dionisio Ridruejo [35] as a movement without a Caudillo and a Caudillo without a movement. Serrano Súñer would be the politician to bring both together. In the process all kinds of complex intrigues and, to some extent, accidents would play an important role, particularly in eliminating the formal head of the party, Manuel Hedilla. An internal crisis provoked by the struggle of different factions within the party—perhaps unexpectedly—facilitated the process. The northern provincial leadership representing the middle-class but progressively oriented sector, as well as the intellectuals, favored Hedilla as national leader. Another faction with support among the Madrid members, who resented the important role played by the provincials, and some of the Andalusian wing more tied to Primo de Rivera by family and friendship than ideology, favored a provisional solution until the announcement of the death of the founder. They constituted a "legitimist" wing ready to wait for the arrival of the Secretary General, Fernández Cuesta, still in Republican Spain, and were fearful that Hedilla would accept the unification. Finally, there were some of the neo-Falangists with a monarchist or Catholic background, who, together with a more apolitical technocratic group, favored Franco. The head of the legitimist faction, a young and aggressive leader of the militia, contacted some of the discontented provincial chiefs and advocated a triumvirate. Hedilla, in turn, to prevent the conspiracy called on April 15 an extraordinary National Council for April 25 to dissolve the leadership junta and formally elect a national leader. On April 16 the conspirators decided to oust him on the basis of his drive for personal power and "excessive and improper propaganda of his person"—the cult of personality, as we would call it today—and presented him with the demand to resign. He rejected the demand, leaving the office in their hands and informing Franco's headquarters of the crisis and the convocation of the Council. The power struggle had only begun, with Hedilla able to prevent the circulation of a note announcing the ouster by the new triumvirate through telegraph or mass media. The threat of violence was in the air; each group feared an attack by armed men in sympathy with the other and mobilized its men. What, according to the pro-Hedilla sources, was an attempt to arrange a meeting with one of his opponents, was according to another interpretation with some good arguments in favor of it, an attempt to arrest them, which ended in shooting. The night ended with the arrest by the police of the participants in the bloody event. On April 18, the National Council convened with half of the members appointed by José Antonio present, since the others were dead or absent—one member had been arrested on account of the events. Hedilla defended himself against the charges of the conspirators and accused them, among other things, of the plan to kill him and forty-seven comrades. He told them that Franco intended to assume the leadership of the party. The vote to elect a national leader was ten for Hedilla, eight blank and four scattered. Hedilla went to communicate the result to Franco, who apparently had just spoken on the radio of the need for unification. On April 19, the Council still elected the new *Junta Política*.[36] On the evening of April 19, Franco sent the decree announcing the unification, which created Falange Española Tradicionalista y de las JONS, to Hedilla.[37] The decree had been written by Serrano Súñer after consultation and approval by Generals Queipo de Llano and Mola. Serrano, himself, has written:

> To be precise it was a unilateral act of Franco, even when there were some previous negotiations with elements in the parties affected whose leading representatives were notified of the intentions of the [military] headquarters.

The next day

> on the occasion of the transcendental decree dictated by the supreme command, the national leader of Falange Española de las JONS, comrade Hedilla, accompanied by . . . visited His Excellency Generalissimo Franco. The Head of State presented to his visitors how much he expects of the *new* organization ordained by him, in the exact service of the new Spanish State, into which, substantively, the norms of the Falange have been incorporated. . . .[38]

This summary announced officially by the party still passed the censorship, but its enemies around Franco started to act and the military in the provinces to interfere with the party, while many of its leaders started to rally to the new power center.

On April 22, Franco appointed half of the members of the "political secretariat or Junta Política of FET y de las JONS," among them Hedilla; three traditionalists who had not been authorized by the regent nor by the exiled leader of the Comunión; a lieutenant colonel who had joined Falange shortly before the uprising; Giménez Caballero, fascist ideologist, who once had been excluded from the party for running on the right coalition ticket in Madrid in 1936; two neo-Falangists, one officer and an engineer who had been associated with Franco's headquarters; together with the former regional head of the party in Sevilla.

Hedilla received the news through the newspaper, and many Falangists urged him to refuse, particularly a group that formed around the sister of the founder and leader of the women's section. Informally, he communicated to Franco his refusal, based on the composition of the secretariat and the way in which the unification had been arranged without previous consultation, except for one very informal feeler. Finally, the option to accept or to go to jail was politely suggested by intermediaries. On April 25, Hedilla was arrested; on April 29, he was indicted; on June 5 and 7 he was tried by a military court on two counts—for the events that led to the death of the Falangist on April 17 and for endangering the unity of the Front—and sentenced to death, a sentence later commuted to life imprisonment. He served until July, 1941, when the sentence was changed into forced residence until 1946. His dismissal from the political secretariat was announced fourteen days after his arrest. Many other Falangists were indicted for "military rebellion" on account of planning a protest in favor of Hedilla. On May 16 the Alphonsine monarchists were incorporated into the party. Already, on April 24, Gil Robles wrote to the representative of the militias of the *Juventud de Acción Popular* that he considered their political activities finished. The Agrarian Party had decided formally to disband. The existence of multiple political organizations in Franco Spain had ended.

The New Political Organization: Falange Española Tradicionalista y de las JONS

To understand the nature of the single party created, "which for the moment would be called Falange Española Tradicionalista y de las JONS," it is best to read the speech of Franco announcing his intentions, the text of the decree, and the recollections of Serrano Súñer.[39] The first two documents have been often quoted in the 1967–1968 discussions about the Movimiento-Organización and in 1969 some of the party reformers demanded its derogation, implicit in the 1966 constitution. The appeal to unity was—legitimately and effectively—made for the sake of the military effort in the name of the dead and of Franco, not of the integrated parties, but also for the building of the new state and its national revolution (but note, not the national-syndicalist revolution). The ghost of the *Unión Patriótica* was exorcised, as was the idea of a government of national unity, when he said, "not a conglomerate of forces, nor government concentrations, nor more or less patriotic or sacred unions. Nothing inorganic, passing or temporary, is what I demand." The essentially flexible conception, which would serve the regime so well and which contrasts with the unchangeability of the program declaration of some totalitarian parties, was stated in these terms:

> . . . A movement more than a program. And as such it is in process of elaboration and subject to constant revision and improvement as reality may suggest. It is not a rigid nor static thing, but flexible. And which—as a movement—has had, therefore, different stages.[40]

As such stages, he was referring to history since the *Reconquista,* the traditionalist resistance to the Europeanizing liberal period, the Primo de Rivera dictatorship as bridge between the *pronunciamiento* and the organic conception of the movements that call themselves "fascist" or "nationalist"; to the JONS and José Antonio, who gave it a modern and youthful dimension and influenced "monarchist and Catholic groups." The speech appealed to everyone with even a gesture to the Western democracies, which were told that the real threat to their empires came not from their neighbors or the nations that demanded a place in the world, but from destructive bolshevism. The three channels of participation, through the functions of family, municipality, and Sindicato, were already contraposed to the "formal" liberal democracy. The preamble of the decree stated:

> Its programmatic norm is constituted by the 26 points of Falange Española [the 27th had been unceremoniously dropped] having to note that since the movement which we lead is precisely that (a movement) more than a program, it will not be a rigid or static thing, but subject, in each case, to the work of revision and improvement that reality advises.

A final paragraph stated that "after the spiritual and material reconstruction, if the needs and the sentiments of the country would advise so, we do not close the horizon to the possibility to inaugurate in the nation the century old regime that shall forge its unity. . . ." Contrary to what many may have thought at the time, thirty-one years later one can argue that no one should have felt deceived. Pragmatism would never allow the Falangist twenty-six points to become the programmatic base of the regime and no legal document—including the text of the unification decree itself in contrast to the preamble—would mention them. The monarchical instauration —note, not restoration—would come in due course, in 1947, but was still to be implemented pending "the needs of the fatherland," obviously to be interpreted by Franco. The functions assigned to the new organization coincided almost completely, except in the language used, with those Sigmund Neumann attributed to the single parties:

> This organization intermediary between the Society and the State, has as principal task to communicate to the State the support [literally the breath] of the people and to bring it [the people] the thought of the State through the politico-moral virtues of hierarchical service and brotherhood.

Neumann formulated the functions of the dictatorial party after the seizure of power:

1. It creates the political elite.
2. It controls and educates the masses.
3. It maintains communication between state and society.[41]

Organizationally the decree called for creation of a "political secretariat or Political Junta"—a kind of politburo to assist the national leader, the head of state, and a National Council. To initiate the tasks, half the politburo would be appointed by Franco (actually ten members) and the other half elected later by the National Council, whose membership was not defined. More specific were the provisions on the unification of all party militias as an auxiliary of the army with Franco as its head and under the direct command of a general of the army, even when promising "political advisors of the command," resembling political commissars. Any hope for an SA or SS had been squelched in the bud. The leadership then proceeded to draft the by-laws of the organization, which were approved by a decree of August 4, 1937 [42] and restated in a more grandiloquent language the ideas of the unification, and defined the leader in these terms:

> He, the Supreme Caudillo of the Movimiento, personifies all its values and honors . . . and assumes in their entire fullness, the most absolute authority. The Leader is responsible before God and History.

Most important, the appointment of a successor was attributed to the Caudillo. The possibility of inner party democracy latent in the original party statutes had disappeared completely and would never revive. A basic difference between the Spanish and other single-party systems was introduced here. Already the original statutes of October, 1934 of FE de las JONS had given the leader the power to appoint the different leaders from the top down.

What disappeared now was the regular election or reelection of the leader by the National Council—which already was really a cooptation procedure, since the forty-eight-member National Council was largely appointed by the leader or those freely appointed by him, like the provincial leaders. The new National Council members were to be appointed and dismissed freely by Franco and would constitute the only political chamber with the function to assist in the legislative process, before the creation of the Cortes in 1942.

The *Consejo,* appointed in October, 1937, had fifty members, who reflected the coalition of forces behind the regime (as shown in Table 5–1).

This elite would not suffer bloody purges, like those in some totalitarian systems, but five would be persecuted and quite a few fell into oblivion. The discontinuity between the party elite of the pre-Civil War, FE de las JONS, and that of the regime was even greater (as can be seen from the data in Table 5–1) and only two would reach a cabinet post, even when in this case the heavy toll of the Civil War has to be kept in mind when comparing these figures with other countries.

The 1937 statutes, modified over the years, did not provide for any elected members until 1955, when fifty councillors were to be elected by the provincial and local party councils, by then representing practically only party and local officials. The elected members were to be part of the 160-member body (the remainder being appointed or ex officio). Even "legal democratization" and "second degree" elections came to the party later than to the state legislature—the Cortes—or even the Sindicatos. The party certainly could not become a channel for political participation even

TABLE 5-1 *Political Background, Continuities, and Discontinuities of the Leadership of FET y de las JONS*[a]

	Pre-Civil War FE de las JONS National Councils		National Councils of FET y de las JONS				Presence of 1937 Council in the 1943 Legislature (I Cortes)
	I 1934	II 1935	I 1937	Changes between 1937 and 1939	II 1939 Continous from 1937	Total	
FET y de las JONS	42	22	7	1	5	8	7
		26	3	−1	2	3	2
			10	−1	8	8	4
New with Falange background						18	
Total FET y de las JONS	42	48	20	−1		37	13
Traditionalists			11	−1	5	8	3
Alphonsine Monarchists			5	−2	3	6	1
CEDA-Catholics			2		2	4	3
Other conservative parties						3	
Military			8	4	6	20	4
Experts, special cases			2		2	5	2
No information			2			15	
Total continuities, respectively 1939 and 1943, of 1937 Council					33		24
Total membership of Council or Cortes			50			100	409[b]

[a]The political background classifications are obviously debatable and some men at different dates should be counted differently. We used their pre-Civil War public identification.

[b]Actually fewer due to multiple incumbencies.

for those identifying with the regime or the Movimiento nor even of its members.[43]

The National Council, after a short period during the war in which it was the scene of some policy debates, would end meeting infrequently and then only to applaud Franco's speeches, except for an attempt of party reform, initiated by Arrese in 1956. This move was condemned to defeat, but to some extent it has been reflected in recent legislation.

The twenty-member *Junta Política* (politburo) created by the Unification decree was conceived as a more active body, but as Serrano Súñer, who was its president from August 1939 until September 1942, writes:

Its labors were rather insignificant, serving only to maintain official contact between the party and the state. In some cases the meetings [it should not be forgotten that the official party, like the national movement itself, was a conglomeration of forces] were strained and even agitated. The political life of the regime resided principally in the Ministries.[44]

The key office in the party became that of the secretary general, who controlled the party bureaucracy and initially the Sindicatos and made most appointments to party offices. The periods of party history to some extent can be linked to the persons occupying that office.[45]

Totalitarianism in the Making?

Once the *Gleichschaltung* [46] of parties and of the party itself in the form of FET y de las JONS had been achieved and victory in the war had been assured, the men of the new organization were tempted to try a *Gleichschaltung* of the society. Or, to be more precise, some men in the new party, particularly some of the Falangists, organization men, activists, and some intellectuals among them might have tried. There is no question that they ultimately failed, even when they made considerable progress in that direction. Why and to what degree did they do so? We would argue that an ideological control of the society, an organizational mobilization of large sectors, a subordination of different institutions and interest groups and, ultimately, the shift of the main decision-making power to the party, were not possible in Spanish society even immediately after 1939. Such a policy ultimately was not acceptable to Franco and did not fit with his own conception of society and politics, with his whole mentality and political style. It therefore could have been carried out only by imposing it on him or against his will, if necessary, by overthrowing him. The men controlling the party, or even those who would have liked to control it with such aims, probably would never have overcome the resistance of other sectors of the society to their goals without the Caudillo on their side. But Franco would never break with the army, the church, experts, and bureaucrats. From our perspective it was not national character or inefficiency that accounts for the failure of totalitarianism, but more structural factors.[47] Our interpretation diverges from that of those who explain the authoritarian, rather than totalitarian, character of the system by the defeat of the Axis, which served the Spanish totalitarians as a model. That defeat certainly facilitated the liberalization of the regime, but we doubt that, except by a direct intervention in Spanish internal affairs by the victorious Germans, the regime would have become totalitarian in the strict sense. That might have required the removal of Franco, and without outside intervention, such removal in the 1940s was almost impossible owing to the almost solid opposition of the army. Even the army leaders, like General Yagüe,[48] favorable to a national-syndicalist revolutionary policy, were ultimately loyal to

Franco and there were no outstanding fascist civilian leaders they might have been tempted to support.

This does not mean that the efforts of *Gleichschaltung* of those sectors of society not closely linked to the church, the bureaucratic elite, powerful economic interests, and above all the army did not go very far and that there were no attempts to even attack those resisting sectors. The working class, which had put its hope in truly revolutionary effort in 1936 under left-socialist, anarchist, and later communist leadership, was totally defeated, its leaders shot, in jail or exile. There was no need to co-opt or control its organizations, as was attempted by the Nazis and fascists, but there was a need to build some organization to integrate the deeply hostile workers into the system. The hostility of conservative sectors to any kind of trade union, the sullen hostility of the defeated, reinforced by the harsh repression in the first years of the regime, and the lack of cadres with labor experience, made the building of Sindicatos a slow and difficult task. Years later Sindicatos would have some success in channeling the representation of the workers at the plant level, initiate some collective bargaining, act as a pressure group for labor, and provide some social services, but it is doubtful that they ever won anything but a passive acceptance of the regime. The emigration of many liberal professionals and civil servants and the more or less enthusiastic acceptance of the regime by those with conservative leanings or those frightened by the proletarian revolution in Republican Spain, all limited the need of party control of those sectors.

The purges after 1939 eliminated the remaining dissidents or potential dissidents but did not affect the limited pluralism among the supporters of Franco. The party's role in those sectors would always remain secondary, since it would have divided the supporters of the regime rather than strengthened it. Power there often went to pro-regime clericals rather than FET y de las JONS activitists. The corporativist ideology of the national-syndicalists led them into a struggle for control of the interest representation of business and an attempt to destroy rival organizations. Many traditional pressure groups opted to enter Sindicatos; others survived by keeping low, waiting for better times; others found support in ministries not controlled by Falangists.

The traditional Chambers of Commerce of Industry, which had been the official bodies organizing business, could survive thanks to the support of the Ministry of Industry and Commerce, even when seriously weakened. The strong organization of Catalan business practically disappeared, and those of the Basque country (less politically compromised) lost their power. Years later business would again create—illegally, but very effectively—some powerful pressure groups free of Sindicatos control and increasingly participate and control the different organizations within Sindicatos.[49] The importance of the big industrial investment banks and the interlocking directorates within industry limited the impact of the *Gleichschaltung*. However, the effort would produce a serious disjunction between formal and informal leadership of the business community. Obviously, business did not have much reason to question the basic outlook of the regime even when it probably felt bitter about many of its policies. A search for contacts within the administration and for some time, corruption, were its responses; it would be privileged but in many respects impotent in formulating policies.[50]

The rural world initially was only the object of an effort of the administration to collect the produce to supply the cities, and nobody could have done much to organize its cooperation to that effect. With the threat of agrarian reform exorcised and a government unable to give much to the farmers but ready to make demands to them, there was not much desire to organize the farmers. The state-controlled Wheat Board (*Servicio Nacional del Trigo*) became the main agent of the state at the village level. Sindicatos in some products helped the state in its task. Only decades later, when a changed market for agricultural products, liberalization of foreign trade threatening some products, the need to export, and increasing scarcity of farm labor changed the rural situation did the *Hermandades Sindicales de Labradores y Ganaderos*,[51] the Brotherhoods of Farmers and Cattlemen, became important to the independent farmers, especially the well to do. Today they are probably the most loyal and influential organization dependent upon the Sindicatos headquarters and an important cog in the machine of the Movimiento. According to some observers, the *Hermandades* were an important factor in recent direct elections by the heads of household of 102 deputies in the 564-member Cortes in more or less competitive and honest elections. However, there was an organization not tinted with leftism that was an important plum for the party and that the ideology obliged it to incorporate: the CONCA.[52] The task was not easy, since CONCA (the *Confederación Católica Agraria,* a confederation of cooperatives, and so forth, of Catholic farmers of northern, north-central, and Levante Spain) was a large, well-established and pro-Franco but non-Falangist organization closely linked with the church. The preamble of the order of September 23, 1941 reflects this difficulty when it recommends "the maximum discretion and respect" in carrying out the law of sindical unity. The implementation of that unity has seriously limited and hampered the emergence of independent interest organizations—"class organizations"— since any association of that type before being approved by the Ministry of Interior requires clearance by Sindicatos, unless the Ministry can ask for and obtain a favorable report from another more influential ministry claiming jurisdiction.

Until monographic research is done on the history of Sindicatos and the economy it will be impossible to say to what extent the party men who were appointed to the top posts in Sindicatos made policies, used their power, and so forth, or the different sectors and groups in the economy used Sindicatos for their own purposes, or ignored it altogether considering their dues as one more tax to support one more bureaucracy. Among the twenty-seven Sindicatos Nacionales and hundreds of suborganizations, over twenty-eight years, we would probably find all these situations. However, the *Gleichschaltung* never achieved a real unity of purpose nor did it aim or achieve for the organization a decisive role in economic development. The activities of Sindicatos in that sphere would not go in any case beyond those of more independent interest groups in Western democracies.

On paper, the control of youth was total, since no other youth organizations were allowed or tolerated. However the monopoly did not represent any wide-spread mobilization of youth under FET leadership. The religious orders boycotted subtly any attempt on the part of the party to gain continued influence upon the upper- and middle-class youth they were educating in their secondary schools (70 per cent of that level of education).[53] In addition there was the difficulty of bringing together youth of different class backgrounds in a status-conscious society with great social and educational inequalities. A late effort to depoliticize the organization and thereby increase its appeal—making it more like the Boy Scouts in the West—encountered resistance in the more ideological local leadership and was not pushed very far.

Ultimately an underdeveloped economy requiring hard work, leaving little time and energy for civic activities, the importance of alternative pursuits to politics, the survival of non-political voluntary associations, the absence of a tradition of joining (except in the autonomist regions), the lack of a tradition of civic-minded activism, the competition of religiously sponsored organizations (of youth, women, charity, and so forth) all put insuperable limits on efforts of social mobilization through organizations linked to the party. One has to add the limited rewards in careerist terms to those involved in the party, given the control of access to real power through other recruitment channels. The social ostracism by important anti-Falangist sectors of society (particularly "society") was another factor. In the case of the women's organization, hanging on to the ideal of unpaid service became another drawback. Much of the effort of early years ended in paper organizations or in depoliticized activities, specifically a weak interest representation before the state bureaucracy.

There naturally remain isolated and frustrated nuclei trying to keep up the faith kindled in the excitement of the Civil War. No one can deny that many of these organizations have performed great services, that some of their leaders were dedicated to their ideals and to their tasks, but the dream of an active society under party leadership ended in defeat. On the other hand, the more or less effective monopoly of the party, together with the much more important monopoly of the church in some areas, and a bureaucratic state of Napoleonic tradition have prevented the free development of initiatives and energies in the more alert and civic-minded sectors of the society. This seems to have been particularly the case in the economically developed linguistic-autonomist regions, while sometimes in the underdeveloped Spain the Movimiento created organizations and activities that would not have been started without the initiative at the center. In a society at the stage of development of Spain, probably only a truly totalitarian party with a strong ideological commitment, under strong leadership, and after complete victory could make an effort of social and political mobilization like the one envisaged on paper in the early 1940s by FET lawmakers.

The following years would witness a long and complex process of transformation of the party created by the Unification and its isolation within the regime and the society. The army protected its interests by assuming command of the militia, reducing it after the war and controlling it. The party statutes of 1937 made all army officers automatically eligible to become militants of the party, a right that would have allowed them to pack the party meetings, but of which they never had to make use. The fearful church hierarchy often warned of foreign neo-pagan influences and "statolatry" and managed to sow suspicion among sectors under its influence. Catholic organizations checked the expansion of the women's organization and the welfare activities of the party, even when for many years they (outside of small elite groups) could not take public stands on political and social problems. The survival of the professional civil service, particularly the strengthening of its elite corps, limited the opportunities for patronage outside party organizations except in a few new ministries and autonomous agencies.

The attempt at totalitarian transformation and control of the society by the new single party—even if it had been serious—was condemned to failure. The party had to share power, in a limited pluralism that made the regime authoritarian rather than totalitarian. This in turn required a process of demobilization [54] of many of those activated in the war and "turned on" by the rhetoric of a national revolution and imperial goals. A number of circumstances made this possible: the death of the founders in the prisons and the battlefield and the low intellectual quality and lack of political sophistication of many second-rank leaders. The identification with the new leadership of many of those who had suffered in Red Spain,[55] added to the war-weariness and the desire for return to civilian life of those who had fought, reduced the political mobilization. The withdrawal from the party of some of the upper class and the educated, who had joined when confronted with the careerism and opportunism, if not corruption, of upward-mobile lower-middle class and marginal people—a reaction that often covered social snobbism as a reaction to the pseudo-equalitarianism imposed as party style—was another weakening circumstance. The limited possibilities for any action in a war-ravaged country, isolated in a world at war, with hunger at the door, repression of the defeated (supported by moral self-righteousness and a spirit of vengeance for real or even imagined and overreported suffering and terror on the other side), plus the bureaucratic injustices of a process like the de-Nazification applied to everyone who had been even living on "the other side," limited any real appeal to the defeated to join. The Falangist idealists often withdrew, kept some of the spirit in small coteries, put their hopes on a future Axis victory, or when the war against the USSR started, went to fight there, often to die on the snowcovered battlefields.[56]

The defeat of the countries that had served as inspiration to the Spanish fascists and the allied pressure after the war forced even further demobilization, the fascist greeting stopped being obligatory, and for a long time the party secretariat was vacant. Franco started recruiting even a larger number of the elite from other political sectors, particularly the ex-Populist Catholics, who he felt would be acceptable to the rising Christian Democrats of Europe and the American church and the collaborationist monarchists. Franco, who often donned the party uniform in the early 1940s, in the early 1950s turned back to the army gray, while his cabinet members appeared increasingly in civilian dress (see Table 5–2).

TABLE 5-2   *Uniforms Worn by Franco and His Cabinet in the First Six Months of 1940, 1945, and 1950*

Type of Uniform	1940		1945		1950	
	Franco	Cabinet	Franco	Cabinet	Franco	Cabinet
Falange blue	44%	44%	35%	25%	—	2%
Falange white (summer)	3	9	3	7.5	—	8
Military	50	12	40	25	87%	6
Civilian garb	3	35	5	55	4	71
Other uniforms (diplomat, admiral, and so forth)	—	—	19	2	9	12
N	(32)	(75)	(37)	(132)	(46)	(49)

Source: Photographs in *ABC* of Madrid.

The weakness of the youth organization and the alienation of many of its more idealistic members limited recruiting into the party. Some of the same factors precluded the emergence of a large discontented or radical second generation. The depolitization of the SEU (*Sindicato Español Universitario*), the student union, which in 1943 became increasingly a dues-collecting and service organization as membership became automatic, was yet another factor, a development that had been foreseen by SEU leaders opposed to obligatory membership. The slow, but relentless, transfer of the propaganda services from party control and later party influence to the state was another step in the same direction.

Ultimately the single party was being reduced to four components: a party bureaucracy—not too large—without prestige or power and with limited funds, a women's organization performing many useful functions with considerable idealism but no ideological autonomy, particularly in view of the ambivalence about feminism growing out of the Catholic and fascist traditions, and a youth organization undergoing frequent shifts in leadership and a limited sphere of influence.

As the party withered away or hibernated in the late 1940s and 1950s, only Sindicatos [57] grew into a giant organization with a large and increasingly influential bureaucracy. There the top positions often went to old party stalwarts, even when under them younger and more professional people gained influence. Coopted industrialists and managers started participating, and at the plant level workers started using the opportunities offered by limited democratization since 1943 to defend some of their interests. The various functions they performed, such as serving as a channel of pressure group activity for economic interests and as an arena for more or less muted and ineffective social protest at meetings, congresses, and so forth, assistance in the case of individual grievances at the plant level, and some of the direct services in the fields of sports, leisure, labor training and finally since 1958, collective bargaining, together with the funds derived from a 2 per cent tax on the total national basic wage bill, have made the Sindicatos a powerful institution.[58] What started in the organization charts of the 1940s as a delegation of the party subordinated to a vice-secretariat became the key organization with the national head of the Sindicatos, José Solís Ruiz, becoming in 1957, also the general secretary of the party and Minister for Party Affairs. The different position of party and Sindicatos is well reflected in the often shabby party offices and the large new building of the Sindicatos in the provincial capitals, the slumbering doormen in the first and the bustle of activity in the second.[59]

Partial Liberalization and Political Demobilization

The need to expand the basis of the regime in the course of the late 1940s and 1950s, together with the international pressure and the increasing complexity of the society, contributed to a growing political pluralism outside the party, one that was limited to those accepting the system, perhaps with some mental reservations. This process had taken place mainly at the top in the cabinet and the central administration, while at the local level the Movimiento organizations probably continued being more dominant and alive.

The increased pluralism implicitly involved a liberalization for sectors of the elite and allowed some of the younger generations, then finishing their studies, to choose among different tendencies to enter a semipublic arena. Liberalization coincided with a total demobilization of the masses, even of those supporting the regime. There were few congresses, mass rallies, torch marches, or activities at party headquarters, left.[60] Party organs like the *Junta Política* and the National Council met infrequently, and no channels for popular participation, even in one-party elections, existed. Only some mass demonstrations—not lacking in spontaneity—at the time of the United Nations sanctions against the regime and the referendum approving the Succession Law [61] gave the supporters of the regime an opportunity to express themselves. The elections to one-third of the municipal council seats of family heads after 1945 did not stir anybody's interest even in the cities, since the candidacies were carefully arranged beforehand. Real opponents did not try (with rare monarchist exceptions) and mavericks were dissuaded or had nothing to offer to an apathetic electorate.

The party had few functions in such a system, even when many of those who had joined in the war days probably continued paying the minimal dues out of a mixture of lack of interest in going to the trouble to drop out, sentimental loyalty, or fear of some undefined consequences. Basically, it was a party without meaningful members, limited to bureaucrats and office holders. On the other hand, those appointed to certain offices—specifically provincial governorships and mayoralties—who were automatically provincial and local heads of the party, were assumed to join upon appointment the Movimiento.[62] Some candidates for such positions refused appointments on that account, while a few did not *de facto* exercise any party functions after their appointment, leaving them to a subleader. In a significant number of cases, mayors were appointed to only state or local office, with the party office of local chief going to someone else. The old Falangists provided only a small proportion of the elite, even at the local level [63] although it is probable that it was at that level where the influence and visibility of the party were most lasting. It was there also where the Movimiento from the beginning had been most open to the entry of newcomers with no ties to the pre-war party.

The Movimiento between World War II and Its Recent Constitutionalization

The Law of Succession in the Headship of State of 1947 had little to say about the Movimiento except to provide for one representative of the National Councillors in the seventeen-man Council of the Realm, and to provide that the king or regent would have to swear allegiance to the principles governing the Movimiento Nacional. Nothing was said about the succession in the leadership of the party, which formally was still a different office from that of the head of the government or of the state. The Movimiento officials, as a group in the elite of the regime, had reason to be concerned about their future. This led to a drive to develop further the open constitution institutionalizing the party. Arrese, appointed secretary general again in February, 1956 (after the liberalizing tendencies of Ruiz-Giménez in education and the lack of control by Fernández Cuesta over threats of violence by Falangists had created a serious crisis which ended in the ouster of both), took this goal to heart.[64] Franco, in a speech in July, seemed to approve of it, and by the end of September a Ley Orgánica (Organic Law) of the Movimiento and a Law Organizing the Government—subject to the constant influence of the Movimiento—were ready for submission to the National Council, to which a law defining the fundamental principles of the Movimiento was added. These proposals provoked a bitter discussion and were rejected in their totality by a significant minority of the National Council members. However, it was the reaction of important sectors in the army and the church that prevented the party and the government from pushing them any further. They fell into oblivion and Arrese resigned, to be appointed head of the new Ministry of Housing in 1957.

His report defending his proposals is one of the most interesting documents about the place of the party in the system. Some of the opponents saw in it an advocacy of return to totalitarianism, others felt it incompatible with the place they wanted to assign to the monarchy, and still others talked about a Yugoslav-type constitution. There is no question that the proposals represented a revolutionary change in the system while insisting on continuity. The report of the *Instituto de Estudios Políticos* supporting it constantly refers to statements of the Caudillo and to his unique historical role and authority. Franco was to be lifelong head of the Movement, but his successor would be "supreme representative of the political communion of Spaniards in the Movimiento, but neither he nor any of his successors would assume any executive political function inside the Movimiento." Pointedly, the *informe* used the expression, "The king reigns but does not govern." The most decisive innovation was Article 17 of the proposed Organic Law of the Movement: "The Secretary General of the Movimiento will be appointed by decree of the head of state at the proposal of the National Council after election within it by secret ballot and majority of votes," with a mandate for six years, and would be member of the cabinet. For the first time in the regime there was a proposal to create real power from below rather than from above.[65] A door was left open to reduce the shock: the whole law would automatically be applicable in the case of succession of Franco, but otherwise he would enact the necessary decrees to apply it progressively and to adapt the present structure to it.

The projected organization of the government provided for the separation of head of government and head of state in the future but left it to the decision of Franco. Afterward the appointment would be made by the head of state—presumably, according to the succession law, the king or regent—after consultation with the president of the Cortes and the secretary general. It provided for questions and interpellations by the Council at the request of its members and for the Prime Minister's resignation after three votes of censure on three different issues with four months between them and with the condition that the sixth demanding it would be in each case different in at least one-third. The no-confidence rule could not be more difficult! Individual cabinet members would have to resign after a no-confidence vote in the Cortes, except if the prime minister wanted to transform the issue into a vote of no confidence to him by a majority of the National Council.

These revolutionary proposals would soon be forgotten. Only a Law on the Principles of the National Movement [66] was passed on May 17, 1958, not too dissimilar to the one proposed by Arrese but without a paragraph on the Movimiento, which added it to family, municipality, and Sindicato as a channel of political participation, and one that stated "through it public opinion is integrated in the foundations of the national community and the peaceful contrast of opinions (*contraste de pareceres*) among Spaniards is channeled." Only years later this expression, with all its ambiguity, would become a keystone of political discussion and incorporated into basic legislation.

After the attempt by Arrese to give the Movimiento a more permanent, institutionalized, and perhaps democratized role in the constitution of the state, a long lull set in and the issue seemed forgotten.[67] Suddenly, in December, 1966, some of the ideas discussed in the Arrese projects and in 1963 at a National Council meeting appeared in watered-down and confused formulation in the new constitution that Franco read to the Cortes.

Belated Constitutionalization: Movimiento in the Ley Orgánica del Estado: Movimiento-Comunión or Movimiento-Organización?

In November, 1966, Franco went before the Cortes and reminded them that it was thirty years before that he had assumed power, and after summarizing his views on modern Spanish history and the achievements of the regime, he turned to propose a new constitutional law, which after approval by the Cortes would be submitted to a referendum. He stated:

> Democracy, which well understood is the most valued civilizing heritage of occidental culture appears in each period bound to concrete circumstances that result in political formulas and different ones in the course of history. . . . Parties are not an essential and permanent element without which democracy cannot realize itself. In the course of history there have been many democratic experiences, without knowing the phenomenon of political parties. They are a relatively recent experiment born of the crisis and decomposition of the organic bonds of traditional society. . . . But the exclusion of political parties in no way implies the exclusion of the legitimate contrast of opinions, of the critical analysis of the solutions of the government, of the public formulation of programs and measures that may contribute to the perfection of the march of the community.[68]

Neither in the speech nor in the text did the Movimiento appear preeminently and some observers, not seeing any reference to FET y de las JONS, gave a wishful interpretation to the "contrast of opinions," expecting the law to open the way for a greater democratization, and perhaps even an institutionalization of conflicting political viewpoints that would weaken the single party. The creation of 108 deputies (two per province) in the Cortes, elected by heads of households, might be considered a democratization, but other features of the law and the supplementary legislation represented an institutionalization of the party without allowing for any real internal democratization or pluralization. The hopes aroused were to be bitterly dashed. The discussion of the legislation regulating the Movimiento [69] made explicit the opposition of staunch supporters of the regime, discrepancies in the Movimiento itself, which, aired by the press, contributed to the malaise that goes with a disappointment. The polemic centered on divergent interpretations of Article 4 of the Organic Law of the State, which defined the National Movement thus:

> . . . the communion of the Spanish people in the Principles cited in preceding article, informs the political system, open to all Spaniards, and for the better service of the country, promotes political life on the basis of an orderly concurrence of criteria.

After the plesbiscitarian approval of the law by the Cortes and a referendum, the issue was debated when the Cortes Commission of Fundamental Laws turned to implement Article 28 that stated that "an organic Law shall establish the norms governing the National Council." The bill proposed by the government was immediately attacked as going beyond the constitutional mandate, since it regulated more than the National Council.

The reading of the debate in the legislature and its reflection in the press provides many insights into the political system. One is struck by the legalism often used (not surprisingly if one considers that many of the participants were law professors and *Abogados del Estado*), by the constant explications of political background stressing both the participation in the Civil War and loyalty to Franco and the diverse political-ideological affiliations then and since, by the personal affect put into some of the interventions, and by the frequent turn to wit and humor to release the tensions building up. However, the most impressive aspect was the amount of dissension expressed and afterward the support for the official proposals when it came to voting—except for a few members who left or occasionally voted against one or another article of the bill—even by those who had just a few hours before argued against them. This lack of civic courage did not pass unnoticed in the press commentary. Certainly, in a totalitarian regime we would not have found the legalism, the clear expression of pluralism, the open attacks against the official position; but in a democracy the false show of unanimity, the contrived and constant efforts to show loyalty to a system one was trying to change basically would not have been necessary. This was an authoritarian regime's policy making in the open. It permitted the system to be discredited, but it was unable to push change beyond a certain point. It could not find a formula that would go beyond the single party, the antiparty party. Instead of opening the door to multiple parties or tendencies within the party, it was to continue to allow multiple tendencies and politics outside the single organization. The hopeless dilemma was often stated in the discussion in which some members noted the impossibility of building a real political force capable of mobilizing the people on the basis of organic democracy without a party or parties.

The vague phrasing of the "communion in the principles"—themselves vaguely formulated—open to all Spaniards of Article 4 of the Organic Law of the State seemed, to those not identified with the Movimiento organization as it had evolved under FET y de las JONS, to open a door for change. Their idea was to create a "complex network of grassroots associations that would be coordinated through the representative channel of the provincial councils which, in turn, would elect the national council." They rejected the bill as smacking too much of the statutes of a single party. They attacked the text that stated, "the form by which that agreement with the principles would be expressed shall be regulated" and went so far as to say, "the national State cannot be built upon a single party, nor would the Spaniards tolerate one party alone taking over the State." A former cabinet member spoke of a club of a few, where some substitute or succeed each other in offices surrounded by the indifference of the people, and an undersecretary spoke of "oligarchic bureaucracies or leadership," and of councils that "transform the Movimiento into a muzzle of public opinion," a comment that produced pandemonium, with the speaker taking back his statement.

Fernández Cuesta put the problem bluntly: "Are we with or against this political system? If we should go to a new one, I accept the amendments proposed; if we shall continue with it they are unnecessary." The defense of the bill argued that to ask that the law should only regulate the Council was to reduce the Movimiento to a parliament, and against fears of party dominance, it stated: "In Spain there has been no single party—such a party controls the State—and here the State always has exercised control." To challenge the opposition that wanted to appear as a loyal opposition, another said: "Here there are no dissidents, here there are supporters of the Movimiento and substituters of the Movimiento." If the Movimiento was to be conceived broadly as encompassing all those supporting the regime—in its own vagueness—as a "communion" the argument of the opponents was that there would be no need for a Movimiento-Organización. This duality of terms would become an established part of the Spanish political language. The character of the party as a "part" of the political life of the regime would force it to become Movimiento-Organización, and even those identified with it would after the debate use these expressions. However the effort to stop its formal institutionalization, leaving the door open for other developments, was defeated the second day after moving appeals to unity and after forty-eight hours of debate on the title of the bill. The debate was fundamentally about the future, as a traditionalist noted the contradiction in which we live, having

. . . confidence in Franco and distrust in the institutions. Some say after Franco the institutions. It sounds well, but if they are born weak they will be swept away after Franco. It is an error to think in one institution: after Franco "the crown," or the *secretaría general del Movimiento.*

The effort to institutionalize political pluralization was clearly stated by one speaker when he said:

My thesis is that the Movimiento should have organizations, not one, but many. The Movimiento as promoter of organizations, but never the Movimiento Organización.

Emilio Romero, participant in the debate and editor of *Pueblo,* characterized those involved when he wrote:

We are faced with an evident political pluralism, which is fruitful and necessary, precisely because it is "sectorized" and not "partisized" and this is the only way the promise of a "contrast of opinions" makes sense.

In this political debate appeared, like a waterspout, a coincidence of opinions that was held up by monarchists of Estoril [partisans of Don Juan], traditionalists of those who cannot go up anymore to Montejurra [meeting place of the Carlists in Navarre], Catholics of the holy house and new Catholics that people ascribe to the Opus Dei. Facing them were personalities active in the cadres of the Movimiento, as organization [I clarify this organization, since this has been the battle horse of the whole debate].

The rector of the University of Salamanca, identified as Opus Dei, proposed an amendment:

To promote and protect the legitimate contrast of opinions and the diversity of thought in politics, without loss of the fundamental unity, the Movimiento constitutes itself into a coordinating body of the circumstantial opinion groups that might form themselves, within it, for the public formulation of programs and critical analysis of the governmental solutions.

He stressed that it had nothing to do with political parties, but was in the spirit of Franco's speech introducing the Organic Law and the function of the National Council in promoting political life in the contrast of opinions. He raised the question of what had been the consequences of the lack of political parties. His answer was political indifference, which has led to a society without concern for public matters, despair, and the politization elsewhere, which is "overflowing the system," for example, of the associations of the church or in the university. Pluralism is inevitable; you only have to see the press after the freedom of the press law. Is the anti-party the only solution? To clinch his point, he asked: "In addition to the statistics of the referendum could we not have those of the membership of FET y de las JONS? Unity and diversity are not incompatible as they are not in the Church." Fernández Cuesta, in answering, could not see how such associations would function without degenerating into political parties. The amendment naturally was rejected.

The next issue was who would elect the two elective *Consejeros Naciona-les* in each province. One set of proposals was to leave it to a group of electors, but there were many disagreements about who should participate in the group: Sindicatos, municipal and provincial councils? Another proposal was to give the suffrage to all party members, while a third favored universal suffrage for all Spaniards over 21. The alignments on this were somewhat different than in previous debates.

The definition of the Movimiento as open to all Spaniards was the main argument for opening the suffrage while—as some argued—being restrictive in the definitions of eligibility. The official proposal was defended as provided of "organic rather than individualistic representation," while a compromise solution suggested that the electorate be limited to those willing to make a statement of loyalty to the principles of the Movimiento. One of the defenders of the bill said, "it pleases no one but it is the only possible solution!" After sixty-three interventions, and a long recess—with only four votes against—the election was assigned to electors elected among the local and provincial councils of the Movimiento (which presumably would be representative, but which many speakers stressed were not). Four members of the committee abstained and six did not vote in agreement with the positions they had defended before.

The next issues were (1) the eligibility for the Council of those occupying appointive office in the province, (2) the degree of linkage between the candidates and the province, and (3) the relationship with the Movimiento, whether "identification" or "vinculation" would be sufficient. The issues at stake reveal much about the regime: the tendency to elect those already holding appointive office, the *nacionalización* of the representation, with the election of persons influential at the center and—again—the broad and vague rather than restrictive definition of the Movimiento. The proposal to accept nomination by a thousand signatures of members fell on deaf ears. Another debate was provoked by the ambiguous role of the secretary general as a member of the cabinet, appointed by the prime minister and leaving office with him, at the same time that he serves as a secretary of the National Council and executor of its decisions.

In summary, the monarchist ex-minister, Vigón, noted that with the law the tendency of the Movimiento toward democratization suffered a change, while the old party secretary general of the Falange and of FET y de las JONS could say with satisfaction, "the present Movimiento is the same as the previous one, adapted to the present moment." The debate proved that the Movimiento could not serve even as an institutional channel for political competition among those supporting the regime and obviously even less so to those who had never fully identified with the victors in the war or who had been born to public life afterwards and felt no need to join its bureaucratized and lifeless structures.

Finally, in July 1968, the National Council approved its rules of procedure.[70] Labadíe de Otermín, who had joined the party as a student before the war, attacked the bill, saying that the Movimiento had its role assured as long as Franco lived, but that no one could know who would succeed him as head of state. Therefore the Council as a collegiate body would have to assume more power. Therefore the general secretariat would have to become the executive organ of this political chamber and not "as today in one way or another [an organ] of the administration [the State executive]." "The general secretariat should be controlled from here and not, as now, the reverse." The Movimiento would have to "stress more and more every day the democratic and collegiate character responding to the pluralist sign of the times. This is necessary if we do not want to end like that ineffective National Council of FET y de las JONS we succeeded." Another member attacked the powerful position in the Council of the cabinet members, another argued for the right to interpellate the government.[71]

The discussion had faint echoes of the Arrese projects, but nothing as revolutionary was suggested in the final plenary public session. However, only 9 of the 101 members voted against the bill. After years of feeble attempts to democratize or liberalize inner party life, this vote confirmed again that the party is only an instrument of the man in El Pardo and in his name, of the secretary general.

On November 16, 1968, after a seven-hour debate, the National Council of the Movimiento approved Article 10 of a new Organic Statute of the Movimiento, which in its paragraph C says:

> Associations in the Movimiento with the purpose to contribute to the formulation of the opinion on the common basis of the Principles of the Movement, at the service of the national unity and the common good, for the concurrency of criteria, in conformity with art. 4 of the L.O.E. and art. 2 of the Organic Law of the Movimiento and its National Council, can be constituted.
>
> These associations will contribute to promote the legitimate contrast of views with full guarantee of the freedom of the person, to make possible a critical analysis of the concrete policy solutions and the ordered formulation of measures and programs directed toward the service of the national community.

In the discussion the proponents of the law stressed that they were not allowing political parties, since there was unity in the ideology and no discipline and exclusionary principles as in parties. Others, however, argued openly for associations that would participate in the electoral process, for a special status for the Carlists—one of the fused groups of 1939—or the use of the old Falange symbols rather than just freedom for the right wing. The old secretary general of the Falange and of FET y de las JONS, Fernández Cuesta, however, argued against associations that could defend ideologies and have political goals, that would be too similar to parties. Others were fearful of a proposed paragraph that would forbid the creation of associations that would claim exclusively values that are the common heritage of the Movimiento, out of fear that it could be used against Falangist discussion groups and the old Falange. The main argument in favor of the bill was to take into account the real pluralism, the real versus the legal country (an expression that has been part of Spanish political discourse since the turn of the century), as a way toward "democracy without parties."

Another debated point was the possibility of regional rather than just local or national associations in view of the regional problem in Spanish politics. The legal formulation, by tying the legality of such associations to the acceptance of the principles of the Movimiento and the emphasis on national unity, severely limited their scope. In formulating the goals for which they can be founded, the law was even more hesitant: to defend professional interests for which there were not yet any organizations, to promote cultural values, "to study and incorporate into social life the doctrine contained in the Principles of the Movimiento," to maintain the ties born in specific historical circumstances and any other recognized by the National Council. Again, in spite of the heated debate, the committee approved the bill unanimously. Even though the unexpected is never impossible in the politics of Franco Spain, the way in which the "associations in the Movimiento" (some commentators add to the Movimiento-Comunión and Movimiento-Organización the Movimiento Asociación, the association within the Movimiento's organizational structure of the more ideologically conscious Movimiento members with a special status) have been regulated makes this halfhearted attempt to democratize and institutionalize even the existing pluralism stillborn.

The remaining debates in the Council meeting reinforced the impression that the bureaucracy of the general secretariat did not want to relinquish any power: the refusal to allow the provincial Movimiento councils—mostly composed of office holders anyway, and in which the "associations" would have only minority representation—to elect their own president rather than having the provincial governor in that position ex officio, was symptomatic. Only the comment by Ballarín defining political pluralism as "the only antidote against economic monopoly, injustice and the misuse of power, because economico-social democracy will never be achieved without political democracy" and that of Labadíe de Otermín that the recognition of the existence of pluralism would bring "the necessary creation of an authentic left," were object of editorial comment and reflect the patient hope of the Falangist left even after more than thirty years of disappointment. For most Spanish society and political groupings the "we will open the doors" of Solís fell on dead ears, while a cartoon in *Pueblo* of two elderly gentlemen talking, with the caption, "look for the bylaws of that party you founded, because I want to see if I organize an association" reflected the basic ambivalence of its authors and the disappointed hopes of finding a functional equivalent for parties. It was not found, but the legal text five years from now, even more belatedly might be used for that purpose. Change at the speed of Franco Spain may be worse for a one-party system than no change.

In the period 1967 to 1968, the party achieved constitutionalization, but was not revitalized, liberalized, or democratized. The power of the remaining machine has in principle been preserved for the future even after Franco, but the organization is as lifeless as ever, without grass roots, internationally isolated. Spanish society is open enough to allow other channels of access to influence and power; few people's livelihood depends upon the party; many in the elite see no future for it, believing it incapable of reform. In 1956 González Vicén in a letter to Arrese had already rightly observed that a revitalized party "not only does not need a leader, but rather finds—and this is even more important—that his presence is damaging for his rule and for the System itself." [72] He was speaking of the future, but the impossibility of modifying the relationship of Franco to the party, of even changing the relationship of the future head of the state to the party and of the government by delegation from him to it, all make a changed relation between party and state and any internal democratization impossible.

A Party without Ideology or Cadre Training

In some parties ideological spokesmen who are not the leaders and often not too respected by them, such as the writers, intellectual magazines sponsored by party organizations, those associated with party schools for cadres, and so forth, play a more or less important role. One cannot say this about the Movimiento. Its syncretic character, the limited pluralism tolerated by the regime, the preeminence of government over party, the machine character of the Movimiento-Organización, all have limited the importance of ideology. Elsewhere we have argued that the regime is based more on a mentality than on an explicit ideology.[73] The basic writings of the founders have been republished—more or less selectively—but except for the works of José Antonio they have not gained much attention. Relatively few Spaniards are likely to have read the interesting fascist essay of Ramiro Ledesma Ramos, *Discurso a las Juventudes de España,*[74] to say nothing of his works as a dissident from FE y de las JONS which until recently have been unavailable. The writings of a confused but sometimes quite brilliant fascist ideologist, Giménez Caballero, are unknown.[75] The elaboration of the party thought after the Unification fell into the hands of law professors,[76] who had little new to say, except to establish some of the similarities and differences between the party and other European fascist movements. Apart from the unexciting efforts of a few professors, the Movimiento had no ideologists. It only had political leaders, officials and journalists.[77]

To understand the present Movimiento-Organización thought, perhaps the most useful work is Carlos Iglesias Selgas' *La vía española a la demo-*

cracia (1968).[78] The neo-Movimiento pseudo-left and pseudo-democratic phrases and occasional criticism of the regime in order to justify a claim for a greater share of power for the Movimiento is well reflected in this work. Infinitely more readable, interesting, and influential were the two books by the editor of *Pueblo* and *Consejero Nacional,* Emilio Romero, *Cartas a un príncipe* (1964) and *Cartas al pueblo soberano* (1965).[79] Written with cynicism and journalistic verve, they reflect well the ideal of continuity of the Movimiento under a monarchy of its making—or a republic if the former were not feasible—combined with a more or less honest desire for social change and some anti-capitalist demagoguery. These themes represented the ideological content remaining after the more ambitious revolutionary, authoritarian, and imperialist phrases of the founders were given up.

In contrast to other single parties and in spite of legal provisions to do so, the Movimiento never created a party school or a research center at its service. The *Instituto de Estudios Políticos* was founded in 1939 [80] as a dependent of the *Junta Política,* to "investigate with political criteria and scientific rigor," the problems of the country in order to advise the party and government. Ultimately it became an intellectual center in the social sciences, publishing books and journals, and organizing some seminars and lectures, but had little to do with the political process and even less with the cadres and bureaucrats of the party. Its director, an ex officio member of many government bodies, could exercise some influence and of the five holding the office, two became cabinet members. A decree which created in 1942 a Higher School of Political Training of FET y de las JONS, dependent on the general secretariat was never implemented.

Before the Unification an ideological magazine, *Jerarquía* (imitating the Italian publication of the same name),[81] was published by a group of intellectuals, a number of whom would end in the opposition, full of enthusiasm for the party and rhetorical grandiloquence. Only five (or according to some sources, seven) numbers were published. There is no equivalent to the many political or semi-intellectual magazines published by different tendencies and local groups in fascist Italy, nor an authoritative ideological magazine like those of the communist parties. In the 1940s, two journals appeared that were more important for intellectual life than for party ideology; of these only one, the *Revista de Estudios Políticos,* survived. The other, *Escorial,* was founded by a group led by Dionisio Ridruejo, ousted from his position as propaganda chief. Its stated purpose was to serve as a:

. . . residence and window of Spanish intellectuals, where some manifestations of the work of the Spanish spirit could congregate and the tasks of art and culture could survive despite the many tribulations and breaks that during years and years have prevented it to live as a conscience and act as an enterprise. And,

. . . we do not think of asking anyone to come here to make lyrical apologies for the regime or to justify himself. The regime is well justified by blood, and what we ask and demand from the men of thought and letters is to come to fill it—that is to fill Spanish life—with their spiritual efforts, their work and their intelligence.[82]

Reminiscing about the effort, Ridruejo notes that from the vantage point of the outside and the present, it had to appear as a "farce, false witness, as merely a maneuver by wise guys to add to and thereby legitimate the cause they served and whose other side was terror." [83] Page to page with authors identified with the regime, occasionally on ideological themes, we find the names of Menédez Pidal, Pío Baroja, Zubiri, Marañón, as well as of some of those men who would become leaders of the intellectual opposition.

The *Revista de Estudios Políticos,* initiated in 1942, became another focus of intellectual pluralism for those interested in the social sciences, law, economics, and history. In later years, it served as an opening to the foreign intellectual scene, particularly under its third director, Javier Conde.

The less clerical tradition of the Falange, the emphasis on public rather than private-church education,[84] and the respect of José Antonio for Unamuno, Ortega, and the 1898 generation, aided the intellectual community in its battle for survival against the worst of its clerico-reactionary enemies.[85] In this sense we find the paradox that in the context of an authoritarian regime a party ideology linked with fascism became a partial and indirect supporter of cultural pluralism. However, with increasing freedom of intellectual expression in recent years and the growing bureaucratization and sterility of the remnant party structures, this temporary alliance has ended.

The Falangist intellectuals, who were no longer active in the Movimiento, contributed some of the best men to the staff of the Minister of Education (coming from a Catholic background), Ruiz Giménez who attempted and failed in an effort of cultural liberalization, a process that indirectly created, in 1956, one of the most serious crises faced by the regime. No less important for the intellectual-ideological evolution of a whole generation that grew up after the Civil War were some of the publications like *Cisneros, La Hora, Alcalá, Destino,* and others, whose funds came from the SEU or other Movimiento organizations. It was in these journals, as in the seminars of the *Instituto de Estudios Políticos,* some *Colegios Mayores,* and in similar circles not linked with the Movimiento, that slowly and confusedly the intellectuals of this generation formulated their alienation from the regime first, the Falangist ideal later, and turned to other positions, often far to the left. In this the history of a Spanish generation has much in common with the one described by Zangrandi in his *Il lungo viaggio attraverso il Fascismo* [86] to which the chapter by Germani in this volume refers.

Falangist ideology did not become a serious object of indoctrination.

The limited efforts in that direction failed dismally owing to the low level of those in charge and the hostility of the society to them. However, the regime's propaganda and the censorship has created a "mentality" pervasive in large sectors of the society based on a one-sided view of the past, a desire for peace and order, and an image of the achievements of the government, that sustains it passively by making difficult alternative appeals. But those few who in the younger generation took the ideology seriously enough to read it (in the late 1940s and early 1950s but not since then) felt compelled to think about the social problems of the country and the discrepancy between the policies of the regime and its programmatic origins. In this way it was a factor of politization in a world of political apathy and conformism, or sullen and terrorized opposition of those defeated.

Party Organizations and Their Membership

Membership in the Movimiento can be through its main male organization, the women's section (*Sección Femenina*), and the youth organization (*Organización Juvenil Española,* OJE, formerly called Youth Front, or *Frente de Juventudes*). Affiliation with them has always been voluntary. It never became as important for success in Spanish society as in the PNF in Italy, which gave rise to the saying, "per necesita famigliare" ("out of family need"). The student organization (*Sindicato Español Universitario,* SEU), founded in 1933, had been highly political until shortly after 1943, when all students were obliged to become dues-paying members. This in the Spanish context inevitably led to depolitization, particularly when it was accompanied by a limited democratization at the class, and later, school level. University turmoil and the consequent legislative changes have led to the *de facto* disappearance of the Movimiento from the university. Among the affiliated organizations some are or were obligatory, like the SEU, the school teachers' organization, and so forth, but almost completely depoliticized, reduced largely to a paper membership and trying to serve as professional pressure groups. They were naturally designed initially as instruments of *Gleichschaltung*. In contrast to fascist Italy, Spain never had such an organization for civil servants. Others represent an effort to link with the Movimiento groups of potential political significance that emerged after the war, like the ex-prisoners in Republican jails, veterans of the Civil War, and the Blue Division. Initially, the army—representing the regime —had tried to discourage the organization of veterans of different units and of the reserve officers—the *alféreces provisionales*—out of fear of the political implications and the potential pressures for various advantages. In the late 1950s an effort was made by the regime to activate the memories of the fight, the comraderie of that time with the purpose to rally support for it.

In the late 1950s, a number of functional organizations loosely tied with the party were created, depending on its *Delegación Nacional de Asocia-*

ciones del Movimiento. To some extent such more or less paper organizations have served to build up some personalities, legitimize or co-opt personalities on the fringe of the Movimiento, facilitate some minor pressure group activity and to link it with much more important international groups of the same type. The imitation of foreign functional organizations to assure Spanish participation in international meetings has probably been more important than any desire to mobilize new sectors of the society or to politicize them.

To our knowledge no membership data of FET y de las JONS have been published nor have surveys asked specifically for them. Therefore it is difficult to make estimates of the proportion of the male adult population belonging to the party or its social composition.

Scattered data [87] suggest a very different penetration of the party in different regions, from an overrepresentation in Old Castile (the *clases medias* Spain, bedrock of the national identity, and core of Franco Spain in the Civil War) to underrepresentation in the poorer interior provinces of *latifundia* Spain. Galicia, despite the fact that it was on the nationalist side in the war, is another weak spot, probably on account of its underdevelopment, which is an obstacle for any form of social mobilization from politics to sports teams. Western Andalusia, where the Primo de Rivera family had some influence before the war and José Antonio was elected in 1933 and tried again in 1936, is another nucleus. Interestingly enough, the Basque country and Catalonia, despite their anti-centralist traditions and their industrialization, are not among the low points of party strength. Perhaps the general tendency to join voluntary associations of all kinds has also favored the party there in comparison to the underdeveloped areas. In terms of place of residence, the party seems to be strongest in villages and small towns (10,000 to 20,000 population) and relatively weak in the cities between 20,000 and 100,000 population, with some strength in the largest cities, perhaps due to the fact that they are (especially Madrid) also the bureaucratic capitals of the country.

Occupationally, the members are disproportionately middle class, particularly middle-level white collar and civil servants, while the unskilled industrial workers and to a lesser extent the farm laborers are underrepresented. The proportion of farmers is probably somewhat lower than in the population as a whole.[88] Small business is also relatively underrepresented and so are the highest managerial and bureaucratic levels. The social basis of the party does not diverge much from that of Catholic Action, the only other nationwide mass membership organization of potential political significance. Catholic Action had greater strength in the business world and the higher professional group, while the party's strength seems to be more concentrated in the white collar middle class and middle-level professionals. The data by subjective class identification for the family, made by the sons, confirm the greater strength of the party among lower-middle-class families.[89]

The women's section claimed a membership of 580,000 members in 1939, which represented 43 per thousand of the female population of 13.5 million.[90] In 1959 the organization reported 207,021 members, not far below the 258,768 affiliated with Catholic Action. These figures represent rates of respectively 13 and 16 per thousand of the female population (15.7 million).[91] A detailed analysis of both organizations by regions shows that there is some correlation of membership in one with membership in the other, indicating a general tendency to join organizations of any kind (which in turn correlates highly with economic development). However, two regions with a high propensity to join voluntary associations, the Basque country and Catalonia, have relatively low membership rates in the SF, largely because of their political traditions and the regional-autonomist nationalism. The women's organization has been able to penetrate in some areas of Old Castile and the southwest with little tendency toward association. Its strength in some of the more secularized areas—despite its emphasis on religion—contrasts with its weakness compared to Catholic Action in those with a strong religious and Carlist tradition, like Navarra and Basque country but also parts of Levante. Essentially, middle-class Spain contributes disproportionately to the organization.

TABLE 5-3   *Youth Organization Membership in December, 1941, by Sex and 1940 Census Population*

	Male			Female		
Age	Members	Population	Per Cent Members	Members	Population	Per Cent Members
7-10	162,738	844,395	19.2%	94,484	833,186	11.3%
10-14	251,197	1,100,649	22.8	126,590	1,093,051	11.5
14-18	150,464	1,020,483	14.7	150,464	1,059,755	19.2
Total	564,399	2,965,527	18.9%	371,538	2,985,992	12.3%

Combined Totals (Male and Female):
Members = 935,937; Population = 5,954,499; Per Cent Members = 15.6%

Source: *Anuario Español del Gran Mundo, 1942,* p. 114.

The Youth Organization, in December, 1941, when it still had a political character it would lose years later, released figures by age and sex that can be related to the population figures of the 1940 census (see Table 5–3). They allow an interesting comparison with those for the Giuventu Italiana del Littorio in 1939 (see Table 5–4). While in Spain 19 per cent of the age group among males and 12 per cent among females belonged to the *Organización Juvenil,* the corresponding figures in Italy were 64.5 per cent and 43.6 per cent. These figures clearly show the different degree of mobilization in the two political systems, even at the height of the totalitarian effort in Spain. Germino gives us the proportion of members in relation to those eligible in nine main provinces of Italy. The lowest percentage in Naples (not surprisingly) was 31 per cent, considerably above the Spanish average of 15.6 per cent.

TABLE 5-4 *Giuventu Italiana Del Littorio Membership, 1939 by Sex and Population*[a]

Age	Male				Female		
	Members	Population	Per Cent Members		Members	Population	Per Cent Members
6-8							
Figli and figlie della lupa	1,546,389			Piccole Italiane			
8-14 Balilla	1,746,560	2,782,032	62.8	Piccole Italiane	1,622,766	2,685,538	64.1
14-18 Avanguardisti	906,785	1,823,353	49.7	Giovani Italiane	441,254	1,765,240	25.0
18-21 Giovani Fascisti	1,176,798	1,332,278	88.2	Giovani Fasciste	450,995	1,287,090	35.0
Total	3,830,743	5,937,663	64.5		2,595,075	5,737,868	43.6

Combined Totals (Male and Female):
Members = 7,891,547; Population = 11,675,531; Per Cent Members = 67.5%

[a]Cohorts calculated according to the 1931 census, a fact that introduces some margin of error.

Source: Dante L. Germino, *The Italian Fascist Party in Power: A Study in Totalitarian Rule* (Minneapolis: University of Minnesota Press, 1959), pp. 73-74.

The Elite of the Regime and the Movimiento:
The Movimiento and Sindicatos in the Cortes

The constitution, approved by referendum in December, 1967, consolidates the Movimiento as part of the regime regulating in title IV the National Council "as the collegiate representation of the Movimiento" with 102 members. It is composed of 55 members elected by 13,175 local party council members, and 12,078 municipal representatives acting as electors: one member per province, irrespective of population or party membership; forty members appointed by the Caudillo; twelve representing three groups (family, local government, and sindical in the Cortes); six appointed by the president of the Council and the party secretary general. These councillors form part of the 548-member Cortes (more or less due to overlapping memberships).[92] The Cortes was created in 1942 as an "efficient instrument of collaboration," with the head of state in the legislative function as "a principle autolimitation for a more systematic institution of power," was initially a rubber stamp for government bills. However, its committees have become increasingly lively arenas of political discussion and expression of interests, occasionally rejecting government bills and often modifying them. The government is not accountable to the Cortes and their appointed president has considerable control of their activities. This is not the place to describe the complex composition and operation of this chamber, with its different elected or appointed sectors. The corporative principle is followed in the election of 25 deputies for professional associations; 150 for the Sindicatos—workers and employers (elected through indirect elections), 113 representing the 9,032 municipalities and 53 provincial councils; 108 representing the "families" elected by 16,415,139 voters (with two *procuradores* per province irrespective of population). Another 110 legislators are ex officio—cabinet, university rectors, and so forth—and 24 of them are appointed by Franco. The "family representation," the only ones directly elected by heads of households and married women with some degree of competitiveness (in 1967, initially, 328 candidates for 102 seats), was a "democratic" innovation of the 1966 constitution. The National Council of the party, therefore, is both a second chamber and part of the national legislature. In addition, the forty appointed *consejeros* occupy a very special position, since after the succession of Franco they shall hold their seats until age 75, and vacancies shall be filled by cooptation by the Council among three candidates proposed by remaining members of the initial forty. It is possible to classify them by their political background (see Table 5–5), something that is not so feasible for the elected members.

Our data allow us to draw a collective biography, if not a political portrait of the whole national Movimiento leadership group. To put it into proper perspective, we could compare it with the other sectors of the

Cortes, particularly those elected more directly, and with the total membership of the legislature, but this will be left for a separate publication.

The members of the National Council, particularly the appointed *consejeros,* come from a somewhat more urban background than do members of other sectors of the legislature, and fewer come from a totally rural background. The elected party leaders—mostly second-level leaders who have made their career in the Movimiento often as provincial governors or in Sindicatos—have a somewhat more rural and small-town background than the appointed *consejeros.* We find the leading figures of the Movimiento-Organización born in the large cities (100,000–500,000 population) to be 28.1 per cent, and those of metropolitan background (over 500,000 popu-

TABLE 5-5   *Political Background of the Forty Appointed Members of the Consejo Nacional in 1968 (classifications are inevitably approximate)*

Political background:	Appointed Members Not in the Cabinet	Cabinet Members	Total Appointed Members
Falangist (*latu sensu*)	19	1	20
Traditionalists	3	1	4
Renovation — Monarchists	2		2
ACNDP	1	1	2
Right-wing Opus Dei		2	2
Military	1	1[a]	2
Experts, with ill-defined background	1	2[b]	3
Difficult to classify due to lack of information	5[c]		5
Total	32	8	40

[a]One admiral classified as right-wing Opus Dei could be added.

[b]One with an Opus Dei identification, the other leaning more toward the Movimiento-Organización with some ACNDP background.

[c]One of them representing Catalan business circles.

lation in 1960) dominant (31.3 per cent). The Movimiento-Organización therefore does not represent, as in the case of the Nazis, the Iron Guard, or the Japanese nationalist extremists, a rural or small-town protest against urban-industrial society, even though elements of such an ideology were not absent in the *Juntas Castellanas de Actuación Hispánica* that Onésimo brought into the JONS. The present elite certainly does not feel any conflict between its background and ideology and the change of Spain into a highly urbanized and increasingly industrial society.

No one will be surprised to find that a large majority of the members of the Cortes have a university or equivalent technical education, that a minority has some secondary academic, technical or professional training, and that practically none has less (1.4 per cent). This is the dominant pattern in European legislatures, even when the proportion with a higher education might be slightly larger than in recent Bundestags and the 1959 House of Commons. The figure is closer to the Italian average for the Chamber between 1948 and 1958 (70 per cent). The number of those with a law degree is large (46.2 per cent) a figure that is larger than that for French legislators from 1898 to 1940 (32.9 per cent) but very close to the 42 per cent among Italian lawmakers in the first four post-war legislatures. The number of those with an engineering or architecture degree (7.7 per cent) is significant, considering the small number of graduates from the *Escuelas Especiales* (higher technical schools) compared with those graduating from the university. The number of the self-educated and those with only primary schooling in Spain is appreciably below the 7.37 per cent in Italy in the four first post-war legislatures. However, the proportion of those with academic secondary education and other middle levels (22.3 per cent) is slightly larger than the figures for similar levels in Italy.

The National Council contingent in the Cortes has a smaller proportion of those with middle-level education and in it the number of those with a legal background is appreciably larger, 64.4 per cent, compared with an average of 46.2 per cent. In fact, among the appointed *consejeros nacionales,* a group in which we find many of the more influential legislators and politicians (even leaving out the cabinet members), the proportion of those who graduated from law school goes up to 71.9 per cent. Together with the cabinet and the twenty-four *procuradores* directly appointed by Franco, this is the group in which the proportion with a military background is largest: 12.9 per cent (compared to 27.8 per cent and 20.8 per cent in two groups mentioned) and 7.3 per cent for the whole Cortes. The National Council group is very different from the Sindicatos representation, in which the number of lawyers is particularly low (27.4 per cent). This is the more surprising if we consider the function of Sindicatos on the employers' side to be a coalition of economic interest groups. The Sindicatos parliamentary group is above average in the number of engineers (something quite understandable if we consider their important contribution to the managerial elite). However, the main difference between both groups—the political and sindical wing of the *procuradores* under the influence of Solís—is that among the Sindicatos deputies, those with only a middle-level academic and middle-level technical or semi-professional education are an important group (36.9 per cent). These are sectors that one could call middle-middle or lower-middle class. The only other sector of the chamber in which they find a place is among those directly elected by the heads of household, even though among them those who attended colleges are more important than those coming from the technical (*peritos*) school.

Like in most legislatures, the representation of the more educated—and therefore middle and upper class—segment of the society is disproportionate (see Table 5–6). Slightly over 2 per cent of the members give as occupation "manual worker"—a figure that rises to 7.6 per cent in the Sindicatos group, but is absent among the National Council members. This

TABLE 5-6   Occupation of the Procuradores in Cortes in 1968

	Total Procuradores in Cortes	Elected Consejeros Nacionales	Appointed Consejeros Nacionales	Total Consejo Nacional	Procuradores for Sindicatos
Farmers	8.4	1.8	3.1	2.0	9.6
Workers	2.3	–	–	–	7.6
White collar employees	4.6	–	3.1	1.0	13.0
Merchants and small business	8.1	3.6	3.1	3.0	10.3
Medium business	2.9	–	–	–	4.8
Larger business and managers (including public enterprise and finance)	20.9	20.0	46.9	28.8	19.2
Brokers, upper commercial occupations	1.6	1.8	3.1	3.0	2.1
Middle-level professions	6.2	5.4	6.3	5.0	13.0
Lawyers	25.9	32.7	34.4	29.7	15.8
Teaching (except elementary)	6.6	9.1	3.1	6.9	5.5
Medicine	4.7	3.6	3.1	4.0	1.4
Other free professions	5.5	3.6	–	2.0	4.9
Engineering and architecture	3.9	1.8	3.1	3.0	4.1
Military	10.6	21.9	12.5	16.9	2.1
Elite civil service	17.5	25.5	31.3	27.7	4.8
Civil servants with university degree but not elite groups	8.9	10.9	3.1	8.9	8.2
Middle- and lower-level civil servants, local government	3.6	3.6	3.1	3.0	2.8
Sindicatos civil servants	2.0	1.8	–	3.0	4.1
Clergy	.7	–	–	–	–
Other	2.7	1.8	6.3	3.0	6.2
No information	1.3	3.6	3.1	3.0	0.7
	(548)	(55)	(32)	(101)	(146)

Bracketed group totals (Elite civil service, Civil servants with university degree but not elite groups, Middle- and lower-level civil servants, local government): Total Procuradores in Cortes 32.0; Elected Consejeros Nacionales 41.8; Appointed Consejeros Nacionales 37.5; Procuradores for Sindicatos 19.9.

proportion is about one-third of that in the legislatures of United Kingdom, France, and Italy and one-half that in Germany in 1957. White collar employees—not in public employment—are twice as often *procuradores* and constitute 13.6 per cent of the Sindicatos parliamentary group.

In a country in which still one-third of the active population is engaged in agriculture, and where the proportion at the time of the establishment of the regime was close to half, the number of deputies who give farming as an occupation is small (8.4 per cent). Among the *consejeros* of the Movimiento, the proportion of farmers is even lower (2 per cent), a somewhat surprising matter when we consider the effort made by the founders of the Falange and the JONS to reach the peasantry, the somewhat ruralist appeals during the war, and the largely rural base of Carlism. Independently of appeal and ideology, the leadership did not come from the peasantry, even when urbanized, and university educated sons of peasants and landowners probably constitute a significant part of the elite. Only among the Sindicatos and local government representatives do we find—naturally—some rural deputies.

Small and medium-sized business is not preeminent among the *procuradores,* even when Sindicatos sends some of them to the chamber. The proportion of those occupying board or managerial positions in large enterprises looms larger (20.9 per cent). Many among them are linked to the nationally owned enterprises and public banks, owing their appointment to them to their political career, rather than their legislative mandate to their connection with business. The proportion of this group is particularly high (40.6 per cent) among the appointed *consejeros nacionales.*

Lawyers, for obvious reasons, have always been overrepresented in Western legislatures. In Spain in the lower house, respectively 54 per cent and 55 per cent of the members elected in 1910 and 1914 were lawyers, with 19 per cent and 24 per cent indicating that they were practicing their profession. To these one would have to add some engaged in legal professions and civil servants with a legal training. In the 1968 Cortes, slightly over one-fourth were lawyers and this number rises to one-third of the National Council—the more political sector of the chamber—dropping to 15.1 per cent among those representing Sindicatos.

Sometimes Spain is described as a military dictatorship, and consequently we would expect a large representation of the armed forces in the Cortes. The proportion is, with 10.6 per cent, certainly higher than in Italy, France and even Argentina under Perón. Among the *consejeros nacionales* the officers are more heavily represented: 21.9 per cent among the elected *consejeros* and 12.5 per cent among the appointed ones. But the proportion certainly is not so high as to make them a major sector in the legislature. The percentage is identical (10 per cent) to that among Turkish legislators between 1920 and 1957, as calculated by Frey for 2,210 legislators. However, the proportion is lower than in Turkish assemblies before 1946 and half of that in the Turkish chamber between 1923 and 1931 under

Ataturk. The clergy, despite its social and political influence in the country, constitutes only .07 per cent of the Cortes, certainly less than its power in the society. However, many laymen identified with different Catholic organizations speak for the church and often are "more Catholic than the few members of the hierarchy" when it comes to religious issues.

The Cortes, in comparison to the House of Commons, has a larger proportion of members over 50 (58 per cent versus an average of 50 per cent in the House) but the proportion is close to that for the German Bundestag. In addition, the proportion of men under 40 seems to be smaller than in the democracies. The *Consejo Nacional* is somewhat, but not much, older than the remainder of the legislature, mainly its appointed members (56 per cent over 55 and 72 per cent over 50).

If we consider the generations represented in the Cortes, we find one-third who at the outbreak of the Civil War were adults (24 years old or over), a large proportion of men in the military age at the time (19 to 23: 23 per cent) while the post-Civil War generations with little or no personal memory of those dramatic days constitute less than one-fifth of the chamber. The Movimiento council has an even larger share of those who were between 14 and 24 when the Civil War started in 1936. They constitute almost one-half of its elected members. This is the front generation—that of the *alféreces provisionales* (the reserve officers who played such a decisive role assuring the victory of Franco), who also provide 65 per cent of the present cabinet. The appointed *consejeros,* who come more often from the groups entering the new unified party in 1937, are from a somewhat older generation, with almost one-fifth having been university students during the Republic. The generational experiences of these legislators will certainly not lead them to question the regime.

In the present legislature we find a considerable number of newcomers (35 per cent of the members) mostly owing to the direct election by heads of household (74 per cent among them being freshmen legislators). Among the four main groups of legislators the number of newcomers was relatively high among the municipal representatives, but considerably less so among those representing Sindicatos. As a major group the National Council has the smallest proportion of freshmen (18.8 per cent), something due mainly to the great continuity in office of the appointed members of the Council, among whom one-half were members of the first Cortes legislature (1943). Even among the elected *consejeros,* continuity was high, with less than one-third newcomers and one-third who were already members in 1955. Obviously, the greatest continuity among the four main sectors of the chamber can be found among the members appointed freely by Franco, among whom already one-third had been in the first legislature. The data clearly show that the Movimiento representation, in the strict sense, has not been the channel for renewal of the elite, but one of its more permanent elements. In fact, only 9.2 per cent of the 196 freshmen legislators are members of the National Council (which constitutes 18.4 per cent of the membership of the Cortes). In contrast, 54.9 per cent of the present *legislatores* who went to the palace on the Carrera de San Jerónimo for the first time in 1943 are now there representing the Movimiento, strictly defined. They in turn represent almost 10 per cent (41 of 424) of that first legislature. To this group one could add the 9.8 per cent of that cohort representing today the Sindicatos. The Movimiento oldtimers do not represent a large proportion of the legislature, but together with Franco's appointees and the cabinet, they form part of the most permanent sector of the Chamber.

In contrast with the continuity of the Movimiento elite at the top we find considerable renewal at the local level among the mayors of 8,994 municipalities, who generally are also local heads of the Movimiento-Organización. A majority of the men heading local government are middle-aged: those 40 to 54 were 57 per cent, those younger than 40, 14 per cent and those 55 and over, 29 per cent. The largest group were between 45 and 49 (22 per cent). The older generation seems to be somewhat more important in the smallest communities, and the eight largest cities are headed by men over 50 years old, as are more than two-thirds of the eighteen cities between 100,001 and 200,000 population. While the men who lived under the monarchy as adults are a minority (14 per cent), those whose adolescence and early adulthood coincided with the Republic form a somewhat larger group (24 per cent); the largest group is constituted by those who were between 18 and 27 in 1940, and who either made the war or grew up after the Franco victory (41 per cent). However, the renewal of leadership is going on: already 30 per cent—even when mostly in middle- and small-sized communities—are men who can have few or no memories of the Civil War and none of the Republic. Few of the present incumbents have been in office for more than 15 years (6 per cent), a significant minority (11 per cent) between 11 and 15 years, one quarter between 6 and 10 years, slightly more between 3 and 5, and 30 per cent less than two years. Certainly the national average of 57 per cent in office less than 5 years suggests no ossification or acute oligarchic tendencies in local government; or if we want to interpret it otherwise, the office of mayor does not seem so attractive as to elicit too great an effort to hold on to it.

The Movimiento: Functional Unit or Survival?

There can be no doubt that in 1937 and in the 1940s FET y de las JONS had an important, even when far from all-important, contribution to make to the regime. It provided it with a dress to show up in the world as something more than a temporary or pure military dictatorship. It contributed symbols and an ideology capable of appealing to large segments of the middle classes, who did not feel that the defense of the status quo or the defense of religion and tradition was sufficient to die and live for; it contributed some policies—a welfare state from above and economic autarchy

—that made sense in a poor country divided by class conflict. Its imperial-ist-nationalism fitted a country that had arrived late in the colonial scram-ble.

Today there is not much left of those contributions: the welfare state idea is generally accepted and largely institutionalized, a neo-liberal capital-ism and the hope to enter the Common Market have replaced economic nationalism (while one form or the other of socialism seems to appeal to others); the hope to integrate the working class ideologically failed, and a limited prosperity, together with depolitization, proved more effective in gaining its acquiescence. The imperialism of a poor country in the era of decolonization sounds ludicrous. The symbols and phrases that gave it re-spectability in pre-1945 Europe are only an obstacle to gaining acceptance in today's world.

Why then maintain and even reactivate the Movimiento? Or has it devel-oped new ideologies and functions? If we read the official literature put out by the Movimiento spokesmen, we certainly find new themes and little ref-erence to many of those of the past, but they are probably too vague to ap-peal to anyone. They are basically shared by almost everyone outside the Movimiento, and the Movimiento-Organización has not provided for spe-cially effective channels to implement them. Economic development, greater equality of opportunity, development of a welfare state, and inter-nal peace, are things almost everyone wants. The more political appeals of the need for greater political participation, opportunity for the contrast of opinions, and guarantee of individual rights sound hollow in view of the realities of the regime and the past ideology and performance of the Movi-miento. The bits of demagoguery and anti-capitalism stand against the suc-cessful reality of neo-capitalism and the real anti-capitalism of the opposition. This is not to deny that the Sindicatos can serve as a more or less successful pressure group for social legislation, unfreezing wages, and so forth. There is no question that Sindicatos perform—at a high cost—a great number of functions: in collective bargaining, handling of grievances at the plant level, a number of social services, and as an arena for discussion of issues for the workers. They also serve the employers as peak organizations for a myriad of more or less effective interest groups and their pressure group activities. But the Movimiento?

It might well be argued that the Movimiento-Organización is a survival and that the only function of its continued existence is to satisfy the vested interests of its bureaucracy, not to offend the sentimental memories of men who had joined in the past, and to avoid the inevitable cost in legitimacy that goes with doing away with an institution that at one point contributed to legitimate the system without putting anything else in its place. How-ever, these reasons would only justify its survival but not the recent consti-tutionalization.

It might be argued that the recruitment of political personnel is the main function, somewhat like that of machine politics, but if we consider the high proportion of civil servants, local notables, the people who over the years held office as governors, mayors, and so forth, the immense majority would have been available anyway. Many joined the Movimiento only after their appointment. In fact a decree of 1943 [93] provided that those becoming *consejeros nacionales* would be considered on that account members of the Movimiento! Recruitment for office would be as easy, if not easier, given the reluctance of many apolitical supporters of the regime to join it, without the Movimiento-Organización. Perhaps the only function of presumably becoming identified with the Movimiento after appointment to some offices is to force people to make a public commitment to the regime. The party that in the Civil War participated as an auxiliary of the army and on its own initiative or that of its local leaders in the repression of the enemies of the regime and even created its own informers service never gained control of the police or the courts judging political crimes, which were staffed mostly by army officers. The limited grass roots organization, inactive membership, dominance of the army—particularly after the war—and the police in security functions have reduced the party's role in this area and that of social control, except in its early days, to a minimum in comparison to other one-party systems.

One of the few reasons for the revival of the organization might be the turn to referendum and elections—municipal and legislative—as a way to legitimize the system, to give it an aura of participation. The turn to them requires a machinery formally separate from those holding office to present candidates, organize the electioneering, and so forth. Rejecting the idea of competitive politics—of parties or voters' associations of some sort—and not wanting to rely only on appointment to office, electioneering, even in low key, requires some kind of organization, particularly at the village and even provincial levels. Even so, it is not clear why a corporative type of representation was not relied on exclusively and why a political chamber based on a different principle was created. This contradiction was noted—insightfully and intentionally—by some of the opponents of the Movimiento-Organiación in the polemics in the Cortes.

Another reason might be found in the need to continue legitimizing the monopoly of the publicly supported youth and women's organizations and "sindical unity," which would be undermined if even a moderate institutionalization of pluralism were carried out. *De facto* there are growing pressures to recognize such pluralism in those spheres, particularly since the Catholic Action organizations, protected by the Concordate from interference, have become more autonomous from the hierarchy and more politically conscious and critical. The rejection of competitive trade unions or competitive factions within Sindicatos is probably vital to the continuity of the regime. Institutionalized pluralism within the Movimiento might be unpleasant but digestible. Institutionalized pluralism within or of Sindicatos, however, would be a real threat. On the other hand, a regime without the Movimiento might be possible, but an industrial society—particularly a capitalist one—without some labor organization would not be.

Many years of coalition politics at all levels, balancing forces, turning to one or the other in crises, countering the threat of one or the other by strengthening its opponents within the system, probably have made the men identified with the Movimiento-Organización indispensable. Undoubtedly for this aspect of Franco's politics the existence of a label for those men, which distinguishes them somewhat from many of his other supporters, facilitates that juggling act.

Ultimately, it seems as if the twentieth century non-party politics were not respectable and that independently of more specific functions, one party seems to look better than no party. It might well be only one more fig leaf for the realities of power for the complex oligarchy that rules Spain.

Obstacles to Real Rather than Only Legal Institutionalization

The Spanish single party has now been in power for almost thirty years —or better, has shared power for most of that period. One could think that this should have led to its "institutionalization," whatever is meant by that vague term. But we would argue that it only has led to its "constitutionalization," the inclusion of its legal monopoly as Movimiento-Organización in the Organic Law of the State and the subsequent legislation. It has not become the main channel of recruitment for political leadership, it is not the source of ideology or policies, its autonomy from the government and the state apparatus is limited, it is not an arena for political discussion by interested citizens, it is not—with minor exceptions—an agency for political socialization of the young. The control of the succession of Franco as head of the state, head of the government, or even as party leader, is not exclusively in its hands,[94] since it ultimately rests in the hands of the Caudillo. If he should not use his power and influence before his death it will be in those of a complex constitutional machinery in which the Movimiento-Organización (to say nothing of the old leadership of the parties unified in 1937) has only a limited share. It has not been able to transform itself into an effective recruiting and patronage organization machine as often suggested for other single parties, even though in the near future, with the creation of more elective offices, it might try to do so. Nor has it become the main area for competition for advantages, from policies to spoils, of different social and economic interests through some *sector* organization like that of the PRI. The regime to some extent has done so through the Cortes, but in it the party and the Sindicatos linked to it represent only some sectors. They have only limited capacity to communicate with those whose interests they purport to represent and articulate. The Movimiento-Organización being based on an apathetic—practically non-existent—individual membership, rather than organizational membership, and lacking an ideology of democratic participation (even of the type involved in democratic centralism) cannot speak for anybody except its officials. In this and many other respects, Sindicatos have a distinctive advantage: they have achieved some degree of institutionalization.

The two main ways toward institutionalization of single parties within an authoritarian system that might have been open in Spain were the institutionalization of *tendencies* (ideologico-political factions or *correnti,* to use the Italian term) and *corporative* institutionalization within the party, along the lines of the ideal model of the PRI. The obstacles for both solutions deserve more detailed discussion.

Institutionalization of Tendencies?

The institutionalization of tendencies was considered under Arrese and in the spring of 1967 and brought up and hesitantly accepted in the fall, 1968 *Estatuto Orgánico del Movimiento.* The continuity with the different ideological traditions submerged by the Unification and the emergence of a variety of tendencies within the agreement on the principles of the Movimiento opened the door to such a solution institutionalizing the *contraste de pareceres* declared legitimate by Franco. To become a reality it would mean competitive elections within the party, among members or leaders, the presentation of different candidates for the post of secretary general for appointment by Franco, and ultimately, perhaps, competition among "licensed" or "tolerated" parties or "voters associations."

Individual pluralism is certainly tolerated and often rampant, but institutional pluralism was ultimately rejected, even within the narrow spectrum of the political elite that would be willing to use the Movimiento-Organización as channel. Not that a real internal democratization and tolerance for pseudo-parties or factions within its institutional framework at this late date would be a promising solution. A number of factors argue against the possibility of both democratization and liberalization within the one-party framework—however elastically manipulated—at this point: the atrophy of party membership and party life and the depolitization of the society as a whole, together with the openly hostile attitude of the highly politicized minorities among students, among some sections of the industrial working class and the linguistic regional minorities. Such groups would not be willing to participate, except perhaps some politically conscious sectors of the working class—mainly communist-controlled—that would use the opportunity for infiltration purposes. Those sectors of the semi-opposition, of the collaborating Catholic groups, of the "pure" traditionalists, the regime-monarchists, who could provide figures and some participants in such an open party with "tendencies" are already there and get as much or more without having to assume public stands and compete for power in an organized way with the need to mobilize a constituency. In addition, their latent constituencies, which today can claim often not to share in the responsibility of the actions of their coopted leaders, might not have that much to gain by coming into the open and facing internal conflicts.

Only an attempt of the Movimiento-Organización machine to monopolize power or curtail severely the power of the other components of the limited pluralism of the regime could lead those elements to favor a greater institutionalization of "tendencies" within the Movimiento. Some of this happened in the debate on the *Ley del Movimiento* and the *Ley de Representación Familiar* in the spring of 1967, but the opportune promise of a number of seats in the Cortes of 1968 that some of the opponents of the bill considered larger than they would have gained in an open competition, given their lack of organizational and financial resources, quickly brought them into line and led to almost unanimous votes on the bill bitterly attacked days before. Institutionalization of tendencies and intraparty democracy based on them despite their actual importance, and potential ideological basis in the history of the regime, as well as faint-hearted legalization, seems to have little chance.

The relative liberalization of the regime by allowing some semblance of a Rechtstaat in the relation of the citizen with the administration; a more active defense of his limited freedoms by the courts; a press [95] that discusses more issues without being allowed to challenge the system much (partly because the much more important television is fully committed to and controlled by the regime); the wider range of freedom for the media of limited diffusion like magazines and even more books; the tolerance for private expression of political dissent, often extended to publication abroad; all have created a political life outside the Movimiento channels that by now no one would be willing to take into such a channel, even if it became honestly open. Even if some of those tolerated channels of semi- or pseudo-opposition were closed or narrowed it is not likely that those having used them would return to even an open Movimiento-Comunión or Movimiento-Organización.

Liberalization—as far as it goes in Spain—has not taken place within the party, nor fully within the regime, but on its fringes, quite in contrast with what apparently has been going on in East Europe, where the Communist Party, party-supported or controlled channels, groups, institutions, have served the process. The persistence of private property of publishing activities may be one important factor in this difference, as well as the continued limited pluralism of the regime from its inception. The fact that many of the semi-opposition and semi-loyal opposition are not convinced that the regime will survive the succession crisis, and with more or less hope or fear, think of a multi-party democracy as a realistic alternative excludes any willingness to use a tainted Movimiento channel for the liberalization process.

The semi-opposition and even real opposition in East Europe knows that a total change of regime, a displacement of the Communist Party from power, is out of the question given the watchful eye on such a development of the Soviet Union and neighboring communist countries less committed to liberalization, and consequently has to put its hopes on transformation of and within the Communist Party or party-related structures. The Spanish regime, basically disliked by its Western allies as an embarrassing survival of the past, does not enjoy that advantage; liberalization is conceivable outside the Movimiento even though not immediately, and therefore, the question arises, why even try to use it? This ultimately means that with a greater initial pluralism, and less emphasis on ideology, the rate of liberalization *within* the regime might end being slower than in the East, the setbacks of the process initiated almost inevitable, and that ultimately the opponents will have to face the question of "if" and "how" to overthrow the regime. Since this was written the declaration of the state of emergency and reintroduction of censorship for three months has confirmed our prediction. The always impending, but always remote, succession crisis unconsciously allows the opposition to avoid the Hamletian question, but an aging Franco or a continuity of the system after his death will confront them with that painful choice. In the meantime the openness and tolerance of the regime allows it to count upon the technical cooperation of many of those politically alienated and hostile who would under no circumstances participate in the Movimiento. The limited pluralism of an authoritarian regime, its a-ideological tolerance, combined with the lack of international support of the non-left dictatorships (despite economic aid and military alliances) by the Western democracies, make an institutionalization of such a single party difficult if not impossible.

Institutionalization through Corporativism or a Sector Organization within the Party?

Another process of institutionalization of non-totalitarian single parties is through the development of corporative elements, that is, interest representation of social and economic sectors combined with patronage and social services. In this respect the opportunities for the Movimiento were and may still be better. Sindicatos, in some of their business sectors, labor at some local levels, and increasingly through its farmers' organizations reflect real interests and have functions, and their representatives in the Cortes and other bodies are often influential. However, the increasing grass roots challenges by the *Comisiones Obreras*—from communists and left Catholics—make that claim more difficult. Important sectors, like the professions and the higher civil service, have not been incorporated (even formally until very recently) and the army never was conceived as a sector, but as a separate institutional realm. The Movimiento-Organización was not, and cannot be, the umbrella of such a corporative structure, even when the regime through the Cortes has to some extent such a structure, not fully unlike the Mexican PRI sectors or some aspects of the Yugoslav chamber system.

However, these interest group corporative structures lost a great opportunity to build a machine structure and patronage and create loyalties, when they left most of the welfare state to the Ministry of Labor and the *Instituto Nacional de Previsión* (Social Security Administration) in the hands of an apolitical bureaucracy. Many other important services that could have linked the corporative-Movimiento structure with the society at all levels, particularly at the grass roots, are in the hands of the various ministries or autonomous agencies (like the *Servicio Nacional del Trigo*— Wheat Board administering price supports; the *Instituto Nacional de Colonización*—Agrarian Development Agency; *Patronato de Igualdad de Oportunidades*—for fellowship aid); and so forth whose clients do not have to show any services to the party. Our impression is that the PRI machinery has been able to link access to public services with party loyalty, in the absence of an independent and universalistic state bureaucracy. At least in an urban context the Movimiento organization has little to offer in exchange for votes or other forms of participation to the masses rather than office holders, even when the regime through the state (not without prodding by the Movimiento-Falangist leaders) has done much for those masses, but as citizens, not as party supporters. The personal link between citizen and the state is not mediated generally through the party or its corporative organizations, but through a relatively impersonal and apolitical bureaucracy which would not be eager to serve as an electioneering or party recruiting agency. There may well be one exception, which the last elections made visible, and that is local government in smaller communities and the official farmers' organization, the *Hermandades Sindicales de Labradores y Ganaderos*. However, with more than 75 per cent of the population living in towns of over 20,000 inhabitants and more than 58 per cent in those with over 100,000 people and with only one-third of the active population in agriculture, these links with the population do not facilitate a machine-type party or corporative system. In a modern bureaucratic state —be it multi-party or single-party—the a-ideological machine politics cannot easily serve as a link between people and the state and benefit in the process of building loyalties. The Mexican development in this respect was possible because the PRI decided on such a course before economic development had reached a certain level, in a still largely agrarian country, and in the absence of a relatively independent professional and universalistically oriented bureaucracy.

Last, but not least, even after many years the origins of the regime in a bloody counterrevolution made and makes the integration of large masses —particularly the working class—difficult if not impossible. This system contrasts with a system like the Mexican, born in revolution, whatever the basic similarity in many social and economic conditions and policies in the two countries.

The ideology and symbols under which a one-party system is born ultimately play a decisive role in the course its institutionalization can take. This is also why Franco, confronted with foreign pressures, toward democratization, could never—even assuming that he would be assured electoral victory—make the plunge into a manipulated or real multi-party system, in contrast with Mexico, Turkey, or recently, Brazil. The Turkish one-party system, despite its desire to hold on to power under Prime Minister Petel and the influences of the fascist model, had been born out of the Young Turks Movement with basically Western liberal-democratic progressive models, the victors of World War I. The Spanish movement was born under the sign of traditionalist, pre-democratic, fascist, and clerico-conservative corporativist ideas, a mixture that offers only limited basis to legitimize democratization and liberalization within the system except on opportunistic grounds. With real difficulties of implementation, as pointed out above, such motives cannot carry the day to take the Movimiento out of its semi-isolation and to break through the vested interests of its present office holders. To make the Movimiento a central and vital institution in the regime, even with all kinds of resources at its disposal, the weakness and fragmentation of its opposition, and the passive acquiescence of most of the population based on its desire for peace and development, seems to be impossible.

The Movimiento in its new form, constitutionally anchored, may last with more or less internal life—less than now is difficult to conceive—as long as the regime. However the survival of the regime does not depend on that of the Movimiento-Organización, even when the Movimiento-Asociación might contribute slightly to it, but so do many other factors. Among them the lack of visibility of real alternative leaders, the fractionalization of the opposition, the fear of disorder, the memories of the Civil War, and the radicalization of opposition segments that consider liberal-democracy as undesirable as the regime contribute as much as the undeniable achievements of Spanish economy and society under Franco and the complex of vested interests of the ruling strata and those of the many co-opted by a modern state machinery.

The Place of a Spanish Single Party in a Typology of One-Party Regimes

As the Spanish system did not turn into a totalitarian regime, we have to ask ourselves into which of the different types of single-party systems it falls. We have attempted to delimit it from both democratic and totalitarian regimes in another paper. Turning to the types of one-party systems that to a greater or lesser extent fall into the authoritarian type, as presented by Clement H. Moore,[96] we may ask ourselves, Is Spain a "chiliastic," "tutelary," or "institutional" one-party system? It is always difficult to operationalize the dimensions in such a typology to proceed to "subsume" the case under one of the typological definitions offered. It might well be that the Spanish system at different points in time would fit more than one type. We would be inclined to consider the two main dimensions: goals and functions as continua, ranging from "total" to "partial" transformation in the goals and greater emphasis on "instrumental" or "expressive" functions. In the days of the Civil War and immediately after victory, the idea of a "total transformation" was felt by many, by some as a real change in the social structure in the form of a "national-syndicalist revolution," by most in creating a new style, a new spirit, a new culture, and a new political system based on a mixture of old and new values and symbols. Nationalism, unity, authority, religious renewal and the rejection full of hatred of class struggle, regionalist claims, and the divisiveness of liberalism and democracy were constantly stressed. The mass demonstrations organized by FET y de las JONS under the slogans of Gibraltar and imperial expansion moved masses of people, as did those following the outbreak of the war with Russia against communism. The rhetorical expressive aspect took preeminence; even the more instrumental aspects of the regime like the autarchy industrialization were justified in such terms. The bifurcation of "us" and "they" against the enemies just defeated was constantly present, while a new national community was—presumably—built for higher and new goals. In that period Spain would probably fit, if not into the totalitarian type, then into the chiliastic.

As the élan of the activists of the party, of the youth and intellectuals who identified with it, decreased when confronted with the difficult and sometimes seamy realities of Spanish life, and with the loss of utopias inevitably linked with the Axis victory, the regime slowly shifted to an increased emphasis on the partial transformation of the economy and the society. If one reads Franco's speeches over time, particularly the end of the year messages and even the one introducing the Organic Law in 1966, one is struck by the constant and probably increasing references to concrete achievements in industrialization, public housing, social security, health services, education, and so forth. The party initially only indirectly participated in this shift, even when Sindicatos very soon built their claim to legitimacy on such achievements. There is no question that the regime would like to consider itself "tutelary," as a modernizing regime. However, the instrumental functions that have achieved much partial transformation of Spanish society—or allowed it to happen—do not seem sufficient to many Spaniards to legitimize the regime forever, even among those not initially hostile to it. Political systems cannot long dispense with the expressive aspects of politics. The constant effort of the regime to create constitutional provisions, particularly for the event of the death of Franco, are an indication of this. The regime defines itself in a continuous and open "constitutionalization" process, as many speeches of Franco prove. If nothing else, the constant use of the term "open process" indicates that the institutionalization has not yet been accomplished. The contradictory and ambivalent components of the Franco synthesis,[97] the coexistence of conflicting and competing legitimizing formulae and their advocacy with more or less precision, plus the enormous pressure coming from the European models leave the outcome uncertain. No one can say if the regime and particularly the Movimiento will be able to shift from the tutelary type or phase into the *institutional* one even when many of the efforts between 1966 and 1968, which we summarized, had just that purpose. We doubt that even those who would favor such a development are confident of success. Our analysis should have made it abundantly clear that we do not believe in its feasibility.

‖ *Notes*

NOTE: The research on which this paper is based has been made possible by a John Simon Guggenheim Memorial Fellowship. I am also indebted to José Juan Toharia and Rocío Terán for valuable research assistance and to Edward Malefakis and Joaquín Romero Maura for their critical reading.

PERSONAL NOTE: The author of this chapter has been close to some of the events and persons discussed in it. In the spring of 1936 I saw my classmates in school write on the walls FE, probably not knowing what it meant. After leaving Republican Spain in mid-October, my mother joined Falange Española de las JONS (not FET) upon arrival in Salamanca in May, 1937, and became very active in *Auxilio de Invierno*—its welfare organization—until the fall of 1939. At 10 years of age, I joined the youth organization of the party, but devoted most of my energies to *Auxilio de Invierno*. This Falangist identification meant a polite rejection by people with CEDA and monarchical backgrounds who initially had received us with open arms as refugees and friends of friends. Cardinal Goma, Primate of Spain, once asked my mother, "How can you be with this rabble?"

Dedicated to my studies, I did not maintain any relation to the party, but in 1943 still participated with feeling in the carrying of a crown to the grave of José Antonio, even when I hesitated in joining the SEU at the University, since I felt deceived by the conservative course of the regime. In 1947, friends of mine at the Law School and the Faculty of Political Science formed a discussion group on political and social problems that formally was illegal even when most innocuous. In 1948, when Javier Conde offered me and two friends who were his teaching assistants in a course on the Theory of Society a chance to join the staff of the *Instituto de Estudios Políticos,* we hesitated, but personal loyalty and the appeal of the program he intended to carry out led us to accept. We made it explicit, however, that we did not identify with the party. A short visit to France in the summer of 1949 led us to question fully the regime.

In 1950, I left for the United States with a government fellowship, and only returned in 1958. Since then I have considered myself in the opposition, but worked with the official youth organization in 1959–1960 on a national sample study, for which its leader gave us complete intellectual freedom, and in other sociological studies with the support of government agencies. As a sociologist, I can interpret the joining of the party by my mother as the logical choice of a person coming from an aristocratic upper-class family, but without any income except that coming from her work, threatened by the proletarian revolution; of an intellectual who had worked with the Republican intelligentsia; and of someone with a background of studies in the social sciences, aware of the deeper causes of the Civil War and the need for social reform that no other party was advocating in Franco Spain. The futility of the effort, together with the milieu developing within the organization—*Auxilio Social*—could not lead to anything but withdrawal late in 1939. Knowing little about Hedilla, who was arrested before our arrival in Salamanca, I remember her having visited Falangist prisoners in jail there. From my position as a democrat who does not believe in any future for the Movimiento and of a social scientist interested in the facts in comparative perspective, I am also sure that this personal experience has added to a better understanding of what Falange and Movimiento have represented in contemporary Spain. One lesson I learned: there can be no government for the people without their full and free participation. Only such participation increases the probabilities of government for the people.

1. On the social structure of contemporary Spain, see Fundación FOESSA (*Fomento de Estudios Sociales y de Sociología Aplicada*), *Informe sociológico sobre la situación social de España* (Madrid: Euroamérica, 1966), based on statistics and secondary data as well as on a national sample survey executed by DATA S.A. under the direction of Amando de Miguel. The cards from that survey are now available from The Roper Public Opinion Research Center for Secondary Analysis. For an annotated bibliography of current Spanish sociology, see Guy Hermet, "La sociologie empirique en Espagne," *Recherche Méditerranèe,* Bulletin of the Centre de Documentation Méditerranèe, Paris, No. 4 (June 1967), pp. 1–45. The Spanish sociological journal, *Anales de Sociología,* is another basic reference. The author is preparing a volume on the social structure of Spain for Random House.

2. This chapter is to be read in conjunction with other publications by the author on contemporary Spanish politics, particularly: "An Authoritarian Regime: Spain," in Erik Allardt and Yrje Littunen, eds., *Cleavages, Ideologies and Party Systems, Contributions to Comparative Political Sociology,* Transactions of the Westermarck Society, X (1964), 291–342, which attempts to provide a theoretical framework for the study of the Spanish political system in comparative perspective. An excerpt of this paper has been reprinted in Frank Lindenfeld, ed., *Reader in Political Sociology* (New York: Funk and Wagnalls, 1968), pp. 128–148. Also in Erik Allardt and Stein Rokkan, eds., *Mass Politics. Studies in Political Sociology* (New York: Free Press, forthcoming)

3. In "Opposition in an Authoritarian Regime: Spain," to be published in a volume on "emerging oppositions," edited by Robert Dahl for Yale University Press, I will explore in detail the nature and problems faced by the opposition under Franco and in so doing will help to explain the problems of stability, transformation, breakdown, or substitution of the present regime, as well as its modus operandi.

4. In "The Inauguration of Democratic Government and Its Prospects in Spain," to be published in a volume to be edited by Alfred deGrazia, I will discuss the prospects for continuity and change of the present regime.

5. Andrew C. Janos, "The One-Party State and Social Mobilization: East Europe between the Wars," in this volume.

6. See J. Linz, "An Authoritarian Regime: Spain," for the definition and analysis of those dimensions.

7. The best source for the modern history of Spain is Raymond Carr, *Spain 1808–1939* (Oxford: Clarendon Press, 1966).

8. There is no adequate study in Spanish or any other language of the Primo de Rivera dictatorship, its origins and policies, nor a scholarly biography of the dictator. The attempt by Ratcliff, *Prelude to Franco,* is inadequate. The only useful sources are the speeches and press notes of the dictator, the memoirs and biographies of Calvo Sotelo, and the writings of enemies of the dictatorship at the time. None of those sources give much information on the UP. For a brief account of its history and "ideology," see José Pemartín, *Los valores históricos en la dictadura española,* with a foreword by Primo de Rivera (Madrid: Publicaciones de la Junta de Propaganda Patriótica y Ciudadana, 1929), pp. 665–687.

9. Speech on November 22, 1966, before the Cortes, introducing the bill of the Ley Orgánica del Estado. See Servicio Informativo Español, *Referendum 1966: Nueva Constitución* (Madrid: SIE, 1966), p. 33. The publication, *Fundamental Laws of the State. The Spanish Constitution* (Madrid: SIE, 1967), contains the texts, useful outlines and "organization tables" of the regime, as well as texts of Franco on the constitution and the Movimiento, but not the text quoted.

10. The Primo de Rivera regime, particularly in its first phase, was a classic example of what Carl Schmitt calls *kommissarische Diktatur.* Carl Schmitt, *Die Diktatur* (München: Duncker and Humblot, 1928, first published in 1921). This type obviously is unlikely to think initially of creating a single party, and when it finally does is most likely to come up with a bureaucratic-type party (in Janos's sense) with the characteristics of an anti-party party.

11. On this point, see Stanley G. Payne, *Politics and the Military in Modern Spain* (Stanford: Stanford University Press, 1967), chap. 10. This work also provides an invaluable information of the role of the army in the origins and politics of the Civil War and its aftermath.

12. It is interesting to note that the idea of the UP crystallized in Valladolid as early as 1923. It was here the movement of the *Unión Nacional*—a league modeled in part after the Cobden Anti-Corn League—initiated by Costa outside and against the two parties of the Restoration had considerable success at the turn of the century. One of the leading reformist critics of parliamentarism and politicians at the turn of the century, Macías Picavea, had been a high school teacher there. In the 1930s it would be one of the main foci of fascism. This relatively important Castillian city was at the time a typical center of what we have called the Spain of the *clases medias* in contrast to the Spain of the bourgeoisie, referring to the non-commercial, non-industrial middle class, the professionals, army officers, and civil servants, the group which in part coincides with the "state bourgeoisie" to which East European writers refer. This class, so characteristic of semi-developed Western societies, was particularly important in Spain. The *clases medias* Spain had a much less class-divided social structure and therefore a "civic" movement across other lines of cleavage was particularly appealing. The idea spread initially to other Castillian towns; Segovia, Santander, and Medina del Campo; and only in 1925 did Primo de Rivera accept the new following. On the *clases medias,* see Juan J. Linz and Amando de Miguel, "Within-Nation Differences and Comparisons: The Eight Spains," in Richard L. Merritt and Stein Rokkan, eds., *Comparing Nations* (New Haven: Yale University Press, 1966), pp. 267–319.

13. On the policies of the dictatorship and some of the debates in the *Asamblea Nacional* see Juan Velarde, *Política Económica de la Dictadura* (Madrid: Guadiana de Publicaciones, 1968).

14. The decree creating the National Consultative Assembly of September, 1927 provided for one representative of the UP per province—that is, 50—among the 331 members, 50 representing the municipalities and another 50 the provincial chambers, 125 representing different corporate groups, interest groups, and intellectual activities, 59 of the state and 56 ex officio (somewhat as in the senate of the constitutional monarchy).

15. Ramiro Ledesma Ramos in his *Discurso a las Juventudes de España* (Madrid: Ediciones F.E., 1939). This was re-edited with the historico-political essays on Spanish fascism he published under the pseudonym Roberto Lanzas until November, 1935; *Fascismo en España? Discurso a las Juventudes de España* (Barcelona: Ariel, 1968). He writes (p. 225): "Primo de Rivera gave Spain seven years of peace—always peace!—in the course of which there was real economic prosperity, but no agrarian reform was carried out—basically the agrarian property continued constituting the main basis of the regime. It never obtained the collaboration of youth, even when the time of the dictatorship coincided with the moment in which for the first time there appeared an effective youthful conscience."

16. On the parties and movements under the Republic, see Juan J. Linz, "The Party System of Spain: Past and Future," in S. M. Lipset and Stein Rokkan, eds., *Party Systems and Voter Alignments* (New York: The Free Press, 1967), pp. 197–282. See pp. 231–264 and particularly pp. 243–249 on the CEDA, pp. 249–251 on the transition from extreme multipartisan to polarized conflict and Civil War. The footnotes give the necessary bibliographic references.

17. See Ledesma Ramos, *op. cit.* The JONS program is reproduced on p. 98 and in *JONS Organo teórico de las JONS: Antología y prólogo Juan Aparicio* (Madrid: Ediciones FE, 1939), pp. 3–4. The appeal of the Conquista del Estado, the first Fascist Manifesto of February 1931, is reprinted in Ledesma Ramos, *op. cit.*, pp. 76–77.

18. The twenty-seven points of Falange Española y de las JONS can be found in Bernd Nellessen and in English in Clyde L. Clark, *The Evolution of the Franco Regime* (3 volumes, no publisher, no date, but declassified in 1956, and with a note that it is not a State Department publication, even when Mr. Clark was associated with it), II, 603–612. Clark's work is extremely useful to anyone studying contemporary Spanish politics since it reproduces basic legal texts for the period 1936–1944, summarizes chronologically events and policies, gives the names of office holders with their dates of appointment and dismissal and sometimes the reasons for the changes.

19. The literature on Spanish fascism *strictu sensu,* has become quite extensive. See Stanley G. Payne, *Falange: A History of Spanish Fascism* (Stanford: Stanford University Press, 1961); Bernd Nellessen, *Die verbotene Revolution, Aufstieg und Niedergang der Falange* (Hamburg: Leibniz Verlag, 1963); Maximiano García Venero, *Falange en la guerra de España: la Unificación y Hedilla* (Paris: Ruedo Ibérico, 1967); Herbert R. Southworth, *Antifalange: Estudio crítico de Falange en la guerra de España* (Paris: Ruedo Ibérico, 1967).

Payne's work is the most scholarly; García Venero gives a wealth of detail, much unknown before, about internal party life, particularly for 1936–1937, from the point of view of a journalist-historian who joined the party before the war and was close to Hedilla and fully alienated from the Franco regime without rejecting his ideological commitments. Southworth was planned as critical footnotes to García Venero, adding useful information and contesting some facts from a hostile position.

20. There is no published study of the CEDA, even though Richard Robinson has completed a thesis at Oxford, to be published soon. José María Gil Robles has published a first volume of his memoirs, *No fue posible la paz* (Barcelona: Ariel, 1968), which provides invaluable information about this period.

21. The JAP is quite critically discussed in Gil Robles, *op. cit.,* chap. 10, pp. 189–209, and the program is quoted on p. 191. "An example of its ambivalence are these programmatic statements: Antiparliamentarism. Antidictatorship. The people incorporates itself into the government in an organic and hierarchical way and not through degenerate democracy." "First reason. Against violence, reason and force." "Prestige of authority. Strong executive power. To prevent rather than to repress."

The real fascists were more decided and poetic in their style when they appealed in the JONS program:

"Substitution of the parliamentary regime by a Spanish regime of authority, that shall be based on the armed support of our party and the moral and material aid of the people."

or in point 6 of the twenty-seven points of FE y de las JONS:

Our State will be the totalitarian instrument in the service of the integrity of the fatherland. All Spaniards will participate in it through their family, municipal and syndical function. Nobody shall participate through the political parties. The system of political parties with all its consequences, inorganic suffrage, representation by factions in conflict and parliament of the known type, will be abolished without pity. (21)

22. The magazine *Acción Española* is indispensable to understanding right-wing thought in Spain—across party lines—in the 1930s. Among the collaborators in the eighty-eight issues published were eight cabinet members and many ambassadors, university rectors, and legislators under Franco.

23. For a biography of Calvo Sotelo, see General Felipe Acedo Colunga, *José Calvo Sotelo* (Barcelona: AHR, 1957) and Aurelio Joaniquet, *Calvo Sotelo: Una vida fecunda, Un ideario político, Una doctrina* (Madrid: Espasa Calpe, 1939). His own writings are interesting: *Mis servicios al Estado* (Madrid: Imprenta Clásica Española, 1931), and a selection edited by Amalio García-Arias, *El Estado que queremos* (Madrid: Rialp, 1958).

24. The literature on the Civil War and its origins fills entire libraries. In English, Hugh Thomas, *The Spanish Civil War* (New York: Harper and Brothers, 1961) and Gabriel Jackson, *The Spanish Republic and the Civil War 1931–1939* (Princeton: Princeton University Press, 1965) are standard. For a critical bibliography from a regime point of view, see Ricardo de la Cierva y de Hoces, *Cien libros básicos sobre la guerra de España* (Madrid: Publicaciones Españolas, 1966), which also includes a reference to the main bibliographic efforts; Juan García Durán, *Bibliografía de la Guerra civil española 1936–1939* (Montevideo: El Siglo Ilustrado, 1964). Gabriel Jackson's *The Spanish Civil War: Domestic Crisis or International Conspiracy?* (Boston: D. C. Heath, 1967) is a reader in the collection *Problems in European Civilization,* with sources reflecting different points of view and an annotated bibliography. The work that best reflects what Republican Spain after July, 1936, meant for Spaniards—not outsiders sympathetic to one or another cause—is Burnett Bolloten, *The Grand Camouflage: The Spanish Civil War and Revolution, 1936–1939,* with an introduction by H. R. Trevor Roper (New York: Frederick A. Praeger, 1968, reprinting a work first published in 1961). The scholarship of Bolloten makes this an indispensable source. Unfortunately there is no similar work on life and politics in Franco Spain.

25. Fernando, Díaz Plaja, *El siglo XX: La Guerra (1936–1939)* (Madrid: Ediciones Faro, 1963), a volume of the collection, *La Historia de España en sus Docu-*

mentos, reproduces basic legal texts, speeches and other documents of the period. See pp. 150–153 for Franco's proclamation on July 17, pp. 154–157 for a typical declaration of the state of war, pp. 174–175 for the first proclamation of the new military junta, the decree changing the flag only a month and a half after the war started. All these documents give evidence of the fundamentally military character of the rebellion and the confusion about future political aims.

26. For the text of this decree of September 25, 1936, published September 28, see pp. 2–3 of Antonio Bouthelier Espasa, ed., *Legislación Sindical Española* (Madrid: Instituto de Estudios Políticos, 1945), I, 22–23.

27. S. Payne, *op. cit.,* p. 146. In April, 1937, General Monasterio, titular chief of the united militias, is said to have stated that there were 126,000 Falangists, 22,000 *Requetés* (traditionalist-Carlist) and 5,000 men from other groups in the militia.

28. On the participation and life of the Falange in the first year of the Civil War, see García Venero, *op. cit.* and Southworth, *op. cit.,* and the sources quoted there. The figures are quoted from an interview of Hedilla on September 26, 1936; see Southworth, *op. cit.,* p. 154.

29. See n. 43 and also Table 5–7 to put those figures into comparative perspective. The fact that FE y de las JONS was *not* a mass membership party nor one of broad electoral appeal before the military uprising was the decisive obstacle for any successful totalitarian ambitions and differentiates it decisively from the PNF and the NSDAP, parties with a large following before taking power.

30. On Gil Robles, the CEDA, and the JAP in the first year of the Civil War, see some information, still insufficient, in Gil Robles, *op. cit.,* chap. 19, pp. 765–802.

31. The work of Dionisio Ridruejo, *Escrito en España* (Buenos Aires: Losada, 1962), provides insight into the motives of those who joined in those years and the process of disillusion in the forties. This semi-autobiographical, semi-analytical work by a former Jefe Provincial, head of the propaganda services of the party, and now active opposition leader could be used to document many of the points made in this chapter. Ridruejo is in many ways the Spanish Djilas. See p. 79 for the text quoted.

32. The party complimentary, partly conflicting account of the antecedents and events leading to the *Unificación* by Payne, *op. cit.,* García Venero, *op. cit.,* and Southworth, *op. cit.,* allow a better understanding of this key event. The accounts are based on sources outside of the inner circle of Franco's headquarters. Serrano Súñer, in *Entre Hendaya y Gibraltar: Frente a una leyenda* (Madrid: Ediciones y Publicaciones Españolas, 1947), gives a very partial—in both senses of the word—account, but one that is invaluable for understanding the political motives and consequences as seen by the man who played a decisive role in creating the new party. The book is also indispensable for understanding the period 1937–1942.

33. There is no biography of Serrano Súñer, except his own very selective memoirs and the book by Angel Alcázar de Velasco, *Serrano Súñer en la Falange* (Barcelona: Ediciones Patria, 1941), devoted to supporting his legitimacy in the party by stressing his personal ties with José Antonio.

34. A study of this elite corps in the Spanish civil service and politics would well deserve a monograph. In the section on the elite of the regime we will refer further to it. In a national study of Spanish youth the prestige rating for an *Abogado del Estado* was 87, compared to 92 for a cabinet member, 89 for a judge of the Supreme Court, 86 for a doctor, 83 for a member of the Cortes. In a sample of Andalusian village elites, ranking eight occupations, his rank was 3.6 in a range that went from a director general in a ministry (assistant secretary), 2.5; bishop, 2.6; director of a firm employing more than 750 persons, 3.3; to 5.9 for the owner of 300 hectares of wheat farmland and 6.5 for a marquis

living off his rents. Among five elite positions the business elite ranked him 2.34 compared to 2.13 for the director of a firm of 750 workers, 2.44 for the director general, and 4.38 for the colonel with regimental command.

35. Dionisio Ridruejo, "La Falange y su Caudillo," *FE* (March–April 1938), pp. 37–38; quoted by Southworth, *op. cit.*, p. 215.

36. For an account of this meeting of the fourth and last *Consejo Nacional* of FE y de las JONS, see Payne, *op. cit.*, pp. 166–168 and chap. 12, pp. 381–389 of García Venero, *op. cit.*

37. On the Unification decree and the preamble, see Payne, *op. cit.*, pp. 168–169; chaps. 13 and 14 in García Venero, *op. cit.*, pp. 391–410; and Serrano Súñer, *op. cit.*, pp. 17–39.

38. Serrano Súñer, *op. cit.*, p. 30.

39. The reading of the text of the speech by Franco and of the decree itself is fundamental in this case as in that of later laws and constitutional laws, particularly since there are really no competent or influential expositions of the Spanish constitutional system—comparable to the abundant literature produced by Italian and German professors—under fascism and nazism, despite the greater correspondence between legal and political reality. The skepticism of even the official intelligentsia, has contributed to this poverty of politico-legal-ideological writings. The official legal texts often are very revealing and deserve more attention of political scientists than a one-sided behaviorism would lead us to expect. A handy summary is *Resumen Legislativo del Nuevo Estado* (Barcelona: Editora Nacional, 1939), Vol. 1, and (Madrid, 1942), Vol. 2. For the party, *Recopilación Sistemática de la Legislación del Movimiento*, published by the *Sección de Organización del Movimiento del Instituto de Estudios Políticos*, with almost 4,000 pages of texts selected from the *Boletín del Movimiento*. A very useful collection of the statements of Franco about the Movimiento is Francisco Franco, *El Movimiento Nacional: Textos de Franco* (Madrid: Ediciones del Movimiento, n.d. but after 1966). For a recent definition (1960), see p. 59. The main post-Civil War laws can be found in *Fundamentos del Nuevo Estado* (Madrid: Ediciones de la Vicesecretaría de Educación Popular, 1943), and the more recent constitutional laws in *Fundamental Laws of the State: The Spanish Constitution* (Madrid: Spanish Information Service, 1967). Many of those texts, up to 1944, have been translated in Clark, *op. cit.* The best Spanish academic analysis of the Constitutional Laws is Rodrigo Fernández-Carvajal, *La Constitución Española* (Madrid: Editora Nacional, 1969).

40. Quoted in García Venero, *op. cit.*, p. 394.

41. Sigmund Neumann, *Permanent Revolution: Totalitarianism in the Age of International Civil War* (New York: Frederick A. Praeger, 1965, second edition of the work first published in 1941), pp. 126–127.

42. The party statutes were strongly influenced by the Italian model. As in Italy and in contrast to the more complex structure of the NSDAP—with powerful heads of different organizations—the party secretary under the direct authority of the Caudillo would emerge as the key official. Both in Italy and Spain the more strictly bureaucratic model of organization was followed, while in Germany the direct and changing relation of a group of "disciples" with a charismatic leader ran counter to bureaucratization, giving the NSDAP a more "feudal" organizational structure.

43. On the first *Consejo Nacional* of FE y de las JONS, see Serrano Súñer, *op. cit.*, pp. 64–65; Payne, *op. cit.*, pp. 184–188, for a list of members; Clark, *op. cit.*, I, 631–635.

There are no adequate data on party membership before the Civil War and it is unlikely that such data exist anywhere. José Luis Arrese in an interview with the author mentioned 8,000 cardholders before the February, 1936 elections; Fernández Cuesta, then secretary general, estimates that the *primera línea*—active militants—were no more than 5,000, in a conversation with Stanley Payne. In his *Falange,* p. 279, on the basis of interviews with local leaders in different provinces and some publications Payne presents figures by province or region. His conclusion is that "by no method of computation could the party's immediate following have been fixed at more than 25,000." The membership is for a population of 24.6 million. See Table 5–7 at end of this chapter for international comparisons.

The data for Italy from Dante L. Germino, *The Italian Fascist Party: A Study in Totalitarian Rule* (Minneapolis: University of Minnesota Press, 1959) and those of Germany from Wolfgang Schäffer, *NSDAP: Entwicklung und Struktur der Staatspartei des Dritten Reiches* (Schriftenreihe des Institutes für wissenschaftliche Politik Marburg, Hannover: Norddeutsche Verlagsanstalt O. Goebel, 1957). The SS, on January 30, 1933, had already 52,000 members (data in Franz Neumann, *Behemoth* [New York: Octagon Books, 1963], p. 546). Even a minor fascist party like the Arrow Cross claimed 8,000 members (for the Party of National Will) in September, 1935, to approximately 19,000 in April, 1937, for a population of 8.7 million. István Deák, "Hungary," in Hans Rogger and Eugen Weber, eds., *The European Right* (Berkeley: University of California Press, 1965), p. 396.

44. Serrano Súñer, *op. cit.,* p. 66.
45. The party secretariat has been occupied by four persons: Fernández Cuesta, Muñoz Grandes, Arrese, and Solís Ruiz, with two of them holding the office twice and an acting secretary general Vivar Téllez. Fernández Cuesta—who had held it under José Antonio, was placed there (1937) by Serrano when he felt that to appoint himself would create too many resentments and that Fernández Cuesta, due to his personality and recent stay in Republican jails, would not create difficulties. He was succeeded (1939) by General Muñoz Grandes, who was considered a pro-Falangist officer even when before the war he had no relation with the party and no interest in ideological issues. He also became the direct chief of the militia of the party. To assist him Gamero del Castillo was appointed vice-secretary general with the rank of minister without portfolio. He had been a leader of the association of Catholic university students who in the spring of 1936 had initiated contacts with the SEU—Falangist student organization—leadership; after the uprising he had become an important figure of the party in Sevilla and participated in negotiations with the traditionalists before the Unification. His background probably made him appealing to Serrano Súñer who at that time assumed the presidency of the *Junta Política.* In addition a Falangist journalist was appointed vice president of the *Junta* with the rank of minister without portfolio. The multiple authority structure and the unclear delimitation of responsibility and the balancing of the background of the incumbents naturally contributed to the ineffectiveness of the party at the height of its prestige. It also allowed Serrano Súñer to play the dominant role as minister of the interior until October, 1940 and of foreign affairs from then until September, 1942 when he also had to give up the presidency of the *Junta Política.* Muñoz Grandes left the party secretariat in 1940. His successor was José Luis de Arrese, married to a relative of José Antonio, who had been arrested at the time of the Unification and later been governor of Malaga. His resignation with ten other provincial governors upon the appointment of an anti-Falangist officer to the ministry of the interior provoked a crisis that Franco solved by bringing three Falangists into the cabinet. Soon the delimitation of the power sphere of the secretary general and the president of the *Junta Política* provoked serious difficulties which might have contributed decisively

to the downfall of Serrano Súñer. Arrese was an honest administrator who reorganized the party, maintained it on a moderate course loyal to Franco, and initiated a shift away from some of the more foreign fascist models and toward a greater emphasis on Catholicism and anti-communism and less on dreams of empire. He outlasted a complex cabinet crisis in 1942 that led to the simultaneous ouster of the pro-Axis minister of foreign affairs and the Anglophile minister of the army and the appointment of a pro-Allied general for the first post and a pro-Falangist one to the second. With the allied victory in 1945 the party became a liability and logically was pushed into the background. In the new cabinet formed on July 20, 1945, Arrese was dismissed and his seat left vacant. A caretaker administration followed under a judge without political ambitions who, according to Payne, considered that the party was without function and might as well be dissolved. The post of secretary general was not filled until July, 1951, when the weak Fernández Cuesta assumed it again. The most representative man of the party for a long period was the Minister of Labor, José Antonio Girón (May, 1941 until February, 1957) who enacted much of the social legislation of the regime and created the national health service, assured job security to the workers, and often contributed to inflationary spirals with some of his wage increases. A crisis provoked by a university conflict led Franco to drop both the liberal Minister of Education, Ruiz-Giménez, and Fernández Cuesta in 1956—following the pattern of Franco to balance cabinet changes—and to appoint Arrese again. His return signaled an interesting attempt to revitalize the party, which we will discuss later; his defeat led to his substitution by José Solís Ruiz in February, 1957. Since then the party machine has been in the hands of this able politician, backslapping, without ideological commitments, whose name does not appear in the early history of the party despite his being 23 years old in 1936. He made his career as provincial governor in the post-war years and as head of Sindicatos. He considered it his task to harmonize conflicting interests avoiding trouble. Under him power shifted from the party bureaucracy—reduced to a minimum—to the bureaucracy of Sindicatos and the complex of interest groups linked to them. The offices of secretary general and *delegado nacional* of Sindicatos for the first time became united in the same person and have remained so to the present. His style was far from the authoritarian fascist drama and ceremonial of the 1940s, but control remained fully in his hands. He would be the first real head of the Movimiento rather than of the old provisional FET y de las JONS.

46. The term *Gleichschaltung* was used by the Nazis to describe the synchronization of all authorities, organizations, associations, and interest groups, achieved by subordinating them to political controls, appointing their officers, assuring party representation, and giving them ideological and policy directives.

47. Such factors also limited the implementation of the totalitarian utopia in Italy despite some other factors—compared to Spain—more favorable to the effort of the radicals in the PNF.

48. See Payne, *op. cit.*, pp. 213–214.

49. On the persistence and reemergence of autonomous business interest groups and their role as seen by the businessmen, see Juan J. Linz and Amando de Miguel, *Los Empresarios ante el Poder Público* (Madrid: Instituto de Estudios Políticos, 1966).

50. On this disjunction between formal and informal leadership of the business community, see the data from a sample survey of businessmen in Linz and de Miguel, *op. cit.*, chaps. 7–8. The problem of the "privileged impotent" business elite in the context of an authoritarian regime is discussed in chap. 4, pp. 116–121.

51. On the *Hermandades*, see Francisco González Sánchez-Girón, *Las Hermandades*

Sindicales de Labradores y Ganaderos. Doctrina Práctica Funcional: Su legislación y formularios, Foreword by José Solís Ruiz (Avila: no publisher, 1960). Juan Martínez Alier, *La Estabilidad del Latifundismo: Análisis de la interdependencia entre relaciones de producción y conciencia social en la agricultura latifundista de la campiña de Córdoba.* (Paris: Ruedo Ibérico, 1968) makes reference to the role of Sindicatos in *latifundia* Spain.

52. The CONCA (*Confederación Nacional Católico Agraria*) was founded in 1912 and in 1933 had 196,255 members.

53. In 1935 Ledesma Ramos *op. cit.,* p. 59, commenting on the efforts of the anticlerical Republican minister of education in favor of a single school, noted that only a state with an "orthodoxy" could sustain it and it would be possible only in a "totalitarian State, be it fascist or bolshevik." It is interesting to note how this left-wing fascist perceived repeatedly the similarity between fascist and communist totalitarianism.

54. On this "demobilization" process see Ridruejo, *Escrito en España,* pp. 122–125. For an extensive quotation, relevant to the distinction between authoritarian and totalitarian one-party systems, see Linz, "An Authoritarian Regime: Spain," pp. 305–306.

55. This point was made by Payne, *op. cit.,* p. 206. David Jato, *La Rebelión de los Estudiantes: Apuntes para una historia del alegre S.E.U.* (Madrid: CIES, 1953), chap. 6 describes the change of mood under the heading "Peace: enemy of illusions."

56. The *División Azul* as escapism of the disillusioned Falangists has been stressed by Ridruejo, *Escrito en España,* pp. 17–18 and Jato, *op. cit.,* pp. 311–319. The latter quotes a farewell letter of one who was to die in Russia, which reflects this alienation.

    This solution was not too different from some of the discontented fascists—including Mussolini's son—who opted for the front in Ethiopia and World War II rather than become members of the *apparat.*

57. On the Sindicatos, in English, see Fred Witney, *Labor Policy and Practices in Spain: A Study of Employer-Employee Relations under the Franco Regime,* Praeger Special Studies in International Economics and Development (New York: Frederick A. Praeger, 1965). Carlos Iglesias Selgas, *Los Sindicatos en España: Origen, Estructura y Evolución* (Madrid: Ediciones del Movimiento, 1965) is a useful summary of the present organization and ideology. For the early years the best source is the legislative collection edited by Boutnelier, *op. cit.* The article by Luis Díez del Corral, "La Ley Sindical," *Revista de Estudios Políticos,* No. 2 (1942), pp. 239–266 is a useful presentation of the ideology at that stage. The early legislation on Sindicatos can be found in English in *The Evolution of the Franco Regime,* compiled by Clyde L. Clark (originally a restricted publication, no place, publisher or date, but declassified by the Library of Congress, 1956).

58. The budget of Sindicatos is a sizable sum, derived from a 1.8 per cent surcharge on the total national wage bill. Apparently the contributions by the rural membership are still to be regulated. According to Iglesias Selgas, *op. cit.* p. 424, the 1965 income was 4,508,220,812 pts., approximately $75 million. In 1964 the total state budget was 66,846,200,000 pts. and that for education 4,980 million pts. The party budget line in the state budget was 102.2 million pts.

    The budgets of the party and Sindicatos are not published in detail like those of the state, and therefore it is not possible to examine the patterns of expenditure, nor, as for the state, the size and salary structure of their officialdom. However, the *Obra Sindical 18 de Julio,* the health insurance fund organized by the Sindicatos to cooperate with the national health insurance system, gave the following figures for *funcionarios del Movimiento,* "civil servants of the Movement," which probably includes those of Sindicatos: 1954, 19,649; 1957, 23,513; 1964, 8,478 of the Movimiento and 18,015 of Sindicatos, adding up to 26,493. (Iglesias Selgas, *op. cit.,* p. 196).

59. A recent front page editorial in *Pueblo* (the newspaper of the Sindicatos) by Emilio Romero, himself *consejero nacional* and one of the more intelligent defenders of the regime, describes the Movimiento today in these revealing terms:

> The minister secretary general is a member of the government [and operates] within the diversity of opinions and sectors in the cabinet. The press and propaganda division is only the administrative and political overseer of a chain of newspapers, magazines and radio stations which live side by side with other private chains of press and radio. It has no T.V. since that belongs to the State.
>
> It promotes sports in general, the youth organization, diverse non-political associations, and the women's section, that carries out cultural training tasks without exclusive dogmatisms.
>
> The Syndical Organization functions under the aegis of the Movimiento, and it is known who constitutes it: employers and workers; there are no discriminations and its achievements are for the welfare of all. Then in the provinces there are nuclei of people of the Movimiento, as there are of other sectors.
>
> The provincial governors and provincial chiefs of the Movimiento are appointed after agreement between the general secretariat and the ministry of interior, and as is logical are of different political groupings. Both ministries also make their influence felt at the local level.

60. The volume by Samuel Ros and Antonio Bouthelier, *A hombros de la Falange de Alicante a El Escorial* (Barcelona: Ediciones Patria, 1940), can give a feeling for the drama, enthusiasm, organization, identification, and emotion that went into the burial of the founder in 1939. The duality of the dead founder— the *Ausente* (absent one)—and Franco as actual ruler has some of the same functions for the regime that the duality of Che Guevara and Fidel Castro has for Cuban and Latin American revolutionaries.

61. There have been two referenda since the 1945 law providing for this procedure, one in July, 1947 to approve the succession law that instaured a monarchy without king and gave a democratic legitimacy to Franco as head of state for life, and another on December 14, 1966 approving the Organic Law of the State. The official figures were: in 1947, 88.6 per cent of the voters turned out and 82.3 per cent voted *yes,* 4.2 per cent *no,* 2.0 per cent voted void; in 1966, 85.5 per cent voted *yes.*

62. The Order of September 21, 1943, granted the *Consejeros Nacionales* the full party membership—*militante*—card. In the Soviet Union this would mean that upon appointment to the Central Committee the member would receive his Communist Party membership card!

63. The *Report to the National Council on the Pre-Projects of Fundamental Laws* presented on December 29, 1956, as a reaction to criticism of the proposals that would revitalize the party and the reference in one of them to "the excessive participation" that the original group of FE y de las JONS might have in the positions in state and Movimiento. Appendix 3 gives the political origin before July 18, 1936 of the elite. Unfortunately we have access only to the data on the proportion of men coming from the Falange, but not the proportion from other groups. See Table 5–8 at end of this chapter.

The figures given by Arrese can be compared with those published by Wolfgang Schäffer on the presence of NSDAP members—by date of affiliation —in the government of Germany and its municipalities on January 1, 1935.

See Table 5–9 at end of this chapter. Even considering only the early joiners, the rates compare favorably with those in Spain. Only in some of the Catholic regions of Germany, was the proportion of party members among the mayors of non-urban municipalities having joined before 1933 comparably low: Württemberg-Hohenzollern, 5.2 per cent; Mainfranken, 7.5 per cent; Koblenz-Trier, 10.3 per cent; and Westfalen-Nord, 12.9 per cent.

These figures given by Arrese have been, in all probability, elaborated using IBM cards on office holders at the general secretariat, which include, among other information, data coded in the following way:

Aside from all politics and without any leaning or tendency
Identified with the regime and the Movimiento without marked tendency
Identified with the regime without marked tendency nor leaning toward the Movimiento
Identified with the Movimiento, and of Falangist tendency
Identified with the Movimiento, and of traditionalist tendency
Identified with the Movimiento, and of monarchist tendency
Identified with the Movimiento, and of demo-Christian tendency
Identified with the Movimiento, and of Republican tendency
Not identified with the Movimiento and of Falangist tendency
Not identified with the Movimiento and of traditionalist tendency
Not identified with the Movimiento and of monarchist tendency
Not identified with the Movimiento and of demo-Christian tendency
Not identified with the Movimiento and of Republican tendency
Not identified with the Movimiento and of leftist tendency
Not identified with the Movimiento and of Marxist tendency

Some of those classifications may be surprising, but I know of a provincial governor speaking favorably of the socialist city councillors in a northern provincial capital; they were elected recently, against his will, but performed their duties with devotion while those he had proposed among the regime forces contributed little and caused trouble. Nothing could make more visible the *limited* pluralism within the regime and even the Movimiento as well as the many shades of identification with them, even among its office holders.

64. On the 1956 Arrese reform proposals and the hostility they provoked in the army and the church among other sectors, see Payne, *op. cit.*, pp. 251–262.

The "Informe del Instituto de Estudios Políticos en relación con los Anteproyectos de leyes Fundamentales sometidos a la Consideración del Consejo Nacional" (24 pp.) is a very interesting document that unfortunately has not been published. The *Proyecto de Bases* submitted by Luis González Vicén to the drafting committee of the Fundamental Laws was circulated in mimeographed form. Both have been available to the author in addition to interviews with Arrese, whose report to the National Council has been published in *Hacia una Meta Institucional* (Madrid: Ediciones del Movimiento, n.d., but probably 1957), pp. 211–226. The defensive tone cannot escape the reader, particularly if he keeps in mind that it comes from the secretary general of the "ruling" party.

65. The projected laws went even further in making the national secretary "politically responsible for his administration" before the Council, and provided that one-fifth or more could introduce a censure motion and that a majority vote could force him to present his resignation to the head of state. For the first time power was to be made accountable to someone else than Franco, certainly not a popular electorate but to a Council with a number of ex officio members, others freely appointed by the head of state and by at least one-half of the 150 elected by the party membership (in a way that remained unspecified even when one article provided for their participation in all elections). Member-

ship was supposed to be open and the automatic membership of army officers and non-commissioned officers was retained.

66. Reprinted in Servicio Informativo Español, *The Spanish Constitution* (Madrid: S.I.E., 1967), pp. 19–25. These principles are today the basic ideological statement of the regime, and anyone wanting to compare the style and program of the Movimiento with the fascist pre-war Falange should compare this document with the twenty-seven-point program.

67. In March, 1963, the National Council was called together, and the discussion centered on the desire to make the National Council a kind of Senate. Franco's closing speech contained a statement to the effect that "our satisfaction cannot excuse us from perfecting those instruments which, conceived a quarter of a century ago, may have lost some of their effectiveness" and recalled the device of the referendum to legitimize institutional changes. A competent observer, Benjamin Welles, *Spain, the Gentle Anarchy* (New York: Frederick A. Praeger, 1965), in chap. 5 on the Falange (see pp. 103–106 for the 1963 *Consejo Nacional*) considered Franco's speech one more step in the loss of power of the party.

68. The speech before the Cortes on November 22, 1966 is reprinted in Servicio Informativo Español, ed., *Referendum 1966: Nueva Constitución* (Documentos Políticos, no. 7, Ministerio de Información y Turismo, n.d.), pp. 29–53; the text quoted is on p. 41. Part of the speech has been translated in *Fundamental Laws of the State, op. cit.,* n. 9, pp. 210–215. Also *The New York Times*, November 23, 1966, p. 18.

69. The Organic Law of 1966 devoted one of its titles to the National Council, "as the collegiate representative of the Movement" defining its functions, its composition, its powers, its presidency as "president of the government, in his capacity as National Leader of the Movement by delegation of the Head of State," and the secretary general and his mandate, which was to be dependent on that of the president of the government. The implementation of its principles was left to successive legislative enactments. The discussions in the Committee of the Cortes and in the National Council of the Movimiento are basic to understanding the role of the Movimiento in the Franco system. Our summary is based on the accounts of the debates in *Pueblo, Ya* and *ABC*, from June 1, 1967, to June 16. The discussion in the National Council of its *reglamento* is in *Informaciones, Ya, ND,* and *ABC*, and between July 27 and 29, of 1968.

70. Summary of the discussion based on newspaper accounts of July 27 to 29, 1968, in *Informaciones, Ya, ND,* and *ABC*.

71. Attacking the possibility of secret sessions, one member argued that if the "contrast of opinions" could not produce itself on the basis of associations but only at the individual level, there should be no limit to the public expressions of the councillors. If a chamber and the plenary sessions to discuss reports requested by the head of state were to be secret, they could not obtain the support of the country, said another.

72. The letter of González Vicén, an "old shirt," has been circulated in mimeographed form. Payne, *op. cit.,* pp. 251–257, quotes it extensively.

73. The distinction between "mentality" and "ideology" has been formulated by Theodor Geiger, in his *Die Soziale Schichtung des deutschen Volkes* (Stuttgart: Ferdinand Enke, 1932), pp. 77–79, and used by me in characterizing the difference between authoritarian and totalitarian systems in "An Authoritarian Regime: Spain," pp. 301–304.

74. The more attractive personality and style of José Antonio has led many students of Spanish fascism to underrate the intellectual contribution of Ramiro Ledesma Ramos. His *Discurso a las Juventudes de España* deserves to be read

by anyone who wants to understand the appeal of fascism in the Europe of the 1930s. Southworth, *op. cit.,* pp. 64–70 corrects this bias. See also Roberto Lanzas (pseudonym of Ramiro Ledesma Ramos), *op. cit.,* written after the split between José Antonio and Ledesma; this was unavailable until its re-edition in 1968.

75. Ernesto Giménez Caballero, *Genio de España* (Madrid: La Gaceta Literaria, 1932, reprinted by FE, 1939).

76. See Juan Beneyto Pérez, *El Nuevo Estado Español: El régimen nacional-sindicalista ante la tradición y los demás sistemas totalitarios,* with a foreword by the Italian minister of justice (Madrid: Biblioteca Nueva, 1939); Luis Legaz y Lacambra, *Introducción a la Teoría del Estado Nacional-Sindicalista* (Barcelona: Bosch, 1940).

   See also the Spanish edition of Mihail Manoilescu, *El partido único: Institución política de los nuevos regímenes.* Intro by Raimundo Fernández Cuesta, trans. Luis Jordana de Pozas (Zaragoza: Heraldo de Aragón, 1938). In the introduction to Manoilescu and in the work of Beneyto we find frequent references to the Turkish Republican Party as the first non-communist single party and its achievements for the nation, but also comments criticizing it for not carrying the idea to its ultimate consequences.

77. Among the leaders, Serrano Súñer, a master politician, wrote a few speeches, and much later his revealing memoirs. Fernández Cuesta limited himself to a few speeches; José Luis de Arrese, professionally an architect, felt more compelled to elaborate the ideas of the Movimiento in works like *La Revolución social del Nacional-Sindicalismo* (1940), *Participación del pueblo en las tareas del Estado* (1944), and *El Estado totalitario en el pensamiento de José Antonio* (1945), a work in which he attempted to disassociate the Movimiento from the fascist influence that had crept in. Some of the ideas that underlie his attempts to reorganize the Movimiento can be found in: *Capitalismo, Comunismo, Cristianismo* (Madrid: Ediciones Radar, 1947), chap. 16. In the same work the reader can find a more complete bibliography. The speeches of his second period as secretary general have been collected in *Hacia una meta institucional* (Madrid: Ediciones del Movimiento, 1957). These works do not commend themselves by their literary brilliance, nor by their originality, nor were they very influential; but they represent a limited and unsuccessful effort to adapt the Movimiento to a changing environment. Recently, the Editora del Movimiento has put out a great number of short books with titles like *Concurrencia de pareceres; Coincidencias y discrepancias en el Movimiento; Configuración Institucional del Movimiento; Evolución política: Democratización y socialización por rutas de unidad,* without authors, which formulate with deliberate vagueness and ambiguity and minimum reference to the past (except to some Franco speeches) the ideas behind the recent effort to institutionalize and revive the party. In the same line we find a collection of speeches of Alejandro Rodríguez de Valcárcel, the present vice secretary of the Movimiento, *El Movimiento y el pueblo español* (Madrid: Ediciones del Movimiento, 1968).

78. Carlos Iglesias Selgas, *La vía española a la democracia* (Madrid: Ediciones del Movimiento, 1968).

79. Emilio Romero, *Cartas a un príncipe* (Madrid: Afrodisio Aguado, S. A., 1964) and *Cartas al pueblo soberano* (Madrid: Afrodisio Aguado, S. A., 1965).

80. The *Instituto de Estudios Políticos* has published the *Revista de Estudios Políticos* since 1942, a number of other academic journals, and a large number of books. Its contribution to the development of the social and political sciences in Spain by publishing both Spanish works and important translations has been notable.

81. *Jerarquía* published, according to Southworth, *op. cit.*, pp. 170–171, four issues between 1936 and 1938.
82. *Escorial* published fifty-four issues between 1940 and 1947. The quotation is from a contemporary prospectus announcing the review. The editors, together with Ridruejo, were Laín Entralgo, future dissident intellectual, a Falangist poet who came from *Cruz y Raya,* a left Catholic magazine, and Antonio Marichalar, who had collaborated in Ortega y Gasset's *Revista de Occidente.*
83. Ridruejo's comments are from his *Escrito en España,* pp. 16–17.
84. On the attitude toward the church see program point 25 of FET y de las JONS, the *Discurso a las Juventudes de España of Ledesma Ramos,* pp. 239–240. FET y de las JONS members of the Cortes often fought some of the most outrageous clerical demands in the field of education. See also Jato, *op. cit.,* for positions taken by the SEU.
85. For an example of the reactionary attack on the intellectuals see Enrique Súñer Ordóñez, *Los intelectuales y la tragedia española* (Burgos, 1937).
86. Ruggero Zangrandi, *op. cit.*
87. In a national quota sample survey of youth between 15 and 21, which excluded only the smallest communities, the respondents were asked for the association memberships of their fathers, specifically in the party and Catholic Action and related organizations. Obviously these data are subject to distortion, owing to the sons' unawareness of their fathers' affiliations. In 1960, a time at which the party had lost its saliency, this may involve an underestimation of party membership, but on the other hand the quota sample executed by members of the youth organization as interviewers probably biased it somewhat toward their inclusion. The sample of 1,318 males included 54 who were sons of members of FET y de las JONS, that is, 4.1 per cent of the households with adolescent children. The comparison between them and the sample as a whole, including them, offers interesting insights into the social composition of the party, particularly when we compare them with the members of Catholic Action, the only other national organization of ideological character. For data on FE membership in 1936 by region see Payne, *op. cit.* pp. 278–279.
88. We have to be careful on this point since our sampling procedure excluded the communities under 3,000 or 2,500, depending on the regions.
89. The data on education shows even more neatly the patterns we discovered studying occupational background. The underrepresentation in the group of those with no primary education is marked, as well as of those with partial or complete secondary education, and even more the middle professionals or incomplete university. The number of those with a scientific university education is relatively low, while those with a humanistic university training—including law—is appreciably higher. In this respect, the party probably differed from the NSDAP, whose appeal was greater in the higher technical schools than in the universities. Despite the "automatic membership" in the party of the army officers and the identification of a significant number of them with it in the course of the Civil War, the number of sons of officers aware of their fathers' party identification is little above the average. Catholic Action is apparently appreciably stronger among the university educated and among the military than the party, while it is lower among those with an academic secondary education and those with only primary school.
90. Payne, *op. cit.,* p. 203.
91. I want to acknowledge the cooperation of the *Sección Femenina* in obtaining these data. The dynamics of recruitment and membership loss of the *Sección Femenina* in the period 1956–1960 are revealing of some of the difficulties encountered by the Movimiento in a period of depolitization and in the absence

of a strong youth organization. The average number joining in all of Spain annually in that period was 3,390, of which 2,033, or 60 per cent, came from the youth organization; 584, or 17 per cent, from a social service period obligatory for all women not working (required mainly of students and those seeking government employment) and only 20, or 0.6 per cent, from the student organization (SEU). Except for 44 (7.3 per cent) who joined directly, the remaining 21 per cent were recruited through various training courses in child care, crafts, folklore, and so forth. In that same period, 1,558 dropped out of the organization. These figures in relation to a total membership of approximately 205,000 clearly show the static character of the organization, which becomes even more notable if we consider the growth of population in the age groups most likely to join and the many socially useful and respected apolitical activities of the organization.

92. The Cortes Españolas have been studied from a legal point of view, with many important documents about their evolution and other factual information reproduced, by the present minister of information and tourism, Manuel Fraga Iribarne, *El reglamento de las Cortes Españolas* (Madrid: Servicio de Información y Publicaciones de la Organización Sindical, 1959). For recent changes in their legal composition, see the *Fundamental Laws, op. cit.,* and "Informe sobre las nuevas Cortes, Análisis jurídico de su composición," in the opposition magazine, *Cuadernos para el diálogo* (Madrid), No. 50 (November 1967), pp. 21–28.

The bibliographical data here presented have been prepared from a variety of sources by DATA S.A., Madrid, a private social research organization. A report by DATA entitled *Quién es quién en las Cortes* has been published by *Cuadernos para el Diálogo* (Madrid, 1969). The author has left a more detailed analysis of this and other elites of the regime for another publication. Some basic biographical data on the mayors of 8,994 municipalities, who (except in the large cities) are generally also the heads of the local party organization, have been analyzed by the author in collaboration with DATA in an unpublished volume, *Estructura y dinámica de los grupos sociales en España,* prepared for the Comisaría del Plan de Desarrollo, Madrid, 1967, on the basis of data generously provided by the ministry of interior.

The data for these international comparisons are from Giovanni Sartori, S. Somogyi, L. Lotti, A. Predieri, *Il Parlamento Italiano, 1946–1963* (Napoli: Edizioni Scientifiche Italiane, 1963); Frederick W. Frey, *The Turkish Political Elite* (Cambridge: The MIT Press, 1965); Darío Cantón, *El Parlamento Argentino en épocas de cambio: 1890, 1916 y 1946* (Buenos Aires: Editorial del Instituto Torcuato Di Tella de Sociología Comparada, 1966); Mattei Dogan, "L'origine sociale du personnel parlementaire français élu en 1951" in Association Française de Science Politique, under the direction of Maurice Duverger, *Partis politiques et classes sociales en France* (Paris: Cahiers de la Fondation Nationale des Sciences Politiques, Armand Colin, 1955).

93. Fraga, *op. cit.,* p. 20.

94. The fact that the party has had to share power with other institutions has not escaped the public. A large national sample survey at the end of 1966 asked the respondents to rate the importance of a number of organizations and groups, from very influential to very uninfluential, in the political life of the country. The answers show the church, the army, and the banks rated above the Falange and the party, and almost equal to the Sindicatos. See Table 5–10 at end of this chapter.

95. The most important step in the limited liberalization process was the Press Law of 1966. On this law and its impact see Guy Hermet, "La presse espagnole

depuis la suppression de la censure," *Revue française de Science Politique,* XVIII, No. 1 (February 1968), 43–67.

96. In this volume.

97. Our perhaps not unbiased, mildly pessimistic view of the future prospects of the Movimiento within the Franco regime obviously is based on certain "futuribles" about Western Europe that correspond to the "surprise free" standard world in Herman Kahn and Anthony J. Wiener, *The Year 2000: A Framework for Speculation on the Next Thirty-Three Years* (New York: Macmillan, 1967). However, in that same volume we find a "twenty-first century nightmare" based on "a new pan-European Movement based on ideas not too far from those of the Movimiento left" (see pp. 339–341). This insightful scenario obviously would make the men of the Movimiento-Organización most happy. A sociologist-political commentator, Amando de Miguel, has seized upon this scenario to analyze what he calls "socialismo nacional" on the Spanish scene within the ranks of the *Movimiento* in two articles in the newspaper *Madrid* (October 17 and 21, 1968).

TABLE 5-7   Party Members (per thousand population) in Spain and Other European countries

Year	Spain FE Total Members	Spain FE Members per 1,000 pop.	Italy PNF Total Members	Italy PNF Members per 1,000 pop.	Germany NSDAP Total Members	Germany NSDAP Members per 1,000 pop.	Germany SS Total Members	Germany SS Members per 1,000 pop.	Hungary Arrow Cross Total Members	Hungary Arrow Cross Members per 1,000 pop.
1919			17,000	0.42						
1920			100,000	2.5						
1922			477,000	11.9						
1925			700,000	17.5	27,117	0.41				
1927			1,000,052	25.6						
1928			1,027,010	25.7	108,717	1.6				
1930			1,040,588	26.8	389,000	5.8				
1931					806,294	12.2				
1932					1,414,975	21.4				
1933			1,415,407	35.4	2,400,000	36.3	52,000	1.3		
1934			1,851,777	46.4						
1935									8,000	0.9
1936	25,000	1.01	2,027,400	50.8						
June	80,000	3.2								
Sept.	590,000	23.9								
1937			2,152,240	53.9					19,000	2.2
1943					6,500,000	99.3				
Total pop. (in millions)	24.6		39.9		66.0		66.0		8.7	
Year	(1936)		(1921)		(1933)		(1933)		(1937)	

TABLE 5-8 *Proportion of Falangists among Office Holders in 1956*

Offices	Total number of Office Holders	Falangists Number	Per Cent
Cabinet members	16	2	12
Under-secretaries	17	1	6
Directors-general	102	8	8
Provincial governors and heads of the party	50	18	36
Mayors of provincial capitals	50	8	16
Presidents of provincial deputations	50	6	12
National Councillors of FET y de las JONS	151	65	43
Procuradores in Cortes	575	137	24
Provincial deputies	738	133	18
Mayors	9,155	776	8
Municipal councilmen	55,960	2,226	4
Total office holders included in sample	66,864	3,380	5.5

Source: José Luis de Arrese, *Hacia una Meta Institucional* (Madrid: Ediciones del Movimiento, n.d., foreword dated 1957), p. 213.

TABLE 5-9 *Presence of NSDAP Members, by Date of Affiliation, in the Government of Germany and Its Municipalities on January 1, 1935*

Offices	Number of Offices	Members of NSDAP	Date of Joining the Party Before September 14, 1930	1930- 1933	After 1933
Heads of state admin- istrative offices	689	62.8%	14.4%	14.4%	34.0%
Municipal offices	51,671	60.7	4.9	15.5	40.3
In cities	2,228	78.2	22.1	25.0	31.1
In non-city municipal- ities (Gemeinden)	49,443	59.9	4.2	15.1	40.6
Total	52,360	60.7	5.1	15.5	40.1

Source: Wolfgang Schäfer, *N.S.D.A.P. Entwicklung und Struktur der Staatspartei des Dritten Reiches* (Hannover: Norddeutsche Verlagsanstalt O. Goedel, Schriftenreihe des Instituts für Wissenschftliche Politik in Marburg, 1957), p. 26.

TABLE 5-10 *Proportion Saying That Different Institutions or Groups Have Much Influence*

Institution or Social Groups	Men	Men and Women[a]	Upper Middle Class Male and Female	Working Class Male and Female
Church	44	38	53	35
Military	42	31	47	28
Banking and finance	35	25	38	23
Falange	31	25	33	22
Sindicatos	30	22	36	19
Businessmen	16	11	14	11
Intellectuals	10	7	17	5
Workers	10	7	14	6
Opus Dei	9	7	18	4
Civil servants	9	6	9	5
Monarchists	4	3	5	2
Carlists	3	2	3	1

[a]Among women, the number of no-answers is large.

6

The One-Party State and Social Mobilization: East Europe between the Wars

|| *Andrew C. Janos*

Introduction

In recent years the party state and various one-party movements have attracted increasing attention among political scientists, replacing such favorites as constitutional government and totalitarianism. The reasons for this concern are obvious. Apart from a number of communist countries on three continents, the majority of African states and a number of other states in the developing areas have turned to this model. At the latest count above one-third of the countries of the world appear to be ruled by more or less effectively established single-party regimes. Statistically, this number is as high or perhaps higher than that of effective two-party or multi-party systems. In other words, the monopolistic party has become a phenomenon of global significance.

Yet, it is not merely the frequency of one-party regimes that has attracted the interest of political scientists, but also the complex reality that is often concealed behind the cloak of monolithic political unity. This reality has sometimes been found puzzling and incomprehensible in terms of classic categories of analysis, including models of totalitarianism. Thus, when the political scientist turns to the single party, he does, above all, search for meaningful concepts and variations around which a body of theory could be built.

The main purpose of this chapter is to join in this search by exploring the past experiences of East Europe with the one-party system. These experiences may be particularly valuable to the political scientist because, in addition to the opportunities for conceptualization and classification, they provide a historical context in which a number of "developing" societies suddenly turned to the organizational model of the monopolistic party. The areawide trend with which we deal here, therefore, may answer some questions concerning the relationship between the one-party state, modernization, and "social mobilization," problems that have specifically engaged the attention of political theory and research. In short, this chapter attempts to answer three general questions: What are the distinctive characteristics of the one-party state—especially in contrast to systems closely resembling it? What major variations can we detect in the overall pattern? How do these variations fit into a general paradigm of modernization?

But while emphasis in this chapter is on generalization, another purpose underlying the selection of the topic has been historical. It reflects the observer's concern with perspective and his conviction that the interpretation of interwar East European politics in the standard literature leaves much to be desired. Although a number of monographic studies have appeared on the subject, few writers have attempted to place the experience in a broader perspective; and those who have were usually too much perturbed by the general decline of political civility in the area to inquire into the deeper meaning of events or to appreciate significant differences in structure and purpose behind the facade of dictatorship that the monopolistic party implies. The fact that many of these systems adopted fascistic labels only further confused the issue, for most observers have been inclined to see them as mere epigones, or parodies of German national socialism or Italian fascism, hardly worthy of independent consideration.

The "Old" Political Order: Political Background to the One-Party State

Despite variations in constitutional form and traditions, the web of relationships and practical arrangements that constituted the *ancien régime* showed considerable similarities throughout the area. With the exception of Czechoslovakia, the political systems were democratic in form but essentially bureaucratic in character. Very early in the process of political development the administrative bureaucracy, or in some cases (such as Yugoslavia and Poland) the military, had emerged as autonomous forces in the political arena. Contrary to popular belief this administrative-military complex, for our purposes "bureaucracy," was not the handmaiden of established social classes or of the national community as a whole, but eventually became an interest group in its own right. Members of the public administration and the military had developed a particular social consciousness. Together with some camp followers, particularly members of professional groups, they became a genuine "political class" or, in Hugh Seton-Watsons' words a "state bourgeoisie" [1] with vested interest in national power and the integrity of state institutions. Although in many instances these groups derived their solidarity and strength from traditional symbols, their political orientation was fundamentally secular, expressed in terms of a liberal anti-clericalism closely intertwined with commitments to modern forms of economic organization and development as the principal sources of national power.

Bureaucratic influence over politics was exercised through parliamentary institutions and resulted mainly from administrative interference with the electoral process. The predominantly rural electorate consisting of agrarian small holders or propertyless elements was highly vulnerable to bureaucratic pressure. Consequently, parliamentary elections were "made" by the prefects or lord lieutenants of the administrative districts, sometimes aided by military units, by means of ballot box stuffing or simple intimidation. In this manner the local administrations, controlled by the minister of the interior in the highly centralized system, would return a large number of deputies friendly to the incumbent government. In exchange, members of the administrative and military establishments were adequately represented in parliament, and the government—though not formally accountable to administrative personnel—could not hope to survive if its policies were grossly injurious to the bureaucratic code of ethics or political expectations. Thus the electoral system provided for a certain reciprocity in politics, not between parliament and the electorate, but between the parliamentary party system and the administrative bureaucracy.

The position of the bureaucracy, while dominant, was not monopolistic. Its sway over elections was never absolute. Besides constituencies subverted by the bureaucracy, there were some rotten boroughs virtually owned by the traditional landowning class or by small cliques of local potentates whose favors or disfavors to the voters could effectively compete with the influence of the bureaucracy. Then, in some instances, the local administration dealt with a tough, independent-minded electorate that refused to succumb to threats and intimidation and, despite administrative pressures, supported their own candidates. As a consequence, the bureaucracy rarely had full political control over the legislature and, in order to rule effectively, it had to enter into political alliances with representatives of diverse economic and corporate interests. Thus, electoral corruption notwithstanding, the political system retained its pluralistic character. The formation of public policy usually entailed bargaining and compromise among major interest groups in the societies, the landowners, banking, industry, the established church, and occasionally the representatives of the urban and rural lower middle classes.

The political instruments of these coalitions were the so-called government parties, the parliamentary caucuses in which the representatives of economic interest groups and the bureaucracy congregated. In some countries these coalitions were relatively stable and so was the institution of the government party. Hungary, for instance, was ruled by the same alliance of bureaucrats, landowners, and financial interests for nearly half a century, even though power relations within the coalition sometimes shifted in the favor of one group or another. During this period the Hungarian parliament was dominated by a single government party under changing labels to indicate certain shifts in "ideology" and public policy. Similarly Serbia, and later Yugoslavia, was ruled by an administrative-military-mercantile coalition represented in the Radical Party, the dominant force in the parliament for nearly three decades. In these countries a one-party regime had been a political reality even before the advent of the modern period, though we should hasten to add that these parties never claimed political monopoly in doctrinal terms; indeed their members would strenuously deny that they occupied a privileged position in the political spectrum. In other countries the ruling alliances were less stable. They broke up frequently and were put together again by coopting new groups and leaving out others. This was particularly evident in Rumania, where in the interwar period parliamentary coalitions lasted only an average of one and a half years. In the decade following World War I, the Rumanian bureaucracy first supported a broadly based national coalition (represented by the People's League), then formed an alliance with urban-industrial interests (in the Liberal Party), and finally turned to an alliance with the representatives of small farmers and medium landowners in the National Peasant Party. In every instance the formation of an alliance implied that a number of machine politicians representing the administrative point of view were incorporated into the team, then the bureaucracy threw its weight behind the party to assure a victory at the polls. As a result of this arrangement the distribution of parliamentary seats was subject to extreme fluctuations.

TABLE 6-1   *Rumanian Elections, 1920-1928 (number of deputies)*

	1920	1922	1926	1927	1928
Liberal Party	17	260	16	298	13
People's League	209	11	292	–	5
National Peasants	44	28	32	49	333
Other parties	99	70	37	40	37
Total	369	369	387	387	388

Apart from the parliamentary party system a degree of integration was maintained among politically relevant groups by common social bonds, fears from the lower classes, and a common allegiance to the person or institution of the head of state. The latter had significant functions in mediating among conflicting groups, averting deadlocks and facilitating the formation of coalitions that eventually would be upheld by bureaucratic rigging in the electoral contest. In Bulgaria, Yugoslavia and Rumania these functions were performed by the traditional institution of the monarchy. Hungary (in the person of Admiral Horthy) and Poland (under Marshal Pilsudski) had quasi-charismatic leaders, military heroes, who were accepted in terms of their personal achievements as authoritative figures by the major groups participating in the political process.

These arrangements had evolved gradually by trial, error, and tacit convention over the half-century period between 1880 and 1930. During these

TABLE 6-2   *The Level of Social Mobilization in East Europe (1930) and in Selected Contemporary Developing Nations (1955)*

	Internal Mail per Capita	Urban[d] Population-5,000	Literacy	Agricultural Population
Austria	59.3%	60.7%	98.0%	27.4%
Czechoslovakia	42.8	47.8	95.3	34.5
Bohemia			97.1	29.7
Slovakia			82.1	60.6
Poland	25.2	27.2	72.9	59.0
Hungary	17.8	36.2	90.4	51.5
Rumania	7.9	20.2	57.0	75.0
Yugoslavia	13.7	22.3	55.0	76.5
Serbia[a]			56.3	80.2
Croatia[b]			68.5	75.3
Bulgaria[c]	6.9	21.4	60.3	80.1
Albania		15.4	30.0	84.0
Cuba		57.0	76.4	42.0
Turkey		25.0	34.3	77.0
Mexico		43.0	56.8	58.0
Egypt		30.0	22.1	64.0
Nigeria		5.0	11.5	74.0

[a]Includes the following Banovinas: Drava, Drina, Morava, Zeta.

[b]The Banovina of Sava.

[c]Relates to 1920.

[d]For the contemporary examples, settlements over 1,000.

Sources: Albania: *Anuari Statistikor* (Tiranë: Republikës Popullore Le Shqipërisë, 1960), p. 53. Austria: *Statistisches Handbuch für die Republik Österreich* (Wien: Bundesamt für Statistik, 1931), p. 127. Bulgaria: *Annuaire Statistique de Royaume de Bulgaire* (Sofia: Imprimerie de l'État, 1935), p. 23. Czechoslovakia: *Annuaire Statistique de la Republique Tchéchoslovaque* (Prague: Orbis, 1932), p. 171 and *Annuaire Statistique* (Prague: Office de la Statistique, 1938), p. 10. Hungary: *Annuaire Statistique Hongrois* (Budapest: Office Central Royal de Statistique, 1932), p. 192; *Statistical Pocket Book of Hungary* (Budapest: Central Statistical Office, 1958), p. 15. Poland: *Annuaire Statistique de la Republique Polonaise* (Warsaw: Imprimerie de l'État, 1930), p. 144; *Concise Statistical Year Book of Poland* (Warsaw: Statistical Office, 1938), p. 28. Rumania: *Anural Statistic al Romaniei* (Bucharest: Directiunea Generala a Statisticei, 1939), pp. 542-543; *Rumanian Statistical Pocket Book* (Bucharest: General Statistical Office, 1960), p. 27. Yugoslavia: *Statisticki Godisnjak 1930* (Belgrad: Drzavna Stampanija, 1933), p. 203; Jozo Tomasevich, *Peasants, Politics and Economic Change in Yugoslavia* (Stanford: Stanford University Press, 1955), p. 304. For the entire area: Dudley Kirk, *Europe's Population in the Interwar Years* (Princeton: League of Nations, 1946), pp. 14, 243, 263; *Progress of Literacy in Various Countries*, (Paris: UNESCO, 1953), pp. 45, 105, 172. For non-European Countries: Karl W. Deutsch, "Social Mobilization and Political Development," *The American Political Science Review*, LV (September 1961), 493-514.

years the system provided a measure of stability, efficiency, and cohesion, at least by the standards of emerging nationhood, a designation applicable to all the countries of East Europe in the period. The evolution of these arrangements was undaunted by impressive constitutional reforms and the introduction of universal suffrage at the end of World War I. The latter event only increased the scope of bureaucratic interference in politics and not genuine popular participation. Its main effect was to increase bureaucratic influence by eliminating from politics local notables whose power had rested on personal ties with a narrow electorate.

Yet hardly had the system reached a degree of maturity in the years following World War I when some of its weaknesses became all too evident in the face of changes that had meanwhile taken place in the underlying societies. During the first decades of the twentieth century the urban population gradually increased and at the same time modern economy and mentality

TABLE 6-3   *The Rate of Social Mobilization in East Europe (1900-1930)*

	1900	1910	1920	1930
Literacy (%)				
Albania				30.0
Bulgaria	29.6	42.2	53.3	78.4
Czechoslovakia			92.6	95.3
Hungary	61.4	68.7	84.8	90.4
Poland			66.9	72.9
Rumania		40.0		57.0
Yugoslavia		43.5	49.5	55.0
Letters mailed (1,000's)				
Bulgaria		26.4	44.4	41.5
Czechoslovakia[a]			630.4	902.9
Hungary			117.0	146.1
Poland			274.6	681.2
Rumania		46.1	45.0	139.8
Yugoslavia			105.7	187.1

[a]Includes all items.

Sources: In addition to Table 6-2 sources see: *Die Ergebnisse der Volkszählung vom 31 Dez. 1910* (Wien: Büro der k.k. Statistischen Zentralkommission, 1914) I, 70-71; *Annuaire Statistique Hongrois* (Budapest: Office Central Royal de Statistique, 1927), p. 169; *Konacni Rezultati popisa stanovistva od 15 Marta 1948 godine* (Belgrade: Direkcija Statistike, 1955), V, 17.

made certain inroads into traditional rural society. For reasons of efficiency as well as national prestige the governments sponsored ambitious educational policies. As a result of these policies, literacy and the level of social communications rapidly increased (see Tables 6-2 and 6-3). The experience of World War I further contributed to the dissolution of traditional values and perspectives in the countryside. As one Hungarian sociologist of the 1930s observed: "It extended the horizons of the village from Siberia to the Pyrenees . . . when they returned they were all changed. . . . Ever since the war France, the Italian people, the Russian winters have become regular conversational topics." [2] The overall effect of these changes was that a substantial segment of the population, both urban and rural, entered the political arena not in the sense of being incorporated in the traditional order, but in becoming available for organization and mass political participation.

From the point of view of the elites, the impact of modernization was aggravated by the apparent failure of economic growth. Following World War I the governments of East Europe initiated ambitious policies of development to create self-sufficient economies and to alleviate population pressures, but the programs were troubled by the shortage of foreign credit and by the difficulties of extracting capital from the impoverished agriculture. Tariffs, taxation, and subsidies proved inadequate in raising the level of investment. Politically, development was impeded by excessive demands made upon scant resources and by the political routine of "paying off" powerful autonomous interests. State intervention notwithstanding, the economies stagnated. In the years between 1924 and 1929, two countries, Rumania and Hungary, experienced brief, spurtlike economic expansion but even in these countries the gains of industrialization were offset by decline in other sectors of the economy. In 1929 as well as 1938, per capita national income in East Europe was at about the same level as in 1913. In two countries, Hungary and Yugoslavia, per capita income actually declined by 17.2 per cent and 20.0 per cent, respectively.[3]

Thus while political awareness increased, the stability of social relations and the level of economic satisfaction declined. Large numbers of people had not only become detached from their traditional way of life, but also could find no real stakes or personal involvement in their new environment. Sociological studies of the period, such as the ones conducted by the Rumanian Professor Gusti or the Hungarian "village explorers," show widespread symptoms of peasant anomie and alienation foreshadowing the rise of mass movements in the East European countryside.[4] Even before, of course, the peasant had rebelled. But the movements of the nineteenth century, or the great rural revolt of 1907 in Rumania, had still been in the nature of medieval jacqueries. They represented the instinctive reactions of an angered, primitive rural mass to deprivations, and were merely aimed at redressing an imaginary balance of their own world and not at reforming society and their own affairs as a matter of political right. This state of affairs now changed, and the best evidence for the changes could be found in the sudden mushrooming of peasant parties and organizations in the early post-war years.

Further social tensions emanated from the problem quite common in backward and developing societies. As a matter of national prestige, institutes of higher learning had grown rapidly throughout the area. At the turn of the century each country could boast of numerous universities and an even larger number of gymnasia and lycées to provide classical and humanistic education. The overall number of students enrolled in the universities was staggering, in comparison both to the pre-war period and to some of the industrially highly developed societies in the post-war world (Table 6–4), and in any case exceeded the absorptive capacity of the backward economies. The students and graduates of the law schools represented the main problem, for the large majority of these expected to find employment in the state administration. In search of solutions, the governments of the day extended the capacity of the bureaucracies to a near breaking point. In Hungary, the combined salaries of military and civilian employees of the state made up 52.7 per cent of the annual budget; in Bulgaria, 39.9 per cent.[5] Notwithstanding these efforts, a large number of university graduates

TABLE 6-4   *The Number of University Students in Selected East and West European Countries, 1913-1914 and 1927-1928*

	University Enrollment	Enrollment in Law	Law Students Percentage of Total
Bulgaria			
1913-1914	2,455	1,349	51
1919-1920	8,677	6,877	78
Hungary[a]			
1913-1914	11,893	5,354	45
1927-1928	12,788	4,893	37
Poland			
1913-1914	13,737	5,942	43
1927-1928	36,364	10,872	27
Rumania[a]			
1913-1914	5,925	3,111	51
1927-1928	29,930	11,438	38
Belgium			
1913-1914	7,907	1,047	14
1927-1928	8,450	1,088	12
Sweden			
1911-1912	6,001	1,118	18
1926-1927	8,856	1,578	16
Switzerland			
1913-1914	11,756	n.d.	
1927-1928	8,765	2,369	28

[a]One should note that between the two dates Hungary's population was halved while Rumania's doubled as a result of territorial changes.

Source: Office Central de Statistique, ed., *Mouvement de la population des universités dans quelques états européns, Statistique des Etudiants de Universités en 1930* (Budapest, 1932), pp. 13-17.

failed to find employment. The universities became the hotbeds of social unrest, and the unemployed intelligentsia naturally tended toward the political arena. There were bizarre symptoms of this illness, like the elections of 1927 in Bulgaria, when 30,000 candidates contested 276 seats in the legislative *Sobranie*.[6] The majority, even in Bulgaria, would turn out to be embittered losers whose political skills would eventually be employed to overturn the prevailing political order.

These latent weaknesses of the systems were suddenly laid bare by the

Great Depression of 1929–1934. For the East Europeans, the crisis meant the collapse of the international grain market, and the sudden cancellation of short-term loans on which their economies had much depended for investment. These two developments made a shambles of the economic concepts of the previous decades. There was massive unemployment in the factories, creeping starvation in the countryside, violent agitation in and around the universities. The traditional social coalition of the ruling classes seemed to be impotent in the face of these developments. They were in turn abused far and wide for stifling progress, for exploiting the lower classes, and for preventing the mobility of the younger generation. It was under these circumstances that a new set of political leaders emerged from within the establishment and made an attempt to restructure the economic, social, and political systems. The pivots of these experiments were to be the civilian and military bureaucracies.

The Bureaucratic Experiment with the Party-State

Before we go any further we will have to make a few remarks concerning the pattern of bureaucratic participation in politics. Though, so far, we have referred to the bureaucracy as a "group," it should be clear that the structure and participation of bureaucratic organizations in politics is different from patterns that one habitually associates with economic interest groups such as landowners or the commercial and industrial bourgeoisie. In contrast to the latter, the bureaucracy is not an aggregate of individuals dealing with one another on an equal footing, but a hierarchy of roles in which the lower echelons are formally responsible to the higher. The will of the military, or of the civilian administration, is therefore not an aggregate of opinions arrived at by free discussion: it is rather a vague consensus, a feeling or "sense" that sometimes develops in the most haphazard manner, without ever being clearly articulated. Bureaucratic interest is defined by a leadership that will frequently be sensitive to the feelings of the rank and file without ever becoming formally accountable to it. On the other hand, one should also point out that hierarchical structure and the lack of accountability do not make the bureaucracies monolithic in terms of perspectives and political interests. At particular times, especially in times of crisis, several factions may emerge and compete for the allegiance of the total organization, reflecting a changing consensus or the diversity of political views among the lower ranks.

In the classic East European pattern, bureaucratic interests were not invariably articulated by administrative or military personnel. Frequently, the bureaucratic point of view was put forward in parliament by professional politicians recruited from the legal profession or from the declining gentry. These politicians used the bureaucracy as a base of operations and in return they catered to the special interests, as well as to the broader national and economic perspectives of soldiers and administrators. Prime ministers like the Bratianus, Pasić, Stambulov, or Bethlen, to name politicians in different countries and periods, were essentially political brokers, intermediaries among landed, mercantile and bureaucratic interests, symbolizing the standing of the bureaucracy in a pluralistic political order. The first casualties of the crisis were these old-style politicians. After 1930 they were gradually replaced by a new type of leader, either a professional soldier or a public administrator (frequently an economic or fiscal expert) representing a new concept of politics and a rapidly changing mood within the military and administrative bureaucracy. This concept and mood pointed toward the attainment of old socioeconomic objectives by new, more efficient political means and may be summarized in four closely related points: (1) economic development and social reform by the all-out mobilization of resources; (2) the political monopoly of the bureaucracy through the abolition of cumbersome parliamentary institutions; (3) the reduction of the economic influence and eventual expropriation of the landed and financial oligarchies; and finally, (4) the mobilization of certain sectors of the lower and lower middle classes by means of mass organization to replace the old, established social classes in the political equation.

This bureaucratic concept of development *cum* political mobilization emerges from the writings of Mihail Manoilescu, an interpreter of contemporary economic and political trends and an advocate of radical reforms for underdeveloped countries, like his native Rumania. An engineer by training, and economist by interest, Manoilescu had won some international reputation as an author, and was one of the rather typical "new men" in East European politics—first, in the capacity of Minister of Commerce and Industry, later, as the Foreign Minister of his country.

The starting point of Manoilescu's theories was economic development, which he equated with industrialization. The peasant farm and traditional estate were antiquated economic structures, unable to provide conditions for national independence and stable social relations. "An agricultural country," he announced in one of his most celebrated essays, "cannot raise itself by increasing slowly and uniformly the income of all its agricultural producers. . . . All the work of progress begins through a center or nucleus of progress and these nuclei are formed by the industries which represent superior productivity." [7] In a country like Rumania, this could be achieved only by the rationalization of production, allocation, and investment. As Henry Roberts observes, Manoilescu saw society, above all, "as a planned work of engineering." [8] "Tomorrow," Manoilescu predicted confidently, "the principles of scientific organization will dominate the whole society and will be applied to the entire system of national production as to a single enterprise." [9] Reorganization, therefore, cannot be restricted to economics but must embrace the entire social and political life of the nation. "In order to exist as a civilized [e.g., developed] state, Rumania must have a political and social form that realizes her energies to the maximum." [10] The specific forms that Manoilescu envisaged were the corporatist society and the one-party state.

Manoilescu's work on the single party followed from a managerial-bureaucratic concern with capacity and efficiency. He saw the single party principally as an instrument of rationalizing the state and the political process. The peoples of the world, Manoilescu stated, were generally tired of inefficiency and the waste of energy that results from poor organization and the futile conflicts of competing political factions.[11] "For this reason, the idea of rationalization makes more and more headway in the soul of the people, and it becomes even a kind of myth. The fact that the term 'rationalization' is not invariably popular, does not change the validity of this proposition." [12] The single party, Manoilescu continued, fulfilled this expectation of rationalism more than any other political institution. The structure of the party was a guarantee of order, its political monopoly assured the stability and continuity of rule, and the idealism of its members secured the political purity of the regime. "It is therefore not surprising at all that the party quickly wins over the population." [13] It is also in this manner that the party acquires the ability to select the best element of the population for membership and can carry out its functions, which Manoilescu listed as the "preparation of public opinion, the political integration of the nation, the defense of the regime, the control over public administration and the development of a new institutional order." [14]

These theories were echoed, or sometimes independently arrived at, by a number of East European statesmen who shared Manoilescu's background and managerial perspective. One of them was Milan Stoyadinović, premier of Yugoslavia between 1935 and 1938. As a young man Stoyadinović studied budgetary theory at the University of Munich, and after graduation he spent two years as an intern in the French Ministry of Finance and the Office of Public Accounts. His experiences there made him a lifetime admirer of French bureaucracy. What impressed him most was that France could exist as a stable and powerful state despite recurrent political crises, a circumstance that Stoyadinović could ascribe to administrative skill and the *de facto* independence of the bureaucracy from cumbersome parliamentary tutelage.[15] These experiences served him well, for at a very young age he became Yugoslavia's Director of the Budget and subsequently Minister of Finance, winning himself a name by the persistent advocacy of fiscal reforms, etatist measures to foster economic development, and programs of expanding the transportation system. Yet his experiences in managing Yugoslavia's finances also convinced him that economic improvement under the Yugoslav conditions was impossible without fundamental changes in the political system. Thus, upon becoming premier, he set out to create a political adjunct to the bureaucracy by following some of Mussolini's organizational precepts. In 1935 he founded the Yugoslav National Community, the first government party in Yugoslav history to be based on mass membership. The organization of the party was to reach down to the village level with intermediary structures in each *banovina* and a National Council at the apex. A hard core of party workers was to wear green-shirt uniforms to serve as the vanguard under the national leader (*Vodya*), a position to be filled by Stoyadinović himself.[16]

In Hungary, similar principles were espoused by the governments of Julius Gömbös and Béla Imrédy. The former was a staff officer of humble social background who, after World War I, made a name for himself by espousing various anti-Hapsburg, anti-aristocratic and anti-Semitic causes. In 1927 he became Under-Secretary of Defense, and the leader of a reformist, authoritarian faction within the establishment. His principal model in these years was Mussolini, whose experiences appeared to demonstrate him the superior efficiency of autocratic government.

Appointed at the height of the depression, Gömbös' first act as premier was to create an informal cabinet of "whiz-kids" (*Sofortfiuk*) to conduct economic policy free from parliamentary supervision, and he staffed it with a number of young economic and technical experts. He then stuffed the government party and the ministries with younger military officers, and eventually, succeeded in purging conservative old-timers from the army general staff. Meanwhile he decided to create a mass base for the regime. While previously the government party had been a mere parliamentary caucus, Gömbös transformed it into a grass roots organization. He established the posts of Party President, Propaganda Chief, and General Secretary. The job of the first was to enforce party discipline. The propaganda department had the obvious function of mobilizing public opinion behind the party. The General Secretary was entrusted with extending the party organization to each of Hungary's 4,000 villages. As in the Yugoslav case, the party was "most completely identified with administration. The Föispán (Lord Lieutenant) of each country became ex officio president of the party's county branch. State officials in rural areas were practically compelled to join the party and become executive officers in it. Village notaries and their superiors, the district magistrates, had to keep card indexes of local party members." [17] Around this cadre was to be built the local membership of "advance guards" (*élharcosok*), whose number under Gömbös allegedly reached 60,000,[18] most of them recruited from the *gutgesinnt* element of the rural smallholding class, and the urban *petite bourgeoisie*. Once this was accomplished, Gömbös stepped forward with his political platform and began to extoll publicly the advantages of the corporatist, single-party state. On June 21, 1935, he expounded his theories, of all the places, in the House of Magnates, where his toughest opponents were to be found. At about the same time, he reputedly predicted to Göring that he would transform Hungary's political structure within two years.[19] But before he could make good on his words, or even before a serious showdown could have taken place, Gömbös became mortally ill and died in 1936.

After a brief power struggle between conservatives and "young Turks" (the self-adopted label of the reformist camp) Gömbös policies were carried forward by Béla Imrédy. A former president of the Hungarian National Bank and a financial expert like Stoyadinović and Manoilescu, Imrédy was selected for the premiership as a moderate, but in September, 1938 he surprised the public by announcing a sweeping program including provisions for the conscription of labor, a near punitive property tax, and an extensive land reform as part of a four-year plan of economic development. Prominently, the program featured anti-Semitic measures, provisions to requisition Jewish property and to restrict the proportion of Jews to 12 per cent in any single enterprise. Economically this law was to serve as an instrument of capital accumulation for economic development. Politically, it was to destroy the power of the "finance oligarchy" and, at the same time, to open up the "pork barrel" to the famishing university graduates who by then had become a major political headache for the governments. Finally, the legislation was to provide the bureaucracy with mass appeal in the absence of genuine ideology. All this was the result of the cold calculation of ends and means. In Imrédy's speeches and writings one would vainly search for the rabid anti-Semitism of a Rosenberg or Streicher. He and most of his entourage were not emotional Jew-baiters for whom anti-Semitism produced some deep, inner satisfaction. Imrédy's anti-Semitism may be described as "managerial," representing an instrumental value in the pursuit of some concrete ends related to national power and modernization.

In two countries, Rumania and Poland, these political principles were, if only briefly, translated into reality. In the former, King Carol II dissolved a hopelessly deadlocked National Assembly and established a regime of the Front of National Rebirth. The organization of the Front followed German and Italian examples, complete with uniforms, membership cards—both innovations in Rumanian politics—and subsidiary organizations for labor, youth, and women. The new party was based on the bureaucracy. Initially, all administrative officials were compelled to enter the Front, and the prefects became the leaders of local organizations.[20] Parliament was to be replaced by a corporate chamber under the guidance of the Front, though this arrangement was discarded in June, 1940 when Rumania, at least in name, became a totalitarian state. With a keen political sense, the king discarded his traditional claims for legitimacy and declared himself as the leader of the Front and of the nation. In this capacity he laid claim to all authority to appoint and dismiss ministers, and to amend the national constitution. The establishment of the one-party regime also portended a new economic policy with emphasis on industrialization. State participation in investment increased, and in 1939, a five-year economic plan was announced. "Thus," as Roberts notes, "the 'royal dictatorship' was not a relapse into old practices or traditionalism but an ultimately luckless attempt to set up a new type of authoritarian regime that showed the political implications of forced industrialization in an agrarian society with great social and economic inequalities. . . . The advent of Carol's dictatorship is intimately bound to the agrarian problem, which in its broadest sense is the reverse side of the question of industrialization." [21]

The Polish experiment of 1936–1939 followed along the same lines, except for the obvious absence of a traditional-ruler-turned-leader and for the greater and more direct participation of the military. In fact, the Camp of National Unity (OZON) was set up by a number of ranking military officers to fill the political vacuum created by the death of Marshal Pilsudski. These officers realized that, in order to survive, their military regime would have to attract a mass following and incorporate it into the political system by organizational means.

The formation of the OZON represented a return to the concept of the party state which the Polish military had rejected when, in 1926, it had opted for the abolition of all political parties. However, the new party state, as its Minister of Propaganda explained, "was not democratic but authoritarian, perhaps totalitarian," though these terms might be construed to mean "conducted democracy." [22] In the new state there would be three political factors: the party, the government, and a "supergovernmental" factor, a national leadership gathered in a Grand Council. In this trio of institutions, it would fall to the party to "consolidate the country and give it a single, organized will." [23] Eventually, Poland would need the equivalent of a Führer or Duce, though how he might emerge remained unexplained. The whole experiment represented an attempt to substitute "organization from above instead of revolution from below" and to attain the triple objective of "military power, economic stability and national solidarity." [24]

As in Rumania, this triple objective served as the "ideology" of the regime, and the logic of military and social needs converged in a policy of industrialization. On the one hand, we have the words of Marshal Smigli-Ridz to the effect that economic policy would have to be fully adjusted to the requirements of national defense; on the other hand, we have the reassurances of Colonel Koc and Finance Minister Kwiatkowski that this course would be socially beneficial, for only large-scale industrialization could end the misery of the peasantry.[25] Thus, beginning in 1938, the OZON government drew up a fifteen-year plan of industrialization, and a special four-year plan for the development of the Sandomierz region in central Poland. In the words of an enthusiastic Polish economist, the purpose of this plan was to develop the country as a whole, to provide it with armament industries located in the geographical center of the country, to provide a larger market for agricultural products, and to find employment for the surplus labor force in the overpopulated eastern provinces.[26]

In the light of this economic program and the accompanying political pronouncements, Poland presents the picture of a dynamic political system moving in the direction of totalitarianism. Yet, underneath this facade of dynamism and unity, there was a reality of political impotence due to the failure of the "colonels" to harness a genuine mass following to their organization. The structure of the single party existed only in form and not in substance. The proclamation of the OZON regime was followed by the creation of an extensive network of 5,000 local cells. But four months after their establishment the membership of the cells consisted merely of administrative personnel, military officers, policemen, and other public employees, including the members of local fire brigades. Apart from this cadre, the OZON handled only 10,000 applications, or two for each local organization, during the first year of its existence.[27] The Polish military leaders had a perfect concept of the relationship between social ends and political means, but the concept itself turned out to be valueless in the absence of genuine sources of mass appeal. For the same reason, they were unable to liquidate powerful vested interests. Their regime was subject to attacks not only from the left, anguished over dictatorship, but also from the right, from the landed and banking circles that had opposed reform policies and the etatist concept of industrialization.

In a seeming paradox, these managerial experiments with mass politics were enveloped in conspiracy and intrigue and were eventually foiled by petty *coups d'état*. Stoyadinović was dismissed by a prince regent jealous of his wife's alleged affection for the *Vodya*.[28] The Rumanian Camp of National Rebirth collapsed when the king departed from the scene. The Polish OZON faded away amidst personal feuds and bickering. Most sensationally, Imrédy was removed by a backroom conspiracy of arch-conservative aristocrats and finance oligarchs who had followed up a secret hint concerning a Jewish ancestor on his family tree.

The fall of these leaders, of course, cannot be merely written off as the result of the cunning plot of a handful of reactionary elder statesmen. These events must be placed within the broader perspective of the fiasco of the bureaucratic concept of mobilization in Hungary as well as in the other countries of East Europe. The civilian and military bureaucracies had shown considerable understanding of the principles of mass politics. They saw the need for a leader, ideology, and organization, and did not lack originality in adapting these principles to local conditions. They failed nonetheless, and the causes of their failure are easy to locate in their lack of appeal to the potentially revolutionary masses. Both civilian and military bureaucracies were tarred with the conservative brush. They were associated with the "old" order in the public mind, and were weighted down by thousands of social ties and personal commitments. They were, in the caustic words of a right-wing critic of the Imrédysts: "the Party of the Right Honourables, the Stellenbosched Ministers, the old school ties, and place hunters," [29] whose revolutionary sincerity was hard to believe. Though the charts and schemes of organization were perfect, the organization itself repelled prospective members. Who would want to join a revolutionary movement whose storm troopers were prefects, county magistrates, and lord lieutenants? For this reason, the parties remained heads without bodies, and elites without the mass base the bureaucracy would have needed to dislocate the political representatives of vested interests. Clearly, the bureaucracies were locked in a vicious circle. In order to break the power of powerful established groups they needed a popular following. But in order to accomplish that they would first have had to destroy well-entrenched interests.

But even more important is perhaps to consider some of the fundamental contradictions inherent in the managerial concept of political mobilization. The *raison d'être* of the experiments was economic stability and development. Yet to accomplish a genuine political breakthrough they would have had to sacrifice some of their original objectives around which the party was to be built. The bureaucracies of East Europe were not only the captives of circumstance but also the captives of their pragmatism and short-range perspective, which followed from the very social role that gave them identity and solidarity. Thus Gömbös or Kwiatkowski's hesitation to follow up radical oratory by the expropriation of landowners and finance capital was not sheer opportunism but concern with short-range consequences as well, such as the decline of agricultural production or the disorganization of the industrial economy.

Another contradiction in the concept existed between bureaucratic identity and the requirements of successful political organization. In its perfect form the managerial ideal calls for detachment, impersonality, and achievement, while a potential mass following often yearns for political community, more willing to accept metaphysics than concrete, empirical solutions. The dilemma was as valid thirty years ago as it is today, raising some general questions concerning managerial capabilities to cope with the problems of political organization and the possibility for a successful synthesis between bureaucratic and mass politics.

The Revolutionary Experiments

The political failure of bureaucracy may be contrasted with the relative success of revolutionary movements that challenged, and in some cases overthrew, the bureaucratic establishment. In the twenty-five years between the two world wars, each of the societies of East Europe witnessed the rise of significant mass movements under Marxist, fascist, and peasantist labels. These movements not only attracted spontaneous and genuine support on the part of significant segments of the population, but in six instances they also established themselves for shorter or longer periods of time. In each case their main political instrument was the monopolistic party organization (see Table 6–5).

These movements were led by groups of people whose social profiles combined marginality and alienation with a high degree of political proficiency. These people, often referred to as the intelligentsia, had been exposed to modern education and through it acquired skills to create and manipulate symbols or, at the crudest level, the ability to communicate with a

TABLE 6-5 *Revolutionary One-Party Regimes in East Europe*

Country	Years in Power	Party	Leader	Highest Vote	Membership	Hard-core
Hungary	1919	Socialist – Communist Workers Party	Bela Kun	–	500,000	
Bulgaria	1919-1923	Peasant Union	Stambulisky	569,000 (53%)	132,000	Orange Guard
Slovakia	1938-1945	National Union	Tiso – Tuka – Mach	520,000 (32%)	60,000	Hlinka Guard
Rumania	1940-1941	Legion of Archangel Michael	Codreanu	438,000 (16%)		Iron Guard
Croatia	1941-1943	Ustasha	Pavelic	–		
Hungary	1944-1945	Arrow Cross	Szalasi	750,000 (26%)	100,000	

frustrated mass population. Education, of course, need not be formal or complete to provide these skills, nor does formal education alone destine an individual to become a radical. The leaders of the revolutionary movements were often the casualties of modernization, people suffering from the trauma of social mobility and rootlessness. There were many among them whose path to politics led through personal failure, downright deviation, or delinquency. But there were also those who started out as models of industry and the paragons of puritanic virtue, people who had emerged from a nameless mass at great effort, only to find the avenues of economic advancement closed by backwardness or to be rejected socially by a narrow-minded, conservative establishment.

Though detailed studies on the revolutionary elites of East Europe are still lacking, most observers agree on the theme of mobility from rather humble social origins. In Rumania, Weber writes, most of the Legionaries came "from the lower middle-class, the sons of wealthier peasants, of priests, of teachers." [30] In Hungary, Deák states, the Arrow Cross men came from rather similar social environments.[31] A further analysis of the social background of seventy-five Hungarian fascist leaders—the candidates of various national socialist groups in the elections of 1939—will show that only nine of them (12 per cent) were members of the aristocracy or the gentry, while in the government party the average representation of these status groups was 38.5 per cent.[32] The "outgroup" character of the Arrow Cross elite is further evidenced by a comparison of their occupational background with those of the candidates of the incumbent (Hungarian Life) party:

TABLE 6-6   *Occupational Background of Arrow Cross and Hungarian Life Elites*

	Land-owner	Peasant	Ex-bureaucrat	Officer	Professional	Business	Other
Arrow Cross	12%	16%	4%	12%	32%	16%	8%
Incumbents	22.3%	—	51.6%		20.3%	5.8%	—

Sources: Based on the *Országgyülési Almanach (Parliamentary Almanac)* between 1922-1939. The names and backgrounds of the candidates for the 1939 election appear in the paper *Népszava,* May 31, 1939.

In several of the revolutionary movements social marginality combined with ethnic marginality. The fact that the supreme leaders of these movements fall into this category almost without exception cannot be dismissed as sheer coincidence. Codreanu's ancestry was Ukrainian and German (his family name having been Zelenski), while Szálasi was born Salosjan from Armenian and German stock. Tiso and Tuka, the leaders of the Slovak National Union, were Magyarone Slovaks: Tiso the erstwhile editor of the Hungarian *Nyitrai Szemle* in World War I, Tuka a professor of law at a Hungarian university who, as his opponents charged, learned to speak

Slovak only at the age of 40.[33] Among the cadres of the Iron Guard, Macedonian Vlachs were said to be especially prominent, while the Hungarian Arrow Cross leadership was overwhelmingly recruited from ethnically marginal elements. The list of 75 parliamentary candidates quoted earlier includes 6 ethnic Germans (Swabians), 21 Hungarians of German parentage, 12 individuals whose names indicate Slovak or Rumanian origin, 6 whose ethnic origin could not be established, and only 33 who were Hungarian by ancestry. In this respect there is a striking similarity between the composition of the parties of the extreme right and left. A comparison of Hungarian communist people's commissars (1919) and fascist leaders (1939) will reveal that both groups were generally recruited from a lower-middle class background, had no connection with traditional status groups, and were ethnically marginal, with the only difference being that in the one case the semi-assimilated element was of German, in the other, of Jewish background.[34]

For these people, torn out of their traditional social surroundings, or insecure about their ethnicity in an intensely nationalistic environment, politics was not an art of the possible, but a matter of personal identity. In the inner world of the Legionary or Arrow Cross man, the pursuit of the chiliastic goal assumed a quasi-religious quality often presented as an alternative of life or death. If the bureaucrat had regarded the party as an instrument of administrative efficiency, the revolutionary looked upon it as the *sine qua non* of national survival. To understand this distinction one must only compare Codreanu's professed motivations with Manoilescu's analysis of the single-party regime, his frenzied desire to "save Rumanians from extinction," his "revulsion and sorrow" felt at the sight of aliens, his "love of the soil" and the binding force of obligation to the dead heroes of national history.[35] The issues of honor and identity were nowhere as clear as in the policies toward the Jews. Whereas the bureaucratic regimes treated the "Jewish question" with cynical detachment as an economic imperative, the revolutionaries introduced into East European politics an uncompromising racial bent. Manoilescu and his companions may have regarded anti-Semitism as an instrument of economic policy, but the Iron Guardists would sing:

Either we drive the Jews away in battle
or else we want to die the hero's death.[36]

The bureaucracies had a vested interest in national power, which in turn defined their objectives as economic development and social transformation. Their view of politics may be described as pragmatic. They searched for instruments to accomplish their objectives and, since "ideology"—a set of moral and metaphysical precepts to justify the choice of means—seemed to be one of the instruments, they consciously concocted or adopted one on an *ex post facto* basis. Typically, as East European intellectuals still remember, they would turn to sympathizers in the academic community with the request to create a doctrine appropriate for their regime. Or else they would simply borrow a few leaves from the German or Italian book. This "ideology," whatever its credibility was for the masses, had a purely ritual function for the elite, and had no effect on its solidarity or identity. Indeed, such solidarities were provided by the organizational context and by the already existing *esprit de corps* of the bureaucracies, whether civilian or military. In contrast, the revolutionary movements were ideological. This is to say, their *esprit de corps* and identity derived not from an established role or social status, but of a chiliastic view of collective destiny and the historical process: a consummatory vision of a perfect society and salvation after apocalyptic struggles. What for the Marxist was the vision of the classless society was for the fascist a society of tribal virtue and racial purity, and for the peasants the fantasies of a bucolic agrarian Arcadia. Central to this imagery was the existence of a demonic enemy: the Jew for the fascist, capitalism for the Marxist, and the urban civilization for the peasant radical. In the ideology of the latter, the city acquired the qualities of the biblical Sodom, and the venom with which it was attacked rivaled Hitler's or Codreanu's anti-Semitic diatribes. Fifteen years before Nuremberg the Bulgarian Peasant Congress urged the physical separation of urban and rural denizens and demanded the imposition of criminal penalties to prevent intermarriage and cohabitation among them.[37] The chief culprit was the commercial class, which Stambulisky once termed as a "band of parasites, lice and bugs . . . to be exterminated . . . so that the peasantry may live,"[38] while the industrial workers were to be rehabilitated and retrieved for the peasant way of life. Whether left or right in conventional terms, these chiliastic fantasies transcended the narrow territorial and ethnic boundaries of the nation. Such peasant leaders as Stambulisky or Ante Radić (the head of the Croatian Peasant Party) ardently believed in uniting the peasants of the world (or at least of East Europe) in a Green International, just as the Marxists wanted to unite all proletarians in a socialist commonwealth. As to the fascists, the nation represented not an end but a means to promote the advent of a broader supranational community, whether the *völkisch* "New Order" in Europe, or the Carpathian-Danubian Great Fatherland of Ferenc Szálasi's dreams.[39]

It is imperative to note, however, that this chiliastic eschatology was closely interwoven with modern concepts of political organization. While the medieval millenarian had expected collective salvation by divine intervention, their most recent counterparts were determined to attain it by sustained political activity by "storming" obstacles, and by defeating the demonic enemy in battle. The Arrow Cross and the Iron Guard were characterized by a single-minded determination to create a new society of utopian qualities and to use empirical means for the attainment of the metaphysical end. The main expression of this determination was the party, or movement representing a synthesis between the principles of a "spiritual community" and modern organization. The bridge between these two antithetical elements was the ideology, the "soul" of the movement that gave the select superior solidarity in terms of the common goal to be achieved.

This ideology was a great source of strength in the formative stages of the movements. Its chiliastic promise harnessed the faithful to the smaller political community and enabled the leadership to apply the "mass line" effectively. It also gave the revolutionaries a zeal and a brutal sincerity that appealed to the broader strata of the population who were tired of social inequities and piecemeal, practical solutions. The bureaucratic parties could not match this in their efforts to mobilize the masses. However, once the revolutionaries established themselves in power, the same ideology became a source of strain. While it had given the movements maximum flexibility vis-à-vis their opponents, it also limited their capacity to solve economic and administrative problems. In the case of Marxism the tension between ideology and power—or on a different level between solidarity and efficiency—was alleviated by the fact that the imperatives of ideology often convergé with those of economic survival. The building of socialist society, after all, assumes and anticipates the existence of complex organization and production. But for the peasant and fascist regimes ideology prescribed the impossible task of dismounting structures that support the modern society and the state in a competitive international environment. Both peasants and fascists made their regimes memorable for a string of measures designed to transform education, economy, and administration in the revolutionary image of the primitive agrarian society. Universities were closed down, the legal profession abolished, qualified personnel purged. Industry and commerce were paralyzed and natural resources squandered to satisfy egalitarian expectations. In the final analysis, they were defeated by *anomie,* by their own norms, which were irrelevant to the concrete situation. As Eugen Weber eloquently remarks in his epitaph on the Iron Guard, "The qualities that gave them some of the strength to act like heroes and martyrs also prevented them from acting in the long-run like sensible men." [40] If the bureaucracies lost out in politics, the weakness of the revolutionaries was in dealing with day-to-day routine in a rational way. They were often paralyzed not by ideology *per se* but by an ideology of a particular kind that had sprung up from the primitive rebellion of East European rural society.

One-Party Regimes: Pluralistic or Totalitarian?

These chiliastic movements were either explicitly totalitarian or else their ideology was such that it fostered intolerance toward opposition and the very idea of pluralism. The fascist and the Marxist parties were avowed protagonists of revolutionary political monopoly, while the peasants, once in power, simply declared that in order to put their political program in effect they would have to rule Bulgaria for at least four decades without interference from other parties.[41] When the rationale of a movement or government is salvation or its secular equivalent, politics will tend to assume a militant character, leaving little room for bargaining and compromise. Yet while the revolutionary movements claimed political monopoly the regimes that emerged under the one-party label fell far short of being monolithic in structure. With the exception of the Stambulisky dictatorship in Bulgaria the regimes were successful in liquidating rival political parties, but at the same time they failed to penetrate powerful social institutions. The survival of organizational autonomy under the monolithic facade of political unity subsequently represented serious threats to the stability and the identity of the party regimes.

In some notable instances the failure of the parties to "break through" the underlying pluralism of social institutions was due to the intervention of external forces. At the beginning of World War II Germany emerged as the principal power in East Europe, and as such she regularly intervened in the domestic affairs of the countries of the area. These interventions were not aimed, as some may have anticipated, to aid the revolutionary right, but to maintain the status quo in an attempt to minimize economic disruption, social dislocation, and political turbulence behind the German lines. Most significantly, Germany threw her weight behind the conservative Rumanian military and actively supported a *coup d'état* against the Iron Guard in January, 1941. In Hungary, too, German foreign policy aided the conservatives and their advice held back the Arrow Cross from seizing power until October, 1944. Similarly, in Slovakia, the Third Reich restrained the radicals of the right and instead of a full-fledged national socialist regime, German policy aimed at maintaining an uneasy balance between revolutionary and conservative forces.

Yet in the majority of the cases foreign relations alone could not explain the structure and dynamics of one-party regimes in the area. More frequently the survival of traditional institutions and interest groups amidst the chiliastic revolution was not the result of external intervention but of the relative weakness of the revolutionary party. Most East European societies, though sufficiently modernized to provide a cadre and membership for a mass movement regime, were sharply divided internally. The politically relevant strata, the cannon fodder of revolutionary movements, were committed to competing revolutionary movements with conflicting programs, identities, and aspirations. In most countries there were rival mass movements of the right and the left, and when the former came to power it felt compelled to seek temporary accommodations with vested interests against its adversaries. Thus in Bulgaria, to take an outstanding example, popular forces were divided in their support between the Peasant Union and the Communist Party, one being the party of the politically mobilized smallholders, the other of workers, artisans, employees, and in general, of the modern, urbanized sectors of society. This division of active political forces created a perennial threat from the left which in turn compelled

Stambulisky to tolerate the autonomy of the army as a counterweight to the Communists. This tolerance eventually proved to be the undoing of his regime.

In Bulgaria (1919–1923) and Rumania (1940–1941) the parties were forced to accept the presence of the army, only to be subverted by its officers. In Slovakia and Croatia there was no military establishment to cope with, but here the parties became reluctant bedfellows of the powerful established church. This association left a deep imprint on the character of the regimes, though in each case in different ways. In the first case political presence of the church led to protracted conflict, subterranean struggles for power, and crypto-politics. In the second it resulted in the fusion of the party with traditional interest groups and a concomitant loss of revolutionary identity.

TABLE 6-7   *A Comparison of Peasant and Communist Strength in Bulgaria (1921-1922)*

	Peasant Union		Communist Party	
Total vote	569,000	(53%)	204,000	(20.2)
Party members	132,081		38,036	
Occupational categories:				
Industrial workers				10.5%
Artisans				17.9
Agricultural workers		2.4%	56.4%	15.0
State employees				8.0
Free professions				4.5
Other				.5
Small property owners:				
−5 Ha. of land	74.0			
5 − 10 Ha. of land	20.5	97.6	—	43.6
10+ Ha. of land	3.1			

Sources: Richard V. Burks, *The Dynamics of Communism in Eastern Europe* (Princeton: Princeton University Press, 1961), pp. 64-67; George D. Jackson, Jr., *Comintern and the Peasant in East Europe, 1919-1930* (New York: Columbia University Press, 1966), p. 168; Joseph Rothschild, *The Communist Party of Bulgaria* (New York: Columbia University Press, 1959), p. 109.

These deviating patterns of political development may be related to conditions surrounding the rise of these two regimes. In Slovakia the one-party state was first set up by a loose alliance of Catholics, nationalists, and conservatives in an attempt to rally the partisans of Slovak independence and, at the same time, to exclude its opponents and other "subversive" elements from the political process. This National Union included the Slovak Populist (Catholic People's) Party, the Slovak Nationals and Agrarians and the representatives of two minuscule middle-class parties. Altogether these groups had controlled some 35 per cent of the Slovak vote in the previous democratic elections. In 1939 the candidates of the National Union ran on a common and unopposed list with forty-eight seats allotted to the former Populist Party and fifteen to their camp followers, a division that roughly reflected the pre-independence electoral of the respective parties. A similar division prevailed in the higher organs of the National Union. The press remained in private hands, with most of the papers under the control of conservative and Catholic business interests.

While the Catholic Church and the National Union were not formally and institutionally connected the hierarchy had always favored Slovak autonomy and had been hostile to the secular Czechoslovak state. In addition, most of the Populist deputies had been Catholic priests. The electoral base of this party had been in the mountainous areas of western Slovakia, where the devout peasantry supported it on purely religious grounds. This circumstance provided considerable clerical leverage over the party and gave the hierarchy access to the political process, especially since the priest-deputy was subject to the discipline of his superiors "in matters spiritual." Yet this discipline was only rarely exercised, for the whole relationship between party and church rested on a subtle reciprocity between the two: the church would deliver the support of the traditional, rural areas in exchange for a policy protective of its institutional interests.

To use terms suggested in Part I of this volume, the National Union had been designated as an "exclusionary" rather than a "mobilizing" party. But this political formula did not square with reality, for the National Union at its various levels also included a number of younger, militant and secular intellectuals who were disenchanted with this concept of political organization and remonstrated that it was impossible "to build a modern Führerstaat . . . with parish priests as its principal protagonists." [42] The leaders of this faction, Sano Mach and Vojtech Tuka (later propaganda minister and prime minister of Slovakia), wanted to follow more closely the German national socialist model, advocated militant racial policies, and hoped to transform the National Union into a mass organization. The radicals became the founders of the paramilitary Hlinka Guard, which they used to perpetrate anti-Semitic outrages and acts of terrorism against the general population. In the winter of 1939 the feud between the two factions of the National Union became so bitter that the Guard threatened to stage a march on Bratislava to dissolve parliament and to sweep from the capital the "small clique of political gamblers" controlling the country.[43] Again on January 21, 1941 Tuka issued a fourteen-point proclamation at Trencianske Teplíce calling for a national socialist regime.[44] To counter these moves the conservatives first attempted to disarm the Guard and discredit it (conservative prelates such as the Bishops of Nitra and Trnava forbade their clergy to become its members and wear its insignia) [45] and to dilute its organization by demanding that membership should be made compulsory for the entire adult male population. The conflict was eventually arbitrated by the Germans, who insisted on the purge of several conservative figures but stopped short of removing President Tiso, or granting the national socialists full control over the government. After this intervention the two factions coexisted uneasily, moving from compromise to compromise, or more accurately, sabotaging each other's policy designs (Table 6–8).

TABLE 6-8   *Political Conflict in Slovakia, 1939-1945: Issues and Outcome*

Nationalism

Conservatives: Slovak autonomy, later independence. National identity based on Catholic religion.

Radicals: Slovakia part of European New Order. National identity based on the concept of Aryanism.

Foreign Policy

Conservatives: A regional alliance of "conservative states" in eastern Europe including Hungary, Croatia, Slovakia, Rumania, and eventually Poland. Reliance on the Vatican and Italy in foreign relations. Neutrality in war.

Radicals: Protective friendship (*Schutzfreundschaft*) with Germany. Hitler "joint Führer" of the two nations. Declaration of war against Soviet Russia and the Allies.

Outcome: Slovakia under increasing German influence. Enters war but her participation is reluctant and thoroughly ineffectual.

Racial Policy

Conservatives: Facilitate Jewish emigration from Slovakia. The definition of Jews on religious rather than racial grounds.

Radicals: Racial definition of Jewry. Expropriation and deportation.

Outcome: First Jewish Law (1939) a compromise in that Jews baptized before 1918 were exempt. In 1941 this clause was changed. In 1940 part of the Jewish population rounded up, but subsequently many of them released. From 1942 to 1944 anti-Jewish measures systematically sabotaged. In the fall of 1944 persecution resumed.

Other Minorities

Conservatives: Hungarian, Ukranian, and German minorities should have instruments of interest representation autonomous from the National Union.

Radicals: Minority organizations integrated with the party except for Germans, who were to gain special status.

Outcome: Minorities retain their autonomous political organizations, Germans granted special privileges.

Social Policy

Conservatives: Free enterprise tempered by Catholic notions of social equity.

Radicals: State controls, redistribution of social resources.

Outcome: Some welfare measures along national socialist lines.

In contradistinction to the Slovak experience, the Croatian *Ustasha* (meaning "insurgent") had its roots not in electoral but in conspiratorial politics. It started out in the 1920s as one of the numerous terrorist organizations that crowded the Balkan scene in the interwar period. As such the *Ustasha* was credited with the assassination of King Alexander of Yugoslavia in 1934. But this particular act tended to bring the organization more disrepute than popularity, and by the outbreak of World War II the *Ustasha* had all but vanished from the political scene. Its leader, Ante Pavelić, and a few faithful followers lived in Italian exile. The home organization had been driven underground and then out of existence.

In its early days the *Ustasha* had no ideology apart from a strong commitment to Croat independence and a cult of violence and terrorism. In later years Pavelić and his associates developed a more elaborate doctrine with emphasis on primitive-tribal motives, the mystique of the soil, and the virtues of the peasant community. Still later in the 1930s the *Ustasha* ideology acquired distinctly national socialistic overtones in that racial motives replaced the traditional themes of religion and culture as the chief sources of national identity. In 1936 Pavelić expounded the amazing thesis that the Croats were not Slavic but Gothic by ancestry, the lost children of the great Teutonic family of peoples, which placed them above the racially inferior Serbs and other Yugoslavs. In the same year, from his Italian exile, Pavelić addressed a remarkable memorandum to the German National Socialist Party in which he further elaborated his thesis and expressed the hope that Croatia would be able to take its rightful place in the new Europe "under the leadership of Germany and her best son, Adolf Hitler." [46] These racial and *völkisch* ideas eventually found their way into the *Ustasha* constitution of 1941. Article II of this document defined Croats as a race distinct from other Southern Slavs, while Article XVI stated: "He who is not of peasant parentage cannot, in ninety per cent of the cases be regarded as a full-blooded Croat." [47]

When a rather whimsical German decision put it in power, the *Ustasha* had a clear-cut ideological identity but no organization framework, experienced cadres, or potential mass following. Pavelić returned to Croatia with fewer than 300 men and was received by a few dubious sympathizers. This confronted him with a serious dilemma. Though Pavelić insisted on developing a one-party state with extensive grass roots organization, the lack of competent and reliable personnel stood in the way of carrying out the plan. Already in 1941 it was evident to diplomatic observers that his cadre was "insufficient for the training and education of an all-embracing organization." [48] It would be imperative, the same perceptive observer noted, to recruit fresh and dedicated membership into the party, though he immediately added that there was little likelihood of success because the *"Ustasha* had not won Croatian independence," and Pavelić was not able to capitalize on the act of liberation.[49] The *Ustasha* cadres were ruefully inadequate even in the capital. The party cell of Zagreb, for instance, entrusted with the organization of a rally to honor Pavelić in the summer of 1941, could round up hardly 200 persons, half of them policemen.[50]

In the absence of a militant cadre, the structure of the party state had to be grafted upon existing organizations. In certain cities, notably in Zagreb and Sarajevo, the *Ustasha* incorporated the paramilitary units of the Peasant Party; in Bosnia several chapters of the Moslem Organization served as the nucleus of the local party. Even more significantly, a number of Catholic associations joined, and the leaders of the Catholic Action were entrusted with the formation of the *Ustasha* youth movement. In the villages, the party had to rely on the local parish for the simple reason that, after the dissolution of the Yugoslav administrative system, the church remained the only visible source of authority. One informant from the backward Dinaric region gave the writer this account of the evolution of *Ustasha*-church collaboration: "The Ustasha-men arrived from Zagreb. They were strangers to the village and region. They would go to the priest who was known to be sympathetic to the new state, and ask him about the 'good' and 'responsible' people in the village." Generally the *Ustasha* would recruit people, recommended by the priest, and would try to use the authority of the local parish to bolster the prestige of the administrative and political organizations. Not infrequently the priest himself would become active in politics. As in Slovakia, the church hierarchy shunned official relations with the party organization, but individual clergymen were to occupy significant political positions, including several posts of the regional chief (*velikij zupan*).

The amalgamation of the party and the traditional-religious groups under the influence of the church had two significant consequences. First, in the domain of ideology there was a rapid shift of emphasis from racial-primitive to "Catholic-crusading" principles, and the party was gradually transformed from a Nazi-type revolutionary into an aggressive, but socially conservative organization. From a structural point of view the fusion implied that many local as well as functional organizations would retain considerable autonomy. The political chiefs of the provinces and villages operated from a political base of their own. Relationships between the provinces and the center were reciprocal and not hierarchical. The provincial chiefs and the former leaders of autonomous organizations were hard to remove from their positions and with the intensification of guerrilla warfare in the countryside, these officials made their own policies or were in the position to set conditions for compliance with the wishes of the Zagreb government. Under these conditions the party amounted to little more than a loosely integrated framework for a number of local chiefs and vested interests united only in their acceptance of Croatian independence and the vague principles of militant political Catholicism.

Conclusions

From this comparison of the political systems the single-party emerges as an organization of the "new type." In contrast to the old congeries of notables that made up the "government parties" of East Europe prior to the world wars, the political experiments of the 1920s and 1930s sprang up around well-articulated goals rather than the principles of pluralism and interest aggregation. The new parties were designed (1) to exclude competing elites but, at the same time (2) to include a mass following and to harness it to the aims and purposes of a solidary elite. The use of the term "party" in conjunction with such monopolistic organizational concept is justified—whether accepted by the participants or not—because the organization rarely aims to be all-inclusive. If it does, the mass membership remains a formality, and the real organization will be hidden behind the facade of the all-embracing national movement, in the form of a narrower, more exclusive group, as was the Orange Guard within the Peasant Union, or the SA within the NSDAP for that matter.

As an organizational "weapon" the party provides a framework for political action that may be put to good use by some, but not by others. In other words, the effectiveness of the party will depend on the character of the leadership and the receptiveness of the mass to their political objectives. The party is—as both Szálasi and Codreanu repeatedly said—only the body, while the "soul" represents an agglomeration of solidarities, purposes and identities. Without this soul the body remains an empty shell, a set of roles, principles, and organizational charts.

The soul of the bureaucracy is different from the soul of the revolutionary, and will produce different political outcomes within the framework of organization. In the first instance the soul is the *esprit de corp* of an already established group whose members have a vested interest in national power and whose identity derives from the institutions of the national state. The established character and identity is a source of both weakness and strength. While there is an obvious advantage in utilizing already existing structures and organized personnel, this advantage may be offset by past associations, commitments and *modus operandi* that diminish the political appeal of the bureaucrat and impede his ability to create political community, the *sine qua non* of operational effectiveness in an apathetic or hostile environment.

In contrast, the revolutionary elites are recruited from all walks of life, with no initial bonds among them apart from common frustrations, hopes, and anxieties. The solidarity of revolutionary elites is not "given" by shared statuses and roles; rather, it develops gradually by the translation of a common state of mind into a more or less explicit set of ideas and visions of a future society. Solidarity, then, derives from ideology, from the ultimate ends closely interwoven with the idea of mission to be carried out on behalf of a mass constituency. It is the ideology that defines the revolutionary as a select group and provides its members with purpose and personal fulfillment, that sets them apart from the bearers of vested interests and the rest of the society. At the same time, the chiliastic perspective absolves the revolutionary from traditional moral restraints, and helps him to draw the mass not only in an organizational context but into a genuine political community.

It appears then that the crucial variable to explain the character, flexibility, and value orientation of one-party systems is a sociological one: the source of solidarities among relevant elites. On the one hand, elites of established status will tend to be more "pragmatic" because they accept the existence of the status group as a value in itself which sets certain limits to the policy objectives collectively pursued. Such status groups may have an ideology, indeed occasionally they will search for one feverishly, but with them ideology remains an instrument, the source of mass appeal, or a language of communication. As a solidarity-building device the role of ideology will be perfunctory. Consequently a status group can "pick and choose" from different ideologies, and it can easily discard them when and where their contents lose relevance or appear to be in conflict with reality. It is only the "marginal" elites whose identity and solidarity depend on ideology which will hang on to utopian premises in apparent irrationality to save the group from extinction.

The established-marginal dichotomy not only explains variations on a pragmatic-revolutionary scale, but also allows us to approach the problem of the dynamics in single-party states and the phenomenon generally described as the "end of ideology." As revolutionary parties seize power and hold on to it for prolonged periods of time, their sect-like character and marginality give way to established status, institutionalized roles, and new sources of social solidarity derived from the institutional context in which they operate. As a revolutionary regime moves from one generation to another, the relevance of the creed articulated by charismatic leadership declines. The marginal man becomes integrated within society as a "new class," and if strains arise between ideology and reality, he will be able to adjust the former without causing irreparable damage to himself and to the group. This problem, however, takes us far away from the East European past and well into the present by raising issues that can be more appropriately studied by observing the maturation and ritualization of communist revolutions.

As instruments of harnessing a mass membership to the purposes of the elite, one-party movements and regimes become relevant only under certain conditions. In traditional social environments where horizons are narrow and the populace largely apathetic, such experiments are out of place unless designed as a mere facade to cover reality or in anticipation of forthcoming social change. The energies of wider popular strata cannot be successfully tapped for political purposes unless society is sufficiently "mobilized," and thus large numbers of people are available for political recommitment. This condition implies political consciousness, competence, and marginality, that is, sufficient awareness of social alternatives, the possession of politically relevant skills, and detachment from meaningful socioeconomic relationships. Only the latter makes an individual genuinely "mobile," enabling him to enter politics as he would enter a religious order, offering full commitment in exchange for personal identity. Sociologically, these conditions are most frequently related to certain aspects of modernization: the rise of a market economy, literacy, and physical mobility. But these conditions become particularly salient when certain discontinuities arise in the process, bringing about severe social, economic and cultural dislocations, or discrepancies between aspirations and reality.

However, social modernization and mobilization represent only necessary, but not sufficient, conditions for the rise and success of the one-party state. As a matter of fact, a closer examination of historical and contemporary examples will reveal that the correlation between the two variables is a rather loose one. The explanation for this is obvious: Modernization may be accompanied not only by discontinuities but by the rise of competitive commitments, in which case revolutionary parties may only be able to capture part of the available human raw material. Thus social analysis will have to go beyond the hypothesis of mass politics and mobilization and attempt to find the differences in tradition, culture, or the sequence of developments that are responsible for the fragmentation of the mass and its availability for different types of revolutionary movements. But then, social insight alone may not always provide us with an adequate answer. Like all other forms of complex social change, the rise and success of one-party systems are the result of the interaction of external and internal forces, an obvious truth that the sociologist is prone to overlook, but the student of politics will have to bear in mind.

These qualifications are particularly relevant in explaining the survival of pluralism in the face of totalitarian tendencies inherent in the ideology of the single party. If and when revolutionary movements seize power in an insufficiently mobilized society, or in a society in which the commitments of the mobilized strata of the population are sharply divided, the new elite may be forced to seek at least temporary accommodations with autonomous groups and organizations. Thus the emerging one-party state will often be totalitarian in ideology and form, but not in reality. On the other hand, the precepts of the revolutionary ideology will militate against bargaining, compromise and reconciliation, and the development of institutional mechanisms for the resolution of conflict. In such political contexts (the term "system" appears to be inappropriate here) tensions between ideology and structure will produce considerable randomness in the political process and may result in recurrent attempts by competing groups to eliminate one another from the political scene. These types of party states are pluralistic *de facto* but not by custom or explicit agreement. This is pluralism by default and not by design. If one may borrow a term from the vocabulary of administrative theory, they are neither pluralistic nor monolithic, but "prismatic." [51] By definition these prismatic configurations of political forces are unstable, and they may be best conceived of as representing a transitional stage in a process of political change. The prismatic condition of a polity may lead to full-fledged totalitarianism, intraparty institutionalization, a multi-party system, or further and complete disintegration, to mention only some of the possible alternatives.

This whole issue underscores the great difficulties involved in the classification of one-party systems. While it is easy and convenient to distinguish political concepts or formulae for such regimes, when turning to structural analysis we will frequently find discrepancies between ideal and real types as well as a great fluidity of political relations among the various components of the regime. Thus the one-party state ought not primarily be approached from the static perspective of systems (suggesting patterned relations and interaction) but from the dynamic perspective of development and decay. Conditions pertaining to these political outcomes are beyond the scope of this chapter. But they may well provide the focus of future research concerning the single-party phenomenon in political science.

‖ *Notes*

1. Hugh Seton-Watson, *Neither War Nor Peace* (New York: Frederick A. Praeger, 1960), p. 161.
2. Zoltán Szabo, *A tardi helyzet* (*The Situation at Tard*) (Budapest: Cserépfalvi, 1936), p. 22.
3. Frederick Hertz, *The Economic Problem of the Danubian States* (London: V. Gollancz, 1948), pp. 213–216.
4. Szabo, *op. cit.,* p. 56.
5. David Mitrany et al., *Economic Development in South-Eastern Europe* (London: Oxford University Press, 1945); also Béla Kovrig, *Magyar társadalompolitika* (Hungarian Social Policy) (New York: Magyar Nemzeti Bizottmány, 1954), p. 97.
6. Joseph P. Roucek, *Balkan Politics* (Stanford: Stanford University Press, 1948), p. 53.
7. Mihail Manoilescu, *The Theory of Protection and International Trade* (London: P. S. King, 1931), p. 30.
8. Henry L. Roberts, *Rumania* (New Haven: Yale University Press, 1951), p. 194.
9. Mihail Manoilescu, *Țaranism și democratțe* (Bucharest, 1922), p. 50.
10. Quoted in Roberts, *op. cit.,* p. 194.
11. Mihail Manoilescu, *Die Einzelne Partei als politische Institution der neuen Regime* (Berlin: O. Stollberg, 1941), p. 42.
12. *Ibid.*
13. *Ibid.,* p. 43.
14. *Ibid.,* pp. 52–85.
15. Milan Stoyadinović, *Ni Rat, Ni Pakt: Jugoslavija izedju dva rata* (*Neither War, Nor Agreement: Yugoslavia between Two Wars*) (Buenos Aires: El Economista, 1963), pp. 30–40.
16. *Ibid.,* p. 352.
17. C. A. Macartney, *October 15: A History of Modern Hungary, 1929–1944* (Edinburgh: Edinburgh University Press, 1962), I, 119.
18. *Ibid.*
19. *Ibid.,* I, 124.
20. Roberts, *op. cit.,* pp. 206–222.
21. *Ibid.,* p. 206.
22. Jan Kowalewski to O. D. Tolishus, *The New York Times,* June 5, 1937, p. 8:5.
23. R. L. Buell, "Political Conflicts in Poland," *Virginia Quarterly Review,* XV, No. 2 (1939), 240.

24. Kowalewski, *loc. cit.*
25. Buell, *op. cit.*, p. 239.
26. Ferdynand Zweig, *Poland between Two Wars* (London: Secker and Warburg, 1944), p. 121.
27. O. D. Tolischus in the *The New York Times,* October 4, 1937, p. 12:1.
28. Stoyadinović, *op. cit.*, p. 606.
29. Szálasi, quoted in Macartney, *op. cit.*, I, 307.
30. Eugen Weber, "Rumania," in Hans Rogger and Eugen Weber, eds., *The European Right* (Berkeley: University of California Press, 1966), p. 569.
31. István Deák, "Hungary," in Rogger and Weber, *op. cit.*, p. 374.
32. Research based on the *Országgyülési Almanach* (*Parliamentary Almanac*) between 1922–1939. The names and backgrounds of the candidates for the 1939 election appear in the paper *Népszava*, May 31, 1939.
33. H. Baerlein, "Inside Slovakia Today," *Nineteenth Century,* No. 127 (March 1940), pp. 309–310.
34. The Revolutionary Governing Council of the Soviet Republic had thirty-five members on March 21, 1919 (commissars and deputy commissars), of whom twenty-one (60 per cent) appear to be of Jewish origin. See the list of members of the Revolutionary Governing Council in Vilmos Böhm, *Két forradalom tüzében* (In the Crossfire of Two Revolutions) (Wien: Bécsi Magyar Kiadó, 1922), pp. 263–264. Right-wing sources usually put this proportion even higher. According to one of these, the Revolutionary Governing Council had forty-five members throughout its four-month existence, thirty-one (68 per cent) of them being of Jewish origin. See Klaus Schickert, *Die Judenfrage in Ungarn* (Essen: Essener Verlagsanstalt, 1943), pp. 193–195.
35. Corneliu Zelea Codreanu, *Eiserne Garde,* 3rd ed. (Berlin: Brunnen-Verlag/W. Bischoff, 1941), p. 19.
36. Codreanu, *op. cit.*, p. 310.
37. Quoted in Joseph Rothschild, *The Communist Party of Bulgaria* (New York: Columbia University Press, 1959), p. 87.
38. *Ibid.*
39. In Szálasi's fantasies, or ideology, Hungary's mission was to establish a multinational state between the Carpathians and the Mediterranean based on the principle of "co-nationalism." The global mission of this state would be to serve as an "equilibrium power" between two world empires, Germany and Japan. See Ferenc Szálasi, *Cél és követelések* (*Aims and Purposes*) (Budapest: Leaflet, Hungarian Arrow and Cross Party, 1935).
40. Weber, *op. cit.*, p. 506.
41. George D. Jackson, Jr., *Comintern and Peasant in East Europe, 1919–1930* (New York: Columbia University Press, 1966), p. 165.
42. Quoted in Joseph A. Mikus, *Slovakia: A Political History, 1918–1950* (Milwaukee: Marquette University Press, 1963), p. 121.
43. Baerlein, *op. cit.*, p. 317. For Mach's denunciations of Sidor and other conservatives see also *The New York Times,* June 5, 1939, p. 6:1.
44. Mikus, *loc. cit.*
45. *The New York Times,* March 5, 1939, p. 36:5; also Mikus, *op. cit.*, p. 128.
46. Politisches Archiv, *Auswärtiges Amt* (1941) (Aktenbestand Büro Staatssekretär: Jugoslawien), Vol. III.
47. Quoted in Eugen Sladovic von Sladoevicki, "Der Unabhängige Staat Kroatien. Eine staats—und völkerrechtliche Behandlung," *Zeitschrift für Osteuroparecht* (1942–1943), p. 15.
48. Politisches Archiv, *Auswärtiges Amt* (1941) (Aktenbestand Büro Staatssekretär: Jugoslawien), Vol. I.
49. *Ibid.*

50. Ladislaus Hory and Martin Broszat, *Der kroatische Ustascha Staat* (Stuttgart: Deutsche Verlags-Anstalt, 1965), p. 65.

51. See Fred W. Riggs, *Administration in Developing Countries: Theory of the Prismatic Society* (Boston: Houghton Mifflin, 1964).

Part III

STRONG AND REVOLUTIONARY ONE-PARTY SYSTEMS

7

The Failure of a One-Party System:
Hitler Germany

‖ *Carl J. Friedrich*

Leader and Ideology

The one-party regime which the National Socialists established in Germany in 1933, led by Adolf Hitler, is distinguished by a number of features which make its case especially interesting to the comparative analysis of one-party systems. It was an attempt to coerce a highly pluralistic and overdivided community into an ideologically unified frame. At the same time, the party had developed over an extended period (ten years) under democratic conditions, competing with other parties for the voters' favor and eventually becoming the largest party, though never achieving a majority.[1] Germany possessed at the time an already highly industrialized economy, though the farmers—mostly peasants—still constituted a very substantial portion of the electorate, about 30 per cent, as against 13 per cent in 1962 (it has since fallen to around 10 per cent). These electoral successes were made possible by an economic depression of unparalleled extent, manifest in about 6 million persons unemployed, approximately 20 per cent of all employables, many of them unprovided for by any social security insurance.[2]

Unlike some other one-party systems, the regime of Adolf Hitler was clearly totalitarian, and the party constituted its core. In spite of the uncertainties that surround the terms "totalitarianism" and "totalitarian dictatorship" in their application to quite a few one-party systems, few would hesitate to apply these designations to the National Socialist regime.[3] In fact, to many students of comparative politics, that regime is archetypical in its totalitarian quality.[4] Nor is there much disagreement on the fact that whatever might be other characteristic features of a totalitarian dictatorship, a

239

single party claiming a monopoly of party-political activity and committed to a totalist ideology is one of them.

Such a party is typically led by one man, the dictator, who is centrally concerned with and in charge of this ideological commitment; he may be the author and interpreter, as Mussolini and Hitler were, or its interpreter, like Stalin and Mao. Hence the identification of the party with its leader is mental as well as emotional, and the nature of this relationship has often been misinterpreted and obscured by calling it "charismatic," when it is more strictly speaking ideological and inspirational.[5] In the case of Hitler, this commitment was particularly strong, because as we just said, he had to found and build the party in competition with other established parties over a number of years.[6] Indeed, Hitler's role, like Mussolini's, was so central to the party's inner life that any analysis of this National Socialist system might really in large part be devoted to a study of Hitler and his immediate entourage: Goering, Goebbels, Himmler, Bormann, and so forth.[7] It is nonetheless proposed here to abstract from the "personal" aspects, important as they are in any historical evaluation; for surely there will never be seen again any man or group closely resembling this collection of psychopaths. Hitler and his lieutenants exhibited, however, a number of characteristics which are typical for the leadership of a totalitarian single party.

"Party ideological unity is the spiritual basis of personal dictatorship," it has been remarked. Unlike military dictators in the past, the totalitarian ruler is both ruler and high priest, thus harking back to the type of leadership found among primitives. Such a leader authoritatively interprets the ideas upon which the movement's revolutionary thrust rests. Something more will be said about such an ideology below; at this point I wish to emphasize that totalitarian leaders do and must insist upon such hierocratic authority. Hitler was particularly striking in this respect. His *Mein Kampf* became the bible of the movement and the party. Laughed at by many intellectuals because of its turgid style and bombastic vocabulary,[8] it contained nonetheless a very destructive action program, highlighted by its virulent anti-Semitism. It has been a recurrent error, of which the writings of Hannah Arendt are symptomatic, to claim that the ideology contained in *Mein Kampf* is merely facade intended to dupe a gullible following. But Hitler's *Table Talk*,[9] no less than his actions, demonstrates beyond cavil that the Fuehrer was in dead earnest, and the same can be said of Mussolini's striking article in the *Encyclopedia Italiana* on fascism.[10] In an established totalitarian system the dictator and his immediate subordinates are *linked* to the party following through their ideological outlook. Of no party was this more true than the National Socialist Party of Hitler. Djilas has written much later, and with reference to a different situation, that "the continuance of ideological unity in the party is an unmistakable sign of the maintenance of personal dictatorship of a small number of oligarchs who temporarily work together or maintain a balance of power." [11] It is striking to see to what extent this held true for the National Socialists; testimony such as that contained in the Goebbels diaries [12] and the records of the trials at Nürnberg is quite convincing.[13]

In contrast to Stalin, Hitler was both leader of the party and head of the government, but while Stalin eventually reduced the role of the party very severely, Hitler sought to maintain the dualism of party and government to the end. To be the leader of his party remained as much his ego projection as to be Chancellor of the Reich. Hence the relation of the party and government, or as Europeans prefer to say, the state, remained equivocal and this dualism affected the party very much, and probably contributed to its failure. Hitler's ideological position was correspondingly perplexing. He exalted the nation, the *Volk;* he deprecated the state. In *Mein Kampf,* Hitler devoted an entire chapter to a discussion of the state. We learn that "the present bourgeois world itself can no longer form any unified picture of the *state* concept" and that "there neither is nor can be any uniform definition of it." [14] The present state is for him "a monstrosity," defended by professors "whose highest task it must be to find explanations and interpretations for the more or less unfortunate existence of their momentary source of bread." After identifying three such conceptions and holding forth about what is the true German nation (not including "German-jabbering Jews") he concludes that culture and values are "essentially based on race" and that "the state must, therefore, regard the preservation and intensification of the race as its highest task." Hence, he exclaims, "the state represents no end, but a means." Only the folkish state, *der voelkische Staat,* is a state worthy of acceptance. "The quality of the state cannot be evaluated according to the cultural level or its power in relation to the outside world, but solely and exclusively by the degree of this institution's value for the nation involved . . . a state can be designated as bad, if, despite a high cultural level, it dooms [sic] the bearer of this culture in its racial composition." [15] This instrumental view of the state, so strongly at variance with German tradition, and indeed with the conception of Mussolini and Italian fascism, this basically *unpolitical* view of government, suggests the inner contradiction of the National Socialist Party regime. The retention of the *Volk* as the ultimate reference point does not alter the fact, of course, that decision-making was concentrated and unlimited at the apex of the official hierarchy, any more than the communist notion of the withering away of the state (really more dramatically the notion *der Staat stirbt ab*) keeps that system from becoming totalitarian.[16]

As compared with this crucial ideological commitment, other features of Hitler's leadership were less relevant to the party, although his style affected and afflicted the entire organization; for all organizations are to some extent moulded in the image of their leadership, and the more autocratic, the more so.[17] There is, however, one issue which needs brief mention, and that is the potency of the leadership. There used to be considerable doubt on this score, many observers believing that Hitler was the instrument of others, especially big business—an interpretation very popular with Marxists.[18] In the opinion of Alan Bullock, however, Hitler exercised absolute power if ever a man did.[19] Documentary evidence, now available in great quantity, confirms this judgment. The position of Mussolini, according to competent observers, was very similar.[20] Such concentration of power in the hands of a single man, though usually considered an advantage, proved a decided weakness. A number of Hitler's gravest errors, such as the attack upon Poland and later upon the Soviet Union, were arrived at without any kind of consultation; the evidence now available suggests that had there been the need for group action, some of these errors might not have been made. Thus, the excessive autocracy of Hitler within and over the party contributed greatly to its failure.[21]

The Meaning of Party

The question may at this point be raised whether a totalitarian leader's following may properly be called a party. It certainly is a different organization from that of a party in a multi-party system; it also differs markedly from parties in some of the non-totalitarian single-party systems, that is, in systems where the party is not committed to a totalist ideology, and where there is no such monopolizing of propaganda and mass communications, of economic and other organizations and of weapons of effective combat usually reinforced by a secret police—these being the outstanding characteristics of a totalitarian regime.[22] For the adoption of the outward form of such a party does not of course mean that their inner dynamic is the same. They do not freely recruit their membership, as other parties do, but base the admission of their members upon tests which are characteristic of secret societies, brotherhoods, and the like. They arbitrarily expel such members without any kind of judicial process. The inner structure, presently to be examined, also differs markedly from that of other parties. Nonetheless, it has seemed to most analysts that these differences are overshadowed by the similarities, and that one is therefore justified in speaking of these groupings as parties.

What then is a party in its most general sense? There has been considerable controversy and theorizing over the years, beginning with Weber and Michels. In terms of functional theory, the following would seem to represent an approximate agreement. It avoids normative or idealizing notions, popular since the days of Burke. A political party is a stably organized group of human beings.[23] It has four major functions: (1) selecting future leaders; (2) maintaining contact between the government (including the opposition) and the people at large; (3) representing the various groupings of the community; (4) integrating these groupings as much as possible. These functions involve securing and maintaining for its leaders the power of governing or ruling the political community on the one hand, and giving to the members of such a party ideological and material satisfactions, benefits, and advantages. In this connection, the political party has the crucial function of ensuring the succession of rulers, when other older forms of legitimacy have ceased to work.[24]

This brief characterization is given here to avoid misunderstandings, and because somewhat differing notions are found in other chapters; this is not, however, the place for engaging in theoretical discussions concerning these differences. It is, however, worth noting that the leadership of the NSDAP was itself very much aware of the sharp difference between a party competing for the voters' favor in a multi-party system, and the single party supporting a totalitarian regime. They often spoke of this distinction in terms of the *Kampfpartei* or party of the struggle, and *Staatspartei* or party of the state. How in fact the new party related to the state will be discussed presently. It would, in view of all the facts, perhaps be more appropriate to speak of a *Herrschaftspartei* or ruling party.[25] The transformation it underwent never quite erased all the traces of its democratic past, although after the purge of 1934 it became much more monolithic. Even so, its large and fairly heterogeneous membership interfered so much with its role as a ruling party that the Schutzstaffeln (SS) or protective guards of Himmler eventually became a serious rival (see below).

Seizure of Power and Gleichschaltung

At the time of the seizure of power after the early March elections of 1933 and the Enabling Act later that month (it is disputable which of these dates may properly be called the *Machtergreifung*) the party had achieved an impressive electoral victory.[26] This is true, even if due allowance is made for the fact that Hitler exploited his position as Chancellor to the fullest and was favored by an "election stunt," the Reichstag Fire, long believed to have been instigated by the Nazis, though in fact the action of an isolated individual.[27] K. D. Bracher has rightly pointed out that most of the measures taken to terrorize the electorate would have been taken anyway, even without the welcome excuse the fire provided. Much to the disappointment of Hitler, the party did not achieve an absolute majority, but the Enabling Act obliterated that defect.[28]

The voter participation was very large, 88.7 per cent, which mostly benefited the NSDAP. Its total support rose from 11,737,000 in November, 1932 to 17,277,000 in March, 1933 out of a total of 39,343,000 votes. If one adds the 3,137,000 of the German National People's Party (Nationalists) who were committed to collaboration with the Nazis, the vote can be said to have been a majority. In view of later distortions by Nazi propaganda and its echoes abroad, it should be pointed out, however, that this majority was in part not a positive vote *for* Hitler and his ideas, but a negative one against the Weimar Republic and the Great Depression. This is particularly true of the non-party voters. As Bracher has rightly remarked, the claim of Hitler and of NS propagandists that this was a "mighty, decisive victory" of their party makes sense only in the perspective of Hitler's insistence, made immediately after the election of March 5 to his cabinet (March 7, 1933) that he considered the election result a "revolution." [29] The notion of legality within the framework of a competitive, constitutional democracy was abandoned in favor of a totalist revolution,[30] involving a "total" destruction of the existing society and its replacement by a new and different one. The party was to be the instrument of this revolutionary transformation.

But since the Germany of the Weimar Republic had been a pluralistic society in every sense of the word, with numerous parties, interest groups, churches and so on, such an undertaking represented a complex task. The instrument which the NS leadership developed for accomplishing the task was the so-called *Gleichschaltung,* that is coordination and subordination, of all organizations. By proclaiming the *Fuehrerprinzip* or leadership principle the basis of all organizations, they meant to suggest that all organizations should follow the autocratic and monocratic pattern which Hitler had developed in the party itself. But whereas in theory at least the Fuehrer was the chosen leader of the *Parteivolk* or party at large, the leaders in all other organizations were "coordinated" by having their leadership selected by party and later governmental authorities. As a consequence, and to some considerable degree by way of anticipation, very large numbers of "opportunists" rushed into the party after March, 1933, the so-called "March hares." This trend was reinforced, of course, by the large number of civil servants who joined and were eventually obliged to join the party. Thus a total of 1,644,818 men and women joined the party between January 30, 1933 and January 1, 1935, about twice the number of members who joined before that date; that is to say, there were two new members for each old one. It will probably never be ascertainable to what an extent these new members really were converts to national socialism, or merely formal *Mitlaeufer.* In any case, there were substantial numbers of these and that makes it very difficult to analyze the extent to which the *Gleichschaltung* became effective; mere recital of the number of Nazis in leading positions does obviously not tell the tale; there were too many "joiners" who had acted on the old principle of "when you can't lick them, join them." [31]

With this warning in mind, the following figures are offered as an indication of what happened by way of coordinating organizations and governmental units with the party process which has been called a "pseudo-revolution." [32] A very considerable number of lower offices in state and local administration changed hands and were occupied by party functionaries. According to the party's own records,[33] 60.7 per cent of all governmental, including municipal, posts were in the hands of party members, but only about a third of these were "old" party members who had joined before 1933. The party scored the most far-flung successes in the municipalities; here 78.2 per cent of all offices were occupied by party members, 47.1 per cent by "old" members. District councillors (*Landraete*) were "old" Nazis "only" to the extent of 28.8 per cent, while in the smaller communes (*Gemeinden,* corresponding roughly to townships) only 19.3 per cent were such (59.9 per cent of these, however, were members of the NSDAP, in other words two-thirds were March hares, as in the cities). In short, the "nazification" in all these spheres of government consisted rather in a formal assimilation than in a genuine *Machtuebernalme* or taking of power. (When the occupation forces took over, after 1945, many of these *Mitlaeufer* shed their NS coloring as readily as they had assumed it.) It was truly coordination rather than conquest which transformed the government into a National Socialist one.

This phenomenon is important for an understanding of the NS one-party regime. It is astonishing to see how relatively few men belonging to the party apparatus became members of the governmental apparatus; only 3.8 per cent of these cadres (the Germans use the rather misleading term *Hoheitstraeger,* employed by the NSDAP) occupied higher posts, such as *Vorsteher* (director) of an office. Schaefer concludes that "the infiltration of state and municipal administration by party cadres was extremely small." [34] It is in line with this finding that among those who occupied such governmental posts, only about a third were genuine activists. Hence we can say in summary that the coordination of cities, townships, and districts was only to a rather limited extent carried out by "politically reliable" men, and as a result the political control by the party was not very effective. However, these officials became eventually rather active party members and thus reinforced the party and provided it with a good deal of the legitimizing appeal which *der Beamte* has for the average German.

A somewhat similar picture is presented to us, when we turn to the interest groups. Since parties were simply dissolved and forbidden (by a declaration on June 22, 1933, the Social Democratic Party was outlawed, as the Communist Party had been, and the rest were soon thereafter),[35] the coordination of the interest groups became the crucial step in the process of subordinating all associational life to the party. Most thorough was the attack on the trade unions. German workers had shown themselves rather resistant to National Socialist propaganda, and hence their stronghold, the "Marxist" trade unions, were destroyed by frontal assault, their property taken over, their functionaries arrested and put into concentration camps or murdered, and a German Labor Front (DAF or *Deutsche Arbeitsfront*) put in their place.[36] This Labor Front eventually became a mainstay of the "corporative" setup by which the National Socialists, like the fascists, sought to provide a facade for the total bureaucratization of German economic life.[37] But it remained a facade, and it is anyone's guess how many of the class-conscious workers whom the German labor movement had indoctrinated ever were converted to National Socialism.

Other interest groups were more deftly "coordinated." After some rather wild excesses in the early months, the top party leadership arranged matters with the existing organizations. Schaefer cites as rather characteristic the story of the coordination of the German Singers' Union (*Deutscher Saengerbund*). A communiqué was eventually issued in connection with an official ordinance which tells the story:

> The formation of special National Socialist choirs and National Socialist Singing Clubs apart from the *Deutscher Saengerbund* is undesirable. . . . Both sides [namely the party and the *Deutscher Saengerbund*] are of the opinion that in order to avoid controversies the boards of such clubs in the districts and provinces be composed of a majority of men who are members of the NSDAP or who sympathize with it, and that no members of such boards are allowed who are opposed to the movement. On this basis the National Office of the NSDAP does not wish that its local cadres interfere in the internal affairs of the *Deutscher Saengerbund*.[38]

This example illustrates what was the pattern of coordination throughout Germany's variegated associational life: provided the leadership became nominally National Socialist or at any rate abstained from making opposition to the regime, they were allowed to continue. This pattern was, of course, particularly important throughout the economy: all the familiar interest groups of industry, agriculture and the other fields of economic activity continued as if nothing had happened except a change in the leadership. One spoke openly of a "protective Nazi" (*Schutznazi*) who mediated between the association and the party.[39] Such men were often "failures" in their particular field who could thus rehabilitate themselves. They served to legitimize the regime by associating it with all the numerous interests and activities in return for being protected against more radical elements.

These radical elements produced a major problem for the NSDAP and Hitler, and eventually were "liquidated" in the sequel to the so-called Roehm Putsch in July, 1934. They had been making opposition since 1930, with a serious attempt at scission being suppressed in 1932, but became more vociferous in response to the *Gleichschaltung* or coordination, which frequently served to perpetuate the status quo by the simple device of making the established leaders party members. It is hardly surprising that this sort of manipulation would anger the "old" party members, particularly those filled with revolutionary zeal and chiliastic hopes for a new dawn. Rather striking statistics tend to show that the remarkably large number of lower cadres were eliminated or left the party by January 1, 1935, namely 18.8 per cent of those who had been members before 1933, over half of them leaders of district, township, and bloc group leaders. There were considerable regional differences, as well as differences in motivation, reported in party statistics. Of the total number of 40,153 constituting the 18.8 per cent mentioned above, 32.3 per cent resigned for professional reasons, 26.3 per cent were dismissed, and 41.3 per cent are lumped together as "other"; one may suspect that it contained quite a few more who were dismissed, as well as other malcontents.[40]

At this point, attention needs be given to the problem of the storm troopers, or SA. During the years of struggle, a substantial intertwining of party cadres and storm troop formations had been the rule. After June, 1934, and the execution of the leaders of the SA, notably Ernst Roehm and his immediate collaborators, these linkages were systematically disentangled, and the storm troopers lost steadily in power and influence. Their place was in part taken by the security guards, or SS, under Himmler, until finally these latter came to assume some of the party functions typical of a totalitarian regime. This development will be discussed below.

With this in mind, one can now more fully appreciate the following figures describing the composition of the "leadership" cadres of the party at the beginning of 1935, that is to say after the great purge of the preceding summer. These cadres (political directing personnel) were composed of 280,916 so-called *Hoheitsraeger* or bearers of sovereignty, meaning persons to whom Hitler had passed on some of the majesty of his position as leader, and who in fact constituted the more strictly political cadres of the party. Besides these, there were 81,859 other party officials (*Amtstraeger*) and 131,889 technical personnel (*Fachamtstraeger*). Thus, these cadres totaled 502,662. Of these 7.3 per cent only had joined the party before 1930, 33.1 per cent between 1930 and 1933, and 59.6 per cent after 1933! [41] These figures, revealing as they are, parallel those for the party as a whole, of the membership of which 129,563 or 5.2 per cent entered before 1930, 719,446 or 28.8 per cent between 1930 and 1933, and 1,644,881 or 66 per cent after 1933. These figures demonstrate the extent to which the party assimilated even in its cadres the "establishment" of the existing society.

This picture must, however, be compared with the situation in the top echelons of the party which is markedly different. All the *Gauleiter* or governors of provinces were men who had joined the party before 1930. There is a regular pyramid to be observed, with the percentage of new men increasing as one descends the ladder from the *Gauleiter* down to the *Blockleiter,* of whom 71.2 per cent had joined the party only after 1933.[42] This situation at the same time necessitated and served to justify the concentration of decision-making in the top echelons, and indeed in Hitler's own hands, and at the same time it was made possible by this concentration. It is part of the process in the course of which the party membership was increasingly excluded from effective participation, as the party passed from a "party for struggle" to a party supporting the state.

Thus the role of the party becomes that of providing a following for the leader. Mussolini once suggested that the party has the function of the capillaries in the body; it is neither the heart nor the head, but provides those endings through which the blood of party doctrine, party policy, and party sentiment is infused into the rest of the body politic. It is clear that such a simile applies more readily to the party membership and its lower cadres than to the upper ranks. In view of such total dependence of the party upon the leader at its head, it could be asserted that the party has no corporate existence of its own. But such an interpretation, with its individual-istic overtones, does not seem to do justice to the highly collectivist and communalistic sense that pervades these movements. For the loss of personal identity is compensated for the party member by a communal identity through which he feels himself merged in a larger whole. Organization-ally, this submergence is expressed in the fascist glorification of obedience, as expressed in Mussolini's well-known formula: "Believe, obey, fight." Linked with these sentiments is the notorious fascist and National Socialist conception of their "style of living." It was proclaimed to be that of the "marching column." [43] The similarity of such a view with that of Lenin as propounded in his famous exposition of the need for iron discipline in a revolutionary party is striking.

The Social Bases of the NSDAP

Such an outlook, at once communitarian and disciplinarian, is radically at variance with the liberal tradition of individualistic tolerance, at times bordering on indifference; for *laissez-faire* is not only an economic, but a general social and ethical philosophy. It is perhaps the most important real difference between communism and fascism, seen as totalitarian movements, that this reaction is understood in class-antagonistic terms by the Marxist, while it is understood in a class-integrative perspective by the fascist and National Socialist. The lower middle class (including the peasants) constitutes the mainstay of these movements, although both stress their working-class ingredient as an antidote, real or presumed, against the class struggle.

At this point, the social composition of the party deserves to be sketched. In Table 7–1 the first three columns show the percentage of the various "professions" (*Berufsgruppen*) in the total party membership; the fourth column gives the percentage of these groups in the total work population; the final column notes the difference in percentage points between the two figures for 1935. It will be seen at a glance that there is a substantial increase (over 25 per cent) from 1933 to 1935 only in the group labeled civil servants.[44]

It is equally clear that only in the worker group is the percentage figure substantially lower in the party than in the population; in view of the large actual number involved, this difference accounts for the larger percentage in the other categories, except for the civil servants. Since the total number of employed was 32,306,074, and of these 2,357,884 or 7.3 per cent were members of the party, it might be interesting to add that of the workers 5.1 per cent belonged to the party, of the peasants 7.7 per cent, while of the civil servants 18.4 per cent and of the teachers even 30.9 per cent belonged to the party. It was clearly not a workers' party, even though approximately one-third of the members were workers.

The picture of the NSDAP as a lower middle-class party is very much more pronounced when one examines the cadres of the party. For here we find that the figures to be compared with those in column (3) in the table are as follows: workers, 23.0 per cent; employees, 22.6 per cent; self-employed, 19.5 per cent; civil servants, 17.6 per cent; peasants, 14.7 per cent; others, 2.6 per cent. Clearly, there are substantially fewer workers, in percentage, and substantially more civil servants, and a goodly increase of peasants.[45] A similar contrast, only still more pronounced, appears when one compares these percentages with those found in the population at large; clearly the lower middle classes together with the peasants constitute the backbone of the NSDAP.

TABLE 7-1   *Social Composition of the NSDAP (percentage)*

Professional Group	(1) 1930	(2) 1933	(3) 1935	(4) 1935	(5) Diff.
Workers	26.3	32.5	32.1	46.3	−12.2
Employees	24.4	20.6	20.6	12.4	+ 8.2
Self-employed	18.9	17.3	20.2	9.6	+10.6
Civil Servants	7.7	6.5	13.0	4.8	+ 8.2
Administrative			9.4	3.7	+ 5.7
Teachers			3.6	0.9	+ 2.7
Peasants	13.2	12.5	10.7	10.0	+ 0.7
Others	9.9	10.6	3.4	1.5	+ 1.9

The fact that the membership and leadership of the party reflected all the divisions of the preceding pluralistic society meant that the party was intrinsically handicapped when it became vital to exhibit a cohesive force. The heterogeneity that afflicted it was further enhanced by a latent conflict of generations. The "old" fighters sought to prevent the rise of younger men for whom the regime was a given. This issue is a current one in autocratic systems, and more particularly in totalitarian dictatorships; it provides one of the reasons for recurrent purges,[46] as was most recently demonstrated by the so-called cultural revolution in Red China. A regime may, as it becomes stabilized, seek to regularize these processes and reduce their violence by making them part of an ongoing process of regeneration. The National Socialist system did not endure long enough to suggest more than an equivocal answer; it seems likely that very severe conflicts would have arisen later. However, the evidence seems to suggest that a party which so nearly mirrored the social groupings of an advanced industrial society and its inherent pluralism, was threatened with disintegration anyhow. This potential threat was one of the factors contributing to the system's failure. Schaefer sums up this aspect rather well, when he writes:

The later characteristic paralysis of the NSDAP and the limitation of its tasks to those of manipulating and controlling the domination of the society was conditioned by the organizationally unstable situation of the top leadership. There could not be any viable plan for its construction right after the seizure of power, because the decisive boundaries between the influence of party and state, which were necessary for organizing such leadership, could not be drawn, because the distribution of power (*machtpolitische Verteilung der Kompetenzen*) between the bureaucracy, the military, the economy, the party and other national-socialist groupings remained uncertain.[47] The Vacuum that resulted from these uncertainties was eventually filled by the SS as will be shown below.

Organization of the Party

We must now turn to the structuring of the organization of the party and its *Gliederungen*.[48] It should be remarked at the outset that this organization is extremely complex, in fact bewildering, in its ramifications. The German inclination to overorganize, which rivals the American propensity in this field, went on a veritable binge. But this luxuriant growth of offices, divisions, sections, *Leiter,* coordinators, delegates, and so forth was, in a way, a particularly striking case of Parkinson's Law; as the party lost power, it proliferated cadres. In any case, we do not, at the present time, know what was the actual influence or power of particular units and offices, since careful and detailed research has been done in only a few cases.[49] Schaefer observed more than ten years ago that "on the basis of present documentation it is not possible to determine the effectiveness of the organizational system." [50] But a certain number of biographical studies have certainly shed a good deal of light on the massive infighting that went on inside the party and reduced its effectiveness.[51]

An attempt has been made to penetrate the jungle of organizational detail by distinguishing between an horizontal and a vertical organization, treating under the latter heading the hierarchical relationships. But such a distinction, valid as such, does not permit us to speak of two distinct organizations; they are aspects of the same structure.[52]

Immediately below the Fuehrer there was the office of the deputy leader, which was divided into twenty suboffices, dealing with internal party affairs, personnel, art and culture, foreign policy, universities, and so forth. But the Fuehrer had also special deputies, such as Alfred Rosenberg, who was his deputy "for the entire intellectual and ideological (*weltanschauliche*) education of the NSDAP." Finally, there were "central offices" (*Reichsleitungsaemter*), also twenty in number, including the Office for Organization (*Organisationsamt*), the personnel office, propaganda office, treasurer's office, and so forth. The universities were represented by a union of academic teachers and a union of students (*Dozentenbund* and *Studentenbund*), not of course organizations controlled by the membership, as the titles might suggest, but also centrally directed offices. Between them and the deputy for universities, a tight ideological control was attempted through the establishment of a veto on all academic appointments and promotions. Other ideological controls were exercised by a censorship commission, which examined all publications that claimed to be National Socialist, and by the press leader of the party, whose office often clashed with the Ministry of Propaganda, in spite of Goebbels' overall control. Another effective office was that responsible for the policy of the communes (*Hauptamt fuer Kommunalpolitik*); it was effectively linked to the organization of the communes, the German Society of Communes (*Deutscher Gemeindetag*) whose president was in fact the director of the office—another typical case of coordination. It incidentally meant the end of communal self-government. Obviously, in all these arrangements, there was ample opportunity for jurisdictional conflict, not only with the government, but within the party. The function of "controlling" the government through these offices correspondingly suffered.

Apart from the offices related to government offices, there existed an entire range of "specialist offices" (*Fachaemter*), which related to associations and interest groups. Schaefer calls them the "veritable core of the party organization for the purpose of social control." [53] They related all social groups to the Nazi regime. Very frequently the head of the office was also the president of the association, so that in a sense the entire group life was linked to the bureaucracy and bureaucratized.[54] By representing the interests vis-à-vis the state, these offices greatly contributed to the intermingling of state and party that was characteristic of the regime, and found symbolic expression in the titles of Hitler: he was both leader of the party and Chancellor of the Reich.[55] At the same time these offices served the basic function assigned by Hitler to the party—in keeping with Mussolini's notion of the capillary—of educating the entire people in the ideology of national socialism.

It is not possible to explore this variegated "corporative" system in detail here,[56] but an illustration or two may be worth giving. Among the main offices, that for educators was, of course, of particular importance. Control was its central preoccupation. The office had "for official purposes, such as employment and promotion . . . to evaluate the political and ideological qualification of educators on all levels." [57] Such an evaluation was made in consultation with the local party organization and was communicated to all governmental offices concerned. However, it is not clear whether the office also concerned itself with educational reforms. Another office of considerable impact was the *Rechtsamt* or Law Office. Again we find that the head of the office is made the president of the NS Union of German Jurists which along with the NS Union of Protectors of the Law (*Rechtswahrerbund*) undertook to line up all persons involved in the administration of justice.[58] The office itself acted as syndic for the party, but it also organized a legal aid office (*Amt fuer Rechtsbetreuung*)—a suboffice of the Law Office. It is highly characteristic of the system of the National Socialists that they had to be so concerned with perverting the legal profession, converting at least outwardly 63,010 German jurists to the extent that they became members of the two Unions just mentioned.[59]

The concern with legal aid is characteristic for two other major party activities, the National Socialist People's Welfare (NSV) and the National Socialist Care for War Victims (NSKOV), which coordinated and centralized numerous private organizations that had previously been concerned with such welfare activities. The huge membership, nearly 4 million by 1935, can be explained by this merging of numerous organizations. The activities of all of them were now credited to the party. It is worth noting that their activities, and more particularly the widely publicized Winter Help (*Winterhilfe*) were tied in organizationally with the party's propaganda activities.[60]

There were, of course, also the usual offices for internal administration one finds in any large organization; one of these, the office of the treasurer, has recently been carefully researched and has been shown to have served an important integrating function supplementary to that of the Fuehrer's own chancellery, although this office was itself rather bureaucratically administered, rigid and unresponsive to the reactions of the mass of the members, hostile to any petitions and much inclined to insist upon strict observance of official channels.[61] These channels constituted an elaborate hierarchy structured in terms of strict subordination and culminating in the leader, whose decisions were unchallengeable in fact and generally accepted as above criticism.[62]

This hierarchy, below the leader and the Reich ministries, that is to say the national level, consisted of five levels: the province (*Gau*), the district (*Kreis*), the local group (*Ortsgruppe*), the cell, and the bloc. A bloc comprised forty to sixty households, or 160 to 240 persons, a cell four to six blocs, that is, 160 to 480 households. The idea underlying this breakdown into very small units was "to make a complete control possible." It also facilitated a continuing pressure through propaganda and intimidation, including a great deal of eavesdropping, spying, and reporting on persons who made critical remarks and complained. The leader of a bloc was considered a "bearer of sovereignty" as mentioned before, and as such he was expected to explain measures of government and party, to moderate and cajole.[63] He was urged not to be overbearing nor to fraternize; he was always to conduct himself as the representative of the majesty of the NS state. It is clear from the detailing of these functions that the capillary function of the party was considered central; the bloc leader was the end point of this system of transmission belts. On the higher levels, this immediate impact upon the populace was lost; here, the party units operated indirectly by integrating the various offices and organizations, some of which we have discussed above. A local group had a maximum of 3,000 households or 12,000 persons until 1937; thereafter it was reduced to half this number, in order to be more effective with the populace at large. Beyond the local group, the functions become strictly organizational, and even at the district level are meant to supervise the governmental offices to some extent. But their primary task, and more especially on the provincial level the task of the *Gauleiter's* office, was to coordinate and integrate the various party offices and organizations. As such, all these levels cooperated in the common task of indoctrinating not only the membership, but the populace at large and making them cooperate in the regime's policies.

The SA and the SS

Anyone who has studied the operation of the party in the Soviet Union and other totalitarian regimes will be struck by the similarity between these several parties, and more particularly their constant effort at producing an "induced" or "manipulated" consensus. Their struggle to secure acceptance of the arbitrary decisions of the top leadership is vital to the maintenance of the system. In many of those subject to such manipulations an illusion of voluntary assent is produced. Some of the measures Khrushchev initiated were strongly reminiscent of the very methods employed by the National Socialists, as indeed of the fascists and earlier Bolsheviks.[64] There was, however, a very basic difference. The National Socialist Party, through its policy of coordination and expansion to include a large number of outsiders, who, of course, made the manipulative functions the more urgent, was bound to become too large to provide any effective partner in the exercise of the core power of the regime, such as are the *apparatchiki* of the Communist Party of the Soviet Union and other satellite states. As a result, the protective guards (SS) assumed this role to an increasing extent. It would originally have been more natural for the storm troopers, who contained many of the old fighters, to exercise this "elitist" function. But this development was forestalled by the Blood Purge of 1934.

It is now fairly clear that this purge resulted from the conflict with the military, reinforced by personal factors.[65] The leader of the SA, Ernst Roehm, an ex-officer, had originally expected to become the head of the military establishment. He tried to have his subleaders co-opted into the army. At the same time, he made himself the spokesman of the more revolutionary elements of the party. As tension rose and the military began to fear a coup by Roehm, and he a liquidation of the SA, Hitler in a lightning action, characterized by ruse and brutality as was his wont, seized the initiative, arrested and executed Roehm and a substantial number of his lieutenants, and then undertook to justify his action by claiming that a plot had been uncovered. All the available evidence points to the conclusion that there existed no such plot, at least not at that time, but that Hitler had come to the conclusion that the SA had lost its usefulness, since it could not be successfully transformed into a more harmless paramilitary organization under its existing leadership, which gloried in the services it had rendered in the period of active struggle against the Weimar Republic. A decree that he issued afterwards to the reformed SA shows clearly that certain moral weaknesses, especially a rampant homosexuality, had also become enough of a scandal to require eradication.[66]

In this lurid drama, Hitler found himself loyally supported throughout by Himmler and his guards (SS). He therefore made the SS into an autonomous organization within the party, directly reporting to him, and providing the party with the firm backbone that a totalitarian regime requires. Himmler took full advantage of this opportunity and succeeded in gradually making his SS an effective rival of the party itself. As contrasted with the heterogeneous party membership, the SS membership was young and filled with zeal for the regime's (Hitler's) ideology; it thus became the unquestioning, enthusiastic support of all the Fuehrer's actions. Eventually, the SS in its three distinct formations came to embody for the masses of the subject populace the genuine Nazi following, especially as it was, through the person of Himmler, closely linked to the terroristic apparatus. It has become quite clear, through a variety of recent researches, that the SS possessed a more radical, indeed fanatic attitude than the average party member or SA man. In course of time, the SS managed to infiltrate various key positions in party and government, especially the military and economic cadres. During the war, and after the abortive plot of the Resistance in 1944, the SS even succeeded in taking over the key controls of the armed forces.[67] It is probably an exaggeration to speak of the Hitler regime as an SS state in fact, but there can be little doubt, on the basis of available evidence, that Himmler planned to make a bid for such a development. Whether Hitler would have been willing to go forward in that direction would seem doubtful in light of his *Table Talk*.[68] That the SS provided Hitler with the opportunity to reduce the role of the party to the kind of instrument we have analyzed above there can be little doubt.

The Problem of Legitimacy

If we finally face the problem of legitimacy, which appears so crucial in one-party systems, and which Clement H. Moore has made the key of his approach, the foregoing suggests the following conclusion. For the population at large, the Hitler regime probably never achieved full legitimacy. His early efforts to secure a widespread recognition of his right or title to rule, which is the core of legitimacy, are discernible in the insistence upon the legality of all his steps—actually not too scrupulously observed, but sufficiently so to satisfy so inexperienced and turbulent a public as Germany possessed in 1933. To reinforce this legal base, Hitler sought as much as possible to give the impression that Hindenburg was authorizing his actions; even before the Blood Purge he visited the old general to receive his blessing for dealing with the "national emergency." [69] Such help as this may have been, and undoubtedly it impressed a substantial number of non-Nazis, disappeared with the death of Hindenburg in August, 1934. Thereafter, Hitler had to rely upon the party for such elusive legitimacy as he might achieve. Broadly speaking, people in a non-traditional and non-religious context are forced to look toward either ideologies or material benefits for determining what is right and hence legitimate.[70] But this ground was, of course, only valid for the party member and follower.

A pseudo-democratic ground was provided by a series of plebiscites Hitler held. The results, though manifestly manipulated in their startling results of 98-99.9 per cent, helped perhaps more abroad than at home, where sarcastic anecdotes undermined their efficacy.[71] The pseudo-charismatic appeal, not rooted in genuine transcendent belief, but in fraudulent claims of a "mission" adorned with much superstitious claptrap, cast a spell over the more simple-minded members of the party but had little effect among the rest of the populace. Altogether, it is important in this connection to bear in mind that political authority, understood as the capacity of a leader for the reasoned elaboration of political decisions, while great among the party following, is very limited among the rest of the populace, and hence legitimacy is likewise bifurcated. Only the actual success of a leader or regime, especially economic and military success, will under such conditions provide legitimacy in the sense of creating a belief that the rulers are entitled to rule. The NSDAP and its leadership had, by providing employment for the unemployed masses, and even a measure of prosperity, secured an important ground for legitimizing its rule. "Legitimate is he who improves the standard of living," may be too cynical a verdict, but it contains a kernel of truth. If to such economic successes there are added foreign policy and prestige victories, such as Hitler was able to achieve in the first few years of his regime, a purely pragmatic legitimacy may result, as de Gaulle has again demonstrated in recent years. His presidency at the same time shows how relatively little such legitimacy depends upon either a party or an ideology. When finally Hitler's armies swept all before them, he was widely accepted in Germany and beyond as the legitimate ruler of Germany, only to lose his legitimacy completely as soon as victories turned into defeat, German cities sank into ashes, and the economy became a shambles.

These brief reflections on legitimacy must suffice to show that the party and the ideology proved feeble reeds in the hour of peril. We have been trying to suggest that the National Socialist experiment was foredoomed to failure. The concessions which had to be made in building the complex and contradictory party organization, because the country the party was meant to rule was already a complex industrial society, the dualism of party and protective guards (SS) which resulted from these concessions, the aggressive racial and foreign policies which the search for demonstrable legitimizing successes precipitated, escalating eventually into vast military conflict with disastrous results—all these tend to show that a one-party system is no solution to the tensions and breakdowns of an industrially developed country. The requirements of such a society extract adaptations which undermine the party's effectiveness as an instrument of rule.

‖ *Notes*

1. Perhaps the best "explanation" of why Hitler came to power is that offered by Theodor Abel, *Why Hitler Came to Power* (New York: Prentice-Hall, 1938), recently republished with slight additions under the title *The Nazi Movement* (New York: Atherton Press, 1965).

2. Franz Neumann, *Behemoth* (Toronto: Oxford University Press, 1942), p. 30, adds 2 million so-called invisible unemployed, and comments: "Only a small fraction received unemployment insurance and an ever larger proportion received no support at all." On the subject of the National Socialist Party, for which we still lack a thorough and detailed overall study, the most satisfactory remains Wolfgang Schäfer, *NSDAP—Entwicklung und Struktur der Staatspartei des dritten Reiches* (Hannover: Goedel, 1956).

3. See the chapters by Clement H. Moore and Samuel P. Huntington in this volume.

4. This viewpoint is particularly stressed by Hans Buchheim, *Totalitäre Herrschaft —Wesen und Merkmale,* (Munich: Kösel-Verlag, 1962). Now also available in English: *Totalitarian Rule—Its Nature and Characteristics* (Middletown: Wesleyan University Press, 1968).

5. A considerable controversy has developed over the problem of charisma. See my article "Political Leadership and the Problem of Charismatic Power," *Journal of Politics,* XXIII (1961), 3–24, placed into systematic context in *Man and His Government* (New York: McGraw-Hill, 1963), chap. 9. See also W. C. Runciman, "Charismatic Legitimacy and One-Party Rule in Ghana," *Archives Européennes de Sociologie,* IV (1963), 148–165. Some of this literature was recently reviewed and synthesized by Ann Ruth Willner, *Charismatic Political Leadership—A Theory* (Princeton: Princeton University, Center for International Studies, 1968). Unfortunately Miss Willner did not trouble to consider my basic critique of the concept. A special application of the concept to Hitler and the NSDAP has been attempted by Joseph Nyomarkay, *Charisma and Factionalism in the Nazi Party* (Minneapolis: University of Minnesota Press, 1967). Nyomarkay includes as usual a belief in divine origin among the characteristics of charismatic leadership. Since such a belief was not shared by all the members of the Nazi Party, let alone the general populace, he is really speaking of pseudo-charisma.

6. See for this Karl Dietrich Bracher's magistral work, *Die Auflösung der Weimarer Republik—Eine Studie zum Problem des Machtverfalls in der Demokratie,* 2nd ed. (Stuttgart: Ring-Verlag, 1957).

7. See Roger Manvell and Heinrich Fraenkel, *Goering* (New York: Simon and Schuster, 1962), and *Doctor Goebbels—His Life and Death* (London: Heinemann, 1960); Helmut Heiber, ed., *The Early Goebbels Diaries* (London: Weidenfeld, 1962); and Joseph Wulf, *Martin Bormann—Hitlers Schatten* (Gütersloh: Mohn, 1962). See also the overall study of Joachim C. Fest, *Das Gesicht des dritten Reiches—Profile einer totalitären Herrschaft* (Munich: Piper, 1963).

8. See Dolf Sternberger, *Storz and Süskind, Aus dem Wörterbuch des Unmenschen* (Hamburg, 1957); and Victor Klemperer, *Die unbewältigte Sprache* (Darmstadt: Melzer, 1966).

9. H. R. Trevor-Roper, ed., *Hitler's Table Talk* (New York: Farrar, Straus and Young, 1953). The German version, ed. Dr. Henry Picker (1951), is distorted by its editing.

10. Besides the Italian original see Michael Oakeshott, *The Social and Political Doctrines of Contemporary Europe* (Cambridge: Cambridge University Press, 1947), pp. 164–179, which is complete.

11. Milovan Djilas, *The New Class* (New York: Frederick A. Praeger, 1957), pp. 37ff.

12. *The Goebbels Diaries,* transl. and ed. by Louis P. Lochner (London: H. Hamilton, 1948).

13. International Military Trials, Nürnberg, *Nazi Conspiracy and Aggression* (Washington, D.C.: Government Printing Office, 1946).

14. Adolf Hitler, *Mein Kampf,* transl. Ralph Manheim (Boston: Houghton Mifflin, 1943), pp. 386ff. (The entire chapter 2 of book 2, which in the German original of 1932 is found on pp. 425ff.)

15. Hitler, *op. cit.,* pp. 394ff. (in the original pp. 435ff.).

16. The common English way of speaking of a "withering away" does not correspond to the more dramatic German *Der Staat stirbt ab.* See Frederick Engels, *Socialism, Utopian and Scientific,* Marxist Library (New York: International Publishers, 1935), II, 69–70; it lays the foundation by relating the origin of the state to private property. Cf. the discriminating critical analysis in Herbert Marcuse, *Soviet Marxism—A Critical Analysis,* (New York: Columbia University Press, 1958), chaps. 5 and 6.

17. See my article "Organization Theory and Political Style," *Public Policy,* X (1960), 44–61.

18. A telling critique of such views is found in Abel, *op. cit.,* pp. 194ff. A Marxist interpretation in a refined and elaborated form underlies Franz Neumann's work.

19. Alan Bullock, *Hitler—A Study in Tyranny* (London: Odhams Press, 1952), p. 367.

20. Dante Germino, *The Italian Fascist Party in Power—A Study in Totalitarian Rule* (Minneapolis: Minnesota University Press, 1959). See also Luigi Salvatorelli and G. Mira, *Storia del Fascismo* (Rome: Edizioni di Novissima, 1952).

21. G. M. Gilbert, *The Psychology of Dictatorship* (New York: Ronald Press, 1950), p. 301, based on the examination of the leaders of Nazi Germany; H. B. Gisevius, *Adolf Hitler* (Munich: Rütten and Loening, 1963). In my *Totalitarian Dictatorship and Autocracy,* 2nd ed. (Cambridge: Harvard University Press, 1965), p. 41, I said: "He (Hitler) came to picture himself as capable of making ultimate decisions in this field (military matters) which proved the undoing of the German army." Cf. Francis H. Hensley, *Hitler's Strategy* (Toronto: Macmillan, 1951), pp. 238–239.

22. Friedrich, *Totalitarian Dictatorship and Autocracy,* chap. 2, esp. at p. 22, modified in my article "The Changing Theory and Practice of Totalitarianism," *Il Politico,* XXXIII, No. 1 (University of Pavia, 1968), 53–76.

23. See my *Constitutional Government and Democracy,* 4th ed. (Waltham, Mass.: Blaisdell Publishing Co., 1968), chap. 20, esp. pp. 442ff. See also Max Weber, *Wirtschaft und Gesellschaft* (Tübingen: Mohr, 1925), p. 167; Harold D. Lasswell and A. Kaplan, *Power and Society* (New Haven: Yale University Press, 1950), p. 159.

24. See my *Man and His Government,* chap. 28.

25. As does Schäfer, *op. cit.,* pp. 24ff.

26. K. D. Bracher, Wolfgang Sauer, and Gerhard Schulz, *Die nationalsozialistische Machtergreifung—Studien zur Errichtung des totalitären Herrschaftssystems in Deutschland 1933–34* (Cologne: Westdeutscher Verlag, 1960); Bracher discusses this problem on pp. 152ff. The legal problems of the Enabling Act have been carefully developed by Hans Schneider, *Das Ermächtigungsgesetz vom 24. März 1933* (Bonn: Bundeszentrale für Heimatdienst, 1961). Gilbert Fergusson, "A Blueprint for Dictatorship—Hitler's Enabling Law of March 1933," *Inter-*

258 | *The Failure of a One-Party System: Hitler Germany*

national Affairs, XL, No. 29 (April 1964), 245–261, was largely based upon the facts and discussion in Schneider's article.

27. Bracher, in Bracher, Sauer, and Schulz, *op. cit.,* p. 82. A special detailed study has been published by Fritz Tobias, *The Reichstag Fire* (New York: Putnam, 1964), with a forceful introduction by A. J. P. Taylor; this book offers a very conscientious and convincing treatment.

28. The results of the elections of March, 1933 are given in the *Statistisches Jahrbuch* for 1930, p. 539 as follows:

(figures in thousands):

Registered voters	46,890
Actual votes	39,343
NSDAP	17,277
Nationalists	3,137
Social Democrats	7,182
Communists	4,848
Catholics (Centre Party)	4,425
Others	2,229

as reported in Schäfer, *op. cit.,* n. 71.

29. Bracher, in Bracher, Sauer, and Schulz, *op. cit.,* p. 135.

30. Arnold Brecht, *Prelude to Silence—The End of the German Republic* (New York: Oxford University Press, 1944).

31. Schulz, in Bracher, Sauer, and Schulz, *op. cit.,* p. 442ff., 476ff., 627ff., and 641ff.

32. Neumann, *op. cit.,* speaks of "counter-revolution," pp. 20ff. Ernst Nolte, *Three Faces of Fascism* (New York: Holt, Rinehart and Winston, 1966) (the original is entitled *Der Faschismus in seiner Epoche*) speaks of a "conservative revolution," pp. 132–133. Bracher, in Bracher, Sauer, and Schulz, speaks of a "pseudolegal revolution," pp. 4ff.

33. Cf. Schäfer, *op. cit.,* pp. 25ff., and the *Parteistatistik* of the National Socialist Party, I, 240ff.; and II, 302ff. To have directed attention to and explored this official party statistics as well as the party's *Verordnungsblatt* (VOBl) is one of the merits of Schäfer's study.

34. Schäfer, *op. cit.* p. 30.

35. Bracher, in Bracher, Sauer, and Schulz, *op. cit.,* pp. 198ff.

36. Bracher, in Bracher, Sauer and Schulz, *op. cit.,* pp. 175ff. Cf. also Neumann, *op. cit.,* pp. 413ff.

37. Friedrich, *Totalitarian Dictatorship and Autocracy,* new ed. (1965), chap. 16; Neumann, *op. cit.,* part 3. For a very pungent treatment of the corporative state see Gaetano Salvemini, *Under the Axe of Fascism* (New York: Viking Press, 1936).

38. Discussed in Schäfer, *op. cit.,* p. 32ff.; *VOBl* (May 13, 1933); Schäfer, *op. cit.,* p. 33; and B. Geismar, *Musik in Schatten der Politik* (Zurich, 1945), pp. 84ff.

39. Schäfer, *op. cit.,* p. 41; *Parteistatistik,* II, 290, as cited by Schäfer. Note also Schäfer's footnotes 118 and 122.

40. *Parteistatistik,* II, 287.

41. *Parteistatistik,* II, 11 and 22.

42. See Schäfer, *op. cit.,* pp. 45–46 for greater detail; also the *Parteistatistik,* II, 52ff.

43. Nolte, *op. cit.,* pp. 421ff.

44. Schäfer, *op. cit.,* pp. 19 and 38, which according to his references are based on *Parteistatistik,* p. 70 and p. 53. Schäfer also refers to his doctoral dissertation in n. 108.

45. Schäfer reports that he gave considerable further detail in his dissertation, already mentioned, and entitled *Untersuchungen zur Entwicklung, Struktur und Organisation der NSDAP* (Unpublished Ph.D. diss., University of Marburg, 1955).

46. See Zbigniew K. Brzezinski, *The Permanent Purge: Politics in Soviet Totalitarianism* (Cambridge: Harvard University Press, 1956).

47. Schäfer, *op. cit.,* p. 48.

48. Alfred Vagts, "Hitler's Second Army," *Infantry Journal* (Washington, D.C., 1943), esp. chaps. 6–13.

49. Ulf Lükemann, *Der Reichsschatzmeister der NSDAP—Ein Beitrag zur inneren Parteistruktur* (Berlin: Ernst Reuter-Gesellschaft, 1963). Cf. also Paul Seabury, *The Wilhelmstrasse—A Study of German Diplomats Under the Nazi Regime* (Berkeley: University of California Press, 1954); and more recently Elke Frank, *The Wilhelmstrasse during the Third Reich: Changes in Its Organizational Structure and Personnel Policies* (Unpublished Ph. D. diss., Harvard University, 1964).

50. Schäfer, *op. cit.,* p. 52.

51. See the works cited in n. 6. The brief sketches in Fest, *op. cit.,* are also very illuminating.

52. Schäfer, *op. cit.,* p. 52.

53. Schäfer, *op. cit.,* p. 57.

54. Friedrich, *Totalitarian Dictatorship and Autocracy,* chap. 16; Neumann, *op. cit.,* pp. 365ff.

55. Friedrich, *Totalitarian Dictatorship and Autocracy,* chap. 3.

56. Neumann, *op. cit.,* part 2, chap. 3; Schulz, in Bracher, Sauer, and Schulz, *op. cit.,* chap. 5. The use of the term *Stände,* literally "estates," was very misleading and has remained a source of confusion in the literature; for the German term *Stand* carried the implication of a measure of participation and control from below.

57. Schäfer, *op. cit.,* p. 59 and references.

58. Schäfer, *op. cit.,* pp. 60–61 and *VOBl* March 20, 1934; February 21, 1934; April 6, 1934 and September 30, 1932, as cited by Schäfer.

59. On perversion see Fritz von Hippel, *Die Perversion von Rechtsordnungen* (Tübingen: Mohr, 1955).

60. Schäfer, *op. cit.,* p. 64.

61. Schäfer, *op. cit.,* p. 68. To cite him: "Die Anlage der organisatorischen Struktur mit ihren tatsächlichen immanenten Kontrollmöglichkeiten enthielt das Wesen der starren, nur durch die Institution handlungsfähigen, aber in ihrem Einsatz geschlossenen Organisation."

62. Much of the literature stresses this point. For a recent restatement in the perspective of the history of dictatorship cf. Eleonore Sterling, *Der unvollkommene Staat* (Frankfurt: Europäische Verlags-Anstalt, 1965), pp. 281ff. For an extreme statement of this position by a German professor of constitutional law see Carl Schmitt, in *Ursachen und Folgen—Vom deutschen Zusammenbruch 1918 und 1945 bis zur staatlichen Neuordnung Deutschlands in der Gegenwart —Eine Urkunden—und Dokumentensammlung zur Zeitgeschichte,* ed. Herbert Michaelis and Ernst Schraepler in cooperation with Günter Scheel, Vol. 10: *Das Dritte Reich—Die Errichtung des Führerstaates. Die Abwendung von dem System der kollektiven Sicherheit,* p. 221.

63. Schäfer, *op. cit.,* p. 72ff.

64. See my article, cited in n. 20 above.

65. The work cited in n. 59 offers in its section VII and more especially on pp. 138 and 221 a most revealing collection of documents leading to the conclusion given in the text and stated on p. 146. See also Schulz, in Bracher, Sauer, and Schulz,

op. cit., pp. 897–972, where the notion of this "second revolution" is fully explored. The problem of SA factionalism is also fully explored by Nyomarkay, *op. cit.,* pp. 110–141.

66. Cf. the work cited in n. 59, pp. 177ff.
67. Gerald Reitlinger, *The SS—Alibi of a Nation* (New York: Viking Press, 1957); and Roger Manvell and Heinrich Fraenkel, *Heinrich Himmler* (New York: Putnam, 1965); Hans Buchheim (contributor and editor), *Anatomie des SS-Staates* (Olten: Walter-Verlag, 1965).
68. See Hitler's *Table Talk* as cited above, n. 8, *passim.*
69. Cf. the work cited in n. 59, p. 195; also Bullock, *op. cit.,* chap. 5, section 6.
70. See my *Man and His Government,* pp. 244ff.
71. Friedrich, *Totalitarian Dictatorship and Autocracy,* pp. 164ff.

8

The Internal Dynamics of the CPSU, 1917–1967

║ *Jeremy R. Azrael*

When Lenin first proclaimed that the Bolshevik Party was prepared to shoulder the entire burden of political power, he was generally considered a foolhardy adventurer.[1] When the Bolsheviks actually seized power five months later, even leading members of the party expected the new regime to collapse within a matter of weeks.[2] Fifty years later, the Soviet Union is still a one-party system, and the Communist Party has just adopted a new program in which it vows to maintain and further expand its leading role.[3] This pledge will not be easy to redeem, but it takes inordinate courage to dismiss the possibility out of hand. Prophecies of the imminent demise of the communist system have once again become common, but the party's monopolistic position still seems quite secure, and the party *apparat* remains an extremely powerful "organizational weapon," deeply entrenched in the most strategic sectors of the economy and society.[4] To be sure, both party discipline and *apparat* control have recently shown signs of significant erosion. All too often, however, these changes are measured against a hyperbolic model of Soviet politics rather than against historical reality. In consequence, there is a widespread tendency to exaggerate both the extent and the rate of change.

For certain analytical purposes, the most noteworthy feature of "classical" Soviet politics may well be their close approximation to the totalitarian paradigm.[5] Nevertheless, the CPSU has never been a complete monolith, and the power of the party *apparat* has always been limited. If recognition of these "shortfalls" blurs useful taxonomic distinctions, it enhances historical accuracy and diminishes the risk of misinterpreting present and emergent trends. At the same time, moreover, appreciation of the fact that the CPSU is only "more or less" unique opens the way for illuminating

261

comparisons with other political parties, including communist parties that diverge from the Soviet model or type. The point is not, of course, to replace analysis with description or to restrict comparison to an account of similarities. It is to identify real differences and to place them in theoretically relevant perspectives. Accordingly, while this chapter will treat "the dictatorship of the party" as an empirical question rather than an explanatory axiom and will underline features of Soviet politics that are common to other one-party systems, the focus will be on the CPSU's unprecedentedly sustained pursuit and extraordinarily effective consolidation of monopolistic political power. The goals that have animated the CPSU have animated other parties as well, and there have been many would-be imitators of Soviet techniques. To date, however, the imitations have proved feeble copies, and efforts to realize similar ends by different means have had dubious success. In short, while the CPSU does not emerge from empirical investigation as either perfectly totalitarian or completely *sui generis,* it does emerge as the embodiment of exceptional political prowess, and any theory of parties that does not recognize and help to explain this prowess is patently defective. If nothing else, this essay should serve to validate these strictures and thereby help to delineate some important conceptual boundaries.

Writing on the eve of the October Revolution, Lenin adduced two basic reasons for answering the question, "Can the Bolsheviks Retain State Power?" in the affirmative.[6] First, he argued that a Bolshevik regime could rally widespread popular support. Second, he argued that a Bolshevik regime could staff the governmental and economic bureaucracies with cadres who were both competent and politically reliable. For many Bolsheviks, however, the question of whether the party could retain power was less important than the question of whether the party could fulfill its programmatic commitments. In their eyes, power was a purely instrumental value, and, in this perspective, Lenin's arguments seemed not only inconclusive but ominous. Thus, Lenin himself acknowledged that popular support was contingent on the party's adoption of such non-partisan and even overtly "revisionistic" programs as "Bread, Land, and Peace." And the stress that Lenin placed on the penetration and effective utilization of established bureaucratic structures was clearly at variance with the Marxist injunction to "smash" the bourgeois state machine and institutionalize communist power on the model of the Paris Commune of 1870.[7] No doubt tactical flexibility was a *sine qua non* for successful revolutionary action, but Lenin seemed ready to compromise basic doctrinal principles. Moreover, the very conditions to which Lenin was responding, the conditions of Russia's backwardness, seemed likely to require further compromises of a sort that would be even more incompatible with the party's ideological goals. It was apprehension on these counts as much as doubt that an insurrection could succeed that made many Bolsheviks reluctant to embark on revolution.[8] Nevertheless, at the moment of ultimate decision, Lenin's policy of Napoleonic "audacity" prevailed.[9]

Events following the Bolshevik seizure of power lent credence to many of the fears expressed by Lenin's critics. After a brief period of left-wing militancy, the revisionism of "Bread, Land, and Peace" gave way to the far-reaching compromises of the New Economic Policy or NEP. The free market was revived; concessions were made to foreign investors; material incentives were restored to their paramount position; and individual peasant proprietorship was actively encouraged. Similarly, "workers' control" and "workers' management" were drastically curtailed, and administrative efficiency, technical rationality, and stringent labor discipline became hallmarks of official policy. In the same vein, the regime granted more authority to holdover "bourgeois specialists" and ordered communist executives to solicit and defer to expert advice. Moreover, these developments were accompanied by definite symptoms of decay within the party itself. In particular, there was a manifest decline of "class vigilance" and revolutionary ardor among the rank-and-file members of the party, and the upper strata of the party showed clear signs of "regrouping" into administrative pressure groups and bureaucratic cliques.[10]

Following the seizure of power, the party was inundated by applications for admission. Careerists and bandwagon followers of all sorts discovered unexpected affinities for bolshevism, and established selection procedures allowed many of them to acquire party cards. Far from enforcing strict admission criteria, the regime was so starved for manpower and so anxious to avoid isolation from the masses that it instructed party screening committees not to be too choosy. In consequence, the party grew from 23,600 in January, 1917 to 576,000 in January, 1921, with the bulk of the new recruits drawn from the non-proletarian elements of the population.[11] Not all of those enrolled during this period were opportunists, of course, but many had ulterior motives, and the vast majority had only the most tenuous grasp of Bolshevik principles. Under the best of circumstances the "tempering" of such cadres would have been a formidable task, and the circumstances of the NEP were anything but propitious. Opportunities for profiteering and bribe-taking were rampant, and many of the newer recruits, as well as a significant number of their seniors, found the temptations too great to resist. But widespread venality was only part of the problem. Even more serious was the fact that many well-meaning communists interpreted the introduction of the NEP as a signal for relaxation and for the transfer of energy from the public to the private sphere. As "political illiterates," they naturally viewed the NEP as a long-term commitment, and they proved no less anxious than their non-party neighbors to acquire land, accumulate consumer goods, and restore peace and decorum to their local communities. Finally, in those cases in which they did initially attempt to play (or to continue to play) a vanguard role, they often found the counterpressure of their neighbors irresistible and gradually reverted to more conventional behavior in conformity with prevailing "petty-bourgeois" standards.[12]

At the upper levels of the party, corruption and "overadaptation" to the NEP do not seem to have been serious problems. Here the majority of cadres were Old Bolsheviks whose personal integrity had been tested by years of underground struggle and whose dedication to the revolution was undiminished by the emoluments of power. After assuming power, however, these elite cadres showed an increasing tendency to interpret their revolutionary obligations in the light of their particular governmental roles and to coalesce accordingly. As early as 1921, Nikolai Bukharin publicly lamented that

> the party as it existed in the period of its illegality, when there was a single psychology and a single ideology, has split into a variety of separate columns. . . . Military workers, soviet workers, trade union workers, and party workers proper have organized together among themselves.[13]

Moreover, some of these groups proved to be highly self-assertive. Thus, Leonid Krasin, the principal spokesman for the "managerial wing of the party," advocated nothing less than a fundamental "restructuring" of the party and demanded that the party replace the "journalists, literateurs, and professional politicians" who presently dominated the Central Committee with experienced "production leaders and economic executives." [14] And, to make matters worse, prevailing personnel practices seemed destined to accelerate the growth of occupational role-consciousness and to intensify such "technocratic" pressure. By 1922, at the latest, official training programs and staffing policies clearly recognized that specialization was essential for effective party control and would become progressively more vital as a result of further modernization.[15] Needless to say, the logic of this position was unassailable. But it was a logic that could only be pursued at the expense of political solidarity within the ruling elite.

The risk that these various developments would demobilize and disarm the party was increased by the extremely hostile reaction they aroused among left-wing fundamentalists and ideological purists. Indeed, a significant number of the dissidents became so desperate that they turned in their party cards and in some cases even killed themselves in protest. Many more became sufficiently alienated to organize an intraparty opposition and eventually to press their dissent to the point where the leadership had little choice but to expel them.[16] If their expulsion was a necessary step in the stabilization of power, however, it also deprived the party of the services of some of its most militant and incorruptible cadres. Nevertheless, despite this loss, and despite the demoralization and "contamination" of many of the cadres who remained, the party did not succumb to routinization. The forces of traditionalism and the forces of rationalism took a heavy toll, but ultimately the party was able to contain them. It managed to establish both a mass base and an administrative superstructure without losing its combat capacity.

The factors that enabled the party to adapt to society while preserving its political independence are relatively familiar, and it is enough to list the most important of them here. In the first place, by the end of the Civil War, Russian society was so debilitated that it was incapable of exerting sustained pressure on the new regime. In addition, the Bolsheviks hastened to destroy all rival parties and to disperse the incumbent leadership of most other important secondary associations. In consequence, when society began to recover during the early years of the NEP, it found its traditional channels of political self-expression blocked. At the same time, the party provided alternative "transmission belts" for political communication and mass mobilization by creating a multitude of auxiliary "public organizations" of its own. In the fourth place, as Lenin had predicted, the party contained enough executive talent to effectively dominate the governmental and economic bureaucracies. And, despite their tendency to "regroup," most of the Bolsheviks who were assigned to high-level state and economic posts remained convinced that party unity was a *sine qua non* for the achievement of their goals.[17] Furthermore, the party leadership took vigorous steps to protect itself against those cadres who did "degenerate" or who sought to use their membership in the party for purely personal ends. Lenin had long since subscribed to Lasalle's maxim that "a party grows stronger by purging itself," and, once the initial stabilization of power was completed, he inaugurated a massive party purge, specifically designed to weed out members who had become too absorbed in their bureaucratic roles or who proved to be too much influenced by "survivals of the past."[18] Finally, as a further measure of defense, the secretarial apparatus of the party was centralized and expanded, and full-time party functionaries were given veto power over an increasing range of decisions, including decisions pertaining not only to intraparty affairs but also to appointments and policies in all politically sensitive fields.[19]

By 1923, it was reasonably clear that the Bolshevik regime had successfully forestalled the threat of imminent routinization. While six years was too short a time for final judgment, there were good grounds for the conclusion that Lenin advanced in one of his deathbed reviews of Bolshevik strategy: "Now there can be no doubt that we have been victorious."[20] It remained to be seen, however, whether the party could survive the crisis of its founder's death. The victory that Lenin celebrated was largely the creation of his own political vision and personal charisma, and none of his lieutenants seemed equally endowed. Moreover, there was little prospect that they would compensate for their individual deficiencies through collective solidarity. In his "last testament," Lenin did his best to insure such an outcome, but the odds were heavily against him.[21] Contrary to common opinion, collective leadership was perfectly compatible with the party's institutional arrangements and entirely legitimate from an ideological point of view. Nevertheless, the presence of intense policy conflicts and personal rivalries among the heirs apparent made the bitter succession struggle that in fact ensued almost inevitable. What is remarkable is that all of the contenders accepted a set of political ground rules that kept the conflict exclusively within the confines of the party and largely within the confines of the party's leading organs. Once again, as in the case of the previously mentioned administrative and occupational pressure groups, the conviction that the party was the only appropriate forum for political activity and the only possible vehicle of socialist construction proved to be a decisive determinant of political behavior. Thus, Trotsky, who was commander-in-chief of the Red Army, did not even consider the possibility of a Bonapartist *coup*, and leaders such as Rykov, who was head of the government, and Tomsky, who was chairman of the trade unions, made no serious attempt to mobilize their non-party "constituents" for factional purposes. This restraint, in turn, virtually insured that Stalin would emerge as Lenin's heir. While all of his rivals occupied high party offices, Stalin alone had concentrated his energies primarily on party affairs, and he completely dominated the party secretariat, the functionaries of which were in a uniquely favorable position to set the agenda of party meetings, to select party officers, to control the recruitment and placement of party cadres, and to determine the victims of the ongoing party purge.

If Stalin's victory in the succession struggle provided an ironic but eloquent reaffirmation of Lenin's vision of a party in which iron discipline was the cardinal virtue and ultimate authority belonged to those for whom politics was a full-time vocation, the "second revolution" that Stalin launched on the morrow of his victory conclusively confirmed Lenin's belief that political power could be used as an instrument of social and economic transformation. Lenin himself probably did not intend so violent an upheaval—any more than he intended Stalin to be his heir. But in the former case as in the latter, the actual outcome was implicit in the premises that he laid down. If Stalin took literally statements that Lenin had put forward metaphorically, this kind of reification followed logically from the view that art was a form of politics and that the full meaning of theory could be discerned only in action.[22] The action that ensued clearly bore the stamp of Stalin's personal brutality, but rapid industrialization and the collectivization of agriculture were both Leninist goals, and it is difficult to believe that they could have been accomplished on any substantial scale without extensive mass coercion. Stalin may have been too eager to make a virtue of necessity, but the necessity in question was an integral feature of Bolshevik doctrine; it was an almost inescapable consequence of the broader theory of historical necessity from which Bolshevik doctrine derived. In this sense at least, the "second revolution" was, as Stalin claimed, a legitimate extension of the first. The violent tactics that had been used against the state in 1917 were now applied throughout the system, and the goal was once again a monopoly of power—no longer merely state power but social and economic power as well.

Like the first revolution, the "second revolution" placed severe strains on party unity and party spirit. If Lenin's "adventurism" provoked anxiety, Stalin's provoked consternation, and many party members proved unable or unwilling to exact the exorbitant costs and sustain the inhuman pressure. At the same time, there was a new group of "left-wing" intransigents who opposed the ideological compromises that once again followed the initial all-out assault—compromises such as the introduction of full-fledged one-man management, the authorization of a steeply graded wage scale, and the decollectivization of small individual garden plots. In addition, economic modernization and the proliferation of bureaucracy strengthened the tendency of party cadres to regroup along functional and administrative lines. This tendency was further accelerated, moreover, by the promotion of younger cadres who had a more professional outlook and were more apt to think of their assignments as steps in a bureaucratic career than as channels for the realization of a revolutionary calling. Furthermore, the rise of these cadres also exacerbated generational conflict. Not only did many party veterans find the outlook of the "new Soviet intelligentsia" uncongenial, but also they feared the better-trained younger men as rivals for their jobs. Finally, and most surprisingly, there was even a resurgence of power-political conflict, including the reappearance of groups prepared to challenge the authority of Stalin himself.[23]

Although these strains had a substantial disruptive impact, the party nonetheless emerged from the "second revolution" as a highly unified force. Indeed, it is probable that there was a net increase in party solidarity between 1928 and 1934. Not only did all of the previously noted restraints on centrifugal impulses continue to operate, and in some cases to operate even more effectively, but also the turn to rapid industrialization stimulated a genuine wave of revolutionary enthusiasm. While there was a great deal of compulsory yea-saying, many party cadres appear to have seen themselves and their fellow Bolsheviks as heroic warriors, mobilized in the cause of progress and committed to a course that allowed no turning back and could only be mastered through iron discipline and unstinting mutual support. It is indicative in this regard that a great many former oppositionists greeted the first Five-Year Plan with full-blown recantations and, on being readmitted to the party, plunged headlong into the task of "socialist construction." In consequence, there was no reason to quarrel with Stalin when he spoke of "the extraordinary ideological, political, and organizational solidarity within the party's ranks"—this at the Seventeenth Party Congress in 1934.[24] However, the Seventeenth Congress was not only a "Congress of Victors," as Stalin dubbed it, it was also a congress of the doomed. The victory celebration was scarcely over when the Great Purge began, thereby adding the "second revolution" to the list of great revolutions that ended by devouring their protagonists.

The devastation of the Bolshevik Party between 1936 and 1938 has been discussed too often to require further commentary.[25] Suffice it to say that Lenin's closest collaborators were shot as spies, that the surviving Old Bolsheviks were wiped out almost to the man, that "responsible workers" in strategic areas were systematically exiled or imprisoned, that there was a wholesale "renewal" of administrative cadres, and that hundreds of thousands of ordinary party members were ruthlessly expelled. For all its arbitrariness and irrationality, however, the Great Purge was a controlled and purposeful holocaust, and, when its fury was finally curbed, the prescribed goal had been achieved: Stalin had established himself as the undisputed leader of the entire country, the supreme Fuehrer or *Vozhd*, whose untrammelled will was the ultimate authority and whose every word was an article not just of law but faith. Nominally, of course, the system remained communist, but both the ideological and the organizational connotations of the term were drastically altered. Marxism-Leninism became a mere rhetorical adjunct of Stalinism, and the conventional description of the USSR as a party dictatorship became a misleading anachronism.

As we have indicated, the political emasculation of the party commenced in the early 1920s and proceeded at an ever-accelerating tempo during Stalin's rise to power. At the same time, many significant, albeit secondary, questions remained open for debate within the party and were decided only after a reasonably thorough canvass of party opinion. With the Great Purge, however, the party *qua* party was relegated to a status scarcely superior to that of ordinary "public organizations" such as the trade unions or the Komsomol. At best, the forms of intraparty democracy and rank-and-file participation in the policy process were transformed into symbolic rites, without decisional content. Elections became vehicles for the demonstration of unanimous assent; party discussions became contests in the affirmation of support; criticism and self-criticism became devices for the institutionalization of cross-espionage and compulsory self-incrimination; and party caucuses became congregations for the worship of J. V. Stalin. Indeed, in many cases the rituals became so hollow that they ceased to be observed at all. Provisions for the regular convocation of party congresses and conferences were regularly ignored; party secretaries were appointed and removed without any pretense of election or electoral recall; and party officials failed to report to, let alone consult with, their constituents for months and years on end. In short, the democratic component in the Leninist principle of democratic-centralism was completely discarded, and unadulterated centralism reigned supreme.

Concurrently with these organizational changes, the requirements for party membership were also relaxed. In particular, from 1939 on, there was no longer any discrimination against non-proletarian applicants, and candidates for membership were no longer required to master the party's program but only to accept it.[26] As a result of these revisions in the party's rules, the way was opened for the uninhibited recruitment of the burgeoning new Soviet intelligentsia on the one hand and the untutored but potentially influential "heroes of socialist labor" on the other. It was the vigorous exploitation of these opportunities, in turn, that was responsible for the party's growth from 2,306,973 members and candidates in 1939 to 6,882,145 members and candidates in 1952.[27] This growth proceeded at an extremely rapid tempo during World War II, and the party's ability to recruit more comprehensively doubtlessly helped the regime to mobilize the population for the desperate struggle against Nazi Germany. By the same token, though, wartime recruitment practices vividly underlined the degree to which the party had ceased to be an ideologically distinctive elite group. Thus, whole military units and civilian shock brigades were enrolled *en masse* under agitational banners that placed far heavier stress on Russian nationalism than on the principles of communism. Indeed, by the end of the war the party had become so "representative" and so "non-partisan" that immediate countermeasures were necessary to preserve even a semblance of continuity with the Bolshevik past.[28] While the party continued to grow at a rapid rate, many wartime recruits were purged, and party committees were instructed to screen new applicants individually and with care. Similarly, the network of party schools and study circles was substantially expanded, and agitators and propagandists were ordered to devote more attention to the inculcation of a communist world view and fervent "party spirit." [29] If these measures indicated a desire to preserve the party's character as an ideologically self-conscious elite formation, however, their significance was purely instrumental. The goal was to make the party a more effective "transmission belt," not to restore its capacity for autonomous or even quasi-autonomous political action.

In contrast to the situation during the pre-purge period, during the post-purge period the decline in the status of the party was paralleled by a decline in the status of the party *apparat*. The *apparat* remained an important instrument of Stalin's rule, and high-ranking *apparatchiki* continued to participate in the policy-making process and to influence important administrative decisions. Following the Great Purge, however, Stalin definitely tended to rely on other political instruments at the *apparat's* expense. Symbolically, this tendency received its clearest expression in 1941, when Stalin took over the premiership and assumed the position of supreme commander-in-chief. While he retained his post as general secretary of the party, Stalin henceforth preferred to be identified by his new titles and to sign joint party-states decrees in his governmental capacity. This preference probably stemmed initially from Stalin's desire to bolster his image as a suprapolitical national leader during World War II. But it persisted after the duration and was accompanied by organizational changes that substantially diminished the *apparat's* span of command and control. Thus, to start at the highest level, the Politburo (Presidium) and Central Committee were superseded by the Council of People's Commissars (Council of Ministers) and other state agencies as arenas for the determination of basic policy.

Within the Politburo and the Central Committee, moreover, Stalin steadily enhanced the prestige and influence of non-*apparatchiki,* whom he promoted in increasing numbers and placed in key positions in the various *ad hoc* groupings (the so-called Sextets, Septets, and Octets) that he substituted for the parent bodies. Similarly, at the operational level, the *apparat's* supervisory powers over state administration and economic management were appreciably curtailed, and *apparatchiki* who tried to subject their governmental counterparts to "petty tutelage" were severely punished. Finally, many of the *apparat's* personnel or *nomenklatura* functions were transferred to the secret police and to the cadres section of Stalin's personnel secretariat, which now became the decisive authority on all high-level appointments, including appointments in the *apparat* itself.

The decline in the *apparat's* political status appears to have been accompanied by a decline in its internal cohesiveness and solidarity.[30] In part, these two developments were directly related, for it seems clear that Stalin's withdrawal from the day-to-day direction of intraparty affairs and the impossibility of redressing the unfavorable balance of institutional power through collective action led the *apparatchiki* to compete more intensively among themselves. Furthermore, this tendency was one that Stalin actively encouraged. Far from trying to enforce monolithism within the *apparat,* Stalin purposely played the leading party secretaries off against each other and stimulated the growth of bitter personal rivalries. These rivalries, of which the most prominent was that between Malenkov and Zhdanov, were never allowed to escalate to the point where they threatened the stability of the system, but they were life-and-death struggles nonetheless, and the dynamics of conflict were such that each of the rivals tended to become the leader of a clique of subordinate secretaries who carried the struggle down to the grass roots.[31] Such factional conflict, however, was only one of a number of sources of growing tension. Additional strains were generated by official personnel policy, which placed increasing stress on the importance of staffing the various committees and departments of the *apparat* with qualified specialists who had worked in the area they were called upon to supervise and could hence perform their supervisory functions effectively, without unduly disrupting normal administrative and production processes. Given continued socio-economic modernization and the regime's continued commitment to ubiquitous, albeit attenuated, *apparat* control, this policy was almost mandatory. But it meant that the process of functional differentiation now began to infect the *apparat* itself, giving rise to discernible splits between "verbocrats" and "technocrats," agricultural specialists and industrial specialists, and so on across the register of vocational or professional concerns. Alongside and intersecting these cleavages, moreover, there were also deep cleavages along hierarchical and territorial-administrative lines.[32] The picture, in sum, was one of extensive fragmentation, with splits reflecting all of the diverse pressures inherent in an organization that was at once despotically ruled, highly centralized, multi-functional, and geographically far-flung. These pressures had made themselves felt even earlier, but their cumulative impact appears to have increased throughout the post-purge period, and they obviously engendered very serious internecine conflicts.

The fact that the *apparat* was in so evident a state of disarray led many observers to discount the possibility of its reclaiming its political primacy in the period after Stalin's death.[33] Skepticism seemed doubly warranted by the composition of the new "collective leadership." The dominant figures in the succession regime, Malenkov, Molotov, and Beria, all occupied governmental posts and were hence extremely unlikely to foster an expansion of the *apparat's* power. Initially, to be sure, Malenkov had held the post of first secretary of the party as well as the premiership, thereby suggesting that the interests of the *apparat* would not be overlooked in the impending reorganization of power and authority. However, Malenkov surrendered the first secretaryship within a matter of days, and his successor, Khrushchev, was relegated to a distinctly subordinate position within the ruling elite. That Malenkov had not been allowed to keep his party post while retaining the premiership was, of course, a reminder that command of the *apparat* was a valuable political asset. But Malenkov's willingness to resign as first secretary without a knock-down struggle indicated that he did not consider such command to be absolutely vital. Moreover, Malenkov was in fact able to maintain his position as *primus inter pares* for well over a year. Nevertheless, as collective leadership broke down and the competition for Stalin's mantle erupted into open conflict, it gradually became apparent that the *apparat* was still the strongest single institutional power base within the system.

Had the redistribution of offices after Stalin's death involved the establishment of overlapping jurisdictions instead of following formal bureaucratic lines, the subsequent succession struggle might well have taken a different course. In particular, the major factional groupings might have cut across institutional lines. However, the decision to place each of the leading contenders for power in sole charge of one of the system's principal bureaucracies, with Beria taking command of the police, Malenkov—the state bureaucracy, and Khrushchev—the party *apparat,* foreshadowed the emergence of quite a different pattern of alignments. Given this decision, the power of the top leaders became heavily dependent on their ability to mold their bureaucratic subordinates into cohesive political constituencies, and the best way to accomplish this task was to downgrade institutionally cross-cutting issues and stress issues of bureaucratic prestige, administrative competence, and organizational independence. In consequence, issues of this latter sort became increasingly prominent on the political agenda and assumed overriding importance at each of the critical junctures in the five-year-long succession struggle that followed Stalin's death. While internal bureaucratic disputes continued to influence political behavior and institutionally heterogeneous alliances often played a major role, the various contenders for power emerged more and more clearly as the spokesmen for particular bureaucratic elites in an intense jurisdictional conflict.[34]

As we have already indicated, when the succession struggle is viewed in this perspective, it qualifies as a major political victory for the party *apparat*. Aided by its strong claim to custody over the principal symbols of Marxist-Leninist legitimacy (an important asset in any succession struggle) and by Khrushchev's skill in mobilizing and deploying its still extensive organizational resources, the *apparat* was able to reestablish both its political primacy and its hegemonial control over the full range of governmental pursuits. It was able to do so, moreover, in the face of resistance not only by the police (Beria) and the managerial elite (Malenkov) but also by the army (Zhukov). Like their predecessors in the 1920s and early 1930s, none of these bureaucratic groupings was prepared to challenge the principle of single party rule as such; they merely rejected the idea that this principle entitled the *apparatchiki* to special political prerogatives or justified interference by the *apparat* in "their" areas of professional expertise and administrative authority. The ensuing conflict was nonetheless severe, however, and the *apparat's* victory was nonetheless decisive. Between 1953 and 1958, Khrushchev and his *apparatchiki* supporters were able to emasculate the secret police, to liquidate the vast majority of centralized state ministries, to oust Marshal Zhukov, and to retire many of Zhukov's military subordinates. Indeed, the trend of developments was so one-sided that one wonders whether the elite groups who had enjoyed the greatest power during the post-purge period had not become so dependent on Stalin's patronage that their capacity for independent action was fatally impaired. In any event, the outcome of the succession struggle strongly suggested that in a direct confrontation with the *apparatchiki* none of the other bureaucratic elites was capable of functioning effectively either as a counterelite or as a factional pressure group or even as a veto group where its own vital interests were at stake.

The *apparatchiki* were doubtlessly aware that their pivotal role in Khrushchev's rise to power did not insure that they would be the primary beneficiaries of his rule. If nothing else, Khrushchev's impassioned denunciation of the way in which Stalin had treated "his" *apparatchiki* served as a grim warning against overconfidence. And, despite his sponsorship of "de-Stalinization," Khrushchev showed a definite tendency to follow in Stalin's footsteps. His tactics during the succession struggle had borne a striking resemblance to Stalin's tactics in the period after Lenin's death, and now that he had disposed of his principal rivals, Khrushchev seemed nearly as determined as his predecessor to consolidate dictatorial power. This goal, in turn, required that Khrushchev too reduce his dependence on the *apparatchiki* who had brought him to power, and in the period following the defeat of the "anti-party group" of Malenkov, Molotov, and Kaganovich (June, 1957) and the ouster of Zhukov (October, 1957), he proceeded accordingly.[35] On the one hand, he made a concerted effort to develop additional sources of power and authority. On the other hand, he launched a direct attack on the power-political capabilities of the *apparat.*

Khrushchev's effort to diversify his political resources took two distinct but complementary forms. In the first place, he undertook to strengthen his personal control over the governmental bureaucracy and to restore state agencies to much of the authority they had lost in the aftermath of Malenkov's defeat. In early 1958, Khrushchev took over the premiership in addition to his post as first secretary of the party, and in the years that followed he presided over a gradual but steady reconstitution of a centralized system of state administration and economic management.[36] While his behavior was strongly influenced by calculations of economic rationality, such calculations had not prevented him from disbanding the ministerial system and dispersing the managerial elite when these actions seemed politically expedient, and it seems clear that his newfound receptivity to the canons of economic rationality was predominantly political in origin. Negatively, he was motivated by the conviction that the managerial elite had been sufficiently chastened by its recent debacle to forgo all thought of opposition. More positively, he saw an opportunity to transform many of his erstwhile opponents into active supporters, grateful for his recognition of their interests and anxious to prove worthy of his continued confidence.[37] His primary objective, however, transcended both these considerations and involved an effort to achieve a more balanced distribution of institutional power. Whereas he had previously sought to insure the absolute primacy of the party *apparat,* he now sought to revive a system of "parallel, competing bureaucracies" in which he, like Stalin before him, was in command of both the party and the state machines and could hence manipulate their conflicts in a way that insured his independence of each.

At the same time that he tried to expand his power institutionally, Khrushchev also tried to create a new pseudo-charismatic "cult of personality." He took great pains to insure that the mass media were controlled by his personal acolytes, and from 1958 on, his appointees directed a burgeoning campaign to build up their sponsor as a major Marxist theorist, a great military leader, and a paragon of political and civic virtue. While the praise of Khrushchev never became as fulsome as the earlier praise of Stalin, it became increasingly extravagant and found increasing expression in *belles lettres,* in academic writings, and in basic political texts.[38] Moreover, thanks to new media such as television and new means of rapid transportation, Khrushchev had an unprecedented opportunity to project his charisma "in person." His frequent "fireside chats" and numerous tours of the countryside deprived him of any aura of mystery, but they produced—or were designed to produce—an eye-witness appreciation of the breadth of his concerns, the scope of his knowledge, the decisiveness of his leadership, and the extent of his ability to resolve issues on his own authority, not only *ex officio* but as an individual, as *the* supreme commander if not, as yet, the *Vozhd.*

As we have indicated, Khrushchev's effort to aggrandize dictatorial power also involved a direct attempt to undermine the *apparatchiki's* capacity for independent political action. One step he took in this direction was to invite large numbers of outside experts and "representatives of the toiling masses," to participate in the proceedings of the Central Committee. In consequence, the authority of the regular members of the Committee, over half of whom were *apparatchiki,* was substantially diluted and the likelihood that Khrushchev's critics would use the Committee as a forum to challenge his leadership was substantially reduced.[39] At the same time, moreover, Khrushchev could take credit for "democratizing" party procedures, thereby strengthening his appeal as a "true Leninist," determined to broaden the arena of political participation and discard the hypercentralism of the Stalinist past.

A second "democratic" innovation that Khrushchev introduced as part of his campaign to curtail the power of the *apparatchiki* was to limit the tenure of most members of party committees to two or three terms and to require that there should be at least a one-fourth to one-third turnover in the membership of such committees at every election. In effect, these changes, which were embodied in the new party rules adopted by the Twenty-second Party Congress (October, 1961), provided for the maintenance of a bloodless permanent purge of leading *apparatchiki,* with exceptions allowed only for those of extraordinary "authority and high political, organizational, and other abilities." [40] Thanks to this last escape clause, Khrushchev and his closest colleagues were presumably safe from the threat of "renewal," but in most cases the burden of proof was clearly on the incumbents, and Khrushchev was in a position where he could use mandatory constitutional procedures to curb the tendency of the leading *apparatchiki* to transform their territorial jurisdictions into enclaves of independent power. Moreover, since "the principle of systematic turnover" was retroactive, he was in a favorable position to break up many existing "secretarial fiefdoms" and to remove many established party functionaries whose political reliability and docility he had reason to suspect. The threat of such action was itself a major deterrent to "undisciplined behavior," and the credibility of the deterrent was greatly enhanced by the fact that the adoption of the new rules was accompanied by a 50 per cent turnover in the membership of the Central Committee.[41]

Alongside these procedural encroachments on the power of the *apparatchiki,* Khrushchev also implemented a number of complementary but far more fundamental structural reforms. To start with, he created a series of new central party organs (the Russian Republic Bureau, the Committee Party-State Control, the Ideological Commission, and so forth) that were headed by members of his personal entourage and that took over a variety of important functions formerly exercised by the Central Committee Secretariat and/or by the provincial party *apparat.* Most importantly, however, in November, 1962, he managed to force through a radical reorganization of the entire party machine. In complete defiance of Bolshevik traditions, the previously omnicompetent provincial and local party committees were divided into specialized committees for agriculture and industry and were instructed to devote themselves to local economic tasks to the virtual exclusion of overall administrative coordination and political leadership. In effect, Khrushchev managed at one fell swoop to multiply the number of party committees, to halve the territorial jurisdictions of the majority of incumbent first secretaries, to transform most local party officials into full-time economic controllers, and to lay the basis for a massive shakeup of party cadres, who were now to be appointed largely on the basis of specialized technical criteria of a sort that most old-line *apparatchiki* could not conceivably satisfy.[42]

It would be wrong to view all of the various measures we have been discussing exclusively from a power-political point of view. Indeed, we have already indicated that the recentralization of the state bureaucracy had much to recommend it in terms of economic and administrative efficiency, the more so as it was combined with a simplification of the planning system and the grant of greater operational autonomy to production enterprises. Similarly, the limitations on the tenure of party secretaries and the expansion of the Central Committee made good sense from the point of view of effective political recruitment and was part of a general effort to cultivate the image of the party as a truly representative body, responsive to the will of its members and genuinely committed to participatory democracy. Again, the bifurcation of the *apparat* was undoubtedly inspired by a desire to provide a safeguard against "abuses" of enterprise autonomy and to "prove" that modernization had not made the *apparat* functionally redundant or historically retrograde. Nevertheless, while none of these factors can be ignored, the primary motive force behind Khrushchev's policy of perpetual institutional change and the force that gave a certain logical coherence to what otherwise ultimately emerges as a set of irrational and mutually contradictory programs was personal ambition, that is, Khrushchev's desire to aggrandize autocratic power.

By 1963 Khrushchev appeared to be in a position comparable to the one that Stalin had achieved within a decade after Lenin's death. While the period 1953–1963 had been full of political conflict, the outcome of the conflict bore little resemblance to the projections of those who had predicted that the death of Stalin would serve as a catalyst to release the pent-up forces of "political modernity" and would hence be followed by the rapid emergence of a pluralistic polity. Not only the administrative specialists of the state bureaucracy and the specialists in violence (the police and army) but the party *apparatchiki* as well seemed to be incapable of defending their interests against the dominant leader. During the period of initial succession, when the rival contenders for power were forced to compete for their support, the various strategic elites had been able to transform Soviet politics into a genuine group process in which active bargaining took place outside the narrow confines of the top leadership itself. Once the immediate question of succession was resolved, however, and the concentration of power crossed a certain (relatively low) threshold, no elite group seemed capable of preserving its political independence, and the stage seemed set for the rapid consolidation of a full-fledged one-man dictatorship.

These were the "lessons" suggested by the trend of developments in the decade after Stalin's death, and even in retrospect it is difficult to question their validity.[43] At the same time, it is clear that Khrushchev did *not* ultimately succeed in consolidating autocratic power and that the indicated "lessons" are valid only up to a point—the point where terror enters the equation and 1934 gives way to 1936. While mass terror on a Stalinist scale is probably unnecessary, enough arbitrary coercion to keep the ruling elite in a state of perpetual uncertainty and fear may well be indispensable. There is some evidence that Khrushchev tried to introduce such a reign of terror by bringing the members of the "anti-party group" to trial on capital charges and that his attempt to do so was thwarted by a coalition of his top lieutenants.[44] Nevertheless, the basic reason for his failure to resort to terror was probably not his inability to overcome the resistance of his lieutenants but his own ambivalence about the desirability of such a course. In particular, he was probably inhibited by calculations of international prestige and considerations of economic rationality. Certainly there is no evidence to suggest that he pressed for a return to terror as vigorously as he might have, and there is no basis for concluding that a more vigorous effort would have necessarily ended in failure. What is clear is that terror was held in abeyance and that its absence played an important part in preventing Khrushchev from realizing his ultimate goal. Unlike Stalin, he did not intimidate his principal lieutenants, and he hence left himself vulnerable to a palace revolution. For a time, he was able to forestall this threat by engaging his lieutenants in mutual competition for status and preferment and by using the technique of permanent reorganization to prevent the formation of stable coalitions. However, when a number of his major policies failed simultaneously in late 1963 and 1964, he discovered that such political manipulation was not enough.

The precise details of Khrushchev's ouster have yet to be revealed. Nevertheless, there is little question that the prime movers were members of the Presidium, and that what was involved in the first instance was, as we have indicated, a conspiratorial *coup d'état*. At the same time, the fact that Khrushchev had alienated virtually every significant elite group in Soviet society was undoubtedly an extremely important ingredient in the conspiracy's success. Of the various elite groups, in turn, the ones whose attitudes mattered most were almost certainly the officer corps and the *apparatchiki*. It was these groups that had saved Khrushchev in 1957, when the "anti-party group" achieved a "so-called numerical majority" in the Presidium, and it is likely that they could have saved him once again. Unlike Marshal Zhukov, however, Marshal Malinovsky offered Khrushchev no support, and, when Khrushchev appealed to the Central Committee this time, he was decisively rebuffed. The Central Committee was still dominated by the old-line *apparatchiki* whom Khrushchev had "betrayed," and they were completely deaf to his present appeals. Whatever hopes or illusions they had entertained earlier, the November, 1962 reorganization had opened their eyes, and their votes thereafter were never in doubt. As one leading *apparatchik* put it, "The Central Committee members stood everything, but they did not stand for or tolerate encroachment upon the party." [45]

If this statement exaggerates the degree to which the *apparatchiki* provided the initiative behind Khrushchev's ouster, it conveys an intensity of feeling that Khrushchev's successors found it advisable to take into account. Accordingly, within a matter of weeks after its assumption of power, the Brezhnev-Kosygin regime authorized the *apparat's* reunification, and this step has since been followed by the abolition of the limits on secretarial tenure, the exclusion of outsiders from meetings of the Central Committee, the liquidation of the Russian Republic Bureau of the party and the Committee on Party-State Control, and the reaffirmation of the *apparat's* right to supervise all spheres of public life. In the economic sector, to be sure, the reestablishment of the ministerial system and the expansion of enterprise autonomy have entailed a reduction in the *apparat's* span of command and control. Despite these measures, however, the *apparatchiki* have once again emerged as a major political force. The fact that power at the top is shared insures them of wide-ranging access to the policy process, while the fact that Brezhnev, the dominant figure in the new "collective leadership" is general (first) secretary of the party insures that their claims and demands get a particularly attentive hearing—a hearing that is the more likely to be favorable because the decision to once again divide power along institutional lines has strengthened their tendency to act as a cohesive group with a strong sense of common interest.[46]

Whether the *apparatchiki* will long be able to maintain such effective access to the policy process is extremely difficult to predict. As long as the present "collective leadership" persists, their continued efficacy seems virtually assured, and it is impossible not to be impressed by the stability thus far demonstrated by the Brezhnev-Kosygin regime. At the same time, the outbreak of a new succession struggle is always possible, and it is easy to imagine such a struggle resulting in a significant decline in the *apparatchiki's* political influence. Certainly this would be the case were there to be a return to full-fledged one-man dictatorship, and it would almost certainly be the case with any redistribution of power that might occur within the framework of collegial rule. In other words, the configuration that provides the *apparatchiki* with the greatest political leverage is precisely one in which power at the top is divided and the dominant figure in the regime occupies the post of general (first) secretary of the party. The fact that this configuration has been so recurrent a feature of Soviet politics, in turn, is testimony to the continuing importance of the *apparat* as an "organizational weapon" and source of authority and power. While the *apparatchiki* have not been able to prevent the rise of autocratic and semiautocratic regimes under Stalin and Khrushchev, they have far outdistanced the system's other strategic elites during periods of leadership competition, and their support has been the principal factor facilitating the suppression of leadership conflict and the emergence of one-man rule. That their success as a support group has each time led to a sharp reduction in their power suggests that their political vision has been extremely limited and that their political effectiveness has been largely dependent on vigorous leadership from above. In the future, however, they may pay more attention to the "lessons" of the past and make a more concerted effort to maintain control over their "representatives" within the top ruling elite. They will be hampered by the ingrained habits and practices of "democratic centralism" but the fact that the leadership has called upon the Central Committee twice in the past ten years for a serious vote of confidence suggests that regularized control procedures may be emerging, and these procedures may well grow stronger and more reliable with time.

If the *apparatchiki* retain an influential voice in the policy process, they will probably also continue to exercise a wide-ranging hegemony over the administrative apparatus of the state. While close political monitoring of administrative behavior may entail increasing social and economic costs, most *apparatchiki* view their supervisory functions as a major source of power, and this view is unlikely to change in the foreseeable future. Nor is it likely that the consequences of the *apparat's* continued involvement in governmental and economic operations will be so dire as to threaten the entire system with disintegration or collapse. At least this is the case so long as the *apparat* avoids excessively petty tutelage and is staffed by men who possess a reasonably high level of technical competence and organizational skill. Both of these conditions, in turn, are likely to be met. As for the first, Krushchev's efforts to "depoliticize" the *apparat* by channeling its energies into the detailed supervision of administrative behavior have probably made the *apparatchiki* more sensitive than ever before to the *political* dangers of overinvolvement in bureaucratic routine. As for the second, the *apparatchiki* are already a well-educated group with broad executive experience, and their qualifications are likely to increase.

By 1967, 91 per cent of the secretaries of district and city party committees and 97.6 per cent of the secretaries of upper-level party committees had higher education, and a significant percentage had become *apparatchiki* after long periods of service as "commanders" on one of the other "fronts" of Soviet life.[47] In contrast to the last years of the Khrushchev era, such prior service is no longer a prerequisite for recruitment, and "practical" criteria are now ranked below "political" criteria in staffing guidelines, but the *apparatchiki* nonetheless appear to be appropriately qualified for their supervisory roles. Although they do not constitute the intellectual elite of the system and often lack refined technical expertise, they

have enough training and experience to subject their administrative counterparts to effective control and to adapt their control techniques to the
most essential "imperatives" of industrial maturation. Over the very long
run, these "imperatives" may require the sort of adaptation that would be
tantamount to abdication or assimilation ("technocratization"), but for the
foreseeable future the *apparatchiki* seem capable both of maintaining their
identity as a group devoted to distinctively *political* goals and of holding
the tendencies toward a "managerial revolution" effectively in check.

If the *apparatchiki's* relationship to the other major elite groups in the
system promises to be relatively fluid, their relationship to the party rank-
and-file seems far less susceptible to change. While there has been a great
deal of talk about a "revival" of intraparty democracy, local party functionaries continue to be appointed from above and the great bulk of the party
membership—which now numbers over 13 million—continues to play only
a marginal part in the determination of official policy. The elimination of
terror has undoubtedly made ordinary communists less reluctant to press
for the removal of party officials who show extreme insensitivity to their
demands, and the necessity to use non-terroristic means of mobilization has
led many party secretaries to show unprecedented concern for the welfare
of their constituents. However, there are still no reliable mechanisms for
enforcing such responsibility, and the atmosphere within the party is still
coercive enough to keep protest to a minimum and restrict demands for
change largely to tangentials. If nothing else, the fact that the party now includes so high a proportion (almost one-third) and so representative a
sample of the younger Soviet intelligentsia leaves little doubt that many
party members would welcome more basic changes.[48] At least among the
younger and better-educated communists, "party spirit" no longer implies
a blind acceptance of fiat rule, and in many cases party membership is
viewed as a necessary compromise, an essential step toward the realization
of professional or personal goals that are recognized to run counter to
official priorities.[49] Nevertheless, the threat of expulsion from the party
and the virtual certainty of a blighted career (an unfavorable *karakteristika*
in the *apparat*-controlled *nomenklatura* files) prevent most of them from
even intimating their more serious reservations, let alone attempting to take
corresponding action. In consequence, other potential dissidents succumb
to the climate of seeming unanimity, and the *apparatchiki* are rarely forced
to accommodate politically unpalatable grass-roots demands.

Recent events in East Europe indicate that the democratization of ruling
communist parties need not always be an entirely illusory process. However, these events also indicate that most *apparatchiki* have tended to resist
such changes to the limits of their ability. And, the ability of Soviet *apparatchiki* to resist far surpasses that of their East European counterparts,
who are much less firmly entrenched, share fewer goals in common, and
enjoy vastly less legitimacy. To achieve the kind of intraparty democracy
that exists in parts of East Europe in the Soviet Union would require ex-

treme pressure from the top leadership, and the leadership is only likely to exert such pressure in response to large-scale popular protest. Faced with such protest, the leadership might well attempt to mitigate opposition by coopting its more moderate critics and providing within-system outlets for the expression of dissent. To do so would alienate the *apparatchiki* and raise the spectre of a rapid erosion of all central control, but in a dire emergency these might seem the best available alternatives.

There is no doubt that political protest in the Soviet Union has recently reached substantial heights. However, it has yet to achieve a mass resonance, and there is little reason to assume that it will soon reach crisis proportions. Given lack of resolute leadership on the part of the regime or a major economic breakdown, there could be a rapid escalation, but neither of these preconditions can be taken for granted and present trends suggest that they are unlikely to obtain. The present leadership at least has demonstrated considerable strength of purpose both in suppressing public dissent and in raising the standard of living. The suppression has not been harsh enough to silence all dissenters, but it has acted as a strong deterrent, and its very "moderation" has helped to prevent a violent reaction. Similarly, its economic reforms have not gone far enough to eliminate serious shortages in consumer goods, but it has managed to keep the "revolution of rising expectations" within tolerable limits, and it has persuaded a great many extremely skeptical citizens that their welfare is one of its principal concerns. In the process, moreover, it has begun to acquire the kind of popular respect that may enable it to repair the torn and tattered fabric of political legitimacy. While there is no prospect of a large-scale revival of ideological faith, many Marxist-Leninist principles have won wide acceptance, and there is a good chance that the regime can capitalize on this consensus and attach it to its own programs, provided that these programs continue to satisfy a broad range of consumer demands. Although increased affluence is often identified as a source of political instability, in the short—and middle—run it is more likely to have a stabilizing effect and to give the regime a freer hand in dealing with its critics.

It is obvious that the preceding paragraphs posit too many contingencies to qualify as anything more than prudent speculation. At the same time, they cover enough contingencies to suggest that the Soviet political system is not necessarily faced with a stark choice between radical "transformation" and rapid "degeneration." [50] Persistence along existing lines is at least possible and perhaps likely. Such persistence will require continual adaptation to new social and economic pressures and over the long run such adaptation may well result in alterations that are far-reaching enough to qualify as system change. Indeed, if one defines the system by certain criteria, such change is virtually inevitable. If the decisive features of the system are the monopolistic position of the CPSU and the political primacy of the party *apparatchiki,* however, a reasonably close approximation of the current status quo may prevail for many years to come.

|| *Notes*

1. N. M. Sukhanov, *The Russian Revolution 1917* (London: Oxford University Press, 1955), pp. 380–381; V. I. Lenin, "Can the Bolsheviks Retain State Power," *Selected Works* (New York: International Publishers, 1943), VI, 250–253.
2. It should be noted that the first Bolshevik government was in fact a coalition government with the left-wing of the Social Revolutionary Party. This arrangement lasted until the middle of 1918.
3. See Charlotte Saikowski and Leo Grediow, eds., *Current Soviet Politics* (New York: Columbia University Press, 1962), IV, 1–31.
4. See Philip Selznick, *The Organizational Weapon* (New York: The Free Press, 1960).
5. See, among others, Carl J. Friedrich and Zbigniew K. Brzezinski, *Totalitarian Dictatorship and Autocracy* (Cambridge: Harvard University Press, 1956).
6. Lenin, *op. cit.,* pp. 250–296.
7. Cf. Jeremy R. Azrael, *Managerial Power and Soviet Politics* (Cambridge: Harvard University Press, 1966), chap. 2.
8. See Merle Fainsod, *How Russia Is Ruled* (Cambridge: Harvard University Press, pp. 77–82.
9. See Lenin, *op. cit.,* p. 292 and "Our Revolution," *Selected Works* (New York: International Publishers, 1943), VI, 512.
10. See Leonard Schapiro, *The Communist Party of the Soviet Union* (New York: Random House, 1960), pp. 213–218, 231–238.
11. See Fainsod, *op. cit.,* pp. 212–213.
12. See, among others, the reports of the Central Control Commission to the Tenth, Eleventh, Twelfth, and Thirteenth Party Congresses.
13. *Desyaty Sezd RKP(b)* (Tenth Congress of the Russian Communist Party), stenographic report (Moscow: Gosudarstvenno Izdatelstvo Politicheskoi Literatury, 1963), p. 255.
14. *Dvenadtsaty Sezd RKP(b)* (Twelfth Congress of the Russian Communist Party), stenographic report (Moscow: Izdatelstvo *Krasnaya Nov,* 1923), pp. 42, 115–116, 120, 142–3, 147.
15. See Azrael, *op. cit.,* pp. 69–71.
16. See Robert V. Daniels, *Conscience of the Revolution* (Cambridge: Harvard University Press, 1960), chaps. 5–10; Leonard Schapiro, *The Origins of Communist Autocracy* (Cambridge: Harvard University Press, 1955), chap. 17.
17. See Azrael, *op. cit.,* chap. 3.
18. See V. I. Lenin, "What is to be Done?" *Selected Works* (New York: International Publishers, 1943), II, 25.
19. See Fainsod, *op. cit.,* pp. 152–171.
20. Lenin, "Our Revolution," p. 512.
21. See V. I. Lenin, *Polnoe sobranie sochineny* (Complete Works), 5th ed. (Moscow: Izdatelstvo Politicheskoi Literatury, 1964), XLV, 343–348.
22. See Leopold Labedz and Max Hayward, eds., *On Trial* (London: Collins and Harvill Press, 1967), p. 208, for Andrei Sinyavsky's view that "Stalin made Lenin's metaphors come true." Sinyavsky goes on, however, to argue that "Lenin is no more responsible for Stalin than language is for the literal putting into effect of metaphors"—this under interrogation by the prosecutor at his trial.
23. See Abdurakhman Avtorkhanov, *Stalin and the Soviet Communist Party* (New York: Frederick A. Praeger, 1959).

24. J. Stalin, *Works* (Moscow: Foreign Languages Publishing House, 1955), XIII, 390.

25. See, among others, Zbigniew K. Brzezinski, *The Permanent Purge* (Cambridge: Harvard University Press, 1956), chaps. 5, 6.

26. *The Land of Socialism Today and Tomorrow* (Moscow: Foreign Languages Publishing House, 1939), pp. 180–185, 199–200. In addition to these revisions in the party rules the probationary period during which one was required to remain a candidate member of the party was shortened.

27. Fainsod, *op. cit.,* pp. 212, 232–239.

28. Embarrassment at the obvious discontinuities may explain why the Nineteenth Party Congress in 1952 dropped the word "Bolshevik" from the party's official name, which now became simply The Communist Party of the Soviet Union.

29. See, for example, Leo Gruliow, ed., *Current Soviet Policies* (New York: Frederick A. Praeger, 1953), I, 116–124.

30. It should be stressed that this decline was relative to the situation in the 1930s, not in the 1920s, during the succession struggle.

31. See, among others, John A. Armstrong, *The Politics of Totalitarianism* (New York: Random House, 1961), chap. 13, 15.

32. See, among others, Robert Conquest, *Power and Policy in the USSR* (New York: St. Martin's Press, 1961), part II.

33. See, for example, Philip Mosely, *The Kremlin in World Politics* (New York: Vintage Books, 1960), pp. 346–347.

34. See Conquest, *op. cit.,* pp. 41–42; Schapiro, *The Communist Party,* p. 552; Roger Pethybridge, *A Key to Soviet Politics* (New York: Frederick A. Praeger, 1962), pp. 45–46.

35. See Carl A. Linden, *Khrushchev and the Soviet Leadership, 1957–1964* (Baltimore: The Johns Hopkins Press, 1966).

36. See Nove, *op. cit.,* chap. 6; Azrael, *op. cit.,* pp. 137–147.

37. Needless to say, not all members of the managerial elite had supported Malenkov during the succession struggle, and it was these exceptions whom Khrushchev gave key posts in the new central agencies he established.

38. For one extremely sensitive reaction to these developments, see Yuli Daniel's explanation of his decision to publish his writings in the West in Labedz and Hayward, *op. cit.,* esp. p. 164.

39. On the composition of the Central Committee between 1961 and 1966, see Yaroslav Bilinsky, *Changes in the Central Committee* (Denver, Colorado: The Social Science Foundation and Graduate School of International Studies, University of Denver, 1967).

40. Saikowski and Gediow, *op. cit.,* pp. 36–37.

41. See Merle Fainsod, "The Twenty-Second Party Congress," *Problems of Communism,* X (November–December 1961), special supplement, esp. x.

42. See, among others, Jeremy R. Azrael, "Politics and Management," *Survey,* No. 49 (October 1963); Richard Lowenthal, "The Revolution Withers Away," *Problems of Communism,* XIV (January–February 1965).

43. For a contrary view, see Jerome M. Gilison, "New Factors of Stability in Soviet Collective Leadership," *World Politics,* XIX, No. 4 (July 1967).

44. See Linden, *op. cit.,* chap. 5, esp. pp. 73–81.

45. *Plenum Tsentralnovo Komiteta KPSS* (Plenum of the Central Committee of the CPSU), March 1965, stenographic report (Moscow: Izdatelstvo Politicheskoi Literatury, 1965), p. 89.

46. The Twenty-Third Party Congress, which met in 1965, restored the old Stalinist title of general secretary in place of first secretary. In addition it renamed the Presidium of the Central Committee, the Politburo.

47. *Current Digest of the Soviet Press,* November 15, 1967, p. 15.

48. *Ibid.,* pp. 10–14.

49. Based on personal observation and private discussions.

50. See, Zbigniew K. Brzezinski, "The Soviet Political System: Transformation or Degeneration," *Problems of Communism,* XV (January–February 1966).

9

Intraparty Conflict in China: Disintegration in an Established One-Party System

‖ James R. Townsend

The disintegration of the Chinese Communist Party (CCP) in the course of the Great Proletarian Cultural Revolution appeared as an unexpected and unprecedented event in the context of the party's relatively stable rule over the Chinese mainland. In the context of one-party systems in general, however, the CCP's decline is much less surprising. Such systems experience great stress as leaders try to perpetuate their party's rule under conditions that differ sharply from those that existed during the initial acquisition of power. In particular, the ruling party must develop effective institutions for governing the society that do not compromise its own autonomy, identity, and monopolistic control over major decisions; and it must somehow control the crisis of leadership succession, above all the first succession in which the departing leader is typically a man who has personified the movement and its ideology.[1]

The CCP could not be immune to these problems. Despite its ability to contain them over many years, and the possibility that it may yet resolve them under a revived and altered system of party rule, the CCP's disintegration has been largely due to their cumulative and combined effects. That is, in its efforts to expand its control over Chinese society, the CCP grew in size and complexity. While it thereby expanded its capabilities with respect to society, it also absorbed a diversity of structures and interests that made the party organization itself increasingly difficult to control through its established appeals and control techniques. Combined with this structural weakness was an emerging crisis of succession, produced by Mao Tse-tung's attempt to mold the CCP permanently in his own image at a time when his age and politics had sharply diminished his authority among his senior colleagues. Whatever its particular characteristics, therefore, the Cultural Revolution is a Chinese version of the crises that institutionalization and succession present for any revolutionary one-party system. The Chinese variant is particularly interesting because it occurs in a system that had shown great potential for establishing itself securely and responding successfully to these problems. Accordingly, the focus of analysis here is to examine sources of strength in the Chinese one-party system and the circumstances that led to a critical decline in this strength.

Viability of the One-Party System

A natural question with which to begin this analysis is whether the Chinese party system, as observed over the years between 1949 and 1965, was truly viable. Is it possible that one-party rule was never as well-established as it appeared to external observers? The answer is negative, but it is instructive to consider the possibility that Communist China might have contained predictable tendencies toward a competitive party system or a no-party system.

The potentiality for a competitive system is easily negated, for there have been no significant non-party groups or institutions which could challenge effectively the CCP's virtual monopoly of power. It is sometimes suggested that power in China is a tripartite arrangement among the party, the state bureaucracy, and the army, and that the latter institutions might be viewed as potential competitors. The problem with this view is that there is no distinguishable non-party military or bureaucratic group with significant influence. Party leadership within these institutions has been thorough and sufficient. This can be seen from staffing patterns at higher levels, and also from the empirical observation that neither of these institutions ever opposed the party in a clear-cut institutional confrontation before the Cultural Revolution.[2]

Other potential rivals have presented even less of a threat to the party. The social strata that wielded real or potential political power in pre-Communist China were uniformly weakened in the early years of the People's Republic. Land reform destroyed the political power of the landlords, while the Five-Anti Movement and the socialization of the economy undercut the strength of industrial and commercial groups. Non-party intellectuals suffered heavy blows through early thought reform campaigns and changes in the educational structure; their surviving political ambitions were smashed in the Hundred Flowers Campaign of 1957.[3]

The CCP has, of course, met some opposition from elements outside the party, but such opposition has suffered from one or both of two fundamental weaknesses. The first is lack of social identity and organizational possibilities. For example, there has been at times substantial discontent, some-times bordering on willingness to engage in physical resistance, among peasants, youth, and less privileged workers. Their opposition, if we may call it that, has been diffuse and scattered, however. Even assuming a sense of class or group grievances that might extend beyond localized settings, there has simply been no possibility of organized resistance because party-controlled mass organizations and communications media have totally preempted the field.

The second weakness has been lack of integration into the mainstream of Chinese society. It is revealing to note that the most significant organized opposition to the party has occurred in minority areas, particularly Tibet and Sinkiang. The strength of resistance here, including some generalized popular support, entitles one to question whether the CCP one-party system truly prevails in these areas. Yet it is also clear that these are special cases, based on ethnic differences and geographic isolation, which must be seen more as a challenge to Chinese claims about territorial and national identity rather than to the Chinese party system. A *Chinese* anti-party movement plainly could not build around this type of opposition.

We may conclude, therefore, that party organization and control has been too strong and pervasive, and has penetrated too far into Chinese society, to permit any possibility of political competition. Any weakness in the party system must be found within the party itself, rather than in external threats. The question that follows is whether the pre-Cultural Revolution system might best be viewed as a no-party system in which the party was actually a front for some particular group, institution or individual, thereby subverting the party's nominal role as the autonomous director of all political activities. Data on the Eighth Central Committee of the party, elected in 1956 with additional changes in 1958, provides clues about this point in the general period (1949–1965) under consideration.[4]

One possibility is that the party has been controlled by a provincial or regional grouping, a suggestion that stems naturally from familiarity with Chinese political history and rests on some basis in fact. Of the 97 regular members of the Committee elected in 1956, 30 came from Hunan and 18 more came from the adjoining provinces of Szechwan and Hupei. Thus, 48 or barely under 50 per cent came from this region; one could add members from nearby provinces and show that the interior provinces of Central-South China have dominated the Central Committee. Nevertheless, the dominance is not overwhelming and is not supported by tangible evidence of this group enforcing its dominance over representatives of other areas. The Central-South group is in fact too loose to be a clique, composed as it is of men from many different provinces, with personal experience divided among provinces outside their region of origin. There can be no doubt that there has been provincial bias in the recruitment of the CCP elite and that this has influenced the character of the party. But this does not prove that a regional group has subverted party organization to its own interests or rendered ineffectual those elements within the party that come from other regions.[5]

Earlier we noted that neither the state bureaucracy nor the army has functioned as a non-party competitor for power because the CCP has absorbed the leadership and control of these structures. One may still ask whether any one of these three hierarchies has held a controlling position within the party as a whole. There is no doubt that the long-term assignment of party leaders to one of these bureaucracies has produced conflicts of institutional identity and interest within the party. Despite such tensions, however, none of these institutions can be identified as the dominant source of authority within the CCP before the Cultural Revolution. A breakdown of functional assignment of regular and alternate members of the 1956 Central Committee shows that the party leadership has been distributed among the party, state and army bureaucracies in a relatively balanced way.[6] Between 1950 and 1962 a gradual shift toward assignment in the party apparatus took place, at the expense of military assignment, but neither this development nor the pattern of intraparty conflicts during the years in question demonstrates that representatives of the party apparatus had assumed a position of sustained dominance over representatives of the state and military establishments.

The strongest argument for viewing the 1949–1965 CCP as a no-party system would be the assertion that the party has been in fact the tool of a small leadership clique, centered around the person of Mao Tse-tung. The advanced age, long association and common experience of the CCP elite are well known. Of the 97 regular members of the 1956 Central Committee, over 70 per cent had joined the Party by 1927 and had been on the Central Committee since 1945 or earlier.[7] After 1935, when Mao achieved command of the CCP, a group of senior cadres dominated the Central Committee and its politburo, occupied the key positions outside the party apparatus and unquestionably served as the source of all major decisions. Death and purges gradually reduced their numbers, yet at the highest level the CCP leadership remained remarkably stable and relatively impervious to the entrance of new members. The critical question is what impact this leadership pattern had on the party. Certainly it placed severe restrictions on upward mobility at the higher levels of the CCP, thereby weakening the party's effectiveness as a recruiter for the political system. Moreover, it compromised formal procedures and checks in decision-making and selection of leaders and administration, since the position of the top elite was virtually unassailable from below. Finally, it raised serious questions about the CCP's ability to survive the demise of the old guard, simply because the identification of communist rule with these personalities appeared to be so complete. The Cultural Revolution has brought all these problems into the open, revealing that the leadership clique's monopoly of power for so long a time had indeed made the CCP a less flexible and resourceful political instrument.

On the other hand, stability within the CCP top leadership was a primary defense for party autonomy, since it reduced opportunities for dilution of party prestige and the infusion of new values and personalities into the command structure. Mao's long association with a group of able and experienced revolutionaries was, in fact, a check on abuse of his personal power. While he was clearly first among equals, the stature of his colleagues was sufficient to prevent the acquisition of truly dictatorial powers for himself. Moreover, the fixed tenure of the leadership never rendered the organization stagnant or inflexible. Although mobility became restricted toward the top, membership at lower levels remained open and could still bring social status and political advancement. Although a small elite made all major decisions, they frequently differed among themselves, encouraged some general party discussion of their conflicts, reversed their policies at times, and allowed lower officials considerable leeway in administering and enforcing their decisions. Although it is now apparent that the passing of the old elite will test the very limits of the system's resources, the choice of Liu Shao-ch'i as Mao's successor—a choice that seemed secure down to 1966—offered for a time the possibility that succession could be channeled through inner-party circles in a way that minimized discontinuities and threats to the party's power and prestige.

To summarize, Communist China until 1965 is legitimately typed as a viable one-party system, in the sense that it showed no signs of transforming itself into a competitive or no-party system. This is not to say that the CCP had no weaknesses, for indeed there were several features of the system that were predictable sources of difficulty. Perhaps the most important of these was the prolonged tenure of the top leadership, which was certain to intensify the problem of succession. Before the Cultural Revolution, however, this seemed to be a condition that would very possibly weaken the party, but not one that would transform it into a no-party system. The distinction between a weak one-party system and a no-party system is admittedly vague. Nevertheless, until the Cultural Revolution erupted there were no grounds for believing that the CCP's actual and potential weaknesses would become so acute as to challenge the identity and autonomy of the party itself.

Sources of Strength

The CCP's ability to maintain a viable one-party system was largely a result of certain conditions that existed at the time of revolutionary victory and extended, in varying degrees, into the post-1949 period. Four such conditions seem to be particularly important as sources of strength in the CCP's struggle to maintain its monopoly of political power.

1. *Tradition of non-competitive politics.* The political history of China offers no serious precedent for a competitive political system in which an opposition is given institutional status. The main thrust of politics, in impe-

rial and "republican" periods alike, was for the dominant political force to eliminate or restrict sharply in their activities any opponents or organizations that might challenge its power. Experimentation with elections and parties in the years following the Revolution of 1911 nourished a tradition of political liberalism among some intellectuals but left no enduring imprint on political patterns. As the frailty of republican institutions and constitutional niceties in the Chinese context became more evident, political actors simply assumed that those groups that controlled the government of China would also monopolize it, or seek to do so. Both the Kuomintang (KMT) and the CCP were fundamentally committed to a one-party system, with competitive politics acknowledged only as a necessary interlude on the road to power. Despite some efforts to forestall civil war by formation of a KMT-CCP coalition government, it is doubtful if any significant number of Chinese ever believed that such a government could emerge and endure. When the CCP gained the upper hand, its rapid implementation of a one-party system was neither a surprise nor, except among a few non-party intellectuals whose "democratic parties" had cooperated with the communists, a disappointment. The effective monopolization of power by the CCP was not antithetical to either the political tradition in which it operated or the expectations of politically conscious Chinese.[8]

2. *Military character of the revolution.* The CCP won control of China by defeating its enemies militarily in a full-scale civil war (1946–1949). Moreover, the communist movement had a pronounced military character from 1927 on, owing to its nearly constant involvement in armed struggle against either KMT or Japanese forces. This military aspect of the communist revolution influenced the strength of one-party rule in two ways.[9]

First, the necessity for armed defense and offense led the CCP to build its own army—an army controlled by party officials, subordinate to party objectives, and thoroughly permeated with party members and ideology. The Red Army became a reliable instrument of the CCP, more than adequate in the long run for the military responsibilities that communist policies placed upon it. As a result, the CCP could win military victory without compromising with non-communist warlords and without coopting into its army large units that were doubtfully loyal to the cause; when new or captured troops were absorbed, the party tried to provide the kind of indoctrination, assignment, and leadership necessary for their integration into this highly politicized army. Total military subordination to the CCP was not always easy to maintain, as recurrent campaigns against the "purely military viewpoint" demonstrated, but on the balance the effort was successful. Thus, after 1949 the CCP faced neither the defection of former military allies, which so plagued Chiang Kai-shek's KMT, nor the risk of opposition from an independent military establishment, which has ended party rule in so many other states. The party entered the post-revolutionary stage with the knowledge that its military arm would strengthen, not weaken, its ability to rule.

Second, the military character of the revolution brought a definitive resolution to the question of domestic opposition. The declared enemies of the CCP were scattered, exterminated, or driven out of the country; non-declared enemies were deterred from opposition by the knowledge that the CCP would respond with military force if necessary and had already demonstrated decisively its military superiority. The survival on Taiwan of the KMT was both disturbing and embarrassing to the CCP, but it also prolonged the climate of confrontation that had nurtured the Red Army's politicization. In effect, the results of the civil war gave the communist government a higher degree of military security than that held by any government of twentieth century China. While this kind of security did not assure the CCP's ability to govern and mobilize the population, it went a long way toward enabling the party to devote its best efforts in this direction. Again, the contrast with the KMT, which was never sufficiently secure from military attack to give full attention to developing its domestic program, is both significant and instructive.

3. *Techniques of political control.* The previous discussion indicates that the CCP's military strength gave it ample opportunity to establish the kind of political system that it wanted. It is equally significant that the CCP had substantial experience as a governing party before 1949 and had faced and resolved, before it came to power, some of the problems that a one-party system encounters. To analyze fully the relevant political techniques and structures that evolved in the Chinese Communist movement is obviously impossible here; to do so would require a thorough discussion of the particular ideological, organizational, and environmental characteristics of the movement.[10] We shall emphasize only the general fact that by 1949 the CCP was both sensitive to and well prepared for the problems of maintaining a system of single-party rule.

Perhaps the critical dilemma for any revolutionary movement that aspires to control of a large and populous area is how to make the movement sufficiently broad and flexible to avoid isolation from society without sacrificing its sense of revolutionary mission and identity. That is, the movement, or the party that leads it, must avoid the kind of doctrinal and political rigidity that makes tactical maneuver difficult and forces all dissidents into roles of opposition; at the same time, it must maintain sufficient autonomy and purity to avoid factionalization and the dilution of its leadership and objectives. The CCP's resolution of this dilemma was seldom easy and never perfect, yet it is clear that from 1937–1938 on it was generally effective in striking the appropriate balance. The resolution consisted of a set of techniques and principles that emerged in the Yenan Period (1937–1945) and were continued, although apparently with decreasing effectiveness, down to the Cultural Revolution. Strong control devices coupled with substantial tolerance of diversity and conflict were the key ingredients in this resolution.

Control was of necessity primary. With respect to society, or the areas under its governance, the CCP established political institutions of its own choice and a monopoly of instruments of force. Through careful assignment and cooptation, it placed party members in controlling positions in all important organizations. The party leadership assumed sole responsibility for advancing major programs and making major decisions. Opposition, in the sense of any challenge to the CCP's dominance, was suppressed. With respect to the party itself, the leadership established a powerful control system that kept close track of members' careers and personal lives and enforced conformity with central decisions. The system placed particular emphasis on ideological indoctrination, coupled with recurrent investigation and "rectification" of members' weaknesses, to maintain a high level of unity, commitment, and performance within the organization.

Nonetheless, the CCP did not let its insistence on control isolate it from the population or stifle all political debate. Efforts to practice doctrinal principles such as the "mass line" and "democratic centralism," despite their ambiguities and limitations, gave at least some support to the CCP's contention that its policies could be influenced by elements outside the top party ranks.[11] Many non-communist groups and individuals participated in governmental activities, while the population as a whole was encouraged to learn about and respond to political programs. The principle of separation of state and party, by which the party would set general policy and supervise the quality of political life, but not monopolize state duties or positions, appeared to place some limits on the scope of CCP activities. Party norms for cadres emphasized willingness to work with and listen to the "masses," in order to avoid psychic or political isolation from the people.

Perhaps most importantly, the CCP accepted the legitimacy of debate within its own organization. Debate was not free from conditions. For one thing, the CCP insisted that the basic premise of democratic centralism be observed, that party members must not openly oppose or sabotage policies with which they disagreed once these policies were approved by authoritative agencies. Another basic condition was that inner-party debate must not take the form of factional struggle. Franz Schurmann has made a critical distinction between "factions" and "opinion groups" within the CCP that is directly relevant to this discussion.[12] According to Schurmann, opinion groups are aggregates of individuals who have in common a "likeness of individual opinion" but have no organizational base for action; the CCP tolerated such groups, both before and after decisions, so long as a minority opinion group did not violate party discipline in an effort to overturn the decision of the majority. Factions are opinion groups with organized force behind them, and have not been tolerated in the CCP because of their potential for splitting the party along institutional, geographic, or personal lines. Through this distinction, the leaders sought procedural guidelines that allowed for genuine policy debate and the possibility of policy reversals, without encouraging the growth of factional conflict and without subverting the party's public image of "correctness" and unity.

The ebb and flow of self-criticism and rectification within the CCP suggests that it has never regarded its resolution of this issue as fixed or perfect. We shall argue later that it was precisely in the area of political control that some of the greatest strains in the Chinese party system became evident. The fact remains that the CCP came to grips with a whole range of issues relating to control of unity and diversity within and without the party before it came to power, and that its ability to compromise between the poles of revolutionary exclusiveness and national inclusiveness was one of its major resources in the building of a new social system.

4. *Leadership of Mao Tse-tung.* One of the most striking characteristics of the Chinese Communist movement is that its acknowledged leader in pre-power years retained his position long after the revolution was won. Mao Tse-tung gained the top position in the CCP in 1935 and has held it ever since, although he gave up the post of head of state in late 1958. The prestige and political importance that derive from such a career, which in a rough way combines the careers of a Lenin and a Stalin, cannot be exaggerated. While Mao's role and ideology have recently become a source of strain within the party, they contributed heavily to CCP strength and stability in earlier periods.[13]

An appreciation of Mao's importance must include at least three points. First, as party leader since 1935 Mao deserves more credit than anyone else for establishing the CCP's successful relationship to its political environment. For example, party-military relations and the mass line style of work, both within and outside of the party, are largely Maoist contributions. However his final years of power may be judged, Mao's practical leadership and visionary guidance were for many years enormous assets to the CCP.

Second, Mao Tse-tung's personal command and writings have served as the formal legitimator of party decisions. The CCP's decision-making process is obscure, but it is plain that Mao's personal position and past writings have provided the definitive justification for most courses of action. This does not mean that the alleged consistency of Mao's "thought" has protected decisions from opposition or future change. It does mean, however, that the party has had an accepted signal for finalizing decisions and for maintaining the appearance of unity, continuity, and revolutionary progress.

Finally, Mao's immense prestige has bolstered the legitimacy of the CCP in its relations with the Chinese population. To be sure, the "cult of Mao" has been designed and imposed by the party, obscuring the extent of the man's "natural" popularity and the possibility of an unfavorable image. However, the cult of Mao is in good part a reinforcement and ritualization of a heroic reputation; there is no evidence that it has been resisted or greeted with cynicism by the people in general, despite some attacks on Mao at higher levels. Mao's ability to attract support during the Cultural Revolution indicates that his popular prestige is undiminished, and that for many Chinese it is he, rather than the CCP, who represents the national will. The disruptive consequences of his split with much of the party command show us how heavily the CCP's leading position in Chinese society relied on its identification with the person of Mao.

Disintegration in the Established System

The discussion thus far has presented some general points about the Chinese party system as it was to 1965, when the Cultural Revolution began. Perhaps it is not wholly accurate to say that the established system endured so long, since the strains that are now revealed so openly had begun to weaken the structure of party rule several years earlier. It is nonetheless significant, and a tribute to its essential viability, that the CCP was able to contain these tensions until 1965–1966 and thereby preserve the possibility of an intrasystemic resolution of its difficulties. With the sudden escalation in the summer of 1966, however, the Cultural Revolution brought at least a temporary rupture in the operation of the established system. We shall first examine the main symptoms of this disintegration and then consider some of its possible causes.

The intensity, duration, and violence of the struggle that has engulfed China since the summer of 1966 is the most dramatic evidence of the system's disintegration.[14] Since the overt phase of the conflict began, virtually every major city has been racked by tense political maneuverings, street confrontations among opposing groups, and in some cases resort to arms. The conflict has stopped short of civil war, has never touched all sections of the country equally at the same time, and has even subsided three times —in the fall of 1966, the spring of 1967, and again in late 1967 and early 1968. Thus far, however, each period of relaxation has been followed by renewed outbreaks; no area of China as yet appears to be truly secure from further conflict.

This pattern of social disorder clearly reflects a decline of the CCP's operative unity and control. There have been indications of party irresoluteness on major issues since the 1950s. It is now ten years since the Party Congress last met in 1958, twelve years since that Congress was convened in 1956. From 1954 to 1962, regular plenums of the Central Committee were held once or twice a year; nearly four years elapsed from the Tenth Plenum in September, 1962 to the Eleventh Plenum of August, 1966, although the Central Committee is known to have met in non-plenary session within that period. Generally, the CCP's record of 1962–1966 was one of significant contrast between actual practice and announced goals and campaigns.[15] Once the divisive issues that these gaps suggest were brought into the open, the long-heralded unity and stability of the top leadership simply vanished. By the spring of 1968, according to one analysis, 34 of the 63 regular Central Committee members active in 1965 had been purged, while 9 more were under attack; of the 72 active alternate members, 27 had been purged and 29 had been sharply criticized; only 9 of the 45 men identified in 1965 as first or second secretaries in regional party organizations were still known to be active.[16] The same analysis indicated that purgees included over half of the membership of the state council, the party politburo and the party secretariat; the party's Military Affairs Committee had also lost three of its seven members in the purge. In terms of leadership personnel, the old system has suffered a shattering blow.

The changes brought by the Cultural Revolution go far beyond loss of old leaders, however, for the party hierarchy no longer dominates the affairs of China. Beginning in early 1967, the Maoists in Peking launched an effort to replace existing authorities in the provinces and major cities with "revolutionary committees" based on a "three-way alliance" among the army, revolutionary rebels, and Maoist cadres. The "seizure of power" by revolutionary committees was not designed to exclude CCP members from the new institutions of authority, but it was in effect a frontal attack on the party's previous monopoly of power. By June, 1968, revolutionary committees had been established in the largest cities and in all but five of China's 26 provinces and regions.[17] The authority held by these committees is neither thorough nor unchallenged, even in those administrative units where they exist, but they are nonetheless an institutional representation of the party's decline.

The People's Liberation Army (PLA) has now emerged as the most powerful organization in China. Although the scope and nuances of its power are indistinct, its influence is unmistakable in both those areas that have revolutionary committees and those that do not. Military representatives now dominate the provincial and regional administration of China, holding well over half of the leading cadre positions at this level. The trend toward military control has been particularly pronounced in those revolutionary committees established after August, 1967. Moreover, within the party Central Committee, military officers have been purged at a lower rate than non-military cadres, so that military representation among the remaining Central Committee members has risen substantially. The PLA has by no means been immune to the purge, but political commissars within the PLA have suffered more than regular military commanders.[18] Throughout the latter half of 1967 and the early part of 1968, the PLA also took precedence over the CCP in official references to the accomplishments and tasks of the Cultural Revolution. The PLA was praised in glowing terms and identified as "the powerful pillar of the dictatorship of the proletariat." The party received scant attention, and that largely of a negative kind; references to it were most frequently calls for "rectifying party organization" and "defeating the handful of top party persons in authority." [19] During the same period, the identification of leading Maoists by party position also declined. As we will note later, efforts to revive the CCP apparently got under way in 1968. There is no doubt, however, that the higher levels of party organization had all but disappeared during the course of 1967.

Finally, the disintegration of the established system is underscored by a significant change in its internal political process, specifically in its use of the purge. The relative stability and unity of CCP leadership has never implied a refusal to use the purge. It is true that the purging of party members has been relatively infrequent since the late 1930s, that it has avoided the bloody and violent excesses associated with it elsewhere, and that generally the CCP has placed more emphasis on the "rectification" and reform of deviant members than on their punishment. However, these are signs of the party's careful application of the purge rather than unwillingness to resort to its threatened or actual use. Some use of the purge may be necessary in any one-party system; without it, the leading party may tolerate too much diversity and conflict. The problem is that the party elite must show its ability to enforce its decisions without decimating or alienating the membership. From 1935 to 1966, the CCP handled this problem effectively. Party discipline was enforced, with occasional purges, but punitive action against members never reached a scale that would rob the organization of essential personnel or support.

Data on purges before the Cultural Revolution is not sufficiently complete to establish hard rules of party behavior, but a few general patterns are distinguishable from known cases.[20] The first of these is that the CCP's treatment of allegedly deviant top leaders (politburo or senior Central Committee members) was cautious and restrained in an effort to minimize the impression of conflict at the top. Preferred treatment of opposition was actually to stop short of a purge if possible. For example, a man identified as an "opponent" by subsequent decisions might simply admit his error, recant in public, and maintain his position; such a case was Teng Tzu-hui, Director of the Party's Rural Work Department, who opposed the "high tide" of collectivization in late 1955 and then admitted his error at the Eighth Party Congress in September, 1956.[21] Or an opponent might be inactivated, subject to later rehabilitation, if he kept his opposition quiet and avoided the stigma of factional intrigue; Ch'en Yün, who has resisted Maoist policies for over ten years and yet still resurfaces from time to time as a senior party official, exemplifies this solution. This is simply to amplify on a point made earlier that intraparty debate and conflict, if kept on the level of "opinion groups," was not grounds for purging. In the case of top leaders, the purge was reserved for real or potential "factions"—opponents who had, and seemed likely to use, an organized base for continued opposition.

In the two main cases of top-level purges before the Cultural Revolution (Kao Kang and Jao Shu-shih in 1954–1955 and P'eng Teh-huai in 1959), considerable restraint was still evident. The party did not identify the purgees until after authoritative decisions on their cases had been made; that is, there was no public campaign against them in advance of their actual downfall, although their vulnerability to a purge might be inferred from indirect references in CCP argumentation and from absence of public appearances. Moreover, the specifics of the charges against P'eng Teh-huai and his associates were not made public at the time; they were not attacked by name, nor was there a lengthy campaign to tarnish their reputations and associations. There was a public accounting of individual errors and punishment in the Kao-Jao affair, indicating the seriousness of their organized opposition to the dominant group in the CCP, but the assault on these men was not exceptionally severe or prolonged.

A second pattern is that purges of lower-level officials showed less caution and restraint. Indeed, in such cases the CCP apparently wanted to dramatize the existence of deviations to threaten higher officials who might be involved and to impress on the party organization as a whole the need for continued vigilance and rectification. Public attacks on individuals sometimes preceded formal announcement of disposition of their cases. The attacks might take on the character of a mass movement, with purgees used as symbols of common failings and with considerable detail on the alleged errors and associations of the purgees.

Finally, in all cases purges appear to have followed a top-level policy decision. They have been a weapon against those who have resisted or attacked an authoritative decision, not a means of shutting off pre-decision debate. This, of course, indicates that the employment and effectiveness of the purge was dependent on the top leadership's ability to mobilize a strong majority behind a particular decision or set of policies. During those periods in which the leadership was divided or uncertain, a purge could not be attempted without risking a violation of the operative guidelines for intraparty control.

The Cultural Revolution represents a significant departure from these earlier patterns. The development of this most recent purge suggests that the CCP's internal political process reached the critical point of strain in May–August, 1966. At some point in that period, the party's established mechanisms for resolving internal conflicts collapsed.

The disintegration of intraparty control actually began following the dismissal of P'eng Teh-huai in 1959. Although the CCP maintained its surface unity in and following this affair, it did so partly by a significant increase in investment of Mao Tse-tung's personal political capital. That is, Mao brought his senior colleagues to his side only by laying his personal position and prestige on the line; he kept them there only by a campaign of personal glorification which made it extremely difficult for other leaders to avoid paying at least lip service to his policies.[22] Even that investment brought limited returns, however. As we noted earlier, actual party behavior in the years down to 1965 persistently violated the intent of Mao's prescriptions. Moreover, despite seeming support for P'eng's dismissal, the affair remained unsettled. P'eng lost his job as Minister of Defense but retained membership on the politburo, with assurances that the party should treat him with "great sincerity and warmth" and help him "recognize and rectify his mistakes."[23] In 1962, he sought a reversal of his purge, allegedly with backing from none other than Liu Shao-ch'i.[24] Officially the repudiation of P'eng was upheld, but it is evident now that the top leadership was too divided to settle the matter once and for all.

The Cultural Revolution began in the fall of 1965, subsequent to a September meeting of the Central Committee.[25] Given the history and depth of party disagreements over preceding years, of which only a portion has been mentioned here, Mao Tse-tung undoubtedly realized from the first that his opposition would include Liu Shao-ch'i, Teng Hsiao-p'ing, and many other highstanding men. It is not certain, however, that he had concluded that his entire opposition would have to be purged, since there was yet the possibility that it might be forced into line. Accordingly, Mao launched his attack on a small group of lower officials who had criticized his policies in 1961–1962. We might interpret the early campaign against this "black gang" as consistent with established practice, in the sense that it was a widely publicized assault on lower-level officials whose actions were demonstrably hostile toward official policy. Presumably, one of its primary functions would be to force top-level sympathizers with the "black gang" to give up their "erroneous" positions and unite with the Maoist "majority." A top-level purge would then be unnecessary, since the opposition would not be punished for earlier resistance if it ultimately recanted and agreed not to obstruct implementation of Mao's policies in the future.

Actually, it is questionable if even the early part of the Cultural Revolution had the "legitimacy" that this interpretation suggests. If the September meeting of the Central Committee had endorsed strongly Mao's call for a fresh campaign, then subsequent actions could be viewed as for or against an authoritative party decision—a legitimate test for deciding whether or not to purge. This degree of unity was lacking, however. At best, Mao initiated the campaign with the active support of some colleagues, the grudging acquiescence of others and the opposition of still others. To the extent that the developing purge did not rest on substantial party approval, it was already a departure from established practice—a case of political adventurism by Mao rather than enforcement of party discipline.

In any case, the breakdown became unmistakable by the late spring of 1966. The campaign against the "black gang," now buttressed by a PLA-backed rectification campaign aimed at senior cadres in general, implicated the CCP propaganda system and the Peking Party Committee headed by politburo member P'eng Chen. P'eng Chen spoiled the scenario by resisting, but on June 3 official sources announced his dismissal and the reorganization of the Peking Committee. At the same time, Mao made clear his intent to extend the Cultural Revolution into a mass campaign to expose and bring down all those who were resisting, or had in the past resisted, his policies. The only salvation for the party system at this point was capitulation by the leading opposition figures. Capitulation, however, meant not only acceptance of the purges to that point—primarily the dismissals of P'eng Chen, propaganda head Lu Ting-yi and army chief of staff Lo Jui-ch'ing

—but also full-fledged support for a combined purge and rectification campaign that promised to shake the authority structure of China to its foundations. Acceptance of the purges was not impossible; they could be viewed as a necessary sacrifice for the preservation of the party. But to Liu Shaoch'i and his colleagues, the escalation of the Cultural Revolution was intolerable. For two months, they tried to restrain and subvert it, hoping that Mao would not insist on a literal fulfillment of his call. This hope was illusory. At the Eleventh Plenum of the Central Committee, held in Peking August 1–12, Mao secured from what was apparently a packed conference two documents that authorized him to go ahead with his campaign, now specifically designed to overthrow "those within the party who are in authority and are taking the capitalist road." [26]

The Central Committee's statements could not conceal that the CCP command was locked in a bitter factional struggle. In fact Mao did not hold a clear majority within the CCP elite. But rather than work through an intraparty debate of indefinite duration to resolve this "contradiction" —an appropriate course under established practice—Mao carried the struggle outside the party organization. To discredit and overthrow those defined as opponents, most of whom still held high party office, the Maoists called for revolutionary mass action and military support. Red Guards, "revolutionary rebels," and the PLA became the Maoists' organizational bases for purging the ranks of the CCP. The personal and public careers of cadres still occupying positions of authority were violently criticized by non-party groups. The resolution of political issues passed from the CCP organizational hierarchy into a much larger and more open political arena in which rival party factions combined with non-party forces in their efforts to maintain or acquire political power. As indicated above, the struggle gradually neutralized or drove from office large numbers of the CCP elite. The precise political results are irrelevant to the present discussion, however. The point is that the Cultural Revolution involved a significant change in the process by which the CCP had previously maintained its unity and control. With that development, the established system of one-party rule ceased to function.

Causes of Disintegration

We turn now to causes of disintegration in the Chinese party system. This subject is manifestly more difficult to penetrate than the symptoms of disintegration, but certain tentative answers can be advanced. The sources of strength in the established system, described above, serve as a useful point of departure for this inquiry.

Two of the system's basic strengths remained essentially intact down to the Cultural Revolution and may, therefore, be omitted from detailed consideration here. The absence of competitive politics or of any serious challenge to the idea of one-party politics was not altered. There was no growth of political opposition outside the party, no infusion of "competitive" ideals from outside the system, and no revival (after 1957) of these fragile pressures within China which might have encouraged a diminution of the CCP's political monopoly. A strong, party-controlled military establishment also endured. The PLA's current power is clearly a change from the past, but it emerged in full force only after the collapse of CCP unity. Neither Lin Piao as an individual nor the senior military staff as a group constituted an anti-party opposition in advance of the crucial events of 1966; their role in these events was supremely important but they cannot be charged with responsibility for the CCP's disintegration. The emergence of military rule—if that is what now exists in China—is a consequence, not a cause, of the Cultural Revolution.[27]

It is, therefore, in the personal role of Mao Tse-tung and the CCP's techniques of control that the decisive changes lie. The role of Mao provides the simplest explanation for the occurrence of the Cultural Revolution. The basic premise of this argument is that Mao suffered a gradual loss of authority in the preceding years, with the result that he could no longer carry the party with him down any path that he wished to take. From 1935 to the purge of P'eng Teh-huai in 1959, Mao was ultimately able to secure Central Committee support for his policies. In the last analysis, he could always carry the day by placing his personal prestige and position on the line. This is precisely what he did in the fall of 1965 in his effort to achieve a true acceptance of the policies he had advocated in 1962–1965. At issue in the campaign against the "black gang" were insinuations about Mao's personal leadership; it was unmistakably clear that continued resistance to his policies would be interpreted as opposition to him personally. Nevertheless, at the critical juncture in mid-1966, a significant number of powerful leaders refused to yield before the invocation of this kind of pressure. Despite Mao's undiminshed national prestige, so amply demonstrated in his ability to muster support during the campaign, the conclusion that his authority among his senior colleagues had declined is unavoidable. A combination of causes contributed to this decline.

First, Mao Tse-tung was certainly less effective as a leader in the 1960s than in the 1950s. Although much discussion of Mao's ill health (not to mention his death) falls in the category of speculation or wishful thinking, advancing age must have taken its toll on his capacity to cope with the demands placed upon him. In addition, his retirement from the chairmanship of the government in late 1958 apparently reduced his involvement in the day-to-day administrative problems of China. By 1965, public adulation of Mao's leadership was a poor representation of his actual influence within the Chinese political elite. Many of his colleagues had reason to doubt that his physical ability, judgment, and knowledge were sufficient to support the authority he had once held.[28] The fact that these men may have fatally underestimated Mao's *power* does not alter this conclusion.

Closely related to doubts about Mao's competence is the question of succession. Whether Mao's partial retirement in 1958 was voluntary or forced, the ultimate result was to establish Liu Shao-ch'i as first in line for the succession and encourage a drift away from reliance on Mao. More generally, the 1958–1965 period brought a growing awareness within the CCP that concrete steps must be taken to prepare for the transfer of authority. "Cultivation of revolutionary successors" and fresh recruitment into the party and youth league became the subject of major campaigns and much high-level discussion. These campaigns, coupled with intensifying glorification of Mao and his "thought," seemed to be aimed at a perpetuation of Maoism in China. From Mao's point of view, this was exactly their objective. But Mao's top aides, who were necessarily most sensitive to the immediate political implications of succession, must have perceived the situation differently. Their primary concern was not the perpetuation of Maoism as such but rather the transfer of Mao's authority from Mao the man to the CCP leadership that would inherit his position. From this point of view, the cult of Mao was a positive advantage so long as it did not suggest any separation between Mao and the party; the CCP could bask in reflected glory as Mao's chosen instrument even while actual leadership was already devolving on the Liu Shao-ch'i–Teng Hsiao-p'ing group. So, too, with the "revolutionary" cultivation and recruitment campaigns, which gave Mao's putative successors an opportunity to prepare organizationally and psychologically for his approaching departure. The point is that the transfer of authority had begun, that mechanisms for assuring a peaceful and orderly change of leaders were evolving. Those who were to benefit from this transition had good reason to believe that a move away from reliance on Mao's personalized leadership was necessary, desirable and to some extent already a *fait accompli*. They could not, therefore, countenance the reactivation of Mao's personal authority, which was initially implicit, and later explicit, in the Cultural Revolution.

Finally, Mao's authority was damaged by his refusal to retreat on the policy issues that dominated CCP affairs over the years between 1957 and 1965. In broad terms, Chinese politics since 1957 have revolved around two basic issues—the Great Leap Forward and the Sino-Soviet conflict. Mao did not force these policies on his colleagues, so far as we can tell, but he clearly identified them as his own. When they produced unfavorable results, Mao could not escape personal responsibility. Publicly, responsibility was denied or diffused, but within the elite Mao suffered a serious loss of confidence. Had he been willing to accept a negative verdict and cooperate with the "revisionist" approach that followed the collapse of the Great Leap, he might have avoided this loss. Instead, he resisted and began a long-term effort to actualize his ideals, an effort that culminated in the Cultural Revolution. By that time, however, many of his colleagues were satisfied that practice had proven them right and Mao wrong. They had no intention of succumbing to his arguments again.

If Mao's loss of authority within the top leadership had not destroyed his national power and prestige, why did he not act sooner against those who were quietly renouncing and undermining his authority? Would a freer use of the purge, perhaps in the 1950s, have averted the crisis of the 1960s? It is important to remember that Mao's leading position, however it was initially secured, came to rest largely on his persuasiveness, statesmanship, and ability to command personal loyalties rather than on coercive power. No doubt he had the power, at least before the 1960s, to construct coercive instruments of personal control, but to do so would have meant a renunciation of his own style of party politics. To consolidate and perpetuate his power in this way might well have accelerated the weakening of his authority, unless he was prepared to go all the way by eliminating all of his old colleagues. However, a purge on the scale of the Cultural Revolution, including so many men of a stature approaching Mao's, would certainly have been traumatic even in the 1950s; one need only reflect briefly on Stalin's example to foresee some of the possible consequences for the party system in this course of action. Ultimately, of course, Mao did call on Red Guards, "revolutionary rebels," and the PLA to buttress his position. But even this act, which was in itself a resort to "factional" struggle techniques as defined earlier, proved to be ineffectual as a means of capturing control over the party structure. By 1966, Mao's high-level opponents were not only unwilling to follow him voluntarily—the evidence of his declining authority; they were also capable of resisting his efforts to secure compliance through force. Despite the CCP's long-standing fear of factions with organized bases of power, the Cultural Revolution revealed a party which had already developed the basic conditions for factional politics. The old patterns of party control, which had given the established system much of its strength, had somehow lost their effectiveness.

In 1949, the CCP's unity and integrity were relatively strong. Unity was a function of common experience and outlook, and a broad consensus about the necessity of transforming Chinese society along socialist lines; integrity was a function of psychological and political distinctness (but not isolation) from society and a determination to ensure party control over the direction of Chinese affairs. Both unity and integrity were maintained by the CCP's flexible control techniques, which allowed some political debate and diversity so long as certain fundamental rules about party discipline and monopoly were observed. These techniques had worked well before 1949 and contributed heavily to the establishment of the Chinese Communist system. Nevertheless, the post-1949 situation posed more acutely than ever before the question of how a revolutionary party should respond to the challenge of governing a huge and complex society.

One choice for the CCP was to become an elitist and exclusive party, to avoid monopolizing leadership of all social organizations, and to content itself largely with directing policy from the top. This choice would encourage a sense of pure national direction, above the partial interests and secondary problems that might divide the administration. However, it would also leave openings for the growth of political opposition and risk inability to implement and supervise policies of far-reaching social change. Had the CCP chosen this path, it might have had only a modest impact on Chinese society.

A second choice for the CCP was to extend its influence throughout society, into every organization, to ensure a party presence wherever important decisions might be made. In effect, the party would become the government. This is ultimately what happened, although the CCP protested for some time that it did not want to assume such a role. The first thrust of party rule in the early 1950s carried it far in this direction. Party organization expanded rapidly, with members everywhere moving into controlling positions as the influence of non-party elements steadily declined. The middle 1950s brought some calls for preserving the independence of non-party institutions, but with the beginning of the Great Leap Forward the CCP explicitly accepted the idea of direct party leadership throughout society. Under the slogan of "politics takes command," the key source of authority at all levels and in all institutions became the party committee.

The expansion of its power gave the CCP great resources for popular mobilization and policy implementation. It also eliminated the possibility of any opposition from extraparty organization. But the CCP had not eliminated political conflict in China. Rather, it had simply absorbed these conflicts into its own organization and had assumed responsibility for resolving them through intraparty processes. As the party grew and became more and more deeply immersed in administrative responsibilities, its membership was transformed in ways that rendered old control techniques less effective, and thereby left the party vulnerable to disintegration.

Part of this change is evident in an altered configuration of CCP membership.[29] Membership grew from 4.5 million in 1949 to 17 million in 1961 and perhaps 20 million in 1965. The scale of recruitment in itself created formidable problems in determining admissions standards, establishing personnel and disciplinary control, and maintaining effective communications; bureaucratization and standardization necessarily followed. Rapid recruitment also altered radically the training and motivation of the membership. In 1949, all party members were by definition "revolutionary cadres" who had taken part in military and political struggles before victory was assured. Their experience and their commitment to a revolutionary movement marked them as men of unusual attributes. By 1961, this pre-1949 group constituted only 20 per cent of CCP membership, while 40 per cent of the party had joined since the Eighth Congress in 1956; projecting these trends, it is likely that in 1966 the original pre-1949 members were less than 15 per cent of the total and that post-1956 members constituted about one-half of the party. In brief, the general character of CCP membership had shifted dramatically away from the earlier one of revolutionary experience and commitment. For those who joined after 1949, whatever their ideological convictions might be, membership meant a sharing of the power, prestige, and upward mobility of a ruling elite.

Growth and administrative responsibility also initiated changes in the social and occupational composition of the party. Members of peasant origin fell from 80 per cent of the CCP in 1949 to 66 per cent in 1961; the percentage of industrial workers as members rose from near zero to 15 per cent in the same period, while intellectual members rose from about 5 per cent to 15 per cent. In 1956, approximately one-third of all intellectuals, about 18 per cent of the workers and only 1.4 per cent of the peasants were members; the path of entrance into the party was plainly shifting toward urban strata. Similar trends were evident in the occupations of the membership. When the CCP came to power, its members were mostly peasants and soldiers; 73 per cent were said to be engaged in agriculture in 1950, while 22 per cent were in the army in 1949. The percentage engaged in agriculture dropped to 58 in 1956, while only around 6 per cent of party members were in the army by 1961.

These scattered figures outline a fundamental change in the meaning and demands of party membership. Before 1949, the party member was typically a soldier or peasant who served the CCP as an unpaid activist, as a "generalist" type of leader at the mass level. After 1949, members increasingly became full-time cadres in the party, government, or mass organizations. They worked in offices that were part of some bureaucratic structure, received a salary, and were subject to selection and promotion through bureaucratic standards and grades. Maoist doctrine was hostile toward this trend, and sought to combat it by recurrent study, rectification, and temporary assignment to lower levels and physical labor (*hsia fang*). Despite efforts to preserve the older "mass line" style of work, however, the bureaucratization and specialization of membership continued.[30] Occupied with countless administrative problems and dispersed among many bureaucratic hierarchies, the membership became less responsive to the ideological and normative appeals and controls that had in the past given it much of its unity, discipline, and identity.

An equally important aspect of this transformation in the CCP was the emergence of "functional systems" in the government of China.[31] We noted at the outset that the placement of party members in key positions throughout all important organizations nullified the possibility of clear-cut conflict between the CCP and the army, state structure, or other organizations. Overlapping party membership brought all conflicts into the realm of intraparty matters, where they could presumably be ironed out through established disciplinary and control practices. However, this solution did not preclude the possibility that party members serving in particular organizations might over time develop loyalties, experiences, and outlooks that would set them apart from comrades serving elsewhere. In the early years after 1949, this problem was apparently insignificant. The traditions of the

CCP, the fact that most senior cadres had combined military, political, and administrative experience, and the shifting of cadres between regions and functional assignments all served to minimize the development of fixed identification with particular lines or places of work. Nevertheless, Barnett observes that by the late 1950s the development of functional specialization had created identifiable systems, which tended to have their own particular orientations and to serve as career assignments for those working in them.

In the unfolding of recent events, it is evident that the CCP "monolith" had partially broken down into a variety of power constellations or bases.[32] How and when these groups developed, or what political role they played before the Cultural Revolution, is not clear. They are almost certainly identified, however, with the growth of functional systems as described by Barnett; that is, they are a product of the emergence of large, bureaucratic structures, which found that they had particular interests to serve and the power to do so. Assuming this to be the case, they are probably a relatively recent phenomenon that had not yet imposed a distinct form of bureaucratic bargaining on the Chinese political process. They had, however, developed sufficient power and autonomy to resist policy trends of which their leaders did not approve. They served as a kind of organizational retreat for their leaders, power bases from which these leaders could defy, and possibly attempt to bargain with, the CCP elite. They were, therefore, potential factions, waiting only on a conflict as severe as the Cultural Revolution to bring them out into the open in full-fledged factional struggle.

The boundaries of these power bases are indistinct but a few general identifications are possible. One group is that which surrounds the party leader and is the most amorphous in structure; its leaders consist of Mao and his close personal associates, and its resources lie mainly in Mao's prestige as translated into individual debts of loyalty and the support of mass organizations such as the Red Guards and revolutionary rebels. Other groups emerge from the functional systems. Those most clearly identified now as participants in the recent factional struggle are the propaganda and educational system, originally headed by Lu Ting-yi; the party organization and personnel system, which was a major source of power for Liu Shao-ch'i and Teng Hsiao-p'ing; a loose grouping within the state structure under the influence of Chou En-lai; and the army. A third major category is the regional power base. P'eng Chen's Peking party structure was the first to be identified in this way, but events since the summer of 1966 have shown that many provinces and almost all major cities have considerable power to resist pressures from the center and to maintain some degree of political autonomy.

Much of the struggle since 1966 can be analyzed broadly in terms of power bases. The conflict began with the party leader's group launching an attack on the propaganda-education base that was supported by Peking.

With the backing of his PLA ally, Mao overcame both of his first targets. Now in control of Peking and the propaganda system, Mao turned on the central party organization and a number of regional bases, of which the most important was Shanghai. All resisted with considerable effectiveness and fought Mao's propaganda media and Red Guards to a standoff. By calling in the PLA as a more active participant in the winter of 1966–1967, Mao turned the tide. Shanghai went over to the Maoist side and the central party organization was neutralized. During 1967, various regional bases became "Maoist," but their cooperation was frequently a *pro forma* move that left power in the hands of local military figures or provincial officials. In the summer of 1967, a leftist clique within the party leader's base attempted a purge of the army. The attempt was abortive, resulting in a weakening of Mao's group and a marked rise in the power of the army. As 1967 ended, the army had become the dominant faction, working in cooperation with many provincial officials and some of the more moderate Maoists in Peking. The struggle had not yet stabilized, however, as there were continued tensions between regions and between the leader's group and some of the more moderate factions within the Maoist coalition.

While this *is* at best a loose description of the events in question, it should illustrate the importance of factional politics in the disintegration of the Chinese party system. The point is not, of course, that Chinese politics now revolves entirely around a struggle among the power bases described. The point is simply that the potential for factional politics had developed so far that the established system, which tried to restrict political conflict to non-factional debate within disciplined intraparty procedures, could not function once a major and controversial decision was forced upon it. The basic structural cause of the CCP's disintegration was the party's expansion of its size and functions, with the result that it came to contain structures too powerful and diverse in interests to be unified by traditional appeals and control techniques. The basic political cause was Mao's attempt to reactivate his personal authority in the service of discredited or at least controversial policies, an attempt that taxed the system's weakened structure beyond its resources.

A final word should be added about the widespread social disorder that has accompanied the Cultural Revolution. The pre-1966 stability of the CCP elite concealed important conflicts and frustrations that were developing at lower levels of the party, and indeed in Chinese society generally. These problems lay mainly in the realm of frustrated upward mobility for cadres, discontent over increasing social stratification and privilege, and contradictions between widely propagated doctrinal principles of social organization and the limitations of actual needs and resources. The Maoists in general, and the Red Guards in particular, have given full expression to such complaints in their attacks on various individuals and institutions.[33] Can we say, then, that the Cultural Revolution is actually a revolution from below, that discontented cadres, students and other "masses" brought about the CCP's disintegration? Generally, pressures from below do not appear to have precipitated the Cultural Revolution, which unfolded initially as a struggle for power at higher levels. However, recognition of diverse and competing interests within Chinese society was certainly related to the growth of political and structural differentiation in the party over preceding years. Moreover, once the split at the top occurred, pressures from below exacerbated the struggle by providing both men and motivations for mass participation in the conflict. Many lower-level officials undoubtedly used the Cultural Revolution to improve their positions; groups of students, workers, and other social groups seized the opportunity to articulate group-specific demands. It is possible that this unleashing of long-restrained frustrations has raised new leaders and issues that will ultimately give a different shape to our interpretations of the Cultural Revolution's significance.

Conclusion

Since the summer of 1966 the Chinese political system has been in suspended disarray. The established pattern of CCP rule has collapsed and a new one has not yet taken shape. Possibly this situation will persist indefinitely, gradually revealing that a no-party system based on military rule has taken root. The longer the present indecisiveness continues and the longer military units exercise *de facto* power, the more difficult it will be to restore effective party rule. It no longer seems far-fetched to imagine a group of younger officers openly asserting their right to govern in the name of order, national defense and reconstruction, and an end to divisive ideological politics.

No-party rule by the army still seems to be an unlikely possibility for the long run, however. A legacy of mistrust of military rule, shaped both by CCP doctrine and the lessons of modern Chinese history, would have to be overcome. Some accommodation with communist ideology would be necessary to pacify the ideologues and provide a sense of continuity in national development. The military leaders would need bureaucratic support to staff an effective government, support which could only come now, after nearly twenty years of communist rule, from men who were at least nominally committed to the party.

Moreover, it would be foolish to dismiss quickly the positive attributes of the one-party system. If our earlier analysis of CCP strength had any merit, it suggests that the party remains the logical vehicle for organizing Chinese society and giving political leadership and planned direction to its development. Chinese experience supports the hypothesis that revolutionary one-party systems become truly "established," in the sense of institutionalization, only with great difficulty. But it also affirms the powerful attractiveness for modernizing elites of a highly politicized but non-competitive party system. It may be instructive to recall Soviet experience here. Although the Soviet Communist Party never suffered exactly the kind of organizational rupture now taking place in China, it nonetheless survived at least two extraordinarily painful crises of succession, crises that also raised fundamental questions about the party's role in society.[34] Perhaps the CCP will prove to be less resilient, but we must concede that the one-party system is not so fragile an instrument as is sometimes suggested.

These comments find added support in tentative steps by the Maoists, beginning in late 1967, to revive the CCP. References to the calling of a Ninth Party Congress, the reappearance of official mentions of leaders' positions in the party hierarchy, and signs of extensive discussions about the role of old party cadres all point in this direction.[35] The difficulty of restoring the CCP's authority cannot be minimized. In July, 1968, it appeared that the Maoists were still bogged down in negotiations over the composition of a Ninth Congress, with no signs that old cadres, military leaders, and the new "revolutionary" elites who have now emerged were able to compromise their differences or overcome their mutual suspicions.

The reestablishment of a one-party system (although certainly a weakened one) still seems to be the most likely alternative, however. The critical question is what kind of party will assume command. There is a strong possibility that Mao will succeed in reconstructing the party under his own nominal leadership. He has purged his major opponents and remains the logical rallying point for all major groups now involved. The CCP, if it is revived in the near future, will therefore be a "Maoist" party; that is, it will proclaim Maoist doctrine and will exert renewed efforts to realize his ideals. However, a revival of a Maoist CCP will necessarily be impermanent. The strongest element in its favor is simply Mao's presence and personality. But even those groups which might accept reunification on Mao's terms must realize that his era of Chinese politics is nearly over; his old system collapsed, and he does not now have the time to rebuild it in enduring form. With Mao's death or retirement, the pressures and conflicts that led to the Cultural Revolution will surface again.

No doubt there will then be some Chinese who will wish to carry on Mao's revolutionary vision, but Maoism without Mao is not a viable alternative. The first crucial question facing Mao's successors will be the construction of a substitute for Mao's authority, both within the party and in its relations with the people. How will the CCP be held together and the people be mobilized for national effort? A "revisionist" CCP is one answer. Political bargaining, ideological flexibility, and material rewards might be the incentives to secure internal cooperation and external support for the party. Another obvious answer is greatly increased reliance on coercive power. Communist China has not yet had a real "Stalinist" period, but some future leaders may see force and terror as the only acceptable instruments for maintaining one-party rule.

‖ *Notes*

The author is indebted to the Center for Chinese Studies, University of California, Berkeley, for assistance and financial support in the preparation of this paper and to Professor Michel Oksenberg for his critical comments.

1. For discussion of these points, see chs. 1 and 2 of this volume.
2. See U. S. Congress, Senate, Committee on Government Operations, *Staffing Procedures and Problems in Communist China* (Washington, D.C.: Government Printing Office, 1963); U. S. Department of State, *Directory of Chinese Communist Officials* (Washington, D.C.: Government Printing Office, 1963) and American Consulate-General (Hong Kong), *Current Background*, Nos. 263, 513, and 752.
3. The Hundred Flowers campaign contained at least a suggestion of political opposition from the "democratic parties" within the United Front, but it was totally suppressed. See Roderick MacFarquhar, *The Hundred Flowers Campaign and the Chinese Intellectuals* (New York: Frederick A. Praeger, 1960).
4. Data on the Eighth Central Committee is drawn from Chao Kuo-chün, "Leadership in the Chinese Communist Party," *The Annals*, Vol. CCCXXI (January 1959); and Donald W. Klein, "The 'Next Generation' of Chinese Communist Leaders," *The China Quarterly*, No. 12 (October–December 1962).
5. So far as members of the Central Committee are concerned, regional ties have probably been weakened by assignment in Peking. In 1949–1950, 120 regular and alternate members were assigned to the provinces and only 51 to Peking, whereas this proportion was exactly reversed by 1962; Klein, *op. cit.*, p. 67. Regional ties may now be more important among lower-level officials than among the top elite.
6. Klein (*op. cit.*, p. 66) gives the following breakdown:

	1949–1959	1962
Party	52	73
Government	55	56
Army	64	42

7. Chao, *op. cit.*, pp. 44–46.
8. See the comments in Lucian W. Pye, "Party Systems and National Development in Asia," in Joseph LaPalombara and Myron Wiener, ed., *Political Parties and Political Development* (Princeton: Princeton University Press, 1966), pp. 376–379. The absence of institutionalized political competition in both imperial and republican China did not, of course, preclude active factional or "bureaucratic" politics within the dominant political structure.
9. See Huntington's comments in ch. 1 of this volume on how the intensity of the struggle for power increases the strength of the one-party system.
10. This task has been done most thoroughly by Franz Schurmann, *Ideology and Organization in Communist China* (Berkeley: University of California Press, 1966).
11. For discussion of this subject, see James R. Townsend, *Political Participation in Communist China* (Berkeley: University of California Press, 1967).
12. Schurmann, *op. cit.*, pp. 55–56.
13. On Mao's life and political career, see Jerome Ch'en, *Mao and the Chinese Revolution* (London: Oxford University Press, 1965); and Stuart Schram, *Mao*

Tse-tung (Baltimore: Penguin Books, 1966). Since Mao's ideas receive little substantive discussion in this chapter, it should at least be acknowledged here that Maoist notions actually *encouraged* some of the trends toward which he later became so hostile. Specifically, it was the idea of "politics takes command" that forced the CCP to take over so many governmental functions after 1957, thereby accelerating the bureaucratization—and disintegration—of party organization. Maoist doctrine has not been the least of the "contradictions" with which the CCP has had to contend.

14. For detailed description and analysis of the Cultural Revolution, see Philip Bridgham, "Mao's 'Cultural Revolution': Origin and Development," *The China Quarterly*, No. 29 (January–March 1967); John Gittings, "The Chinese Army's Role in the Cultural Revolution," *Pacific Affairs*, Vol. XXXIX, No. 3–4 (Fall and Winter, 1966–1967); Chalmers Johnson, "China: The Cultural Revolution in Structural Perspective," *Asian Survey*, Vol. VIII, No. 1 (January 1968); Franz Michael, "The Struggle for Power," *Problems of Communism*, Vol. XVI, No. 3 (May–June 1967); and Charles Neuhauser, "The Chinese Communist Party in the 1960's: Prelude to the Cultural Revolution," *The China Quarterly*, No. 32 (October–December 1967).

15. See Neuhauser, *op. cit.*

16. *The New York Times*, June 25, 1968.

17. *Ibid.*, June 3, 1968. The provinces that had not yet set up revolutionary committees were Fukien, Kwangsi, Yunnan, Tibet, and Sinkiang.

18. For details, see Jürgen Domes, "The Cultural Revolution and the Army," *Asian Survey*, Vol. VIII, No. 5 (May 1968), esp. pp. 360–363.

19. For example, see the joint editorials of *Jen-min Jih-pao, Hung Ch'i* and *Chieh-fang Chün Pao* for October 1, 1967, and January 1, 1968; texts in *Peking Review*, October 6, 1967, pp. 15–19, and January 3, 1968, pp. 10–13.

20. For documentation on the main purges in China between 1949 and 1965, see *Documents of the National Conference of the Communist Party of China, March 1955* (Peking: Foreign Languages Press, 1955); *Second Session of the Eighth National Congress of the Communist Party of China, May 1958* (Peking: Foreign Languages Press, 1958); and *Eighth Plenary Session of the Eighth Central Committee of the Communist Party of China, August 1959* (Peking: Foreign Languages Press, 1959). See also the following analyses: David Charles, "The Dismissal of Marshall P'eng Teh-huai," *The China Quarterly*, No. 8 (October–December 1961); Schurmann, *op. cit.*, pp. 56n, 214–216, 267–278, 353–361; and Frederick C. Teiwes, "The Purge of Provincial Leaders 1957–1958," *The China Quarterly*, No. 27 (July–September 1966).

21. *Eighth National Congress of the Communist Party of China* (Peking: Foreign Languages Press, 1956), II, 182–83.

22. Charles, *op. cit.* The significance of P'eng's purge for the Cultural Revolution does not rest simply on the "procedural" problem that the Central Committee was not truly unified in favor of his dismissal. P'eng had attacked the communes and the Great Leap Forward, defended the professionalization of the PLA, and favored maintenance of close relations (at least for military purposes) with the Soviet Union. In retrospect, therefore, his position became a classic of Chinese "revisionism." The party's inability to agree on his disposition was directly related to a fundamental policy cleavage that Mao ultimately chose to resolve by force.

23. "Resolution of the Eighth Plenary Session of the Eighth Central Committee of C.P.C. Concerning the Anti-Party Clique Headed by Peng Teh-huai," August 16, 1959, excerpts in *Peking Review*, August 18, 1967, pp. 8–10.

24. *Hung Ch'i* editorial, No. 13, 1967, text in *Peking Review*, August 18, 1967, pp. 18–20, 35.

25. See Bridgham, *op. cit.* and Neuhauser, *op. cit.,* for details.

26. "Decision of the C.P.C. Central Committee Concerning the Great Proletarian Cultural Revolution," August 8, 1966, and "Communique of the Eleventh Plenary Session of the Eighth Central Committee of the Communist Party of China," August 12, 1966, texts in *Peking Review* August 12 and 19, 1966.

27. Gittings, *op. cit.* The rise of military (and Lin Piao's) influence can be traced back to the early 1960s and was directly related to the opening up of the Cultural Revolution, particularly in giving Mao the backing necessary for his attack on the opposition. However, the Cultural Revolution is not adequately explained as a consequence of a drive for power on the part of Lin Piao or the PLA.

28. Judgments about Mao's authority are difficult to substantiate, but the Cultural Revolution has uncovered much evidence that indicates that Mao was treated with much less respect after 1958. For example, Mao is reported to have said that he was forced to resign in 1958, and that thereafter Liu and Teng treated him like a "dead parent" and relegated him to a "second line" position. Some of the "black gang's" writings were assuredly personal though indirect attacks on Mao, published in open sources. In 1965, P'eng Chen and Lu Ting-yi said that Mao must be criticized like anyone else. See Bridgham, *op. cit.,* p. 17; Michael, *op. cit.,* pp. 13–14; and Neuhauser, *op. cit.,* pp. 27–30.

29. The following data is taken from J. M. H. Lindbeck, "Transformations in the Chinese Communist Party," in Donald W. Treadgold, ed., *Soviet and Chinese Communism: Similarities and Differences* (Seattle: University of Washington Press, 1967); and John Wilson Lewis, *Leadership in Communist China* (Ithaca: Cornell University Press, 1963), pp. 108–120.

30. For detailed discussion, see A. Doak Barnett, "Social Stratification and Aspects of Personnel Management in the Chinese Communist Bureaucracy," *The China Quarterly,* No. 28 (October–December 1966); and Ezra F. Vogel, "From Revolutionary to Semi-Bureaucrat: The 'Regularisation' of Cadres," *The China Quarterly,* No. 29 (January–March 1967).

31. A. Doak Barnett, *Cadres, Bureaucracy, and Political Power in Communist China* (New York: Columbia University Press, 1967), *passim,* but especially pp. 6–9, 431–432.

32. The CCP leadership was never truly monolithic, of course. Possible divisions and factions within it have been observed for many years, although never with general agreement on precisely where the divisions lay and who was involved. For analysis of pre-Cultural Revolution "factions," see J. Chester Cheng, "Problems of Chinese Communist Leadership as Seen in the Secret Military Papers," *Asian Survey,* Vol. IV, No. 6 (June 1964); Harold Hinton, "Intra-Party Conflicts and Economic Policy in Communist China," *World Politics,* Vol. XII, No. 4 (July 1960); John W. Lewis, *Chinese Communist Party Leadership and the Succession to Mao Tse-tung* (Washington: Department of State, 1964); and Roderick MacFarquhar, "Communist China's Intra-Party Dispute," *Pacific Affairs,* Vol. XXXI, No. 4 (December 1958).

33. For a stimulating analysis of group conflict in China, and its role in the Cultural Revolution, see Michel Oksenberg, "Occupational Groups in Chinese Society and the Cultural Revolution" (Paper prepared for the Year in Review Conference, University of Michigan, Center for Chinese Studies, 1968).

34. See ch. 8 of this volume.

35. For analysis of this point, see Charles Neuhauser, "The Impact of the Cultural Revolution on the Chinese Communist Party Machine," *Asian Survey,* Vol. VIII, No. 6 (June 1968); and "China's Communist Party: Orphan of Mao's Storm," *Current Scene,* Vol. VI, No. 4 (March 1, 1968).

10

Tunisia: The Prospects for Institutionalization

‖ *Clement H. Moore*

It is too early to know whether Tunisia's single-party system, established in 1956, will long survive its founder, Habib Bourguiba. The system may become institutionalized, however, as a by-product of concerted efforts of political and social mobilization which, while corresponding to Bourguiba's strategy of modernization, seem to constitute recipes of political decay in most transitional settings.[1] For in Tunisia the concentration and expansion of power for the sake of modernization has the unintended consequence of fostering specialized interests and young leadership—replacing the intermediaries Bourguiba destroyed and the veteran politicians he retired—with a stake in the party as an institution conferring legitimacy and respectability rather than as an organization implementing strategy. The very scope of its power and the inclusiveness of its mobilized bases suggest that the party can continue to absorb the social transformations it has unleashed, even while acquiring institutional respectability.

Other single-party experiences in Africa pretty much confirm Huntington's view that prospects for institutionalization vary inversely with social mobilization, defined by such indices as communications, urbanization, literacy, and mass education, all of which presumably enhance the level of demands and stresses placed on political systems. Indeed, the "mobilization system" analyzed in the flush of independence by observers of West African politics a few years ago has become an almost empty category.[2] The one-party regimes of the victorious nationalists could not extract enough resources to sustain their visions of radically transforming society by organizational methods. As party cadres disappeared into ex-colonial bureaucracies and as new party-state officials suppressed internal party opposition, one-party states seemed destined to become no-party states.[3] At best the

311

party survived as a flexible machine that "maintains solidarity among its members by appealing to their self-interest while allowing for the play of factions and for recurrent reconciliation." [4] Ironically it could be argued that single parties have the best chances of survival in the least mobilized, most backward societies, such as Mali and Tanzania, rather than in countries like Ghana with greater resources, where, as a result, "an inflationary process of demand-formation is likely to develop." [5] In very backward societies revolutionary blueprints affecting the modern sector of the economy cause little disruption. Just as flexible machine politics may favor economic and social stagnation, prolonged stagnation, as in Liberia (or parts of the American South), may facilitate their institutionalization. On the other hand, it is more difficult today than fifty years ago to halt the spread of new ideas and demands among elite strata, at least, of even the most isolated backwaters of the Third World.

Sharing in Mediterranean civilization from ancient times and permeated by modern currents of thought since the early nineteenth century, Tunisia could hardly avoid modernization and the "social mobilization" that modernization connotes. But Bourguiba has positively encouraged not only economic planning but also communication, literacy, and mass education—to which he adds his own frequent speeches and continual party exhortations designed to escalate demands as well as to elicit sacrifices. Comparisons with Ataturk's Turkey, a relatively successful single-party experiment, are perhaps more instructive than those with floundering experiences in contemporary sub-Saharan Africa. Social mobilization was far more restrictive in Turkey. From 1927 to 1950 the percentage of the population in school increased from 3.7 to 8.3. The increase in Tunisia from 1956 to 1967 was from 6.7 per cent to 25 per cent. Despite some governmental and party efforts to stem the tide of impoverished or dissatisfied Bedouins into the cities, the percentage of people living in towns of over 20,000 population more than doubled from 1956 to 1964, reaching 23 per cent. Turkey did not experience the problem to the same degree, for in 1955 only 18.2 per cent of its population was urbanized.[6]

The limited modernization of Turkey permitted Ataturk virtually to exclude the masses from politics while bringing full political participation only to an elite of modernized intellectuals, professionals, and civil servants. Thus it was much easier for the Republican People's Party to foster consensus on modernizing goals. The masses were brought into the political process only after 1946 when a two-party system emerged. As Frey has suggested, "The fact that the process has been able to be divided into two phases, rather than compounded by being telescoped into one, may partially account for the relative Turkish success compared with most other 'emergent' nations." [7] Tunisia, on the other hand, has faced the more difficult task of managing, indeed positively encouraging mass political participation without undermining the elite's modernizing consensus.

Yet Tunisia's potential resources to meet new demands were and remain modest by any standards. Per capita income is approximately that of Ghana.[8] Inheriting a French colonial infrastructure, independent Tunisia was possibly more economically developed than the Turkey of 1922, but it was also more dependent upon foreign assistance and had no significant industry. Even Tunisia's pride, a substantial and politically talented western-educated elite, was probably smaller in numbers in 1956 and certainly less experienced in administration than the comparable Turkish elite of 1922, although the scope of party and governmental activity has been greater in Tunisia.

In fact the one economic index that makes Tunisia's mobilization efforts appear practicable, at least in the short run, in contrast to those of the mobilization systems in Africa that fail to live up to their rhetoric, concerns the scope of governmental activity. The Tunisian political system is able to extract a far greater proportion of gross national product than other contemporary or former non-Communist one-party systems. The total government budget amounted to 32 per cent of the GNP in 1967. Comparable figures in other African one-party states, and presumably Ataturk's Turkey, range from 15 to 25 per cent, with richer countries like Ghana and Ivory Coast at the lower end of the scale.[9] Since 1957 Tunisia has also received more than half a billion dollars in aid and credits from the United States alone. Hence it has been possible for the government not only to spur economic growth at an annual rate approaching 4 per cent,[10] but also to stimulate new demands, mainly through mass education and political mobilization, while at least partially satisfying them.

Whether or not Tunisia is ultimately successful in its efforts to become the Switzerland of Africa depends on long-term economic considerations outside the scope of this paper. What is politically fascinating, however, is how the system is able to mobilize widespread sectors of the population both socially and politically—that is, instill them with new demands—while containing them within the framework of a coherent, organized single party.

The Instrumental Ideology

The Destour Socialist Party's institutional capacity to absorb mobilized individuals and groups is largely the product of its history. Founded in 1934 under the name of the Neo-Destour Party, itself an offshoot of an older party dating back to 1920, the PSD is the oldest nationalist party in Africa. Like India and the Philippines, Tunisia was fortunate in having "a colonial administration which is willing to permit and *to contend with* a nationalist movement for many years, thus furnishing the time, the struggles, the slowly increasing responsibility which are the ingredients of institution-building." [11] Mere longevity, however, even coupled with a plausible claim of "victory" over the colonial power, does not ensure vitality after the independence honeymoon. In addition to age—and more important than the formal structures periodically suppressed by the French authorities—the Neo-Destour had acquired an operative, or "instrumental," ideology that shaped the goals and priorities of the party elite while reenforcing its cohesion vis-à-vis not only France but "backward" and "retrograde" indigenous mentalities.

"Destour Socialism," the body of political and economic doctrine codified since 1961, when Bourguiba launched economic planning, will be *déjà vu* to anyone familiar with "African Socialism" as it has been articulated in other French-speaking African countries. The claim made recently by a party editorialist that Tunisians have "understood perfectly the laws of evolution of human societies" [12] also has that familiar hollow ring. Vaguely stating that "the bases of our socialism are not necessarily those of scientific socialism," the official resolution on Destour Socialism passed by the party's most recent congress goes on to enumerate its "principles." Elevating the individual's intellectual and material level should be the ultimate goal of all collective effort. Socialism does not mean class warfare; rather, the "method of the party consists in rallying all wills in order together to attain socialist objectives." Moreover, "State intervention is not an end in itself. It becomes necessary if the private sector proves inadequate, neglectful of the general interest, or badly managed." For "the management of private property is a social function, necessarily tied to the general interest and having to contribute to achieving national objectives . . ." [13]

That society should be transformed by rational engineering; that social tensions can be overcome through Bourguiba's "dialectical methods" of persuasion; that Destour Socialism in the words of the Planning Minister is, more than a doctrine, a veritable "faith"; that these phrases are reechoed as a veritable catechism by an elite of ministers and party managers; and that Destour Socialism is being restudied, rearticulated, refurbished by an "ideological commission" inside the party: all this recalls other self-conscious efforts to construct an ideology—ranging from Ataturk's "Six Arrows" to African "communitarianism" and "ujmaa." Nor are Bourguiba's "pragmatism" and explicit rejection of doctrinaire ideologies peculiar to Tunisia.

What is impressive about Destour Socialism is that it closely reflects actual policy, that objectives are limited and realistic, that it was codified only after extensive economic planning was well under way, and that, unlike a number of ghost-written African ideologies, it nonetheless has deep roots in the indigenous political culture that gestated before independence. Aristide Zolberg has suggested of African one-party ideology that "as a map of the political world, it provides relief from strain even if reality differs greatly from the formulations it contains, as . . . . it does," and that "in the creation of this map Africans are involved in an activity which closely resembles a religious ritual . . ." [14] His analysis is based on the hypothesis that these ideologies are expressive responses to the cultural strain caused by the breakdown of traditional order and the political actors' consequent need of a conceptual reorientation, whether or not they also face severe social dislocations and experience psychological tensions.[15] But cultural strain was far less severe in Tunisia after independence than in most new nations because the problems involved in adapting Islam to the modern world had been confronted and largely resolved before independence by a self-confident, modernizing elite. Thus Destour Socialism is not only more closely attuned to reality but also less necessary for reassuring politicized Tunisians than, say, the "revolutionary socialism" preached by neighboring Algerians who continue to suffer intense cultural strain. Long before Destour Socialism was invented, Tunisians had discovered their political map, so that the new code is more a set of shorthand symbols for socializing newly mobilized strata, for transmitting the underlying operative ideology of the political elite, than a rhetoric or ritual for the latter. Verbalism is less pronounced in Tunisia than in any other Arab country.

The handful of young French university graduates who founded the Neo-Destour distinguished themselves from the older party they contested by their more active political tactics of mass mobilization against an intolerable colonial situation. But in fact, by virtue of their activism, they were able to transcend the apparently conflicting outlooks of those who wholeheartedly accepted the multifaceted modernization of Tunisian society imposed by the French presence with those who rejected colonial domination in the name of traditional Tunisian Islamic values and harked back to a golden age preceding the French Protectorate established in 1881. The combative young nationalists could attack foreign domination more effectively than the traditionalists, and hence capture while reinterpreting the Islamic imagination, by using modern techniques of agitation and appealing to the "liberal France" admired by a growing number of French-educated Tunisians.[16] The Neo-Destour did not in the thirties create political culture *ex nihilo,* but it did articulate, render politically operative, and eventually through "victory" legitimate strands that were already present. The Neo-Destour did not deliberately codify an ideology—even "Bourguibism" as a set of tactics for eliciting favorable concessions from the colonial power was only a term coined by French journalists after independence— but Bourguiba and his colleagues elaborated an operative synthesis of French radical socialism and "Jacobin" Islam [17] that defined Tunisia as a Mediterranean (rather than exclusively Arab) nation-in-becoming that would be modern and francophile as well as independent and Muslim. Even before independence, the party elite more or less agreed on such controversial issues as educational and Islamic legal reform that have divided most Muslim nationalist elites. For protracted conflict not only with the French but also with traditionalists in their own society had served to clarify Neo-Destour objectives and to identify nationalism with modernization. Further, the combination of agitation and rational persuasion used to win independence were tactics the elite could agree to apply to their own society in future "battles against economic and social backwardness." Hence, subsequent "mobilization" and rational economic planning were outgrowths of the colonial experience.

Without survey data it is impossible to determine how widely the Neo-Destour synthesis was shared or to specify the number of Tunisians who really "understood" Bourguiba and other top party leaders or to what degree. Probably most of the party's 100,000 members in 1954 had little understanding of the elite's objectives, apart from independence, or tactics, apart from the need for discipline. Abstract concepts meant little to an uneducated, largely tradition-bound audience; rather, nationhood was personified by the "Supreme Warrior," Bourguiba, his trials and tribulations in French prisons with which one could identify and which marked successive phases of the nationalist "struggle." But the party elite's modernizing outlook was both more explicit and more widely shared in Tunisia at independence than in comparable African contexts or in the Turkey of 1922. This would explain why it was more possible in Tunisia to continue mobilizing masses with less risk that such mobilization might reawaken traditionalist forces and undermine the elite consensus on modernization.

The consensus that Ataturk had to create after taking power already existed in Tunisia by independence. Bourguiba himself reflected as much as he expressed the modernizing aspirations of Tunisia's French-educated elite. Even in the 1930s this elite was no longer confined to traditional notables; indeed, by making their education available to other strata, the French precipitated a social revolution. Peasant sons of the Sahil, a coastal region south of Tunis noted for its many old villages, olive groves, and industrious freeholders, outnumbered the sons of the traditional bourgeoisie and aristocracy of Tunis in French universities and modern professions. The new arrivals were more open to modern ideas than sons of notables with a vested interest in the existing order (for the French used old families to legitimate their rule) or the pre-colonial order (for some notables had been excluded).

The Neo-Destour reflected their commitment both to French cultural and economic innovations and to radical political change. The party's leadership was predominantly from the Sahil, and its first congress was held at Ksar-Hellal, in the very heart of this region. Rapidly the party acquired the allegiance of Muslim students in French lycées, colleges and universities—irrespective of their traditional social status. The original Destour Party from which the younger leadership broke away managed to persist until 1957, but the Neo-Destour succeeded by 1937 in discrediting it in the eyes of the French-educated elite. Yet the older party's existence was a helpful source of negative identification; its verbal intransigence could be contrasted with the Neo-Destour's instrumental view of politics as a process of reasoning with and educating the "retrograde" mentalities of both traditionalists and colonialists—and sometimes, in fact, of its own mobilized and intransigent rank and file as well.[18] With independence the modern party won a decisive victory against the traditionalists.

Long before the final victory, however, the party attracted the more radical and zealous of the traditional Zitouna University students and the graduates of modern Quaranic schools, especially in the Sahil, that dispensed with different emphases a wholly Arabic education. These groups were better trained than the Gallicized top leadership to staff the party's lower echelons and make the necessary connections between elite objectives and the residual Islamic culture of the conservative masses. Dedicated and competent local and intermediate leadership, fully comprehending and committed to the purposes of the modernizing elite, probably continues to be the party's major organizational asset that makes possible a high degree of mobilization. During the two decades before the party acquired governing responsibilities, thousands of activists assimilated the cognitive map and practical experience necessary for carrying on the political pedagogy that Bourguiba deems the essence of both modernization and nation-building. His ideology could be instrumental because it had acquired an audience, a cohesive party cadre.

The Inclusive Framework

Bourguiba and other top party leaders, schooled in French republican values and unsympathetic to communism, had no explicit conception of single-party government. But political influence and high government position after independence almost invariably presupposed an active party past. The party's mission was deemed "permanent" in 1959; it was increasingly elaborated at party congresses and National Council meetings; in the most recent formulations, the PSD is "Center of gravity of the republican regime and essential motor of the organs of State," and an amendment passed in 1967 constitutionally recognizes the party.[19] Rather than narrowing its social bases like most ruling parties, however, the PSD has broadened them, both by incorporating most Tunisians who by virtue of their education and personal inclinations might aspire to important political roles and by developing its local organization.

A highly inclusive national movement, the party easily eliminated its rivals. The Tunisian Communist Party, which won only 7,890 out of 597,-907 votes in 1956 elections to the National Constituent Assembly, was harmless and hence tolerated until a plot on Bourguiba's life was used as a pretext to ban it in January, 1963. The original Destour Party stopped publishing its newspaper and simply ceased functioning in 1957. A number of "traitors" and former "collaborators" of the French Protectorate were prosecuted by a revolutionary tribunal, expropriated, denied political rights, and in some cases imprisoned but subsequently pardoned. The only serious opposition to Bourguiba came from within his party. Salah Ben Youssef, the second in command, broke with his leader in October, 1955, just five months before independence, over the issue of France's continued influence in Tunisia.[20] Intransigently rejecting compromises Bourguiba had accepted, Ben Youssef appealed to a wide spectrum of public opinion at a time when the party was just recovering from three years of colonial repression.

Most of the party's veteran cadres and top leadership remained loyal to Bourguiba and his policy of Franco-Tunisian cooperation rather than to the Youssefist alternative of pan-Maghrib and pan-Arab solidarity and renewed struggle with France at the expense of modernization. But Ben Youssef's initial successes—his ability to sway the crowds and eventually to provoke a virtual civil war—revealed the vulnerability of the party in its hour of victory. Coming from the island of Djerba, he had the support of most fellow Djerbans, who controlled much of Tunisia's commerce. He also had the support of traditionalist religious opponents of the Neo-Destour, other members of the decaying elite of old Tunis families, land-owners fearful of agrarian reform, radical urban youth, especially in Tunis, some of the 3,000 nationalist guerrillas as well as urban terrorists whom the Neo-Destour had organized against the French, and tribesmen in the Center and South who were always ready in national disputes to take sides against their traditional rivals. The party's sustained effort of mass organization can be partly understood as a response to potential Youssefism, though Ben Youssef himself was in exile from 1956 until his assassination in 1961.

Bourguiba therefore had to build up the party as well as staff the new state with party cadres after independence. The double task rapidly led, as in other African countries, to an overlapping of party and state structures, for there were not enough experienced leaders to staff two separate organizations and, moreover, the activities of the party had to be coordinated with official state policies at all levels. In 1958 the party's forty-one federations, elected by the party branches, were replaced by commissioners appointed directly by the Political Bureau for each of Tunisia's fourteen governorates. In 1963 the governors became ex officio presidents of new party Committees of Coordination elected in each province. Party officials claim today that relations with the state have "gone a stage beyond symbiosis." Yet they have prevented the party from becoming just another government bureaucracy, for a certain functional differentiation is retained. The party is supposed to "interpret the aspirations" of the masses and to coordinate a broadly based process of consultation that legitimates important policies, as well as to explain and marshal support for governmental decisions.

The PSD has developed a fairly elaborate administration connecting the national and provincial levels, but the "bureaucratism" that has plagued similar parties, such as the Algerian FLN, has been kept to a minimum. There are only 160 full-time party employees, including stenographers and chauffeurs as well as the party director and general secretaries of the provincial Committees of Coordination presided over by the governors.[21] This figure undoubtedly does not include many Tunisians with minor governmental jobs who are "detached" part time for party service, but the party apparatus remains relatively small, considering the all-embracing importance of the PSD in Tunisia's political life.

To a much greater extent than other African parties, the PSD encompasses Tunisia's political process. The hypothesis of a "residual sector" that modern politics does not penetrate in West Africa would be difficult to verify in Tunisia.[22] The subsistence economy outside the domain of the West African party-state's allocative authority, for instance, is rapidly diminishing in Tunisia under the combined impact of a very intensive colonial situation and the implementation since 1961 of extensive economic planning. In the sphere, too, of personal status, the impact of the Tunisian party-state has been enormous. Bourguiba was the first Muslim leader to promulgate, shortly after independence, a new family code that abolished polygamy and marked a radical break with the traditional *shari'a* in matters of marriage and divorce. An appendix to the code passed in 1959 concerning laws of inheritance was an equally audacious innovation. More recently a family planning program has made modest headway. That such reforms can be undertaken—with fair prospects of implementation—is a tribute to the grass roots organization of the PSD.

The party in 1967 had roughly 400,000 members, almost twice as many as in 1961 and four times as many as in 1954. Mere numbers, of course, are not significant. In 1957, for instance, the party claimed 600,000 members, a claim that was plausible considering the atmosphere of party "victory" at the time and the personal disadvantages of not having a party card. Members then may have indeed constituted three-fifths of the adult male population (female membership has never constituted more than a negligible fraction of the total), but membership meant little. With most of its experienced cadres drafted into government, the party was poorly organized and overextended, with too many badly managed local branches that had to be cut back the following year when commissioners were introduced. Ten years later, however, the party had accumulated almost as many branches as in 1957 under considerably improved local leadership. While the grass roots of most African party-states have atrophied, there were more than one thousand territorial branches in Tunisia in 1965.[23]

Becoming a party member does not require the sort of ideological conversion associated with more exclusive vanguard parties.[24] Indeed the party was unable to implement its decision in 1964 to distinguish "militants" from mere members, for the criteria of militancy were too vaguely drawn, and discrimination would not only have divided the party community but perhaps hindered internal mobility and the rise of younger elements. The "militant" is simply anyone who is a "good citizen contributing to the development of production and the strengthening of socialist convictions" and "has proved devoted to executing party directives" for at least three years.[25]

In practice, however, the party retains its cohesion though it is open to virtually everybody. At the local level it sustains an intense level of activity by providing a semblance of democratic participation and allowing branch leaders to articulate local interests and play a role in managing local affairs. Yet a hierarchical chain of command permits leaders at all levels to locate and promote "militants," judged by their organizational performance. Destour Socialism is sufficiently concrete to provide applicable criteria. For instance, in a standard questionnaire distributed each month to its branches by a provincial Committee of Coordination, one branch executive committee answered that the "best Destourians of the month" were an adult "who has succeeded in persuading people to work in the cooperative" and a youth "who has persuaded several parents to send their daughters to school." [26] Both examples were local illustrations of Bourguibist "reasoning" for agreed objectives of modernization. The party constantly activates individuals, but it also channels their participation into "constructive," organizational pursuits. The extension of the scope of government in independent Tunisia has created an increasing need for "rational persuaders" and hence greater scope for sustained party activity.

The increased scope of politics, however, has entailed a correspondingly greater functional load upon the political system. More interests seek outlets of expression under the impact of economic planning and other spheres of governmental activity designed to project Tunisia into the modern world. As the interests become more complex and as more individuals become capable of expressing them, the party's aggregative load increases. Is there not a double danger that individuals flood the party framework with their demands while groups materialize and try to escape the framework?

It is not likely that the party can continue for long to mobilize new groups and individuals; retrenchment is more likely as disenchantment with economic planning sets in. "Permanent revolution" requires a steady increase of available resources, but Tunisia's small size and low level of economic development limit the resources available to any conceivable regime, and these limits have probably already been reached. Both the party's tutelary ideology and its inclusive social bases preclude the sustained sort of mobilization associated with totalitarian ideologies and more exclusive bases.

On the other hand, the pattern of mobilization to date, associated with Destour Socialist economic planning, suggests that the party may be able to contain the forces it has already unleashed in a viable set of institutions. Of particular significance are (1) how the party has dealt with sectorial or professional groups whose interests are touched by economic planning, (2) how it contains regional pressures and primordial loyalties that accompany an increasing politicization of society, and (3) how it has renewed its own cadre. With respect to each of these problems, the party's responses are enhancing its own legitimacy as a framework of political action for the community.

Manipulating Interest Groups

With respect to sectorial groups, the party has consistently attempted to manage organizations of its own. Shortly after World War II and mainly in response to communist organizational efforts, the Neo-Destour created associations representing business and handicrafts (UTAC) and farmers (UGAT) and delegated some of its cadres to help Ferhat Hached organize the General Union of Tunisian Workers (UGTT). These "national organizations" were supposed to be functionally specific interest groups; in fact they closely cooperated with the party and shared its political objectives, for the country's independence was conceived to be a necessary precondition for satisfying specific interests.

After independence the party prevented these groups from becoming autonomous. UGAT was eliminated in late 1955 when some of its leaders sided with Salah Ben Youssef; the party simply established a new farmers' union, UNAT, in the abandoned offices of UGAT, and thereby set a precedent for controlling the national organizations. UTAC, rebaptized UTICA (Tunisian Union of Industrialists, Merchants, and Artisans) to encourage small Tunisian industry, was slightly "renovated" in 1961 as the party pushed economic planning, but most union officials prudently accepted official policy and advocated modernization of private enterprise "within the framework of the Plan." Only the UGTT posed serious problems of party control.

Tunisian-run trade unionism had a tradition dating back to Mohammed Ali's efforts in 1924 to found an autonomous union. Founded in 1946, the General Union of Tunisian Workers under Ferhat Hached had developed strong organizational loyalties independent of the party. Though French terrorists assassinated him in 1952, the union constituted an independent power base in 1956, when its new leader, Ahmed Ben Salah, tried to pressure his fellow Neo-Destour leaders to adopt progressive economic policies. Like the Youssefist leaders of UGAT, however, Ben Salah was less concerned with any functionally specific interests of workers than with broad issues of power and policy. His major goal, with independence won, was to provide "new content" to party programs, perhaps through an organic fusion of the two organizations.

After he refused Bourguiba's offer of a minor ministry and openly attacked the latter's conception of modernization as pedagogy, Ben Salah was removed from the trade union leadership. Individuals close to Bourguiba easily played upon internal personal rivalries to engineer a scission within the UGTT, then reshuffled the leadership to resolve these differences. The new trade union leader, Ahmed Tlili, was also a leading member of the party's fifteen-man Political Bureau, thereby apparently ensuring harmony between the two organizations. Tlili, however, had controversial political aims that others inside the party shared. While subordinating the union to the party, he wished also to subordinate Bourguiba and his personal entourage to regular party controls—as an institutional precondition for achieving specific worker interests, he could argue to the workers, just as Ferhat Hached had once advocated political emancipation.

The party engineered Tlili's removal in 1963, just as economic planning under Ahmed Ben Salah was getting under way. The two men were bitter personal rivals; moreover, Tlili objected to the comprehensive planning that Ben Salah had eventually succeeded in persuading Bourguiba to accept. Again, it was easy for the party to manipulate elections within the UGTT, for the union had long been internally divided between supporters of Ben Salah, of Tlili, and of his successor, Habib Achour, the veteran trade unionist who had originally launched the scission against Ben Salah. Much less of a politician than his two rivals, even though he had been a member of the Political Bureau since 1957, Achour was a bread-and-butter unionist and also the founder of cooperatives predominantly owned by UGTT members. Under his leadership the UGTT directly opposed Ben Salah's efforts to manage the economy, including its cooperative sector. Though the UGTT withdrew its objections to the devaluation of the dinar in September, 1964, public disagreements in one-party Tunisia never went unpunished. The following summer, with Achour jailed, justly or unjustly, in connection with an accident in one of his cooperatives,[27] the UGTT leadership was almost totally reshuffled, and a governor (after resigning his post several weeks before the congress) who had not been active in the union since 1956 was made general secretary.[28]

Transparent party control of the national organizations, accompanied by policies that have attacked the economic interests in turn of each of their constituencies, has resulted in an obvious decline in their activities and membership. Serving mainly to relay the message that special interests must subordinate themselves to the general interest, the national organizations were allowed little scope to play autonomous roles in articulating specific interests. UNAT was never more than a paper organization with central headquarters, and little activity could be observed outside Tunis. UTICA and UGTT seem to have lost much of their membership.[29] Occasional wildcat strikes suggest that the trade union has lost touch with the rank-and-file workers, especially in the phosphate mines, though there have been many more spontaneous strikes in neighboring Algeria, where the trade union is less supervised than in Tunisia. The fate of the national organizations suggests that the political cohesion needed for increasing the scope of governmental activity may undermine the party's aggregative function by suppressing the interests that are to be aggregated. If this were true, it could perhaps be concluded that the "mobilization" engendered by economic planning was threatening to outrun the system's organizational capacities to absorb it.

Yet even the UGTT, given Tunisia's low level of economic development and general unskilled work force, was never really a functionally specific interest group; moreover, its leaders, even Habib Achour, devoted more resources to diffuse political goals or to enhancing their personal power than to professional trade union objectives. The "decadence" of the UGTT began in 1957, not 1963 or 1965, and it probably reflected a general slackening of political fervor after independence more than the repression of concrete worker grievances. Most general union policies, too, had become governmental ones by the early 1960s. By tethering the UGTT and other interest groups the party has exchanged a slight loss in political infrastructure for enhanced cohesion based on agreements to increasingly specific and concrete policies. Moreover, the party has attempted to recoup losses in infrastructure by devising new channels of interest articulation within the party.

Over Tlili's opposition the party, as early as 1961 when economic planning became official policy, quietly began to extend its very embryonic network of professional branches in various public and private enterprises. Originally designed as a means of controlling the UGTT, they seem to have displaced the union as a framework for syndical as well as political activity, though a nominal separation of function remains. In the words of a party editorialist, these branches "permit the introduction into the minds of every official, every worker, every technician, of the intimate conviction that he accomplishes a social act and takes part in the construction of a new society. . . ." Available evidence suggests that the approximately 250 branches include almost as many workers and employees as the UGTT and organize all politically sensitive sectors such as railroads and mining.[30] Party officials claim that the branches mitigate class tensions and thus promote Bourguiba's vision of social harmony, in that workers and managers jointly run them in many enterprises. As the party trains more cadres, the branches are developing more complex structures and increasing their activities. The branch leaders seem as a group to be younger, more educated, and to have joined the party more recently than those of the geographically based branches.[31] Thus, as the professional branches proliferate—they already outnumber the other branches in the city of Tunis—they may alter the balance of power within the party in favor of cadres most attuned to the problems of economic planning raised by Destour Socialism.

Possibly professional branches will also articulate the interests of small farmers, merchants, and artisans in the new cooperative sector more effectively than UNAT or UTIC. The party has not yet attempted to organize special branches for small commercial groupings that have recently been imposed upon the shopkeepers, Djerbans for the most part, but some large wholesale groupings already have professional branches. In the countryside the producer and service cooperatives created since 1963 in themselves constitute a substantial organizational effort, though few party branches have as yet been formed.[32] Rather, interests are articulated, if at all, through the planning administration, which retains tight tutelage over the cooperatives.

In addition to aggregating interests through its regular channels, the party coordinates an exhaustive process of consultation within the administration and among various constitutional organs such as the National Assembly and the Economic and Social Council. Virtually every Tunisian with economic experience, whether or not he had a party card, was consulted about the Three-Year and subsequently the Four-Year Plan. Despite their lack of economic expertise, party officials have created specialized national commissions and coopted both leading administrators and interested private citizens. Since 1965 the party has sponsored a series of economic seminars. Harmony between the party and government is of course assured by overlapping leadership, and Planning Minister Ahmed Ben Salah, for instance, devotes considerable time to his responsibilities as assistant general secretary of the party. But the party's aggregative role is credible: the seminars and commissions it sponsors really are considered more important than the exclusively governmental or constitutional organs of decision-making. Specialized party commissions are being attached to the technical sectorial commissions inside the Planning Ministry that actually draft planning proposals.

Though the party is not Tunisia's unique aggregator, economic planning has enhanced rather than diminished its role. The PSD remains highly inclusive by reorganizing the groups it eliminated as autonomous political forces and by coopting their former leaders into the new framework. The new consensus on economic planning facilitates the task of aggregation, for disputes are expressed in a technical vocabulary and concern specific economic goals and implementation rather than questions of broad principle. As interests become more specific, the process of consultation coordinated by the party has better chances of being institutionalized. Factions related to those discussed in connection with the UGTT persist within the party, but they may reach compromises more easily as differences become related to specific details of policy as well as to the broader problem of Bourguiba's succession.

Regionalism and Decentralization

Since Tunisia is a small, linguistically and ethnically homogenous country, social mobilization has not produced the intensified primordial loyalties that threaten national integration in other partially mobilized societies.[33] Regionalism is nevertheless a factor in Tunisian politics, especially among the students. Bourguiba and a disproportionate number of top party politicians come from the Sahil, the party's historic stronghold. A decade ago Sahilian preponderance could be justified on grounds of educational achievement as well as political qualifications, and hence militants accepted not only a national but a provincial leadership that was disproportionately Sahilian. Today it is less easy to explain to students, for instance, why half of the offices of their union, UGET, should be held by Sahilians when students from this region, once a majority, now constitute only one-fifth of the student population.[34] Greater equalization of educational opportunity, broader extension of the party's geographic base, and historic rivalries between different regions such as Tunis and the Sahil all contribute to a problem of regionalism, muted during the independence struggle, that has reappeared on the Tunisian political scene.

Regionalist sentiments are of course officially forbidden. The deputy to the National Assembly represents the nation, not his constituency (though in fact all but three deputies come from the governorate that elected them).[35] The suppression of the party federations in 1958 eliminated any possibility of the Federation of Tunis joining other outlying provinces (including Tlili's Gafsa) in attempting to impose more internal democracy upon Bourguiba (and other Sahilians) within the party. The system of party commissioners, giving militants designated by the Political Bureau direct tutelage over the branches, placed a disproportionate number of Sahil militants—both commissioners and assistants they could designate— into the provincial party machines of other regions having fewer reliable cadres. The administrative apparatus of governors and their delegates was naturally also composed of party veterans selected for their political experience rather than their regional origins and hence was similarly weighted. Even in the mid-1960s almost half of the forty governors and general secretaries of Committees of Coordination still come from either the Sahil or neighboring Sfax.[36] Five of the thirteen general secretaries in 1967 were not natives of the provinces they supposedly represented; four of them were from the Sahil or Sfax. As it connotes "retrograde" traditionalism, regionalist sentiment is either suppressed or officially ignored.

However, the historic conflict between Tunis and the Sahil, reflected in earlier battles between the original Destour and the Neo-Destour, was mitigated after independence by many marriages that occurred between successful Sahil politicians and daughters of the old Tunis families. The new political class assimilated non-political aspects of the more sophisticated subculture of the old elite.[37] Moreover, as traditional values, suitably reinterpreted, were adapted, scions of old families, even those associated with previous Zitouna opposition to Bourguiba's modernism, were reintegrated into the official community and even offered positions in party commissions.

Regional tensions are also mitigated partly by a commitment to "balanced development," which means that new industries are allocated to backward regions where they are to be "poles of development." More important perhaps, in conjunction with economic planning, has been the party's stress on developing regional political infrastructure. The Committees of Coordination, elected since 1963 by delegates from the party branches of each province, have considerably intensified party activity at this level by including some two thousand local party members and experts in their network of commissions, subcommissions, and seminars. One close observer has concluded that this group, together with the much larger but over-lapping group of branch leaders, constitutes "the core of Tunisia's political system, in the sense that hardly any basic articulation or aggregation of interests can take place without their participation." [38] The fact that the ten to twenty members of the Committees of Coordination are elected every two years also ensures that the regional and local levels are closely intermeshed, even though the elections are carefully supervised by higher party authorities and by the governor who, personally appointed by Bourguiba, heads both party and government in his province.[39]

Local and regional politics are increasingly tied into national politics. In the early 1960s regional conferences of cadres would occasionally listen to a visiting member of the Political Bureau and ask him questions, but linkages with the center consisted primarily of directives from Tunis transmitted by the party commissioner and his staff. Administrative decentralization meant only that the governor represented the whole central government, was empowered directly to supervise and coordinate the activities of the ministries' external administration in his province, and was given central funds, in addition to a very small regional budget, for executing certain types of projects. Critical administrators in Tunis have suggested that greater decentralization of this sort would merely mean greater power for the governor, who would be accountable only to Bourguiba. But a real, though controlled, diffusion of power to the regions is also occurring. The economic commissions of the Committees of Coordination have acquired an important voice in elaborating provincial investment plans included in the annual national economic budget. The party is attempting to rationalize its economic consultations by vertically integrating the discussions of its specialized regional and national commissions. Eventually regional economic councils are to participate in preparing the national investment budget and thereby influencing allocations among the different ministries. Presumably greater regional influence will enhance the importance of the Committees of Coordination and further institutionalize the party. It may also damp regionalist sentiments among junior members of the national elite by giving them a concrete outlet.

Changing the Guard

Administrative and political decentralization are related to the rejuvenation of Tunisia's leadership, in that most of the governors and general secretaries of the Committees of Coordination appointed since 1964 constitute a younger generation of leadership recruited from UGET and the party youth since independence. The increased emphasis upon professional branches points in the same direction, though youth are also encouraged to present themselves for office in the territorial branches. Indeed, constant infusion of youth into offices at all levels of the party has been one of Bourguiba's most notable achievements, counterbalancing the natural aging of the party cadres injected into the less flexible state administration at independence. His advocacy of economic planning further promoted a young generation of technocrats when established administrators were blocking the mobility and initiative of more qualified new arrivals.[40]

Even at the apex of the party, turnover has been striking since 1934. Of the original five-man Political Bureau, only Bourguiba remains in political life. An additional two (Mongi Slim and Hedi Nouira) of the ten members elected in 1948 now serve on the Political Bureau. The turnover has been great even since independence, despite the fact that the eleven elected in 1955 were mostly of a generation that had risen in the party since World War II. In addition to the two veterans, Bahi Ladgham is the sole survivor of this group; he is general secretary of the party and a leading candidate for Bourguiba's succession. The two assistant general secretaries, Ahmed Ben Salah (the other leading candidate) and Habib Bourguiba Jr., are much younger leaders who entered the Political Bureau in 1962 and 1964, respectively. The director of the party, Mohammed Sayah, comes from an even younger generation; he was a student leader until 1962.

The "iron law of oligarchy," with its corollary of aging party leadership, does not apply to autocratic Tunisia. Rejuvenating party leadership at all levels is one of Bourguiba's personal axioms, partly as a means of ensuring his own personal power but also because he wishes to maintain the party's youthful image and perhaps senses fresh recruitment to be an organizational requirement. The rejuvenation of top leaders has been relatively easy: before independence they died, retired, or disagreed with Bourguiba and opted out of the struggle, and since independence Bourguiba as president of the Republic has been able to exercise his virtually unquestioned authority to retire people early and promote younger ones rapidly. As president he appoints and dismisses ministers at will, thus largely determining who within the Political Bureau had real influence, and he occasionally uses more direct methods. At the most recent congress the Bureau was enlarged to include thirty-two elected members, all the previous members, all other ministers not otherwise included, and all the governors.[41] Then Bourguiba selected fourteen of them to join him in the new "Praesidium." After a few months of semantic confusion, the latter body became known as the Political Bureau, while the enlarged Bureau was renamed the Central Committee.

Possibly Tunisia's small size helped Bourguiba to avoid generating too much bitterness among top leaders retired early, for there were always a plethora of prestigious yet unimportant positions to retire them to—obscure embassies, the National Assembly, a variety of administrative positions in the public or semipublic sector, and of course the party's Central Committee. In a much larger state, such as China, the number of honorific positions presumably would not be correspondingly larger. Moreover, leading actors whom Bourguiba had excluded from the stage were, with the sole exception of Salah Ben Youssef, recalled for new performances. Thus within a few months of his elimination from the UGTT Ben Salah was appointed to a minor ministry and subsequently called upon to carry out the policies he had originally advocated. Mohammed Masmoudi, who had sponsored a newspaper that even went so far as implicitly to criticize the Supreme Warrior, was twice dismissed from and twice recalled to top governmental and party posts. So great was Bourguiba's prestige that he could manage his lieutenants as he saw fit.

At lower echelons, however, his influence was limited to appointing the governors and encouraging them together with his party director to insure mobility within the regional and local party structures. Under the commissioner system the party had removed militants and former guerrilla leaders who did not adapt to the party's new roles in support of the government; most of them were given land, petty concessions, or jobs in the National Guard, and the reconversion of the party was accomplished relatively successfully by 1960.[42] But economic planning necessitated a subsequent reconversion, for, even at the local level, some understanding of economic problems as well as general enthusiasm was needed if the party was to fulfill its pedagogical and aggregative functions.

Changes among governors and general secretaries of the Committee of Coordination set the tone for the reconversion. As Rudebeck has pointed out, "youth, academic training, and political awareness have been emphasized at the expense of purely practical experience and long service to the party."[43] Only one of the party veterans appointed governor in 1956 held office in 1967. While only two of the incumbents in 1961 had completed secondary school, at least eight of the twelve governors six years later had university education.[44] Nine of them had backgrounds either in UGET or party youth activities. Eight of the general secretaries in 1967 also had university degrees, and at least six of them had been active in UGET or the Neo-Destour Youth, whereas the corps of commissioners and even the general secretaries first elected in 1963 had tended to be party veterans having little education. Moreover, there were only two governorates in 1967 where neither official had a university degree, and both governors, former scout leaders, had the proper image of youth and efficiency.

Other members of the Committees of Coordination tended to be slightly older and much less educated than the ones the Political Bureau designated to be general secretary. Even so, almost half of the Tunis Committee had university backgrounds, and the governors, secretaries, and party directors encouraged the election of similarly young, educated members. The turnover was great: only 47.1 per cent of 189 members elected in 1965 had belonged to the committees elected in 1963.[45] Often veteran militants, though displaced, were kept on various subcommittees or informally consulted, for younger leaders are inclined to respect their experience and quasi-religious dedication to the party; they in turn seem to accept Bourguiba's constantly reiterated theme that the elders must give way to younger elements armed with skills more appropriate for the new economic crusade. Constant consultations, ceremonial expressions of party brotherhood, an Islamic respect for education, and modest payoffs to the elders seem to relieve generational strain among the party cadres.

Renewing branch officials and stimulating economic discussions and activities at the local level have been more difficult tasks, though the Committees of Coordination have extensive disciplinary powers. Branches are supervised in carrying out local projects of economic or social import. Elections can be somewhat influenced, but they are not rigged. No data are available about recent changes in composition of the branch executive committees.[46] But the party has encouraged young, educated members to take up local duties in their native village even if they work in Tunis, just as Bourguiba insisted even to one of his ambassadors and Political Bureau members that he take charge of his native municipal council.[47] Building new professional branches has also been a way of giving promising young members important responsibilities. The decision in 1964 to grant the party's Tunisian Union of Youth the right to elect its own local leaders further stimulated mobility, for the youth leader is a member of the branch executive committee.

Moreover, the party in the mid-1960s has devoted substantial organizational efforts to recruiting youth, after a sharp decline of the Neo-Destour Youth in earlier years. Some 30 per cent of the university and secondary school students belong respectively to the party and the *Jeunesse Scolaire,* a section of the Tunisian Union of Youth (UTJ).[48] One-seventh of the primary school children are involved in another section of the UTJ. In addition, half the party's regular membership consists of Pioneers in the UTJ who are further divided into young rural people, young industrial workers, and young public officials; and 10,000 of the rural youth are annually trained in labor brigades to qualify for jobs in the new agricultural cooperatives. Student survey data suggests that the party is ensuring its future, despite occasional student unrest and the articulate opposition of a small radical minority to party-controlled student unionism. In a fairly representative, randomly selected sample of 500 students surveyed in 1966, 55 per cent belonged to UGET, 28 per cent were party members, and 50 per cent had been members either of the *Jeunesse Scolaire* or Neo-Destour Youth before entering university. Only 18 per cent of students having neither present nor past political affiliations desired to become militants or exercise future political responsibilities, whereas roughly half of the others indicated such political aspirations. The secondary school affiliations seemed especially important in engendering not only political interest and aspirations but also loyalty to the party. Thus the third of the sample expressing a lack of sympathy for the party was only half as likely as the other two-thirds to nurture political aspirations. Moreover, UGET seemed to attract even the politically ambitious students who were party critics and thereby contain them within the one-party system and foster institutional loyalties.[49]

The Conditions of Institutionalization

Drawing upon the work of Philip Selznick, we assume that any organization, to develop into an institution, must acquire a flexible ideology, a clearly identified elite to sustain it and provide leadership, and "contending interest groups, clustering around various aspects of the organization's program and the values it represents, both inside the organization and among its external clients." [50] In addition to being a weapon valued for the purposes it pursues, the organization, to be an institution, must be valued for what it is. By contending within its framework, interest groups can acquire a stake in its procedures and thus confer an intrinsic value to the organization. By denying interest groups, on the other hand, the organization remains a mere weapon, bereft of the complex deliberative procedures that accompany the aggregation of interests. Any intrinsic value is fragile, based on a shared mythology rather than concrete activity.

As with organizations generally, so with the parties of established one-party systems in particular: to become the central political institution, conferring legitimacy to the system on the basis of what it is as well as what it does, the party must acquire complex procedures for aggregating interests and, indeed, selecting top political leaders. Hence the need not only for a clearly identified elite but a flexible ideology, one that combines the tutelary capacity to define goals with an administrative one to accept procedural routines and conflicts of interest.

Obviously institutionalization cannot occur in Tunisia until Bourguiba retires from the scene. Charisma is incompatible with routine party procedures. Adulation of the Supreme Warrior appears to be the party's prime mission, and the personality cult has increased, if anything, in recent years. Despite a rationalized structure at lower levels, the party at the top is a patrimonial system. Once, when queried about his role in the Tunisian political system, Bourguiba replied, "System, what system? I *am* the system." Even the party statutes passed in 1964, calling for less frequent meetings of the party's top deliberative organs, are implemented, like previous ones, only in the president's convenience. The Central Committee, in theory the "executive organ of the party," in practice was unimportant, though Bourguiba arbitrarily expanded its membership in August, 1965 (in utter disregard of the statutes). Ironically this was the party organ mandated, if the need arose, to designate a new party president and thus partially answer the crucial question Bourguiba himself has raised: "If today legitimacy is not in doubt by reason of my presence at the head of the party and the State, will it be the same when I disappear?" [51] As a close observer of Tunisian politics in 1965 concluded, Bourguiba "continued to prefer his own methods of consultation and decision-making, although publicly analyzing the need for a structured and institutionalized system." [52] More recently, he decided he would again amend the constitution so as to appoint his own successor.[53]

Yet his personal rule has made it possible for the party to become an institution conferring legitimacy and stability to Tunisia's political system after he retires. While undermining the party's old network of federations and national organizations, Bourguiba expanded the scope of the political system, generating new networks of interest and support. Through his exercise of personal power he has succeeded in transforming Tunisia's structure of demands, in fostering more functionally specific interests in place of the national organizations and regional federations. His autocratic leadership has moreover permitted a healthy renewal of the party cadre.

Indeed the PSD, even while becoming Bourguiba's personal instrument, has molded and rejuvenated an elite set off from other Tunisians primarily by its concrete organizational experience rather than social status, family ties, or any of the other particularistic standards prevalent in less developed one-party systems. Though ideological conversion does not accompany party membership as in more exclusive systems, the party is identified with a distinctively modern subculture that it continuously reinterprets and rearticulates in routine pedagogical activities. In a loose sense all patriotic Tunisians are considered Destourians, whether or not they have a party card, but party activity defines their degree of political acculturation.

The ideology of Destour Socialism, moreover, is a flexible one capable of defining organizational goals but also of instilling a respect for administrative procedures—indeed, of political procedures, for Destour is the Arabic term for "constitution," one of the nationalists' traditional goals, just as "socialism" in Arabic connotes participation. Western constitutionalists may bemoan the lack of "politics" in single-party systems, the submersion of "the political" into administration. With Tunisia in mind, one observer of African single-party states has suggested that their passion for uniformity precludes meaningful political socialization. The new participant

> is being pressed to forego both the social and psychological constructs that enable him to relate affairs in remote contexts to his life, to imagine how the unforeseen might be resolved, and to relate new information and experience to continuing developmental efforts. . . . Denied the structural device of social differentiation, possibly by his own deep desire for social equality, the new participant is also deprived of the psychological anchors of issues, candidates, and party identification.[54]

Yet it is by no means clear how such constructs could be psychological anchors in an Islamic culture stressing consensus and community and the equality of all believers. The host of intermediaries that the party has laboriously constructed within its organizational structure would appear to be more effective substitutes for the mechanisms of social and regional differentiation that it destroyed in order to increase its scope of power.

It must be admitted, however, that mobilization occasionally taxed the organization's capacity to absorb it. In December, 1966, for instance, student demonstrations triggered by a banal incident expressed latent dissatisfactions within UGET against party control.[55] To subsequent demonstrations, in March, 1968, the regime overreacted by bringing to trial more than one hundred students and sentencing some to as much as twenty years of hard labor, furthering the gap between frightened elders and a radical student minority. The party was also unable to channel the violently anti-Zionist crowds who on June 5, 1967, the day Israel launched its six-day war, set fire to the British Embassy, a synagogue, and Jewish shops. Top authorities were deeply shocked by the irrational explosion, recalling Youssefist outbreaks and signaling diffuse resentment not only against Israel but also against economic austerity at home. Mass education was also creating problems; even before the riots Bourguiba expressed concern for the many dropouts, "destined to crime and debauchery." [56] The party's extensive organization does not ensure that a rootless youth will not step up crime and violence in the overpopulated capital. And in the not too distant future, the expanded university may produce an unemployed intellectual stratum if the jobs predicted by economic planning do not materialize.[57]

Still, the organization seems adequate insurance for the regime. Unhappy students may demonstrate, and city dwellers may occasionally riot, but they do not have any organized capacity for sustained opposition. The party controls access to all social bases of power, whether urban workers, the salaried middle class, petty entrepreneurs, or peasant cooperators. Tunisia's 20,000-man army and security forces might tip the scales decisively in any power struggle, but the struggle would have to occur inside the party, and the victor, to be legitimate, would have to be recognized by the party.

The blurring of politics and administration—a consequence of the expanded scope of politics—may be a condition of institutionalization in single-party systems. For then "apolitical" interests can coalesce and contend with one another, thereby acquiring a stake in and conferring value to the procedures devised to aggregate them. Political factions no longer contend overtly for influence in the "monument without cracks" that Bourguiba has erected. But economic planning, while spelling the end of traditional party factions, has enhanced rather than diminished the party's role as aggregator, by increasing the amount of deliberation accompanying decision-making at all levels of the system. These activities in turn mark a growing functional distinction between party and state, despite increased structural overlap signified by the governors' and ministers' ex officio positions in the party. Only because they manifest themselves in a "technical" guise in the planning process can interests be expressed and aggregated; if they connoted political division, they would be suppressed.

Already, however, relationships are developing between technical interests and politicians who contend for the succession or future influence when Bourguiba retires. Only then might technical and political linkages achieve full expression in party organs and only then would political actors have a sufficient stake in party procedures for the PSD to constitute a legitimate as well as effective framework of political activity. Then just possibly Tunisia might prove to be of the few contemporary illustrations of Montesquieu's oft-quoted maxim that in new societies it is "the heads of republics that make the institution; it is then the institution that forms the heads of republics."

‖ *Notes*

1. See Samuel P. Huntington, "Political Development and Political Decay," *World Politics,* XVII (April 1965), 386–430.
2. See David E. Apter, *The Politics of Modernization* (Chicago: University of Chicago Press, 1965), chap. 10, for a discussion of the "mobilization system."
3. Immanuel Wallerstein, "The Decline of the Party in Single-Party African States," in J. LaPalombara and M. Weiner, *Political Parties and Political Development* (Princeton: Princeton University Press, 1966), pp. 201–214.
4. Aristide R. Zolberg, *Creating Political Order: The Party-States of West Africa* (Chicago: University of Chicago Press, 1966), p. 160.
5. *Ibid.,* p. 149.
6. The above statistics were drawn from F. W. Frey, "Education: Turkey," in R. E. Ward and D. A. Rustow, eds., *Political Modernization in Japan and Turkey* (Princeton: Princeton University Press, 1964), p. 218; L. Carl Brown, "Tunisia," in James S. Coleman, ed., *Education and Political Development* (Princeton: Princeton University Press, 1965), p. 159; *L'Action* (Tunis), October 30, 1967; Samir Amin, *L'Economie du Maghreb* (Paris: Editions du Seuil, 1966), I, 29; Bruce M. Russett, et al., *World Handbook of Political and Social Indicators* (New Haven: Yale University Press, 1964), p. 52.
7. Frederick W. Frey, *The Turkish Political Elite* (Cambridge, Mass.: The M.I.T. Press, 1965), p. 43.
8. Russett, *op. cit.,* p. 296.
9. Zolberg, *op. cit.,* p. 132.
10. From 1960 through 1965 Tunisia's annual growth rate was almost 6 per cent; but it declined to 1.8 per cent in 1966, mainly as a result of the weather, and on October 27, 1966, Bourguiba announced a cutback in investments projected in the Four-Year Plan (1965–1968). A higher rate was expected for 1967.
11. Huntington, *op. cit.,* p. 422.
12. *L'Action* (Tunis), August 12, 1967.
13. Parti Socialiste Destourien, *7e Congrès,* Bizerte, October 19–22, 1964 (Tunis, November 1965), pp. 83–86.
14. Zolberg, *op. cit.,* p. 65.
15. See Clifford Geertz, "Ideology as a Cultural System" in David E. Apter, ed., *Ideology and Discontent* (New York: The Free Press, 1964), esp. p. 64.
16. For a good historical account see C. A. Micaud, et al., *Tunisia: The Politics of Modernization* (New York: Frederick A. Praeger, 1964), esp. Leon Carl Brown's Part I.
17. J. Berque uses this term in his *Maghreb entre deux querres* (Paris: Editions du Seuil, 1962).
18. Bourguiba explained at the first Neo-Destour congress held after Tunisia had

gained full independence that he had needed a highly disciplined party "to silence the demagogues and be obeyed and understood by the rank and file"; see his speech of March 2, 1959, summarized in Clement H. Moore, *Tunisia Since Independence* (Berkeley: University of California Press, 1965), p. 98.

19. Law no. 66-67 of November 28, 1966, established a Council of the Republic consisting of the party's fourteen-man Political Bureau and the remaining members of the government. See *Journel Officiel,* no. 51, p. 1672. On July 26, 1967, a constitutional amendment to Article 51 passed its final reading. It calls for the Council of the Republic to designate a successor to the president of the Republic in case of the latter's death or incapacity. The National Assembly then elects the new president to complete his predecessor's five-year term. Apparently the Assembly is expected to ratify the choice of the Council of the Republic. See *L'Action* (Tunis), July 28, 1967.

20. For details see Moore, *op. cit.,* pp. 61–70.

21. Interview with Mohammed Sayah, Director of PSD, July 21, 1967; as for the Algerian FLN, see Boumedienne's speech, July 20, 1965.

22. Zolberg, *op. cit.,* p. 133.

23. For this and much other useful information about local and regional party structure in the mid-1960s, see Lars Rudbeck, *Party and People: A Study of Political Change in Tunisia* (Stockholm: Almqvist and Wiksell, 1967). There were slight increases in the numbers of party branches depicted in his table, p. 142, describing the situation at the end of 1965.

24. New members, however, must take the following oath: "I swear by all-powerful God and his sacred book to act in accord with the principles of the Destour Socialist Party and to stay faithful to the Party all my life. I take God as witness to the sincerity of my declaration." See *7e Congrès, op. cit.,* p. 101. The practice of oath-taking appears to have been discarded after independence but was subsequently reintroduced. It suggests the close connection between political and religious faith for most Tunisians. One might also note that a survey of university students mentioned below on p. 36 indicates that the more religious students tend also to be more interested in politics and loyal to the party—all this despite the fact that the party has tried to modernize religious conceptions.

25. *7e Congrès, op. cit.,* pp. 93–94.

26. Rudbeck, *op. cit.,* p. 172.

27. For this and other details about the domestication of the UGTT in 1965, see Eqbal Ahmad "Trade Unionism," in L. C. Brown, ed., *State and Society in Independent North Africa* (Washington: Middle East Institute, 1966), pp. 185–190, and Rudbeck, *op. cit.,* pp. 186–200.

28. Only eight of the twenty-five Administrative Commission members elected July 31, 1965, by the congress had been members of the old Commission. This body in turn elected a nine-man Executive Bureau, only one of whose members had belonged to the previous one.

29. Possibly the 10,000–15,000 members claimed to Rudbeck (*op. cit.,* p. 42) by a UTICA official in 1965 did not really mean that UTICA had lost members since 1961, when a different official claimed 20,000 members to me (Moore, *op. cit.,* p. 164). But UGTT membership seems to have declined substantially. The claims of 185,000 and 150,000 in 1955–1956 may have been exaggerated, but Rudbeck was told (*op. cit.,* p. 199) that the UGTT had only 50,000 members in 1965. Apart from sponsoring an annual national seminar and attending international meetings, the leadership appeared to be inactive in 1967. In 1968, however, it claimed 170,000 members, attracted by government and union efforts to increase fringe welfare benefits for the rank and file.

30. Quoted by Rudbeck, *op. cit.,* p. 140; see also pp. 166–167, 180, 199, for discussions of the professional branches' extension and scope of activity.

31. See Rudbeck's *op. cit.*, tables 17–19, pp. 149–150, based on a sample of forty branches for which he was able to collect data.
32. *La Réforme Agraire,* 1967, an anonymous pamphlet written by administrators of the agricultural division of the planning ministry for a UGTT seminar, claims that between 1962 and 1966 more than 300,000 hectares were transformed into producer cooperatives and that an additional 320,000 hectares would be converted in 1967 and 1968 (pp. 226–227). The most delicate political problem to date has been extending service cooperatives in the Sahil to renovate olive orchards. More than one hundred farmers in Msakken were jailed for protesting against inclusion in such a "cooperative" in 1964, for they feared the government would take away their trees. A drought delayed ambitious government plans to uproot old trees, and it is not clear whether the party has really succeeded in convincing its historic stronghold of the cooperatives' virtues. Rather, an authoritarian governor was uprooting arbitrarily selected areas and creating "pilot zones" that were expected to have eventual demonstration effect.
33. For a general discussion of primordial loyalties and national integration, see Clifford Geertz, "The Integrative Revolution: Primordial Sentiments and Civic Politics in the New States," in Geertz, ed., *Old Societies and New States* (New York: The Free Press, 1963).
34. In the survey discussed below, p. 36, the 103 out of 497 students who came from the Sahil included half the student leaders of the sample.
35. Interview with the General Secretary of the National Assembly, August 8, 1967. In the previous Assembly thirteen deputies did not come from the constituency where they were elected; see Moore, *op. cit.,* p. 187.
36. Rudbeck, *op. cit.,* p. 111.
37. See Jean Duvignaud, "Classes et conscience de classe dans un pays du Maghreb: La Tunisie," *Cahiers Internationaux de Sociologie,* XXXVIII (1965), 185–200, esp. 196.
38. *Ibid.,* p. 133.
39. Furthermore, a new unit, the *daira* or district committee which corresponds to administrative subdivisions of the governorate, consists of the branch presidents of the area who are supposed to meet once a month with a representative of the Committee of Coordination. Though meetings are not in practice as frequent as the party statutes prescribe, they help to interrelate local and regional activities.
40. See Mustapha Zanouni, "Le rôle de l'administration dans l'execution du Plan," *Aspects et Perspectives de l'Economie Tunisienne* (Tunis), (March–April, 1962).
41. Theoretically thirty-two members were elected by the congress, but these included the fourteen members of the previous Bureau, whom Bourguiba insisted had to be elected.
42. Several former guerrilla leaders, however, were involved in the plot on Bourguiba's life in December, 1962, that also included some Youssefists, at least five army officers, and an assistant commissioner of the party.
43. Rudbeck, *op. cit.,* p. 103.
44. There were only twelve governors because one governorate had been abolished in 1959 and one governor was in charge of two governorates in 1967. The following information is pieced together from Rudbeck, *op. cit.,* pp. 104ff., Moore, *op. cit.,* p. 128, and interviews with party officials in July–August, 1967.
45. Rudbeck, *op. cit.,* p. 121.
46. Rudbeck's data for 1965, (*op. cit.,* p. 150) would suggest spectacular increases in the cadres' general education since 1960, but my data (Moore, *op. cit.,* p. 153) and his are for very different samples of branches.
47. Tunisia's 136 municipal councils, elected by universal suffrage, include roughly two-fifths of the country's population and significantly extend the scope of local politics, though virtually all council actions are subject to the approval either of

the governor or central ministries. See Municipal Decree of 14 March 1957, Article 50, published in *Loi Municipale* (Tunis: Imprimerie Officielle, 1960). Rudbeck, *op. cit.,* p. 155, confirmed that council membership and branch membership only overlapped in part, for only 5.7 per cent of his sample were councillors, instead of the 10 per cent to 15 per cent one would expect if all councillors were branch officials. Since 1957 municipal elections have been strictly one list affairs, and efforts in 1966 to liberalize party nomination procedures seemed very tentative. Branches were permitted to "nominate" candidates at general assembly meetings, and then the Committee of Coordination selected the final list from among the names put forward by the branches. Rudbeck, *op. cit.,* p. 159, seems mistaken in claiming the branches had the last word. For the best, though perhaps overly pessimistic, account of Tunisian local government, see Douglas E. Ashford, *Local Government and National Reform* (Princeton: Princeton University Press, 1966). For recent trends see also my paper, "From Sheikh to Cell: The Evolution of Local Government in Tunisia" (Mediterranean Social Science Research Council, V General Assembly, September 12–16, 1966), mimeographed.

48. Membership figures of the *Jeunesse Scolaire* provided by the same party official have varied considerably; Rudbeck, *op. cit.,* pp. 202–203, was given the figure of 50,000 in late 1965 at just about the time I was told 40,000. In the summer of 1967 the same official claimed only 27,000—or almost precisely 30 per cent of secondary school students. The university student wing of the UTJ was formally abolished in 1966, for the party appeared no longer in need of a special organization to control UGET, the student union. But the party official explained that students remained organized, for they elected lists of party candidates to compete in UGET elections. In fact some party students who lost the "pre-elections" broke party discipline to run in the general elections—with the result that 30 per cent of the delegates to UGET's 1967 congress were non-party or opposition elements.

49. The actual data have not yet been published, but some results are summarized in C. H. Moore and A. R. Hochschild, "Student Unions in North African Politics," *Daedalus* (December 1967). Rudbeck's smaller survey, *op. cit.,* pp. 222–248, suggests similar trends.

50. Ernst B. Haas, *Beyond the Nation-State* (Stanford: Stanford University Press, 1964), pp. 95; see also P. Selznick, *Leadership in Administration* (New York: Harper and Row, 1957), pp. 14–15.

51. *Le Monde,* April 28, 1966.

52. Rudbeck, *op. cit.,* p. 102.

53. *Le Monde,* Jan. 30, 1968.

54. Douglas E. Ashford, *The Elusiveness of Power: The African Single-Party State* (Ithaca: Cornell University, Center for International Studies, 1965), pp. 25, 29.

55. Two students were hauled off for police questioning after having an argument with a bus driver. Other students started demonstrating at party headquarters when news of the incident reached them, and the following morning the university underwent its first general strike.

56. Bourguiba speech, March 1, 1967.

57. The demand for qualified cadres was estimated to be greater than the supply for the years 1965–1968. See République Tunisienne, Secrétariat d'Etat au Plan et à l'Economie Nationale, *Plan Quadriennal, 1965–1968,* III, 30. However, school dropouts would produce a serious oversupply of petty employees.

Part IV

PATTERNS OF ADAPTATION
IN ONE-PARTY SYSTEMS

11

Political Socialization of Youth in Fascist Regimes: Italy and Spain

|| *Gino Germani*

Fascism: Form and Substance and Their Impact on Youth's Political Socialization

The main concern of this analysis is to identify some of the consequences of the basic aims of fascism and of the particular political form this regime may assume in the political socialization of youth. Special attention will be given to university students, a segment of the population highly susceptible to political elite recruitment and training.

I will attempt to define the "basic aims," that is to say, the historical, social and political meaning of fascism, in terms of a broad model, covering different possible types of fascist movements and regimes. These movements are likely to acquire a mass basis, often causing a fascist regime to emerge in those countries in which all or most all of the following conditions are met.

1. The transition towards a modern industrial society has been initiated under some sort of "capitalistic" form.
2. The process has advanced beyond the initial steps and the society may be considered located within the "middle range" of modernization. Such a range is conceived here as rather large, including both more and less advanced countries, and a variety of possible configurations resulting from the coexistence within each society of more and less advanced stages, in terms of the partial processes which compose the total process of economic, social, and political modernization.[1]
3. In terms of this component, the society must have been, at least for a period of time, under a regime of representative democracy.

339

4. The process of modernization was initiated more on the basis of a revolution "from above" than under the conditions created by a revolution "from below" (of the "bourgeois-democratic" variety).
5. The process of national integration has been delayed, or at least has failed to reach an adequate degree of consolidation.
6. The interclass and intraclass conflicts related to stresses and strains induced by the transition have reached a high level of intensity, or at least, their resolution has become exceedingly difficult.
7. The "primary" mobilization of the lower classes [2] is advancing at a fast rate and is perceived as a serious threat, beyond democratic control, by the various sectors of the elites.
8. The "crisis of the middle classes" [3] is reaching a most acute phase, as these strata feel particularly threatened by the rise of the lower class, by the danger of material and/or psychological status loss, and by the growing concentration of economic power in the higher class (such as "big business" and in certain cases, big landowners).
9. In those countries in which the middle classes have suffered the effects of particularly traumatic changes, their "displacement" and "availability" may cause their mobilization ("secondary mobilization") through political movements which provide a mass basis for fascism. Where this process is lacking, the rise of a fascist regime will require the intervention of other forces, usually the military. But, the middle class will still provide, in one form or another, a substantial support (perhaps through acquiescence) for the emergence of the regime and its consolidation.

Under these circumstances some form of fascist regime is likely to be seen as a solution to the threatening and unresolved conflicts. Typically the fascist solution consists of a compromise between the various components of the higher class, particularly between the "declining" rural sector and the "emerging" industrial bourgeoisie. Other powerful sectors composing the "establishment" also intervene: the church, the military, the monarchy and the aristocracy (where it exists), and those segments of the intellectual and professional elites and of the political class more closely connected (in terms of common ideologies, interests, life styles, and social origins) with the other components of the "establishment." Though the dynamic factor in their alliance is the aim to induce the forced "demobilization" of the lower class, the compromise tends also to reach a truce (and if possible a lasting peace) in the intra-elite, intra-high class conflicts. Thus the basic *raison d'être* of the regime is to consolidate a state of affairs considered able to enforce, for a considerable period of time, both lower class "demobilization" and a moratorium on all those aspects of modernization that may threaten the interests of the coalition, even at the cost of prolonged economic and social stagnation. Since this arrangement may fail to protect the interests of the middle classes or to help solve their "problem" in a rational way, some other "substitute satisfactions" may be given to them, in terms of stability, nationalistic goals, prestige symbols, and rituals.[4]

Fascism, defined here in terms of its main functions in a given social context, may assume different political forms compatible with such functions. It may be suggested that the specific kind of political system, and its ideological expressions, will be determined by several internal (national) and external (international) factors:

1. the ideological climate predominant at the national and the international level at the period in which the regime is established;
2. the position of the country within the international system, the characteristics of this system in terms of economic, political, and military power differentials among nations and the current international cleavages and conflicts;
3. the degree of modernization (economic, social, and political), already achieved by the society (within the "middle range" broadly defined as mentioned above);
4. the characteristics of the culture and of the social structure and especially of the stratification system, as it has emerged from previous transition, and as shaped by other long-run historical factors;
5. the nature of the coalition causing the various segments of the high class and elites, and its composition;
6. the role of the middle classes (varying from a dynamic one, as a mass basis for the fascist movement, to a rather passive participation in support of the regime);
7. the role of the army (to a great extent determined by historical sociocultural factors mentioned in (4) above).

"Classic" European fascism, in the countries where it succeeded in consolidating itself over a relatively long period, has assumed the form of a one-party *totalitarian* state. Such was the case in Nazi Germany and in fascist Italy. Another form assumed by fascism is the *authoritarian* state. Other European cases of aborted, or at least short-lived, fascism may have assumed peculiar variations of the authoritarian form. Finally, in Latin America, since the 1930s (and with increasing frequency in the last decade), another form of "military" fascism or, more precisely, of a military functional substitute for fascism, has been attempted. This type of regime, if it achieves some stability, may assume an authoritarian rather than a totalitarian form.[5]

A suitable definition of the "totalitarian" state (as an "ideal type") has been proposed by Friedrich and Brzezinski. It consists of a "syndrome" of six interrelated traits: (1) an official ideology "covering all vital aspects of man's existence, to which everyone is supposed to adhere, at least passively"; (2) a single mass party typically led by one man, the "dictator"; (3) a system of terroristic police control; (4) a complete, or nearly complete technological monopoly of control of all effective means of mass communication; (5) a similar control of all effective means of effective armed combat; (6) a central control and direction of the economy.[6] Another aspect, especially important in the context of this analysis, is the type of consensus demanded by the system. Although for the masses passive conformity may be acceptable, active ideological identification and participation is required of a minority within the party, especially the elite and the segment of the population out of which the future elite will be recruited. In adopting this definition it is of the utmost importance to stress the distinction between the "historical meaning," that is, the *substance* of fascism, and the political *form* it may assume. On the one hand fascism may assume forms other than the totalitarian without losing its "substance"; on the other, regimes with an entirely different "historical meaning" may adopt the totalitarian form.[7]

Franco's Spain presents some of the traits of the totalitarian state. However, many observers are convinced that this regime cannot be considered "totalitarian," or at least that in its evolution since the end of World War II the totalitarian components have been increasingly obliterated. At the theoretical level, Linz has advanced a model of the "authoritarian state," which in his opinion is much more valid for the Spanish regime than the totalitarian model. Authoritarian regimes—in Linz's formulation—"are political systems with limited, not responsible, political pluralism; without elaborate and guiding ideology (but with distinctive mentality); without intensive or extensive political mobilization (except for some points in their development), and in which a leader (or occasionally a small group), exercises power within formally, ill-defined limits, but actually quite predictable ones." [8] This model may prove to be very useful in the analysis of other regimes as well.[9] But the same provisoes already emphasized regarding the distinction between "substance" and "form" must be observed. The basic aims and the historical meaning of Franco's regime are typically fascist. That its political form may be characterized as authoritarian is certainly relevant, but no more (and perhaps even less) than its fascist substance.

All fascist regimes make deliberate efforts to internalize, from their beginnings, at early stages those values, attitudes and beliefs considered essential for the maintenance and future of the system. To this purpose they may use all the available agencies of socialization that can be effectively manipulated: the family, the educational system (from pre-school to university), physical and military training, leisure time, sports and other voluntary and compulsory associations, some of them especially organized for political indoctrination. All this is in addition to the control of the mass media, and to the predominating climate in a fascist regime, no matter what political form it may assume. The scope of these efforts and their effectiveness are certainly much wider in totalitarian than in authoritarian systems; and they may also vary between countries, under the same political form. But the general hypothesis may be advanced that in fascist regimes, the basic *raison d'être* and its totalitarian *or* authoritarian form tend to reinforce each other in introducing conflicting demands on the process of political socialization. These contradictions usually do not, however, emerge at the earlier stages of the individual's developmental process, that is, in his childhood or adolescence, but later on, when political socialization becomes prominent at the conscious level and indoctrination and political training assume a more open and deliberate fashion.[10] The conflicting demands posed on youth are likely to initiate stresses and strains usually leading to apathy, and in those individuals with a higher propensity for political involvement, to active or passive forms of deviations, or to total rejection of the system's ideologies and basic aims.

Two closely interrelated aspects of these internal contradictions will be examined here: the conflict between proclaimed ideals and the basic aim of lower class demobilization, and the contrast between the views to foster an active participation of youth, and the necessity of maintaining totalitarian controls. In the first place, the "basic aims" of lower class demobilization and status quo protection on behalf of the ruling coalition, class with the proclaimed "revolutionary" ideals of the regime, especially social justice, good jobs and welfare for all members of the national community, and the construction of a "new order" far superior to liberal capitalism or to materialistic communism. This is true not only in the totalitarian form, where an elaborate ideology is formally enforced, but also in the authoritarian state. In this case the regime must use all available means to exalt its alleged achievements and to continue to impress on the population the greatness of the benefits it bestows upon them. Even if the regime's ideology is not as elaborate as it is in the totalitarian case, the same themes are stressed and, especially in dealing with youth, revolutionary slogans are similarly emphasized. In Spain, as will be shown, the official party played the most important role in the political indoctrination of university students, and the emphasis on the "social goals" of the "movement" (or the single party) quite closely approached the Italian example, even if the party itself in fact played a comparatively minor role within the institutions and the politically powerful groups of the regime.

The second aspect is more clearly seen in the totalitarian form, although it is by no means lacking in the authoritarian. It stems from the clash between certain methods required to induce youth mobilization and the need to maintain a strict control on all dangerous deviations, not only from the party line, but above all from the basic aims of the regime. As has been predominant, although passive conformity is often sufficient for the mass of the population, leaders and potential leaders—such as the university students—must show an active ideological identification and a genuine political consciousness. In order to reach this goal, considerable scope must be allowed for youth's spontaneity and creativity, which are, however, likely to lead to deviations, heresy, and even rebellion, especially in conjunction with the first aspect already mentioned: the contrast between the "facts of life" under the regime and its proclaimed achievements and ideals. Hence, there is a permanent contrast between an "instrumental liberalization" limited to students' political expression, and control and repression of heresy and deviation.

In the authoritarian case, although mobilization was not a basic requirement for the maintenance of the regime—at least after consolidation—a similar internal contradiction could be observed with regard to the political socialization of students. Two factors intervened in the Spanish regime. In the first place, because the official party was in charge of the political socialization of the student, some efforts at mobilization were made. The resulting dilemma of "criticism *versus* discipline" showed a striking similarity to the Italian case. Secondly, the "limited pluralism" of the authoritarian regime (such as monarchic, Catholic, and falangist tendencies) introduced some liberalizing effects likely to stimulate the possibility of deviations and heresies in contrast not only with the official image upheld by the regime, but also with its basic aims. In fact, even if the more heterogeneous composition of the ruling coalition determines the "limited pluralism" which defines in Linz's terms the authoritarian version, such "pluralism" cannot extend beyond the limits and the interests of coalition itself, that is, *it still must operate within the system*. Outside it, the rigid suppressive controls of the authoritarian regime operate as efficiently and oppressively as any totalitarian-like type of control.

The consequences of these inner contradictions in the process of youth's political socialization seem to lead to a typical pattern in the development of the individual's political attitudes and also a progressive change in the reactions of the successive generations as time elapses, the regime becomes older, and its "revolutionary" origins are removed more and more into a distant past. Individuals' idiosyncratic traits and biographic events play a role in this process at the personal level. Likewise internal and external changes and events exercise an impact at the system's level. Most of the analysis will be devoted to describe the processes in a fascist-totalitarian regime: Italy. An illustration of the fascist-authoritarian case will be provided by a brief consideration of the Spanish regime.

The Totalitarian Organization of Youth under Italian Fascism

In contrast with nazism and other forms of totalitarianism both left and right, Italian fascism has been studied more from the historical viewpoint than from that of the behavioral scientist. In fact, it may be said that sociological analyses of fascism are very scarce, and the same is true with regard to political science. Recently contributions by historians have been somewhat enlarged with a sociological approach both in terms of facts and conceptual framework. It remains true, however, that the rich empirical material offered by two decades of fascist rule has seldom been used by sociologists or political scientists. And this is even more true of the specific aspect considered in the present chapter, an aspect which so far historians, too, have neglected.[11]

Although interpretations of fascism by Italian and foreign scholars vary rather widely, the facts themselves, as described in most historical accounts, fit quite closely the fascist model used in the present analysis. The reader is, therefore, referred to the relevant literature on the subject.[12]

Perhaps even more than other similar systems, Italian fascism shows a central concern for youth. In the case of Italy, not only was the mobilization of youth a basic requirement for the continuity of the regime itself, but the content of the ideology and the tradition of the fascist movement incorporated the glorification of youth as one of its essential myths.

The first youth organizations were created by the Fascist Party long before its accession to power in October, 1922. After its consolidation in 1926 the regime transformed it into an official institution of the Italian state, by creating the so-called *Opera Nazionale Balilla* (ONB). In 1929 the ONB was placed under the jurisdiction of the Ministry for National Education. However, this change was more formal than real, since the same person remained leader of the organization, and the party was able to maintain effective control.[13] In any event, eight years later another reorganization again placed the ONB (now called GIL, *Gioventù Italiana del Littorio*) under the direct control of the party national secretary.[14]

Since its creation, the youth organization has attempted to cover in one way or another all aspects of life according to the party creed. Physical and military training were given special emphasis, but thorough ideological indoctrination and above all the deliberate and systematic attempt to shape the young mentality according to fascist ideals, was the essential purpose of the youth organization. Obviously the whole educational system had been changed in content and method to serve the same purposes from kindergarten to university, but the ONB and the GIL were, so to speak, the more specialized organs to create the fascist man, and to replace the old-fashioned mentality with the new "fascist style," according to the widely diffused expression of the party jargon. This unity of purpose was enforced through the continuous and effective interaction between state and party, the mobilization and ideological indoctrination of teachers at all levels of the educational system, and the efficient operation of negative and positive controls. Also, the formal organizational structure underwent several changes reflecting the underlying interpenetration of the educational system and the youth formations. The "school charter" (*Carta della Scuola*), issued as a parallel of the "labor charter" (*Carta del Lavoro,* the basic document of the Corporate State), simply gave a more thorough expression to this unity, which in any case had been enforced with all the means at the disposal of the regime, since the period of its consolidation in the middle 1920s.

The youth formations included children, adolescents, and young adults of both sexes, from age 6 to 21 (or up to a maximum of 28 for university students and graduates), classified in various special formations by age and sex groups. As in all totalitarian parties, membership in the Fascist Party was not open [15] and all new members were recruited through the youth organizations. These operated at the same time as a mechanism for training and for selection of new party members. In an annual ceremony performed with the usual "Roman" ritual, the so-called Fascist Levy (*Leva Fascista*), all members of the youth organizations moved a step up in the age-graded units, and those who had reached the maximum age within juvenile formations were promoted to party membership.

Of the various formations and components of the youth organizations I am concerned here only with those more directly related to the political education of *young adults* and *elite training* and *selection*. The specific institutions involved in these tasks were the Fascist University Groups (*Gruppi Universitari Fascisti,* GUF), and to a lesser extent the Young Fascists (*Fasci Giovanili de Combattimento,* FGC). The former included university students from age 18 to graduation, or even after that, but up to a maximum age of 28; the latter received all the *Avanguardisti* (at age 18) and passed them to full party membership at age 21. Other central institutions which intervened directly in the political training and the selection of the elite were the *Littoriali,* the schools for political training, and the National Institute for Fascist Culture (*Istituto Nazionale di Cultura Fascista,* INCF). Less directly involved but still participating—in addition to the whole school system at all levels—was, it is important to remember, the Ministry of Popular Culture. Finally I must mention the press, published by and for the youth, especially college students.

The *Littoriali* were similar to a congress or convention coupled with a competition, held every year in a different city, attended by students representing all the Italian universities (that is their respective GUF), the representatives themselves being selected through local competitions and meetings (the *prelittoriali*). Both at the national and at the local level, the competitions were conducted through oral and written presentations to be discussed by all participants under the leadership and the supervision of special commissions of "experts" in the various fields. These committees of experts were usually composed of university professors and also of nationally known artists, writers, journalists. The topics covered the humanities, art, natural and social sciences. But in all topics, the accent was on politics and ideology, from the point of view of the organizers, the party leadership and the young participants themselves, though this coincidence, as it will be shown later, occurred to some extent with different purposes. Though "Young Fascists" were also admitted and later on the *Littoriali del Lavoro* (Labor *Littoriali*) provided a parallel institution for young workers, the importance of the *Littoriali* was restricted to the intellectual and political elite, specially recruited among university students.

The Schools for Political Training (*Corsi di Preparazione Politica Per i Giovani*) constituted the highest and the formal training and selection ground for party and government leadership. Less specific methods of selection took place from the very first year of a youth's admission into GIL, among children and adolescents who were evaluated and selected for special training within the various organizations. Another form of selection took place within the *Littoriali*. But the schools were meant to produce graduates who were expected to begin a formal political career. These schools were established by the party in all provinces. There were strict standards for admission, which was open, at least theoretically, to members of "Young Fascists" as well as to members of GUF (that is, persons without college education were also eligible). Enrollment was limited to a maximum of one hundred students for each provincial school. The courses lasted two years and included both theoretical and practical training, through visits, participant observation, and actual work in provincial party and state organizations. The "decisive characteristic for admission"—indicated the party directives—"will be a passion for politics and a gift for organizing, previously shown by aspirants." [16] Finally, in Rome, a National Center for Political Training was organized, for those who demonstrated the higher capacity of command. Again a limited number were admitted (one hundred), through very strict selection, and the Center was considered the highest stage in fascist political education. Among other schools and courses, which were highly diffused among the universities and other institutions, mention must be made of the *Scuola di Mística Fascista* (School of Fascist Mystique), created in Milan, under the sponsorship of the GUF, which occupied an important place in the educational system for leadership training.

Aimed primarily at the *fascistization* of the higher culture and at the permanent mobilization of intellectuals, the National Institute for Fascist Culture also had an important role in the shaping and selection of the political elites during the regime's existence. It was a subsidiary organization of the party and maintained sections in all the Italian provinces, with some one hundred thousand members. It controlled a number of organizations and institutes for cultural activities and higher learning and scholarly research, and a considerable array of publications.

As noted earlier the entire school system had been transformed to serve the purpose of a totalitarian education. In addition to this general penetration of fascist ideology, and the attempt to politicize all aspects of the curriculum, many courses, lectures and seminars specially devoted to political training were included at all levels of education, but especially in the universities. In fact, an entirely new type of school was added to those already existing in the Italian universities: the Department of Political Sciences (*Facoltà di Scienze Politiche*).[17]

Finally another important mechanism for elite training was the students' press. The GUF had its own national magazine, but, in addition to this, provincial branches had their own organs; also a considerable number of journals and small publications of different kinds mushroomed everywhere in Italy, in formal or informal connection with the youth formations. Obviously, all the press was completely fascistized, both in terms of personnel and orientation, and of very efficient internal and external control. The "little" magazines of the fascist students did not escape this general framework. However, they were in a rather special situation, probably because they were considered "safer," being under the direct supervision of the party and the GUF and also in view of their functions in elite training and formation. This function was never formally recognized but it was clear enough to the party leadership. For these reasons, although there were rigid limits (which led sometimes to the suppression of certain publications), the range of possible variations was a bit larger than for the rest of the press.[18]

The various special organizations and institutions I have enumerated were created at different times and underwent several reforms during the two decades of fascist rule. The very first to appear were the GUF. Created in 1920, they were never formally included in the ONB or the GIL, but constituted a special branch of the party, under the direct supervision of the national and provincial party secretaries. This was a special situation expressing the privileged position of the students within the fascist system. The Young Fascist groups were created in 1931, under the direction of the party. Later they were incorporated into the GIL. The first *Littoriali* met in 1934, and the Schools for Political Training in 1935. The Institute for Fascist Culture had existed since 1925, though its scope was considerably enlarged in following years. As will be shown later, these successive additions, expansions, and modifications not only expressed the growing concern of the regime for the real effectiveness of elite training and selection but were also the consequence of the fascist leadership's dissatisfaction at the result of their efforts. It was an expression of their partial failure in building a fascist elite.

Effectiveness and Limitations of Totalitarian Education

The failure of totalitarian education could not be seen at the open behavior level, but only at a deeper level, and in relation with the purpose of obtaining not only conformity or even some enthusiasm but also active participation involving initiative, spontaneity, and sincerity. Obviously this failure was never recognized as such by the regime or its leaders, but it can be observed clearly enough from the discussions conducted among fascists, and on the basis of other evidence.

These limitations, which showed clearly some of the strains inherent in a totalitarian system, will be considered in the last section of this chapter. Some mention must be made first of the more manifest results. From this point of view, the fascistization of the young generations appeared as accomplished not only in the official image maintained by the fascist leadership but also to neutral, outside observers, and even antifascist emigrés, during the regime and after its downfall. This is true both in terms of size and of organizational membership and in terms of open behavior and surface attitudes.

From the point of view of statistical growth, it must be said that prior to 1939 (when membership became formally compulsory), the party never reached total affiliation of all the individuals within the age groups covered by the youth reformations. But the proportion affiliated was very high and reflected the degree of incorporation of the population into a modern urban structure more than it did the efficiency of the party and youth organizations. In the mid-1930s, affiliation for all age groups (between 6 and 21 years) varied from more than 70 per cent in the more modern and urban northern provinces, to above 30 per cent in the less urban and more traditional provinces in the south. However, the coverage was much more complete for younger age groups everywhere in the country. For instance, among those 6 to 14 years old, the proportion affiliated was as much as 90 per cent in the north and fom 50 to 60 per cent in the south.[19] For Italy as a whole in 1937 the *Balilla* (6 to 13 year old formations) represented nearly 70 per cent of the age group, and the *Avanguardisti* (14 to 17), some 60 per cent. But, as one fascist observer remarked, in separating those who attended school from those who did not, it was precisely among the latter that most of the non-affiliation occurred. In fact, more than 90 per cent of the individuals actually enrolled in schools were also affiliated with the corresponding youth formations. Also it must be noted that these figures include both sexes, and that female affiliation was much lower, especially in the higher age groups.[20] In fact, after the late 1920s, affiliation of children and young people with party organizations had become practically automatic, even if theoretically it was not yet compulsory. This was especially true for the middle and higher social strata, where affiliation was considered absolutely normal among those attending high school and college, and certainly approached the 100 per cent level. When compulsory membership was established, it really acquired the same status as primary education (which had always been compulsory, at least according to the law, in the pre-fascist era). Another fact pointing to the same conclusion was the existence of compulsory military training, which, as established by fascist law, began at the age of 8. In agreement with the central principle of the School Charter the obligation to attend school and to participate in the GIL applied to all individuals from their childhood, and was considered as a public service or duty inherent in their status as citizens of the fascist state. In this way, it was recognized, the "public and political orientations" of juvenile life represented the basic instrument for building the whole personality along national values.[21]

Also, from the point of view of ideological, political and psychological character building, no less than in terms of simple numerical affiliation, or physical and military training, it seemed that fascism had succeeded in the goal of shaping the nation's youth in its own fashion. "Most competent observers . . . today agreed that the youth emerging from these groups in the 1930s were enthusiastically Fascist, and the younger generation was one of the bulwarks of Fascist strength." [22] Italian historians and other scholars unanimously recognize the impact of fascism on youth. The penetration of the regime and its ideology among youth is considered as a most serious achievement in fascistization, which had a series of consequences for the future.[23] Even those who think that this task was only partially successful among the older generations regard the result obtained among the young as a remarkable success.[24]

It is more difficult to speak, on the basis of the available documentation, of the nature of the process of fascistization. However, even though lacking any systematic research, it is possible to advance some tentative generalizations on the basis of literary material and autobiographic accounts. These generalizations are limited to the youth belonging to urban middle strata, especially students, since very little or nothing has been published concerning the working class and the rural sectors.[25]

Two aspects emerge as main components of the process of fascistization among youth: negative factors inducing conformity, and positive factors generating active response. Among the first is the fact that the totalitarian way of life was perceived as *normal,* with very few exceptions, by the new generations, including those born around 1910 or later. This "normality" meant that the regime was taken for granted and that for most youngsters the question of alternate possibilities was the result of a discovery reached after years of slow maturation. The realization that fascism "could not have been," coming as a result of a long critical process, is a common theme in these autobiographical accounts.

It was not a mere question of information. Getting information, of course, was not easy; this depended a great deal on the family background of each individual. But, with some exceptions found among those born in families of opposition leaders or activists, it seems that the older generations did not communicate with the younger ones. The general climate of fear and conformity was the main reason. Another factor is that by and large the middle-class social environment was not particularly hostile to fascism; on the contrary, it was precisely this sector which provided the movement with most of its mass basis.[26] More important than the lack of information was a general negative attitude towards the "old" world contrasting with positive attitudes towards the "new" world of fascism.

The image of the old world was one of decadence, sickness, weakness, national humiliation; the image of the anti-fascist—if it existed at all—was one of an old person, defeated and trying to disguise his dissent under a thin veil of outside conformity. Militant anti-fascism, and the underground movement, which existed and was operating, failed to reach the great majority of the population. "Anti-fascism was archeology," and the general crisis of democracy, the attitudes of European powers towards fascism, and the critical years following the Great Depression were a confirmation of these feelings. On the other hand the normality of being a fascist and behaving according to the expectations and the requirements of the regime was greatly reinforced by the fact that all careers, even the more modest jobs, depended on membership in the party or in some of its subsidiary organizations. In an age of widespread unemployment, especially among white collar workers and professionals, the need for a job was one of the most powerful mechanisms of totalitarian control. This control was probably much more powerful than fear of repression, or police terror: in fact, in most cases it did not operate simply under the form of a direct threat—though this threat was always present, and certainly felt by everybody—but as something beyond discussion, natural and normal as registration in the school or any other bureaucratic requirement. The family operated here as a powerful instrument of conformity, even when the older members were not fascist. The normal preoccupation for the future of the children involved pressure for conformity in so vital a matter as their work future. The value system, according to which family solidarity is considered as having higher priority than political duties, or abstract and ideological principles, was certainly another factor generating conformity.[27]

Among the *positive* factors of youth fascistization, the more obvious is the monopoly by the party of all political activity. Thus the party became the only channel for political expression for those who felt the call of politics. On the other hand, because of pervasive politicization generated by the totalitarian system, other callings removed from politics but involving some type of organization also had to be expressed through quasi-political channels. For this reason not only the urge for political expression and the potentialities for political leadership, but also any other strivings towards self-realization in the fields of literature, the arts, journalism and the like, had to be expressed through the organizations of the party and the regime. The party (and its subsidiary organs) represented all the forms of association and public life. But monopolization by itself could have done little more than attract ambitious young men in search of a rapid career. In fact a number of young fascists fell into this category, and the accusation of careerism (*arrivismo*) returns again and again in the discussions on the "youth problem," as it was called at the time.

More important for the active mobilization of youth was the promise of fascism as a revolution. In the first place fascism was asserted to be a *movement* whose final goals were not stated once and for all, but could be redefined by the new generations. Fascism had to be something living and not crystallized, and youth represented the dynamic factors for permanent renewal, or better, for *permanent revolution*. As presented to the young generations, fascism was not reaction or tradition, but *future*. This future was presented in terms of social justice, of a change of the economic system to replace capitalism, and even as a form of a freedom far superior to democratic pluralism. The theme of nationalism was also important but operated more in terms of conformity and superficial rhetoric than as a dynamic factor. Social justice, the development of the corporate state, the building of a new society, along with freedom and choice, were the themes that mostly attracted the young. Because of these promises many believed themselves fascists, only to discover later that "their fascism" did not really exist. This is the process found more often in the autobiographical material, and it coincides with the development of the youth problem as seen from contemporary fascist sources It is here that fascism's contradictions emerge. The basic mechanisms used by the party to insure the continuity of the regime by generating the creative participation of the young and by promoting the emergence of an authentic political elite (that is, not merely a bureaucracy of *arrivisti*), included two main components: on one side the promise of a social evolution of the regime in terms of social justice and drastic changes in the economic order, on the other the promise to the young generations to exercise an innovating role through criticism, circulation of ideas, and actual change of institutions and men. But both components—social change and liberalization—contrasted sharply with the basic aims of the regime. The former was blocked by the persistence of its initial *raison d'être,* the defense and preservation of the major vested interests in the existing social order and the demobilization of the lower classes. Once this possibility was eliminated, any liberalization would become the source of dangerous deviations and an immediate threat to the stability of the regime. Thus through all its history the party policy towards youth never managed to escape this inner contradiction. The more successful the "dynamizing" mechanisms, the more the party was compelled to restrict or to eliminate them. As the incoming generations successively discovered that the promised future did not really exist and became aware of this inherent limitation, their "long journey through fascism" [28] came to an end: passive conformity or open rebellion were the only outcome of the process, and it depended on the interplay between personal circumstances and external historical conditions which way was chosen.

Internal and External Sources of Dissent and Military Resistance

Militant anti-fascism and underground activities were always very much alive under the totalitarian regime in Italy. Though until 1941 or 1942 their effectiveness in penetrating the majority of the population was greatly checked by the positive and negative controls of the regime, it provided the basic cadres and the ideological motivation for the military guerrilla resistance from 1943 to 1945. The Resistance resulted from a mass of mobilization involving hundreds of thousands of partisans in the mountains, the countryside, and the cities.[29] But this popular uprising, which in its guerrilla units was composed mainly of young people, would not have been possible without the increasing alienation and active disaffection created under fascism not only among the older population, the survivors of the pre-fascist era, but also—and above all—among those born (or at least polit- ically socialized) under the new regime.

I have indicated in the inner contradictions of the regime a source of what could be called the *internal* origins of dissent among youth. But these were not the only factors which fostered opposition. Other factors, external to the totalitarian system, were also in operation. Both sources tended to interact and to combine, especially at the final stage of each individual evo- lution from alienation and dissent to the "discovery" of anti-fascism and the transition to a militant opposition. In fact external factors, which were usually neutralized by the totalitarian climate, could be transformed into a precipitating factor in the *crise de conscience* leading to anti-fascism, only after the internal contradictions had induced some maturity and a realistic approach in terms of political awareness.

Before we proceed further some words must be devoted to these "exter- nal" factors and the way they operated among the young. Only in a minor- ity of cases do these factors seem to have operated alone, without a period of maturation *within* fascism, at least during the "normal" totalitarian rule, before 1943, and the beginning of the armed resistance. It is impossible to assess their respective weight as causal factors in producing dissent. Family background is frequently mentioned in the autobiographical accounts as having been very important. But we have seen that family influence oper- ated in both directions (dissent and conformity), and in fact, in some cases, even a family tradition of active opposition and leadership was not sufficient to prevent an initial acceptance of fascism among the young. An- other source was religion, not in terms of Catholic organizations or the church as an institution,[30] but in terms of religious beliefs. School also seems to have operated, though only occasionally, as a vehicle of the old in- tellectual tradition, so inimical to any form of autocracy and oppression.[31] As for any other "island of separateness" [32] surviving in Italy from the pre-fascist past, the monarchy, the army, the church and whatever was left of the old bureaucracy, they operated mostly in generating conformity, not dissent. It is true that their interests did not coincide completely with those of the regime, and that fascism, which they had considered as a weapon useful for attaining lower class demobilization, went beyond their initial in- tention. But up to the last moment they were clearly aware that their own fate was linked to that of the regime. In any case institutions like the army or the monarchy could produce a palace coup—as they did in 1943—when everything was lost, but were completely unable and unwilling to generate resistance when the regime seemed strong and successful.[33]

An important source of deviation is to be found in individual idiosyncra- sies. Any peculiar trait strong enough to produce a feeling of being differ- ent could, in the overwhelming climate of conformity, generate one of two opposite reactions: deviation or overconformity. In the autobiographies there are many instances citing dislike or unfitness for sports, physical disabilities, or a particularly strong introversion or shyness as an initial factor which in time would result in some sort of political dissent.

So far, I have discussed factors external to the regime, but internal to the social structure. Other important sources of dissent were also originated by external events. In this sense the more important are the Spanish war, the persecution of the Jews, and the alliance with nazism and the war. The intervention in Spain made a deep impression on youth. For the first time anti-fascism presented a very different image, that of a fighting force, openly defying the regime. For the first time also, radio broadcasts from Spain and other places abroad could break the complete isolation in which old and young Italians alike had remained for a long time.[34] Anti-Semitism contrasted with basic values in the culture; and the alliance with the Nazis was perceived as a tremendous threat to the integrity of the nation, and went against deeply felt national traditions. It was ironic that the alleged contrast between fascism and nazism (especially in 1934 and 1935) was a cause for favoring fascism. All these events are mentioned as precipitants in the transition towards conscious dissent and active opposition. The Palace coup and outbreak of guerrilla activities must be considered as the final blow that triggered mass mobilization against fascism and its Nazi ally.

The "Youth Problem"

Within the restricted scope of the present chapter, I will attempt now to summarize a process which provides a vivid illustration of the contradictions between participation and control in the framework of a totalitarian structure rigidly limited in its further evolution. This process is the history of the so-called youth problem, which made its appearance soon after the consolidation of the regime and the emergence of the totalitarian organization, and persisted under different labels, throughout and well to its end.[35]

The youth problem involved, in the first place, the need to create a new political elite. But how was this possible under the conditions of a totalitarian state? The danger of alienation was perceived as soon as the first crop of young people educated under fascism began to appear. In 1927 a fascist writer observed an alarming decrease of political interest among youth.[36] A few years later, in 1930, apathy and indifference were seen as a major trait among Italian youth. Just as in Moravia's first novel, *Gli indifferenti* (*The Indifferent Ones*), a serious moral crisis was affecting the young.[37] At the same time a well-known writer (also fascist) imputed "estheticism," "epicureanism," "sadness," "lack of enthusiasm" to the typical young man of his day.[38] Despite the great interest of the regime in the new generations, they maintained their "bourgeois" style.[39] Again, in the years following, the same accusations return: apathy, indifference, conformity, senility. "Today's youth only aspires to imitate the old man: its rebelliousness has disappeared"; [40] "Italian youth sleeps. Everywhere apathy, degeneration, nihilism." [41] Or perhaps anti-fascism? "Those who work within fascism especially in close contact with the young cannot avoid a persistent fright-ful doubt, the doubt that the older ones, those who have remained farther away from fascism, are not the remnants of the pre-fascist world, but are to be found among the young generations, of those who should have ac-quired a fascist mentality . . . though a minority has acquired a real fas-cist style of life, the great majority is submerged in apathy and lack of in-terest in all the important national problems. And this apathy is made much deeper by the fact that it is disguised under a completely different ap-pearance, as pure faith, discipline, perfect political orthodoxy." [42] This contrast between appearance and reality was seldom perceived by foreign-ers, or even by anti-fascist emigrés. Yet it was one of the most striking symptoms of the inner contradictions of the state. Another common accu-sation concerned *arrivismo* as the only, or the predominant, motivation among the young. [43] On the other hand it was recognized that the youth problem was to a great extent a problem of unemployment. The unrest ob-served among youth—their "generalized protest"—stemmed from their marginality with regard to the party and the regime leadership, because of the monopoly of the old men in all offices. [44] This problem was seen as closely connected with the need to modify the composition of the bu-reaucracy, which, despite the extensive purge, was composed mainly of per-sonnel trained in the old days. More generally, the question was one of gradually easing out the old generation, socialized under the past order, and replacing it with the "new fascist man." [45]

It was recognized that all these problems (except the question of unem-ployment, which was mentioned but never discussed, as it was a conse-quence of economic stagnation) were really aspects of the central issue: how to generate the active mobilization of youth and their creative participation in the regime. Confronting the problem of alienation and the difficulty in molding an adequate educational policy, *Crítica Fascista* correctly identi-fied the cause as an "ingrained defect of our political structure." This was written in 1932. [46] Whereas *even* the United States and Latin America had a system for elite replacement (the spoils system), fascism had none, de-spite the hierarchic principle. [47] Many solutions were considered and re-jected, but the need for some type of liberalization and mobilization through free choice and limited elections from below was again a recurrent theme. Periodic meetings were proposed but severely criticized. [48] But that discus-sions in one form or another were essential was generally recognized. The need for the "circulation of ideas," for free criticism, was reiterated for many years, after its first expression in the late 1920s. An underlying ambiva-lence between the realities of totalitarianism and the need for real dyna-mism characterizes many of these expressions. The comparison of Italy to a Prussian barracks (*caserma Prussiana*), an imprudent remark even for a fascist, was severely condemned by Arnaldo Mussolini (the brother of *il Duce*) in *Popolo d'Italia*. [49] Another article on the conformity predominant in the press, suggestively titled "The Kingdom of Boredom," generated a storm of replies and counterreplies.[50] Though nobody discussed, as noted, the need for a strict control of the press, and its complete fascistization (which was, of course, achieved), at the same time many wanted the press to offer some variety and some positive functions of criticism and control. A curious theory was suggested by a well-known journalist, Longanesi, who considered that it was within the spirit of fascism "to take the risk of criticism," that is, to risk jail if criticism was not accepted by the party.[51] The permanent dilemma between freedom and discipline, although disguised under the usual jargon, was clearly recognized as the central issue in the problem of youth. "Hierarchic discipline does not exclude personal responsibility"—especially at a time when the regime has been consolidated.[52] Discussion is a "fascist obligation." [53] Those who oppose discussions and interpret discipline too narrowly are an obstacle to the development of the revolution.[54] Discussion is a mechanism for developing maturity in the young and for fostering their dynamic role in the party.[55] Conformity and alienation can only be avoided by discussion, by heresy.[56] The claim for an "orthodox heresy" (*una eresía ortodossa*) provides an amusing illustration of the ambivalence and confusion of these polemics.[57] And the jargon of "pure act idealism," would have permitted worse contradictions. Others saw discussion as a means of propaganda.[58] The need for higher intellectual culture and a reorientation of the university was also stressed.[59] But how could this need for discussion be satisfied within the totalitarian framework? There was some request for a return to "fascist normality," to forms of "legitimate" discussions.[60] But though Bottai and other leaders had sometimes spoken of a new deal and a revaluation of individualism possible after the regime's consolidation,[61] nobody dared to approve the kind of "normality" implied in that request. In fact discussion was to take place only *within* the party and *among real fascists,* under the "supreme guidance of the Duce and the State"; [62] other types of discussion with non-fascists, or (even worse) with anti-fascists, were barred forever. It was really a problem for police control. Such was the opinion of the "liberals" among fascist intellectuals. Freedom of the press was just "fantasy," an idle dream of unrealistic people.[63] What then? A certain awareness of the lack of realistic solutions did exist, as in a candid article published in 1932: it is impossible to return to "liberalism," but the young need an alternate solution to the now obsolete liberal system. The only suggestion to reduce marginality and apathy was in terms of "occupational opportunities" within the party.[64] Also the other aspect of the problem of youth, the one related to the "circulation of elite," the participation of the youth as a "rejuvenating" and dynamic factor in the life of the party to avoid sclerotization and bureaucratization,[65] revealed analogous ambivalence and inner contradictions.

Again the appeal for a "return to normalcy" was expressed in relation to the system of elite selection. The dictatorship was necessary but it was also "necessarily transitory," and a return to elections within the party should be a solution for the problem of youth. This extraordinary thesis (in fascist times) was followed by an editorial comment stating "Everything authorizes (us) to believe that this state of necessity which from 1925 on, led the organs of the regime to adopt authoritarian forms and methods, has now used up its reasons, and ought, today, to be replaced by a system in which political forces have a larger range of movement [*un piú largo respiro*], and a greater range of possibilities [*un piú amplio gioco*]." [66] This type of expression may have been related to the recurring rumors of a possible liberalization of the regime. However, not only did such liberalization never materialize (the contrary was true), but the same sectors gave a very different meaning to these aspirations. In fact, the return to "electoralism" was considered completely alien to fascism; instead, the idea of extending the "aristocratic" principle of hereditary succession combined with the "hierarchic" principle of selection from the top was seriously proposed. In any case choice from below should be limited to "minor offices." This request was usually linked to a possible development of the corporate state, and it meant to allow direct elections for workers and owners' representatives at the plant level.[67] But again this quite modest suggestion—though formalized in the law—was never put into practice. It really went beyond the ideological and structural possibilities of the system. In any case this "playing" with several possible developments in terms of liberalization as well as in terms of social justice certainly functioned as useful manipulating mechanisms for the mobilization of the young. The principle of the single party, the elimination of any possible sources of pluralism even within the party, was reaffirmed both in the discussions and in the concrete steps taken to solve the problem of youth.[68] In the first place, the totalitarian form of fascism was solemnly reaffirmed by Mussolini and the party secretary. Criticism had to be "well-inspired" and the role of the single party was strengthened.[69] On the other hand, the concrete steps taken aimed more at the appearance than at the substance of the problem, with the exception of the *Littoriali.* Thus the creation of the Young Fascists (as a subdivision of the ONB) had the purpose of recreating the spirit of "squadrism," a return to the origins. But this was more in the uniforms than in anything else. The problem of participation was "solved" by issuing party instructions to the press to accept collaboration from youth.[70]

The only solution offered by the regime was the creation of a special privileged situation for the students through the *Littoriali,* more tolerance for the "little" journals, combined with a mixture of police repression and integration by cooptation into jobs and minor offices. But it was a short-lived solution, because these *ersatz* could not provide a lasting expression to the mobilization of youth.

Certain consequences of the first *Littoriali,* in 1934, came as a real shock to the party leaders. In the first place, the spontaneous reemergence of pluralism added several contrasting qualifications "to the pure and clear simplicity of the term 'fascism,' belonging to different and opposing orientations." [71] The old parties seemed to reappear: collectivists versus liberals, Catholic versus free thinker and atheist, monarchists against communists.[72] Non-conformist tendencies appeared even clearer in discussions on arts and literature. The *magnum opus* of the corporate state (the Labor Charter) was declared "obsolete." [73] In the following years the situation, at least during the formal sessions, tended gradually to change, perhaps because of increasing controls by the Committees. But in 1935 the same deviations were noted in the fascist press, with discussions between Catholic, collectivist and other orientations. Preference for a leftist answer in terms of social justice, and even drastic reforms concerning private property, were observed with apprehension.[74] This tendency was also noted in the pre-*Littoriali,* in the provinces.[75] In later years a considerable decrease in deviation seemed to have taken place. Though the students seemed to be fascist, they lacked "passion," their fascism was "different"; "a cold rationalism and a certain ironic skepticism" were clearly observed. A tendency towards surface conformism, especially through an escape into technicalities, could be noted. Other observers noted considerable lack of interest and information on political problems.[76] But it is known that most of the more significant activities occurred behind the scenes, in informal contacts between participants. In this sense the *Littoriali* involved a real mobilization of the young elites, but a mobilization which did not favor active incorporation into the party and the regime, but precisely the opposite, since it operated as a precipitant in the anti-fascist *crise de conscience.* All the available evidence confirms this generalization and in this respect, fascists and anti-fascists seem to coincide. "They were the occasion for the first spontaneous emergence of a critical consciousness, and of opposition" and the meeting ground for potential and actual anti-fascists; they were deliberately used both by those who still believed in the possibility of an internal evolution of the regime, and by the underground.[77] Within the anti-fascist movement the only groups that became interested in the new generations were *Giustizia e Libertá* (a liberal socialist movement), and the Communist Party. But until the mid-1930s, there was a great resistance, based on ethical reasons, against undergound members' joining fascist organizations. However, in many cases the students themselves formed their own clandestine groups and tried to contact the underground.[78]

The Schools for Political Preparation met with complete failure. One year after their creation they were considered nearly useless and demands and suggestions for reform became very frequent.[79] They could produce only bureaucrats, not leaders. The creation of a political consciousness was beyond their reach.[80]

The privileged position enjoyed by the youth press was another factor favoring active participation, but as in the case of the *Littoriali* it could lead to unacceptable deviations, and in fact the suppression of "little" magazines became very frequent. Their orientation was ordinarily "leftist," that is, they attempted to bring to the extreme logical consequences the social elements apparently included in the official ideology. A return to "origins," to the "leftist" initial party program of 1919 (soon abandoned), was also used by the communist underground, and "naively" by young fascists. But the corporativist promise failed completely, and instead of real reform the regime could only provide verbal attacks against the bourgeoisie and its style. At the end of the 1930s and in the early 1940s, the external factors accelerated the conversion of the young generations, a process which finally resulted in fusion with the underground movement in the great popular uprising of the armed resistance in 1943–1945.

It is impossible to affirm that without the defeat, the fascist regime could have been destroyed. The evidence shows, however, the existence of strong disintegrative factors whose impact cannot be evaluated on the basis of present knowledge.

These factors were the expression of the inherent contradictions between mechanisms for control and mechanisms for elite mobilization. The contradiction could have been neutralized, perhaps, if the structural and ideological framework of the regime had permitted an evolution in terms of social goals. But this was impossible, given the persistence of vested interests inimical to any attempt to eliminate the "lower class demobilization" and the protection of the interests of the coalesced elites which had been the prime movers in the rise of the new regime.

Political Socialization of Youth in Fascist Spain [81]

There is little doubt that Spanish society in the early 1930s had most or perhaps all the traits required for the emergence of a fascist regime, as enumerated in the first section. These facts, described by many writers, led to a typically fascist solution.[82] The main differences with "classic" fascism were the role of the army, the nature and composition of the established elites' coalition, the form acquired by the mobilization of the middle classes, and the hispanic historical-cultural setting.[83]

These peculiarities probably contributed to the regime's evolution toward the authoritarian form, although during the first decade the totalitarian components were much more pronounced.[84] It was, however, during this early period that the regime's youth organizations were established and the educational system at all levels thoroughly reformed in accordance with proclaimed totalitarian purposes. The formal institutions followed the Italian pattern rather closely. The first youth organizations were organized by the Falange, before the Civil War. In fact the Falange and its student sector, the SEU (*Sindicato Español Universitario*) were, in the words of one of its prominent leaders, one and the same thing, since the Falange was born with "the mark of the university youth." [85] In 1937 Franco unified the Falange (which in the pre-Civil War years had merged with another Fascist party, the JONS (*Juntas Ofensivas Nacional-Sindicalistas*), with the Carlist (*Comunión Tradicionalista*), creating the single party (or "movement" according to the official jargon), as "the basis of the Spanish state." One of the basic services assigned to the new official party was the Youth Organization (*Organizaciones Juveniles Españoles,* OJE). The Militia, including the University Students premilitary service, and the SEU were obviously part of the Falange.[86] Soon after, the SEU was reorganized in accordance with the new legal status of the single official party. Following the totalitarian pattern, it was strictly hierarchical in its organization, with all authority concentrated at the top and delegated to appointed representatives at the provincial, university, school, and course levels. In 1939 the SEU absorbed the student's branch of the Carlists and the Catholic Students Confederation, while all other student organizations were suppressed and the creation of new ones forbidden. As a section of the official single party the SEU effectively monopolized all the students. A University Militia in charge of student premilitary service was also created in 1940. It included special sections, like the so-called *primeras lineas* (First Lines), who were Falangist activists having already completed their military service. The only difference with the Italian university militia was that the army maintained some control over it through the national and regional chiefs, who were regular army officers. The same year an organization, similar to the Italian GIL, was also created: the Youth Front (*Frente de Juventudes*). It was intended to unify all the youth organizations (that is the OJE and the SEU) under the same framework. The OJE was divided into several groups according to age, from seven-year-old boys and girls up to the age of military service. Those admitted to the University automatically became members of the SEU. Its prime missions, as emphasized in the law, were the molding of members to make of them party militants, and the initiation of all the youth of Spain into the political doctrine of the movement. Special schools were established for the training of instructors to serve in the Youth Front. In the view of Falange and SEU ideologues, the *Frente* was intended to increase their impact on the population and especially "to implant a strong national Catholic-syndicalist spirit in the new generations." However, when finally established, the new organization was much more limited in scope than envisaged in Falangists' aspirations, and the SEU remained pretty much in the same isolation from the rest of the youth as before.[87] It will be remembered that this situation also prevailed in the Italian GUF. In 1943, SEU membership became automatic for all students at the universities, and the following year this obligation was extended to all other post-secondary education centers.

Since the very beginning of the Civil War the regime devoted great attention to education: drastic purges of personnel continued for many years, as well as strict permanent control of teachers' recruitment and political orientation, censorship of texts, and uniform adoption of specially written textbooks. New principles to remodel the entire educational system at the primary, secondary, and higher levels, both in content and methods, and to stress religious and political indoctrination, were for the first time formulated in the 1938 law. In following years a series of reforms were introduced to stress control of teachers, ideological content of teaching, and other aims of the regime. Since the end of the Civil War the Falange and the Ministry of Education were expected to cooperate particularly in the control of the members of the youth organizations. A Falange representative was included in all provincial Commissions for Education and the Falange also created its schools and was put in charge of the students' camp. In 1942 dissatisfaction with the effectiveness of political indoctrination conducted by SEU in the universities led to the creation of the *Colegios Mayores Universitarios,* a revival of boarding schools existing in the seventeenth and eighteenth centuries. "The obvious advantage of the system was that of bringing all university students together in state supervised dormitories." [88] Religious and political education were among their important aims. The Falange was in charge of political education. And, more in general, the church, the army and the Falange were given a prominent role in the universities. The 1943 law stressed the state control and the "indoctrination of the students in the principles of National-Syndicalism." The SEU was also in charge of all the services and the welfare of the students, in addition to their political control, the university militia, and sports. In fulfillment of the university law of the previous year, compulsory political indoctrination courses were established in 1944. This task was obviously allocated to the SEU, and it was considered a primary mission of higher education. The Blue Division sent by the regime to fight the Russians in 1941 was overwhelmingly composed of university students, SEU members. The large voluntary recruitment among students proved—in the opinion of a Falangist writer—that bureaucratization had not yet suppressed the revolutionary spirit of the Civil War, in which some 60 per cent of SEU members had died, according to Falangist estimates.[89]

No one will dispute that during the first ten years, since 1936, a full-fledged fascist "totalitarian" structure was being established in Spain. To the complete control of youth organizations and national education one must add the no less complete control and manipulation of all the mass media and all relevant sectors of the society, particularly the lower classes. Negative control through police, repression, and extreme terror, during the Civil War and after, is well known, and there is no need to describe it here. The famous Law of Political Responsibilities and all the legislation following it led to the violent suppression of opposition to the regime. In fact, even after the Civil War, and for many years after its end, the degree of terror in Spain was much greater than at any time in Italy, except during the German occupation in 1943–1945. In the universities the SEU imposed strict conformity to the Falangist orthodoxy.[90] It is true, however, that despite the strict ideological control forced on the professors, most of them had a Catholic origin, a fact which produced some consequences in later years, when it helped to introduce the first cracks into the monolithic structure of the university. In any case it must be kept in mind that the church, being part of the fascist coalition, had a strong vested interest in the system, and these sources of deviation were really limited to a few intellectuals among the Catholics.[91] (New political tendencies in the young clergy were to appear much later.) At the level of higher learning, an Institute of Political Studies was established, similar to the Italian national center for political training. It was at the same time a "training school for party workers, and a general study center for ideology and new projects of every sort." Later, as the regime approached the authoritarian form, the institution lost its importance, and even became a "center of convert Fascistic liberalism." [92] This was a consequence of the illusions entertained by some of the party ideologues on the possibilities of a Falangist left, entirely similar to the Italian fascist left, and equally doomed to failure by the rigid requirements of the regime's basic aims.

The impact of the Allies' victory and the destruction of the fascist regimes in Europe obliged the Spanish government to abandon its more visible totalitarian traits and to introduce some liberalization, which in the opinion of most observers was mostly external, since the positive and negative controls, propaganda, indoctrination and terror continued.[93] The year 1945 was the most dangerous for the regime: both the opposition in exile and the internal underground renewed their activities, including guerrilla outbreaks. But the policy of the great powers was not in favor of any positive action, and very soon the Cold War contributed to the consolidation of the regime. By 1949 the guerrilla and other internal opposition groups were crushed, and later on the international isolation of the country came to an end, with the establishment of American military bases in the peninsula, and the admission of Spain into some international organizations.

From the second half of the 1940s the new generations politically socialized under the new order had appeared on the national scene. It may be said that the effects of the negative and positive controls operating on youth led to the same results as in the Italian experience. Fascistization *was* successful.

These results seem to have been reached even if discrepancy existed between the ideal image provided by the formal system—as crystallized in norms, regulation, ideology—and the everyday reality. Most Spanish observers emphasize this discrepancy between the appearance of the official structure and the reality of life; so that a great many of the legal prescriptions were in fact systematically violated or simply considered nonexistent in actual practice. In fact we find a similar discrepancy between appearance and reality in the Italian case too. Nonetheless the fascist climate pervaded the whole society. The regime was now the normal, taken-for-granted social environment of everyday life. To accept the system, as if it always had existed, was simply the obvious thing. At the same time routinization and bureaucratization impeded the formation of a genuine political consciousness, ideologically oriented in accordance with the movement, or when some political awareness did arise, it led to deviations, heresy, and final rejection. Ridruejo describes the evolution of youth during the first decade after the end of World War II as a succession of four phases, which bear a striking similarity to the process incurred under the Italian fascist regime:

> In analyzing the development under an unconformist consciousness among youth, in its various possible expressions in the last ten years, one could observe a succession of four stages:
> 1. impatience to replace the various echelons of the Movement hierarchy already filled by people no longer young;
> 2. disenchanted comparison between the Movement's ideals and its concrete achievements, especially in the social realm;
> 3. an attempt to bring about a revival of these *same* ideals of the Movement, through the formation of informal groupings, opinion trends, or disguised deviationist organizations;
> 4. an open rupture with party discipline and its ideology, and the opening of new possibilities, created by the youth itself, and necessarily limited by the scanty clandestine information and a desperate search for guidance.[94]

Thus, exactly the same alternative paths appeared in Spain as had been observed among the Italian youth: alienation for the great majority, expressed in apathy, or passive conformity and increasing deviations leading to rebellion for the few who possessed a higher propensity towards politics. Among the great majority—wrote Lain Entralgo in 1955—two overwhelming interests predominated: "profession and fun," and among the few, open differences with the official indoctrination but still without any positive content, in a state of "availability." [95] Around 1946 the leadership of the SEU had to be replaced by younger people, and the organization stressed its social service, welfare, and students' professional needs more heartily. Politization and strict ideological control, however, did remain, being taken care of by the special section within the SEU, the *primera linea*, a "real political police within the University." [96]

The growth of youth dissatisfaction, and increasing deviation, *within* the movement can also be observed through the students' magazines, many rather short-lived, since sooner or later they reached the limits of ideological heterodoxy permitted even under the "liberalized" and "limited pluralistic" authoritarian regime. Among the more representative "little" magazines may be mentioned: *La Hora, Alférez, Alcalá, Juventud, Laye.* The major themes discussed in the Falangist youth press were exactly the same as those found in their Italian equivalents: pessimistic diagnosis of the situation of Spanish youth, its apathy, hedonism and indifference; careerism; the need for criticism, but at the same time the strictures of official control and the dilemma between criticism and disciplines; efforts to recapture the original Falangist ideologies, translated into two main problems—claim for freedom and individual rights, on one side, and for social justice and a truly new social order on the other; the boredom of, and the weariness with the eternal stereotypes of official propaganda; and the shocking contrast between the official image and dire reality.[97]

In drawing the "Balance of One Generation," the generation of those who had gone through the university after the end of the Civil War, a Jesuit priest in 1947 sadly commented on the "cold" and "egoistic" alienation of students and graduates alike. In another article, youth's "indifference and apathy" and the need for a "dynamic minority" to revive the original ideals of José Antonio (J.A. Primo de Rivera, founder of the Falange) were pointed out. Also noted was the "hegemony of the quiet ones," the typical student, who had "all the required party cards in his pocket, and refrains from any comment lest he may offend the powerful. All his ideals are a good salary and no risks." Present youth, says another writer (also in 1947), has no purpose, only a "sordid pragmatism." [98] Five or seven years later little had changed: "Our generation has lost all its political ideals," and even religious ones; there is no vitality. The students lack personality. "One must recognize," said the Rector of the University of Santiago in one address, "that our movement which began with the total politization (of youth) has achieved their total de-politization." The same charge that youth had turned old—so frequent in Italy—was heard in Spain. *"Alcalá* is an expression of old age, not of youth," "Boredom" reigns in the "massified, lonely, disenchanted youth," affirms another article, which, incidentally, started a long polemic on the "problem of youth." [99] The causes of this state of affairs were certainly clearly recognized, although often disguised: too much propaganda, too many slogans, myths, and too little freedom. "If everyone is obliged to have the same ideals, all such imposed ideals will end up being rejected." "Peace is not an end in itself"; it must be used to reach the always promised and never realized "revolution." "When fathers are too bossy (literally: *cuando los padres son patrones*), the sons turn out to be servants"; "Peace must be dialogue, not monologue." [100] In the 1950s the causes of youth's apathy are more openly discussed: we have football instead of politics, because politics are not possible; "there have been fifteen years of parades, now we must start walking"; "it would be dishonest to talk about things which cannot be changed" or to talk revolution when revolution is not possible. The mystique of the past has been reduced to a series of prohibitions and permissions; youth was always considered not a subject but a passive object. To the charges of lack of clarity in youthful thinking, a precise answer was given: "If we (the young) are confused, it is because all doors and all windows have been kept closed, thus we may only have obscurity. . . ." [101]

As in Italy the solution was to stimulate a more critical attitude among the young, the possibility of an "internal opposition," or, in the words of a young Italian fascist, "an orthodox heresy" (this same expression was actually employed). But the same precautions had to be observed to maintain criticism within the system. From one side criticism had to be stimulated. On the other it could lead to deviation and even rebellion. Since the regime was now established, there were no reasons to maintain the same prohibitions, for instance it should be permissible to admire pre-Civil War writers and thinkers, "whom until then, it was sin to remember." In any case criticism was really a "form of collaboration." The need was "to unite on the essentials, to dissent on the details." "Heretics are necessary" and "the rulers must not fear youth's lack of conformity since this is the only way to avoid falling into a fatal stillness." "Politics being an eternal transition," there was need for innovation, for more imagination. Above all, there was "need to recover certain eternal truths such as freedom and individual rights, a true contact with reality, without propagandistic inflation." The revolution should be discussed, not merely accepted; "the real revolution is simply to tell the truth." [102] This appeal for freedom was usually justified as a revival of the original ideology of the Falange. The same support was given to emphasizing the need for social reform, presented as an unaccomplished goal of the "revolution." *Alférez* in 1947, and again *Alcalá* in 1955, insisted on "drastic solutions for socio-economic problems," "better social distribution of wealth and income," "accomplishment of the revolutionary social ideals of 1936." [103] Finally, as in fascist Italy, the youth press noted the complete failure of the "courses for political training."

By the mid-1950s this timid internal deviationism may be considered to have been exhausted, students' politization increased, and deviation turned into open rebellion. Ridruejo and other observers agree that 1956 represents a key turning point in the evolution of Spanish youth.[104] Both internal and external factors explain the new trends and the growth of open anti-fascist tendencies among youth, despite the fact that the authoritarian control was still rather strictly enforced outside of the "limited pluralism" and despite the various attempts at "liberalization." I will not deny that these attempts were not a factor in the politization of the students and in the rise of more open forms of deviationism and finally opposition. In any case, from a functional point of view, they were the counterpart of the "liberalizing" attempts often repeated under the Italian regime. It must be granted, however, that they were directly related to the nature of the ruling coalition, and to its looser structure in comparison with the Italian case. For instance, the limited possibilities opened to the "liberals" to operate within the university and to influence the new generations were a consequence of the changes in the cabinet that occurred in 1951. At that time— once the regime had achieved a new strength, after the post-World War II crisis—Franco policy was one of equilibrium between Falangist, monarchist, and some liberal influence.[105] But the participation of the liberals like Ruiz Gimenez, Minister of Education, may have been an important factor in widening the range of choice among the students. Quite symptomatically, a few years later, when the first serious disruption of discipline occurred in the university, Ruiz Gimenez was dismissed.

On the other hand, one must remember the deep changes taking place in the Spanish society: some economic developments, internal and external migrations, urbanization, changes in the occupational structure—from a still predominantly agrarian labor force toward modern industry and services. These changes had their impact on the social stratification and on the volume and composition of the student population. Second, after the experience of the preceding decade, the new generations could not doubt the rigidity of the system, its impermeability to real reforms—in terms of either democracy and political freedom—or in social and economic aspects.[106] In fact the original "basic aims" of the regime had not changed, perhaps they were slowly being adapted to the new characteristics of the society and to the emerging power groups originated through these changes. On the other hand, external factors were also important: Western Europe had reemerged from the catastrophe to reach its highest levels of prosperity; Europe was moving fast under democracy while Spain remained backward and segregated. The increase in international contacts with Europe and the rest of the Western world eased at least the isolation and obscurity which had suffocated preceding generations.

The rise and growth of a militant anti-fascist consciousness among the Spanish students is not easy to describe and summarize. For one thing it is still an unfolding process, taking place under the permanent threat of the repressive controls of the authoritarian state which continues, as always, to defend the system and its basic aims as they are. Even if political unrest and political and social protest have a degree of visibility which was unthinkable in the past in fascist Italy, still, it must find its expression in clandestine or semiclandestine groups and movements, when—as often occurs —their nature and ideologies go beyond the "limited pluralism" allowed by the system.[107] For the purpose of the present analysis a few brief observations may be sufficient. In the first place the internal evolution of some segments among the young Falangists, secondly, the struggle within and against the SEU, and finally the rediscovery of the contemporary, democratic, old and new leftist ideologies. It is known that it is precisely the so-called Falangist left which turned out to be the main source for the present most extreme leftists. This evolution went on slowly in the beginning, accelerating in the late 1950s.[108] Given the official monopoly by the SEU of all organizational activities in the universities the students tried first to achieve its democratization, gain its control and eventually use it as a framework for anti-regime political expression and action. This attempt failed, since despite the frequent reorganization of the syndicate to give it some semblance of democratic control, the government did too little and too late. In any case, the attitudes of student activists was now one of open rebellion. By 1964 the SEU was virtually destroyed, and the students had formed new free professional organizations in all the universities as well as a national federation. The rediscovery of the ideologies and the emergence of numerous political groups occurred to a large extent outside the old underground and the opposition-in-exile. "We had no teachers, and the few things we managed to know, we learned directly from reality," says the organ of the new University Socialist Association, created in 1957.[109] Although all the main ideologies have reappeared (from the New Left to the Demo-Christians) an increasing radicalization to the left seems to characterize the Spanish students, together with their connections with other similar political groups in the country. (It must be remembered that the students' movement had, since the early 1950s, always been favorably affected by working-class protests.)

The evolution of the Spanish students under Franco's regime shows a process strikingly similar to the one in fascist Italy. The totalitarian or the authoritarian form assumed by fascism did not seem to alter the nature and the consequences of the contrasts between mobilization and control, or between the rise of a genuine political involvement and the rigid defense of the basic aims of the regime.

Summary and Conclusions

I have attempted to analyze the problems confronted by fascist regimes in performing two of the functions of any political system: (1) how to generate and maintain among youth the type of consensus and participation required by each particular system; and, more especially, (2) how to socialize and train that segment of the new generation out of which the regime expects to recruit its future ruling elite, the elite intended to replace one day the present incumbents of power. Since fascism has been defined as a phenomenon which under given conditions *may* occur somewhere at an *intermediate stage* of the transition towards modernity, the mechanisms usually found in pre-industrial society are no longer available. The type of consensus and the motivation to participate—especially for the potential elite—cannot rely any more *solely* on spontaneous mechanisms of socialization into traditional *beliefs*. Instead, active indoctrination into the regime *ideologies* is required.[110] Also, passive conformity, although perhaps sufficient under the authoritarian form, fails to meet the need of elite recruitment and training in both authoritarian and totalitarian fascism. But if active consensus and dynamic and creative participation is required, then the kind of mechanisms demanded by this type of political socialization will generate an acute conflict with other requirements, rooted in the basic aims, and the very *raison d'être* of the fascist regime itself, both under authoritarian and under totalitarian form. The conflicting demands generated by these two sharply contradictory sets of requirements may generate different reactions: high participation actively supporting the system, or some form of cynical "careerism" and "bureaucratization" of leadership, apoliticism, active or passive deviationism, and active or passive opposition to the system. In this aspect, a typology of responses may be constructed in terms of two main variables: (1) propensity for political participation, and (2) acceptance of the system.

The scheme presented in Table 11–1 may be helpful in summarizing the evolution of youth—that is, the successive emerging generations—in both fascist regimes examined in this chapter.[111] Such evolution seems to have passed through four stages. The first stage corresponds to the period of struggle to establish the regime. During it the degree of political involvement for the young is likely to be higher than normal (in terms of the level prevailing in each national political culture), and the population (including the young) will be highly polarized in favor of or against the rising fascist movement. In the second stage, once the regime has been consolidated and the first generations politically socialized under the new order are emerging, the propensity for political involvement will tend to be much lower, in fact, depolitization may prevail. At this level of leadership the regime will

TABLE 11-1 *Typology of Responses of Youth to the Conflicting Requirements of Political Socialization in Fascist Regimes.*

Degree of Propensity for Political Involvement or Participation	Degree of Acceptance of the Regime			
	Full Acceptance	Indifference, Neutrality or Lack of Ideological Commitment	Partial Rejection	Total Rejection
High	active supporters ideal leaders	political "careerists" bureaucrats	active deviationists	active opponents (underground and resistance members)
Low	passive[a] supporters	apoliticals	passive deviationists	passive defeated

[a]These terms were employed by Amando de Miguel, "Institutional Norms of the Spanish Youth" (unpublished MS); they were located, however, in an entirely different conceptual context.

fail to create a loyal and dynamic elite. Instead it will recruit more and more bureaucrats and young people motivated only by personal ambitions. In the third stage, as efforts are made to recreate the original spirit of the movement in order to give new motives for loyal active support by youth, the politically involved young will tend toward some form of deviationism. Finally, in the fourth stage, many young people finally realize that the regime cannot be changed from the inside, and the minority of the young with a high propensity for politics will turn increasingly toward a total rejection of the system and toward active opposition. The transition from stage to stage will be accelerated or delayed according to the impact of international events, changing ideological climates, and the rate and nature of the process of modernization. Other factors, such as emigration [112] or degrees of political skillfulness of the regime's leadership may also introduce wide variations.

According to the assumptions on which this analysis has been formulated, this model on the evolution of youth should be applicable *to any fascist regime, under authoritarian or totalitarian form.* The possibility of testing it on other cases, however, is rather restricted by the fact that only in the Portuguese case has the regime lasted through a number of generations entirely socialized under its rule. Fascisms in Eastern European countries either aborted or were too short-lived for a test of this kind. The same may be said of nazism, whose "normal" generational succession was interrupted too early by the outbreak of the war. As for the validity of the model in the case of the "functional substitute for fascism" now emerging in some Latin American countries, it is obviously too early to draw any conclusion. In any case, however, I think that this model should be modified on several aspects. Two main reasons suggest such modifications. In the first place, they are not based on the secondary mobilization [113] of an important sector of the population, but on the role of the army. Secondly, at least until now, their goal seems to be more the passive acquiescence of the population than their active participation into a political movement. In fact the attempt appears to be the establishment of a *no-party system.* Under these circumstances, the young, particularly the students, are likely to be alienated or strongly opposed to the regime from its very start.[114]

For other reasons, the analysis of which cannot be formulated here, the model does not seem valid without important modifications in the case of *non-fascist* authoritarian or totalitarian regimes. As I have emphasized, the basic aims of fascism, its historical meaning, are the main factors in blocking its future evolution, and the fulfillment of the social and political ideals which in the beginnings of the movement play a decisive role in attracting youth. But authoritarian or totalitarian systems based on the "primary" mobilization of lower strata, oriented toward some model of modernization and nation-building, may retain the enthusiasm of youth for a longer period. They have a "future," even if such future may often involve an open conflict with the oligarchic bureaucracy, which usually turns out to replace the founding revolutionary elite. *The potentialities of a regime as "future" rather than anything else seems to be the more general factor involved in the loyalty and the active participation of youth*—a future, however, which—at least in our modern world—cannot be conceived as a mere reiteration of the past but as a continuous creation, as "permanent revolution."[115]

|| *Notes*

This study was made possible by a grant from the Comparative International Program, Department of Social Relations, Harvard University. I also want to acknowledge the important collaboration of persons and institutions which have in one way or another greatly facilitated my work. In this respect I must mention especially the Archivio Centrale dello Stato and Dr. Costanzo Casucci for his help in surveying the context of this archive, and among many persons, Dr. Renzo de Felice, Prof. Juan Linz, Dr. Ruggero Zangrandi, Dr. G. Silvano Spinetti, Dr. J. Pinillas de las Heras, Dr. Alberto Acquarone, Professor Camillo Pellizzi, Dr. Agostino Nasti, Dr. J. F. Marsal. However, I am solely responsible for the contents of this chapter.

1. This proposition is based on a model in which the total transition is perceived as composed by three main processes (economic, social, and political modernization) and many partial processes within each of the three main components. Although main processes and partial processes are intercorrelated, this relationship is far from perfect. Each component and main and partial process may have different rates of change and may occur in different sequences under varying historical, cultural, and social conditions. This variety introduces considerable differences and peculiarities in the transition of each country. G. Germani, "Stages of Modernization in Latin America," paper delivered at the LASA meeting in November, 1968 in *Studies in Comparative International Development,* Vol. V (1969–1970), forthcoming.

2. The concept of social mobilization used in this analysis has a very different content and meaning from the same term as used by K. Deutsch and others. It is based on a general theory which distinguishes different "moments" or phases within the process and different types. Mobilization is defined here as a process of social change, and its different "moments" (which may take place simultaneously or successively), are: (1) a state of integration (within a specific structural pattern); (2) a process of breakdown or disintegration (affecting some aspect of the existing structure); (3) release of individuals (and/or social groups); (4) response to such release, taking the form of either withdrawal or availability (the latter corresponding to *psychological mobilization*); (5) objective mobilization, consisting in an active response, characterized by new forms of participation (including decision, opinion, consumption patterns, and so forth) neither expected, nor regulated by the preexisting structure, and often resisted by powerful segments of the society; (6) reintegration of the mobilized groups or individuals, through either their final adaptation to the pre-existing social structure, or through changes in this structure, or more often through a mix of both processes. Integration exists when a society is characterized by a "sufficient" congruence between three levels: norms, internalized attitudes, environment (that is, actual circumstances related to the requirements of norms and attitudes). Two main types of mobilization may be distinguished: "primary mobilization" is the process by which non-participant traditional sectors are being incorporated into some form of modern participation (political, social, economic, and so forth); "secondary mobilization" is an increase in forms and intensity of participation (in particular political participation), in sectors which have been already for a long time incorporated into the national society but have remained —or have become—apathetic or non-participant in some particular sphere of behavior (for instance politics, the typical example here being the middle-class non-voter): G. Germani, "Social Change and Intergroup Conflict" in I. L. Horowitz, ed., *The New Sociology* (Oxford: Oxford University Press, 1964). A revised version appears in *Sociología de la Modernización. Estudios Teóricos y Aplicados a América Latina* (Buenos Aires: Paidos, 1969), chap. 3. The application to the rise of fascism may be found in Germani, "Fascism and Class," in S. J. Woolf, *The Nature of Fascism* (London: Weidenfeld and Nicholson, 1968).

3. This "crisis" corresponds to a particular "transitional stage" in the course of the

transition toward a modern advanced structure, (according to the "capitalistic" model). A comparison between the middle classes in the present situation in the more advanced Latin American countries and the European experience in the inter-war period (in relation to this interpretation of fascism) may be seen in *Sociología de la Modernización, op. cit.,* chap. 7.

4. In this definition I have taken into account the many factors suggested in the vast literature on fascism. This particular definition is, however, based on a general theory of fascism partially formulated in *Sociología de la Modernización, op. cit.,* chap. 7. The relevant sources have been mentioned in the books and articles quoted in the preceding notes. To these references I should like to add A. F. K. Organsky, *The Stages of Political Development* (New York: Alfred A. Knopf, 1965).

5. The more advanced countries in Latin America are passing through a situation in many aspects comparable to that of the Latin European nations in the 1920s and 1930s. However, the different structural configurations characterizing the Latin American societies, the difference in the ideological climate and other internal and international factors are likely to generate other—as yet unknown —forms of fascism, or some "functional substitute" for it. Until now, though the "crisis of the middle classes" remains a key factor as much as it was in the European cases, the lack of strongly traumatic experiences has prevented the occurrence of the "secondary mobilization" of these strata, and their role in a mass fascist-like movement. Nonetheless, the middle classes, through their present ambivalence and incoherence, are contributing, in conjunction with the Latin American equivalent with the conditions enumerated in the text, to the required political and social context favorable to the emergence of some sort of "fascist" solution. The dynamic factor here is provided by the military, and their intervention replaces the mass movements of "classic" fascism in establishing regimes likely to achieve and to maintain the demobilization of the lower classes and the protection of the higher class from the risks involved in certain aspects of modernization; see Germani, "Social Change and Intergroup Conflict," chaps. 1 and 8.

6. C. J. Friedrich and Zbigniew K. Brzezinski, *Totalitarian Dictatorship and Autocracy* (Cambridge: Harvard University Press, 1956), pp. 9–10. The definition has been summarized.

7. Failure to recognize this essential distinction has often led the theory of totalitarianism to misplace, in the same category, socioeconomic systems that are entirely different in terms of this historical meaning: for instance, systems aiming at the demobilization of the lower class with systems expressing the primary mobilization of these same classes.

8. Juan J. Linz, "An Authoritarian Regime: Spain," in Erik Allard and Yrjo Littunen, eds., *Cleavages, Ideologies and Party Systems* (Helsinki: The Academic Book Stores, 1964).

9. Incidentally, it may be added that the Spanish case is particularly interesting for the Latin American context in so far as, to some extent, it approaches emerging fascist regimes in those countries.

10. I use the term "socialization," which seems to have a stronger connotation than "education" or "training," in order to stress also the impact of the total climate pervading the society, the subtle influences of everyday life and the various agencies of socialization operating in youth and adult life. But, as this analysis is focused on youth, it will not refer to family and school (except college and higher education). Also, no effort will be made to compare the problems of political socialization in democratic or non-authoritarian societies, with those examined here. For an overview of the general problem of political socialization reviewing research up to 1959, see Herbert H. Hyman, *Political Socialization*

(New York: The Free Press, 1959); on political socialization in children, Robert D. Hess and Judith V. Torney, *The Development of Political Attitudes in Children* (Garden City, N.Y.: Doubleday & Company, 1968), (This research is limited to the United States). A recent review of the literature on political participation of youth and some findings on present Italian youth may be found in Guido Martinotti, "La Partecipazione Política dei Giovani," in *Quaderni de Sociología,* XV (1966), 334–386. In recent years the literature on students' politics has been growing at a fast rate. See for instance S. Martin Lipset, ed., *Student Politics,* special issue of *Comparative Education Review,* Vol. 10, No. 2 (1966), and *Daedalus,* issue on *Students and Politics* (Winter 1968).

11. The regime's contradictions inherent in the political participation of youth were described by this writer from the militant anti-fascist prospective in G. Germani, "Dodici anni di Educazione Fascista," in *L'Italia del Popolo* (Italian daily published in Buenos Aires), December 23, 1934. The problem of generations in recent Italian history has received some attention, but I know only one sociological contribution: Renato Treves, "Il Fascismo e il Problema delle Generazioni," in *Quaderni di Sociologia,* XIII (1954), 119–146.

12. Only the most important sources will be given here: Luigi Salvatorelli, *Storia d'Italia nel Periodo Fascista* (Torino: Einaudi, 1964); Alberto Acquarone, *L'Organizzazione dello Stato Totalitario* (Torino: Einaudi, 1965); Angelo Tasca, *Nascita e Avvento del Fascismo* (Bari: Laterza, 1966); Ernesto Rossi, *Padroni del Vapore e il Fascismo* (Bari: Laterza, 1966), Vol. I; Paolo Alatri, *Le Origini Fascismo* (Roma: Editori Reuniti, 1961); Renzo de Felice, *Mussolini il Rivoluzionario* (Torino: Einaudi, 1965) and *Mussolini il Fascista* (Torino: Einaudi, 1966). See also references mentioned in n. 2 and n. 4.

13. There were tensions between the party and some sectors within the Ministry of Education, but in any case these originated in the increasing role of the fascist youth organization in the normal routine of the educational system. In fact this allocation of jurisdiction served the purpose of helping the process of "fascistization" of the school more than that of giving it control of the youth organization.

14. For a more detailed description of the youth formations under fascism see Dante L. Germino, *The Italian Fascist Party in Power* (Minneapolis: The University of Minnesota Press, 1959), chap. 5; Acquarone, *op. cit.,* pp. 264 ff.; D. S. Piccoli, *The Youth Movement in Italy* (Roma: Novissima, 1936) (describes the organization until 1935); Achille Starace, *Gioventù Italiana del Littorio* (Milano: Mondadori, 1939). For some early description, see Herbert W. Schneider, *Making Fascists* (Chicago: The University of Chicago Press, 1929); Herman Finer, *Mussolini's Italy* (New York: Holt, Rinehart and Winston, 1935).

15. There were several exceptions to this rule, in special periods, through the two decades during which affiliations were open to older people. Usually contingent political reasons were the main factors which caused these temporary reopenings of the party membership.

16. Piccoli, *op. cit.,* pp. 61–64.

17. Salvatorelli, *op. cit.*

18. A list of the youth press is given in G. Silvano Spinetti, *Difesa di una Generazione* (Roma: OET, 1948).

19. Germino, *op. cit.,* pp. 74–75. It must be remembered that the Nazi youth organization never reached this level of affiliation.

20. Bernardo Giovenale, "La Gioventù Italiana del Littorio," *Critica Fascista,* XV (1936–1937), 404–405.

21. Editorial comment of *Crítica Fascista,* "La Carta della Scuola e la sua Etica," XVIII (1938–1939), 130–131.

22. Germino, *op. cit.*, p. 82.
23. Salvatorelli, *op. cit.*, 426ff; Acquarone, *op. cit.*, 264ff.
24. See also works quoted in n. 4. Among contemporary observers, one must note the book by Blondine Olivier, *Jeunesse Fasciste* (Paris: Gallimard, 1934).
25. The considerable documentation existing in the archives, especially in the State Archives, has been receiving some attention in the last few years and it is being used in the most recent historical works. A preliminary exploration conducted by the writer in the State Archives did not reveal any important material on the topic. It is possible, however, that a more systematic research could produce some relevant data. The only possible procedure for more reliable information would be a sample survey among people belonging to the relevant age groups. After 1945 and especially in the last few years there have been several contributions by noted intellectuals and political leaders through autobiographic and literary essays, novels, and, in most cases, brief answers to inquiries made by literary or political magazines. The publications used in the present chapter are the following: Humanitas, *Autobiografie di Giovani del Tempo Fascista* (Brescia: Morcelliana, 1947); G. Silvano Spinetti, *Difesa di una Generazione* (Roma: OET, 1948); Ezio Antonini, ed., *La Generazione degli Anni Difficili* (Bari: Laterza, 1961); Aldo Capitini, *Antifascismo tra i Giovani* (Trapani: Celebes, 1966); Ruggero Zangrandi, *Il Lungo Viaggio attraverso il Fascismo* (Torino: Einaudi, 1947, and second enlarged edition, Mursia, 1967); Alfredo Signoretti, *Come Diventai Fascista* (Roma: Volpe, 1967); Luigi Preti, *Giovinezza, Giovinezza* (Milano: Mondadori, 1964); Giorgio Amendola, *Comunismo, Antifascismo, Resistenza* (Roma: Editori Riuniti, 1967); Eugenio Curiel, *Classi e Generazioni del Nuovo Risorgimento* (Roma: Edizioni di Cultura Sociale, 1955).
26. The predominant middle-class recruitment of fascism, during its early years and during the regime, is well known.
27. I am not inclined to explain these attitudes in terms of a peculiar Italian "familistic culture," or by using the hypothesis of an "amoral familism" as advanced by Edward Banfield in *The Moral Basis of a Backward Society* (New York: The Free Press, 1958). To what extent is this priority of family over political values not a universal response under totalitarian stability and normality?
28. This is the title of one of the autobiographical accounts, quoted in n. 16.
29. More than 300,000 partisans participated in actual fighting. The number of those killed in combat was 44,720, and disabled veterans number more than 21,000, according to the official figures of the Italian government. See Roberto Battaglia, *Storia della Resistenza Italiana* (Torino: Einaudi, 1964), p. 561.
30. All the Catholic organizations for youth (and adults alike) had been dissolved or neutralized by being limited to strictly religious roles. The conflict with the church concerning their youth formations (Catholic Action, Catholic Youth, Catholic Scouts, and so forth) which took place between 1928 and 1931 had ended with a nearly complete withdrawal of the church. In the following years, as in those preceding the Concordat and the conflict, the church behaved as part of the Italian establishment, reinforcing and using the regime. Not only the Pope but also cardinals and bishops called Mussolini the Man of Providence. At the time of the Ethiopian war and even more during fascist intervention against the Spanish Republic, the Vatican enthusiastically supported the regime. There were even signs of fascistization of the liturgy, with the so-called "Fascist Masses." Obviously many Catholic laymen and also priests did not become fascist. Some of them participated in the underground movement before 1943, or were active among the emigrés. But the manifest official position of the church was one of support, at least until the outbreak of World War II. It had been observed that the church received considerable advantages from the

Concordat of 1929, but it is also true that its privileged position was not used to undermine the regime while it remained strong and its end was not in view. The Catholic organizations probably exercised a role in preparing a Catholic elite for eventual succession in the long run, but in any event this activity was encapsulated and did not affect the consequences of its overt action among the majority of the population, which tended to generate conformity and consensus. See Acquarone, *op. cit.,* p. 293ff.; Germino, *op. cit.,* chap. 5; Salvatorelli, *op. cit.,* chap. 7; Richard Webster, *La Croce e i Fasci* (Milano: Feltrinelli, 1964).

31. The regime had inherited from the pre-fascist era the educational system, and —what is more important—its personnel. As indicated elsewhere in the text all precautions had been taken to prevent any open expression of disaffection and to control as much as possible the behavior of the teachers. Though a long standing intellectual tradition could not be easily cancelled, it was sufficiently neutralized most of the time. As mentioned in several autobiographies, as perceived by the young, a gesture of conformity often destroyed years of honest, but passive and covert, dissent.

32. This is the expression used by Friedrich and Brzezinski, *op. cit.,* chap. 6.

33. The monarchic-military coup of July, 1943 found the regime already dead because of the combined impact of external defeat and internal disintegration. The attempt by the higher hierarchy of the party to replace Mussolini occurred independently from the Crown initiative. The anti-fascist underground was extremely active in the last two years, and the great strikes in Milan and Turin in 1942 were a clear expression of the changes.

34. The autobiographical reports are also confirmed by other sources. See Alberto Acquarone, "La Guerra di Spagne e l'Opinione Pubblica Italiana" in *Il Cannochiale* Nos. 4–6 (1966).

35. Most of the material for this section is drawn from *Critica Fascista* and some other fascist periodicals (in addition to the autobiographical literature already quoted). *Critica Fascista* was one of the most influential political journals of the regime. Its director, Giuseppe Bottai, an outstanding member of the fascist hierarchy, was also its most prominent ideologue. Bottai, considered by some observers as inclined towards the so-called fascism of the left, always insisted on the alleged social goals of the movement and favored some liberalization (within the boundary of the party line). However his actual political action remained always loyal to the regime, at least until its cause was definitely lost, in 1943. See his memoirs, G. Bottai, *Vent'Anni e un Giorno* (Milano: Garzanti, 1949).

36. Gherardo Casini, "La Classe dirigente, Propositi e Fatti" in *Crítica Fascista,* V (1927), 304. *Crítica Fascista* will be indicated hereafter as *C.F.*

37. G. Lombrassa, "L'Indifferenza Male del Mondo," in *C.F.,* VIII (1930), 8–9.

38. Antonio Aniante, as quoted by *C.F.,* VIII (1930), 130.

39. *Il Tevere* (a Roman daily newspaper), May 1930.

40. "Senilità," in *Il Saggiatore,* December 1931.

41. *Vampate,* January 1931.

42. Giorgio Radetti, "Svecchiare," in *Vita Nova,* as quoted in *C.F.,* X (1932), 30.

43. One of the first and most widely discussed denunciations of the entire youth problem as a matter of "careerism" among youth was published by Camillo Pellizzi, a well-known intellectual, in the daily paper of Bologna, *Il Resto del Carlino,* December 14, 1928. The ensuing discussions included many more themes, among others one which again became a recurring topic in the following years: the contrast between generations within and outside fascism.

44. An alarming unemployment among youth was denounced by *C.F.,* VIII (1930), 69; the same theme may be found in the publications *Provincia* (Aosta),

Azione Corporativa (Turin), as quoted in *C.F.*, VI (1928), 250, and others.

45. The party had become for the old a defense of vested interests, criticized Germano Secreti in "I Giovani e il Partito," *C.F.*, VI (1928), 282–284; the same author spoke of a "generalized protest" generated by this "resistance to youth." He insisted on the need to replace the old generation. The same stand, as means of eliminating the remnants of the *ancien régime*, was taken by Gioacchino Contri, "I Giovani e il Regime," *C.F.*, VII (1929), 211–213; Carlo Giglio, "I Giovani e l'impiego," *C.F.*, IX (1931), 453–454. These requirements were reiterated in the most important dailies, such as *Popolo d'Italia* and *l'Impero*, as quoted in *C.F.*, VI (1928), 201–202.

46. Dogana, "Documenti," *C.F.*, X (1932), 30.

47. Gioacchino Contri in *Il Resto del Carlino,* as quoted in *C.F.*, VII (1928), 250.

48. Editorial comment, "Un regime di Giovani," *C.F.*, VI (1928), 201–202. G. Secreti, "I Giovani e il Partito," *C.F.*, VI (1928), 282–284.

49. *C.F.*, VI (1928), 342.

50. "Il Regno della Noia," *C.F.*, VI (1928), 301–302, 332–333.

51. L. Longanesi, "Libertà di Stampa Fascista," in *L'Italiano,* February 1929.

52. Discussion between Bottai and Casini, "Polemiche," *C.F.*, VIII (1930), 82.

53. G.D.L., "Necessità della Polemica," *C.F.*, VI (1928), 230.

54. *C.F.*, VI (1928), 303.

55. As quoted from *L'Assalto* (Bologna), on several occasions, *C.F.*, VI (1928), 303; *C.F.*, IX (1931), 171; *C.F.*, XI (1933), 117–118.

56. Dogana, "Conformismo ed eresia," *C.F.*, XII (1933–1934), 330; "Eresie di Giovani e Conformismo di Vecchi," *C.F.*, XII (1933–1934), 191.

57. Dogana, "L'Eredità del Fascismo" *C.F.*, XI (1933), 390–391. Also a quotation from *Totalità* on the need for "heresy."

58. *Roma Fascista,* December 1929.

59. G. Bottai, "Fascismo e Cultura," *C.F.*, VII (1928), 441–443; "Parole al vento. Fascisti si diventa," *C.F.*, XIII (1934–1935), 89–90.

60. *C.F.*, VII (1929), 336.

61. Editorial comment, "Il Problema de Domani," *C.F.*, VII (1929), 429–430.

62. G. Gamberini, "Il Problema di discutere," *C.F.*, VIII (1930), 103–104, and *C.F.*, VII (1929), 379.

63. Agostino Nasti, "Liberta di Discussione e Publica Sicurezza," *C.F.*, VIII (1930), 119; comments in *C.F.*, VI (1928), 342.

64. Ugo de Vita, "Funzioni della gioventu: impiego dei giovani," *C.F.*, XI (1933), 143–144.

65. Giuseppe Bottai, "Funzione della Gioventu," *C.F.*, XI (1933), 81–82; Dogana, "Necessita dei Giovani" *C.F.*, IX (1931), 170 (to avoid routinization, mediocrity).

66. D. Montalto, "La Libertà e i Giovani," followed by comments, *C.F.*, VII (1929), 312–313.

67. Camillo Pellizzi, "Il Problema dell'autorita," *C.F.*, VI (1928), 202–203; Stefano Mario Cutelli, "Il Problema dei Giovani," *C.F.*, VII (1929), 232–234. The problem was also discussed in many other party publications and it was often related to as "a sort of diffuse *malaise* among the more aware elements of fascist youth." "L'elezionismo nella vita del partito," *C.F.*, VI (1928), 302. Ten years later it was recognized that the hierarchic system, which finally and coherently (with fascism) prevailed, "had its costs." Enzo Capaldi, "Il problema dei Capi," *C.F.*, XVIII (1939–1940), 100–102.

68. Agostino Nasti, "Partito Unico e Libertà di Discussione," *C.F.*, VIII (1930), 179–180. Luciano Inganni, "Il problema dei partiti nel Regime Fascista," *C.F.*, VIII (1930), 323–324; Manlio Pompei, "Azione del Partito," *C.F.*, IX (1931), 43; "Fascismo Unitario" (editorial comment), *C.F.*, IX (1931), 161–162.

69. B. Mussolini, "Punti Fermi sui Giovani," *C.F.*, VIII (1930), 43; and "Appunti per il Terzo Tempo," *C.F.*, VII (1929), 367; Circular of the Secretary of the Party on discussions within the Young Fascist organization, *C.F.*, IX (1931), 66. The topic was commented by the major press.
70. *Foglio d'Ordini del PNF*, November 1934.
71. Giuseppe Bottai, in *C.F.*, May 15, 1934.
72. *Il Secolo Fascista*, May 1934, p. 145.
73. Agostino Nasti, "Ancora dei Littoriali," *C.F.*, XII (1933–1934), 212.
74. Ugo d'Andrea, "I Littoriali della Cultura e dell'Arte," *C.F.*, XIII (1934–1935), 277–279; Ugo Manauta, "I Littoriali," *Lavoro Fascista*, May 1, 1935.
75. *Corriere Padano*, March 14, 1935.
76. Agostino Nasti, "Orientamenti dei Giovani," *C.F.*, XVII (1938–1939), 185–186; Editorial Comment, "I Littoriali dell'anno XVIII," *C.F.*, XVIII (1939–1940), 194–195; Vincenzo Buonassini, "Dopo i Littoriali dell'anno XVIII," *C.F.*, XVIII (1939–1940), 230–231.
77. See especially, Humanitas, *op. cit.;* Antonini, *op. cit.;* Preti, *op. cit.;* Amendola, *op. cit.;* Curiel, *op. cit.;* Also, R. Rossi, "Come si formo nei Littoriali una opposizione giovanile al regime," *Incontri*, Nos. 1 and 2 (1954).
78. Amendola, *op. cit.;* Zangrandi, *op. cit.;* Curiel, *op. cit.;* (Eugenio Curiel, a member of the clandestine Communist Party, became director of a provincial organ of the GUF).
79. Gianni Granzotto, "La formazione di una classe dirigente," *C.F.*, XV (1936–1937), 254–256; Enzo Capaldo, "Classe dirigente e corsi di preparazione política," *C.F.*, XV (1936–1937), 370–373; Editorial comment, "Il Centro di Preparazione Politica," *C.F.*, XVI (1937–1938), 82–83.
80. Giuseppe di Nardi, "L'ordinamento dei corsi di preparazione politica," *C.F.*, XVI (1937–1938), 4–5.
81. This section on Spain must be considered as a first approach to a complex problem. It is based on very limited sources—documentary material and interviews—and lacks the first-hand knowledge of the society that provides a firmer basis to the Italian case study.
82. A particularly enlightening interpretation of the social and political context of the emergence of fascism in Spain is provided by Dionisio Ridruejo, *Escrito en España* (Buenos Aires: Losada, 1964), especially pp. 53–91. Ridruejo, a former prominent member of the Falange, gives a detailed analysis of the relevant social classes, in particular the elites, the middle classes, and the proletariat. The description of the specific conditions leading to the mobilization of the middle classes (what he calls *el macizo de la raza*, the "rock of the race") is very illuminating. See also Stanley Payne, "Spain," in Hans Rogger and Eugene Weber, eds. *The European Right* (Berkeley: University of California Press, 1966); Hugh Thomas, "Spain," in S. J. Woolf, ed., *European Fascism* (London: Weidenfeld and Nicholson, 1968); Herbert L. Matthews, *The Yoke and the Arrows* (New York: George Braziller, Inc., 1958); Stanley G. Payne, *Falange* (Stanford: Stanford University Press, 1961); Hugh Thomas, "L'Eroe nella Stanza Vuota" in *Dialoghi del XX: Fascismo Internazionale, 1920–1945*, No. 1 (April 1967). (This is the Italian edition of the journal, *Contemporary History*.)
83. According to Ridruejo, *op. cit.*, though the military assumed a leading role in the *alzamiento*, the rebellion against the Republic would not have been successful without the mobilization of the middle classes.
84. That during the first decade after the outbreak of the Civil War the totalitarian components were rather important is acknowledged by Linz, *op. cit.* For a detailed chronology of this evolution after 1945 see "El Largo Camino" in Ignacio Fernandez and José Marynez et al., *España Hoy* (Paris: Ruedo Ibérico, 1963). (This is a special issue of the journal *Ruedo Ibérico*.)

85. The SEU was created at the end of October, 1933, less than one month after the organization of the Falange. It was really the same act. See David Jato, *La Rebelión de los Estudiantes* (Madrid: CIES, 1953), p. 62.
86. Statute of the Falange Españo la Tradicionalista y de las JONS, in Clyde L. Clark, *The Evolution of the Franco Regime* (Private Publication of the U.S. State Department, n.d.), Appendix, I, 67ff. Except where otherwise indicated all factual information on youth organization and the party (up to 1950) is drawn from this source. Clark's book consists of two volumes plus three volumes of documents.
87. Payne, *op. cit.,* pp. 208–211; Jato, *op. cit.,* p. 308.
88. Clark, *op. cit.,* I, 403.
89. Jato, *op. cit.* p. 313.
90. Antoniano Peña, "Veinticinco Años de Luchas Estudiantiles" in *Horizonte Español 1966* (Paris: Ruedo Ibérico, 1966), II, 170–171.
91. *Ibid.*
92. Payne, *op. cit.,* p. 221.
93. The more important institutional additions were the so-called *Fuero de los Españoles* (Spaniards' Bill of Rights), municipal elections, law of succession, declaration of monarchy as the form of the Spanish state, and the referendum. But this "liberalization" did not involve any real change in terms of individual rights, political freedom, and democratic participation. Municipal elections and referendums were a farce (96 per cent "yes" for the regime). The repression continued with few changes. The influence of the Falange, which seemed to diminish, was really increasing. For instance, the new Law of Primary Education, passed in 1945, defined as its primary goal infusion of the fundamental principles of the "Movement" into young children. Clark, *op. cit.,* II, 504ff.
94. Ridruejo, *op. cit.,* p. 216.
95. Report of Pedro Lain Entralgo, as Rector of the Universidad Central (quoted in Ridruejo, *op. cit.,* pp. 214–215). For the meaning of "availability," see n. 2.
96. Peña, *op. cit.,* p. 171. This observation is confirmed by an orthodox Falangist, Jorge Jordana Fuentes, who in 1952 recognized that the students perceived the SEU as the "policeman of the university." Appendix in Jato, *op. cit.,* p. 342.
97. The review of the Spanish youth press had been limited to two magazines: *Alférez,* of Catholic hispanic orientation, (published from 1947 to 1949) and *Alcalá,* published by SEU in Madrid and Barcelona (the only period considered here is the 1952–1955 period).
98. M. J. Llanos L. J., "Balance de una Generación," in *Alférez* (March 1947), A. A. Miranda, "Figuras del Patriotismo," and J. I. Tena Ibarra, "Llamada de Servicio," *Alférez* (April 1947); Gambrinus, "Hegemonía del Pacato y otras notas," and J. M. García Escudero, "La Generación de los Hermanos Menores," *Alférez,* September 1947.
99. Luis Legaz y Lecambra, "Sobre los Deberes del Universitario," *Alcalá* (August–October 1953); J. A. Garcia Madariaga, "En Alcalá no hay Jóvenes," *Alcalá* (March 1952); J. Castex Anaya, "Así es nuestra generación Universitaria," *Alcalá* (March 1952); Gonzalo Saenz de Buruaga, "Juventud Española," *Alcalá* (January 1955).
100. Gambrinus, "La crítica como colaboración," *Alférez* (July 1947); Gambrinus, "La Juventud como obligación," *Alférez* (August 1947).
101. J. M. de Llanos, C.J., "Quién tiene la culpa?" *Alcalá* (November 1952); "Lección del Rector de Salamanca," *Alcalá* (March 1953); M. Ortuño "El Papel de los jóvenes" *Alcalá* (January 1954); Buruaga, *op. cit.;* Buruaga, "Algo Más sobre la Juventud Española," *Alcalá* (March 1955).
102. R. F. Carvajal, "Educación y Casticismo," *Alférez* (June 1947); Gambrinus, "La crítica como colaboración"; Gambrinus, "La Juventud como obligación";

"Puntos de Política" (editorial, September 1947); "Profesión Política" (editorial, December 1947); G. Sanz de Buruaga (article quote in n. 98).

103. *Alférez* (editorial, December 1947); *Alcalá*, J. J. Fuente (National Chief of the SEU), "Lo que Esperamos de 1955" (January 1955).

104. Ridruejo, *op. cit.* p. 219; Pena, *op. cit.* pp. 178–179; Payne, *op. cit.*, p. 248.

105. In the cabinet formed in July, 1951, Franco used three distinct components designed to neutralize each other: the resurrected Falangists neutralized the monarchists, and the liberals performed the same function with regard to the Falangists. "But this political game—really designed to support Franco—had the consequence of facilitating the politization of the University and the emergence of new political generations opposed to the regime." See *El Largo, op. cit.*, p. 24.

106. In 1956–1957 the Falange made its last attempt to exercise a decisive influence in the reshaping of Spain during and after Franco. These attempts, which in the intention of some Falangists would have produced a democratization of the regime and a turn to the left, were in fact limited to establish some form of constitutional monarchy, with limited popular participation. However, even this more modest reform was rejected, the Falangist ministry's Arrese had to resign, and the new government nominated in 1957 practically eliminated the Falange's influence. See Payne, *op. cit.*, pp. 253–267; Ridruejo, *op. cit.*, pp. 117–119.

107. Despite the periodical recurrence of highly publicized measures of "liberalization," freedom of the press, individual political rights and freedom of association are not recognized by the existing laws, nor by the actual practice of police controls and repression. Though some of the political crimes are now under civil jurisdiction, military jurisdiction is still applied to a wide range of actions considered "against the security of the state." Fines, obligation to live in assigned cities or places, arrests, and long prison sentences are the risks normally confronted by political opponents, not to mention the serious problems created by economic and social forms of ostracism affecting them. Even death penalties have been applied in recent years. For the years 1958 to 1961 the Bulletin of the European Committee for Amnesty reported that some 600 persons had been condemned by the special political tribunals, with an average of five-year sentences. This is only a small fraction of all the people arrested, confined, fined, or obliged to exile abroad. See "El Largo Camino"; "El Imperio de la Ley en España"; "Terrorismo"; "1963: Represión y Terrorismo"; "Julian Grimau: el muerto de la paz"; in the two volumes of I. Fernandez de Castro and J. Martinez, *España Hoy, op. cit.* See also an interesting account of the repression and life in the Spanish prisons by L. Ramirez, *Nuestros Primeros Veinticinco Años* (Ruedo Ibérico, 1964). The drastic restrictions introduced in January, 1969, abolishing all the liberalizing measures of the last decade, including parts of the Fuero de los Españoles, were a hard reminder of the fascistic nature of the regime. Their proclaimed "temporary" duration does not modify this meaning.

108. Peña, *op. cit.* p. 175.

109. *Ibid.*, p. 179. As in the Italian case the historical opposition, the *emigrés* and, with some exceptions, pre-Franco parties failed for a long time to recognize the deep changes occurring among the new generations.

110. A distinction is introduced here between "beliefs" and "ideologies." The former are traditional in nature insofar as they belong to a social setting that lacks *controversy*, not because such controversy has been suppressed (the authoritarian or totalitarian case), but because there is a "natural" unanimity created spontaneously by early socialization mechanisms. *Ideologies* are the expression of a climate of controversy, in which individuals are required to make certain choices between conflicting opinions (*ideologies*). Ideologies may appear where

public opinion (defined in terms of the eighteenth century model) does exist. In modern authoritarian or totalitarian society, it is this model which prevails, though the "choice" open to the citizen is a one-way choice, a "forced choice." This theory, based on a particular typology of social action, may be found in Germani, *Política y Sociedad en una Epoca de Transición* (Buenos Aires: Paídos, 1962), chap. 3.

111. It must be noted that the two variables included in the scheme are really *continua*. The division into four or two values is a mere simplification.

112. The case of Portugal gives strong support to the hypothesis of the role of selective emigration in diminishing the internal opposition potential of the youth.

113. See n. 2.

114. This is the case of the Argentinian and the Brazilian present military regimes.

115. Perhaps the current "students' revolution" can be interpreted in terms of a perception of the industrial society (West and East), as a dead end of history.

12

Established Revolution Versus Unfinished Revolution: Contrasting Patterns of Democratization in Mexico and Turkey

‖ *Ergun Özbudun*

The Party of Revolutionary Institutions (PRI) in Mexico and the Republican People's Party (RPP) in Turkey are the prototypes of non-totalitarian modernizing single-party systems which appeared in a great number of new nations in the post-World War II era of decolonization. Similarities between the Turkish and Mexican single-party experiences undoubtedly warrant a comparative study of the two systems, and their differences make such a comparison even more worthwhile for a broader understanding of single-party systems in general.

Turkey and Mexico represent two typical examples of modern tutelary regimes that consciously attempted to modernize their traditional societies and polities largely by means of induced (government-directed) change. In both countries, the tutelary regimes were the products of convulsive national revolutions. In both countries, post-revolutionary order depended on a single-party system, and authority was effectively concentrated in the party leadership. In both countries, a constitutional facade based on liberal democratic norms masked authoritarian operational structures. Ideologically, both Mexican and Turkish single parties were highly nationalistic, strongly anti-clerical, and development-oriented. Under both tutelary regimes, significant social, economic, and political modernization was accomplished. Moreover, this was done without resort to totalitarianism or to any rigid ideological framework. In fact, a high degree of pragmatism and ideological flexibility characterized both systems. In both countries, the military played a dominant role in the early phases of the revolution; but gradually, it lost its political power to the new civilian political institutions created by the revolution. Finally, both countries moved, in due course and in their own ways, toward a more pluralistic political system and a greater distribution and reciprocity of power.

If these similarities between the two single-party systems are significant, so are the differences. In Mexico, after a decade of bloody civil war in which more than a million Mexicans lost their lives, the problem of peaceful succession has finally been surmounted. The last serious threat of violence occurred in 1935 when ex-president and one-time strong man Calles moved unsuccessfully against President Cárdenas; since Cárdenas, Mexico has been a post-revolutionary society. In Turkey, by contrast, fifteen years of multi-party rule came to an abrupt end with the military coup of 1960. The civilian governments that followed the military interregnum of 1960–1961 were faced with two open, and a number of abandoned, attempts at coup. The last four Mexican presidents have been civilians, whereas the last two Turkish presidents have been military commanders. Thus, while the post-revolutionary political system of Mexico displayed a high degree of stability based on widely shared goals of the Revolution, the past two decades of multi-party rule in Turkey witnessed the weakening of the Kemalist unity and the resurrection of severe pre-Kemalist intra-elite conflict, which produced "simultaneous stagnation and instability." [1]

The different paths the two revolutions have followed are also reflected in the different fates of the two single parties. In Mexico, the existence and reasonably free operation of opposition parties have not challenged seriously the dominant position of the PRI so far. In each presidential election that the PRI has contested, it has won a minimum of 75 per cent of the ballots cast. In the last two Mexican presidential elections of 1958 and 1964, the party's candidates, Adolfo López Mateos and Gustavo Díaz Ordaz, polled respectively 90.4 per cent and 89 per cent of the popular vote, compared to about 10 per cent of the *Partido de Acción Nacional* (PAN), the strongest opposition party.[2] Distribution of seats in the national Congress also attests to the domination of the PRI. In the 1958 elections, the PRI obtained 153 out of 162 seats (94.5 per cent) in the Chamber of Deputies and all the seats in the Senate. Indeed, the PRI felt so secure about its virtual monopoly that a recent constitutional amendment deliberately sought to assure the opposition parties an increased representation in the legislature. Under this change, any national party gaining 2.5 per cent of the total vote for the Chamber of Deputies would receive a minimum of five deputies, with additional seats for each additional 0.5 per cent of the vote, up to a maximum of twenty seats. Thus, in the 1964 elections, only two candidates of the PAN and one of the *Partido Popular Socialista* (PPS) were elected to the Chamber by direct popular vote, and the

new electoral scheme entitled the minor parties to party deputies as follows: PAN, 18; PPS, 9; and PARM (*Partido Auténtico de la Revolución
Mexicana*), 5.[3]

By contrast, the Turkish single party, the RPP, lost power to its major
rival, the Democratic Party (DP), in the first genuinely free general election it contested in 1950 and has been reduced to an almost permanent minority party since then. It received 40 per cent of the votes in 1950, 35.3
per cent in 1954, 40.9 per cent in 1957, 36.7 per cent in 1961, and 28.75
per cent in 1965. Throughout this period, the RPP has been out of power,
except for the years 1961–1964 when it participated in the coalition governments. Between 1950 and 1960, the DP ruled the country with comfort-
able electoral and parliamentary majorities (only in the 1957 election did
the percentage of its popular majority fall a little below 50 per cent). Although the DP was dissolved by a court order under the military regime
of 1960–1961, its successor, the Justice Party (JP), was able to become a
major partner in the first civilian coalition government that followed the
military interregnum. In 1965, the JP became the governing party of Turkey with a clear popular majority of 53 per cent.

This enormous difference in the present popular strength of one-time single parties provides a good vantage point from which to study and compare
the Turkish and Mexican patterns of political development. Why has the
Mexican PRI been able to retain its domination, while the Turkish RPP
was voted out of office as soon as the Turkish voters obtained an opportunity to do so? What are the sources of strength of the PRI in comparison to
the weaknesses of the RPP? Do these differences reflect a fundamental dis-
similarity in the courses the two revolutions have followed? And what
broader implications can be drawn from this comparative analysis for the
study of single-party systems in general?

One can argue, of course, that democratization of the single-party system in Mexico simply has not gone as far as in Turkey and that the Mexican elections are essentially an "affirmation of authoritarianism." [4] It has
been suggested, for example, that toleration of the opposition parties in
Mexico does not indicate a readiness on the part of the PRI leaders to turn
over power to the opposition should the latter ever become a majority.
Some scholars have even expressed doubts about the true nature of the
Mexican opposition parties, maintaining that the legally recognized parties
(PAN, PPS, PARM) are in fact mere instruments of the governing party,
used and paid by it to provide a democratic facade.[5] Charles Haight, for
example, observed that "over the self-styled and legal opposition parties
there hangs a sizeable cloud of suspicion to the effect that they are merely
a directed opposition, in more or less clandestine relationship with the
government." [6] Whether this is true or not, it is certain that the Mexican
opposition parties are not allowed to depart radically from the established
operating norms of the political system. If they do, "They may find their
political party outlawed, as did General Henriquez Guzman after the 1952

election, or their business hampered by labor difficulties, or themselves in jail, as David Alfaro Sequeiros of the Communist Party did for several years until granted amnesty after the 1964 presidential election." [7]

Now, it is true that the leaders of the present Mexican regime have not so far been confronted with the "acid test" of surrendering power to their opponents after being defeated at the polls (if this is indeed an acid test of democracy). It should also be admitted that the Mexican political system has not yet evolved into a full competitive system, open not only to "loyal" opposition parties but to the extremist ones as well. Nevertheless, this is hardly a convincing explanation of the different patterns of political development in Turkey and Mexico. For one thing, despite the existence of a measure of intimidation and fraud in the early Mexican elections, the overwhelming victories of the PRI certainly cannot be attributed to such electoral manipulations. Martin Needler, for example, observes that "today . . . unfair electoral practices are met with probably no more frequently in Mexico than in the United States, and the PRI gains its victories fairly and squarely." [8] Clarence Senior argued in the same vein that "the basis of the revolutionary victories seems to be the same as that of the Democrats [in the "solid South" of the United States], in spite of fraud, violence, and antiquated voting procedures. Violence is decreasing steadily and a new electoral code which may help reduce electoral skullduggery was recently adopted. The 1940, 1946, 1952, and 1958 federal elections were held with little more trouble than Kansas City or Chicago elections of recent memory." [9]

Similarly, the loyalty of the opposition parties cannot be taken as decisive evidence of the authoritarianism of the Mexican political system. The relatively moderate positions the opposition parties tended to take in recent electoral campaigns are attributable less to their fear of repression than to their desire to capture as large a following as possible. Robert Scott has convincingly argued that the Mexican opposition parties are faced with two alternatives: either they adopt doctrinaire and extreme programs, thus limiting themselves to a very specialized role and a very special clientele, or they move toward the center and resemble the PRI in order to maximize their mass appeal.[10] Furthermore, it should be remembered that the limited range of party competition does not necessarily preclude the possibility of a governmental turnover. After all, the Turkish multi-party system from 1946 to 1960 was an extremely limited one in the sense that both right and left parties (even relatively moderate ones) were excluded from the race, leaving the competition open only to the center parties. Finally, even though extremist tendencies were not given a free hand to organize politically in both countries, freedom of press and of expression has been undoubtedly much greater in Mexico than in Turkey.[11] In short, to explain the continued domination of the RPI in contrast to the electoral failure of the RPP by the more authoritarian methods of the former simply will not do.

In fact, the dominant position of the PRI is due, more than anything else, to its immense popular strength. This, in turn, derives from the party's identification in the popular mind with the widely shared goals of the Mexican Revolution and from the fact that it "represents the policy preferences of the vast majority of Mexicans." [12] But before explaining why and how this has happened in Mexico and has not happened in Turkey, it would be worthwhile to discuss another possible explanation based on the political-cultural characteristics of the two nations.

One recent study of these Mexican characteristics is that by Professor Scott, who argues that the dominant political subculture in Mexico is the *subject* political culture. Scott estimates that about 65 per cent of Mexicans can be classified as *subjects,* as opposed to 25 per cent *parochials* and 10 per cent *participants.* Prevailing subject norms include, for example, dependency, lack of self-esteem, search for miracles, weak ego-image, *machismo* (the cult of masculinity), authoritarianism, and the norm that weakens associational sentiments and inhibits collective action. These subject norms are implanted mostly by pre-adult experiences, but adult workplace experience does little to counter such early authoritarian and anti-social influences. These subject norms, Scott argues, are consistent with the authoritarian operational political structures and inhibit the move toward a more participant political system. "The predominant subject political norms are satisfied by the strong emphasis on effective government output performance made possible by the development of central authority structures." [13]

Qualifications to these findings of Scott are to be found in the study of civic cultures by Gabriel Almond and Sidney Verba, who argue instead that Mexicans display a relatively high level of subjective political competence (that is, orientation to participation), even if such a sense of participation exists mainly on an aspirational level and is unmatched by actual performance. Furthermore, this high level of aspirational political competence is combined with a conspicuously low level of subject competence. "In Mexico," Almond and Verba argue, "the balance between subject and participant orientations is heavily weighted in the direction of the participant." [14] Even if we assume that the Mexican political culture is a typical case of subject political culture, such a cultural pattern cannot be said to preclude categorically the development of an opposition against an authoritarian government. If anything, Turkey seems to be closer to a subject political culture than is Mexico, yet it was in Turkey that the tutelary single-party system came to an end by popular vote, not in Mexico where participatory orientations are considerably more developed.[15]

In discussing the different fates encountered by the Turkish and Mexican single parties, I shall now concentrate on three main variables: the pattern of interests, the pattern of power, and the pattern of policy.[16] These variables are certainly interrelated, but for the sake of convenience, I shall examine them separately.

The Pattern of Interests

In the study of revolutions, the most pertinent questions to be asked are perhaps the following: Who led the revolution? Who provided its mass support? Who ultimately benefited from it? Against whom was it directed? What were the interests (or rather the alliances of interests) involved? Seen from these perspectives, the Turkish and Mexican revolutions clearly differ from each other.

Although opinions vary as to the social bases of the Mexican Revolution, probably the most convincing answer will be that the Revolution was initiated by the urban middle class, and its crucial mass support was provided by the peasants and urban workers. In fact, under the Díaz dictatorship (1876–1910), both the intellectual and commercial elements of the growing urban middle class were denied easy access to top positions in their respective fields, administration and business. The former was dominated by the dictator's personal favorites and by a small group of technocrats known as the *científicos,* while the latter came to be increasingly dominated by foreigners. Thus, the businessmen's demand that "Mexico be returned to the Mexicans" was added to the quest for political participation of the urban intellectuals.[17] The old regime, which was based on a coalition of the landed aristocracy, the church, and the army, conspicuously lacked the adaptability to accommodate the demands of such urban middle sectors.

An equally important component in the revolutionary coalition was the crucial support of the peasants and urban industrial workers. One reason for this support may be seen in the policies followed by the old regime, especially under Díaz. Although the Díaz government heavily stressed modernization and material progress, this was by no means progress in an egalitarian sense. Under Díaz, wealth was concentrated in ever fewer hands while the poverty of the rural masses increased. In Charles Haight's words, "The economic condition of the majority of the Mexican people in 1910 was poor and lowly to a degree that was remarkable even for a country famous for centuries as providing a classic example of social inequality." The concentration of land ownership in the hands of an exceedingly small minority was carried "to heights that had few equals in the history of any other epoch or any other nation." [18] Thus, "by 1910 approximately 97 per cent of the total arable land of the country had fallen into the hands of approximately 835 families." [19] This continuous absorption of small estates by *hacienda* owners not only robbed the small farmers of their properties but also reduced them (as rural wage workers) to virtual slavery or feudal servitude (*peonismo*) in their relationships with the great landed proprietors. The *hacendado*'s monopoly of land was also supplemented by a monopoly of force. Díaz had constituted an elite corps of mounted police, known as the *rurales,* the main function of which was "to hunt down any-one who threatened the rights of property in the countryside." [20] Thus, with the backing of the *rurales,* and eventually of the army, the *hacendado* could with impunity punish or even kill the recalcitrant *peon.*[21]

The peasants' plight was largely shared by the urban proletariat. Despite considerable headway made in industrialization under Díaz, the emergent class of industrial workers was forced to work at a subsistence level. Strikes were repressed by the army with extreme brutality. As L. Vincent Padgett notes, little of the new prosperity engendered by industrialization "touched the workers of the factories, the mines, and the railroads. The urban day laborers and the peons and Indians of the countryside continued in the same miserable circumstances. There was the same institutionalized exploi-tation of workers through the company store, impossibly low wages, and the long work day. Stratification was made more rigid by use of foreigners as skilled workers, technicians, and managers." [22] This condition of per-sonal and economic servitude that bound factory workers to their employ-ers, known as *fabriquismo,* was certainly among the causes of the Mexican Revolution.[23]

Thus, the Mexican Revolution from its earliest years found peasants and workers among its most ardent supporters. The famous revolutionary motto *tierra y libertad* (land and liberty) characteristically combined the middle class's desire for liberty with the peasants' yearning for land, sym-bolizing the revolutionary alliance between these two classes. It is true that the urban middle-class elements in the revolutionary coalition did not origi-nally have much interest in land reform. For example, Francisco Madero, "the Apostle of the Revolution" and the first revolutionary president, had barely included land reform in his platform. But the peasants made it clear that they wanted *both* land and liberty. Thus, in 1915, even such a conservative revolutionary as Carranza, himself a large landholder and a former senator under Díaz, had to issue an agrarian reform decree not dissimilar to the proposals of the radical Zapata and to grant the funda-mental demands of the organized labor. This was a clear indication of the fact that the contribution of the peasants and workers to the revolutionary cause was simply too great to be ignored.[24]

Workers and peasants not only played a crucial role in the formative years of the Mexican Revolution, but they also remained active partici-pants in the revolutionary coalition after the violent, civil war phase of the Revolution ended in 1920. On several critical occasions they put their weight behind the men and the programs that were more representative of their group interests, and in each of these cases their intervention seems to have changed the course of events. For example, in 1923 three generals (Sanchez, Estrada, and Adolfo de la Huerta),

disappointed by Obregón's choice of Calles to succeed him as Presi-dent . . . gathered the greater part of the army to their cause, which seemed certain to be victorious. . . . But then unusual things began to happen; organized *ejidatarios* cut Estrada's communication lines, sabotaged his supplies, and even formed diminutive armies which attacked his rear. It soon became clear that Estrada's army was not going to be able to "hold" rural areas at all; then President Obregón marshalled a new army out of a few detachments of troops that had remained loyal, volunteers from the *ejidos,* and "labor battalions" of Mexico City union members, took to the field, and defeated Estrada. . . . For this result, Mexico had to thank the labor battalions and especially the organized peasants. So labor and the *ejidatarios* gave substance to their claim for an equal voice with the military in the councils of the Revolution.[25]

A similar, although this time unarmed, confrontation took place in 1936, when ex-President Calles broke with President Cárdenas and threatened him openly. Then "a so-called Proletarian Defense Committee rallied to the side of President Cárdenas immediately." This show of organized strength was one of the principal factors that forced Calles to retire from politics and leave the country.[26]

It would appear from this discussion that peasants and urban workers constituted an integral element of the Mexican Revolution. Together with the urban middle class, they were clearly the revolutionary forces in the Mexican society. The revolutionary alliance between the middle class and the lower classes determined the present power structure and the pattern of policy of Mexico. Indeed, it seems that this is the only type of alliance that makes possible the emergence of a political system that is at once stable, progressive, and democratic—certainly a very rare combination in developing countries. Most of the fundamental differences between the Turkish and Mexican patterns of political development can, I think, be explained by the different nature of the revolutionary coalitions in these two countries.

The Turkish Revolution, like the Mexican, was led by the urban middle class. However, while the Mexican Revolution was purely a domestic event, the Turkish Revolution was, at the same time, a war of national independence. As such, it was not directed against a particular social class, but against foreign enemies and their Turkish collaborators. After the Greek invasion had been repulsed, the revolutionary leaders, in their efforts to secularize the country, moved against the religious establishment whose sources of support were widely diffused throughout all social strata. Consequently, the Turkish Revolution always remained a political, rather than social, revolution; and it did not produce such clearly identifiable coalitions of interests as did the Mexican Revolution.

This does not mean, however, that there was no discernible pattern of interest-coalition in the Turkish Revolution. Very briefly, this coalition was between the military-bureaucratic-intellectual elite at the national level and many small town and rural notables at the local level. Frederick Frey has shown, in his excellent study of the Turkish political elite, that the military-bureaucratic element was dominant at the level of national legislature during the single-party era, but that there was also in the Assembly a sizable group of locally based deputies.[27] This finding probably reflects accurately the relative strength of the two distinct elements in the RPP coalition: the national military-bureaucratic elite was the major partner, but the local notables, most of whom were undoubtedly large landholders, also wielded considerable influence. This influence was naturally greater at the local level than at the national level. Thus, although the owners of large estates constituted a relatively small contingent in the National Assembly, they generally dominated local governments and the local levels of the RPP apparatus.

This ruling coalition denied the lower strata of the Turkish society (namely, the incipient urban proletariat and the great mass of agricultural workers and smallholders) any effective share of political power. Herein lies the most basic difference between the Turkish and the Mexican revolutions: Unlike those in Mexico, the Turkish peasants and workers did not become an integral part of the Revolution; and while the landed aristocracy was effectively broken by the Mexican Revolution, their nearest Turkish counterparts, the local notables, became influential, even if junior, partners in the governing coalition of Turkey. In short, while the urban middle class led both revolutions, it allied itself with fundamentally different groups in each country. The difference in the social bases of the revolutionary coalitions set divergent paths for the two revolutions and deeply affected both their power structures and policy outputs. However, before comparing Turkey and Mexico in these terms, it may be worthwhile to explain why the revolutionary middle class in Turkey chose to ally itself with the landed oligarchy instead of with rural and urban lower classes.

This question becomes all the more important in view of the fact that the Turkish military-bureaucratic elite seemed at that time to possess sufficient freedom of action to turn the political revolution into a genuinely social one. It can be argued indeed that this national political elite had been largely independent of the economic elite from the Ottoman times. Unlike some developing countries, the Turkish army and the civilian bureaucracy had no strong ties with the landed oligarchy. Neither this unorganized landed oligarchy nor the incipient business groups were politically strong enough at a national level to make the military-bureaucratic elite an instrument of their class interests. On the contrary, as I have shown elsewhere, the bulk of the Turkish officer corps was (and still is) recruited from the lower middle class and the salaried middle class.[28] Therefore, the alliance between the military-bureaucratic elite and the landed local oligarchy should not be viewed as the inevitable outcome of their identical interests, but as a result of a deliberate and relatively free choice on the part of the former.

This choice was encouraged partly by the circumstances of the Turkish War of Independence and partly by the nature of the "modernization" program the revolutionary leadership envisaged for Turkey. The local nobility had, on the whole, made a significant contribution to the War of Independence. In many parts of the country, the local notables had formed the nucleus of the local branch of the "Defense of Rights Association," which was the political arm of the nationalist movement. Thus, the RPP, which was based on the already existing organization of the Defense of Rights Association, continued to reflect the wartime alliance between the national elite and the landed local nobility. But perhaps a still more significant factor in that alliance was the nature of the Kemalist conception of modernization. Modernization (or Westernization), as was understood by the RPP leadership, involved mainly the adoption of Western political and cultural institutions with no radical change in the social structure. The local nobility, being relatively well-educated and exposed to Western civilization, was more likely to support such a program than the more traditionally oriented peasant masses, provided that the Revolution did not touch the sources of their local power. Thus, an implicit tradeoff materialized between the two groups. The local nobility supported the modernization program of the national military-bureaucratic elite, in return for which it was allowed to retain its land, status, and local influence, as evidenced in the conspicuous absence of any real land reform under the Republican governments.[29]

The main losers in this tradeoff were the peasants. They also had fought heroically in the War of Independence, even if they were motivated less by truly nationalistic feelings than the desire to defend their homeland and religion against "infidel" invaders and to save the Caliph from the hands of the enemy (the latter remained the officially proclaimed goal of the nationalist movement until the final victory). But the peasants did not represent an articulate and organized force to press their demands for land and better standards of living on the revolutionary government. Perhaps they were not even aware of such a possibility. It is clear that the Turkish Revolution did not have the peasant leaders and heroes of the Mexican Revolution, such as Zapata and Villa. Furthermore, when the foreign enemy was defeated and the national leadership began to launch its secularizing reforms, the tradition-bound peasant masses became more apathetic, if not openly hostile. Their failure to grasp the meaning of and to support the Westernization program pushed them further away from the locus of political power.

Here again we find an important difference between Turkey and Mexico. In pre-revolutionary Mexico, the church had become an object of popular hatred because of its strong ties with the politicians of the old regime and with the aristocratic land system. The Mexican church not only had been "the country's largest single landowner and largest single banker" but also preached submission to the civil authorities, to the *hacendado,* the factory owner, and the mine superintendent.[30] Therefore, the anti-clerical attitude and secularizing reforms of the Mexican Revolution had genuine popular support. By contrast, Islam has never been such an oppressive force in

Turkey, and while the Sultan-Caliph and the heads of the official religious hierarchy in Istanbul collaborated with the occupation powers, many local religious leaders in Anatolia strongly supported the nationalist movement. The First Grand National Assembly (1920–1923) contained a large group of clerics (at least 17 per cent of all deputies).[31] Thus, the lack of support among the Turkish peasants for the secularist policies of the Republican governments is quite understandable from their own point of view. But it is equally clear that this was one of the factors which led the national leadership, thoroughly determined to secularize the society, to stretch its hand to the local nobility instead of attempting to enlist peasant support.

Our discussion so far has shown that the Mexican and Turkish revolutions differ from each other in terms of their social bases. The Mexican Revolution carries many characteristics of the peasant revolutions, while the Turkish Revolution is much closer to the model of the "revolution from above," although admittedly neither of them is a pure or ideal type.[32] Let us now consider how this difference has affected the pattern of power and the pattern of policy in each country.

The Pattern of Power

The structure of the Mexican PRI clearly reflects the combination of social forces which made the Revolution.[33] Before examining the present "sector organization" of the PRI, however, it will be necessary to say a few words on the historical development of the party. Briefly, three phases can be discerned in the development of the Mexican "official" party. It was formed in 1929 by the outgoing President Plutarco Calles to meet the crisis of presidential succession. From 1929 through 1937 it was known as the National Revolutionary Party, PNR (*Partido Nacional Revolucionario*), and was personally dominated by Calles until the accession of Cárdenas to the presidency in 1934. "Unlike its official successors, the original PNR was not highly centralized; instead it was an amalgam of local political machines and of various agricultural, labor, and other interest associations, backed by the silent but ever-present force of the military." [34] Although agrarian and labor groups were included in this loosely organized political apparatus, it was not before the consolidation of power by Cárdenas that the foundations of the present sector organization were laid. During the presidential term of Cárdenas, the party was reorganized on a functional rather than a geographical basis, under the name of the Party of the Mexican Revolution, PRM (*Partido de la Revolución Mexicana*). In this second phase of its development (1937–1946), which may appropriately be called the period of "corporate centralism," the party's structure was divided into four functionally based "sectors"—agricultural, labor, popular, and military. Under this scheme, the party's candidates were to be apportioned among the sectors before each state or national election, except the presidential one.

The sector organization or, in actual practice, the sector's leadership, then named individual candidates for the offices allotted to it. The individuals so nominated then were supported in the campaign and at the polls by the combined efforts of all four sectors. . . . Presidential nominations also reflected a corporative tendency. Selection of the revolutionary party's candidate at the national nominating convention required the support of a majority of the sectors, at first three of the four and later, when the military sector had been dissolved, two of the three sectors.[35]

In this corporate structure, each sector had its own hierarchy reaching down to the state and local levels. The agricultural sector, represented by the *Confederación Nacional Campensina* (CNC) where all *ejido* farmers were automatically enrolled, was based on local peasant leagues. Similarly, the basic labor sector unit was the local union (or confederation of local unions), and for the popular sector the local political association. This organizational pattern remained almost unchanged until 1946, with the exception that the military sector was dissolved in 1940 and those officers who wished to stay active in the politics affiliated themselves with the popular sector.

Starting from the mid-1940s, a third phase in the life of the official party (having changed its name to that of the *Partido Revolucionario Institucional,* or the PRI) can be discerned. This phase involved attempts, especially by the middle-class elements of the party, to put an end to sector political power. Opponents of the sector organization argued that the system could neither accommodate many interest groups, which remained outside the party sectors, nor facilitate popular participation in the decision-making process. Consequently, party rules were changed in 1946, and while the three sectors were kept as basic organizational divisions of the party, party primaries were substituted for the sector designation of the candidates, thus stripping the sectors from the main source of their political power. However, the new nominating system did not last long. Faced with increasing intraparty conflict and great labor dissatisfaction with the reorganization, the party leadership had to restore the nominating powers of the sector organizations in 1950. The sector system persists today in a slightly modified form adopted by the 1960 party rules, which tended to increase the power of the party's own hierarchy at the expense of the sector organizations.[36]

Much had been, and can be, said for and against the corporate organization of the PRI. It has been maintained, for example, that this organizational pattern tended to discourage popular participation in politics. It may also be true that the dual representative-administrative role of the sector leaders sometimes led them to neglect their representative function and to demonstrate a lack of loyalty to the organizations which originally gave them political power.[37] Furthermore, the corruption of the sector leaders cannot be checked easily, since their position as the head of a particular interest association is strengthened by the position they simultaneously occupy in the party hierarchy.[38]

However, I believe that the sector system, even with all its shortcomings, did not discourage but encouraged popular participation in politics (if by "popular" participation we do not exclusively mean "middle-class" participation). The corporate structure of the party gave an incentive to the sector organizations to conduct recruiting drives, because the more members the organization had, the greater its bargaining power within the party. This led to a marked expansion in the proportion of the population represented when decisions were made.[39] Through sector organization, workers and peasants obtained a direct voice in the highest party councils. They could even dominate these councils, at least numerically, if they chose to act together. To this should be added the moral satisfaction and the sense of political competence the Mexican workers and peasants received from belonging to the official party. As Professor Scott commented, "to many politically aware Mexicans, membership in a farm organization, a labor union, or a 'popular' organization is tantamount to membership in the revolutionary party that governs the country; for most, this is a satisfactory solution to the problem of political action." [40] In short, the corporate structure of the party has favored the underprivileged groups, namely the peasants and the workers. The main thrust for the abolition of the sector system came, therefore, from the middle-class elements; conversely, the loudest objection to this change was voiced by the labor sector, leading to the break with the party by Vicente Lombardo Toledano, a prominent labor leader, and by some labor groups in 1946.[41]

However, the influence wielded by the agricultural and labor groups through sector organization should not conceal the growing importance of the middle sectors in the PRI. Especially in the past two decades the popular sector, the representative of the middle sectors, has been becoming stronger and stronger in the revolutionary coalition, and gradually changing the "collectivist, proletarian orientation" of the party under Cárdenas.[42] The popular sector (*La Confederación Nacional de Organizaciones Populares,* CNOP) is clearly overrepresented in the national and state governments. "By the latter 1950s its membership in Congress and other elective posts roughly doubled the highest figure from any other organized sector of the Revolutionary Coalition." [43] In 1955, a full 62.9 per cent of the PRI candidates for the Chamber of Deputies were middle-class professionals. Thus, Scott observes that "for all its early amorphism . . . today the urban middle class plays an important role, probably an increasingly important one, in Mexican politics. . . . In spite of its relatively small numbers . . . the Mexican middle class very nearly equates in political power with the mass farm and labor interests combined, particularly as most of the bureaucracy and leadership of the functional interest associations representing these interests, as well as the government bureaucracy, come from middle-class rather than working-class ranks." [44]

The growing influence of the middle class in the revolutionary coalition has, no doubt, significantly affected the policies followed by recent Mexican governments, giving them a more centrist character. But the other partners in the coalition, the peasants and the workers, have by no means been reduced to an insignificant role. The present power structure of Mexico reflects a relative balance between the interests of these three classes. The corporate structure of the party appears to have contributed to the maintenance of this balance by consciously organizing the masses and thereby preventing a complete domination by the middle sectors.

In contrast, the Turkish single party, the RPP, deliberately chose to remain a cadre party, an elite organization. Indeed, the structure of the RPP reminds one of the European liberal parties rather than the twentieth century totalitarian and authoritarian single parties.[45] The party hierarchy was dominated by the military-bureaucratic-intellectual elite at the national level and by the landed local nobility at the local level.[46] Interestingly, the RPP leadership made no notable effort to broaden the party's popular base and to enlist the support of the masses, concentrating its attention on the small Westernized elite.

This cadre party structure accorded well both with the composition of the revolutionary coalition and the nature of the party's philosophy, the main components of which were nationalism, rationalism, secularism, anti-clericalism, and eventual political democracy. Thus, philosophically as well as organizationally, the RPP was closer to the liberal tradition than to any type of modern collectivism. As Professor Frey rightly points out, the immediate goal of the revolutionary leaders was not to fundamentally improve the peasant's lot or to grant him increased political power. The Ataturk Revolution exploited the basic bifurcation between the educated elite and uneducated masses, rather than deploring it or immediately attacking it. The essence of the Turkish Revolution is that it concentrated on the extension and consolidation of the precarious beachhead won by the Westernized intellectuals, to make it secure beyond all possible challenge. "It was not . . . a revolution 'from the bottom up'—an attempt to remold the society by starting with the peasant masses." [47]

Given the social bases and the philosophical goals of the Turkish Revolution, no wonder that the RPP remained essentially an elite organization. Though this organizational pattern might have suited the task at hand temporarily, in the long run it proved disastrous for the party. Neglected peasant masses were increasingly alienated from the RPP. Furthermore, neither element in the RPP coalition was in a position to command much popular sympathy. The intellectual elite had been handicapped by the perennial communication gap between the educated, Westernized elite and the uneducated, traditional masses. The authoritarian and extractive methods of the bureaucracy further increased the popular alienation. Thus, in the typical peasant image, the RPP came to be identified with the tax collector and the conscription officer. Many of the landed local notables, on the other hand, were often highly exploitative and despotic in their relations with the peasants; and these local notables gradually lost whatever touch they might have had with the peasant masses as they began to identify with the national elite and to imitate Western ways of life. To summarize, unlike the Mexican, the Turkish single party was totally unsuccessful in organizing and absorbing the peasants and giving them a sense of participation in the political system.

It is interesting to note that the RPP was no more successful in appealing to the business community. Although the official party policy of *étatisme,* which was introduced in the 1930s, was anything but a systematic and coherent leftist approach, it is quite understandable that the businessmen felt more secure with the DP, which openly advocated economic liberalism. The restrictive measures of the World War II years (especially the property tax of 1942) and the reluctance of the party to recruit business elements into significant political roles increased the alienation of this group from the RPP. Thus, the DP, from its inception, found particularly strong support in the business community.

The Pattern of Policy

Some of the most interesting dissimilarities between the single-party governments in Turkey and Mexico are to be found in their policy outputs. Very briefly, the revolutionary Mexican governments have, on the whole, followed policies that assured them the continued support of a large majority of their population, whereas the policies of the Turkish revolutionary regime served mainly the interests of the two partners in the RPP coalition (that is, the military-bureaucratic elite and the local notables) and were met with indifference, if not hostility, by the peasant masses. Obviously, considerations of space preclude the possibility of extending this comparative analysis to the whole range of public policy. I would rather concentrate, therefore, on certain selected policy areas that are particularly germane to the present study, namely land reform and labor legislation.

A glance at the Turkish Constitution of 1924 and the Mexican Constitution of 1917 clearly indicates the magnitude of policy differences in these areas, although constitutional norms are by no means wholly reliable guides to the actual practices. The Turkish Constitution was unmistakably in the tradition of the nineteenth century liberal constitutions. It stressed political democracy and guaranteed the classical civil rights, but maintained a total silence on social rights, which by that time had already found their way into some modern constitutions (for example, the Weimar Constitution). Consequently, whatever has been done by way of social reform under the RPP rule in Turkey has been accomplished not through but in spite of the Constitution. No better evidence than the 1924 Turkish Constitution can be found to demonstrate the lack of interest by the RPP leadership in comprehensive social reforms.

By contrast, the Mexican Constitution of 1917 is commonly referred to as the most socially advanced constitution of its time. Two articles of this document (articles 27 and 123), especially deserve attention. Article 27 vested in the nation the original ownership of the lands and waters contained within the national territory as well as the direct ownership of the mineral resources. The same article specifically provided that necessary measures could be taken to divide up large landed estates. Similarly, Article 123 provided "the most advanced labor code in the world of that day," recognizing the right to unionize, the right to strike, an eight-hour work day, minimum wages, and the right to rest, as well as many other social rights.[48]

The crucial fact, however, is that these constitutional norms were closely conformed to in actual practice. Indeed, land reform in Mexico can be hailed as the single most important achievement of the revolutionary regime. Much has been written on the Mexican land reform, the details of which need not, therefore, be treated at length here.[49] However, a unanimous judgment that emerges out of these analyses is that the Mexican land reform significantly improved the lot of the Mexican peasants. To give a few illustrations, the grand total of land distributed by the end of 1964 amounted to 59.5 million hectares.[50] The number of landowners showed an astronomical increase of 6.750 per cent between 1910 and 1950.[51] In the year 1910, 88.4 per cent of the agricultural population were *peons* and fewer than 60,000 persons or communities could claim any sort of title to land, whereas by 1950 about 3.3 million persons, most of them heads of families, were legally landowners, either as *ejidatarios* or private farmers.[52] Moreover, despite the post-Cárdenas shift of emphasis from the *ejido* system (communal ownership) to small private holding, and occasional slowdowns in the distribution of land, land reform in Mexico has never come to a standstill. Thus, President López Mateos (1958–1964) greatly revitalized the land reform, disproving the more conservative thesis that land susceptible of distribution had become very scarce. Land distributed under the administration of López Mateos amounted to 16 million hectares, or more than one-third of the total amount of land distributed between 1915 and 1958, ranking second only to the Cárdenas period.[53]

Critics of the Mexican land reform frequently assert that the distribution of land under the revolutionary governments could not completely eradicate gross inequalities in land ownership. *Latifundios* (large private estates) still exist in underpopulated regions. Legal provisions limiting the size of the private plots have sometimes been evaded, resulting in "the accumulation of land and the formation of agricultural corporations of a capitalist type." Thus, argues a prominent Mexican author, Pablo González Casanova, "from a form of exploitation close to slavery (*peonage*), the transition is made to capitalist forms of exploitation."[54] On a countrywide basis, Cline observed that very large holdings (over 800 hectares), owned by 0.06 per cent of all the private landholders, amounted to 31.86 per cent of the privately owned rural lands, whereas about 90 per cent of the private landholders owned less than 20 per cent of such lands. The average annual income of private smallholders with plots under 5 hectares (82.5 per cent of all private agriculturists) was only 352 pesos in 1950; at the other extreme, very large holdings mentioned above provided their proprietors with an average annual income of over 1 million pesos.[55] As for the *ejidos,* the critics assert that a large proportion of *ejidatarios* received small parcels (an average of 6.4 hectares apiece), or else land of poor quality. Clarence Senior compares the resultant problem of *minifundia* to "the action of a captain who allows a lifeboat to be loaded far beyond capacity." [56]

Although these criticisms contain a great deal of truth, a realistic appraisal of the Mexican land reform should be based not on what could have ideally been done, but on what has actually been done. Granting the incompleteness and certain other shortcomings of the land reform in Mexico, we can argue with safety that it brought about a substantial improvement in the standards of living of the peasant masses. Mexican peasants not only benefited materially from the distribution of land, but also were saved from a degrading condition of virtual slavery in the hands of the *hacendados.* Even as vehement a critic of the inadequacy of the land reform as P. G. Casanova admits that "the feudal structure of Mexican rural life has disappeared" and "the colonial economy has been broken." [57] Politically, there is no doubt that the land reform played a most important role in assuring the allegiance of the peasants to the revolutionary regime. In fact, as Haight observes, agrarianism "possesses the deepest emotional attraction for the Mexican people, many of whom may be neutral or hostile to other aspects of the [revolutionary] movement." [58]

Land reform is, probably, *the* major policy area where the Turkish and Mexican patterns of development diverge most clearly. In contrast to the Mexican experience, land reform had been absent among the primary goals of the Kemalist regime and, when at last a seemingly sincere effort in this direction was made toward the end of the single-party rule, it met with total failure. It should be admitted, however, that the distribution of land ownership in Turkey has never been so inequitable as in pre-revolutionary Mexico. This was due, in no small part, to the Ottoman land tenure system, which vested the original ownership of land in the state, and limited the rights of the temporarily appointed fief (*timar*) holders to the collection of taxes and the supervision of peasants under their jurisdiction. Therefore, there was no feudal landed aristocracy in the Ottoman Empire, except in certain areas (for example, east and southeast Anatolia) where the authority of the central government could not be effectively extended. However, starting from the seventeenth century, the land tenure system of the Empire degenerated rapidly. Local notables (*âyan*) increased their wealth and power through leasing state-owned lands, which ceased to be assigned to fief holders. "Later, in the eighteenth century, the leases were made for lifetime and prior rights to the leases were granted to the sons of the lessees." [59] Finally, with the adoption of a land law (*Arazi Kanunu*) in

1858, which substituted private ownership of land for state ownership, the local notables were able to concentrate in their hands the legal ownership of large portions of state-owned lands through bribery, usury, tax farming, violence, and intimidation.[60]

Thus, the distribution of land ownership in Republican Turkey has presented far from a balanced picture, even though a majority (72.6 per cent) of farming families hold some land. According to a survey made in 1952, 1.5 per cent of agricultural families hold 24.8 per cent of total cultivated lands, while 75.4 per cent of agricultural families hold only 29.4 per cent of such lands.[61] Similarly, the Second Five Year Development Plan states that 3.71 per cent of the agricultural holdings amount to 33.5 per cent of the total cultivated areas, while 68.78 per cent of the agricultural holdings (under 5 hectares) hold only 24.8 per cent of such areas. Distribution of income among agricultural holdings conforms to the same pattern: while about one-fourth of total agricultural income goes to 68.78 per cent of the agricultural holdings, about one-third of total agricultural income is gained by only 3.71 per cent of such holdings.[62] Finally, village inventory studies conducted in twenty-six provinces by the Ministry of Rural Affairs demonstrated that defects of the land tenure system were more acute in those provinces. Thus, one-third of total cultivated areas is held by only 4 per cent of agricultural families, while about one-third of such families hold only 3 per cent of cultivated areas.[63]

The fact that there was no attempt at land reform in Turkey until 1945 should not be interpreted as a sign of indifference of the Kemalist regime to the plight of the Turkish peasants. Ataturk's famous slogan, "The peasant is the master of the country," cannot be easily dismissed as mere rhetoric. On the contrary, Ataturk unequivocally stated in his last annual message to the Grand National Assembly that he expected the Assembly to pass a land reform bill. "It is an absolute necessity," Ataturk continued, "that every Turkish farming family must own the land on which they work and depend. The construction of the fatherland on solid foundations depends on this principle." Although this recommendation was not acted upon during the early years of the Inonu administration, the time finally seemed to have become ripe for a land reform in the mid-1940s. President Inonu, who already had expressed his support for "radical" agricultural reforms in 1936 before his departure from premiership, became even more impatient with the irresponsible pursuit of profit by large landholders during the World War II years. Finally, in 1945, a Land Reform Bill was submitted to the Assembly by the government.[64] The bill provided that private holdings in excess of 500 hectares (and in regions where land is insufficient, those in excess of 200 hectares) would be expropriated to be distributed to the landless and land-short peasants. A still more radical provision was Article 17, which stipulated that properties cultivated by sharecroppers, tenants, and agricultural workers would be subject to expropriation, irrespective of the size of the plot, to be distributed to those who cultivated it; in such cases, the original landowner would be entitled to retain a piece of his land (a minimum of 5 hectares) three times the size of the plot each grantee received.[65]

National Assembly debates on the proposed bill show, perhaps better than anything else, the nature of the RPP coalition. While the military-bu-reaucratic-intellectual wing of the party strongly supported the measure, representatives of the local nobility vehemently opposed it. The normally docile single-party Assembly witnessed, for the first time, a genuine and pro-tracted controversy. In fact, only Inonu's determined intervention seems to have saved the bill. Reportedly, Inonu was very much involved in the land reform attempt; he personally helped draft the famous Article 17, and let the rumor spread that he would have no connection with a party that did not want to pass the Land Reform Bill. Finally, in June, 1945, the law was passed by the Assembly. But for all practical purposes, it was stillborn. The RPP government did not have the courage to apply its radical provi-sions in the face of strong intraparty and extraparty opposition by the landed oligarchy. In fact, the newly established Democratic Party was suc-cessfully exploiting the land reform issue defending the interests of the large landholders; interestingly, two of the founders of the DP, Adnan Menderes and Refik Koraltan, had voiced strong criticism against the law during the National Assembly debates. And a great number of RPP members were ei-ther openly opposed to the law, or gave it only nominal support. Conse-quently, many provisions of the Land Reform Law remained on paper. In particular, the expropriation provisions concerning private property were barely applied, the area thus expropriated amounting to only 3600 hec-tares. In August, 1945, the Minister of Agriculture and the chief architect of the Land Reform Law, Şevket Raşit Hatipoglu, had to resign and cu-riously enough, was replaced by one of the foremost opponents of the re-form, Cavit Oral, himself a large landowner. The deathblow to the Land Reform Law was finally administered in 1950 when the law of 1945 was amended by the Assembly on the proposal of the RPP government. The amendment abolished Article 17, thereby limiting, in essence, the land to be distributed to that owned by the state and pious foundations (*vakif*). The only land reform attempt of the RPP thus ended in a total failure.[66]

A second policy area that clearly differentiates the Turkish and Mexican single-party systems is labor policy. As indicated above, the Mexican Con-stitution of 1917 laid the basis for a progressive labor policy in Mexico.[67] In return for its active participation in the Revolution, the Mexican labor class was rewarded with Article 123 of the Constitution, which granted al-most all the fundamental demands of organized labor. Moreover, Mexican governments have, on the whole, been consistent in their pro-labor policies. Among the more recent gains of the Mexican working class, one may cite the substantial expansion of the social security program in the 1950s and the adoption of a profit-sharing system in 1962.[68] As Professor Cline has summarized very well, "the modern labor movement formed part of the militant Revolution; therefore, from the outset it has had an honoured place in social and economic circles, assured by Article 123. . . . There has never been an anti-labour Government in Mexico since 1917; conversely, there has never been an anti-Government labour party or programme of consequence." [69]

The Turkish labor class, on the other hand, has not been nearly as lucky as its Mexican counterpart. The first labor law of the Republic, passed in 1936, was modeled on the labor law of fascist Italy. It denied the workers the right to unionize, and declared strikes illegal. It was not until the passage of the Trade Unions Act in 1947 that the right to unionize was recognized, but even this law did not grant the workers the right to strike. Unions were frequently closed, and their leaders jailed, whenever they were suspected of leaning to the left. Trade unionism, naturally, could not flourish under such adverse conditions. Thus, in 1950 there were only eighty-seven labor unions in Turkey with a total membership of 76,000.[70] The Turkish workers had to wait until the 1960s to obtain those social rights (including the right to strike) their Mexican comrades had won almost a half century before.

Conclusion: Contrasting Responses to Democratization

As the present analysis would have already indicated, the continued domination of the PRI in Mexican politics comes chiefly from the fact that the revolutionary governments in Mexico have succeeded in pursuing policies that have brought substantial tangible benefits to the urban and rural working-class masses. Another important element in the popular strength of the PRI is its success in effectively organizing these masses, thereby giving them a strong sense of participation in the political system. Almond and Verba's insightful findings presented in *The Civic Culture* support these arguments. They observed that the Mexicans score high in subjective political, or citizen, competence (that is, perceived ability to affect governmental decisions through political influence), even if few of them actually attempt to exercise such influence. To put it differently, participation does exist at an aspirational level, if not yet in actual practice. The authors of *The Civic Culture* also observed that the Mexicans, although apparently not satisfied with the ways in which policies are implemented (output alienation), display a high level of "system affect," or pride in their political and governmental institutions—in fact, higher than both the Germans and the Italians. And it is precisely this kind of affect that contributes most to democratic stability. As Almond and Verba argued,

> satisfaction with governmental output may lead an individual to support his political system, and high levels of such satisfaction are therefore likely to foster political stability. For long-run stability, on the other hand, a more diffuse sense of attachment—one that is less closely tied to performance—may

be more significant. Satisfaction with political output usually varies with system performance. The more diffuse sense of attachment to the system (or what we have called system affect), though in the long run not unrelated to specific output, can be expected to be a more stable kind of satisfaction.[71]

In view of this situation, we may predict that the PRI will retain its virtual monopoly in the foreseeable future, unless the growing influence on the party of the middle sectors and the consequent rightward shift of policy reach a point where the agricultural and labor sectors (or either of them) may decide to break away—a development which, at the moment, seems rather unlikely, in view of the considerable adaptability demonstrated so far by the PRI leadership.[72]

In contrast to the Mexican experience, the Turkish RPP paid dearly for its lack of concern for the masses, manifested both in its organization and its policies. To some extent, of course, the elitist pattern of power and the essentially conservative social policies of the RPP were dictated by the social structure of the revolutionary coalition in Turkey. But I would strongly argue that this particular type of coalition was not rendered inevitable either by the organic ties between the national military-bureaucratic elite and the local nobility, nor by the inherent conservatism of the former. On the contrary, there is abundant evidence in recent Turkish history that the military-bureaucratic elite is not at all hostile to social reforms and social justice. President Inonu's attempt at land reform, risking to alienate powerful elements in his party, is a good case in point. Supporting evidence may be found in the military coup of 1960, which was carried out by the same national elite and, as I argued elsewhere,[73] was unmistakably oriented to social reforms. Finally, the opening to the left of the RPP in the mid-1960s may be interpreted as a conscious choice made by the bureaucratic-intellectual wing of the party to break away from their old partners, the local nobility, and to search for new allies among the lower classes.

All this leads me to conclude that the national elite's original choice of partner was largely dictated by the kind of reforms they envisaged for Turkey. For a reform program stressing secularism and positivism, their only possible ally would naturally be the relatively Westernized local nobility, not the traditional peasants. But had they given priority to social reforms over secularizing reforms, they could conceivably have built a coalition similar to the Mexican one. The RPP was faced with a similar choice in 1945 between land reform and immediate democratization. In the months following the inauguration of land reform legislation and of a multi-party system, it became readily apparent that both aims could not be achieved simultaneously; for the Democrats were successfully capitalizing on the discontent of the numerically weak but socially, economically, and politically influential local nobility. Consequently, the RPP leadership chose to sacrifice land reform, once again refusing to accord top priority to infrastructural change.

It remains possible, of course, that the recent efforts of the RPP to build a coalition between reform-minded intellectual-bureaucratic elements and the urban-rural lower classes might eventually succeed. In fact, the leftward shift in party policy led to an intense intraparty struggle and to the resignation of many local notables, who formed the Reliance Party in the spring of 1967. However, in the following midterm elections of June, 1968, the overall percentage of the RPP vote did not fall, thus indicating that the party might have compensated for its loss by starting to gain ground among the lower classes. But evidence on this point is inconclusive; and, even if this measured optimism is justified, the RPP is still a long way from power. For one thing, the essentially negative image of the party among the peasantry may take many decades to overcome. Furthermore, the strong influence of the ultraconservative small-town elites (land-owning, commercial or religious) on the bulk of the peasantry will constitute another major obstacle in the party's drive to form a winning coalition.

However, the ambivalent attitudes of the RPP governments toward social questions led to a paradoxical situation, which continues to intrigue almost every observer of Turkish politics. It is true that the DP represented, and greatly benefited by, the legitimate discontent of the masses with the RPP regime. But this popular reaction was canalized and led by groups whose interests were more inherently adverse to those of the masses than were the interests of the military-bureaucratic elite: business groups which were uneasy about the RPP's *étatisme;* many local notables who either had remained outside the RPP or were recently alienated from it because of the attempt at land reform; [74] and, finally, the religious leaders, who had never forgiven the RPP for its secularist policies. (Note the similarity to the sources of support of the Mexican PAN.) Thus, the DP was supported by such strange bedfellows as the rural and urban lower classes on the one hand, and the businessmen and many local notables on the other. Paradoxical though this coalition may seem, it proved to be electorally unbeatable in the last two decades.

Unfortunately for the long-neglected Turkish masses, however, the conservative character of the DP (and now JP) leadership precluded any serious attempt at social reform. Moreover, the frustration of the bureaucratic-intellectual elite both with the conservative policies of their rivals and with their own, seemingly permanent, exclusion from power pose a major threat to the stability of the multi-party regime. After all, the coup of 1960 was, in essence, an outburst of this frustration, and nobody can say for sure that similar outbursts will not happen again. Thus, while in Mexico a revolutionary coalition between the middle and lower classes resulted in a regime that is stable, progressive, and increasingly democratic, the failure of the RPP to create such a coalition seems to have brought Turkey to an impasse marked by instability, conservatism, and potential authoritarianism. Professor Scott has aptly called the Mexican Revolution "the established revolution." If we were to follow the current fashion of qualifying revolutions, the most appropriate term for the Turkish Revolution might well be "the unfinished revolution."

‖ *Notes*

1. Frederick W. Frey, *The Turkish Political Elite* (Cambridge: The MIT Press, 1965), pp. 391ff.
2. Howard F. Cline, *Mexico: Revolution to Evolution, 1940–1960* (London: Oxford University Press, 1962), p. 166, Table 31; L. Vincent Padgett, *The Mexican Political System* (Boston: Houghton Mifflin, 1966), p. 68; Martin C. Needler, "Changing the Guard in Mexico," *Current History*, XLVIII (January 1965), 27.
3. Padgett, *op. cit.,* pp. 80–81; Robert E. Scott, "Mexico: The Established Revolution," in Lucian W. Pye and Sidney Verba, eds., *Political Culture and Political Development* (Princeton: Princeton University Press, 1965), p. 370.
4. For a skeptical view concerning the fairness of Mexican elections, see Philip B. Taylor, Jr., "The Mexican Elections of 1958: Affirmation of Authoritarianism?" *Western Political Quarterly*, XIII (September 1960), 729, 742. Taylor argues that "Mexico seems to be a smoothly running authoritarian regime. . . . In all fairness it must be concluded that the possibility of a truly honest election in Mexico is still very scant indeed."
5. Padgett, *op. cit.,* p. 81.
6. Charles H. Haight, "The Contemporary Mexican Revolution as Viewed by Mexican Intellectuals" (Unpublished Ph.D. diss., Stanford University, 1956), pp. 66–67.
7. Scott, *op. cit.,* pp. 379–380.
8. Needler, *op. cit.,* p. 26.
9. Clarence Senior, *Land Reform and Democracy* (Gainesville: University of Florida Press, 1958), p. 43.
10. Robert E. Scott, *Mexican Government in Transition* (Urbana: University of Illinois Press, 1964), pp. 176–181.
11. Haight, *op. cit.,* pp. 15, 65, 101–109.
12. Needler, *op. cit.,* p. 27. Almond and Verba's cross-national survey also indicated that 85 per cent of the Mexican respondents supported the PRI to some extent (Cited by Scott, "Mexico: The Established Revolution," p. 333, n. 3).
13. Scott, "Mexico: The Established Revolution," *passim;* quotation is from p. 389.
14. Gabriel A. Almond and Sidney Verba, *The Civic Culture* (Boston: Little, Brown, 1965), *passim;* quotation is from p. 364.
15. Frey, for example, compares the subjective political competence (perceived political efficacy) of the Turkish peasants with the similar data on Mexico presented in *The Civic Culture*. Turkish peasants score higher than the Mexican respondents in local efficacy, but lower in national efficacy. Furthermore, the use of groups to influence the decisions of local and national governments is an almost unknown strategy to Turkish peasants. Thus, as opposed to 20 per cent to 28 per cent of Mexicans, only 1 per cent of the Turkish villagers said they would enlist others in their efforts to influence the government, an overwhelming majority preferring to act alone. It should be noted, however, that the data presented in *The Civic Culture* were collected only in towns of over 10,000 inhabitants, whereas the Turkish data concerned only peasants. See Frederick W. Frey, "Five Nations Plus One: Comparative Survey Research on Political

Efficacy" (Paper delivered at the Annual Convention of the American Association for Public Opinion Research, Excelsior Springs, Mo., May 1964).

16. For this framework of analysis, see Samuel H. Beer, "The Analysis of Political Systems," in Samuel H. Beer and Adam B. Ulam, eds., *Patterns of Government: The Major Political Systems of Europe* (New York: Random House, 1962), pp. 3–68.

17. John J. Johnson, *Political Change in Latin America: The Emergence of the Middle Sectors* (Stanford: Stanford University Press, 1958), pp. 128–131; Raymond Vernon, *The Dilemma of Mexico's Development: The Roles of the Private and Public Sectors* (Cambridge: Harvard University Press, 1963), pp. 54–55; Haight, *op. cit.,* pp. 313–320; Scott, *Mexican Government in Transition,* pp. 56–58, 77, 83. Frank Tannenbaum, however, maintains that the Mexican Revolution was primarily lower-class and agricultural in character, and was opposed by the urban middle class: *Peace by Revolution: Mexico After 1910* (New York: Columbia University Press, 1966), chap. 11.

18. Haight, *op. cit.,* p. 111.

19. Padgett, *op. cit.,* p. 186; Senior, *op. cit.,* pp. 15–16. Similarly, Casanova notes that in 1910 "88.4 per cent of the agricultural populations were *peons . . .* only 0.02 per cent were owners of plantations." See Pablo González Casanova, "Mexico: A Semicapitalist Revolution," in Ignacy Sachs, ed., *Planning and Economic Development, Studies on Developing Countries,* (Warszawa: PWN–Polish Scientific Publishers, 1964), I, 174–175.

20. Padgett, *op. cit.,* p. 20.

21. Senior, *op. cit.,* pp. 17–18; Cline, *op. cit.,* pp. 21–22.

22. Padgett, *op. cit.,* pp. 164–165.

23. Haight, *op. cit.,* pp. 2–3.

24. Senior, *op. cit.,* pp. 22–23; Padgett, *op. cit.,* pp. 24–25; Hung-chao Tai, "Land Reform in the Developing Countries: Tenure Defects and Political Responses" (Unpublished paper, Center for International Affairs, Harvard University), p. 25. A very good account of the bloody conflict between revolutionary radicals (Conventionists) and revolutionary moderates (Constitutionalists) is given by Robert E. Quirk, *The Mexican Revolution, 1914–1915* (New York: The Citadel Press, 1963). The civil war of 1914–1915 between the two wings of the revolutionary forces was won by the Constitutionalists. But interestingly, through presidents who succeeded Carranza, the ideas of the Conventionists established themselves ever more firmly as the basis of government programs. As Professor Quirk said, "The inarticulate, militarily ineffectual Zapata accomplished in death what he could not win in life," but "the victory of Carranza and his Constitutionalist armies on the battlefield brought no similar triumph for the political ideas of the First Chief." His liberalism "was, after all, an anachronism in twentieth-century Mexico. The future belonged to the mentality of the Convention" (*op. cit.,* pp. 292–293).

25. Martin C. Needler, "The Political Development of Mexico," *American Political Science Review,* LV (June 1961), 310.

26. Scott, *Mexican Government in Transition,* p. 129.

27. Frey, *The Turkish Political Elite,* chaps. 5–6.

28. Ergun Özbudun, *The Role of the Military in Recent Turkish Politics,* Occasional Papers in International Affairs, No. 14 (Cambridge: Harvard University Center for International Affairs, November 1966), pp. 28–29.

29. For a similar explanation, see Turan Günes, "C. H. P. Halktan Nasil Uzaklaşti," *Yön,* I (December 20, 1961), 14.

30. Senior, *op. cit.,* pp. 18–19, 59–60.

31. Frey, *The Turkish Political Elite,* p. 183.

32. For this classification of revolutions, see Barrington Moore, Jr., *Social Origins*

of Dictatorship and Democracy: Lord and Peasant in the Making of the Modern World (Boston: Beacon Press, 1966), chaps. 8–9.

33. My discussion of the organization of the PRI relies heavily upon Professor Scott's excellent account: *Mexican Government in Transition,* pp. 115–181. See also Padgett, *op. cit.,* pp. 47–62; Cline, *op. cit.,* chap. 15.

34. Scott, *Mexican Government in Transition,* p. 122.

35. *Ibid.,* p. 131.

36. *Ibid.,* pp. 139–144; for the organizational changes introduced by the 1960 rules, see Padgett, *op. cit.,* pp. 51–60.

37. Scott, *Mexican Government in Transition,* p. 25.

38. For a case example, see Padgett, *op. cit.,* pp. 114–120.

39. Needler, "The Political Development of Mexico," p. 311. Frank R. Brandenburg, on the other hand, dismisses the role of the PRI in the policy-making process, claiming that the official party is essentially an arm and instrument of the presidency, *The Making of Modern Mexico* (Englewood Cliffs, N.J.: Prentice-Hall, 1964), chap. 6.

40. Scott, *Mexican Government in Transition,* p. 174.

41. *Ibid.,* pp. 141–142.

42. Cline, *op. cit.,* p. 155.

43. Padgett, *op. cit.,* p. 125.

44. Scott, *Mexican Government in Transition,* pp. 81–83, 193–194.

45. For a similar view on the RPP, see Maurice Duverger, *Political Parties* (New York: Wiley, Science Editions, 1963), pp. 276–278.

46. For the national leadership, see Frey, *The Turkish Political Elite, passim.* Unfortunately, there is no similar comprehensive study of the local cadres of the RPP in the single-party years. However, Frank Tachau observed in the province of Adana that wealthy landowners tended to concentrate in the RPP, "Provincial Party Organizations in Turkey" (Paper presented to the Conference on Social Growth and Democracy in Turkey, New York University, May 27–29, 1965), pp. 14–15.

47. Frey, *The Turkish Political Elite,* pp. 40–43; also his "Political Development, Power, and Communications in Turkey," in Lucian W. Pye, ed., *Communications and Political Development* (Princeton: Princeton University Press, 1963), p. 313; see also Lewis V. Thomas and Richard N. Frye, *The United States and Iran* (Cambridge: Harvard University Press, 1952), p. 72.

48. Senior, *op. cit.,* p. 30; Haight, *op. cit.,* pp. 233–234; Cline, *op. cit.,* pp. 137–139.

49. See, for example, Senior, *op. cit., passim;* Cline, *op. cit.,* chap. XXII; Padgett, *op. cit.,* chap. 8; Eyler J. Simpson, *The Ejido: Mexico's Way Out* (Chapel Hill: University of North Carolina Press, 1937); Nathan L. Whetten, *Rural Mexico* (Chicago: University of Chicago Press, 1948).

50. Padgett, *op. cit.,* p. 195.

51. Senior, *op. cit.,* pp. 27–28.

52. Casanova, *op. cit.,* pp. 174–175; Haight, *op. cit.,* p. 185; Senior, *op. cit.,* pp. 27–28; Cline, *op. cit.,* pp. 216–218 and Table 45. Tai has shown the considerable decline of land concentration in Mexico, calculating the Gini indices for 1930 and 1960. Decline in Gini index, in percentage, is 27.64 for this period. See Tai, *op. cit.,* p. 92, Table 6.

53. For land reform under Lopez Mateos, see Padgett, *op. cit.,* pp. 194–200.

54. Casanova, *op. cit.,* p. 182.

55. Cline, *op. cit.,* pp. 218–221.

56. Senior, *op. cit.,* p. 209; Cline, *op. cit.,* pp. 211–212; for a full discussion of favorable and unfavorable appraisals of the agrarian policies of the revolutionary governments, see Haight, *op. cit.,* pp. 190–230.

57. Casanova, *op. cit.,* p. 178.

58. Haight, *op. cit.,* p. 186.
59. Halil İnalcik, "The Nature of Traditional Society: Turkey," in Robert E. Ward and Dankwart A. Rustow, eds., *Political Modernization in Japan and Turkey* (Princeton: Princeton University Press, 1964), pp. 47–48.
60. Şevket Süreyya Aydemir, *İkinci Adam* (Istanbul: Remzi Kitabevi, 1967), II, 303–310.
61. *Gelir Dagilimi Araştirmasi* (1963) (Ankara: T. C. Başbakanlik Devlet Plânlama Teşkilâti, September 1966), p. 34.
62. *Kalkinma Plani, İkinci Beş Yil, 1968–1972* (Ankara: T. C. Başbakanlik Devlet Plânlama Teşkilâti, 1967), pp. 239–240, Tables 118, 119. See also *Gelir Dagilimi Araştirmasi,* pp. 39, 59.
63. Gürgân Çelebican, "Türkiye'de Toprak Reformu" (unpublished paper), p. 19.
64. For the events leading to the submission to the Assembly of the Land Reform Bill, see Aydemir, *op. cit.,* pp. 320–345.
65. *Çiftçiyi Topraklandirma Kanunu,* No. 4753, Düstur, XXVI, 1169–1182.
66. Kemal H. Karpat, *Turkey's Politics: The Transition to a Multi-Party System* (Princeton: Princeton University Press, 1959), pp. 117–125; Aydemir, *op. cit.,* pp. 345–349.
67. On the labor and labor policy in Mexico, see Padgett, *op. cit.,* chap. 7; Cline, *op. cit.,* chap. XXIII; Haight, *op. cit.,* pp. 233–251; Marjorie R. Clark, *Organized Labor in Mexico* (Chapel Hill: University of North Carolina Press, 1934); Vicente Lombardo Toledano, "The Labor Movement," *The Annals,* CCVIII (March 1940), 48–54; Horace B. Davis, "Numerical Strength of Mexican Unions," *Southwestern Social Science Quarterly,* XXV (June 1954), 48–55; Joseph A. Kahl, "Three Types of Mexican Industrial Workers," *Economic Development and Cultural Change,* VIII (January 1960), 164–169.
68. Padgett, *op. cit.,* pp. 167–176.
69. Cline, *op. cit.,* p. 222.
70. Karpat, *op. cit.,* pp. 74, 109, 312–316; Aydemir, *op. cit.,* pp. 357–363.
71. Almond and Verba, *op. cit., passim,* esp. pp. 185, 202–203, 310–311, 363–364; quotation is from p. 192.
72. Linda Mirin, however, argues that "Mexican society is currently ready to adjust to such a change. . . . In the longer run, it seems almost inevitable that a genuine political party, the product of a growing if still containable factionalism, will arise from within the PRI and will offer policies coherent enough to survive early defeats, yet reasonable enough to form the basis for a workable two party system." "Mexico's PRI: How much Democracy" (Paper presented to the Conference on The Evolution of Established One-Party Systems, Timber Cove, California, April 5–7, 1968), p. 27. On the future of the PRI, see also Needler, "The Political Development of Mexico," p. 312; Cline, *op. cit.,* pp. 171–172; Taylor, *op. cit.,* pp. 740–744.
73. Özbudun, *op. cit.,* esp. pp. 22–26.
74. Some anthropologists argue, in fact, that the Turkish rural communities generally display a bipolar power structure. Thus, if one local faction belongs to the government party, the rival faction will be inclined to associate itself with the opposition. In the single-party years, the reigning factions had already identified themselves with the RPP; those who opposed them (generally lesser notables) were, therefore, committed to the DP. "This analysis implies that the DP in fact captured the support of most of the local oppositions which existed in every town and village in Turkey." See Paul Stirling, *Turkish Village* (New York: Wiley, Science Editions, 1965), pp. 281–282; also Dankwart A. Rustow, "The Development of Parties in Turkey," in Joseph LaPalombara and Myron Weiner, eds., *Political Parties and Political Development* (Princeton: Princeton University Press, 1966), p. 123.

13

The Kuomintang and Modernization in Taiwan

║ *Hung-chao Tai*

The most obvious political consequences of modernization, Karl W. Deutsch has suggested, are the continuous "expansion of the politically relevant strata" and the increasing demand by the people for expansion and improvement of governmental services to satisfy their needs.[1] Under these conditions, Deutsch has written elsewhere, the political system must seek to maintain stability and to augment its capabilities. Stability and capabilities are mutually dependent. Stability can be maintained when the rising needs and expectations of the people are not unduly frustrated but fulfilled, at least partially, through the growing capabilities of the government.[2] The growth of governmental capabilities requires, as does the entire modernization process, the existence of "an environment in which uncertainty has been reduced and planning based on reasonably safe predictions is possible."[3] The political requirement of modernization, then, is an adaptable political system capable of continuously absorbing and managing the demands generated by modernization "with relatively few eruptions and breakdowns."[4]

As seen in the evidence to be presented below, Taiwan over the last decade and a half has been undergoing rapid modernization, the most salient aspect of which is fast and steady economic growth. To what extent has modernization affected the functioning and evolution of the Kuomintang (KMT), or the Chinese Nationalist Party, which has maintained since 1945 a preponderant presence at all levels of the governmental system on the island? Has the KMT responded to the challenges of modernization with flexibility and adaptability? If one answers these questions in the light of the organizational structure and the composition of national leadership of the party, the KMT does not seem to have been much affected by the impact of modernization. Thus, some have taken the view that the Kuomintang exhibits a high degree of political rigidity in sharp contrast to the dynamic economic growth on the island.[5] However, if one accepts the formulation suggested above that the political system capable of meeting the requirements of modernization over an extended length of time is of necessity adaptable, one may infer that insofar as Taiwan has experienced both modernization and stability for the last fifteen years, there must have been observable changes in the political system. Indeed, one would find upon close examination that the KMT did show a capacity for innovation and adjustment.

As in the case of any other established one-party system, KMT's central objective remains persistently the preservation of its dominant power position. Its adaptations to a changing economic and social environment are, therefore, manifested only in such areas as its leadership perceives to be most conducive to the achievement of this central objective.

The Kuomintang as an Established One-Party System

The Legacy of the Kuomintang

The conditions under which a political party emerges and the crisis situations that it subsequently goes through, to paraphrase two political scientists, shape its structural and functional characteristics and influence the pattern of its future evolution.[6] In an analysis of the adaptations of the KMT in Taiwan, the party's historical experiences take on special significance. For, with its origin dating back to the last century, the period of KMT rule in Taiwan occupies only a minor part of its history. The legacy of the party considerably conditions the manner of its response to modernization, and only against this legacy can one meaningfully assess its present adaptations.

A dominant and persistent characteristic of the KMT as shaped by history is that the party has been and is conceived to be revolutionary. It was to overthrow the Manchu monarchy that Dr. Sun Yat-sen founded the two parental bodies of the KMT: the *Hsing Chung Hui* (The Society for Rebuilding China) in Honolulu in 1894 and the *Tung Meng Hui* (The Society of the Common Cause) in Tokyo in 1905. After the creation of the Kuomintang in 1912, the first year of the Republic of China, the party launched the Second Revolution, a revolution against the monarchy-revival movements and regional warlordism. Soon, following the conclusion of its northern expedition against the warlords in 1928, the KMT engaged intermittently in a two-front battle: the internal one against the communists and the external one against the Japanese. Before the end of the Chinese-Japanese war in 1945, the Kuomintang had recently renewed fighting against the communists. Its defeat in 1949 terminated its rule on mainland China, to which it avows to return.

With these prolonged experiences of armed struggle, the party leadership has continuously identified revolution as the major means to achieve its aims. Evidently, in the political vocabulary of the KMT, revolution does not always mean a massive movement to overthrow the established political order; for the KMT was itself in power on the mainland in the two decades following 1928. In the light of the KMT history, the party leadership apparently understood revolution primarily as a military means to establish and safeguard its rule over all of China. It was Dr. Sun who first emphasized the indispensability of an army to the achievement of the party's objectives. And it was Dr. Sun who began in 1924 to form a KMT army by creating the Whampoa Military Academy with Chiang Kai-shek as its first commandant.

This action proved to be a momentous one, profoundly affecting the future evolution of the KMT. Within one year after the death of Dr. Sun in 1925, Chiang gained prominence both in the party and in the army. Subsequently, as the party faced the challenges of the warlords, the communists, and the Japanese—the kind of challenges that could be met only with a reliance on the military—its leadership gravitated toward Chiang; and the graduates of the Whampoa Military Academy became one of the most important forces controlling the KMT, the national and provincial administrations, and, of course, the army.

A revolutionary movement and a military establishment may be said to share one common characteristic: the concentration of power in the hand of the man who holds the highest command. The fact that KMT was conceived as a revolutionary organization dominated by the military created an inevitable trend toward the personalization of power. Reinforcing this trend were certain conditions prevailing in the early years of the republican era. The revolution of 1911 toppled the monarchical rule, but the traditional Chinese political culture, characterized by people's habitual acceptance of one man, the emperor, as the source of all political authority, proved to outlive the Manchu dynasty. Dr. Sun was late to recognize, and Chiang Kai-shek emphatically believed, that under a republican system personalization of power by the leader of the KMT was indispensable to the consolidation of the disparate forces within the party and, more importantly, to the party's claim to national power. In the first few years following the creation of the KMT in 1912, Dr. Sun repeatedly and painfully came to appreciate the fact that the party's vitality and revolutionary vigor were seriously weakened by the dilution of the party ranks with politicians seeking political fortunes. To meet this internal crisis of the party, Dr. Sun set out in 1914 to centralize power in his hand by assuming the newly instituted office of *Tsung-li* (Director-General). Subsequently, when the party constitution was adopted in 1924, it provided Dr. Sun with almost unlimited authority, stipulating that all party members should follow the direction of *Tsung-li,* who, as the chairman of both the National Congress and the Central Executive Committee, had the right to make final decisions on matters brought before either body.[7]

Following the death of Dr. Sun, Chiang Kai-shek gradually carried forward this tradition of personalization of power. To secure his position as the political successor of Dr. Sun, and to consolidate a disintegrated nation, Chiang found "actually no alternative course of action available to him, once supreme power was in hand, than to continue to hold it. . . . To exercise power as he must, Chiang had to rely, in the absence of institutional loyalty, on personal loyalty as a means to assure himself of the absoluteness of his power and the effectiveness of his authority." [8] In 1938, ten years after having actually ruled the KMT, Chiang formally became the party leader by assuming the office of *Tsung-tsai,* a position practically identical with that of *Tsung-li.*[9]

Party Structure, Functions, and Ideology in the Mainland Period

Though Kuomintang's origin can be traced to late last century, it was not until 1924 that the party's institutional structure took a definite and permanent shape. The First National Congress of the party, held in that year, adopted a new charter and a program of sweeping reorganization. Then allied with the Soviet Union, the KMT borrowed in this reorganization effort Soviet experiences. According to the late Tsui Shu-chin, a prominent party official, Soviet influence was evident in the following aspects of the reformed party structure.[10] First, KMT membership was open to only those who pledged to carry out party decisions, actively participate in party primary organizations, and regularly pay dues. Second, a pyramidal party structure, parallel to the government hierarchy, was established. With "small groups" as its base, the party built up by cooptation its local, provincial, and national organs. At the top of the party, an elected National Congress served as the supreme organ, which discharged its functions between sessions through the Central Executive Committee which it elected. Third, "party groups" were formed in social organizations whereby party influence was to be exerted and execution of party policies facilitated. And fourth, control committees responsible for enforcing disciplines among the rank and file were established at all levels of the party organs.

In addition to these features borrowed from the Soviet Union, the KMT exhibited peculiar organizational characteristics of its own. Unlike its Soviet counterpart, which included a large number of proletarian elements, the KMT consisted primarily of politicians, the military, and intellectuals. It was a cadre party designed to facilitate the exercise of power. Moreover, as Chiang Kai-shek reached the apex of power, his leadership gradually showed a paternalistic tendency. Chiang's deference to Confucianism, reliance on personal loyalty for political control, and, above all, prolonged exercise of power in both the party and the government led him and a substantial number of his followers to believe that party policies and national interests were inseparable from his personal convictions. To the rank and file and the party leader alike, the former's obedience to the wishes of the latter was conceived to be a personal dedication to the cause of the party and the nation. Party cohesion was maintained largely through this personal bond between the leader and the membership.

In addition to reshaping the party structure, the First National Congress formulated a basic program for "national revolution and reconstruction." [11] To carry out this program the Congress prescribed three periods: "(1) the period of military dictatorship; (2) the period of political tutelage; and (3) the period of constitutional government." With the conclusion of the northern expedition in 1928, the KMT came to power, marking the end of the first phase. The period of political tutelage, which then began, lasted toward 1948. In that year the third period began; the national government was reconstituted under the constitution that had been adopted the previous year.

During the period of political tutelage, which coincided with almost the entire length of the KMT rule over the mainland, the party performed a number of functions. First, it sought to legitimize its exclusive rule on the basis of its historical accomplishments and of the paramount need to meet the exigencies of the day—the two-front challenges coming from the communists and the Japanese. Without having to rest its rule on popular consent, the KMT did not encourage electoral participation. Second, its commitment to political tutelage was interpreted in practice to mean the supremacy of the party over the government. In every administrative division of the nation, the appropriate party committee constituted the center of power, guiding and supervising the parallel governmental agency. Third, it served as an instrument for political recruitment and training. From its membership came almost all governmental leaders, key civil servants, and military officers. With an extensive system of training institutions offering political education to these people, it ensured their ideological conformity with, and subordination to, the party leadership. And fourth, as the repository and interpreter of the official ideology, it endeavored not only to propagate Dr. Sun Yat-sen's teachings as a political doctrine to which the rank and file of the party must subscribe, but also to make them a set of national values to which all people should adhere.

Among Dr. Sun's extensive writings it is his work *The Three Principles of the People* (*San Min Chu I*) that the KMT has consistently identified as the essence of its ideology. Consisting of a series of lectures Dr. Sun delivered in 1924, this work deals with three subjects: the Principle of Nationalism (*Min Chu Chu I*), the Principle of Democracy (*Min Chuan Chu I*), and the Principle of People's Livelihood (*Min Shen Chu I*). Of these three principles the last one is the most significant. In this principle Dr. Sun offered his own interpretation of the evolution of human history; thus it was regarded as the philosophical foundation of all his writings. In terms of its policy content, this principle espouses equalization of land ownership and the regulation of capital. With respect to the former, Dr. Sun proposed to retain private ownership, to abolish landlordism in rural areas through a land-to-the-tiller program, and to accrue the increased land value in urban areas to the government through taxation or public purchase of the under-valued land. With respect to the regulation of capital, Dr. Sun stressed the need for the development of national capital and the limitation of private enterprises. By developing national capital he meant "state operation of in-dustries, state control of capital, and state ownership of profits." These in-dustries would encompass all major transportation, mining, and manufac-turing enterprises. "When . . . [these industries] are all developed, profits from them each year will be immense; and under the system of state con-trol, they will be shared by all the people. In this way capital will be a source of blessing to the people in the country, not a source of misery as in some foreign countries, where capital is concentrated in private hands." [12] Small enterprises that were not monopolistic in character, Dr. Sun believed, could be left to private individuals. What Dr. Sun proposed was, in essence, a planned, mixed economy with the public controlling the major share. In theory, this aspect of the Principle of People's Livelihood much resembles British Fabianism; and, indeed, there was some occasional acknowledg-ment by the KMT of the affinity of the two economic theories. In practice, although the principle was not carried out by the KMT on the mainland, the party has repeatedly reaffirmed its theoretical significance and made nu-merous pledges to implement it.[13]

The Initial Phase of the KMT Rule on Taiwan, 1945–1949

Following its transfer from Japan to China in October, 1950, Taiwan was placed under the authority of a military governor. For two years both the national government and the KMT, preoccupied with the civil war on the mainland, paid relatively little attention to the developments on the is-land. The first Governor-General, Chen Yi, was proven to be an extremely incompetent administrator, and his policy of exclusion of the natives from the government was highly unpopular among the islanders. Chen Yi's in-eptitude not only antagonized the native population but also provoked ten-sions between the latter and the mainlanders who came to the island after World War II. On February 28, 1947, an almost island-wide revolt broke out which led the national government to resort to force for the restoration of order. In May, 1947 Chen Yi was removed, and a civilian, Wei Tao-ming, became governor of the reformed Taiwan Provincial Government. To pacify local discontent, Wei began to admit large numbers of natives into his administration. However, in the meantime, the unsettling conse-quences of the civil war reached the island. The influx of the mainlanders began in earnest, while communist underground agents, capitalizing on local dissatisfaction with the government, started a vigorous drive to infiltrate the island. In January, 1949, when the KMT had suffered severe military reverses on the mainland, Chiang Kai-shek appointed General Chen Cheng governor of Taiwan, apparently paving the way for the eventual removal of the national government to the island.

In his short term as governor, Chen Cheng concentrated his effort on stabilizing the island's political and economic conditions. He suppressed communist activities, reformed Taiwan's currency to ward off the impact of inflation on the mainland, and introduced the 37.5 per cent rent reduction program, the first phase of Taiwan's land reform. In December, 1949 the central government and the national headquarters of the Kuomintang moved to Taiwan, and Chen became Premier the following year.

Thus, during the first years of the Chinese rule of Taiwan, the KMT had little party activity locally. It set up a provincial committee but made no serious effort to recruit the indigenous elements. It was only after the arrival of the party's national headquarters that the KMT began to develop its local strength and to seek actively natives as its members.

Modernization and Challenges

The political and economic instabilities that marked KMT's initial rule in Taiwan persisted for several years after the arrival of the national government. It was not until the early 1950s, when the KMT had recovered from the shock of defeat and when the United States had resumed its full support of the Nationalist government, that the island began to embark on a path of rapid modernization.

Economic Development

With the launching of a series of land reform measures in 1949–1953 and the commencement of the first of several four-year economic plans in 1953, Taiwan's economy has been growing at a fast pace. Maintaining a higher growth rate than any other Asian country except Japan, Taiwan almost tripled its productive capacity in fourteen years. "Measured in constant 1964 U.S. dollar equivalents, Taiwan's GNP rose from $879 million in 1951 to an estimated $2.4 billion in 1965." [14] And, in spite of the very high rate of population growth, its per capita GNP rose in the same period from $106 to $187, at an annual compound rate of 4.2 per cent.[15] These accomplishments reflect the emergence of a self-sufficient and self-sustained economy, warranting the discontinuation of American economic aid in 1965. The overall pattern of economic growth of Taiwan in 1952–1964 can be seen in Table 13–1.

Accompanying its quantitative expansion, the economy also showed three important structural changes. First, measured by the industrial origin of national domestic product and by the occupational distribution of the

TABLE 13-1 *Growth of Taiwan's Economy, 1952-1964[a]*

Economic Indicators	1952 Amount or No.	Index	1958 Amount or No.	Index	1964 Amount or No.	Index	Average Annual Growth Rate in % 1953-1964
GNP in constant 1963 prices (in million NT$)	37,933	100	57,992	152.9	90,645	239.0	7.52
Per capita income in 1963 constant prices (in NT$)	3,618	100	4,457	123.2	5,753	159.0	3.98
Agricultural production index[b]		100		151.9		197.6	5.94
Industrial production index		100		190.0		422.4	12.8
Industrial production index, by private and public sectors							
private sector		100		245.9		719.3	17.9
public sector		100		170.5		326.6	10.4
Factories	9,966	100	12,289	123.31	27,540	276.34	8.84
Profit-making non-agricultural firms[c]	68,000[d]	100[d]			227,000	333.82	10.57
Business corporations[c]	1,000[d]	100[d]			11,000	1,100	22.12
International trade (in U.S.$ 1,000):							
total	326,507	100	397,218	121.7	873,511	267.5	8.55
exports	119,527	100	164,433	137.6	463,110	387.5	11.95
imports	206,980	100	232,785	112.5	410,401	198.3	5.87
Annual foreign private investment arrival[e] (U.S.$ 1,000)	816	100	2,669	327.0	17,330	2,123.8	29.00

Sources: Except as noted otherwise, the data of this table come from China, Executive Yuan, Council for International Economic Cooperation and Development, *Taiwan Statistical Data Book 1965* (Taipei, Taiwan, China, 1965), (hereafter referred to as *Taiwan Data Book 1965*), pp. 11, 13, 22-23, 38-41, 49, 115.

[a]Except indicated otherwise, 1952 is the base year (index: 1952=100). For most of the period under review, 40 New Taiwan (NT) dollars are roughly equivalent to one U.S. dollar. Data for 1964 are preliminary.

[b]Including crops, forestry, fishery, and livestocks.

[c]Neil H. Jacoby, *U.S. Aid to Taiwan: A Study of Foreign Aid, Self-Help, and Development* (New York: Frederick A. Praeger, 1966), p. 92.

[d]1951 (Index: 1951=100).

[e]Jacoby, op. cit., p. 291.

employed population, there has been a notable shift from an agricultural to an industrial economy. Second, in industry the private sector had decisively replaced the public sector as the dominant component. And third, with the expansion of both the volume of foreign trade and the number of trading nations, and with the fast increase of foreign investment, Taiwan's economy has gradually become an autonomous unit of the world market, liquidating the economically dependent status it had possessed in the period of the Japanese rule and before.[16] These structural changes of Taiwan's economy in 1952–1964 are illustrated in Table 13–2.

TABLE 13-2   *Structural Changes of Taiwan's Economy 1952-1964*

Economic Indicators	1952		1958		1964	
	Amount or No.	Per Cent	Amount or No.	Per Cent	Amount or No.	Per Cent
Distribution of net domestic product by industrial origin (in NT$ million): Total	13,050	100	32,850	100	77,002	100.00
Agriculture	4,595	35.2	10,403	31.7	19,667	25.5
Industry (including construction)	2,930	22.5	8,588	26.1	25,445	33.0
Services	5,525	42.3	13,859	46.9	31,890	41.5
Private and public output as % of industrial production		100		100		100
Private output		42.7		51.8		62.1
Public output		57.3		48.2		37.9
Distribution of employment (1,000 persons)	2,936	100.0	3,178	100	3,710	100
Agricultural	1,792	61.0	1,813	57.1	2,010	54.2
Non-agricultural	1,144	39.0	1,365	42.9	1,700	45.8

Source: *Taiwan Data Book 1965*, pp. 7, 14, 42.

Social Development

In Taiwan the effective mobilization and utilization of the physical and human resources for rapid economic development was accompanied by changes toward a society of rising literacy, industrialization, and urbanization. At the same time the island experienced a proliferation of social organizations and business firms, a high geographical mobility (and with it high occupational mobility), and an increasing exposure by the populace to mass communication media; these developments reflect a tendency toward greater differentiation of social structure and the emergence of a rational innovational personality.

TABLE 13-3 *Incremental Social Changes in Taiwan 1952-1964[a]*

	1952		1958		1964		Total Increase in 1952-64, in %
	No.	Index	No.	Index	No.	Index	50
Population (in 1,000 persons)[b]	8,128	100	10,039	123.5	12,257	150	50
Civic organizations							
Organizations	2,219	100	3,984	179.5	4,937	222.0	122.0
Membership	557,694	100	1,292,404	231.7	1,703,330	305.4	205.4
Newspaper cirulation[c]							
Total copies			350,000[d]	100[d]	750,000[e]	217[e]	117[f]
Reader per 1,000 Literate population			69[d]	100[d]	103[e]	149.3[e]	49.3[f]
Radio audience[g]							
Total sets	51,001	100	339,108	665	1,070,904	2,066	1,966
Average sets per 1,000 families	34	100	188	553	555	1,632	1,532
Passenger traffic[h] (in million persons)	163	100	358	219.6	473	290.2	190.2
Medical personnel[i]							
Total medical personnel	11,613	100	15,610	134.4	21,664	186.5	86.5
Persons served by medical personnel	700		643		566		

Source: Except as noted otherwise, the source of information is *Taiwan Data Book 1965*, pp. 4, 6, 19, 62, 153.

[a]Except as indicated otherwise, 1952 is the base year (index: 1952=100).

[b]Excluding armed forces and foreigners.

[c]Neil H. Jacoby, *U.S. Aid to Taiwan: A Study of Foreign Aid, Self-Help, and Development* (New York: Frederick A. Praeger, 1966), p. 303. The base year is 1957 (index: 1957=100).

[d]1957.

[e]1963.

[f]1957-1963 period.

[g]Jacoby, *op. cit.*, p. 304.

[h]Including only railroad and highway traffic. For intercity travel by train, bus and air, 1951-1964, see Jacoby, *op. cit.*, p. 306.

[i]Including physicians, pharmacists, nurses, and midwives.

Tables 13–3 and 13–4 indicate the main directions of social changes in Taiwan.

Political Development

While Taiwan has made uniformly impressive gains in the realm of economic and social developments, its record on political development has been one of uneven accomplishments. This record may be examined with respect to electoral participation and the political role of interest groups.

TABLE 13-4 *Distributive Social Changes in Taiwan 1952-1964*

	1952		1958		1964	
	Number (1,000)	Per Cent	Number (1,000)	Per Cent	Number (1,000)	Per Cent
Population distribution by Taiwanese & main-landers,[a] total	8,128	100	10,039	100	11,884[b]	100[b]
Taiwanese	7,478	92.0	8,943	89.1	10,349[b]	87.1[b]
Mainlanders	650	8.0	1,096	10.9	1,535[b]	12.9[b]
Urban-rural population distribution,[c] total			9,000[d]	100[d]	12,300	100
Urban			2,800[d]	31[d]	4,300	35
Rural			6,200[d]	69[d]	8,000	65
Distribution in agricultural population,[e] total	4,257	100	4,881	100	5,649	100
Full owners	1,598	38	2,975	61	3,769	67
Part owners	1,113	26	1,132	23	1,154	20
Tenants	1,546	36	774	16	726	13
Literacy[f] Total population aged 6 or over	6,384	100	7,821	100	9,871	100
Literate, number and as per cent of total	3,694	57.9	5,404	69.1	7,653	77.6

Source: Taiwan, Taiwan Sheng Ti Fang Tsŭ Ch'ih Chih Yao Pien Chi Wei Yuan Hui, *Taiwan Sheng Ti Fang Tsŭ Ch'ih Chih Yao (Compendium on Self-Government in Taiwan)* (Taichung, Taiwan, China, 1965) hereafter referred to as *Compendium.*

[a]*Compendium*, p. 168. At the end of 1946, over one year after Taiwan was transferred to China, the population distribution was as follows: Total, 6,090,860 (100 per cent); Taiwanese, 6,059,139 (99.48 per cent); and mainlanders, 31,721 (0.52 per cent). Ibid.

[b]1963.

[c]Neil H. Jacoby, U.S. Aid to Taiwan: A Study of Foreign Aid, Self-Help, and Development (New York: Frederick A. Praeger, 1966), p. 104. Urban population refers to residents in cities with 25,000 or more people.

[d]1955.

[e]Taiwan Data Book, 1965, p. 19.

[f]Ibid., p. 6.

Since 1948 there has been no popular selection of members of the national representative institutions. These institutions include the National Assembly (the agency responsible for amending the constitution and for electing the president and the vice president), the Legislative Yuan (the law-enacting organ), and the Control Yuan (the agency exercising the power of administrative impeachment). The National Assembly, which

TABLE 13-5 *Distribution of Party Strength among Elected Political Offices in Taiwan, 1967*

	Elective Positions	Year elected	Total	KMT		YCP		CDSP		Independents	
				No.	Per cent	No.	Per cent	No.	Per cent	No.	Per cent
National Govt.	National Assembly, delegates	1947	1521[a]	1333[b]	87.64	85[c]	5.59	56[c]	3.68	47	3.09
	Legislative Yuan, members	1948	493[d]	443[b]	89.95	13[c]	2.63	13[c]	2.63	24	4.89
	Control Yuan, members	1948	84[e]	70[b]	83.30	5[c]	6.00	2[c]	2.4	7	8.30
Provincial & Local Govts.	Provincial Assembly, members	1963	74	61	82.43	1	1.40	0	0.00	12	16.00
	County magistrates and municipality, mayors	1964	21	17	81.00	0	0.00	1	5.00	3	14.00
	County and municipal assemblies, members	1964	907	670	73.87	5	0.55	2	0.22	230	25.40
	Village and townships,[g] heads	1964	319	295	92.48	–	–	–	–	–	–
	Village and township assemblies,[g] members[h]	1965	4776	2355	49.30	1	–	2	–	2418	50.70

[a]The total number of seats elected in 1947 was 2,961; of these 1,521 were active members residing in Taiwan or abroad as of 1963. *China Yearbook, 1964-65* (Taipei, Taiwan, China: China Publishing Co., n.d.), *passim.*

[b]T. C. Chang, "The Kuomintang's Alliance for Freedom," *Free China Review,* XIV (January 1964), 30.

[c]T. C. Chang, "Minority Parties Challenge the KMT," *Free China Review,* XIV (September 1964), 10.

[d]The total number of legislators elected in 1948 was 760; 493 were active members residing in Taiwan or abroad as of 1963. Same source as that in n. a, above.

[e]The total elected membership was originally 180; 84 were in Taiwan as of 1963. Same source as that in n. a, above.

[f]*Compendium, passim.* There have since 1950 been numerous elections at the provincial and local levels. The distribution of party strength remained virtually the same throughout all these elections.

[g]Including county-controlled municipalities.

[h]Chosen on the basis of non-partisan contests.

TABLE 13-6 Voter Participation in the Latest Taiwan Provincial and Local Elections[a]

Elected Offices	(A) Date of Election	(B) Population	(C) Eligible Voters	(D) Actual Voters	(E) Participation Ratio (D)/(C) X 100	(F) No. of Seats or Offices	(G) Number of Candidates
Provincial Assembly	April, 1963	11,439,787	5,236,896	3,626,952	69.26	74	123
County magistrates and municipal mayors	April, 1964	11,984,970	5,387,450	3,719,969	69.05	21	47
County and municipal assemblies	January, 1964	11,723,572	5,336,985	4,096,606	76.76	907	1,563
Village and township heads[b]	1964[b]	9,355,064[c]	4,115,621[c]	3,192,040[c]	77.58	319	580
Village and township assemblies	1964-1965	9,335,687[c]	4,117,992[c]	3,086,926[c]	74.96	4,776	8,510
Hamlets and precincts heads	1961-1964[d]	10,955,429[c]	4,870,638[c]	3,031,641[c]	62.24	6,548	10,395

Source: Compendium, pp. 316, 423, 537, 611, 654, 671-672.

[a] Prior to the elections of 1968.

[b] Elections were held in different months. Information does not include data on a small number of villages and townships that elected their heads in 1965.

[c] Data exclude urban residents and voters.

[d] In certain areas the latest elections were held in 1965.

elected KMT Director-General Chiang Kai-shek to the presidency in 1948, has since renewed his term three times—in 1954, 1960, and 1966. The Executive Yuan (the Cabinet) has since 1949 been under the exclusive control of the KMT without participation by other parties.

The lack of popular election at the national level is contrasted to the numerous elections held at the provincial and local levels. Except the governor, who is appointed by the Executive Yuan, all chief executive officers and members of legislative assemblies in the provincial and local government system have since 1950 been directly chosen by the people. Table 13–5 shows the distribution of political strength among the KMT, the two minority parties—the Young China Party (YCP) and the Chinese Democratic Socialist Party (CDSP)—and independents at all but the lowest levels of the government structure in Taiwan.

With respect to the provincial and local elections, a number of points deserve special mention. KMT's overwhelming lead in these elections has not contributed to a diminution of voter's interest in electoral participation. As illustrated in Tables 13–6 and 13–7, voter turnout in all elections has been consistently high.[17]

TABLE 13-7 *County and Municipal Elections: Voter Participation Ratio (actual voters as percentages of eligible voters) 1950-1964*

| | Elective Positions | |
Year	Magistrates and Mayors	Members of Assemblies
1950-1951	75.77	80.73
1951	82.40	
1952-1953		79.72
1954	74.85	
1954-1955		78.88
1957	78.20	
1958		78.31
1960	72.49	
1961		73.83
1964	69.05	76.76

Source: *Compendium,* pp. 410, 414, 417, 420, 423, 456, 472, 488, 505, 521, 537.

Upon close observation of the electoral data, one may also discern that in the limited number of metropolitan areas, competition between the KMT and independents was markedly keen and that at the grass roots level in rural areas there were very lively political contests.

An analysis of the KMT performance in the elections at the level of Taiwan's 21 administrative divisions may reveal the increasing electoral competitiveness in metropolitan areas. Of these 21 administrative divisions there are 5 municipalities—Taipei, Keelung, Taichung, Tainan, and Kaohsiung—which, with one-fourth of the island's total population, constitute metropolitan areas, and 16 counties that may be classified as non-metropolitan areas. In all 5 elections held since 1950 in which the chief executive officers of these 21 administrative divisions (metropolitan areas: mayors;

non-metropolitan areas: country magistrates) were chosen, the KMT was able to achieve almost total victory in the non-metropolitan areas, winning from election to election 15 to 16 of the 16 county magistrates. But it faced serious challenges from independents in the metropolitan areas, having never been able to control all the five municipal mayors; and in the 1964 mayoralty election the KMT won only 2 out of the 5 contested offices (independents won in Taipei—the national capital—Keelung, and Tainan).

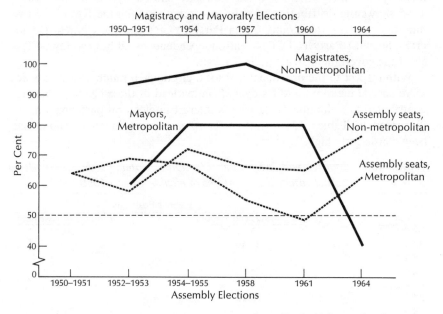

Source: Data for this figure are from *Compendium*.

FIGURE 13–1. Divergence of KMT Strength In Nonmetropolitan and Metropolitan Areas: County and Municipal Elections, 1950–1964

The assembly elections in these 21 administrative divisions showed a similar tendency. Of the six elections held in 1950–1964, only in the first two was KMT's electoral performance better in the metropolitan areas than in the non-metropolitan areas. Since the third election, in 1954–1955, an opposite trend has prevailed; and in the 1961 election, while the KMT retained a majority of the total seats of the sixteen assemblies in the non-metropolitan areas, independents—combined—held a larger share of the total seats of the assemblies in the five metropolitan areas. This discrepancy in the KMT's electoral strength in metropolitan and non-metropolitan areas can be graphically demonstrated in Figure 13–1.

Preliminary data on the 1968 elections, in which members of the provincial assembly and the chief executive officers of counties and municipalities were chosen, indicate the following distribution of popular votes: Of the total 556,676 valid ballots cast in the four metropolitan areas (municipalities), KMT candidates received 298,074, or 53.55 per cent; and the non-KMT candidates 258,602, or 46.45 per cent. Of the total 3,123,797 valid ballots cast in the 16 non-metropolitan areas (counties), KMT candidates received 2,367,941, or 75.80 per cent; and the non-KMT candidates 755,856, or 24.20 per cent.[18] Thus the KMT was doing better by 22.25 per cent in the non-metropolitan than in the metropolitan areas.

There are a number of explanations for the differing electoral performances of the KMT in the metropolitan and non-metropolitan areas. First, as is common among countries where the electoral process is relatively free and open, metropolitan areas usually experience greater political competitiveness than do other areas. For it is in the metropolitan areas that the residents have a higher literacy rate and a greater accessibility to the mass communication media. Second, the rapid urbanization in Taiwan's metropolitan areas has greatly intensified popular demand for public services, which often exceeds the government's capacity to meet it. Urban discontent can be a ready source of political strength for the opposition candidates. In Taiwan's metropolitan areas, the poor people who complain about unemployment and housing shortages, and the small merchants who have problems with licensing and taxing matters, become the targets of political appeal of the non-KMT candidates.[19] In the countryside, in contrast, the KMT's land reform programs and agricultural development policies have materially improved farmers' well-being and have earned for the party the good will of the rural residents. And the characteristics of KMT's competitors also help explain why the party faces a greater challenge in the metropolitan areas. Since the two non-KMT parties are extremely weak, politicians competing with KMT candidates are overwhelmingly independents. These politicians are islanders who, having achieved success in business and in the professions, possess considerable economic means. Maintaining neither organizational nor personal ties among themselves, they rely primarily on their individual strength and effort to win political offices. While their wealth facilitates their campaign effort, the security of their professions enables them to run the risk of political defeats. According to a recent compilation of biographies of sixty-four most prominent islanders, there were no less than thirty-three who occupied influential positions both in the government and in private practices. The political positions that they held ranged from chief executive officers at the county and municipal level to presidency of the Legislative Yuan in the national government. In the business and professional community, many of these men were board chairmen of industrial or commercial corporations; some were in the practices of medicine, law, and journalism.[20] By and large, they were concentrated in the metropolitan areas.

One further note on Taiwan's electoral participation relates to the increasing political involvement by rural residents. Facing no serious challenge from the countryside, the KMT encourages such involvement; rural residents, realizing that KMT's nomination for political offices is tantamount to election victory, eagerly compete within the party. Table 13–6 already showed that in the various elections at the village and hamlet levels, from 62.24 per cent to 77.58 per cent of the eligible rural voters voted. With the influence of landlords sharply dwindling after land reform, small owner-farmers and tenants have been elected—for many of them, the first time—to numerous political offices. A recent detailed survey of several rural townships indicates that in the early 1960s there had been a rise by 30 per cent to 40 per cent of farmer voters since the land reform of 1949–1953. In most instances 80 per cent of owner-farmers, part-owner-farmers, and tenants voted in elections.[21] The United Nations reported that in 1948 to 1962 owner-farmers serving as "heads of hamlets and neighbourhoods" increased from less than 5,000 to some 17,000, and that the number of all types of farmers elected to "various offices and representative bodies in community and local organizations increased fourfold from 8,830 . . . to 35,413" in the same period.[22]

With their increasing electoral participation, the rural people also displayed a concerned attitude toward those who held local offices. For some time, the citizens exercising the right of recall of public officials were all rural residents.[23] As a number of American observers have noted, these developments, with the energetic stimulation of the Chinese-American Joint Commission on Rural Reconstruction (JCRR), have considerably "improved the capacity of local institutions to articulate the interests of the rural population. . . ."[24]

The rapid pace of economic and social transformation in Taiwan and the high level of political participation at the provincial and local levels cannot but lead to the proliferation and differentiation of interest groups. As already indicated in Tables 13–3 and 13–4, there has been a very fast rise of civic organizations and profit-making business enterprises. A further examination of relevant data reveals that the number of commercial, manufacturing, and professional organizations quadrupled in eighteen years, increasing from 435 in 1947 to 1,732 in 1965; and in 1965 these organizations had a total of 205,444 firms, factories, or individuals as members.[25] Labor organizations at the county and municipal levels rose from 27 to 694 in 1946–1965; and their membership from 9,221 to 312,107 in the same period.[26] Agricultural organizations also increased in number and variety; the more important ones include the farmers' associations, the irrigation associations, and the farm-tenancy committees. All these associations operate on an island-wide basis with their officers elected by landlords, owner-farmers, tenants, and farm laborers.[27] Of these rural organizations the farmers' associations appear politically most influential. In 1953–1965 their membership increased from 589,299 to 845,658; in 1965 there were 23,480 delegates, 4,515 directors, 1,266 supervisors; and among these various elected offices, owner-farmers and tenants constituted the overwhelming majority.[28] On the basis of their growing organizational strength, these associations have gained a significant share of elective offices in the government. As a JCRR officer pointed out recently,

> Although they are organized primarily for social and economic development in rural areas, the farmers' associations offer the best opportunity for training local leaders in parliamentary procedures and in self-help activities. . . . [In 1964] five of the sixteen county magistrates, one of the five municipal mayors, eleven of the seventy-four members of the Provincial Assembly, over forty percent of the township office heads, and thirty percent of the members of the county and city assemblies were former elected officers of the farmers' associations.[29]

In contrast to the farmers' associations, the labor and business organizations have not been politically active. The primary function of these organizations is to cater to the social and economic needs of their membership. In the case of labor unions, the political quiescence is partly due to their relatively small numerical strength and partly due to the lack of well-developed organizations. In the case of businessmen, they prefer to channel their influence through individual contacts with government officials rather than through their associations. As noted earlier, many successful industrialists and business executives have become politicians. Others have gained access to the middle-rank policy makers and work with them directly in regard to matters affecting business interests.[30]

The Challenges

As a goal, modernization is what every developing society seeks to achieve, but modernization is also a process creating tensions. In a society experiencing modernization, there are inevitable conflicts between demands for equitable sharing of the fruit of an enlarged national wealth, on the one hand, and requirements for continual economic growth, on the other; between the heightened aspirations for increased political representation and the limited availability of public offices; and between the fast-rising popular demand for public goods and services and the slowly growing governmental capacity to meet them. To any political system these dichotomous developments present challenges. To the KMT the task of meeting these challenges is perhaps particularly exacting, for the party's capacity of response is limited and complicated by two special constraints.

The first relates to KMT's considerable preoccupation with the policy of recovery of the mainland. In view of the existing balance of power between the Nationalist and communist regimes and the former's prolonged absence of serious actions against the latter, many regard this policy as unrealistic and meaningless. To the KMT leadership, however, this policy is of substantive importance. Given the unpredictable events on the mainland, and given the fact that Chiang Kai-shek's total, unswerving dedication to this policy has decisively shaped the party's mentality, the KMT leadership does accept this policy as realizable. In order to fortify its will to carry out this policy, the KMT believes it necessary to continuously stress its "sacred mission to fight Communism and to deliver the mainland brethren from the tyrannical rule." In a sense this policy has been elevated to the status of an ideology, an unquestionable national value. It is in the light of this added ideology that the KMT gives meaning to its policies of reconstruction of Taiwan. But it is also this new ideological commitment that sets limits to KMT's capacity of response to the challenges of modernization. Thus, though it has a vital stake in continuing the present pace of economic growth, it must shoulder an enormous military burden, amounting to roughly 80 per cent of the central government's annual budget.[31]

The second constraint on the KMT's response to the challenges of modernization concerns the relations between the mainlanders and the native islanders in Taiwan. Though the mainlanders and all the natives except the mountain aborigines share common Chinese ancestry, the political blunders committed by the administration of Governor Chen Yi during the first days of the KMT rule, caused much tension between the two groups of people. The revolt in February, 1947 and the subsequent mishandling of the incident by Chen Yi left an unfavorable imprint in the ethnic relationships. While this situation has been much improved, there are new issues for the KMT to grapple with. The economic development of the island has a much greater favorable effect on the native propertied class than on the bulk of the mainlanders, who by and large derive their income from government services. The intensified political participation in the provincial and local governments has brought natives to dominate the elected offices, whereas the mainlanders are concentrated in the national government, in which the center of power is located. Under these circumstances the tasks which the KMT ought to perform are indeed challenging. It must ward off, within the resources of the government, possible economic discontent among the salaried mainlanders, who share with it the common aspiration of returning to the mainland; but the government has already been subject to considerable budgetary strain because of the military burden and of administrative overstaffing. The KMT must also provide increasing representation in national politics for the natives who are locally powerful and economically influential but whose concerns are primarily with the development of the island.

The Adaptations of the Kuomintang

To respond to the challenges of modernization, the KMT has shown in varying degrees adaptations in three areas: party structure, functions, and ideology.

Structural Changes

Kuomintang's organizational pattern and principles of the mainland period remain operative in Taiwan today. The structural changes that did occur appear to be few and insignificant.

In 1950 Chiang Kai-shek created a Central Reform Committee to reorganize the KMT in the light of the party's recent defeat and its future needs. Though having made a number of policy decisions with regard to land reform and local self-rule, the committee did not effect any major institutional changes. In 1952, following the party reform, when the Seventh National Congress of the party was held (the first one on the island), the traditional party structure was revived. The Congress renewed Chiang's term and elected a Central Committee and a Central Advisory Committee with 32 and 48 members, respectively. Chiang, possessing the same powers as before, governed the party with the assistance of the Central Standing Committee, which the Central Committee elected. The Eighth National Congress, held in 1957, increased the membership of the Central Committee to 50, created the office of deputy director-general, and elected Chen Cheng, the then vice president and premier, to the post. Since Chen's death in 1965 the post has been left vacant. The Ninth National Congress, held in 1963, further increased the membership of the Central Committee to 75 and that of the Central Advisory Committee to 144. The Central Standing Committee, whose membership has been fairly stable over the years, is now composed of 19 members. Among these 19 members are Vice President and Premier C. K. Yen, Defense Minister Chiang Ching-Kuo, Governor of Taiwan Huang Chieh, and Speaker of the Taiwan Provincial Assembly Hsieh Tung-ming. Of the 75 members of the Central Committee, one-fifth are men with prolonged military background or senior officers on active duty, six of whom are on the Central Standing Committee.[32]

With respect to the changes in party membership, the fragmentary nature of published information inhibits an adequate account. The following statistics are generally known.[33] First, the party membership has been rising rapidly, increasing from 282,000 in 1952 to 509,000 in 1957 and to 667,000 in 1963. Second, of the total membership in 1963, 150,000 (or 23 per cent) were farmers and laborers; and 56,000 (or 9 per cent), businessmen. Thus in terms of distribution of membership by profession, one-third of the total belonged to social and economic groups; the unaccounted two-thirds were in all probability composed of politicians, civil servants, and the military. And third, though the KMT was predominantly a mainlanders' party, the growth of islander membership was nevertheless impressive. From 1945 to 1963 the natives in the KMT grew by 205,000, equaling 80 per cent of the total KMT membership in 1952. This reflected KMT's intensive drive to enlist the Taiwanese as members.

Functional Adaptations

In contrast to the lack of major structural changes, the KMT has manifested it ability to make functional adaptations. These may be grouped into three categories: political participation, legitimation, and integration.[34]

POLITICAL PARTICIPATION   While maintaining a rigid control in the national government, the KMT embarked on an untraveled path when it introduced to Taiwan local self-rule in 1950. Having no prior experience with representative government, the KMT had from now on to seek a popular mandate for its rule in the provincial and local governments.

The KMT's electoral strategy consisted of several aspects. First, it sought to create an image of popular government. Through extensive publicity campaigns it encouraged maximum voter turnout at election time. In spite of occasional irregularities, the numerous elections held so far have generally been free and fair, as attested by the ability of independents to win repeatedly important contests in metropolitan areas. Second, it entered practically all major contests for offices beyond the bottom layer of the government. As the electorate was composed of largely Taiwanese, the KMT actively sought natives as its candidates, using its vast organizational and financial resources to secure their victory. On the average, the islanders supplied about 85 per cent of KMT's candidates in provincial and local elections.[35] Third, it occasionally supported friendly independents by refraining from contesting the offices they were seeking and by lending them its assistance in the campaign. This support of independents, which was limited in scope and generally restricted to non-metropolitan areas, was in part a matter of political necessity; for in certain places the party may not have qualified candidates of its own. In part, this also reflected a KMT concern that its continuous sweeping electoral victories might undermine the democratic image it tried to create. Fourth, with respect to the other two political parties—The Young China Party and the China Democratic Socialist Party—the KMT as a rule tolerated their electoral participation but sought their defeat in those contests in which the KMT candidates participated. Plagued with serious factional disputes, and lacking organizational strength and financial power, neither party has been able to challenge the KMT. And fifth, the KMT seeks to confine electoral campaigns to issues of local concern, permitting no candidates to engage in activities in conflict with "the constitution, interests, and fundamental policies of the nation." [36]

The surety with which the KMT won most of the electoral contests has understandably led to an intensified intraparty competition for nomination. At present the party's national and provincial headquarters, through some form of consultation with the membership, select and decide on candidates to be nominated. These party organizations have frequently faced the problem that the members seeking nomination were locally powerful but were not fully qualified for the posts they were seeking. When they were refused party nomination, they entered the contests on their own. This was particularly true when the party supported independents. This defiant action by certain KMT members obviously diverted votes from the party-supported candidates, sometimes leading to the latter's defeat. In response to this problem the party has either permitted its members to participate freely in elections without nominating official candidates or expelled members who entered elections against party-supported candidates.

LEGITIMATION   In every country where a one-party system operates, the ruling party faces the need for continuously justifying its exclusive claim to power. When such a system is involved in the modernization process, political legitimation takes on special significance; the ruling party's success in effectively mobilizing the human and physical resources for peaceful reconstruction of the society depends to a certain extent on some popular acceptance of the existing power pattern as appropriate and on people's willingness to carry out government's decisions.

As it can no longer rely on its historical accomplishments to justify its present power position, the KMT must find new bases in Taiwan to enlist popular acceptance of its rule. KMT's initiation of local self-rule can be viewed as one of the first attempts to create identification of the population with the government. As a consequence of this measure, there is the exclusion of the military from the provincial and local government. This is a development wholly departing from KMT's previous experiences, and, moreover, not fully reconciled to the requirements of the initially anticipated military offensive against the mainland. That the KMT was willing to allow this to happen indicates a conscious effort to improve its political image.

In the realm of the economy the KMT adopted a number of measures that have strengthened its political position. First, it decided to deemphasize the public sector of the economy and to encourage private enterprises. Second, despite continuous official statements to the contrary, it was determined to develop the island's resources for peaceful uses rather than to create a war-oriented economy. And finally, the KMT allowed the agencies—both Chinese and American—in charge of economic development a measure of freedom and political independence that no other public agencies enjoyed. This made it possible for rational economic planning and effective management of economic growth. The political effect of these KMT economic policies is clear. A vigorously expanding economy and a substantially improved living standard, which these policies helped bring about, have nurtured among the people a feeling of satisfaction with the existing state of affairs.

The land reform programs implemented in 1949–1953 represent another major KMT measure of political legitimation. Conscious of communist use of land reform in the past as an instrument to win over the peasants on the mainland, and apprehensive of communist attempts to exploit the rural situation in Taiwan, the KMT deemed it imperative, at the time when the civil war came to a close, to take immediate steps to improve the life of the island's farmers. Thus Chen Cheng, the principal architect of Taiwan's land reform, observed that a defective tenure system

> provided the Communist agitators with an opportunity to infiltrate into vil-
> lages. It was one of the main reasons why the Chinese mainland fell into
> Communist hands. On the eve of rent reduction [in 1949] . . . the villages
> on this island were showing signs of unrest and instability. It was feared that
> the Communists might take advantage of the rapidly deteriorating condition
> to fish in troubled waters. But with the implementation of rent reduction, the
> livelihood of the farming population was immediately improved. The Chinese
> Communists were effectively deprived of propagandistic weapons by a new
> social order that had arisen in the rural areas.[37]

The highly successful results of land reform have won for the KMT a great deal of rural good will and developed among the farmers a vested interest in the government's agricultural program.

Recognizing that its failure in the past to play an effective social role had contributed to the defeat on the mainland,[38] and appreciating the political necessity to meet the rising popular demand for public services today,[39] the KMT became aware that it must cease to be a mere governing instrumentality. It must become also an agency directly involved in economic and social transformations. This awareness has led the KMT to initiate a series of social welfare programs, the most important of which include the construction of publicly financed "national housing" units, the mobilization of the armed forces to develop "model social communities," the creation of a cabinet commission to provide for job retraining and employment, and the extension of free education from six to nine years.[40]

In addition to these governmental measures, the KMT has initiated some welfare programs of its own. It established in 1952 an island-wide network of community service organizations to serve as "a bridge linking to the people" and "to improve the party's social relations."[41] In 1962 it launched an annual "uniting for serving the people program" under which it mobilized the resources of itself, the government, the army, and the public to provide the needy with free meals, medical care, educational and recreational facilities, and unemployment relief assistance; the program also helped small merchants resolve their problems with taxation and licenses.[42] Soliciting the good will—thus, the votes—of the indigent through these various programs, the KMT performs today a function like that of American and British political parties in a past age. To the KMT, which has been accustomed to governing the people, the task of serving them became a completely new experience. Its willingness and readiness to perform this task reflects not only its functional adaptability but also, in the process of adaptation, perhaps its perception of the changing nature of the party.

POLITICAL INTEGRATION   To maintain the cohesiveness of the political system operating in Taiwan, the KMT has been concerned with two sources of tension. As is normal with any political system, one source relates to the ongoing competition for leadership positions and the divergence of views in the formation of policies. The other source, peculiar to the KMT, concerns the differing, and often competitive, aspirations of the islanders and the mainlanders. During its mainland rule, the KMT was known to have a number of factions, among which the principal ones were the C. C. group (the conservative wing, controlling the party's organizational apparatus), the Political Science group (the liberal wing), and the Whampoa group (consisting of the early graduates of the Whampoa Academy). Today these groups appear to have lost much of their cohesiveness and influence. In the period of party reform in 1950, Chiang Kai-shek manifested a strong aversion to the feuding of these groups, which he considered a main cause of the defeat of the party on the mainland. Subsequently, with Chiang's constant warning against the revival of factional disputes, these groups have apparently given up the effort to maintain close-knit organizations within the party. Some of the leaders of these groups have retired, gone abroad, or died. While other leaders may still be represented on the Central Committee and the Central Standing Committee, they appear to participate in these high party organs as individuals, maintaining no coordination among themselves. The waning of the factions of the party seems to have strengthened KMT's traditional approach to the resolution of internal conflicts. In matters of appointing top party and government posts and of formulating high policies, party Director-General Chiang Kai-shek possesses near absolute authority, using personal intervention and appeal to remove differences and to soften discontent. It is this charismatic and paternalistic quality of leadership that furnishes the basis of unity among the high echelons of the party and the government.

To retain the confidence of both the islanders and the mainlanders and to improve the atmosphere for their cooperation, the KMT has to adopt specific measures to meet specific demands. With respect to the islanders, KMT's policies consist, essentially, of a substantial improvement of their economic position and a differentiated response to their political aspirations. The shift of the weight of the economy from the public to the private sector has understandably benefited the natives.[43] And "the average inhabitant of Formosa [clearly] . . . enjoys a higher living standard" than the mainlander.[44]

In the realm of politics, the KMT has secured for its islander members the major share of the elected provincial and local offices, a share corresponding roughly to the natives' proportion in the population. Natives also were staffed in large proportions in provincial and local administrative positions.[45] In regard to natives' access to the national power, the KMT has followed a cautious approach. For, as one observer has pointed out.

"the Chinese leaders did not wish to absorb a large number of Chinese from one province into a government intended to rule all of China."[46] It has admitted so far only a few natives to high party and government positions. In the party, of the seventy-five members of the Central Committee four are Taiwanese, two of whom are on the nineteen-member Central Standing Committee. In the national government, islanders occupy the offices of the Speaker of the Legislative Yuan and the Minister of the Interior. To give Taiwanese a greater representation in the national government, the KMT has been contemplating holding elections in Taiwan to fill vacancies left open in the Legislative Yuan, the National Assembly, and the Control Yuan.[47]

With respect to the mainlanders, the KMT has concentrated its effort at improving the life of the two key groups of people: the functionaries of the national government and the retired servicemen. In recent years the government has made three upward adjustments of the pay scale, adding NT $2.5 billion to the public outlay.[48] Already straining the government's financial resources, these increases in salary for the government employees have not kept pace with the rise of private income. But for a number of reasons the mainlander functionaries are apparently contented with their economic life. They recognize that the salary increases they have received are what the government can realistically provide. Many who have been with the national government for several decades also often make it a habit of comparing their present fate in Taiwan with their plight during the Chinese-Japanese war in the 1930s and 1940s and consider that there has been much improvement of their well-being since. Some also derive a sense of satisfaction from the high ranks that they hold in the central government.

Through a cabinet Assistance Commission for the Retired Servicemen, the KMT had resettled as of 1966 a total of 156,845 veterans in 99 government-created productive enterprises and cooperative farms throughout the island.[49] This program proves to be a highly successful adventure both economically and politically. In 1966, with a total revenue of over NT $1 billion from these economic undertakings, the veterans had an average income better than what some governmental workers earn today.[50] The veterans, intermingling with natives through business dealings and social activities, also constitute a stabilizing factor in local communities and the countryside.

While recognizing that the measures adopted by the KMT do not meet in full their respective needs, the islanders and the mainlanders deem it possible for further improvement of their well-being. Moreover, both groups realize that such improvement requires their increasing mutual acceptance and cooperation. For the reality is that whereas the mainlanders are in the position to make basic decisions in regard to the islanders' future economic welfare and access to national power, the already improved economic and political position of the islanders enable them to influence to a certain extent how the mainlanders make these decisions. These conditions, coupled with the mixing of the young in schools and in the increasing instances of cooperative business undertakings of the two groups, have made the ethnic tension that once constituted an acute internal problem of the island recede "into the background." [51]

Ideological Adjustment

If United States aid is obviously a crucial factor in bringing about a rapid economic development in Taiwan, what is not as obvious is the influence the United States exerted on the KMT to change its economic policies and ideology.

Although anti-Marxist in its philosophical tenet, KMT's Principle of People's Livelihood has a certain socialist orientation. Having never seriously implemented this principle during the mainland days, the KMT was quite disposed, in the initial period of its rule in Taiwan, to translate the principle into reality on the island. The transfer of many Japanese enterprises to the Chinese government had already placed a major share of Taiwan's economy under public management, and the military exigencies of the day might justifiably require a stringent government control of the rest of the economy.

From the point of view of the United States, such a disposition was economically unsound. American aid agencies believed that "a shift from state to private ownership would contribute to the operating efficiency of . . . enterprises, hasten over-all economic development and decrease the [government's] financial burden in subsidizing [public] activities." [52] Behind this belief also "lay the political aim of demonstrating the superiority of free economic institutions as instruments of social progress." [53] Thus, through a combination of several measures—exhortation, participation in economic planning, and manipulation of availability of development funds—the United States has been able to bring about basic changes in KMT economic policies.[54]

As Neil A. Jacoby has observed, "By far the most important consequence of U.S. influence was the creation in Taiwan of a booming private enterprise system." [55] In addition, the United States was instrumental to the liberalization of economic regulations, the lessening of foreign exchange control, and the creation of conditions and machinery for a market-oriented economy.

Ideologically, these changes may be considered permissible developments under KMT's Principle of People's Livelihood. For this principle envisages a mixed economy that is composed of public and private sectors. It should be noted, however, that this KMT ideology, in its original formulation as well as in its subsequent reaffirmations by the party, signifies "state operation of [major] industries, state control of capital, and state ownership of profits." The emphasis is clearly placed on the public sector. But in contrast to this original concept, today in Taiwan "there has been an evident trend in the government's policy toward continuous expansion of free economy and promotion of private enterprise." [56] Seen in the light of this development, it is evident that the KMT has modified its economic philosophy, substituting an enlarged private enterprise system for an expanded public economy as its professed policy objective.

Conclusion

For the KMT there are two basic values to be preserved: its dominant power position and continuing modernization. While the latter may be subordinate to the requirements of the former, prolonged experience with modernization will build a momentum of its own, which can hardly be curtailed without giving rise to undesirable political consequences. To preserve both values, the KMT deems it necessary to show adaptability and flexibility. However, the adaptations of the KMT exhibit themselves unevenly in the party's structure, function, and ideology. KMT's introduction of local self-rule, assumption of responsibilities for economic and social transformations, and promotion of political and social integration have compelled the party to perform a host of new tasks. That it has been able to perform these tasks with varying degrees of success indicates that it is functionally innovative and adjustable. Ideologically, the party showed a change in the realm of economic policy; such change is significant and has contributed to the dynamic growth of the island's economy, which, in turn, perhaps helped initiate the whole process of modernization.

The KMT has shown the least change structurally. The organizational pattern and principles operating in the mainland period persist in Taiwan. This dissonance in the structural and functional changes of the party can be explained by reference to the durability of the party leadership. Having long been accustomed to the established rules and procedures, the leadership cannot perceive any need to change them. The high party echelon also holds the view that the preservation of the existing power structure is essential to the island's stability, on which KMT's political hold depends. To the leadership, therefore, a combination of the structural integrity and functional adaptability of the party seems the best way under the circumstances to secure the party's political preponderance and to insure continuing modernization. One may speculate that in the long run, as the populace participates more actively in the political process, and as modernization further intensifies popular demands upon the political system, KMT's ability to preserve stability and to respond effectively to challenges of the continually changing economic and social environment will require structural adjustments of the party as well. Evidently one needed adjustment would be a broadening of the social foundation of the party by bringing in more members from the business, labor, and agricultural interests. At the same time the KMT must provide a mechanism through which the competing demands of these interests can be mitigated and reconciled. Perhaps the experiences of the PRI in Mexico, which are discussed elsewhere in this volume, may be most instructive for the KMT.

In many aspects the PRI and the KMT are remarkably similar. As inheritors of revolutions that occurred only a year apart, both parties had experienced a period of internal strife before they were consolidated into instruments of governing; both have maintained a preponderant position in the electoral process; and both have perceived themselves to be the agents of modernization. One primary difference between them clearly lies in the sphere of institutional arrangements. Whereas the KMT remains dominated by politicians and the military, the PRI has integrated the campesinos, laborers, and other "popular" elements into its structure. For three decades the official party in Mexico has consistently retained its political hegemony, preserved stability for the country, and maintained a fast-growing economy. In no small measure, these accomplishments are due to the fact that the PRI has, by integrating social groups into its organization, converted the potential sources of challenge to its rule to forces actively sustaining its modernization effort.

‖ Notes

1. Karl W. Deutsch, "Social Mobilization and Political Development," *American Political Science Review,* LV (September 1961), 497–498.
2. Karl W. Deutsch, "Toward an Inventory of Basic Trends and Patterns in Comparative and International Politics," *American Political Science Review,* LIV (March 1960), 39; cf. Samuel P. Huntington, "Political Development and Political Decay," *World Politics,* XVII (April 1965), 405–410, and Lucian W. Pye, *Aspects of Political Development* (Boston: Little, Brown, 1966), p. 75.
3. Pye, *op. cit.,* pp. 41–42.
4. S. N. Eisenstadt, "Breakdowns of Modernization," *Economic Development and Cultural Change,* XII (July 1964), 347. Cf. David E. Apter, *The Politics of Modernization* (Chicago: The University of Chicago Press, 1965), pp. 56 and 66–67; and Manfred Halpern, "Toward Further Modernization of the Study of New Nations," *World Politics,* XVII (October 1964), 177.
5. See, for instance, Melvin Gurtov, "Taiwan in 1966: Political Rigidity, Economic Growth," *Asian Survey,* VII (January 1967), 44–45; Joyce K. Kallgren, "Nationalist China: Political Inflexibility and Economic Accommodation," *Asian Survey,* IV (January 1964), 638–645; and Mark Mancall, ed., *Formosa Today* (New York: Frederick A. Praeger, 1964), especially Mancall's "Introduction" and John Israel, "Politics on Formosa."
6. Joseph LaPalombara and Myron Weiner write: "Historical crises not only often provide the context in which political parties first emerge but also tend to be a critical factor in determining what pattern of evolution parties later take." "The Origin and Development of Political Parties," in LaPalombara and Weiner, eds., *Political Parties and Political Development* (Princeton: Princeton University Press, 1966), p. 14.
7. See Chang Chi-yun, *Tang Shih Kai Yao (The Concise History of the Kuomin-*

tang) (Taipei, Taiwan, China: Chung Yang Kai Tsao Wei Yuan Hui Wen Wu Kung Ying Shê, 1951), I, 275–276.

8. Pichon P. Y. Loh, "The Politics of Chiang Kai-shek," *The Journal of Asian Studies,* XXV (May 1966), 447.

9. See *Chung Kuo Kuomintang Ti Chiu Tsu Chüan Kuo Tai Piao Ta Hui Tê Chi* (*Summary of Records of the Ninth National Congress of the Chinese Nationalist Party*); hereafter referred to as *Summary of Records* (Taipei, Taiwan, China: Chung Yang Wen Wu Kung Ying Shê, 1964), p. 39.

10. Tsui Shu-chin, *Sun Chung-shan yü Kung-chan Chu-i* (*Sun Yat-sen and Communism*) (Hong Kong: The Asia Press, 1954), pp. 37–38.

11. For the complete text of the Declaration of the First National Congress of 1924, see Leonard S. Hsü, *Sun Yat-sen: His Political and Social Ideals* (Los Angeles: University of Southern California Press, 1933), pp. 119–141.

12. Quoted in Tsui, *op. cit.,* pp. 438–440.

13. Aside from the KMT Declaration of 1924, which first officially embraced this economic policy, the most important document attempting to lay down detailed plans for its implementation is the "Chinese Economic Reconstruction Program" submitted by Chiang Kai-shek to the Third National Congress of the KMT in 1936. Stressing that "economic development must . . . be planned . . . and must rest on a basic theory," the program stated, "The basic theory of the Principle of People's Livelihood is to develop national enterprises, . . . while at the same time controlling private capital and equalizing land ownership. Chinese economic principles are not those of *laissez-faire* nor of promoting the class struggle. . . ." See Chang, *op. cit.,* IV, 2049–2053.

14. Neil H. Jacoby, *U.S. Aid to Taiwan: A Study of Foreign Aid, Self-Help and Development* (New York: Frederick A. Praeger, 1966), p. 85; cf. Robert F. Emery and Henry F. Lu, "Economic Trends in Asia in 1966," *Asian Survey,* VII (November 1967), 808; and *The New York Times,* January 19, 1968, p. 68.

15. Jacoby, *op. cit.,* pp. 85–86.

16. Referring to Taiwan's rapid expansion of foreign trade in 1967, an economic officer of the American embassy commented in Taipei: "For the first time in its history, Taiwan's welfare depends on its ability to compete in the world market. . . . This is new, and it will have a profound effect." *The New York Times,* January 19, 1968, p. 54.

17. The level of voter participation in Taiwan is comparable to that of a number of Western democracies and higher than that of most of the developing countries. See Bruce M. Russett, et al., *World Handbook of Political and Social Indicators* (New Haven: Yale University Press, 1964), Table 4, pp. 84–87. Electoral participation in Taiwan is voluntary. There are neither fines against absentees nor such subtle pressures as commonly employed in Communist countries to induce the people to vote.

18. *Central Daily News* (hereafter cited as *CDN*), April 22, 1968, pp. 1 and 3. In 1967 Taipei was elevated to the status of a "special city," under the direct control of the Executive Yuan; no election was held in the city in 1968. Thus in 1968 there were only four metropolitan areas in which elections were held.

19. See Jacoby, *op. cit.,* p. 112 and Allan B. Cole, "Political Roles of Taiwanese Enterprisers," *Asian Survey,* VII (September 1967), 651.

20. Yu-fu Pu, *Taiwan Fêng Yün Jên Wu* (*Notables of Taiwan*) (Hong Kong: Hsin Wen Tien Ti Shê, 1962).

21. See Yen-tien Chang, "Land Reform and Its Impact on Economic and Social Progress in Taiwan; in memory of [the] late Vice President Chen Cheng," *Industry of Free China,* XXIII (April 1965), 36–38.

22. United Nations, *Progress in Land Reform, Fourth Report* (New York, 1966), p. 155. For a breakdown of all the elected offices occupied by farmers in 1955, see

China, Taiwan, Taiwan Provincial Government, Department of Civil Affairs, *Taiwan Tu-ti Kai-Keh (Land Reform in Taiwan)* (1957), p. 81.

23. See China, Taiwan Provincial Government, Department of Civil Affairs, *Taiwan Hsuan Cheng (Elections in Taiwan)* (1960), pp. 317–319.
24. John D. Montgomery, Rufus B. Hughes, and Raymond A. Davis, *Rural Improvement and Political Development: The JCRR Model* (Washington, D.C.: Agency for International Development, 1964), p. 7.
25. Taiwan, Taiwan Sheng Ti Fang Tsû Ch'ih Chih Yao Pien Chi Wei Yuan Hui, *Taiwan Sheng Ti Fang Tsû Ch'ih Chih Yao (Compendium on Self-Government in Taiwan);* hereafter referred to as *Compendium* (Taichung, Taiwan, China, 1965), p. 869.
26. *Ibid.*, pp. 885–888.
27. For a description of the organizational structure of these associations, see S. C. Hsieh, "Farmers Organizations in Taiwan and Their Trends of Development," *Industry of Free China,* XX (December 1963), 23–38; and Taiwan, Provincial Government, Department of Agriculture and Forestry, *The Reorganization of Farmers' Associations in Taiwan* (Taipei, Taiwan, China, 1950), pp. 43–51.
28. *Compendium*, p. 896.
29. M. H. Kwoh, "Brief Statement of Farmers' Associations in Taiwan," (Taipei, Taiwan, China, 1966), p. 74. Quoted in Richard Hough, *AID Administration to the Rural Sector: The JCRR Experience in Taiwan and its Application in Other Countries,* AID Discussion Paper No. 17 (Washington, D.C.: Agency for International Development, 1968), p. 27.
30. Cf. Cole, *op. cit.,* pp. 650–651.
31. Using the Harrod-Domar model to estimate the impact of the military burden on Taiwan's economy, Neil H. Jacoby estimates that without this burden, Taiwan's GNP might have increased 22 per cent more than what was actually achieved in 1952–1965. Jacoby, *op. cit.,* p. 124.
32. China, Hsing Chêng Yuan, Hsin Wên Chü, *Kuomintang Chiu Chüan Ta Hui (The Ninth Congress of the Nationalist Party)* (Taipei, Taiwan, China, 1963), pp. 38–39; and *CDN,* November 24, 1967, p. 1.
33. See *Summary of Records,* pp. 88–89. Membership figures were given in round numbers.
34. The use of these categories of party activities as points of analysis is conceptually inspired by LaPalombara and Weiner, *op. cit.,* pp. 14–19 and 339–418.
35. This is an estimate based on information in Table 13–5, above, and *Compendium,* pp. 317, 407, 538, and 656.
36. In 1960 a group of Taiwanese, as well as a few mainlander politicians, began to organize the China Democratic Party with the intention to offer programs that would potentially challenge some of these restrictions. These politicians had expressed in varying degrees their doubts on the KMT's policy of recovery of the mainland; they also attempted to base the party's future strength on the Taiwanese. Viewing these developments as likely to lead to a questioning of its basic policy goal, and to an injection of the unfortunate issue of racism into the political process, the KMT became opposed to the formation of the party. The organizers of the party abandoned their effort.
37. *Land Reform in Taiwan* (Taipei, Taiwan, China: China Publishing Company, 1961), pp. 47–48. Cf. Hui-sun Tang, *Land Reform in Free China* (Taipei, Taiwan, China: The JCRR, 1954), p. 31.
38. Thus Chiang Kai-shek told KMT members in 1949: "We must frankly admit that our Party has done more for the political phase of our National Revolution than for the economic and social phases. Many of our members speak for social reform in theory, while in practice they rarely go into the heart of society and work for social improvement. Thus they incurred the criticism of being 'leftists

in thought but rightists in action.' " *President's Statement to All Members of the Kuomintang, September 1949* (Taipei, Taiwan, China: China Cultural Service, 1954), pp. 22–23.

39. There is evidence suggesting that KMT's loss of strength in recent elections in the metropolitan areas was partly due to a sizable number of protest votes from the poor. See Jacoby, *op. cit.*, pp. 112–113.

40. See *CDN*, August 1, 1966, p. 1; September 21, 1967, p. 3; and October 12, 1967, p. 12.

41. *Summary of Records*, pp. 1, 16.

42. The KMT estimated that the total value of these services performed in 1962–1967 amounted to NT$218 million. See *CDN*, May 30, 1967, p. 3., and January 9, 1968, p. 3.

43. According to one estimate, "More than 60% of all production in the island's growing economy is in private hands, and about 80% of private enterprisers are Taiwanese." Cole, *op. cit.*, p. 645. In one government-sponsored conference on economic development held in 1961, to which chief business executives of the island's major private firms were all invited, there were eight mainlanders and thirty natives who held positions as corporation board chairmen or presidents. See *Yangmingshan Hui-tan Shih Lu* (*Records of the Yangmingshan Conference*) (Taipei, Taiwan, China, n.d.), pp. 73–85.

44. Karl L. Rankin, *China Assignment* (Seattle: The University of Washington Press, 1964), p. 202.

45. For example, of the total of 191,162 persons (not including 9 foreigners) employed by the provincial government in 1965, 119,613 (62.57 per cent) were islanders and 71,549 (37.43 per cent) were mainlanders. See China, Executive Yuan, Directorate-General of Budgets, Accounts, and Statistics, *Statistical Abstract of the Republic of China, 1966* (Taipei, Taiwan, China, 1966), p. 732.

46. Jacoby, *op. cit.*, p. 112.

47. *Tsu Kuo I Chou* (*China Weekly*), November 12, 1967, pp. 4–5.

48. Included military pay increase. *CDN*, October 12, 1966, p. 1; and May 31, 1967, p. 3. See also *Free China Weekly*, March 26, 1967, p. 1.

49. *Tsu Kuo I Chou*, March 12, 1967, p. 7.

50. *Ibid.*

51. *The New York Times*, August 9, 1967, p. 5. See also Cole, *op. cit.*, pp. 648–649.

52. U.S., The Comptroller-General, *Report to the Congress of the United States: Examination of Economic and Technical Assistance Program for the Government of the Republic of China (Taiwan), Fiscal Years 1955–1957* (mimeographed, August 1958), p. 22.

53. Jacoby, *op. cit.*, p. 137.

54. For a brief description of the measures employed by the United States to lead to the desired changes in Chinese policies, see *ibid.*, pp. 134–137.

55. *Ibid.*, pp. 137–138.

56. Concluding statement of the Yangmingshan Conference on Economic Development. See *Yangmingshan Hui-tan Shih Lu*, pp. 4, 22. Cf. The Kuomintang Platform adopted at the last National Congress in 1963. *Summary of Records*, pp. 43–44.

14

Group Politics in Communist Society:
A Second Look at the Pluralistic Model

‖ *Andrew C. Janos*

Introduction

For some years the study of communist political systems has been undergoing radical changes. Whereas before the methodological premise underlying research was that communist systems were in many respects unique and that they displayed novel political characteristics—themes that had been carefully woven into various models of totalitarianism—now political scientists clamor for a more comparative approach, hoping to gain new insights by applying categories to the study of communism that have been derived from the experience of Western and developing societies.

One can but welcome this new trend, for it promises to enrich not only communist studies but, through a process of empirical testing, also the broader theoretical framework of political science. Yet at the same time one should also guard against possible pitfalls, above all against those of mechanical adaptation. To be sure, some categories of analysis may be highly suggestive in the context of communism, but others may be too parochially "Western" or otherwise areabound to be useful in explaining communist politics. Indeed, unless handled carefully and critically these constructs may easily lead to erroneous conclusions and mistaken inferences.

These dangers, it seems to me, loom especially large in the resurgent attempts to adopt group theories and various models of pluralism as the main paradigm of politics in communist societies. While in the past the policy process in communist countries was relatively neglected as a subject of inquiry—usually in favor of leadership structure, policy outputs, and political controls—or else explained in terms of the personality of an omnipotent leader and his relations to an obedient party, more recently experts began to discover conflicting interests, pressure groups, and pluralistic trends.[1] Even though most writers cautiously emphasize the "imperfect" or "incipient" character of pluralism in communist societies, the current tendency in the field points away from the earlier monolithic concept of totalitarianism. In the words of a major protagonist of the new school,

> The totalitarian concept which excludes group interest and conflict is no longer an appropriate means of analyzing Soviet politics. . . . A new model of Communist politics is thus slowly emerging as a result of changes that have occurred since Stalin's death and of the shifting perspectives of both western and Communist analysts. The model of a totalitarian system in which a single party, itself free of internal conflict, imposes its will on society and on all social groups, is being replaced by a model that takes account of conflicting groups that exert an influence on the making of policy by the party.

The same author declares that in their present, transitional stage communist systems can perhaps be best described by Dahl's expressive term—as "polyarchies." [2]

This quotation, while obviously not totally representative of the new trend, may still be taken as our point of departure because it raises some of the major problems that need critical examination before we may accept the pluralistic or group concepts as models of communist politics. It is, of course, obvious to all but the most superficial or biased observer that in the past few years communist governments have shown increasing responsiveness to their societies by anticipating and screening potential demand. But whether such responsiveness can invariably be described as the result of "group politics" is another question. In any case, the assumption that the politics of communist societies is explicable in terms of a single model, and that the earlier totalitarian model ought to be simply substituted by a new one, is a somewhat startling recommendation, especially because it is being made at a time when the political diversity of communist countries has already become a journalistic and academic commonplace. Furthermore, it may be necessary to raise questions not only concerning the general validity but also concerning the dimensions and variations of group politics. Even though we may detect groups in some communist societies, the structure of these groups and the context in which they operate may be responsible for significant deviations from the pattern we tend to associate with group politics in Western, industrial societies.

Dimensions of the Group Model

In order to develop these themes and place communist and non-communist systems in comparative perspective, let us briefly outline the group model and the categories of analysis relevant to it. In terms of this model, "inputs" into the system originate from several (at any rate more than one) aggregates of individuals who cluster around some common purpose that reflects their socioeconomic position, religious beliefs, or primary affiliations. The "outputs" of the system, on the other hand, are "authoritative allocations of value" that reflect a synthesis of conflicting group interests as well as power relations among the major competitors. The more powerful a group, the greater the share it is likely to receive from the common pie. Using this model, the pattern of public policy allows us to draw inferences concerning the structure of interests and the distribution of power in society. Conversely, if we know the structure of competing interests and the groups representing them, we should be able to predict the content of binding decisions with some measure of accuracy. The utility of the group model is that it serves as a link between social structure and "authoritative allocations" explaining how and why the total social environment leaves its imprint on daily politics.

To carry the discussion one step further we will have to consider the dynamic aspect of pluralism and distinguish among three alternative modes in which groups bargain and pursue their interests. The first of these modes, persuasion (or lobbying), involves an attempt to attain one's goal by rational argument, the essence of which is that a particular course of action is in the interest of both of the parties involved. Persuasive tactics aim at an authoritative allocation without reference to either resources that the parties may possess or to negative consequences that one of the parties may suffer if the demand for an allocation is not satisfied. Persuasion is the principal way in which the average lobbyist operates in a parliamentary system, pleading with the authorities that a particular policy decision would be in the "common good" or "national interest." The quintessence of persuasive tactics is expressed in the celebrated slogan: "What is good for General Motors is good for the country." The second mode of action relevant to this analysis is the exchange (or proffered exchange) of political commodities in a manner analogous to activities in the economic marketplace. A good example of this mode of action would be the case of a group of businessmen offering to invest in a strategically located foreign country in exchange for tax or tariff benefits. The essence of the ensuing "deal" is that it has been entered into freely by both parties, and accepted by them as only one of many possible options. The emphasis is still on common interest as it flows from the exchange of political support for an authoritative allocation. In contrast, pressure refers to a mode of action in which the options of one of the parties are limited (or threatened to be limited) to two undesirable alternatives. In the case of pressures one party states a desired objective that involves costs for another, specifying simultaneously consequences that may follow in the event of noncompliance.[3] Pressure may be applied in a number of ways of which the most common are threats to withhold resources or cooperation or cause a third party to do the same. In modern, industrial societies, however, pressures become most frequently operative through the existence of institutionalized forms of accountability.

The *ultima ratio* of groups in such societies is to threaten to withdraw their electoral support from incumbent authorities, or else, to use their resources in a way calculated to bring about the same result. Since not all groups have the capacity to bring about this result or to make other threats effective, not all interest groups may properly be described as "pressure groups." Indeed, it may be advisable for our purposes to distinguish empirically between pressure groups and other politically interested groups, or lobbies.

The effectiveness of these modes of action and the general relevance of the group model assumes a number of conditions. First, in order to compete politically, groups must possess a degree of integration. While it is possible to speak of a group, as indeed sociologists do, in terms of the objective reality of roles and affiliations (and predictable responses to environmental stimuli), politically groups become active only if their membership possesses a degree of collective awareness as well as a network of communications, however rudimentary, through which interests may be clarified, formulated, and articulated. In the absence of these conditions we have, in Ralph Dahrendorf's words, only "quasi-groups" with "latent interests" [4] that become politically relevant only through the perceptions of decision-makers. Secondly, the groups must be autonomous, a condition that obtains in the absence of accountability to outside authority (at least in relation to the issues that are subject to political bargaining in any given situation) and a degree of self-containment with respect to (1) the internal structure and arrangements of the group, (2) its resources, and (3) most critically, with respect to formal or informal group leadership.[5]

The last step in our conceptual enterprise is to establish potential variations in the group model in terms of the character of the groups and the context in which they participate. Here I will suggest three politically significant categories. To begin with, groups should be differentiated in terms of their "representativeness." This term should not be taken to mean that the group possesses a democratic constitution or that the leadership is formally accountable to the rank and file; representativeness implies only that a degree of reciprocity exists between leaders and led derived from a common goal that, in turn, flows from the social roles or fundamental beliefs of the membership. In "representative" groups leaders may command, but their authority to do so flows from their ability to perform in accordance with collective expectations. This type of relationship is common in modern associations as well as in traditional communities or corporate organizations organized around specific social roles and interests arising out of them. On the other hand, such reciprocity does not exist in charismatic relationships where the leader's authority rests on effect and not on performance, nor for that matter in mercenary groups where the membership follows the elite as long as the latter performs a specific, contractually established obligation. In general, members of such "non-representative" groups respond to positive or negative incentives unrelated to the goals pursued by the leadership. Thus in a political arena populated by non-representative units, the link between social differentiation (the social roles of the group membership) and the content of public policy will be a weak one.

Another variation that obtains is in terms of the purpose or "inclusiveness" [6] of groups participating in the political process. The "non-inclusive" group arises from multiple affiliations and is typified by associations in modern, industrial societies created with the aim of pursuing specific goals. In contrast, the "inclusive" group, typified by the medieval corporation, tends to dominate all aspects of its members' lives, aiming not so much at participation in the formulation of public policy but at the separation of the various spheres of society from one another and from the political sphere. The corporatist concept of interest representation is a passive one, centering around the ideas of the *pouvoirs intérmediaires,* and while corporate organizations may step outside its prescribed boundaries and act as modern interest groups, such forms of political participation will rarely have their roots in consensus and will be apt to generate political tensions. In addition, distinctions will have to be made between group models in terms of the political context in which the groups operate. In one type of system, autonomous groups exist both *de facto* and *de jure,* that is, the existence of competing groups is guaranteed by custom or contract. The competing groups, while pursuing conflicting objectives, are willing to accept the inevitability of conflict, the fundamental justice of the case of the opponent, and his right to defend his interests. This "political formula" generally finds institutional expression in independent tribunals that guard over the autonomy of the groups and the observance of the rules of the game, in bodies of mediation and arbitration, and in parliamentary-type institutions for the orderly aggregation of interests. In other systems groups may exist *de facto* and compete effectively, yet their existence is not guaranteed by either internalized or legal norms. If this is the case, relations among groups will be unstable and the outcome of the political process will tend to be highly unstructured and random. On these grounds, therefore, we will have to distinguish between "reconciliation" systems and fragmented societies.[7]

Politics and Society: Variations on the Communist Theme

Having presented our theoretical equipment, let us now turn to communist reality and see how these systems fit the various categories of the model. For the sake of simplicity, and because of the writer's qualifications, this discussion will be restricted to the Soviet Union and the communist states of East Europe. Taking these under investigation it will soon be evident that, in terms of our variables, they will fall into three broad categories.

In the first category of systems we will find the Soviet Union, Rumania, Albania, East Germany, and Bulgaria. In these five European communist societies the integration of groups is too low to be meaningful; the prevailing political formula does not recognize the principle of social autonomy, and the groups that exist in the form of structured associations are hierarchically subordinated to the party-state. True, the much publicized and significant economic reforms have decentralized management and increased its scope of control over the allocation of resources. But the reforms, often quite explicitly, stopped short of the principle of full autonomy and the establishment of autonomous economic units in which management would be accountable to the plant or to some corporate body of workers rather than to the political authorities. Political control over social communications, above all over the mass media, is effective and extensive enough in scope to prevent the crystallization of political groups around socioeconomic roles. Even strategically located individuals, such as writers, scientists, or industrial managers, find it impossible to act in a concerted fashion. The last, according to a recent and exhaustive study on the subject, "on occasion have functioned as a fairly cohesive political action-group." Yet, the same author continues, "The group activities of the Soviet managerial elite have never been accorded political legitimacy," and as a consequence, "collective action on the part of the managers has been a high-risk enterprise likely to evoke a terroristic response from the political leadership." [8] An observer of the much publicized Rumanian "deviation" comes to the same conclusions. Writing of the recent party congress in that country he states that "the political elite's greatest fear relates to the appearance of 'spontaneous elements' . . . . If there is any theme throughout the speeches delivered at the *NPC* [National Party Congress], it is that of concern with the abolition and denial of uncontrolled autonomy." [9] This does not, of course, preclude conflict or bargaining, particularly on the levels of local economic and political organization, but the bulk of transactions between society and political authorities does not represent group pressures but rather individual lobbying and protest. Characteristically, but not surprisingly, grievance procedures in these societies emphasize and encourage individual complaints—in the form of letters to the authorities or to the editors of journals—while at the same time discouraging group action and collective protest by treating them as acts of insubordination and rebellion.

Moving on to a second category of regimes we may list the remaining members of the Soviet bloc in East Europe: Hungary, Poland, and Czechoslovakia. In these three countries political groups have emerged time and again over the past decade to challenge the policies of the governments or pressuring for specific concessions. The professional organizations or *ad hoc* groupings of students, intellectuals, and workers (the various discussion clubs, the workers' councils and writers' unions), aided by an independent-minded press, have left a significant mark on politics, and at times even succeeded in controlling the course of political developments. In at least one country the established church has maintained a considerable freedom of action and has used it to mobilize public opinion not only in the defense of religious institutions but also in promoting particular policies in opposition to the government.

These examples of group politics have frequently been cited in the pluralist literature and elsewhere as manifestations of the regimes' "liberalism." The contrast with some of the more "orthodox" or "hard-line" regimes is indeed striking, but the "liberal" adjective may be misleading. While it is true that groups have emerged in public life and have periodically exerted considerable influence on the political process, such influence has not been the result of any conscious design or ideological consideration but of the temporary weakness of the ruling parties. One should not fail to realize that, in the last analysis, the existence of "interest groups" and a "free press" in these countries has been most precarious, controlled by political exigencies rather than by constitutional guarantees or legal covenants. The words of a Czechoslovak writer illustrate this point: "At the moment censorship exists on paper but not in practice. However, in theory, the censor can clamp down tomorrow. . . . What is important is to get a law today to remove censorship and guarantee the freedom of speech and assembly. This is a necessary condition to any liberalization." [10] In the absence of such laws the regimes in question remain liberal only *de facto* without bestowing legitimacy upon collective political participation. Looking back into the past, the Petöfi Club, the Crooked Circle, the writers' unions and workers' councils of Hungary and Poland, so often quoted as evidence for "pluralism," were at one time influential organizations. But where are they now? They were destroyed, together with other spontaneously established associations, in the moment when the ruling parties felt strong enough to do away with inconvenient political opposition. And herein lies the essence of group politics in contemporary East Europe. Even if we may speak of "incipient pluralism," or less convincingly of "polyarchy," this pluralism has a spurious quality; the groups participating in politics have a highly unstable character, their life is ephemeral, and their impact on politics random and incidental.

More than that, the ruling parties of these countries have established a considerable record of hostility not only toward opposition groups but toward the very idea of social autonomy and collective bargaining. Thus while two of the aforementioned three regimes have accepted thoroughgoing reforms of the economic system involving the decentralization of economic decision-making, they have rejected the idea of economic "self-management" and the autonomy of production units from the central authorities in most explicit terms.[11] Similarly, the idea of autonomous trade unions serving as instruments of interest representation have been turned down as "highly inappropriate at the present stage of development." [12] Instead of being granted autonomy, the unions were "strengthened" and assigned new functions of economic and political control, including controls over management and pricing practices, while their members were urged to shun special interests, concern themselves with the common good, and guard against economic particularism and opportunism.[13] The autonomy of other social organizations and institutions is subject to similar limitations. Attempts at emancipating youth organizations from the party have been angrily rebuffed by the political leadership, and the much-vaunted autonomy of institutions of higher learning remains severely restricted by the maintenance of political controls over the appointment and removal of academic personnel.[14] Most recently in Czechoslovakia these principles appear to be subjected to serious review, but as of writing (May, 1968) the outcome of this review is still uncertain. In the other countries all outward signs indicate a further ideological hardening with respect to autonomy and the institutionalization of political bargaining.

One East European country, Yugoslavia, so far represents a special case and a category by itself. Often regarded as the representative example for post-Stalin communism in East Europe, the Yugoslav system is actually unique among its neighbors, because it is the only one to accept without qualifications two significant political principles: the legitimacy of special interests and the autonomy of social organization. These two principles are firmly rooted in the successive Yugoslav constitutions of 1952 and 1963 and are embodied in various institutions of administrative and economic "self-management," of which the best-known and most characteristic are the workers' councils and the communes. In both of these institutions the principle of autonomy prevails not only concerning the allocation of resources but also in relation to powers to exercise control over management and local administrative personnel. Moreover, it is important to point out that the autonomy and rights of these institutions appear to be effectively protected against political encroachments by an increasingly independent judiciary.[15] Last but not least, the existence and autonomy of economic and administrative organization is given adequate recognition in an elaborate parliamentary structure, based on a hierarchy of corporate chambers.

There is no doubt in the mind of this writer that these autonomous groups have a considerable impact on the quality of Yugoslav life and that the institutional structure represents a very significant advance from an earlier pattern of dictatorship in that country. At the same time, however, one must also raise the question whether and to what extent these arrangements permit or encourage the representation of interests, bargaining, and participation in the formulation of public policy. Clearly, from the point of view of the latter, the system has major weaknesses stemming from a concept of parliamentarianism that outlaws combination for the promotion of public policy in the name of "direct democracy," and insists on rotating parliamentary personnel, a practice which precludes the formation of legislative groups with institutional loyalties and sufficient bargaining experience. But above all, the political authorities maintain strict controls over the electoral process. Although the nomination of candidates to public offices takes place at the grass roots level, the Trade Union Syndicate (in the case of the workers' councils) and the Communist League (in communal, republican and federal elections) retain discretionary powers to screen the candidates politically and to eliminate the "enemies of socialism" from the electoral competition. This means that the government, while accepting the principles of autonomy and bargaining as legitimate, insists on determining who should bargain and on behalf of which group. This pattern of politics is closer to the one prevailing in the corporatist states of the interwar period or to that of the classic autocratic state than to the political process in modern, industrial democracies. In practice, group autonomy and the institutional order are not so much instruments of interest articulation and aggregation but of conflict resolution in areas that are not deemed to be strategic by the regime. They represent, in the words of an authoritative study, "an experiment in the settlement of the great bulk of public and economic matters at a level close to the undertaking and without involving political decisions." [16] As such their real function is not to incorporate new social strata into the political process, but rather to "de-politicize" society by drawing a line between the active and passive concerns of the ruling party. This aspect of Yugoslav politics is best summarized by Adam Ulam in his essay on the essence of Titoism:

> In the classical Communist pattern, the average citizen is made aware of the political importance of every social act. . . . In Tito's Yugoslavia, on the contrary, there is a very elaborate set of devices and institutions designed to persuade the citizen that most of his activities are not connected with politics. . . . In his activities as producer or as a member of the commune, the citizen is allegedly performing objective economic and administrative tasks, not fulfilling a set of directives laid down by an oppressive political authority. Politics is the business of the League of Communists, and the average citizen is relieved of the presence and pressure of Big Brother; indeed, he is asked not to notice that Big Brother exists.[17]

The Group Model and Elite Politics

But if there is no genuine give-and-take and group competition in most communist societies, would not the pluralist model of group politics be applicable to the study of relations among the ruling elites? The parties are, so it has been stated, no longer "monolithic." Instead of serving as the tool of the totalitarian dictator, today they represent a meeting ground of diverse ideas and are often divided into competing factions that perform some of the functions of a multi-party system in an open society. Like competing political parties, factions may represent broad policy alternatives and put forward, in effect, alternative slates of contenders for high political office. To support the argument, writers on the subject generally point out well-known examples of "liberal" and "orthodox" or "pro-Soviet" and "pro-Chinese" factions in East European parties. Or else they call attention to the presence of coteries of leading individuals (such as the Pulawy and Natolin groups in the Polish party) whose solidarity and political goals derive from a common ethnic or organizational background. Moreover, as at least one in-depth study of Soviet decision-making in the Khrushchev period has demonstrated, pressures for policy changes may emanate from the lower and regional echelons of the party organizations, frequently resulting in compromise or the scaling down of initial policy objectives.[18]

The analogy between a multi-party system and intraparty factionalism is an attractive one, but before we can accept it as a working hypothesis we have to point out some major differences of context that derive from the nature of the political formula, more specifically, from the stern Leninist injunction against faction. Without exception, communist parties throughout the world still rigidly subscribe to the precept that caucuses and policy groups are politically dangerous to the stability of the regimes, and the "liberal" Yugoslav party is as anxious to enforce it as any one of the hard-boiled Stalinists of the area. Less than two years ago, at a time of sweeping political reforms, President Tito upheld the Leninist maxim, asserting that "its abandonment would mean the dissolution of the League of Communists into various *factions* guided by *different interests* [italics added]." [19] In a similar vein Edvard Kardelj, no orthodox communist himself, denounced the idea that party members might be "organized in groups on grounds of similar interest as in the case of bourgeois states with a multi-party system." [20] Thus the Yugoslavs together with other reform-minded parties maintain a strict distinction between "democratization" and "liberalization," distinguishing between the right to express opinions and the right to combine for their effective political promotion.

A second major aspect of the political formula to which the parties adhere in their internal organization is the principle of hierarchical organization. In accordance with the Leninist concept of democratic centralism (and its Stalinist interpretation) officials of the ruling party are *de facto* accountable not to the lower, but to the higher echelons in the organizations. Relations within the structure must be understood principally in terms of sub- and super-ordination. Autonomy, as T. H. Rigby points out in one of his incisive articles on Soviet politics, arises by default and not by design: it is the usual concomitant of succession crises or of weak, hesitant leadership at the center. Consequently, "pockets of autonomy" tend to disappear once firm leadership is restored.[21] Normally, therefore, the politics of communist parties is the politics of organizations and not of autonomous groups. This is not to say that communist parties are immune from conflict and internal competition. But the conflicts that arise are fought out or resolved in a hierarchical context, which gives politics a special quality.

The scope of organizational politics will be limited even in an "open society" principally by the threat that, as a last resort, a stubborn subordinate may be relieved by his superiors. If all other means fail, for instance, the President of the United States can dismiss a recalcitrant general (MacArthur) or department head, a step he can never take against the leadership of the National Farmers' Association or the National Association of Manufacturers. But in an open society the subordinate appears to have at least two powerful weapons that make pressures on his superiors occasionally

tem in East Europe vitally affected the character of its leadership. Far from constituting the autonomous political bodies typically implied by the very notion of the "ruling party" in a revolutionary one-party system, the East European ruling parties were reduced to the unenviable status of "derivative totalitarian parties," [19] that is, mere appendages of the CPSU. If before the purge of ostensible "Titoist" elements following upon Stalin's excommunication of Tito in 1948, signs of revolutionary creativity had been highly suspect, afterward they became an invitation to liquidation. Even so modest an attempt at revolutionary improvisation as "domesticism," that is, the perfectly natural proclivity to adjust revolutionary perspectives the better to deal with distinctive domestic situations,[20] fell victim to the mechanical adoption of the Soviet model of the "construction of socialism" with scant regard to its applicability under different national conditions.[21] Indeed, implementation of the Soviet model often dictated something akin to nihilism in matters of national culture. Negating all particularistic impulses were the imperatives of Soviet Communist ideology or, to be more precise, Marxism-Leninism-Stalinism, as the ideology was known in those days. With the accent so heavily on Stalinism, it is scarcely surprising that professional ideologists were in such short supply within the East European ruling elites and apparently so little required to spell out any special claim to regime legitimacy. Only in Yugoslavia, where after 1948 Tito's regime faced the necessity of justifying its isolated existence, was the situation different and this was very much a case of the exception that proved the rule.

Small wonder, then, that under such circumstances genuine charismatic leadership was so notably absent everywhere except in Yugoslavia or that the attempt to endow East European leaderships with a kind of derivative charisma predicated upon the personality of Stalin should have so largely missed the mark. True to the style of the treatment he meted out to subalterns inside the Soviet Union, Stalin knew well how to shift signs of his personal favor so as to institutionalize insecurity within the satellite elites. The result was bureaucratic leadership, conditioned to and dependent upon orders from Moscow, staffed by men drawn mainly from working class and lower-middle class background who have been quite appropriately described as "tough, resourceful, intellectually indifferent, and *supremely opportunistic practitioners of the revolution.*" [22]

This is not to say that the "we" of the East European revolution were only "tough," "resourceful," and "opportunistic." To leave matters at that might well be to suggest an immediate point of comparison with Mexican experience, but it also would be to fail to take account of the distinctive psychology of important elements of the East European revolutionary one-party system's social support. This support included certain members of the intelligentsia who were both mesmerized by the phenomenon of total power in its application for purposes of social change and also freshly endowed with material perquisites, and segments of the newly urbanized industrial class who were comparably favored with a degree of material privilege and the promise of more to come once "socialism" had been attained. All such elements were joined with the party elite and its *apparatchiki* in a common psychology of regime legitimacy. It was not merely an explicit revolutionary ideology that sustained their common allegiance but rather two quite specific components of that ideology. The first of these was the commitment to "proletarian internationalism." In practice, this meant nothing less than unconditional loyalty to the Soviet Union, but acceptance of so onerous and seemingly improbable a commitment was greatly facilitated as much by genuine admiration for Soviet accomplishments in the "construction of socialism" as by real awe at the imposing nature of Soviet power. The second, scarcely less important component was "Stalinism" itself. Official practice increasingly pushed the cult of Stalin's personality to the point of deification, but no matter the lengths to which it may have gone, adulation of the Soviet leader did serve to forge a sense of personal identification with Stalin, the man behind the "ism," as both the source and the symbol of revolutionary victories. Manifestations of the psychological hold of "proletarian internationalism" and "Stalinism" throughout East Europe were legion but the phenomenon was never more strikingly, if ironically, illustrated than at the July, 1948, Yugoslav Party Congress, called to ratify the Yugoslav Party's defiance of the Cominform's anti-Tito resolution, at which Tito proclaimed, "Long live the Soviet Union! Long live Stalin!" and the delegates took up the chant, "Stalin-Tito-Party"—in that order.[23]

Taken together, the absence of real party autonomy everywhere except in Yugoslavia, and the resultant internationalist-personalistic psychological basis of regime legitimacy during the Stalinist phase of communist power in East Europe help illuminate the deeper roots of the major political crisis that erupted in the area shortly after the Soviet dictator's death. Clearly the momentous events of 1956 cannot simply be chalked up to a misguided relaxation of Soviet control after Stalin's demise. To be sure, the Soviet dictator's successors at once set out to ameliorate the consequences of Stalin's rule abroad no less than at home. Among other things, they accepted domestic autonomy where, Stalin's efforts notwithstanding, it had actually been established, that is, in Yugoslavia and China. Moreover, recognizing the socioeconomic costs of the revolutionary transformation in East Europe and understandably desirous that the ruling parties there broaden their narrow base of popular support, Moscow did call for a slackening of the revolutionary pace and a relaxation of the worst features of terroristic police control. Still, these developments by themselves need not necessarily have precipitated a major political crisis. Rather, as Richard Lowenthal has pointed out, any adequate explanation of the crisis of the mid-1950s must take account of the convergence of this relaxation with a "triple crisis of authority," involving Khrushchev's disclosure and disavowal of Stalin's crimes, the prior involvement of many satellite bosses in the anti-Tito phase of these crimes and the uncertainty of the succession crisis in the Soviet Union itself.[24] In other words, not only did the Soviet center of the East European revolutionary one-party systems fail to produce a new leader capable of replacing Stalin as the focus of personal loyalty; worse yet, by denouncing Stalin, it unwittingly destroyed a crucial component of the legitimation of the East European revolution, thereby rendering its practitioners the more vulnerable to popular recrimination and made that very outcome the more certain by acting both to curb the inculcated programmatic instincts of the East European communist elites and to call into serious question their ingrained methods of rule. It would indeed have been astounding if all this, in turn, had failed to unloose currents highly damaging to the internationalist component of regime legitimacy in East Europe. Although the immediate consequences varied from country to country, wherever cleavages opened up within the ruling elite, resuscitated social forces, articulating pent-up mass discontent as well as group grievances, threatened the stability and even the survival of one-party rule. In 1956, of course, it was Hungary that provided the most dramatic example of the linkage between what Paul Kecskemeti has aptly characterized as an "elite" process of disarray and a "mass" process of disaffection, necessitating Soviet armed intervention to salvage a revolutionary one-party system on the verge of total disintegration.[25]

Paradoxically, the events of 1956 at once served to make the problem of the institutionalization of domestic one-party rule most urgent and at the same time rendered any immediate practical solution of the problem highly unlikely. The historical moment itself was scarcely a propitious one for novel experimentation designed to accommodate resurgent social forces whose demonstrated restiveness, all ruling communist elites had good grounds for believing, could only be accommodated at the risk of an undermining if not an overthrow of party rule itself. Moreover, the primary imperative of the moment, at least as Khrushchev saw it, called for institutionalizing *international* communist unity and the formula he hit upon contained crucial elements that for the short run tended to inhibit the emergence of more pluralistic, better institutionalized *domestic* communist regimes. For one thing, Khrushchev's stress on the ideological bonds of international unity presupposed a rejuvenation of Marxism-Leninism not just in theory but also in practice and the latter consideration implied a resumption in the revolutionary transformation of domestic society. Thus, without renouncing either the principle of domestic autonomy or the possibility of institutional diversity, Khrushchev strove to gain acceptance of concrete limitations on both in the interest of fidelity to a single common road to socialism, the one blazed by the Soviet Union. At first, Khrushchev's post-1956 reconstructionist efforts were buttressed by a mutual alignment of interests between the Soviet leadership and the East European political elites based upon their common antipathy to ideological revisionism, which seemed to threaten domestic dictatorships everywhere within East Europe as well as Soviet hegemony over the area. Gomulka may have harbored certain reservations about the implications, but Tito alone held himself aloof from this alignment. While at that time combatting his own internal revisionists, Tito refused to sign the 1957 Moscow Declaration acknowledging Soviet leadership and subsequently sought to justify his separatist course in the 1958 Yugoslav party program. As a result, Yugoslavia became a major target of the anti-revisionist campaign, and whatever practical suggestions Yugoslav domestic experience might have proffered the other East European leaderships were thus automatically ruled out.[26]

Yet, given the mixed and at bottom deeply contradictory tendencies of the Khrushchev era, the period of the late 1950s and early 1960s witnessed not only attempts at resuming the revolutionary transformation of domestic society but also the first tentative steps in the direction of established one-party rule in East Europe. The latter were, of course, most notable in Gomulka's Poland. Even while cracking down on the social forces (especially the critical intelligentsia) that had facilitated his own return to power in the teeth of initial Soviet opposition and doing this in such a way as increasingly to stamp his regime as "illiberal," Gomulka nonetheless did institute limited reforms designed to encourage greater popular participation in local government and a somewhat more active role for the national parliament, the *Sejm*. This, in turn, created some meaningful scope for the activity of other political groups, although the substance of overall party control was not diminished in any significant respect. More strikingly yet, despite Soviet stress on the desirability of agricultural collectivization, the Gomulka regime accepted the collapse of Polish collectivization that had occurred in 1956 and evinced no particular taste for a renewed revolutionary onslaught against the countryside. Significantly, the justification advanced for the stagnant party rule which was at the core of the distinctive Polish "road to socialism" was undertaken as much in terms of traditional nationalist geopolitical appeals as in terms of Marxist-Leninist ideology.[27]

Elsewhere in East Europe the emphasis was different. Although full-scale revolutionary onslaught by the party against society, as this had occurred in the Stalinist period, was neither advisable nor necessary, revolutionary exertions had still to run their course. Through the employment of varying degrees of persuasion and brute force, more or less complete agricultural collectivization was accomplished, first in Bulgaria (1957), then in Czechoslovakia (1959), next in East Germany (1960) and, finally, in Rumania and Hungary (1961–1962). In the late 1950s heavy industrial development, along lines reminiscent of the Stalinist order of economic priorities, dominated economic planning in Czechoslovakia, Hungary, East Germany and, of course, Rumania. Under the Chinese banner of a "great leap forward," Bulgaria embarked on a truly ambitious if ill-conceived effort at revolutionary mobilization. East Germany proclaimed its intention of "catching up with and surpassing" the Federal Republic of Germany in economic development. In 1958, its leadership instituted a "culture revolution" (under much tighter party supervision than the subsequent upheaval bearing a comparable designation in China) and, for some months immediately after the erection of the Berlin Wall in 1961, reverted to terroristic practices that seemed to pit the party irrevocably against society. In Czechoslovakia, the successful termination of agricultural collectivization, together with major strides in the socialization of the professions and the expropriation of small tradesmen and artisans, culminated in the promulgation of the 1960 Constitution, which proclaimed Czechoslovakia to be a full-fledged socialist state.

Much as his aspirations may have been matched by many East European elites' short-term views of their own self-interest, Khrushchev's manifest desire to have all the East European communist states pursue the forward march to socialism along the lines recommended by Soviet experience was doomed to ultimate failure. In retrospect, it seems clear that Khrushchev's vision fell victim less to its basic incompatibility with his own willingness to grant some scope for domestic autonomy and institutional diversity than to the gradual erosion of the Soviet Union's overall political authority in the course of its protracted but indecisive conflict with China. The repercussions of the Sino-Soviet dispute, Albania's substitution of Peking's tutelage for that of Moscow and Rumania's studied self-assertion, are too well known to require recapitulation here. The steady if uneven process of desatellization proffered unprecedented leeway for internal political reform throughout East Europe as a whole, although, of course, it did not always guarantee that individual ruling elites would necessarily see fit to embark on that course. Ironically, perhaps, wherever such efforts were seriously contemplated, they could, as Khrushchev's Chinese critics were repeatedly quick to point out, draw some inspiration from certain Khrushchevian tenets. For even while striving to revivify ideological perspectives on the essentials of the proper road to socialism and the construction of full-scale communism, by first rejecting the Stalinist doctrine of the intensification of the class struggle and later introducing the concept of the "all people's state," Khrushchev contributed a potentially significant doctrinal justification to any future attempt at transition from a revolutionary to an established one-party system. It was under such an ideological dispensation that a Kadar could embark on policies aimed at reconciliation between the party and the Hungarian population or a Lakatos, in the otherwise basically restrictive political atmosphere of Czechoslovakia under Novotny, could call attention to the persistence of group interests under socialism and the need to find the proper institutional mechanisms to reconcile them.[28] With the introduction of various national schemes aimed at thoroughgoing economic reform in the mid- and late 1960s, all these problems and a host of related issues have become increasingly topical. Everywhere in East Europe, with the exception of the rather special case of Albania, the revolutionary one-party systems initially installed under Soviet aegis and fitfully reconstructed under waning Soviet influence can now be said to have gone into final eclipse. What is far less certain, however, is whether, given the legacy of revolutionary experience in particular countries, better institutionalized and more pluralist regimes can, in fact, establish themselves as viable alternatives.

Reflecting on the broad contours of the background and development of the East European one-party systems to date, it is difficult to feel any great confidence about the possibility of a successful outcome. What one specialist on East Europe has labelled sheer "historical givenness" [29] may well serve to legitimate a relatively stagnant party rule, buttressed by the necessary minimum of police control and yet productive of a modicum of economic well-being and even a gradual improvement in the standard of living. Yet that one factor alone cannot guarantee efficacious institutional adaptation to new social conditions nor rule out the possibility of serious political instability in the wake of any major institutional reforms. Indeed, by unloosing a train of unforeseen political consequences, these very reforms, to the extent to which they may prove genuine, may even serve to unhinge any prior sense of "historical givenness."

III

As noted at the very outset of this chapter, various aspects of the basic problem of how best to institutionalize one-party rule forged in revolutionary dynamics have been accorded quite explicit recognition by a number of East Europeans themselves, including Yugoslav, Czechoslovak, and in a somewhat more guarded vein, Hungarian commentators.[30] But even where, as in the Soviet Union itself, open discussion of such matters is still frowned upon, official practice nonetheless suggests a groping awareness of the need to come to terms with a complex socioeconomic reality quite at variance with earlier revolutionary expectations. At stake throughout East Europe (and for that matter in the Soviet Union as well) is an entire complex of fundamental considerations involving the role of the party, the character of political leadership, the nature and accommodation of social forces, the scope for popular participation and, overriding them all, the fate of ideology and the crucial question of regime legitimacy.

Spared the kind of party-organized, ideologically motored, and foreign-influenced revolutionary upheaval experienced in East Europe, the Mexican political system has not had to face the distinctive and potentially intractable institutional problems of the East European revolutionary aftermath. To recall what has been discussed earlier, Mexico's dominant "institutional" party emerged at the behest of an individual aspirant for national leadership at a time of revolutionary exhaustion. From an incipient personal machine and potential "civic militia at the service of the Duce," the Mexican party evolved into a highly complex quasi-corporatist structure, housing spokesmen for the country's major organized socioeconomic groups. At the same time, the party became ever more intimately linked less to any particular presidential incumbent than to the chief executive office itself. In the course of this process, the power of the presidency naturally expanded, but popular acceptance of the centralization and concentration of political power was greatly facilitated by virtue of the observance in actual practice of the principle of limitation of presidential tenure to a single six-year term. The entire system was further buttressed by the opportunities it provided for popular participation, both through mass membership in functional socioeconomic groupings affiliated with the dominant party and through regularized elections conducted in at least a nominally competitive atmosphere thanks to the presence of the other, minor parties. Never consigned any special "commanding" role over either government or society by an official ideology, so vague and diffuse in its general nationalist-reformist appeals as always to have commanded popular acceptance more widespread than the distinctive sources of social support for particular Mexican administrations, the dominant Mexican party has both contributed to and profited from the overall sense of legitimacy which, so far at least, has permeated the entire Mexican political system.

Given the tremendous differences in historical experience and political culture between Mexico and East Europe, the exact replication of the entire complex of institutional features and political processes characteristic of the Mexican political system may well be ruled out as highly unlikely. The more pertinent question, therefore, is whether one can now identify or envisage the future emergence of certain specific Mexican traits or else their functional equivalents in East Europe. To answer that question with an unqualified negative would be to overlook some suggestive evidence to the contrary proffered by recent East European developments. To answer it with an unqualified affirmative would be to draw from that evidence inferences that may well prove to be unwarranted.

The evidence in question can best be reviewed in terms of the main lines of the general argument that can be adduced for a "Mexican" evolution of the East European party systems. Based on the plausible assumption that the initial revolutionary model is no longer applicable, the case emerges somewhat as follows.

In the first place, as the forcible transformation of society according to ideological blueprint recedes into the past, the original revolutionary ideology itself becomes increasingly obsolescent. Ideological "erosion" in the East European environment has been a much-remarked phenomenon. Wherever the old revolutionary rationale for party rule is still invoked, one is struck by the ritualized character and substantive emptiness of the formal ideological pronouncements. By contrast, over the years that have elapsed since the initial Soviet-Yugoslav break, the Titoist rationale for rule has evidenced a remarkable capacity for creative adaptability to changed post-revolutionary circumstances. Nor has Yugoslavia been entirely alone in this experience. In Rumania, Marxism-Leninism has been administered a strong infusion of nationalism at the hands of the successive Gheorgiu-Dej–Ceausescu leaderships. For the short run, this has doubtless strengthened the dictatorship and steeled it for the tasks of domestic "construction," especially in the industrial sphere, upon which the regime is still embarked. In the longer haul it may well provide a quite serviceable basis for a reconciliation between the regime and the Rumanian population as a whole. To the extent to which precisely such a reconciliation has been stressed elsewhere, it has already been accompanied by a deliberate downplaying of the revolutionary facets of official ideology. A good illustration of what is involved was provided by Kadar when he consciously reversed the elements of an earlier formulation by announcing that "whoever is not against us, is with us." Even those East European regimes commonly regarded as utterly "orthodox" in their ideological commitment have also found it advisable to sound much the same note. All of this suggests the desirability, if not quite the inevitability, of a rationale for one-party rule much more in keeping with changed realities, that is, a rationale predicated less upon irrelevant chiliastic expectations than upon presently developing institutions—in other words, something functionally akin to the "ideology" of the Mexican Revolution.

Postulation of this kind of development, of course, presupposes certain additional corollaries. Among other things, it assumes the institutionalization of political power on a more secure basis than before. As concerns the top leadership, one need not necessarily anticipate the emergence of the chief executive office as the prime locus of political power, as in Mexico, much less the imposition of a fixed limitation in time on the exercise of personal leadership in the Mexican manner. Rather, it can perhaps be argued that a collective leadership that effectively divides power may serve as a functional substitute, the more so to the extent to which such an arrangement may be subject to the further check of more or less regularized procedures, possibly within the top party bodies, for the replacement of individual leaders without major disruption of the entire system. While the evidence to date has been so scanty as to leave this line of argument largely hypothetical, those who wish to do so may interpret the transition in Czechoslovakia from Novotny to Dubcek or even the ouster of Khrushchev and what is known of the operation of Soviet collective leadership since then in this light.

In any case, institutionalization of the top political leadership seems more likely to follow than to precede a reformulation of the role of the party. Measured against the standards and actual practices of Communist Party rule in the period of revolutionary onslaught against society, a number of significant changes seem to have ensued. Gone are the days when the party served as the relentless motor of social change with all-pervasive functional control over every last facet of administration and social life. What now appears on the agenda is a much less ambitious role for the party as the ultimate repository of political power and the immediate source of practical policy based upon its mediation and integration of the competing claims of various social groups.

Even the least reform-minded communist states, while stressing the separate identity of the party and the state and still insisting upon the primacy of the former over the latter, have had to respond to the latent tensions between emergent functional autonomy and residual political authority. This is the gloss that must be put on Soviet practice, under Khrushchev, of holding enlarged plenary sessions of the party Central Committee to include representatives of functional groupings otherwise outside the sphere of such party deliberations.[31] It is also the interpretation that can be advanced for the notable change toward the managerial-technical in the sociological makeup of the entire political elite just below the top leadership that has occurred in recent years in East Germany.[32] Even the recent changes in Rumania, which seem to point in an entirely different direction, can be similarly interpreted. At first glance, the 1967 Rumanian fusion of party and state positions ("a single comrade in the leadership should take care of a specific field of activity, both in the party and the state spheres") bespeaks a concentration of power in some ways suggestive of an updated version of the authoritarian regimes familiar from interwar East European experience. Yet, it is important to note that this Rumanian innovation confers important decision-making prerogatives upon members of the fused party-state apparatus in their capacities as technical specialists rather than party functionaries.[33] It may thus serve to ameliorate the inherent tension between the party *apparatchiki* and the managerial elite and even create unprecedented leeway for the *tecnicos* over the *politicos,* to borrow the Mexican terminology for a comparable phenomenon.

To be fully effective, the institutionalization of communist political power obviously requires much more than merely the accommodation of highly specialized technocratic interests. What is needed is a reformulation of the role of the party so as to take account of the existence of a wide variety of different group interests and numerous sources of legitimate social conflict. This much has been tentatively acknowledged in Hungary and even more decisively so in Czechoslovakia, where the reformist appeals of the Dubcek regime centered on the promise of a thoroughgoing redefinition of the "leading role" of the party so as to provide meaningful channels for the expression of individual and group aspirations and their eventual satisfaction. As concerns this crucial aspect of institutionalization, Yugoslavia has long led the way, in theory at least. As early as 1952, the Yugoslav Party, then newly rechristened the League of Yugoslav Communists, began to speak of its "educational" rather than "commanding" role. A few years later, in answer to domestic critics such as Djilas, who had come to advocate evolution into a multi-party system, Yugoslav spokesmen proclaimed the goal of a "non-party socialist democracy." Despite institutional innovations and some promising provisions of the 1963 Yugoslav Constitution, practical implementation of so vague a formula was to prove at best halting, until Tito's decision to embark on the bold economic reforms of 1965 begged the issue of the entrenched hold of the party *apparatchiki* more urgently than ever before. The 1966 purge of Aleksandar Rankovic, boss of the secret police and Tito's presumed heir apparent, signalled a green light for critical discussion of truly far-ranging political reform. Indeed, the Draft Theses on party reorganization, currently under consideration, envisage a complete and final break with Leninist theory and practice. Not only is the League of Yugoslav Communists supposed to relinquish its position as "the center of state authority" and thus undergo a "divorce from power" but its internal processes are also to be reformed so as to transform it from a "political party in the classical sense" into a "broad political organization embracing all social forces which accept the socialist foundations of society," one which allows "conflicts of interest to be freely expressed and democratically resolved." [34] *Mutatis mutandis,* that formulation could scarcely come closer to expressing the official theory of the dominant party in the Mexican political system.

Whether the representation of group interests will actually take place directly within the Yugoslav party structure itself remains to be seen. An equivalent to Mexican corporatist practice in the communist states, it can be argued, need not necessarily require this. Rather, one can envision group representation within parliamentary bodies and/or the executive agencies of government. Czechoslovak theorists, notably Lakatos, have advocated the former, and comparable ideas have emerged from recent Hungarian discussions on the nature of "socialist democracy." [35] In Yugoslavia itself, an elaborate institutional framework for parliamentary corporatism already exists in the form of a National Assembly with five chambers, four of which are functional in character, and similar although less complex corporatist structural arrangements at the republican and provincial levels. In Rumania, the recent party-state fusion included a provision possibly pointing in the second direction, that is, toward functional representation within the government, in that the leaders of the mass organizations (Union of Communist Youth, National Union of Agricultural Cooperatives, the trade unions and others) are now to become cabinet members.[36] Irrespective of the institutional forum in which it may be expressed, genuine corporate representation obviously depends upon real group autonomy and democratic processes in the selection of group leadership. On this score, too, there have been some encouraging signs, if not yet in Rumania, then at least in Hungary, Czechoslovakia, and Yugoslavia.[37] If Mexican experience is any guide, however, the transition from mass organizations as "transmission belts" to genuinely autonomous groupings will be as ticklish as it is crucial. Where sector, or social group, leaderships are called upon to play a dual representative-administrative role, the strains are bound to be enormous and the opportunities for party manipulation of individual leaders virtually unlimited.

A final element in the case for the Mexican evolution of the East European party systems concerns the development of real popular participation not only through functional groupings but also in the electoral process. In place of electoral competition between parties (the dominant party and the minor opposition parties as in Mexico), a measure of genuine popular participation may, perhaps, be achieved through the device of multiple candidacies for at least some positions. This practice has existed for some time in Poland, where, however, elections are still considered by official apologists as "semi-plebiscitary" in character.[38] More recently, it has been introduced in Hungary, albeit with a warning by Kadar that "it is necessary and unavoidable that the Communists will be the majority in the leading bodies of state power."[39] In experimentation with multiple candidacies, as in so many other respects, Yugoslavia must once again be considered far ahead of all the other communist countries. While still not permitting any expression of opposition in the form of alternative programs, Yugoslav electoral practice has come to feature genuine competition for office and meaningful involvement of the population in both representative and corporate nominating processes. Each successive recent election (1963, 1965, 1967) has witnessed an increase in the number of contested seats at all electoral levels.[40] This has doubtless facilitated the desired entry of much new blood into public life, but it is also noteworthy that in the 1967 elections there were certain instances in which old partisan heroes competed against younger technocrats and "the party supported the latter but the voters gave their vote to the former."[41] All told, recent Yugoslav elections, especially those of 1967 which produced examples of electoral campaigning "as vigorous as any seen anywhere," can well be said to "show a definite trend toward increased public participation at all levels."[42] Moreover, this increase in public participation has been accompanied by a reanimation of parliamentary life itself. In keeping with the official encouragement of "democratic self-management" throughout Yugoslav society, the entire complex five-chamber Federal Assembly has shown signs of becoming an active arena of debate, and this has also been true of representative-corporatist structures at other levels of government. Indeed, on one recent occasion, the Government of Slovenia felt obliged to tender its resignation as the result of an adverse vote on a draft health insurance bill.[43] In the lengths to which these developments have gone, Yugoslavia currently constitutes a case unto itself. For purposes of argument, however, the Yugoslav example and the fragmentary evidence proffered by other East European party systems may be accepted as indicative of the plausibility of the eventual development of a more general trend toward popular participation in the political process. To the extent to which this trend actually materializes, one may grant that it may well impart an additional important element of legitimacy to the entire system.

How, then, to weigh all the available evidence and evaluate the general argument for a Mexican evolution of the East European single-party systems? In considering the pros and cons, it is well to bear in mind the apt observation of Zdenek Mlynar, Secretary of the Legal Commission of the Central Committee of the Czechoslovak Communist Party and leader of a team of specialists appointed in 1966 to study "the development of the political system in socialist society." "What is involved," Mlynar has observed, "is the entire concept of a political regime, which cannot be defined by structural analysis alone." [44]

"The entire concept" of the "political regime" in East Europe is obviously in flux and may presently be best described as post-revolutionary and yet still pre-institutional. In this situation, it is important, as Lakatos has warned, to distinguish between reforms that have the effect of making political manipulation more efficient and those which may actually serve to place public policy more nearly within the control of society.[45] At issue is the crucial matter of viable institutional guarantees to assure that new or rejuvenated structures will really function according to their promise. While the transitions away from a Stalinist-type leadership at the top may constitute a necessary condition, clearly it is not yet a sufficient one. For as another Czech intellectual of the reformist persuasion, Milan Hubl, has aptly noted, "The experience of many a socialist country, for instance after 1956, has demonstrated that . . . it would be naive to pin all hopes on the quality of work of a single, new, 'better' leader without drawing conclusions from previous experience and without furnishing certain firm institutional guarantees." [46] What Mlynar himself had in mind goes one logical step beyond this by stressing free play for an informed public opinion as perhaps the single most urgently needed condition for meaningful reform of institutions and structures.

In this connection, it is significant that the Action Program presented in April, 1968 by the Czechoslovak Party under Dubcek's leadership explicitly acknowledged the desirability of "firm guarantees against a return to the old methods of subjectivism and high-handedness from a position of power" and endorsed the development of "forms of political life that will insure the expression of the direct say and will of the working class and all working people in political decision making." [47] While tantalizingly vague on how this could be achieved without surrendering the party's monopoly of power, the same program promised a number of quite concrete freedoms, including, notably, freedom of expression, unhampered by political censorship of the communications media. Were these promises to be fulfilled in Czechoslovakia or anywhere else in East Europe, they would contribute to the perpetuation of a political climate far more open than any in Mexico, with its partially if indirectly controlled management of public opinion. To the extent to which the same promises go unfulfilled or are actually retracted, they threaten a return to the kind of popular apathy which, while it may facilitate stagnant party rule, will not only work against implementation of the economic reforms now so badly needed in East Europe, but will also inhibit genuine political institutionalization.

The basic question, therefore, boils down to this: Are firm institutional guarantees, including such matters as genuine group autonomy and free play for public opinion, really at all compatible with the preservation of single-party rule in the communist states? Is it indeed possible, as one Western writer has queried with respect to Hungary, "to dispel popular apathy and indifference by substantive reform without diluting the inner cohesion of the party and weakening its monopoly of power?" [48] And, if not, one is entitled to pose the additional conundrum: Is it really possible to dilute the inner cohesion of the party and weaken its monopoly of power so gradually or else to such a limited extent that the essential foundations of the one-party system are not entirely destroyed in the process?

One dramatic answer to these questions might be for ruling communist parties "to adjust gracefully to the desirability and perhaps even the inevitability" of their own "gradual withering away." [49] In Yugoslavia, at least, this line of thought is no longer anathema; indeed, it finds expression in the Yugoslav party's own current Draft Theses. Yet is it a wholly satisfactory or even very realistic answer, especially for Yugoslavia itself? The very same Draft Theses polemicize against the objection, obviously raised within the Yugoslav political elite, that implementation of such novel proposals might lead to the disintegration of "society, [state] authority, and the Party." Although dismissed by Yugoslav proponents of "democratic self-management" as inconsequential, this kind of objection deserves to be taken on its merits. After all, if the party is still to serve as an integrative and innovative mechanism, it is hard to see how it can perform these crucial functions and yet also wither away. As concerns Yugoslavia itself, the matter is particularly pressing, given that country's regional differences and traditional nationality animosities. So far, it has been the party, or to be more precise, its top leadership in the person of Marshal Tito, which has furnished the necessary integrative leadership. No doubt it has been Tito's very success in integrating quite divergent interests, both political and regional, placating the conservatives while encouraging the reformers and all along balancing the competing claims of different nationalities, that over the past twenty years has imparted such an ambivalent character to the Titoist regime and involved it in "constant shifts from concession to restriction, from reform to relapse, from progress to reaction." [50] At the present moment, the reformers have apparently won the upper hand and may be well on the way to destroying permanently the influence recurrently exerted by the hidebound party *apparatchiki*. If they really do succeed in "divorcing from power" a party that with the exception of its central bodies is bereft of any nationwide organization, the urgent question will then become whether other political structures have been sufficiently institutionalized to withstand the inevitable centrifugal pulls. Those who purport to see stabilizing propensities against the threat of national disintegration by virtue of the emergence of coalition politics along republican lines and the possible strengthening of this tendency as a result of certain integrative aspects of the Yugoslav economic reforms [51] will find their assessment put to the acid test only after Tito has departed from the scene.

Short of withering away, which no ruling Communist Party other than the Yugoslav has seriously contemplated, prospects for adapting the party's "leading role" to what various communist theoreticians now acknowledge to be "the new state of social development" are so beclouded by difficulties so peculiar to their distinctive domestic and international setting as to call into serious question the entire case for attempting an analogy with Mexico. Some of these difficulties—such as those relating to leadership stability and succession, group autonomy and representation, and popular participation—may be considered institutional in character, but they all come into common focus on the key question of the legitimacy of the East European political system itself.

It is one thing to note the widespread erosion of revolutionary ideology and to prescribe the desirability of an institutional rather than an ideological rationale for one-party rule. It is quite another to expect this development to come to fruition without the intervention of seriously disruptive consequences. To understand the multiple and contradictory roles played by ideology in the contemporary East European scene is immediately to appreciate why this should be the case. To be sure, the need for ideology, in the earlier sense of a coherent doctrinaire system to motivate and justify the transformation of domestic society, has largely declined, hence all the manifest signs of its apparent erosion, in the decline of revolutionary ideological fervor on the part of the East European regimes (save Albania) and their evident lack of concern for the cohesion of Marxist-Leninist doctrine. Yet, having been installed on the basis of the revolutionary ideology, the communist political elites often find themselves beholden to the principle of continued "ideological guidance" as an instrument not of revolutionary change but rather of national and social discipline.[52] To the extent to which the practice of "ideological guidance" permits and indeed demands continued domination by the party bureaucracy, it acts as a major brake on genuine political reform. Where, however, "ideological guidance" and party bureaucratic control are relaxed, ideology may play another, equally disruptive role. Revisionist exposition of revolutionary ideology, especially at the hands of critical communist intellectuals who may reason their way back from Leninism through Marxism to original liberalism can readily become a guide not for the institutionalization of one-party rule but rather for its dismantlement. Individual examples of revisionist conclusions drawn from revolutionary ideology are legion. One need not tarry over such outstanding individual cases as that of the Polish Marxist philosopher, Leszek Kolakowski, or the East German natural scientist and veteran party member, Robert Havemann, both of whom have run afoul of their respective party leaderships and in so doing, incidentally, helped reinvigorate their respective party's concern for the control function of official ideology. A much more pointed recent illustration of the corrosive touch of revisionist Communist intellectuals is provided by recent developments in Czechoslovakia where they played a key role in the broad coalition, including economic reformers, Slovak nationalists, and more pragmatically oriented members of the party hierarchy, that ejected Novotny and replaced him with Dubcek. In the course of this transition in leadership, the critical intellectuals served to instruct the public at large about the dictatorship's suppression of rights and the means thought necessary to prevent any such recurrence. More interesting still, there also occurred an escalation of the intellectuals' own demands on the system. To cite one typical case in point, consider the example of the group of party intellectuals drawn from various academic disciplines while Novotny was in power to study the institutionalization of the Czechoslovak political system. Whereas in September, 1967, the team's leader, Mlynar, regarded it as "premature to talk about proposals introducing institutional changes,"[53] only a few months later, his aide, Pithart, called for "the autonomous working of political parties appealing to voters with their own independent lists of candidates, and real freedom of speech," that is, in effect, a multi-party system, as what he termed "the subsistence minimum for Czechoslovak democracy."[54] Nor was Pithart alone in demanding a dismantlement of the single-party system. The active revival of other political parties, long mute captives of the communists within the National Front, and the emergence of quite new political groupings such as the clubs of "committed non-party members" testify to the trend, which was not really different from what had occurred in Poland and Hungary in 1956. As for the intellectuals, what happened may be summarized, using Gordon Skilling's terminology, as an escalation from "specific" to "fundamental" and, in some cases, to "integral" opposition to the one-party system.[55]

It may, perhaps, be countered that the foregoing only argues for the imperative necessity of cutting off the critical intelligentsia from significant political participation if post-revolutionary Communist Party rule is to be effectively institutionalized. Precisely this, of course, occurred in Gomulka's Poland and a similar fall may be in store for Czechoslovakia's critical intellectuals. Yet, taken on balance, it is highly questionable whether Gomulka's Poland constitutes a very persuasive casestudy in effectively institutionalized one-party rule. With the *pays réel,* as represented by the Catholic church officially conceded to be "a perpetually competitive ideological force juxtaposed to the party and the state,"[56] and the party hierarchy itself plagued by infighting bearing only the most tenuous relationship to the aspirations of the country's major social forces, Gomulka's Poland rather strikes one as a case study in stagnant and frustrated one-party rule. As Michael Gamarnikow has observed, "The alienation of the Polish party hierarchy from the nation has been a fact in Poland for more than two decades, except, perhaps, for a brief period during and after October, 1956."[57] It should be noted that the two decades in question span both the revolutionary and the post-revolutionary periods and the brief exception corresponds to the one phase in Polish communist history when the critical intelligentsia was free to give voice to the aspirations of the nation. Were the suppression of the intellectuals now to ensue in Czechoslovakia where they have been so instrumental in exacting promises of real institutional guarantees against the abuse of power, it is safe to predict that the regime's prospects would suffer no less severe a setback.

If the intellectuals throughout East Europe today constitute a major political force, something which has always been true historically, then it is important to note yet another salient aspect of their present-day universe. In his structural-functional study of the European communist states, Ghita Ionescu concludes that there are two "irreversible trends" presently at work throughout the area. The first of these he identifies as "the increase of pluralization" within individual countries and, the second, as "the tendency of the European Communist states to become more European and less Communist." [58] Leaving aside the arguable question of whether or not these trends are "irreversible," they are, in fact, interconnected. For in addition to the intelligentsia's propensity to draw revisionist-democratic conclusions from the ideological legacy and indeed reinforcing it is their more general orientation toward West European political culture. "The European of today," to cite the thought of a Slovak intellectual, "wants to share in the decisions . . . to elect his leadership and afterwards, according to the actions of the leadership, laud, or criticize, or replace it by another leadership; in a word he wants the constitutional principles, which declare that 'the people are the source of all power' to be turned into daily and concrete practice, and [on this basis] to exercise his right of choice, control, and responsibility." [59] Given the experience of Communist Party rule, the past abuse of dictatorial power, and the inevitable recriminations that it has left in its wake, the pull of West European political culture is less toward institutionalized single-party systems than toward a resuscitation of multi-party parliamentarism. For a significant segment of East European public opinion, as guided and instructed by the critical intelligentsia, it may well be that, as the most recent Yugoslav exponent of a two-party system has put it, "historical experience has demonstrated the limited value of the one-party system." [60]

Needless to say, the political universe of the ruling party elites is a quite different one. While lower level party functionaries typically evince a quite understandable concern for the personal perquisites of power and react instinctively against efforts to dilute the party's political monopoly in the interest of institutionalization, traits that have been shared within the top leadership, the latter's preoccupations are not thereby exhausted. Rather, to the extent to which the Soviet Union is still able to exert hegemony over particular states in East Europe, and so far only Yugoslavia, Albania, and Rumania seem for different reasons to be reasonably secure in their separate roads, the political universe of even the most pragmatically inclined party hierarchs must at least to a certain extent continue as before to center in Moscow. As long as the Soviet Union, in turn, is governed by a leadership that itself feels constrained to emphasize "ideological guidance" and party primacy, it can always react adversely to institutionalization abroad that may seem to threaten the party dictatorship at home. The consequences of any direct Soviet intervention, such as has occurred in Czechoslovakia, seem destined to redound unfavorably upon the prospects for a more pluralistic, better institutionalized Communist Party rule not only in the country involved but elsewhere as well.

In sum, then, the case for a Mexican future for the East European party systems has to be judged in the light of the specific historical and political conditions pertaining to Mexico on the one hand and each individual East European country on the other. The institutional future, if such it is to be, of the East European party systems remains to be worked out in terms of a multiple set of stresses and strains posited by the quest for genuine political pluralism as against the hold of residual party power, further compounded in the case of most East European countries by divergent international pulls, toward West European political culture on the one side, toward the Soviet on the other. If this were not so, or even if the international context of internal political change were a less important factor than it is, one would be entitled to feel far greater confidence in drawing firm Mexican conclusions from those facets of the available East European evidence that do seem to suggest such an inference. What is missing in East Europe, however, is the ideologically unencumbered, historically untainted ruling elite, together with the relative lack of political sophistication and relative degree of international insularity that accompanied the maturation of the Mexican political system.

Indeed, as Mexico itself enters more fully into the era of world history, it may well be pertinent to ask whether its one-party system can long survive in its present form. The system's various shortcomings have for some time been apparent to favorably disposed commentators as well as critics, both Mexican and foreign. The argument that PRI's long established dominance has begun to brake socioeconomic progress as well as inhibit political development can draw upon a substantial if diversified list of particulars. There is, as Gonzalez Casanova points out, the recalcitrant phenomenon of "marginalism," that is, the system's failure to deal at all adequately in political terms, not to mention economically, with the considerable marginal population of Indian rural, and in some cases, urban poor and the marginal population's resultant inclination to violence.[61] There may be, as Raymond Vernon has argued, a serious question about the scope for the initiation of policy available to the president, whose office has been so well-institutionalized as to render its incumbent beholden to a myriad of veto groups.[62] There is also, as Robert Scott has noted, the restriction on group autonomy and individual initiative that comes from excessively centralized political control and the absence so far of effective responsible opposition politics.[63] Finally, one may add, there ought to be some question about the long-term viability of those diffuse political values, the distinctive "Mexican Proposition" of which Brandenburg makes so much,[64] and the related consideration of the durability of the political elite's consensus on those informal rules of the game upon which the Mexican system has so vitally depended for its successful operation. There have been instances in the past when disappointed aspirants to the presidency or dissident factions have ventured beyond the normal confines of the extended "revolutionary family" to establish political parties of their own. Should that recur in the context of a weakened elite consensus, the disaffection of those social groups that already exist at the "margin" or the dissatisfaction of others at the center of national political life might well provide a significant basis of ongoing political support upon which to base the kind of personal or factional power aspirations that have previously gone unrequited in their dissidence. The consequences for the Mexican one-party system as it has functioned up to the present should not be difficult to imagine.

In the light of their distinctive political dynamics and separately problematic futures, perhaps the question "Is Mexico the future of East Europe?" should be recast to read "Is Mexico the future of Mexico?" For the moment, perhaps the most that can be said on either score is the thought expressed by Mlynar in response to a question concerning the work of his Czechoslovak study group.[65] Asked whether his term's work could be properly categorized as futurology, he had to admit that at best political science was only a small part of that much broader field.

‖ *Notes*

1. *Politika* (Belgrade), October 31, 1967.
2. Zbigniew K. Brzezinski, "The Soviet Political System: Transformation or Degeneration," *Problems of Communism*, XV (January–February 1966), 1–15.
3. Cf., for example, Brzezinski, *op. cit.*, p. 14.
4. Cf. Frederick C. Barghoorn, *Politics in the USSR* (Boston: Little, Brown, 1966), p. 215.
5. David E. Apter, *The Politics of Modernization* (Chicago: The University of Chicago Press, 1965), pp. 394–396.
6. Frank Tannenbaum, *Mexico, The Struggle for Peace and Bread* (New York: Alfred A. Knopf, 1951), pp. 60–61.
7. Robert E. Scott, *Mexican Government in Transition* (Urbana: The University of Illinois Press, 1959), p. 101.
8. Tannenbaum, *op. cit.*, p. 53.
9. "Mensaje del Presidente Plutarco Elías Calles," in *Historia del Partido Oficial*, Primera Parte, *Política*, III, No. 7 (March 15, 1963), xiii. (Since 1963, *Política*, a bi-monthly leftist news magazine, produced in the format of *Time* magazine, has been publishing the texts of major documents relating to the historical evolution of the "official party.")
10. Scott, *op. cit.*, p. 9.
11. Frank Brandenburg, *The Making of Modern Mexico* (Englewood Cliffs, N. J.: Prentice Hall, 1964), p. 144.
12. L. Vincent Padgett, *The Mexican Political System* (Boston: Houghton Mifflin, 1966), p. 48.

13. On the latter point, see Raymond Vernon, *The Dilemma of Mexico's Development* (Cambridge: Harvard University Press, 1963).

14. Cf. Brzezinski, *op. cit.,* esp. pp. 14–15.

15. This simplistic but essentially misleading interpretation is found in virtually all apologetic treatments of the Mexican system. For one such treatment, see Martin C. Needler, "The Political Development of Mexico," *The American Political Science Review,* LV, No. 2 (June 1961), 308–312.

16. Robert J. Shafer, *Mexico, Mutual Adjustment Planning* (Syracuse: Syracuse University Press, 1966), *passim.*

17. Padgett, however, strikes a slightly different note. While admitting the presence of "the arbitrary factor," he nonetheless tends to feel that "the process (of nomination) described in the (party) rules is usually followed even if this does not eliminate situations in which decisions are made for candidates with credentials inferior to their rivals." Padgett, *op. cit.,* p. 59.

18. Carl J. Friedrich and Zbigniew K. Brzezinski, *Totalitarian Dictatorship and Autocracy,* 2nd ed., rev. by Friedrich (New York: Frederick A. Praeger, 1965). For an attempt to update the original analysis in terms of more recent developments, see Carl J. Friedrich, "Totalitarianism: Recent Trends," *Problems of Communism,* XVII (May–June 1968), 32–43.

19. The phrase "derivative totalitarian parties" is Richard Lowenthal's and has been applied by him to the non-ruling parties under Stalin's control of the international movement. See Lowenthal's *World Communism* (New York: Oxford University Press, 1966), p. 240.

20. For a definition and discussion of the phenomenon of "domesticism," see Zbigniew K. Brzezinski, *The Soviet Bloc: Unity and Conflict,* rev. ed. (Cambridge: Harvard University Press, 1967), pp. 51–58.

21. To be sure, even after 1948–1949, the internal processes and domestic politics of the satellite states were not susceptible of total coordination down to the very last detail. Two of them, Poland and Rumania, managed to hold on to a small measure of what might be termed "marginal autonomy" in the implementation of policy; a third, Bulgaria, by being more Stalinist than Stalin, can be said to have practiced a kind of "inverted autonomy." See Brzezinski, *The Soviet Bloc,* p. 146.

22. Andrew Gyorgy, "The Internal Political Order," in Stephen Fischer-Galati, ed., *Eastern Europe in the Sixties* (New York: Frederick A. Praeger, 1963), p. 165, italics added.

23. Vladimir Dedijer, *Tito Speaks* (London: Weidenfield and Nicolson, 1953), p. 381. For a good discussion of the psychological impact of Stalin's excommunication on the Yugoslav elite at the time, see Adam B. Ulam, *Titoism and the Cominform* (Cambridge: Harvard University Press, 1952), *passim.*

24. Richard Lowenthal, "Schism Among the Faithful," *Problems of Communism,* XI (January–February 1962). Cf. also Melvin Croan, "Communist International Relations," in Walter Laqueur and Leopold Labedz, eds., *Polycentrism* (New York: Frederick A. Praeger, 1962), pp. 9–19.

25. Paul Kecskemeti, *The Unexpected Revolution* (Stanford: Stanford University Press, 1961).

26. The influence of the Yugoslav workers councils had at one time been significant, but it diminished markedly after Hungarian workers soviets played such a remarkable role in the 1956 uprising. During his visit to Yugoslavia in 1963, Khrushchev remarked that the Yugoslav councils merited study, but his remarks were not carried in the Soviet press. John C. Campbell, *Tito's Separate Road* (New York: Harper and Row, 1967), p. 133.

27. Cf. Adam Bromke, *Poland's Politics: Idealism vs. Realism* (Cambridge: Harvard University Press, 1967).

28. M. Lakatos, "On Certain Problems of the Structure of Our Political System," *Pravny Obzor* (Bratislava), I (1965), and his "Some Problems of Socialist Democracy from the Viewpoint of the Citizen's Position in Our Society," *Pravny Obzor,* III (1966). For a general discussion and analysis, see H. Gordon Skilling, "Interest Groups and Communist Politics," *World Politics,* XVIII, No. 3 (April 1966), 435–451.

29. Carl Beck, "Bureaucracy and Political Development in Eastern Europe," in Joseph LaPalombara, ed., *Bureaucracy and Political Development* (Princeton: Princeton University Press, 1963), pp. 299–300.

30. On Hungary, see Paul Lendvai, "Hungary: Change vs. Immobilism," *Problems of Communism,* XVI (March–April 1967). For Czechoslovakia, cf. Morton Schwartz, "Czechoslovakia: Toward One-Party Pluralism," *Problems of Communism,* XVI (January–February 1967).

31. Cf. Brzezinski, "The Soviet Political System," p. 11.

32. Cf. Peter Christian Ludz, *Parteielite im Wandel* (Köln and Opladen: Westdeutscher Verlag, 1968).

33. "Rumania Revamps the Role of Party and State," Research Department, Radio Free Europe, December 13, 1967.

34. "Draft Theses Concerning the Reorganization of the League of Communists of Yugoslavia," *Kommunist* (Belgrade), April 27, 1967, as quoted in Slobodan Stankovic, "Yugoslav Party Reform Entering New Phase," Research Department, Radio Free Europe, May 2, 1967.

35. Lendvai, *loc. cit.,* esp. pp. 11–14.

36. "Rumania Revamps the Role of Party and State," *loc. cit.,* p. 3.

37. Developments have gone furthest in Yugoslavia, especially with respect to the trade unions. See "New Role for Yugoslav Unions," *East Europe,* XVII, No. 8 (August 1968), 41–42.

38. Jerzy J. Wjatr and Adam Przeworski, "Control without Opposition," in Institute of Philosophy and Sociology of the Polish Academy of Sciences, Department of Political Sociology, *Studies in Polish Political System* (Wroclaw: The Polish Academy of Sciences Press, 1967), p. 139.

39. *Nepszabadsag,* November 29, 1966, as quoted in Lendvai, *op. cit.,* p. 14.

40. R. V. Burks and S. A. Stankovic, "Jugoslawien auf dem Weg zu halbfreien Wahlen," *Osteuropa,* XVII, No. 2–3 (February–March 1967), 131–146.

41. Slobodan Stankovic, "Yugoslav Elections Analyzed," Research Department, Radio Free Europe, April 25, 1967, p. 1.

42. Slobodan Stankovic, "Elections in Yugoslavia: Final Results," Research Department, Radio Free Europe, April 27, 1967, p. 5.

43. Slobodan Stankovic, "Government of Slovenia Has Resigned," Research Department, Radio Free Europe, December 7, 1966.

44. "Democracy Today and Tomorrow," *Pravda* (Bratislava), October 25, 1967, trans. in Radio Free Europe, *Czechoslovak Press Survey,* No. 1977 (263), p. 5.

45. M. Lakatos, "Some Problems of Socialist Democracy from the Viewpoint of the Citizen's Position in Our Society," *Prayny Obzor* (Bratislava), III (1966). Cf. the discussion in S. Riveles, "Czechoslovak Writer Calls for Free Elections," Research Department, Radio Free Europe, April 20, 1966.

46. Milan Hubl, "Socialism for Us," in *Kulturny Zivot,* January 5, 1968.

47. "Excerpts from Reform Program of the Czech Communist Party," *The New York Times,* April 11, 1968.

48. Lendvai, *op. cit.,* p. 16.

49. Brzezinski, "The Soviet Political System," p. 15.

50. Slobodan Stankovic, "Titoism—Twenty Years After (Part Four)—Ideological Revisionism," Research Department, Radio Free Europe, July 11, 1968, p. 6.

51. Alvin Z. Rubinstein, "Reforms, Nonalignment and Pluralism," *Problems of Communism*, XVII (March–April 1968), 31–41, esp. 40–41.
52. Cf. the incisive analysis of Richard Lowenthal, "The Soviet Union in the Post-Revolutionary Era: An Overview," in Alexander Dallin and Thomas B. Larson, eds., *Soviet Politics Since Khrushchev* (Englewood Cliffs, N.J.: Prentice Hall, 1968), p. 7.
53. "The Development of the Political System in This Country. Docent Mlynar Interviewed," *Student,* September 27, 1967, Radio Free Europe, *Czechoslovak Press Survey* No. 1971 (243, 248), October 17, 1967.
54. P. Pithart, "Political Parties and Freedom of Speech," *Literarni Listy,* No. 17 (May 29, 1968); Radio Free Europe, *Czechoslovak Press Survey* No. 2097 (177, 178), July 8, 1968.
55. H. Gordon Skilling, "Opposition in Communist East Europe," publication forthcoming in Robert A. Dahl, ed., *Emerging Oppositions.*
56. Jerzy J. Wjatr, "The Hegemonic Party System in Poland," in Institute of Philosophy and Sociology of the Polish Academy of Sciences, *op. cit.,* p. 121.
57. Michael Gamarnikow, "Eastern Europe—Light at the End of the Tunnel," *Interplay,* May 1968, p. 33.
58. Ghita Ionescu, *The Politics of the European Communist States* (New York: Frederick A. Praeger, 1967). Cf. Melvin Croan, "Political Science and Eastern Europe," *Survey,* No. 48 (April 1968), pp. 156–158.
59. Gustav Husak, "An Old Anniversary and New Hopes," *Kulturny Zivot,* January 12, 1968.
60. Stevan Vracar in *Gledista* (Belgrade), No. 8–9 (August–September 1967), as cited in Slobodan Stankovic, "Yugoslav Theoretician Advocates Two-Party System for Communist Countries," Research Department, Radio Free Europe, October 6, 1967.
61. Pablo Gonzalez Casanova, *La Democracia en Mexico* (Mexico, D.F.: Ediciones Era, 1965).
62. Vernon, *op. cit.*
63. Robert E. Scott, "Mexico: The Established Revolution," in Lucian W. Pye and Sydney Verba, eds., *Political Culture and Political Development* (Princeton: Princeton University Press, 1965) and Scott, *op. cit., passim.*
64. Brandenburg, *op. cit.,* chap. 1.
65. "The Development of the Political System in This Country," pp. 5–6.

16

Yugoslav Party Evolution: Moving beyond Institutionalization

‖ *M. George Zaninovich*

Introduction

Apparent at the outset as regards the Communist Party in Yugoslavia is the dramatic change that has taken place since its first ascent to power. Although not clearly manifest in the top leadership structure as such, these changes become easily visible in the League's self-image with respect to the range of acceptable party roles, in addition to its complex of organizational-administrative forms expressed through the years. Although there has been much vacillation since World War II as to direction, the trend seems clearly to move toward further institutionalization and wider acceptability of the Yugoslav League of Communists. An important concomitant of this institutionalizing process has been the growing legitimacy of the League within the context of the Yugoslav system; as will become clear in the discussion that follows, the process of institution-building and the widespread popular legitimacy of the party organization must work hand in hand. Furthermore, as the institutionalizing of the League in this sense proceeds, the more apparent also the trend toward a multi-organizational (multi-party?) system based upon internal Yugoslav complexity.

The process of institutionalizing a party depends upon the relation of that organization to other viable structures within a society as well as to its broader cultural and normative context. More generally, institutionalization focuses upon the maintenance of effective mechanisms that allow the party as an organization to adapt and survive over time as new problems and situations are encountered. Central also to the institutionalizing process is the ability of the party as an organization to lock into the wider normative fabric of a society in order to generate a viable basis for its legitimacy and generalized acceptance.[1] The institutional component of the party must have a capability of outliving the fixed ideology that founds the movement, the specific manifestations of its organizational structure, and any particular leader who may dominate it for a time. Metaphorically, the institution as a primary attribute lives on, while various secondary attributes (that is, given program, specific structure, or single personality) pass away. In addition, as institutional attributes develop in the party organization, a higher tolerance of internal diversity and conflict would also be expected. Consistent with this, decentralization of the organizational apparatus would occur as more regard is demonstrated for locally grounded and lower level leadership elements. What this suggests also is that the organizational tasks of a party would be increasingly delegated with its gaining of stature as a generally accepted institution and the expansion of its basis of legitimacy. Similarly, with institutionalization the base and the scope of participation would tend to expand, with active elements in party affairs reflecting both higher educational qualifications and higher socioeconomic status. Finally, a timely and telling aspect in the institutionalizing process involves the general routinization of change within the party organization (as well as in the wider society), and in particular that form of change that bears directly upon leadership succession. The overriding factor in institutionalization can be defined as a growing reliance upon rule-oriented behavior and predictable control functions, since this serves to reduce levels of anxiety and ambiguity, to minimize the arbitrary nature of decision-making, and to maximize environmental predictability both for the member and the citizen. In general, the institutionalizing process calls for the strengthening of a self-perpetuating component as over against other aspects of a party organization, a component whose primary function is to maintain the continuity of experience for the membership and to reinforce its voluntary adherence.

The substance of this chapter addresses itself to the changing nature of the Yugoslav party system in light of events that have transpired within the broader framework of Yugoslav society. It is presumed here that the institutional development of the League hangs in rather large measure upon the wider socioeconomic setting of which the League is merely a part. Therefore, the evolution of the Yugoslav party must be examined by looking at other aspects of the environment as well—namely, political-structural innovations, economic reforms, new ideological content, the impact of external events, and recent Yugoslav politics. The analysis will proceed by observing the degree to which the Yugoslav League has reflected the attributes of an institution as specified above—namely, a less intense and fixed ideology, a greater flexibility of organizational expression, a growing legitimacy among the wider population, a depersonalization of leadership roles, a higher tolerance of diversity and conflict, a more prestigeful status for its membership, a growing routinization of leadership change, and an increased emphasis upon predictable, rule-oriented behavior. The basic thesis argued here is that the Yugoslav League of Communists has progressively displayed such attributes, and that it can be said that over the years it has developed from a simple organization into a Yugoslav institution. In fact, the Yugoslavs argue that, by developing into an accepted, institutionalized League organization, they in one sense pass "beyond institutionalization," in that League goals and functions may become fully absorbed by the wider fabric of Yugoslav society. From an ideological standpoint, the prevalence of these attributes gives evidence for the Yugoslav that "the dictatorship of the proletariat" can be terminated and that formal party structure as such may "wither away." More recent events in Yugoslavia—in particular, the stress upon the "divorcing of party from power" thesis—holds radical implications for the changing nature of the overall system. It is also clear that such a principle merely represents the logical culmination of trends that have existed within Yugoslavia for some time, trends that move progressively toward separating the League from its governmental base. The irony of the Yugoslav party is that, as it continues to become institutionalized and as its base of legitimacy expands within Yugoslav society, it also increasingly promises to "wither away" such that Yugoslavia might eventually be characterized as a *non-party system*.

Historical Aspects

The popular base that the League of Communists now enjoys in Yugoslavia in some sense has a source in the interwar period. Having been awarded a legitimacy at the founding of the Kingdom of Serbs, Croats, and Slovenes at the end of World War I, the Yugoslav Communist Party immediately proceeded to capture its share of the popular vote in 1920 at the first national elections. The Yugoslav party managed to garner fifty-eight seats in the Constituent Assembly and approximately 12 per cent of the popular vote; only two other political parties in the country managed to capture more seats in the Constituent Assembly than did the Communist Party.[2] A factor that may have contributed to the large communist vote was that most ethnic minorities could find no party that effectively represented their interests; accordingly, for many it meant a choice between the prevailing Serb or Croat parties, on the other hand, or the Communist Party, with its ethnic indifference and cross-regional posture, on the other. This early political success revealing a popular base in support of a Marxist-related party in Yugoslav society provides the groundwork for subsequent party acceptability and institutional growth.

Following upon the success of the Yugoslav Communist Party at the electoral polls, the royalist government of King Alexander took immediate steps to deprive it of its formal legal status. By a cabinet decree of December, 1920, the Yugoslav government banned all activities of the Communist Party in Yugoslavia.[3] As a result, the Communist Party was driven underground, where it continued to carry on a vigorous life, which became especially manifest among intellectual circles in major Yugoslav universities. It was in fact from these university circles that much of the Communist Party elite was drawn during World War II and the post-war era. Although the membership of the Yugoslav party at the outbreak of World War II was rather small, many of its leaders had their roots and experience in student-activist groups that plagued the royalist Yugoslav regime. An aspect with implications for subsequent party institutionalization that emerges during this time is the sense of camaraderie among student activists at these university centers. Furthermore, these ties among "old friends" were subsequently to play a very significant role in the effectiveness and the cohesian of Yugoslav party leadership. The relative success that the Communist Party experienced between the wars provided some historical ground for arguments in support of party legitimacy that were to be used later.

The period of resistance during World War II in Yugoslav party evolution (that is, the "national-liberation struggle") provides the first opportunity for the growth of viable institutional components. The primary contribution of this period was the generating of shared norms and traditions based upon the resistance experience that extended beyond the narrow confines of Communist Party members themselves. From the standpoint of party institutionalization, this served to liberate the party from any charge of narrow ethnic parochialism; the Communist Party was viewed as "Yugoslav" in the broadest sense, and the traditions that were defined during the resistance experience incorporated all Yugoslav peoples. To become a partisan or "a fighter against the invader" it was not necessary to specify that one was a Serb, Croat, Slovene, Muslim, or whatever; neither was it necessary to declare oneself specifically as a communist.[4] Furthermore, the bonds that developed between comrades-in-arms from many ethnic groups under fire confronting a common enemy—namely, the German invader—took on an especially meaningful aspect. This type of cooperation in the face of death and threat from the invader tended to reduce feelings of ethnic animosity and separatism, while it also served as an exceptional base upon which to construct normative appeals for countrywide solidarity on the part of the League. Such a tradition and experience (that later takes the form of the partisan myth of solidarity) served not only to bind together leaders of the communist movement, but also helped consolidate the lower echelon, non-communist rank and file as well. The partisan wartime experience was invaluable as the normative groundwork (that is, as the underlying historical-experiential referent) upon which the subsequent institutionalization of the Yugoslav Communist Party might develop.

In addition to its normative base, a number of organizational elements began to emerge that became relevant for later party institutionalization. The first of these are the widespread, regionally based "national-liberation committees" that formed the local bases and units for partisan resistance operations in various parts of the country.[5] The effect of this was to establish a primitive local governmental network that would later contribute to pressures within Yugoslavia for a decentralized system of authority. In this respect, the national-liberation committees served to reinforce the institutional principle within the Communist Party that local (as well as lower-echelon) leadership elements must be honored if the party organization in general is to exist. The second major element concerns the AVNOJ (Anti-Fascist Council of the National-Liberation of Yugoslavia), which constituted an early parliament of sorts that brought together representatives from the network of national-liberation committees across the country.[6] In this respect, the authority structure that was to give support to Communist Party activity and organization began to take shape while the struggle against the German invader was still in progress and as yet unresolved. What becomes relevant here for subsequent party institutional development is the convergence of three key components—the party organizational apparatus, the normative-historical rationale for the exercise of party power, and the incipient local governmental structure. There was also the suggestion that even during the resistance a system of representative institutions and a conception of decentralized decision-making had been championed by the Communist Party. These three components taken together provided the Yugoslav communists with a basic self-perpetuating capability that later was to contribute to the process of institutionalizing the party organization.

The years of partisan warfare for the Communist Party had given it a solid cadre of experienced, dedicated members who had won state power by what they saw to be their own efforts. From the very beginning partisan literature deemphasized the role of Western military aid as well as the importance of Soviet armed forces in Yugoslavia, and in turn had somewhat exaggerated the contributions of Communist Party leadership to the success of the resistance struggle. As a central aspect of their legitimacy, the Yugoslav partisans stressed the fact that they represented the only Communist Party in Europe that had come to power by its own effort and in its own right. The Yugoslav sacrifice during World War II had served to dramatize a political founding that was unique among all socialist countries; a critical factor as regards legitimacy was that the "heroes" of the struggle viewed themselves (and were viewed by others) in the first instance as Yugoslavs and secondly as communists. This view also found its relevance later in that it was to provide the basis for effective post-war state authority as well as an argument for widespread acceptability of Communist Party leadership. The partisan war resistance was central to Yugoslav party institutionalization in providing the basis for the acceptability of the party among the wider population through a political founding myth that served to dramatize the creation of a "new Yugoslavia."

Party-Administrative Phase

Following upon the war period, the strongest single force that could guarantee integrated effort within Yugoslavia was the Communist Party. Since it had gained considerable prestige and notoriety as the leader of the resistance movement, the Yugoslav party immediately took upon itself the role of main bulwark of the Popular Front. Although in theory a coalition of the Communist and other "anti-fascist" interwar parties, the Popular Front was effectively dominated and manipulated by its communist elements as a means by which to mobilize widespread support.[7] The party leadership adroitly employed the Popular Front as the organizational instrument through which to expand its general following, just as it used words such as "partisan" and "national liberation" to strengthen its legitimacy by representing itself as an "all Yugoslav" institution. Finally, the heroic image cast and the dramatic mood created by the personality of Tito and his comrades during their epic-making resistance (exploiting the charismatic dimension of political founding) also helped the Communist Party to widen its popular base.

With respect to its organization, the Yugoslav party possessed administrative structures in each republic and local region that paralleled its countrywide system. The Communist Party unofficially controlled the federal administrative system even though a party member did not always formally head every relevant bureaucratic section. During this early phase, the administrative structure of the Communist Party was steeply hierarchical, including a paramilitary aspect that grew out of the partisan resistance. In general, the task of the Communist Party was viewed simply as the direct, administrative control of all relevant aspects of Yugoslav society in terms of a fixed Marxist model and based upon a centralized buraucratic system. Although some basic steps had already been taken as regards Communist Party legitimacy and institutionalization, the structure of the party tended for a time to remain classically democratic-centralist with strict adherence to the Soviet model. It is clear that during this phase the party leadership felt·that there was only one properly communist organizational form, and that version had its unquestioned source in Moscow as the Third Rome.

With the creation of the new Yugoslav state after World War II, the Communist Party initially placed great reliance upon narrowly organizational-administrative controls. In retrospect, even the average Yugoslav will today refer to this experience as the "administrative period" during which the party dogmatically and inflexibly tried to make of Yugoslavia the model satellite simply to please the Soviet Union.[8] In fact, the regard held by Yugoslav leaders for Stalin and the Soviet system was slightly less than full religious adulation and spiritual reverence. The figure of Stalin loomed as a hero-legislator (with Tito his appointed vicar) through whose inspiration and guidance a new socialist society based upon the Soviet model would be established. As a result, the Yugoslav communist state became the model satellite with an unwavering commitment to a strictly orthodox version of Marxist ideals; all sectors of Yugoslav society and economy were to be pushed as rapidly as possible in order to realize the Marxist vision. The Yugoslav party sought to found its authority upon narrowly organizational attributes (that is, inflexible, orthodox ideology, rigid, hierarchical structure, and strong, individual personality) as well as in elements that lay outside of specifically Yugoslav national experience. In short, what this meant was that Yugoslav party leaders had in effect turned away from seeking (for the moment at least) the expanded institutional base for party authority among the populace that the partisan experience had already in part established. The result was increasingly heavy reliance upon purely organizational-administrative instruments of control such as the secret police, the military, and the bureaucracy, as well as upon related aspects such as charismatic, personalized leadership, and dogmatic ideological forms. For our purposes, the significant aspect of the Soviet-Yugoslav break in 1948 was that it created a need for the Yugoslav party to seek its supports in sources other than the bureaucracy, firm Marxist dogma, and the secret police. In short, this event was instrumental in forcing the party to generate an institutional context that would link it up more closely with the broader Yugoslav populace. Three basic value-elements became relevant with respect to subsequent developments in strengthening the institutional base of the Communist Party—namely, the established integrity of local leaders and organizations, the grounding of a normative frame of reference in a shared historical experience, and the mass participatory ethic that resulted from widespread "Yugoslav" partisan activity—all of which contribute directly to the policy of decentralization as integral to the Yugoslav socialist system. In general, the development of the League that follows after 1950 indicates the growing attempt by its leaders to ground popular support (that is, legitimacy) for the party within a broader Yugoslav experiential context. As a result, those forces that could press the Yugoslav party toward greater institutionalization were greatly strengthened.

The existence of an external environment, which may loom either as threatening or supportive, may also serve to accelerate the institutionalizing and legitimizing process of a Communist Party. For the Yugoslav case, the dramatic break with the Soviet Union in 1948 provided the needed catalyst to intensify the process that could transform the party from a simple organization into a widely accepted institution.[9] Up until this time, the major legitimizing component that the Yugoslav communist regime parlayed was playing the role of "the best communist satellite," which meant, however, that it always followed the lead of the Soviet Union with a touching devotion and that it usually sought acceptability in Moscow. The significance here is that support and legitimacy are found external to the Yugoslav intra-societal context, such that it would be difficult to confer upon the party the status of a specifically "Yugoslav" institution. The major consequence and significance of the Soviet-Yugoslav break was the creation of a need to seek out new and more viable moorings for the legitimacy and popular acceptability of the Yugoslav party within the confines of its own society. Most generally, this triggered the development of what has come to be known as "national communism" which, in its broadest implications, signifies that the party should establish its legitimacy in terms of its own national culture, its internal environment, and its own historical experience. The outcome for the Yugoslavs was to generate a number of strategic concepts designed to reinforce the identity of the party with Yugoslav society (for example, "the independent road to socialism"), in addition to stressing the specific or unique features of the Yugoslav environment (that material conditions in Yugoslavia are specific to it). The results of such reformulations were to broaden domestic party support and to open the door for the acceptability of the Communist Party as a peculiarly Yugoslav expression. In particular, the myth dramatizing the "independent road" thesis has in fact served the convenient dual function of consolidating supportive forces at home while withstanding pressures from the great powers abroad. Another specific function of this concept has been to disarm Western critics by employing it as a symbol of liberalizing policies as well as decentralization within Yugoslavia.[10] For the Yugoslav populace as a whole, this meant that the party might become less rigid ideologically, more flexible in its organizational expression, more tolerant of differences in perspective, and more predictable (that is, rule-oriented) in its overall activity. The basic principle conveyed here is that institutionalizing a Communist Party within a *national* society requires a basic gesture that seems to undercut the *international* aspects of the communist movement.

Another effect upon the Yugoslav institutional environment stemming from the Cominform split touched upon the issues of debureaucratization and decentralization, involving thereby an attack upon the fixity of organizational forms in Soviet communist experience. Since the Yugoslavs had severely berated the Soviet regime for its intransigent statist and over-centralist system (and, in general, for its cumbersome bureaucracy), the Yugoslav response domestically was precisely to experiment with and to contrive new socioeconomic forms that were designed to remedy such organizational ills.[11] This resulted in the Yugoslav system of worker self-management which reflected the principle of direct economic democracy and a largely decentralized, more flexible system of decision-making. Ultimately, these principles of decentralization and workers' democracy found concrete expression economically in the workers' councils system and politically in the commune as the local governmental-territorial unit. The major effect of these institutional innovations was to expand the participation and the involvement of the Yugoslav citizen in both the polity and the economy; it also meant that the privilege of actively controlling the destiny of Yugoslav society was not to remain solely with the members of the Communist Party but was to be extended to "working people" everywhere in Yugoslav society. From the standpoint of the Communist Party as the overriding Yugoslav organization, this meant that, although it would retain the responsibility for general supervision of Yugoslav society, it would most likely have to relinquish its direct, administrative control functions. There was indeed a sense in which the Yugoslav party would be expected to serve Yugoslav society rather than simply to administer and control it.

Given these incipient trends in the early 1950s toward democratizing and decentralizing the environment, the special privileges of party members also tended to be curtailed to some degree. As a result, individuals other than Communist Party members became more eligible for as well as more successful in holding public office. Fully up until 1952 and the Sixth Congress, however, the Yugoslav party on the whole continued to play the classical Marxist or Soviet-style role of directing nearly all political, social, and economic life in the country; in short, the party for the most part remained organizationally and ideologically inflexible. Despite the early resolutions of the Fifth Congress on the Cominform dispute, and the serious disaffection with the Soviet Union, the Yugoslav party still for a time insisted upon its strict Marxist orthodoxy and retained its well-centralized structure. In the words of Rankovic, the party's statutes were "a copy of the statutes of the Soviet Communist Party." [12] At this point the need was felt to start applying similar liberalizing principles to the party itself that had been advocated for Yugoslav society at large. The process of party institutionalization begins to gather more effective force as these internal liberalizing trends in Yugoslavia become increasingly apparent.

The Transitional Phase

Major changes in Yugoslav party structure and function began to occur at the Sixth Congress in 1952—namely, a basic decentralization of its organizational system. A specific practical effect was that local Communist Party secretaries were ordered to give up many of their positions as heads of local governmental bodies, an occurrence which in some measure foreshadows the much later development of striving to "divorce the party from power." In addition, party functionaries in republics were given more authority and autonomy to determine official Communist Party stands in their regions than previously. Designated anew the League of Communists of Yugoslavia (consistent with its debureaucratized self-image), the party was no longer to be "the immediate operational guide and directive-giver neither in economic nor in government and social life." It must rather contribute to development through "its own political and ideological activity" and by working "in all organizations, agencies and institutions for adoption of its line and standpoint, or standpoints of its individual members." [13] Here it was suggested that the League might limit its function to political education and the setting of basic guidelines, while other socioeconomic organizations were to be charged with the more immediate and concrete problems of direction and control. In fact, the choice of the designation "league" as opposed to "party" itself reveals the desire of the Yugoslav communists to deemphasize the strictly organizational attributes of the socialist movement.

Coupled with decentralization, membership in the League was also made somewhat easier to obtain while special privileges of party members were progressively curtailed. Furthermore, the old Popular Front was resurrected and designated anew the Socialist Alliance, a move consistent with the League's desire to expand the basis of its mass support. Given the context of decentralization, the rejuvenated Popular Front was expected to become more involved in many aspects of social direction and control that were previously assumed by the Communist Party alone. In order to assure coordination and ideological unity, however, the leadership of the League and that of the Socialist Alliance remained essentially one and the same. The withdrawal tendency of the League (that is, trying to create a more subdued role for itself) marks an important transition from, on the one hand, the status of an organizational party involving a resort to direct measures of administrative control to, on the other, that of an institutionalized party that indirectly permeates various aspects and levels of society and seeks to exert controls unobtrusively.

The leadership of the Communist Party by 1953 became painfully aware that it might have loosened things up a bit too rapidly. As a result, the warning was issued that League members must not abandon their leadership over the working masses; a tendency was also noted that members seem to lose themselves in the Alliance and leave the nominating process to the "wild movement of events." [14] There was a suggestion that the League as yet had not developed the institutional strength (for example, having its end-goals generally accepted) and the popular legitimacy that would permit it to enjoy the luxury of extensive relaxation of direct controls. In June, 1953 at the Brioni Plenum the party attempted to slow up this disintegrative process by a tightening of administrative discipline within the League of Communists. With respect to the wider society, this resulted in the introduction of a larger number of party "actifs" into various governmental departments, in conjunction also with the training of new and better party cadres in newly established League "higher schools of political science." This renewed old-style party approach to supervising Yugoslav society meant a slight and brief revival of more direct involvement and control by League members at all levels of governmental operation—that is, it involved a reversion to an earlier party organizational form. In addition, the League began to expel some of its members, a process which, after the Djilas affair, was considerably accelerated. Here it might also be noted that the arguments of Djilas merely represent the full logical extension of the then prevailing trends as regards the debureaucratization of both government and party within Yugoslavia. By June, 1956, party membership declined to 635,984, which was its lowest point since 1950, as compared to a high of

779,382 recorded for June, 1952.[15] This narrowing of the League membership base dramatically reflects the temporary reversal of the party institutionalizing process in the Yugoslav case. The Communist Party leadership had perhaps allowed things to move too quickly and too early as regards turning the League membership loose (presuming also thereby that the party had attained sufficient institutional status) without adequately securing itself within the broader context of Yugoslav society. Tragedy of course marks any such period of rapid change, experimentation, and then sudden reversal—and Djilas thus becomes the convenient sacrifice to somewhat incautious attempts at liberalizing the structure of the League.

The changing governmental-organizational setting in Yugoslavia also bears upon the transformed nature of the Communist Party role. With the basic commitment to debureaucratize and decentralize, to return the factories to the direct control of the working people themselves, a need arose to give concrete effect to the principle of expanded citizen participation both in formal governmental institutions and in socially owned economic enterprises. The Fundamental Law of 1953 served to give fuller effect to citizen participation by establishing a legislative system in which "producers" themselves could place delegates in governmental assemblies.[16] The principle of direct producer (that is, worker) representation became manifest within the governmental complex of institutions by creating a special "council of producers" at various levels. This basic law also holds implications for the diminished role of the League, since the principle of *direct democracy* (that is, involvement of citizen-producers directly in the governmental structure) suggests that the mediating and interest-aggregating function of the league would eventually become superfluous. The stress upon direct producer and economic-group (that is, functional) representation in the parliamentary system still becomes more strongly expressed in 1963 with the creation of "chambers of working communities" within the Federal Assembly.[17] In this way, the parliamentary system became structurally geared to concrete but broadly defined socioeconomic functions expressed through the various chambers—namely, economic, education and culture, social welfare and health, and organization-politics. The impact of such a system was to further deemphasize and to question the Communist Party as the *only* appropriate instrument for achieving direct and efficient control of the Yugoslav sociopolitical environment. It also gave added impetus to the institutionalizing process by further gearing the League into the popular context and the newly emerging socioeconomic forces of Yugoslav society. This new system has meant that the elected delegate to a legislative body must, in the first instance, increasingly commit himself and work in terms of the substantive context of his own chamber and, only secondarily, behave on the basis of the narrow interests and ideological concerns of the League. In effect, the League was increasingly compelled to view its interests in broadly societal terms and to define its Marxist ideology more pragmatically—both tendencies being identifiable as attributes of growing party institutionalization. A concrete added result has been to generate cleavage-lines in terms of socioeconomic (rather than ideological) issues along which tension and competition among Yugoslav party factions might be expressed; this also gives evidence that conflict tends to focus more on broader societal concerns and less upon narrower League issues. Finally, it has intensified the trend in the direction of a diffuse, widely accepted institutionalized League, in contrast to a more tightly controlled, organizational Communist Party within the Yugoslav system.

The steady removal of pressure by the League upon elements in Yugoslav society was explicitly recognized by theorists as a new phase in socialist development. This trend has been expressed in the formula that, with a newly transformed socioeconomic base (and, in particular, the social self-administration of the working people), the further relaxation of the general environment could be permitted. Logically, this relaxation of controls must follow since a major effect of new socioeconomic forms and experience also involves the transformation of basic political and governmental superstructure, which means that new and more appropriate political-administrative forms must be generated in the light of new socioeconomic experience (that is, the workers' councils system). Stated otherwise, as the League redefines its role and develops a range of institutional attributes, the nature of the parliamentary system and other governmental forms must also change, namely, by expanding the arena of direct citizen participation and by allowing conflict to be resolved by means of political competition within the governmental structure. In practice, these developments have also meant that the League no longer felt the need strenuously to press for the affirmation of its basic goals, with the presumption that direct involvement in self-administration by the working people was fully adequate to reinforce them. In short, Yugoslav society as a whole no longer reflected the need to be constantly and forcibly mobilized by the League as an organization;[18] in fact, League members have felt more and more confident that the party has developed into a basic Yugoslav institution in that its norms and goals are being acknowledged by and grounded in the socioeconomic experience of the bulk of the Yugoslav citizenry. This also suggests that the process of the past twenty years in Yugoslavia is considered by many as being irreversible, a view which betrays a certain security taken by the Yugoslav party leadership in its socialist achievements.[19] Consistent with these trends, the 1958 party program had stated that the League "will gradually, in the long run, disappear with the developing and strengthening of ever more inclusive forms of immediate socialist democracy."[20] It would seem, therefore, that the institutional base of the League was felt to be secure enough to permit the gradual dismantling of some time-worn organizational aspects of the party structure; thereafter, it would follow that the control and the administration of all aspects of Yugoslav society are to be increasingly taken over by the working people themselves. It meant also that Communist Party dogma was viewed as less relevant, that party membership was regarded more highly by the general populace, and that some promise existed for routinizing changes in political leadership. Apart from a slight reversal a bit later that reasserted the League's role as a vigorous and active guide of Yugoslav socialist development, the pattern indicated here defines the overriding trend as regards the party role since the 1958 congress.

Further underscoring the institutionalizing process, in February, 1958, the party central committee had sent a letter to League organizations denouncing "dictatorial methods," special privileges, and the practice of favoritism.[21] With the Seventh Congress, which took place in 1958, a still less direct and openly administrative role for the League of Communists had been stressed with a renewed vigor. While formally the overall guiding role of the League (especially as regards basic socialist principles) was to remain unchallenged, in practice the Socialist Alliance and other organizations were charged with assuming more direct responsibility for moving the Yugoslav system toward socialism. Furthermore, local governmental bodies, workers' councils in enterprises, and producer representation in assemblies—all such institutions kept increasing in prestige among the Yugoslav populace as well as in the scope of their authority. Greater stress upon professional competence, upon legal and formal governmental channels, and upon "socialist legality" (rather than upon narrow party loyalty) had the effect of circumscribing the League of Communists as the only or primary factor relevant to Yugoslav political life. The League also tried to involve larger numbers of people in its lectures, classes, and schools (that is, in political education) as a means of instilling socialist principles and broadening the institutional base of the League among the Yugoslav citizenry. Progressively, the emphasis upon formally governmental (rather than narrow party) channels of communication, in addition to a stress upon the Socialist Alliance, trade unions, and other organizations, encouraged the view that the League had become a "honor society" of sorts that merely sets the broadest guidelines for the Yugoslav system. As a consequence, the formal governmental structure at nearly all levels has tended to assume both more importance and more legitimacy among the populace.[22] Following directly upon these trends, the orthodox Yugoslav Marxist has had (more or less continually) to point to a certain laxity in enthusiasm of League members for active work in local organizations. Such official pressure for active participation and involvement at all levels by Yugoslav party members was seen as necessary in order to maintain the overall *but* indirect guiding role of the League.

A number of international aspects that contribute to expanding the institutional base of the Yugoslav Communist Party should also be noted. Ever since the break with the Soviet Union, the pattern of Yugoslav foreign policy has been to cultivate relations with Third World nations and to stay clear of entanglements with either major power bloc.[23] The result has been that members of the League of Communists in attendance at international conferences are viewed (and also see themselves) more as representatives of Yugoslav society than as devotees of a world communist movement. Over the years the boycott of the Yugoslav League by various Communist Party sponsors of international meetings (for example, the Havana world conference on revolution, or recent Budapest meetings on Marxist ideology) without question strengthens such a disposition. In fact, the attacks of "revision" to which the Yugoslav party has been repeatedly subject over the years also contributes significantly to its domestic support and serves to legitimize the League as "Yugoslav" above all else. The Yugoslav insistence upon its special and unique form of socialism, which remains unencumbered by Communist Party interest and policies elsewhere, would further reinforce such legitimacy and expand its authority base.

Internally, the effect of these trends over the years has been to make of the League an institution that quite properly and acceptably speaks for Yugoslav national interests. Furthermore, these factors also contribute to the gradual process of party institutionalization, in the sense that norms and goals pursued by the League and those expressed by the Yugoslav populace at large must gradually but surely converge. The result is that members of a more fully institutionalized party become, as it were, "creatures" of a Yugoslav national society rather than being ideologically or organizationally bound as instruments serving a communist world cause.

Current Party Trends

Recent events within Yugoslavia point to a further redirection of the role and nature of the League of Communists, a redirection that in fact suggests that the party may be moving "beyond institutionalization" or toward a withdrawal from active political life. Certainly a major change suggested in the Yugoslav system relates to the principle of separation of the League from active political power.[24] Although the full implications of such a policy are currently uncertain, it remains consistent with the thesis that the League of Communists should merely provide ideological guidelines and involve itself ever less so in the direct administration and control of public affairs. Here the growing legitimacy and the increasing status of the League develops to a point that encourages the transfer of specific control functions to non-party, citizen-based organizational bodies.

The operational effect of this separation of "party from power" requires that an individual may not hold a position of authority *both* in the League and in the governmental structure, although it is expected that government officials would for the most part also be members of the League of Communists. The result seems to suggest that the League as a bureaucratic, direct-control instrument would tend to "wither away," with the presumption that the existing consensus on socialist principles is sufficiently ingrained (that is, the party is adequately institutionalized, to justify such a radical venture). Furthermore, this move to fully divest the League of direct-controlling power underscores the new role of communists in Yugoslav society as a sort of overriding Brahmanic caste, in that they immunize themselves from the "dirty business" of politics and become the exclusive (and priestly) guardians of socialist morality. They in effect acknowledge that the Yugoslav populace has been prepared to freely accept the League as that institution specifically charged with defining broad ideological guidelines, without requiring the traditional application of direct administrative controls and secret police harassment in order to secure such a residual but critical role for Yugoslav communists. Here then it is presumed that social groups will be able to pursue their own interests and be "political" (without the direct assistance of the League) within the context of a broadly based Marxist commitment. To presume that the authority structure of the League and the government need not parallel one another betrays a confidence by League members in a widespread acceptance of the party as a basic Yugoslav institution. This capability of attaining the status of a Yugoslav institution for the League also indicates a clear grounding of its goals and activity in Yugoslav socioeconomic experience and culture.

A far-reaching set of *Draft Theses* concerning the reorganization of the League (although in fact anticipated to a large degree) seems to follow in the wake of the recent resignation by Rankovic as vice president of Yugoslavia.[25] The basic motive underlying these League reforms relates to applying the principles of self-management and direct democracy that are believed to exist in Yugoslav society at large to the narrower confines of the League itself. A more specific theme focuses upon the abolition of "the 'personal' union between the leading forms of the League of Communists and the government," which means that leading political figures in Yugoslavia would not be permitted to hold positions of power both in the government and in the League.[26] The result would be to put the League of Communists above both politics and government in the sense of existing as a *non-party* (that is, non-organization) or above-factions type of Yugoslav institution; in this regard, the League would function primarily as the caretaker of the socialist morality and Marxist principles that underlie Yugoslav society in general. Such a proposal also has the effect of further depersonalizing leadership functions as well as routinizing the process of change (that is, making it publicly knowable and predictable for the citizenry) within the overall political arena. However, the "divorcing of the party from power" requires from the other side that individual communists become more active politically *as individuals* since the direct party control aspect in Yugoslav society would be gradually eliminated.[27] Here then the issue that might be raised with respect to one-party as against multi-party systems is felt to be resolvable in favor of a *non-party system,* in which the "working people" and *their* organizations involve themselves directly in political life. The insistence by the Yugoslavs that they are working toward a non-party system provides us with an illuminating symptom of the institutionalizing process that has been at work in Yugoslavia. In this respect, as the League of Yugoslav Communists becomes more of an institution (that is, as acceptance of its norms, goals, and style pervades society), it would also tend to become less of an organization, shedding itself of political-administrative control functions. Such developments also look forward to the decreasing role that any given, single personality such as Tito would have to play in maintaining the life of the League of Communists. In fact, the federal law relating to nonsuccession to political office in Yugoslavia serves as a structural device designed to militate against the predominance of a single personality as a basis for perpetuating the party organization. It serves in effect, therefore, to underscore the necessity for predictable, routinized change in leadership, and in general to accelerate the growth of depersonalized, rule-oriented behavior in Yugoslav society.

The second major factor expressed in the *Draft Theses* that relates to party institutionalization is the principle that direct democracy must now also be applied to the internal workings of the League itself. In carrying this out, the practical operation of the League of Communists as an organization would be based upon the same rules and norms of procedure (with individuals also possessing the same rights therein) as would exist in other organizations in Yugoslav society. In this respect, the League of Communists becomes less a privileged or "secret" organization of like-minded believers, and would become more fully integrated into the general social practice and the normative fabric of the Yugoslav system. The gulf between the League of Communists and the wider Yugoslav populace in this respect narrows as party institutionalization grows. As regards this internal democracy of the League, the *Draft Theses* now being considered stress the fact that open debate and criticism must also be encouraged; more concretely, it is suggested that personal and collective resignation from the League of Communists might be honored without the normally expected punitive measures. What this seems to point toward is the development of a system of accountability in which members could legally resign as a form of protest against the policies that the League may be currently pursuing. The League of Communists, increasingly confident of its status as a Yugoslav institution, feels that it might absorb any ill effects that stem from internal differences and minority dissent. As of the moment, it is difficult to say precisely what the concrete outcome of any such reforms might be, or which of the various debatable theses will be effectively implemented by future League congresses or central committee plenums. In any event, the basic thesis of "divorcing the party from power" and the internal democratization of the League are of and by themselves quite revolutionary in implication, while they also add considerable force to the institutionalizing process and strengthen the general acceptability of the League.

The recent April, 1967 elections in Yugoslavia also seem to have far-reaching implications for the increased liberalization of Yugoslav society as well as for further institutionalizing of the party. Relevant aspects of these elections include the encouraging of socioeconomic or workers' organizations to put forth as many political candidates as possible, the giving of concrete effect to the provision of nonsuccession (that is, rotation) of political offices, and the stimulating of greater participation by younger and more qualified candidates in general elections.[28] First of all, it appears that of the newly elected members of both the federal and republican assemblies only a handful are carryovers from previous legislative bodies. But what is even more important, those individuals who were selected for key governmental posts (for example, president of the Federal Assembly) reveal the emergence of a new younger bevy of Yugoslav leaders. Both of these developments in fact give evidence that the principle of rotating political offices has been relatively effective in the Yugoslav system. A major by-product of rotating political office has been to depersonalize Yugoslav leadership roles —that is, to emphasize the position that is being held rather than the person who holds it. Furthermore, it demonstrates that the continued life of the League of Communists must be grounded in its general acceptability as a Yugoslav institution with publicly acceptable and routinized procedures for change, rather than relying upon the possibly arbitrary use of strictly political-administrative controls or the uncertain charisma of a few of its "old-time" leading personalities. Second, the recent Yugoslav elections have apparently expanded the level of involvement in the political process by the Yugoslav citizenry in general as well as by various socioeconomic and quasi-political organizations. Consequently, a considerably larger number of elections than was previously the case were multi-candidate and were in fact heatedly and competitively contested; [29] even at the federal level we find that approximately 25 per cent of the available legislative seats had more than one candidate in the running, a proportion that becomes even greater at the lower commune level of government. A thought provoking by-product of this more interested citizen participation in Yugoslav elections has been the loss of assembly seats by well-regarded League members in highly competitive political campaigns to candidates not officially sanctioned by the League. As a result, the configurations of elective governmental bodies tend more accurately to reflect the conflict lines that exist out in Yugoslav society, while heated political debates, acknowledged opposition groups, and divided votes on critical issues are becoming commonplace in the Yugoslav Federal Assembly. Here then we find the conjoining of the institutional attribute of an expanded participatory base with those of routinized procedures for sociopolitical change and increased tolerance for diversified viewpoints. Finally the April, 1967 electoral campaign has resulted in salient changes in the basic sociological makeup of the Yugoslav leadership structure, which has served to enhance the prestige of the League member. Generally, the elections have favored the younger and better educated over the older with more experience, and thereby have resulted in establishing the vanguard of a more sophisticated, educated, and youthful leadership element within the League.

In one sense, recent political events within the Yugoslav system merely reflect the gradual change that has taken place in the sociological composition of League membership. It has become clear over the years that the educational level of League members has increased, that there has been a dramatic reduction in the number of peasants, that the various professional groups are more strongly represented, and that the average age of League members has also tended to drop.[30] Here again, with respect to further implications for institutionalizing the League, those elements in Yugoslav society that have acutely vested interests in preserving the system (that is, those who receive the economic payoffs) have been more inclined to gravitate to and become stronger forces within the League of Communists. The Yugoslav leader in this sense increasingly becomes an integral part of the more general society, in addition to being more acceptable to the populace as a whole, and in particular being viewed as more reliable or predictable in his public acts. Despite these sociological changes in its membership composition, the League has still maintained the necessary strategic ethnocultural balance in its leadership composition in order to assure the representation of major national groups within the country. Given the long history of problems in Yugoslavia relating to strife among national groups, such a policy affords an eminently reasonable tactic for holding ethno-cultural conflict in check. This also reflects a dimension related to the depersonalization and routinization of sociopolitical change in Yugoslavia, expressed however in terms of an official de-ethnicization of conflict lines in order to minimize irrational (emotive) sources for making political demands. If these two factors are considered together (the continued professionalization of League membership, on the one hand, and the retention of a desired strategic balance of ethno-cultural groups, on the other), then it would seem that a foundation exists for providing the legitimacy among the wider populace that the League needs to assure its acceptability as a Yugoslav institution. Furthermore, if we take into account the three factors mentioned earlier—namely, the accelerated and routinized turnover of political leadership, the expanded participation of the Yugoslav citizenry, and the growth of a more acceptable, better educated leadership element—then it would also seem reasonable to expect a major change in both the nature and the role of the Yugoslav Communist Party. In general, such events as those that have recently transpired in Yugoslavia indicate that the League has developed the overriding institutional attribute of absorbing and adapting itself to new elements that emerge in Yugoslav society.

Two other factors of recent origin that have contributed to the changing nature of the Yugoslav party role should be briefly mentioned. First of all, the economic reforms of July, 1965 have further strengthened and expanded the autonomy of decision-making power in the local commune, in addition to that of the socially owned (that is, workers' council) economic enterprise system. In other words, these economic reforms have put still more of the administrative-control functions directly in the hands of assorted organizations not immediately related to the Yugoslav party. Such a trend is of course fully consistent with the basic theme of the "withering away" of the Communist Party organizational apparatus and reflects the theme that the League may be passing "beyond institutionalization." Second, the ideological posture of the League of Communists has become increasingly flexible, even to the point of tolerating what appears to be an "opposition" Marxist theoretical movement within Yugoslavia.[31] Furthermore, it could be argued that the progressively adaptable posture of the Yugoslav party on Marxist ideology (that is, its conscious attempt not to be dogmatic) has contributed much to the development of the League as an acceptable Yugoslav institution. We have seen that both a less rigid ideology and a generally increased tolerance of internal diversity can contribute to the growth of an institutionalized one-party system. The remarkable thing about the Yugoslavs is their apparent talent for deciding to introduce suspiciously "capitalist" elements (for example, inviting foreign capital to invest in the country), and yet at the same time justifying these very same moves within the framework of Marxist ideological jargon. In short, the Yugoslav Communist Party has been quite creative over the years in their uses and adaptation of a basic Marxist vocabulary, refusing all along to be unreasonably bound either by its Moscow-based dogmatic form or simply by its long tradition.[32] The League of Communists has been persistent in demonstrating a progressively more flexible ideological posture, a feature that has been defined as being integral to the process of party institutionalization. Significantly, due to such a tactical adaptation of Marxist ideals, the League of Communists has improved its capability for survival as a basic Yugoslav institution.

The Yugoslav communist regime has quite properly been described as experimentalist and innovative in its style. What follows from this posture is the increased level of tolerance for internal diversity in addition to a dynamism of organizational forms found in the Yugoslav system. However, it would be a mistake to presume that any such innovation has its source only in top League echelons or, for that matter, that Tito himself represents a sort of modern-day "innovating monarch." Quite to the contrary, the experimentation and innovation that is found in Yugoslavia has its source in and accurately mirrors the conflict lines that the Yugoslav environment itself projects onto the political scene. For example, the major liberalizing step taken by the 1965 reforms found its strongest proponents among both Slovene and Croat elements, who insisted that the profit stemming from economic activity should be retained by the region that produces it—namely, that such profit should be kept within Slovenia and Croatia for investment in new productive forces. The ouster of Vice President Rankovic may, on the other side, be viewed as the League's response to the attempt by elements in the Serbian regional party to block the carrying out of these new economic reforms. What this in effect demonstrates is that Tito himself does not in fact innovate, but rather that he permits innovation by his willingness to listen and respond to group demands. Accordingly, the source of change and innovation in Yugoslav society must be sought not in the League itself but in the contours of the more general environment—namely regional-territorial divisions, economic-group competition, ethno-religious variation, and intraparty factional cleavage. In this respect, and quite understandably, the League of Communists would further consolidate its status as a Yugoslav institution as it effectively responds to demands for socioeconomic change and innovation that have their source within the broader context of Yugoslav society.

Conclusion

A number of observations suggest themselves as the result of this general survey of Yugoslav party evolution. On balance, it becomes rather clear that the League of Communists (even as its name would seem to signify) moves progressively toward becoming a Yugoslav institution, if this can be contrasted to its continued existence simply as an organization seeking to assure the survival of a communist movement. The League has become an institution in the sense of linking its own norms and its goals (having also modified them in so doing) with those that exist within the larger Yugoslav context, such that the continued life of the League as a Yugoslav institution also symbolizes the effective survival of the Yugoslav system as a whole. The Yugoslav party also manifests insitutional attributes in its willingness to adapt to new problems and situations, in its rather modest degree of ideological dogmatism, in its attempt to routinize leadership change through the principle of rotating political office, and by its general adaptability as regards organizational forms. The underlying irony of the Yugoslav case is that the ideologically avowed purpose of the League is to make itself obsolete as an organization—that is, to generate both norms of behavior and organizational forms within the wider socioeconomic system that will sustain the broad societal goals and norms of the League itself.[33] In this respect, then, as the Yugoslav Communist Party continues to develop the attributes of an institution, it would also tend increasingly to withdraw from its active role as the organization primarily concerned with directing political-administrative affairs. Stated somewhat differently, the path to the "withering away" of the League might be defined otherwise as the process of institutionalizing the Yugoslav party organization. Or, even more dramatically, the League of Communists would enter a phase of party development that might be defined as moving "beyond institutionalization" or a retirement from active political control. At this juncture, then, the League would in effect become a non-party, non-organizational expression of an overriding Yugoslav political self-awareness having the implicit but full endorsement of the society as a whole.

From still another standpoint, as the institutionalization of the League of Communists continues, there also appears to be a proliferation of suborganizations under the overriding umbrella of the Yugoslav party. What seems to be suggested here is that, as the League gains its increased legitimacy

and acceptance as a Yugoslav institution, it will become easier for a number of other sociopolitical organizations to emerge (based upon either regional or economic ties) as acknowledged and accepted purveyors of the
range of interests expressed by the Yugoslav population. In effect, the process of transforming the League from an organization into an institution as
defined here conduces to the growth of a multi-organizational (multi-
party?) internal Yugoslav environment. In other words, and more simply,
as the Yugoslav party voluntarily withdraws from active political involvement, organizations *other than the League* will be expected to assume those
organizational tasks that it had once exclusively performed. It would seem
reasonable to expect, at least from the general theoretical standpoint, that
as a Communist Party becomes progressively institutionalized, the probability of the growth of infra-organizations which assume active and meaningful
political roles would be enhanced.

A final point worthy of some attention touches upon the problem of the
Titoist succession in the Yugoslav political scene. Here it is clear that the
accelerated process of party institutionalization within Yugoslav society
largely coincides with the attempt by Tito to prepare the groundwork for a
post-Titoist era of Yugoslav socialism. This has already been mentioned as
regards the legally prescribed rotation of political offices (excepting Tito),
as well as in terms of the appearance of a new, younger, better educated
leadership group. For a Tito (or for any leader with a strong personality),
it often seems well advised to encourage the Communist Party to develop
those institutional attributes (for example, a normative linkage with the
wider population, specific rules placing limits upon the privilege of leadership, and so forth) that might work toward the effective preservation of
what the party has accomplished in the past. In short, the charisma that
Tito has employed to bring order and change to Yugoslavia must be transformed into a widely accepted routinization of sociopolitical change and
into generally rule-oriented behavior once the master himself departs from
the political scene. The simple organizational party with its direct-control
style of operation would not have the ability to guarantee the extension of
its past achievements into the future; on the other hand, the fully institutionalized party with its grounding and its legitimacy deeply imbedded
within widely held societal norms would be more likely to possess the capability of perpetuating the achievements of the "founding elite." Furthermore, a leader such as Tito seems to have been well advised in trying to
reduce potential threats to the institutionalized party emanating from powerful and competing organizational-administrative entities—namely, from the
secret police apparatus and the Yugoslav military establishment. If the
events that have transpired within Yugoslavia over the last two years are
considered (for example, the ouster of Rankovic and the demise of the secret police), then it seems that Tito has followed the strategy of trying to
undermine competing organizational forces in order to preserve the institution of the League. In order to perpetuate the achievements of the found-

ing elite, and to assure the survival of the League as a widely accepted Yugoslav institution, Tito has felt it prudent to strengthen citizen-related governmental organizations rather than to rely excessively upon quasi-military administrative-control instruments such as the army and the secret police. However, in the final analysis, given the rather severe ethnic cleavage lines that currently pervade Yugoslav society, the judgment whether the League of Communists has in fact attained the status of a self-sustaining institution must await the uncertain aftermath of Tito's death.

Notes

1. For a fuller discussion of the process of institutionalization than can be effectively pursued here, see David Easton, *A Systems Analysis of Political Life* (New York: John Wiley & Sons, 1965), pp. 289–310; S. N. Eisenstadt, *Essays on Comparative Institutions* (New York: John Wiley & Sons, 1965), pp. 40–57; Robert Michels, *Political Parties* (New York: Dover Publications, Inc., 1959), especially pp. 185–201, 205–214, 226–231, 365–392; Clement H. Moore, "Tunisia after Bourguiba: Liberalization or Political Degeneration?" in *Political Modernization in the Near East and North Africa* (Princeton: The Princeton University Conference, 1966), pp. 72–74. A related discussion as regards changes in the Yugoslav party, placed however within the wider context of Yugoslav societal transformation, is also found in M. George Zaninovich, *The Development of Socialist Yugoslavia* (Baltimore: The Johns Hopkins Press, 1968).

2. Ivan Avakumovic, *History of the Communist Party of Yugoslavia* (Aberdeen: The Aberdeen University Press, 1964), pp. 43–44.

3. In addition, the National Assembly passed a Law on the Protection of Public Safety and Order in the State (August 2, 1921) which threw the communist delegates out of the Assembly and provided special measures for dealing with all activities and propaganda against the state. Julijana Vrzinic, *Kraljevina Srba, Hrvata i Slovenaca do Vidovdanskog Procesa* (*The Kingdom of Serbs, Croats, and Slovenes to Vidovdans Law*) (Beograd: Rad, 1956), p. 109; Radoljub Colakovic, Dragoslav Jankovic, and Pero Moraca, eds., *Pregled istorije Saveza komunista Jugoslavije* (*Survey of the History of the League of Communists of Yugoslavia*) (Beograd: Institut za izucavanje radnickog pokreta, 1963), pp. 69–77.

4. As a result, spokesmen for the new Yugoslav state, such as Vladimir Dedijer, spend much of their time discussing the foundation of the new Yugoslavia as a dramatic, national epic that brought "all Yugoslav peoples" together. In so doing, these writers contribute significantly to the myth of political founding that stands at the foundation of the authority of the Yugoslav Communist regime. Dedijer, *Tito* (New York: Simon and Schuster, 1953), pp. 115–118. In addition, see Josip Broz-Tito, *Borba za oslobodjenje Jugoslavije, 1941–1945* (*Struggle for the Liberation of Yugoslavia, 1941–45*) (Beograd: Kultura, 1947); Vladimir Dedijer, *Dnevnik* (*Diary*) (Beograd: Jugoslavenska Knjiga, 1951).

5. The critical role played by these "national-liberation committees" during the partisan resistance phase are outlined by Ferdo Culinovic, *Stvaranje nove Jugoslavenske drzave* (*Creation of the New Yugoslav State*) (Zagreb: Grafickog zavoda Hrvatske, 1959), pp. 104–144.

6. *Ibid.,* pp. 192–212.

7. The Popular Front rapidly expanded its membership until by 1948 it approached the 7 million figure; today the average Yugoslav will in fact joke, somewhat cynically, about everyone being a member of the Socialist Alliance (the present designation of the Popular Front), even "house pets." In addition, the Communist Party of Yugoslavia had indicated rather astonishing growth immediately following World War II—namely, from 140,000 members in 1945 to 530,000 by 1949. George W. Hoffman and Fred Warner Neal, *Yugoslavia and the New Communism* (New York: Twentieth Century Fund, 1962), p. 197.

8. The concern of the Yugoslavs has been expressed repeatedly over the years as regards the ills of "centralist" as well as "statist" tendencies which seem to plague most communist societies. For example, see Ante Fiamengo, "From Statism to Self-Management," *Socialist Thought and Practice,* No. 25 (1967), pp. 50–62.

9. For relevant documentation and analysis concerning the Soviet-Yugoslav split, see Robert Bass and Elizabeth Marbury, eds., *The Soviet-Yugoslav Controversy, 1948–58: A Documentary Record* (New York: Prospect Books, 1959); Adam B. Ulam, *Titoism and the Cominform* (Cambridge: Harvard University Press, 1952).

10. Moma Grujic, "Posledni kongresi Komunistickih partija u Socijalistickim zemljama" ("Recent Congresses of Communist Parties in Socialist Countries"), *Sociializam (Socialism),* No. 1 (1963), pp. 75–84.

11. As a matter of fact, the Yugoslav critique of the Soviet Union on this score was largely the result of the astute perceptions and the boldness of Milovan Djilas. The general theme of "the new class" indeed has its source in the general Yugoslav (as well as the specifically Djilas) experience of criticizing the Soviet communist elite for vested interests as "a class" in existing constellations of power. Djilas, *The New Class* (New York: Frederick A. Praeger, 1957).

12. *Politika,* November 9, 1952.

13. *VI kongres Komunisticke partije Jugoslavije (Savez komunista Jugoslavije)* (*The VI Congress of the Communist Party of Yugoslavia [The League of Communists of Yugoslavia]*), stenographic reports, November 2–7, 1952, p. 427.

14. *Borba,* September 19, 1953.

15. Hoffman and Neal, *loc. cit.* For more complete statistics on the changing nature of membership in the Yugoslav Communist party, see Milos Nikolic, *Savez komunista Jugoslavije u uslovima samoupravljanja (The League of Communists of Yugoslavia under Conditions of Self-Management)* (Beograd: Kultura, 1967), p. 748.

16. *New Fundamental Law of Yugoslavia* (Beograd: Union of Jurists of Yugoslavia, 1953). For an integrated version of the Yugoslav constitutional system as of 1957, see *The Constitution of the Federal People's Republic of Yugoslavia,* intro. by J. Djordjevic (Beograd: Union of Jurists Association of Yugoslavia, 1960).

17. See Edvard Kardelj, *The New Yugoslav Federal Assembly* (Beograd: Federal Assembly Series, 1964); *The Constitution of the Socialist Federal Republic of Yugoslavia* (Beograd: Secretariat for Information of FEC, 1963).

18. Prvoslav Ralic, "Samoupravljanja i drustvena kritika" ("Self-Management and Social Criticism") *Socijalizam,* No. 4 (1963), pp. 145–149.

19. Najdan Pasic, "The Self-Contradictions of State Capitalism and Circumstances of the Class Struggle," *Socialist Thought and Practice,* No. 6 (1962), pp. 63–87.

20. *Program Saveza komunista Jugoslavije (Program of the League of Communists of Yugoslavia)* (Beograd: Kultura, 1958), p. 219. In addition, see *Yugoslavia's*

Way: The Program of the League of Communists of Yugoslavia (New York: All Nations Press, 1958); and, for a more recent analysis of the role of the League and its members, "The Third Plenum of the Central Committee of the League of Communists of Yugoslavia," *Socialist Thought and Practice*, No. 5 (1962), pp. 101–102.

21. *Komunist*, February 28, 1958.

22. Vojin Hadzistevic, "Menjane drustvenog polozaja radnicke klase Jugoslavije" ("The Change in the Societal Situation of the Working Class of Yugoslavia"), *Socijalizam*, Nos. 5–6 (1963), pp. 44–46.

23. The basic Yugoslav posture in relation to Third World nations is outlined by Milan Draskic, "The Tripartite Meeting and the Asian Situation," *Socialist Thought and Practice* No. 24 (1966), pp. 152–159. Furthermore, studies have demonstrated that Yugoslav voting patterns in the United Nations tend to fall within the Afro-Asian group of countries. Bruce M. Russett, "Discovering Voting Groups in the United Nations," *The American Political Science Review*, LX (June 1966), 333–335.

24. Krste Crvenkovski, "Divorcing the Party from Power," *Socialist Thought and Practice*, No. 22 (1966), pp. 23–28.

25. For relevant materials and related discussions on recent developments concerning party reorganization, see *Komunist*, June 29, 1967; Mijalko Todorovic, "Reorganizacija Saveza komunista i objektivna potreba radnicke klase" ("Reorganization of the League of Communists and Objective Needs of the Working Class"), *Komunist*, July 6, 1967.

26. Crvenkovski, *op. cit.*, p. 43; *Komunist*, July 27, 1967.

27. In this context, however, Yugoslav leaders are raising doubts about the capability and the dedication of the League member, which represents nothing more than a strategy to encourage more active involvement in politics and organs of self-administration by individual members of the League. *Komunist*, July 27, 1967.

28. Edvard Kardelj, "Responsibility for the Elections," *Socialist Thought and Practice*, No. 25 (1967), pp. 18, 26–27.

29. Furthermore, recent analysis of the earlier 1965 elections have shown that trends which have now become quite clear in the April, 1967 elections (for example, multi-candidate, competitive contests) were in fact already beginning to appear. For example, see R. V. Burks and S. A. Stankovic, "Jugoslawien auf dem Weg zu halbfreien Wählen?" *Osteuropa* (Stuttgart), XVII (1967), 131–146.

30. Perhaps the most dramatic change is reflected in the reduced number of peasants in the Yugoslav Communist Party. While in 1946 they constituted 46.4 per cent of the membership, by 1966 they only comprised 7.8 per cent of party members. During this same span of years, although the percentage of workers had not increased appreciably (from 30.3 per cent to 35.6 per cent), for the third category designated as "official employees" (that is, governmental bureaucrats) the increase in numbers has been quite marked (from 15.5 per cent to 41.1 per cent). In addition, the education-skill level attained by Communist Party members has also risen strongly over the years. While in 1958 only 12.4 per cent were classified as "highly qualified" and 50.4 per cent as "poorly qualified," by the year 1966 the former comprised 28.8 per cent and the latter merely 30.2 per cent of the membership of the League. Finally, in terms of the age structure of the Yugoslav party in 1966, only 4.8 per cent were listed as more than 56 years of age, while 71 per cent were 40 years and younger, with only faint memories of directly experiencing the partisan war of resistance. Nikolic, *op. cit.*, pp. 757–760, 775–777, and 780.

31. In 1964 a group of young intellectuals at the University of Zagreb established a journal of sociopolitical criticism called *Praxis*. Generally, this group holds that Marx was first and above all else a social critic and a humanist, and feels

strongly that the earlier writings of the "young Marx" have been largely ignored by later communist theorists. They maintain that certain institutions can be abandoned (even the one-party system) *if* it is clear that they violate the humanistic premises of Karl Marx. The first number of *Praxis* appeared in September, 1964, and it has been published ever since on a regular bi-monthly basis.

32. And thus: "It may also be that within that which is called 'Marxism' there are many variations within a unified standpoint. There may even be many Marxisms, but the 'Marxists' still use a single language that allows them to understand one another, even if in their disagreements." Henri Lefevre, "O Nekim kriterijima drustvenog razvoja i socijalizma" ("On Some Criteria of Social Development and Socialism"), in Danilo Pejovic and Gajo Petrovic, eds., *Smisao i perspektive socijalizma* (*The Spirit and Perspectives of Socialism*) (Zagreb: Hrvatsko filozofsko drustvo, 1965), p. 14.

33. Accordingly: "The discussion has already shown that there is a consensus of opinion against the concentration of functions in the League of Communists and in other social and state bodies, as it inevitably strengthens the tendencies towards bureaucracy and monopoly. . . . Sharp criticism has also been levelled against the tendency to identify persons with forums [i.e., organizations]. . . . I only wish to say that we are reforming the League of Communists precisely in order to strengthen its ideological influence on our social development and trends. Our objective is *not a communist party but a communist society* [Italics mine]." Mijalko Todorovic, "Reorganization of the Leading Bodies of the League of Communists of Yugoslavia," *Socialist Thought and Practice*, No. 24, (1966), pp. 47–48.

17

Conclusion: Authoritarianism, Democracy, and One-Party Politics

Samuel P. Huntington

Clement H. Moore

Democracy exists where the principal leaders of a political system are selected by competitive elections in which the bulk of the population have the opportunity to participate. Authoritarian systems are non-democratic ones. Authoritarian and democratic polities have existed throughout history. In the modern world, however, strong one-party systems are the principal form of authoritarian politics, just as strong plural [1] party systems are the principal manifestation of democracy. Yet clearly the relation between authoritarianism and one-party politics and democracy and plural party politics is not a necessary one. The possibility exists that under certain conditions a one-party authoritarian system could evolve into a democratic system or into another type of authoritarian system.

For purposes of analysis it is useful to identify six types of political systems on the basis of number of parties and degree of democracy. No-party systems, authoritarian and democratic, usually exist only at relatively low levels of social mobilization and political development. Democratic plural party systems are few in number but varied in makeup, with the United States, India, and Chile representative examples of the two-party, dominant-party, and multi-party variations. Plural party authoritarian systems are rare, since the existence of more than one significant party (and we here exclude pseudo-parties created, as in Iran, to furnish a democratic facade for an authoritarian system) usually means a fair amount of competition between those parties. Colombia, however, has two organized parties, which have agreed not to compete with each other and have thereby attempted to remove from the system the characteristic that, ac-

509

cording to our definition, makes it a democracy. The functional consequences of this arrangement, as was pointed out above on p. 16, in many ways resemble those of a one-party system. Both the revolutionary and exclusionary one-party systems discussed in this volume have, with a few exceptions, belonged in box B of Table 17–1. What factors will determine whether they remain in that box or shift into one of the other categories, particularly one of the democratic ones?

TABLE 17-1 *Authoritarian and Democratic Party Systems*

	Authoritarian	Democratic
No party	A. Ethiopia	D. Lebanon
One party	B. Soviet Union	E. ??
Plural party	C. Colombia	F. United States
		India
		Chile

The differences between exclusionary and revolutionary one-party systems reflect differences in political mobilization. Exclusionary systems emerge in partially mobilized societies deficient in political resources. Within the society, one social force has achieved a relatively high level of political mobilization, the other principal social force a relatively low level of mobilization. Even if the political leaders have an ideology aiming at closing the original bifurcation, they cannot accumulate the power required to assimilate or to obliterate the subordinate social force. Therefore either the ideology will be chiliastic, that is, expressive and inoperative, or it will be tutelary, that is, operative but aiming at only a partial transformation of society. Ataturk, to be realistic, had to exclude the peasants, just as ethnic and religious oligarchies have to combine ideology and organization to hold down the opposing and subordinate social force. Social-economic modernization and the eventual political mobilization of the subordinate social force thus lead to the breakdown—as in Turkey—of the exclusionary system and to the emergence of a plural party system. In becoming democratic, the system ceases to be a one-party system.

This alternative seems the most likely long-term prospect for most exclusionary single-party states. There are, however, at least three other possibilities. Conceivably, an exclusionary, one-party system could maintain its position for an almost indefinite period in the future, assuming it could slow down social change and develop effective mechanisms of repression. Or, such a system might be overthrown and displaced by a revolutionary single-party. Or, conceivably, the resort to sheer repression could take the form of a military-police displacement of the party as the source of legitimacy and "retrogression" to no-party authoritarianism.

Revolutionary one-party systems confront an even broader range of potential evolutionary paths. A revolutionary system involves, at least in theory, the full participation in the system of all elements in the society.

The aim of the system is not to maintain differential participation but to promote universal participation. The evolution of an exclusionary system requires either an end to the bifurcation or the creation of a more effective repressive machinery to maintain it. The evolution of the system is thus shaped primarily by the process of modernization and the political consequences of that process. The evolution of a revolutionary one-party system, on the other hand, is less affected by the process of modernization since the most important political consequences of that process have already been brought to a culmination in the revolutionary upheaval that brought the system into being. The evolution of revolutionary systems is thus likely to be influenced as much by the reemergence of distinctive cultural traditions and patterns of behavior unique to the particular society as by the more general processes of modernization. Old forms are given new meaning; old practices are put to new uses. Thus, in Mexico, sectoral or "pillar" structuring of power, which in the traditional society had been manifested in the church, army, and oligarchy, was recreated after the revolution with the organization of the revolutionary party into labor, farm, popular, and military sectors. In Yugoslavia, the nationalities issue reasserts itself as the dominant problem of post-revolutionary politics even as it had been in the pre-revolutionary days. In Poland traditional anti-Semitic tendencies reappear in a communist context. Somewhat similarly, democratic tendencies appear to develop the greatest strength in Czechoslovakia, the one post-revolutionary system with a significant pre-revolutionary democratic experience. Thus, it seems reasonable to postulate that once a revolutionary system has become firmly established, the very process of institutionalization will involve reintegration into the revolutionary system of at least some political forms and practices characteristic of pre-revolutionary politics. The probabilities that a revolutionary one-party system will move from box B into any one of the other possibilities outlined in Table 17–1 hence may be significantly affected by the nature of the pre-revolutionary society.

A second major factor influencing the direction in which these systems may evolve comes, of course, from the international environment. Students of comparative politics at times treat political systems as if they evolved in relative isolation from each other and hence were susceptible to comparison but not to mutual influence. In the current world, however, the political evolution of states is often decisively affected by the system of international incentives and constraints. The contemporary international climate tends to encourage a rhetoric of revolution and nationalism at the same time that the more concrete influences of the major powers restrict the options open to many small power statesmen. For many countries Brezhnev's doctrine of "limited sovereignty" is a controlling fact of political life. American policy has drastically reduced, if not eliminated, the probability of another revolutionary one-party system emerging in Latin America. Soviet policy has imposed limits on the extent of democratization in East Europe.

External influences hence may make it impossible for Latin American countries to get into box B and for East European ones to get out of it. Where the tendencies within the society conflict with the dominant tendencies in the international system, the result is likely to be military intervention by the major power in overt or covert forms.

A third factor affecting the democratization of a revolutionary system will be its level of institutionalization, that is, the extent to which the revolutionary system has moved through the phases of transformation, consolidation, and adaptation, and thus acquired many of the characteristics of an established one-party system. Evolution from one phase to another is not a painless or inevitable process. The problems of the transition can lead to the breakdown of the single-party system and possible retrogression to no-party forms of authoritarianism. Both Cuba and China, for instance, in the mid-1960s confronted in dramatic fashion many of the problems involved in the transition from the transformation phase to that of consolidation. In both cases, the top leadership (Mao, Castro) tried to resist the "routinization" of the revolutionary experience. The result in China was the Cultural Revolution; the result in Cuba was a somewhat similar effort at mass mobilization in 1966–1968 undermining the power of the bureaucracy, which had played a leading role between 1962 and 1966. The consequence of these efforts to hold off routinization was a disruption of the party organization in China and the reinforcement of the continuing failure to develop a strong, autonomous party organization in Cuba. In both countries, also, the weakening of authority structures led to the military reappearing on the scene as a major political force. In China the army clearly became the one source of stability and effective authority amidst the otherwise prevalent violence and civil strife, and its leader emerged as the leading contender for the succession to Mao. In Cuba in 1966 and 1967 the military commanders associated with the guerrilla movement similarly emerged as a dominant force within the government. In 1962, for instance, 55 per cent of the members of the Cuban National Directorate had army titles and 28 per cent occupied positions in the army and security forces. In 1967, 69 per cent of the members of the Central Committee had army titles and 51 per cent were directly engaged in military or security work. Correspondingly, the proportion of top leaders involved in economic work declined from 44 per cent in 1962 to 20 per cent in 1967. "Apart from the obvious decline of the PSP," observes one scholar in analysing these shifts, "the most striking thing is the rise in the importance of the army." The explanation for this change lies, as it also does in large part in China, in "the fact that these men were loyal to the government—of almost unquestioning loyalty." [2] In both societies, however, the increase in military power as a result of the efforts of the top leadership to head off the process of consolidation also increases the probability that military leaders and the army will play a major political role after the death of the top leader. Revolutionary one-party authoritarianism that is not consolidated in institutional structures may well be displaced by military authoritarianism.

Institutionalization of the party is thus a necessary condition for democratization to occur within a single-party system. If the system has achieved its revolutionary goals, if the initially opposed social groups have been liquidated or assimilated into the party, if the party's constituency has become coterminous with society, institutionalization becomes possible. Under these conditions, in fact, the single-party system will be unstable and illegitimate unless institutionalization occurs. On the other hand, this process is not inevitable, and it is a necessary but not sufficient condition for democratization.

With institutionalization, the principle legitimating one-party rule changes. The party is no longer valued as an organization for what it does or for the ideological goals it may achieve, but rather for what it is. Infused with value, the party organization becomes a party-institution. Legitimacy derives more from the structure than from the achievements of valued goals. The party develops sacrosanct procedures, and it is these that legitimate policies and leaders, not the ideological "correctness" of their decisions. The only ideology, in short, is of the expressive, administrative sort, tolerant of a wide variety of goals. The good administrative communist is distinguished not by this scientific world outlook and strategy but "his readiness to recognize the views established institutionally."

However tolerant of diverse goals, the administrative outlook does not necessarily imply democratization. To become a party-institution, the party must be of intrinsic value to all social forces capable of political participation, but institutionalization logically entails neither the liberalism nor pluralism of modern democracies. In Yugoslavia the freedoms of groups and individuals are fully tolerated only in spheres the regime has determined to be apolitical. In residual sectors of uncertainty and political choice, the party retains tight organizational control. The administrative outlook need not predispose party leaders to favor democratization in these sectors. Rather, what is good for the organization is perceived as good for the society, irrespective of the wishes of the organization's clients.

Institutionalization in Yugoslavia, however, may undermine organizational control and lead to the disappearance of residual sectors of decision-making that the League still monopolizes. This would mean evolution towards a no-party democratic system (box D). Zaninovich has stressed the trends in this direction, while Janos has analyzed the limitations on pluralistic politics in contemporary Yugoslavia. Presumably the party must satisfy its various clients if they are to accord it the respect and deference due to a governing institution. Perhaps the only way to insure this respect is to institutionalize the free participation of groups and individuals in the system. The party-institution might then be comparable to the constitution of a modern pluralist democracy.

In the real world, however, the institutionalization of a single-party system cannot mean the withering away of party organization or the abolition of politics. Though power must be dispersed and autonomous groups tolerated in growing fields of choice, clients can be made to accept the institution as legitimate even though it retains organizational controls over the political process. It would be unrealistic to expect the rulers of any single-party system to destroy their own instrument of power. Rather, in an institutionalized system the leaders have authority because they have "something added," namely the power to make decisions in the residual sector of political choice beyond the arenas of a pluralistic bargaining.

Can there be democracy in such a system or must it be authoritarian? Neither Yugoslavs, Tunisians, Czechs, nor Mexicans have produced procedures and mechanisms inside the party whereby the bulk of the population has the opportunity to participate in the selection of principal leaders through competitive elections. The communist ones are more likely than the non-communist ones to develop such procedures, but common to the four political cultures is the distaste for overt political conflict and "factions," which characterizes other single-party cultures, with the possible exception of China. Does such a cultural trait preclude meaningful competitive elections for top political leaders? In this respect Czechoslovakia, with an antecedent democratic tradition, would be more likely to devise procedures than Yugoslavia, if the Soviet Union would permit it to do so.

No modern systems are perfectly democratic, just as none, not even the "totalitarian" variant, are purely authoritarian. No form of modern political organization affords all citizens equal opportunity to participate in the selection of top leaders. In plural party systems the nominating procedures of the major parties benefit some individuals and strata to the detriment of others. In a complex modern society a pluralism of dispersed inequalities may be the best a democrat can hope for. Probably there can be as much or as little democracy in an established one-party system as in a stable plural party system. Still, the number of parties makes a difference in how democracy is organized. In the established one-party system, however much the party has become an institution insulated from most routine decisions, there can be only one publicly identified group of men who express the good of society as a whole—not two groups or more, as in plural party systems. Though plebiscites are possible, it is the party, not the people, that chooses the top leaders. The bulk of the population can participate only indirectly in the selection of these leaders, to the extent that the party attempts to be responsive to their representatives. There cannot be direct accountability. Within an inclusive institutionalized party, however, procedures may be as democratic as, say, among American Democrats or British Tories. The style of authority will reflect styles in other related spheres of social interaction.[3]

In societies such as France and Russia, which inherited strong autocratic traditions, multi-party systems may present more obstacles than single-party systems to the devolution of authority. The French party system never overcame a strongly centralized bureaucracy; the Bolsheviks did. Established one-party systems possibly permit more bureaucratic decentralization than multi-party systems. The institutionalization of a one-party system, indeed, is a process whereby the party devolves its functional overload upon a variety of governmental and autonomous or quasi-autonomous groups. As the scope of politics in the grand sense decreases, political participation increases. In France and Yugoslavia depoliticization has different connotations. In France it means disenchantment with traditional parties; in Yugoslavia it means greater opportunity for citizens to participate in local and regional councils and a variety of groups deemed apolitical. In both cases and perhaps more generally in modern society it is associated with official and unofficial efforts to revise the dominant style of authority, by strengthening functional groups and institutions rather than the formal structures of government. In established single-party systems, as in France, it is possible that styles of authority developed in apolitical structures may spill over into the political arena. Democratic procedures evolved in Yugoslav local councils, for instance, may be carried into the party. But the process of adaptation is likely to be erratic.

The shift from authoritarian to democratic single-party politics could impose costs on the system that outweigh its benefits. In the first place, of course, intraparty democracy would provide an unfamiliar and disruptive challenge to the existing leadership. The problems of adjustment from an essentially bureaucratic, cooptative political system to a more egalitarian, electoral one would be considerable. Over time this structural change would result in a significant change in the character of the political leadership, producing a leadership less capable of dealing with the ordinary, day-to-day problems of a complex, specialized, and bureaucratic society, but more capable of introducing fundamental changes and of responding effectively to major crises. In a bureaucratic system the stress is inevitably on continuity; bureaucratic personnel systems reproduce their own; there are fewer dramatic breaks between one style, direction, or generation of leadership and another. Electoral competition, in contrast, opens up the possibility of such changes. It also tends to insure that the leadership that regularly emerges will be less skilled in the ways of bureaucracy and in the ways of exercising control over bureaucracy than would be a leadership which is itself the product of a bureaucratic political structure. A shift to electoral competition, in short, is likely to enhance the autonomy of functional groups and to reduce the effectiveness of political controls over specialized bureaucracies.

Electoral competition is also likely to reopen communal cleavages in many societies. Authoritarian single-party systems, particularly communist ones, have been strikingly successful in integrating into their systems diverse ethnic, racial, and religious groups. Membership in the system is defined in class and political terms rather than those of nationality, language, or race. In a revolutionary one-party system, the political leaders have a direct interest in combining an open appeal on non-communal, ideological grounds with a *de facto* policy of balanced representation of all communal groups in the party structure. The creation of communist systems in plural societies such as the Soviet Union, Yugoslavia, Czechoslovakia, and North Vietnam was in each case accompanied by generally successful efforts to secure an initial reduction in communal antagonisms. Much of the success of the Yugoslav Communist Party in the 1940s, for instance, was based on the fact that in contrast to the Serbian Cetnici and the Croat Ustase, it appealed to and incorporated elements of all Yugoslav nationalities. The party, in turn, created a Yugoslav state, which rested on the principle that there was no Yugoslav nationality.

The shift from a revolutionary to an established single party is likely to open the way for reintensification of some communal rivalries. The autonomy granted to functionally specific bureaucratic structures and groups contributes to a general loosening up of the system and hence permits greater self-assertion on the part of nationality and racial groups. The widespread introduction of electoral competition is likely to exacerbate these tendencies. The democratization trend in Czechoslovakia coincided with the reemergence of tensions between its two major nationality groups. Party primaries in Tanzania stimulated tribal appeals. Competition in local elections in Yugoslavia similarly produced some blatant and many *sub rosa* appeals to ethnic loyalties. Electoral competition at the national level where so much more would be at stake could well threaten the national unity of this and other multi-communal societies.

This danger of disruption from democracy, however, may well be counterbalanced by the danger of stagnation without it. In multi-party systems built on liberal foundations, parties and individuals have the freedom to interpret and articulate the values of the society in response to new problems, whereas in authoritarian single-party systems the party must curtail this freedom, allowing only leaders and intellectuals inside the party to infuse administration with purpose. Single-party systems may allow much participation, some pluralism, but little liberalism. So far as they remain revolutionary, they may adapt to new problems by transforming society. But so far as they are institutionalized, they may tend to drift and fail to respond to new problems unless the top party leadership is exceptionally enlightened or fortunate.

Authoritarian one-party systems are less able than democratic systems to tolerate breakdowns of ideological consensus, for they afford fewer safety valves of dissent and possibilities to build new consensus. They also seem inherently more conservative. They correspond, in fact, to Saint-Simon's vision of the modern world, for they signal the functional division of political labor. The top leaders are administrative managers. They coordinate a decentralized and dispersed empire of specialized agencies and functional groups originally created by the party. All the actors in the empire share the administrative outlook of the top leaders, and in modern society they may have a greater capability than the political actors of multi-party systems to stimulate consensual and specialized political participation by the masses. So far as the empire of groups corresponds to modern society and expresses and responds to its specialized needs, the institutionalized single-party system can produce legitimate and effective government. In fact one-party systems are more appropriate to modern society than multi-party systems, if all that modern society requires of the political system is a functional division of political labor. Mass participation stems mass alienation, while functional channels serve the distinctive, specialized needs of modern society. On this view, indeed, electoral competition and the variety of parties in other systems becomes superfluous just as partisan ideology is no longer relevant to the problems of modern society.

But the ritualized ideology of party priests is even less likely to prove relevant to a modern society of routine sinners. Originally a response to no longer recognizable problems, revolutionary ideology is less flexible and adaptable to new problems than the open clash of partisan purposes and political ambitions. If dialectic in the Marxist sense is no longer a practical guide to political activity, dialectic in the Socratic sense is as relevant to modern as to classical culture. Many problems of modern society are subject to administrative solution or regulation, but the essence of modernity is perpetual change, which constantly generates new social tensions and political problems. Any ideological consensus in modern society is apt to be more fragile and transient than the consensus of traditional society. Yet an authoritarian one-party system depends upon a semblance of likemindedness and ideological consensus.

Perhaps most established single-party systems, assaulted by the new problems and groups of modern society, will remain undemocratic and fail to develop a political formula whereby power is dispersed and group autonomy encouraged. Modern society in the abstract is no less congruent with authoritarian rule than are traditional or transitional societies. But the post-revolutionary party, no longer justified by an ideologically inspired mission, will be threatened with a legitimacy crisis. The most likely response is institutionalization in an authoritarian rather than a democratic direction, appealing to a corporatist rather than a competitive tradition. Such government seems capable of handling routine problems but uninspired and fearful of new ones. It could, like the dinosaur, become too big, complex, and ineffective to survive long in a world of change.

‖ Notes

1. We use the term "plural party system" to describe all types of party systems in which there is more than one significant party. This category thus encompasses two-party, dominant-party, and multi-party systems, as defined above on pp. 5–6.
2. Jorge Domínguez, "The Politics of the Institutionalization of the Cuban Revolution: The Search for the Missing Links" (Unpublished paper, Harvard University, 1968), pp. 83–84.
3. See Harry Eckstein, *A Theory of Stable Democracy*, Research Monograph No. 10 (Princeton: Princeton University Center of International Studies, 1961).

Index